Luminos is the open access monograph publishing program from UC Press. Luminos provides a framework for preserving and reinvigorating monograph publishing for the future and increases the reach and visibility of important scholarly work. Titles published in the UC Press Luminos model are published with the same high standards for selection, peer review, production, and marketing as those in our traditional program. www.luminosoa.org

Discrimination at Work

Discrimination at Work

Comparing European, French,
and American Law

Marie Mercat-Bruns

Translated from the French by Elaine Holt
With a Foreword by Christopher Kutz

UNIVERSITY OF CALIFORNIA PRESS

University of California Press, one of the most distinguished university presses in the United States, enriches lives around the world by advancing scholarship in the humanities, social sciences, and natural sciences. Its activities are supported by the UC Press Foundation and by philanthropic contributions from individuals and institutions. For more information, visit www.ucpress.edu.

University of California Press
Oakland, California

© 2016 by The Regents of the University of California

This work is licensed under a Creative Commons CC-BY-NC-ND license. To view a copy of the license, visit http://creativecommons.org/licenses.

Suggested citation: Mercat-Bruns, Marie. *Discrimination at Work: Comparing European, French, and American Law*. Oakland: University of California Press, 2016. doi: http://dx.doi.org/10.1525/luminos.11

Library of Congress Cataloging-in-Publication Data

Names: Mercat-Bruns, Marie, author.
Title: Discrimination at work : comparing European, French, and American law / Marie Mercat-Bruns ; [Elaine Holt, translator].
Other titles: Discriminations en droit du travail. English
Description: Oakland, California : University of California Press, [2016] | "2016 | Includes interviews with American professors of law. | Includes bibliographical references and index.
Identifiers: LCCN 2015038337| ISBN 9780520283800 (pbk. : alk. paper) | ISBN 9780520959583 (ebook)
Subjects: LCSH: Discrimination in employment—Law and legislation—Interviews. | Lawyers—United States—Interviews. | Discrimination in employment—Law and legislation—United States. | Discrimination in employment—Law and legislation—France. | Discrimination in employment—Law and legislation—European Union countries.
Classification: LCC K1770 .M4713 2016 | DDC 344.01/398133—dc23
LC record available at http://lccn.loc.gov/2015038337

24   23   22   21   20   19   18   17   16
10   9   8   7   6   5   4   3   2   1

CONTENTS

Foreword — *xi*
Preface — *xiii*
Introduction — *1*

1. History of Antidiscrimination Law: The Constitution and the Search for Paradigms of Equality — 9
2. Antidiscrimination Models and Enforcement — 29
3. Disparate Treatment Discrimination: Intent, Bias, and the Burden of Proof — 61
4. From Disparate Impact to Systemic Discrimination — 82
5. The Multiple Grounds of Discrimination — 145

Appendix — *247*
Notes — *257*
Index — *359*

To Benoit, Adrien, Florence, and Alexandra

Without common ideas, there is no common action, and without common action men still exist, but a social body does not. Thus in order that there be society, and all the more, that this society prosper, it is necessary that all the minds of the citizens always be brought together and held together by some principle ideas.

—Alexis de Tocqueville, *Democracy in America*

FOREWORD

Christopher Kutz

It is my pleasure to introduce Professor Marie Mercat-Bruns's work to an American audience in this translation. While the topic of antidiscrimination protections in employment law is of course of very great intrinsic interest, it has a much greater symbolic reach, and I hope that with this translation, Mercat-Bruns's brilliantly conceived project will find a global audience. For the idea of antidiscrimination is, as Yale Dean Robert Post says in this book, another face of the ideal of the citizen-worker and the attributes of that citizen-worker that are above or below the notice of the state. The conception of the citizen-worker is under tremendous pressure, both in Europe and the United States, arising from a new sentiment among citizens in all advanced democracies that salient aspects of one's identity and humanity need not be covered or closeted in public, nor are they appropriate bases for rejection or refusal. The law and philosophy of antidiscrimination is, in other words, the law and philosophy of the democratic citizen.

Mercat-Bruns makes this link herself in her introduction when she discusses the ways in which the *Charlie Hebdo* and Kacher market murders put racial and religious identity at the center of public debate, even more so, perhaps, than did the later debates about who precisely was Charlie and who was not. The republican ideal of the sexless, raceless, secular citizen has been fractured under the pressure of social and economic exclusion, religious targeting, and the surge of both National Front and cross-cultural politics.[1]

---

1. As this volume moves into press, France, and its attendant conceptions of Frenchness, have been rocked even more radically by the Daech attacks on the café and club youth culture of Paris. Again the attackers included self-evidently alienated French citizens of the *banlieue*. The need to understand the social and economic pressures of difference in French life could not be more acute.

While the issue of home-grown Islamist extremism and flourishing anti-Semitism is by no means unique to France or the republican model—and it strikes this observer as curious that there is much less talk of the failure of the German, Belgian, or British "models" of the citizen—there is one aspect of French political and legal culture that really is peculiar among multicultural democracies, and that is the deep-seated commitment to formal over substantive equality in legal privileges and rights. The commitment to formal equality, which is considerably offset by France's strong commitment to social solidarity and labor protection in economic terms, is a direct product of the republican ideal. And so the lessons of America, as it has struggled with an overly formalistic conception of equality, may be of great help to French scholars, judges, and lawmakers as they adjust a conception of citizenship that has worked best in the more demographically homogenous France. I have no doubt that *Discrimination at Work* has already been read profitably in France because of its reconstruction of a nuanced republicanism.

The really interesting feature of Mercat-Bruns's project, however, is how much it has to show American lawyers, scholars, and judges. For just as the neutral republican citizen ideal is under pressure in France, the identitarian conception of citizenship in progressive American legal thought is under pressure in the United States through a rhetoric of "color-blindness" and anti-antidiscrimination that bears much in common with republican ideals. While the move to color-blindness at the Supreme Court and Court of Appeals level is largely deplored by the scholars Mercat-Bruns interviews, many of whom have played important roles in constructing and furthering American antidiscrimination legal doctrine and theory, the trend is unlikely to disappear. And so this book provides an opportunity for a fresh dialogue between two points of view on equality and antidiscrimination, which is of great and immediate interest on both sides of the Atlantic.

This brings me to the most distinctive feature of *Discrimination at Work*: its use of interviews with leading American legal scholars to illuminate the roots and trends of U.S. antidiscrimination law and their relevance for French law. Of course, collections of thematic interviews have been published before; however, such collections always pose a risk that the interviewees will end up scattering themselves across the pages with a range of disparate points and interests. In this book, however, Mercat-Bruns provides a structure to harmonize these voices by holding them tightly to the themes she has put forward in the volume. Mercat-Bruns presents her interlocutors as partners in a conversation about her specific topics, and the result is a fusion of their insights with her own conception of the law. The casualness of the interview format makes her book enjoyable as well as readable, providing a window into the relation between compassion and analysis in the work of Mercat-Bruns as well as that of her interlocutors. Bravo to all.

PREFACE

The "Why" and the "Who" of This Book

THE "WHY"

The interactive format of this book requires some explanation in terms of methodology. Why choose to interview American scholars in order to discuss American, European, and French law on discrimination at work? This method is generally uncommon in law, but comparative law always entails a more contextual analysis of issues.[1]

How could a comparative study successfully bridge the gap between countries with such distinct legal heritage? I have always felt it difficult to convey a stimulating analysis of foreign law, even though comparative law is so insightful on topics such as discrimination. Furthermore, law is a practice in every country and the most vivid examples come from cases that tell stories. How could I expose these narratives in a transatlantic perspective?

Social science provided a key to this challenge. Surveys and interviews are commonplace in sociology.[2] Fieldwork through the use of questionnaires and semistructured interviews can enhance knowledge in a particular sphere, drawing from the qualitative experience and data of those interviewed. Outside the realm of social science, I also discovered that journalists like Bill Moyers have written books based on interviews on various topics, comparing the perspectives of different experts in the field.[3]

Why not try this in comparative law to help clarify the historical construction of legal concepts like equality and antidiscrimination and their interpretation and their critique outside of formal legal sources? Intuitively, I began seeking out ways to integrate interviews with those who applied and taught discrimination law in the United States. This approach allows readers (lay or expert) to make up their own mind on themes that can involve very different grids of analysis of law. The questions can vary a little from one expert to another according to their area of expertise.

I interviewed American scholars who had contrasting points of view on discrimination at work, and then I took advantage of this dialogue to pinpoint how similar questions were dealt with in France and Europe. In this way, readers do not end up with a dogmatic, unilateral view of discrimination at work but an open-ended debate and different solutions and queries on the relevant issues raised. Readers are empowered to draw their own conclusions on the subject. In a globalized world, issues of discrimination are pervasive and antagonizing, but a universal debate thrives on what constitutes effective policies of enforcement.

The next challenge was to choose the right sample of experts. In social science, the point of entry is important. Through my PhD experience on a comparative study of aging and the law in the United States and France, I had met outstanding American law professors who were either familiar with discrimination law or who reflected in a critical way on concepts of equality and liberty. Using a social science technique called snowball, or chain, sampling, I relied on such contacts to recruit other experts in the field among their acquaintances. Most of the experts I selected had been named several times by their colleagues, and this cross-referencing confirmed the need to include them.

As a result, the fifteen professors I interviewed do not necessarily cover all topics in employment discrimination, but they illustrate some of the essential trends in the field and a network of thinkers among the elite in American academia. Sometimes they even respond to each other in the book. This mechanism of co-opting does not necessarily restrain the debate since the interviews are themselves a pretext for the comparative study. The dialogue is almost an excuse to think out of the box and question French and European law by distancing myself from the way the French and European usually frame the debate.

This justifies the pedagogical format of the book. The comparative perspectives presented after each set of interviews are grouped within an overarching theme. The structure follows the traditional table of contents found in law books useful to researchers, students, and laypersons. It targets the main issues of antidiscrimination law. This study starts with the legal construction of concepts of equality and antidiscrimination and covers the contours of disparate treatment and disparate impact discrimination to finish with the different grounds of discrimination.

THE "WHO"

Before presenting the biographies of the scholars I interviewed, let me summarize what attracted me most in the first pieces I read by them and give examples of their seminal articles that illustrate the critical view of antidiscrimination law that

I needed to enrich the transatlantic comparison. Susan Sturm's work on diversity and "The Architecture of Inclusion" offered a creative perspective on equality and institutional change.[4] I was also struck by Martha Minow's groundbreaking work on new ways of framing concepts of equality: *Making All the Difference: Inclusion, Exclusion, and American Law*.[5] Robert Post explained brilliantly the underpinnings of antidiscrimination law in his article "Prejudicial Appearances: The Logic of American Antidiscrimination Law."[6]

I discovered Reva Siegel through her historical work with Jack Balkin that covers equal protection and the role of civil rights groups: "Principles, Practices, and Social Movements."[7] David Oppenheimer's work on the theory of negligence and discrimination is central to understanding certain aspects of the nature of discrimination law in practice.[8] Christine Jolls, from the perspective of behavioral economics,[9] and Linda Krieger, from the perspective of a legal practitioner interested in social psychology,[10] attracted my attention with their in-depth work on implicit bias, absent in the French debate on discrimination law. Richard Ford's book *Racial Culture: A Critique*[11] and Janet Halley's book *Split Decisions: How and Why to Take a Break from Feminism*[12] draw from a critical legal studies perspective and offered me great insight on the limits of antidiscrimination law. Julie Suk, from a comparative perspective, allowed me to revisit the interaction between stereotypes, antidiscrimination law, and work-family conflict.[13] Vicki Schultz enlightens brilliantly the relationship between sexual harassment and sex segregation of the workforce.[14] Ruth Colker's work on the history of disability discrimination in the United States was decisive to understanding the construction of disability law in the United States.[15] Finally, in order to develop an interdisciplinary perspective on discrimination in the field of employment, the debate had to include the work of two sociologists: Frank Dobbin in his book *Inventing Equal Opportunity*[16] as well as the extensive research of Devah Pager and her studies on racial bias in recruitment.[17]

Before turning to the interviews, brief biographies of the scholars are needed to show the scope of their work in the field of equality law. In addition, the appendix of the book covers a couple of more intimate conversations with some of them on what motivated them to investigate discrimination law and includes links to more extensive versions of their biographies.

Ruth Colker

Ruth Colker is the Distinguished University Professor and Heck-Faust Chair in Constitutional Law at the Moritz College of Law at the Ohio State University. She received her AB in Social Studies from Harvard (cum laude) and her JD from Harvard Law School. Before joining the faculty at Ohio State, Professor Colker taught at Tulane University, the University of Toronto, the University of Pittsburgh, and in the women's studies graduate program at George Washington University.

She also spent four years working as a trial attorney in the Civil Rights Division of the United States Department of Justice, where she received two awards for outstanding performance.

Her primary research interests are special education, disability discrimination, and LGBT issues. Professor Colker is one of the leading scholars in the country in the areas of constitutional law and disability discrimination. She is the author of twelve books, two of which have won book prizes. She has also published more than fifty articles in law journals.[18]

Frank Dobbin

Frank Dobbin received his BA from Oberlin College in 1980 and his PhD from Stanford University in 1987. Dobbin, a professor of sociology at Harvard, studies organizations, inequality, economic behavior, and public policy.[19] With Alexandra Kalev, he is developing an evidence-based approach to diversity management. Innovations that make managers part of the solution, such as mentoring programs, diversity taskforces, and special recruitment programs, have helped to promote diversity in firms, whereas programs signaling that managers are part of the problem, such as diversity training and diversity performance evaluations, have not. These findings have been covered by the *New York Times*, the *Washington Post*, the *Boston Globe*, *Le Monde*, CNN, and National Public Radio.

Chai Feldblum

Chai Feldblum received her BA in Ancient Studies and Religion from Barnard College and her JD from Harvard Law School. She is currently on leave from her position as a law professor at Georgetown University Law Center and is serving as a Commissioner of the Equal Employment Opportunity Commission (EEOC). Nominated to the post by President Barack Obama in September 2009, she was renominated and confirmed by the Senate to serve a second term ending on July 1, 2018. A former law clerk to First Circuit Court of Appeals Judge Frank M. Coffin and Supreme Court Justice Harry A. Blackmun, Professor Feldblum has worked to advance the rights of persons with disabilities and the rights of lesbian, gay, bisexual, and transgender people to health-care and social security benefits in employment-related contexts. She played a leading role in drafting and negotiating the Americans with Disabilities (ADA) Act of 1990 as well as the ADA Amendments Act of 2008. She also helped draft and negotiate the bill prohibiting discrimination based on sexual orientation as well as various medical privacy bills and regulations. Professor Feldblum has written numerous articles and books on sexual orientation, morality and the law, disabilities rights, and the practice of law in a legislative advocacy context. In 2003, Professor Feldblum founded Workplace Flexibility 2010, a policy enterprise focused on finding common ground between employers and employees on workplace flexibility issues; she co-directed it until 2009.

Richard Ford

Richard Thompson Ford is the George E. Osborne Professor of Law at Stanford Law School. He received his BA from Stanford and his JD from Harvard Law School. An expert on civil rights and antidiscrimination law, Richard Ford has distinguished himself as an insightful voice and compelling writer on questions of race and multiculturalism. His scholarship combines social criticism and legal analysis,[20] and he writes for both popular readers and for academic and legal specialists. His work has focused on the social and legal conflicts surrounding claims of discrimination and on the causes and effects of racial segregation. Methodologically, his work is at the intersection of critical theory and the law. Before joining the Stanford Law School faculty in 1994, Professor Ford was a Reginald F. Lewis Fellow at Harvard Law School, a litigation associate with Morrison & Foerster, and a housing policy consultant for the City of Cambridge, Massachusetts. He has also been a Commissioner of the San Francisco Housing Authority. He has written for the *Washington Post*, the *San Francisco Chronicle*, the *Christian Science Monitor*, and *Slate*, where he is a regular contributor.

Janet Halley

Janet Halley is the Royall Professor of Law at Harvard Law School. She has a PhD in English Literature from UCLA and a JD from Yale Law School. She is the author of *Split Decisions: How and Why to Take a Break from Feminism* (Princeton 2006), and *Don't: A Reader's Guide to the Military's Anti-Gay Policy* (Duke 1999). With Wendy Brown, she coedited *Left Legalism/Left Critique* (Duke 2002), and with Andrew Parker, she coedited *After Sex? On Writing Since Queer Theory* (Duke 2011). She is the coeditor with Kerry Rittich of a collection of essays entitled *Critical Directions in Comparative Family Law* (58 American Journal of Comparative Law 753, 2010), and the author of "What is Family Law?: A Genealogy," published in 2011 in the *Yale Journal of Law and the Humanities*. Her current book projects are *The Family/Market Distinction: A Genealogy and Critique* and *Rape in Armed Conflict: Assessing the Feminist Vision and Its Law*.[21] She was recently awarded the Career Achievement Award for Law and the Humanities by the Association for the Study of Law, Culture and the Humanities. She teaches Family Law, Gender and the Family in Transnational Legal Orders, Gender in Postcolonial Legal Orders, Trafficking and Labor Migration, and courses on the intersections of legal theory with social theory.

Christine Jolls

Christine Jolls is the Gordon Bradford Tweedy Professor at Yale Law School, a chair previously held by Nobel Laureate Oliver Williamson. She is also the Director of the Law and Economics Program at the National Bureau of Economic Research (NBER). Previously she served as a law clerk at the Supreme Court of the United States in the chambers of Justice Antonin Scalia and at the United States Court of Appeals for the District of Columbia Circuit to Judge Stephen F. Williams. Professor Jolls received her JD, magna cum laude, from Harvard Law School and her PhD in Economics from MIT, where she was a National Science Foundation Graduate Fellow. She earned her undergraduate degree at Stanford University, where she was elected to Phi Beta Kappa in her sophomore year and won the Robert M. Golden Medal. She has published numerous research articles on behavioral economics, employment law, privacy law, and other fields of law, in reviews, including the *Harvard Law Review,* the *Stanford Law Review,* and the *American Economic Review/Papers and Proceedings.*[22]

Linda Krieger

Linda Hamilton Krieger is a professor of law and Director of the Ulu Lehua Scholars Program at the University of Hawaii, William S. Richardson School of Law. She received her AB at Stanford University in 1975 and her JD at the New York University School of Law in 1978. A former federal employment discrimination litigator, she joined the faculty at the University of California, Berkeley, School of Law in 1996. Her scholarship centers on interdisciplinary perspectives on antidiscrimination law and policy and on judgment and decision making in law and public policy.[23]

Martha Minow

Martha Minow is the Morgan and Helen Chu Dean and Professor of Law at Harvard Law School, where she has taught since 1981. An expert in human rights with a focus on members of racial and religious minorities and women, children, and persons with disabilities, her scholarship has also addressed private military contractors, management of mass torts, transitional justice, and law, culture, and social change. She has published more than 150 scholarly articles and books.[24] Following nomination by President Obama and confirmation by the Senate, she serves as Vice-Chair of the Board of the Legal Services Corporation.

A Phi Beta Kappa graduate of the University of Michigan and the Harvard Graduate School of Education, Minow received her law degree at Yale Law School before serving as a law clerk to Judge David Bazelon and Justice Thurgood Marshall of the Supreme Court of the United States.

David Oppenheimer

David B. Oppenheimer is Clinical Professor of Law and Director of Professional Skills at Berkeley Law. Following his graduation from Harvard Law School, Professor Oppenheimer clerked for California Chief Justice Rose Bird. He then worked as a staff attorney for the California Department of Fair Employment and Housing, prosecuting discrimination cases, and was the founding director of the Boalt Hall

Employment Discrimination Clinic. He has published articles on discrimination law in the *Pennsylvania Law Review,* the *Cornell Law Review,* the *Columbia Journal of Human Rights Law,* the *Berkeley Women's Law Journal,* the *Berkeley Journal of Employment and Labor Law,* and *Droit et Cultures.*[25]

Devah Pager

Devah Pager is Professor of Sociology and Public Policy at Harvard University. Her research focuses on institutions affecting racial stratification, including education, labor markets, and the criminal justice system. Pager's research has involved a series of field experiments studying discrimination against minorities and ex-offenders in the low-wage labor market. Her book *Marked: Race, Crime, and Finding Work in an Era of Mass Incarceration* (University of Chicago, 2007) investigates the racial and economic consequences of large-scale imprisonment for contemporary U.S. labor markets.[26] Pager holds masters degrees from Stanford University and the University of Cape Town, and a PhD from the University of Wisconsin-Madison.

Robert Post

Robert Post is Dean and Sol and Lillian Goldman Professor of Law at Yale Law School. Before coming to Yale, he taught at the University of California, Berkeley, School of Law (Boalt Hall). Dean Post's subject areas are constitutional law, First Amendment, legal history, and equal protection. He has written and edited numerous books, including *Democracy, Expertise, Academic Freedom: A First Amendment Jurisprudence for the Modern State* (2012); *For the Common Good: Principles of American Academic Freedom* (with Matthew M. Finkin) (2009); *Prejudicial Appearances: The Logic of American Antidiscrimination Law* (with K. Anthony Appiah, Judith Butler, Thomas C. Grey, & Reva B. Siegel) (2001); and *Constitutional Domains: Democracy, Community, Management* (1995).[27] He is a member of the American Philosophical Society and the American Law Institute and a fellow of the American Academy of Arts and Sciences. He has an AB and PhD in History of American Civilization from Harvard and a JD from Yale Law School.

Vicki Schultz

Vicki Schultz is the Ford Foundation Professor of Law and the Social Sciences at Yale Law School, where she teaches courses on employment discrimination law; proving discrimination in social science and the law; workplace theory and policy; work, gender and the law; and feminist theory. She also runs the Workplace Theory and Policy Workshop and the Work and Welfare group, interdisciplinary groups that explore economic and other forms of inequality.

Schultz has written and lectured widely on a variety of subjects related to antidiscrimination law, including workplace harassment, sex segregation on the job, work-family issues, working hours, and the meaning of work in people's lives.[28] Schultz's work has been influential in scholarly circles in both law and the social sciences; her work has also been cited widely by courts and the national news media (the *New York Times Magazine,* the *New Yorker, Ms. Magazine).* She has appeared on *NewsHour with Jim Lehrer,* the *CBS Evening News,* ABC's *World News Tonight, Good Morning America,* and National Public Radio. Schultz is a past president of the Labor and Employment Section of the Association for American Law Schools and a past Trustee of the Law and Society Association. A former trial attorney at the United States Department of Justice, Civil Rights Division, Schultz began her academic career at the University of Wisconsin Law School where she became interested in sociological approaches to law. She has a BA from the University of Texas and a JD from Harvard.

Reva Siegel

Reva Siegel is the Nicholas de B. Katzenbach Professor of Law at Yale Law School. Professor Siegel's writing draws on legal history to explore questions of law and inequality and to analyze how courts interact with representative government and popular movements in interpreting the Constitution.[29] She serves on the board of the American Constitution Society and on the General Council of the International Society of Public Law. She has a BA from Yale College, an MPhil from Yale University, and a JD from Yale Law School.

Susan Sturm

Susan Sturm is the George M. Jaffin Professor of Law and Social Responsibility and the founding director of the Center for Institutional and Social Change at Columbia Law School. She received her BA from Brown University (magna cum laude) and her JD from Yale Law School. Her areas of teaching and research include institutional change, structural inequality in employment and higher education, diversity and innovation, employment discrimination, public law remedies, conflict resolution, and civil procedure. She has published numerous articles, case studies, and books on "the architecture of inclusion," institutional change, transformative leadership, workplace equality, legal education, and inclusion and diversity in higher education.[30] She collaborates with a wide variety of organizations and networks involved in initiatives aimed at increasing full participation, including Syracuse University, Imagining America, Rutgers Future Scholars, Liberal Arts Diversity Officers (LADO), University of Michigan, the American Commonwealth Project, the Reentry Education Network, the Criminal Justice Consortium at Columbia University, the Kirwan Institute, and Harvard Business School. Her research on strategies for facilitating constructive multiracial interaction in police training is featured on the Racetalks website (www.racetalks.org). Professor Sturm was one of the architects of the 2008 national conference

"The Future of Diversity and Opportunity in Higher Education." She is currently cochairing a working group on Transformative Leadership, as part of a Ford Foundation-funded project, Building Knowledge for Social Justice. She is also currently the principal investigator on a Ford Foundation grant awarded to develop the architecture of inclusion in higher education.

Julie Suk

Julie C. Suk is a professor of law at the Benjamin N. Cardozo School of Law–Yeshiva University in New York City, where she teaches comparative law, employment law, and civil procedure. Professor Suk recently served as Chair of the Association of American Law Schools (AALS) Section on Comparative Law and the Section on Employment Discrimination. Before entering law teaching, she clerked for Harry T. Edwards on the U.S. Court of Appeals for the DC Circuit. She obtained an AB summa cum laude from Harvard in English and French literature, a JD from Yale Law School, and a DPhil in Politics from Oxford University, where she was a Marshall Scholar. Professor Suk is a leading scholar of comparative equality law. Her research has developed a transnational perspective on the theory and practice of antidiscrimination law. Professor Suk's articles compare European and American approaches to a broad range of problems, including the stakes of criminal, civil, and administrative enforcement of antidiscrimination norms, the state's role in mitigating work-family conflict, the law of Holocaust denial and hate speech, and constitutional limits on race-consciousness and affirmative action.[31] Her current research examines race and class quotas in Brazil and gender quotas in Europe.

ACKNOWLEDGMENTS

I would like to thank the eminent scholars who provided insight and expertise by accepting to be interviewed and were very supportive during the whole process of publication, including the American translation. I am immensely grateful to Ruth Colker, Frank Dobbin, Chai Feldblum, Richard Ford, Janet Halley, Christine Jolls, Linda Krieger, Martha Minow, David Oppenheimer, Devah Pager, Robert Post, Vicki Schultz, Reva Siegel, Susan Sturm and Julie Suk.

Introduction

Today, *discrimination* is not a popular term: it reflects past, present, and future wrongs. In our postmodern—and, presumably, postracial—society, the concepts that inspire are *equality, liberty, empowerment, capabilities.* Those words make people sit up and listen. But Islamophobia, police brutality, antigay hate crimes, unequal pay, sexual harassment, transgender bias, denial of disability rights, and pregnancy discrimination are also sharing the headlines. This book seeks to provide a comparative transatlantic framework of analysis and revisit the question of discrimination in employment in a pragmatic, critical way. The workplace is a strategic venue for confronting discrimination.[1] The setting of this book is a dialogue between a Franco-American academic and her colleagues from the United States.[2]

As Justice Ginsburg recalled in the *Ricci* case,[3] in cases of discrimination, regardless of the country, "context matters." Today, in and outside of employment, context is often vivid and sometimes tragic. In the United States, multiple issues are being raised. Consider the *Fisher* case on diversity in university admissions,[4] the *Wal-Mart v. Dukes* class action sex-discrimination lawsuit,[5] the *Hobby Lobby* case on religious rights of companies,[6] and the racial quagmire[7] surrounding the deaths[8] of Michael Brown in Ferguson and Eric Gardner in New York.[9] Fifty years after the Civil Rights Act[10] and Martin Luther King's "I Have a Dream" speech, where does the United States stand in tackling and solving issues of discrimination based on different grounds (sex, race, gender, disability, religion, age, etc.)?[11] Is Europe in a better place?

How can we understand France's reaction to the Charlie Hebdo and kosher supermarket assassinations and the kamikaze attacks in Paris, when, at the same time, its government bans the full-face veil[12] and promotes a secular republic? How do second- and third-generation sub-Saharan and North African young men and women cope with a color-blind model of equality by assimilation? On a higher level, European law has strived to reach the goal of antidiscrimination and equality. What can we say about the pattern followed by the law, its implementation, its enforcement and dilemmas in the workplace on the Old Continent? Today is an opportune time to compare the American and European legal frameworks that have shaped the concepts and grounds of discrimination. We now have enough experience on both continents to explore a variety of topics, ranging from the historical and constitutional dimensions of antidiscrimination law to its enforcement by independent bodies, and to critical comments on the specific issues raised by former or current civil rights specialists and policy makers.

Can the law be multidimensional on this issue? Today, the focus of research is on individual biases—often implicit, as Devah Pager demonstrates,[13] but sometimes explicit—with the concept of microaggressions gaining prominence in the workplace[14] and on campuses.[15] Smoking out systemic discrimination in educational institutions, employment, and public policy is also of paramount importance, as Susan Sturm recommends.[16]

In a more global view, should we pursue our struggle for antidiscrimination, or should we privilege human rights law, which can offer a less stigmatizing approach to the problem?[17] Should we be skeptical about "rights talk" in general, as Richard Ford and Janet Halley suggest?[18] Does it always target entrenched economic subordination and follow principles of justice?[19] Is antidiscrimination law efficient?[20] Can we interpret legal norms through the more incisive lens of social psychology, as Linda Krieger explains,[21] or of behavioral economics, as Christine Jolls's work indicates?[22] Does enforcement of antidiscrimination law require a global policy, a powerful public agency? Do advocacy groups transform the debate on equality in unanticipated ways, as Reva Siegel describes?[23] Will promoting the more positive discourse on diversity or the affirmation of liberties make the difference?

Litigation in antidiscrimination law reflects cultural differences on religion and gender in Europe and the United States. The influence of colonization and the welfare state in Europe are reflected in antidiscrimination law and its application. Can French and European case law still learn from American thoughts on the foundations of equality law and its development? Can the United States draw from EU innovative judicial arguments on indirect discrimination? How does the American idea of intersectionality translate into the perception of multiple discrimination in Europe[24]? Can we confront systemic discrimination in a transnational perspective? Academics and legal practitioners in the United Kingdom, Belgium, South Africa, Canada, and Australia are also developing new ways of thinking about discrimination in law.[25]

This book attempts to describe the challenges in antidiscrimination law rooted in respective geographical and technical contexts to brainstorm ideas originating from both sides of the Atlantic.

DISCRIMINATION CHANGES FORM BUT LINGERS ON EACH SIDE OF THE ATLANTIC

Discrimination is about facts. Sometimes, stories of injustice have happy endings in which rights are vindicated:[26] think of Lily Ledbetter, who discovered upon retirement that she had been receiving a lower salary than male colleagues in similar positions with the same career path. The Lily Ledbetter Fair Pay Act, the first law signed by President Obama, provides that the 180-day statute of limitations for filing an equal-pay lawsuit regarding pay discrimination resets with each new paycheck affected by that discriminatory action.[27] Julie Suk argues that antidiscrimination law is not always transformative: it is path dependent and even counterproductive when it focuses only on individual bias.[28]

The nature of discrimination might also have changed, becoming either more subtle or more invidious. It is rare for employers to discriminate overtly in the United States or in France. Discrimination is now either hidden or stems from unconscious bias. Finding evidence of discrimination is therefore more complex. It can also be inconspicuous when it permeates collective practices, such as general testing, dress codes, professional evaluations, and physical examinations, which seem facially neutral but disproportionately exclude women, workers with religious practices, older workers, and others. Moreover, employer evaluations of good job performance can be based on standards that monitor all types of job behavior and reject a more flexible view of "gender performativity."[29]

Discrimination is invidious in new ways when microaggressions create a hostile environment in the workplace and affect the dignity of the employee because of a monolithic view of the status of the worker and the protection of his or her rights. Hostile-environment harassment can produce a collective form of discrimination[30] and, as Vicki Schultz observes, a sex-segregated workforce,[31] even in the absence of the more traditional pressure for sexual favors. Discrimination based on age or disability is of a more technical nature and requires guidelines,[32] and, as Ruth Colker observes, mediation can be preferable to litigation in reasonable accommodation cases in the United States[33] and job reassignment cases in France.

THE STRUCTURAL AND ENVIRONMENTAL CAUSES OF DISCRIMINATION ON EACH SIDE OF THE ATLANTIC

Both Europe and the United States are facing discrimination on different scales. On a micro level, Robert Post explains that some forms of individual bias will always exist,[34] not always related to the core inequalities in the workforce, linked to historical subordination based on race, origin, and gender. On a larger scale, new attempts to combat systemic discrimination are being implemented through similar procedures in France and the United States: territorial affirmative action plans in schools[35] and efforts to balance gender representation on executive boards.[36] Is it possible to detect the personal experience of discrimination and expose its link to a wider practice of exclusion? Events in 2014 and 2015 illustrate that discrimination is rooted in structural and environmental causes linked to the way the State has or has not dealt with "difference" in general, as reflected in policies on immigration, ethnic groups,[37] religion,[38] social security benefits, criminal prosecution, and welfare. We might be at a turning point. Today, models of equality and liberty on both sides of the Atlantic are challenged by a lack of social cohesion[39] and community values[40] in each country and a globalized world where the interpretations of these models can vary. Most often, the need for public order and national security takes precedence over the risks of racial and ethnic profiling.

LAW AMONG OTHER TOOLS TO FACE A CONTINUUM OF INSTITUTIONAL CHANGES

Once the eradication of all discrimination is recognized as a myth, the question is whether to accept that the law cannot always prevent arbitrary decisions from being taken by people who have economic power in employment. Can we promote "inclusive equality" in all institutional settings, from the educational realm to the job market?[41] Critical thought allows us to acknowledge the risk that the prevailing dogma of universal rights, as Richard Ford names them,[42] can also perpetuate certain modes of subordination. Janet Halley has demonstrated that certain modes of subordination simply replace other forms of subordination.[43] Moreover, Martha Minow's "dilemma of difference"[44] between formal and substantive equality will always exist. Either we ignore difference, or we take it into account. The only way out is to focus on the framework in which difference is constructed.[45] It requires a relational view of difference to follow Chai Feldblum's project and subvert the standard norms by which the majority evaluates the minority.[46] In what way can the victims of discrimination strive for active and constructive participation in society rather than only seek remedy? In what way can this recognition touch those who are most often disenfranchised at the intersection of multiple forms of subordination?[47] Law is only one of the tools used against discrimination in the workplace, notwithstanding the various ways companies manage to internalize legal norms, as Frank Dobbin points out.[48] Soft law, often a product of corporate social responsibility in France and the United States, collective bargaining in Europe, and informal networks between employers, colleagues, and clients can also constitute factors of inclusion or exclusion in employment.[49] If equal opportunity as a paradigm prevails, the difficulty will then be to reconcile very different interests in the firm, as Chai Feldblum demonstrates.[50] In France, the issue is also to distinguish individual difference between French citizens over recognition of group membership, seen as a sign of dangerous multiculturalism.

The tensions raised now by the aspiration to equality on both sides of the Atlantic beg the question, why should we compare antidiscrimination law, and why compare at all? The current attraction of our different common law and civil law legal systems to fundamental rights justifies the specific focus on antidiscrimination. This book's particular form, based on inspiring interviews of scholars, brings these issues to life.

WHY COMPARE ANTIDISCRIMINATION LAW?

Antidiscrimination law is worthy of attention as a relatively new field in Europe dealing with fundamental rights in the national and international legal order. The universal nature of equality and antidiscrimination (its companion principle) and the mass of laws and precedents they have inspired have prompted us to reflect, through a comparative perspective, on the actual scope and relevance of these principles and in the specific context of certain countries. What we learn from legal traditions and doctrinal commentary is that although there is no absolute consensus on antidiscrimination law, it is consistently linked to strenuous efforts to regulate the employment market and achieve increased transparency in selection decisions in employment and education.[51] At times, these rules fail to follow the logic of more comprehensive yet segregating systems, such as those specific to welfare states. American scholars also turn a critical eye to the possibilities and limits of this body of law, while France in particular and Europe in general attempt to preserve social rights and promote employment without undermining social cohesion. Everywhere, globalization and its challenges have impacted employment law,[52] regardless of the country's model, and this can be perceived in the writings of American scholars, who have been led to closely examine antidiscrimination law with respect to these global changes, echoed by the International Labour Organization and its 1998 Declaration on Fundamental Principles and Rights at Work.[53] An international doctrine also exists and furthers thought about the various antidiscrimination models in use internationally.[54]

The field of antidiscrimination is also appealing because it encourages the use of a comparative approach to analyze the wealth of positive law while critiquing it.[55] The interviews and observations in the following chapters combine an anthropological vision of antidiscrimination law, in which the person is placed at the center of the constructed system, with an undeniable inclination of these scholars and the author to see law as an instrument of varying effectiveness in a comparative setting. As Gillian Hadfield says: "It may be true that there is an 'untranslatable abyss' between the law of one place and the law of another—just as there is between one person's experience of a strawberry and another's—but this does not mean that we have no business seeking to understand why law here produces this effect and law there produces that effect."[56]

INTERVIEWS WITH AMERICAN SCHOLARS AS A SOURCE OF INSPIRATION FOR VIVID COMPARISONS

An analysis of antidiscrimination law[57] integrating insights drawn from conversations with foreign scholars, mostly law professors, breaks away from the conventional framework of comparative studies.[58] This approach, consisting of dialogues followed by comparative observations, marks a departure from traditional comparative-law exercises[59] relying exclusively on written sources while, at the same time, maintaining some similarities with them.

Generally speaking, comparative law exercises are not accorded the same legitimacy as the comparative methods employed in the observation of international law, despite an increasing interest in the scope of equality in transnational law.[60] In these pages, conversations with American scholars[61] serve as an opportunity to address specific questions about the development of American norms that are stirring debate in European and French law.[62] Since the adoption of Article 19 of the Treaty on the Functioning of the European Union[63] and Directives 2000/78 and 2000/43, antidiscrimination law has experienced an unprecedented expansion in the Member States.[64] Scholars observing American law since the 1960s can share their more distanced views of intertwining notions: equality, antidiscrimination, direct and indirect forms of discrimination, evidence of discrimination, and discrimination grounds.

Another valuable aspect of the book is related to the fact that American scholars do not constitute a uniform group as French doctrine has been considered traditionally. In France, *French doctrine* denotes the "people, the group of authors who write in the area of law" as well as the "opinions of these authors."[65] A "doctrine" is said to be defined as much by what it is not as by what it is, notably, "the opinion generally expressed by those who teach Law, or even those who do not teach, but write about Law. This is where doctrine and jurisprudence diverge."[66] This traditional definition of doctrine conveys the idea of a community of people at a distance from the law, which constitutes their sphere of observation.[67] Any debate tends to focus on the extent to which French doctrine influences law and can be considered a source of law in its own right.[68] Despite their roots in common-law tradition, American academics also exercised a powerful influence at the end of the 19th century.[69] Inspired by Dean Langdell of Harvard Law School,[70] they created "their own exegetical school of law, which professed to deduce abstract principles from the examination of a few carefully selected higher court decisions." They nevertheless turned away from this approach in the 1920s, forming the legal realist movement[71] and "drawing abundantly from the other social sciences, in the exact opposite manner from the French." As a result, their science of law drew closer to the social sciences and even began to resemble "a social science . . . infused with all the others, while dogmatics became no more than a method of legal analysis, competing alongside methods borrowing from anthropology, philosophy, psychology, literature, economics." The consequence of this change was a shift of authority. According to Jamin and Jestaz, American law professors see themselves as academics and "do not claim to form an ensemble which as such has weight over the development of law—but this does not hinder them from exercising influence as individuals. They are intellectuals who reflect on law, as others reflect on economics or sociology."[72] Interviews bring out their different points of view.

Furthermore, interviewing makes it possible to quickly pinpoint difficulties encountered by American courts in applying or interpreting rules and concepts in both constitutional and statutory contexts. Although seldom used in law, this direct source of information and analysis by scholars rapidly puts into perspective the potential trends in European and national law—law, case law, and the positions of scholars and players in the judicial arena in Europe and France.[73] By conversing with outside observers, we can better gauge the amount of resistance or, on the contrary, creativity employed in applying antidiscrimination concepts and proving discrimination in national and European law. The strong influence of case law in discrimination cases debunks the preconceived idea of the need for judicial precedent to grasp the subtleties of complex forms of discrimination, deeply rooted in the assessment of facts.[74]

These conversations simply provide inroads to comparative reflection: the interview excerpts, sorted by theme, are followed by comparisons and some broader questions they raise about national and European law. By forgoing the numbers-based approaches to comparative law currently in vogue—more concerned by the countries in the sample than the quality of the necessary analyses of each country[75]—this book prompts thought on comparative methodology and the functions of comparative law.

Much has been written on the complexity and challenges of comparative law, whose value must be defended again and again.[76] In her notable article on "the subversive function of comparative law," Horatia Muir Watt explains how comparative law can be seen as a critical reading of law in France, while other countries, such as the United States, prefer a critical doctrine that deconstructs law by favoring a more economic or contextual analysis rather than by making international comparisons.[77] Both approaches come into play in these interviews with American scholars, the majority of whom are members of critical movements: foreign scholars share their critical readings of positive law, inspiring equally critical comparisons from an international perspective.[78] Comparing employment antidiscrimination law (whose chief leitmotif is the fight against bias) offers the added benefit of freeing us from the inherent bias involved in analyzing foreign or domestic law. Interviews help to flush out these biases by supplying an immediate response, sensitive to history and context, to written analyses of sources of foreign law.[79] In addition to offering a functional approach,[80] this comparative method eschews the current trend of opposing common law and civil law systems with the aim of demonstrating that one (the system originating in common law) engenders a more efficient economy. In fact, the interviews will reveal that antidiscrimination law, which pervades every system today, is much more complex than this argument, and the leximetric studies promoted by certain international organizations, would have us believe.[81]

More generally, the approach I have taken aligns with comparative studies allowing us to take a step back in our legal analysis and use greater discernment in designing our comparative methodology. However, I wish to point out certain risks associated with this comparison of antidiscrimination law based on conversations with the doctrine. Sometimes this dialogue emphasizes issues of special concern to the American scholars being interviewed that are not closely relevant to European judicial debate and vice versa. Professor Pierre Legrand tells us that "comparing means being willing to bring out differences"[82] and that the comparative method is based only on a subjective perception of differences.[83] I have indeed made a point of following these comparative interviews with my own personal observations: they refine and tap into foreign ideas and analyses from a French and a European point of view. Without these observations, we might have been left with a mere presentation of American doctrinal commentary and analogies with how equivalent notions are interpreted in Europe, without shedding any light on fundamental differences in our legal, social, and cultural systems. Although similarities may be drawn between certain notions from either side of the Atlantic, it is not my purpose to reignite the debate over the circulation of ideas or the transplantation of legal mechanisms or systems.[84]

This comparative method is also a valuable learning opportunity. It shows how American scholars repeatedly draw inspiration from interdisciplinary thinking to illuminate their ideas, the scope of law, and its underpinnings. Using this approach, equally well-suited to comparative law,[85] we discover that antidiscrimination law enforcement cannot overlook economic, cultural, sociological, and historical factors and how they are changing, since they contribute to the construction or negation of a person's identity with respect to the principles of equality and antidiscrimination in each country.

As I explained in the preface, this book draws from a careful selection of interviews of fascinating scholars, professors in law or sociology. This book is essentially about the meaning of antidiscrimination, the grounds of discrimination, and the diversity of critiques of fundamental rights in employment in light of comparative, international, and constitutional law. These amazing scholars have covered a wide spectrum of dilemmas posed by the equality paradigm in France and Europe.

1

History of Antidiscrimination Law
The Constitution and the Search for Paradigms of Equality

Was the Constitution and its interpretation the driving influence and inspiration of antidiscrimination law? In the conversations that follow, American scholars help to deepen our understanding of the climate that produced antidiscrimination law in the United States, evoking the political and social events that shaped its uneven construction, sometimes advancing, sometimes resisting its development, and providing a cultural lens through which to understand the expansion of this law in Europe.

I. THE ORIGINS OF ANTIDISCRIMINATION LAW

The constitutional interpretation of the U.S. Supreme Court has played a pivotal role in the civil rights movement, hastening the country toward the Civil War with the landmark *Dred Scott* decision in 1857,[1] then legitimizing racial segregation laws with its "separate but equal" decision in 1896,[2] before finally introducing a more practical way to deal with inequality and paving the way for antidiscrimination protection[3] with the *Brown v. Board of Education* decision in 1954.[4] American activist organizations have also spurred antidiscrimination initiatives forward, while support from the Equal Employment Opportunity Commission (EEOC) and trade unions has been irregular, sometimes promoting but sometimes hindering the expansion of antidiscrimination law.

In Europe, the recognition of discrimination emerged from a different background, but lessons learned from the American experience can enrich the current debate in Europe over the role of the French equivalent of the EEOC, the Defender of Rights[5] (formerly HALDE), and what employee representative bodies and trade unions should be doing to manage diversity. With the introduction of a new form of judicial review in France (called *question prioritaire de constitutionnalité*) enabling individuals to challenge laws that infringe their constitutional rights, as well as recent European case law on fundamental rights, the opportunity is ripe for a closer American analysis on the influence of constitutional jurisprudence on antidiscrimination law. This question is essential for European authorities, such as the European Union (EU) and the Council of Europe, who are developing and interpreting fundamental human rights norms and do not always know how much deference European judges must show in considering national views on the meaning of equality: what are the pros and cons of imposing this fundamental right in international law? Should they be aware of certain limitations to the application of constitutional norms and nondiscrimination as a fundamental right?

In the following excerpt, David Oppenheimer talks about the development of constitutional case law on nondiscrimination.

MARIE MERCAT-BRUNS: *Do you think employment discrimination law has succeeded in its goals?*

DAVID OPPENHEIMER: To a substantial extent, I think it has, although not nearly to the extent many of us had hoped for in the 1960s and 1970s. The view of most legal academics and most lawyers who represent plaintiffs in discrimination cases is that the law has failed. And I think in reaching that conclusion, my colleagues and friends have seen the glass as half empty. I look at that same glass, and I see it as half full.

There's much yet to be accomplished, and I worry about whether it will be accomplished, particularly given this Supreme Court. But at the same time, I think the law has accomplished a great deal in transforming our society. There have really been two transformations: a transformation through antidiscrimination and a transformation through diversity.

I'll develop on antidiscrimination transformation. I think that between 1964, when the Civil Rights Act was passed,[6] and 1978, when the *Bakke* decision was handed down,[7] there was an enormous change in the views of the American public with regard to discrimination and antidiscrimination law and the rights of minorities. If you go back into the 1950s, when the civil rights movement was becoming an important force in the United States, leading up to the 1964 Civil Rights Act, there was enormous white resistance, some by those who simply believed in white supremacy and some by those who held strong biases. There was a significant group who believed in white supremacy, especially in the southern United States. And there was a very substantial group who may have espoused a belief in equality but didn't really believe that black Americans were equal to whites in terms of intelligence or honesty or morals or ethics or loyalty or patriotism, who held very strong prejudices against black Americans.

By 1978, there had been a real transformation in American culture. Public expressions of racism were generally not tolerated in most parts of white society. Prejudice was still very strong but it was diminished, and it was probably far more subconscious or unconscious prejudice than conscious. You began to see a big difference in polling results between questions that asked explicitly about antiblack views and questions that more creatively uncovered those views.

In 1954, there was little white support for civil rights legislation. By 1964, there was support but there was also opposition. By 1978, most white Americans at least said that they thought there should be antidiscrimination legislation. There was still a significant minority who were just outright bigots. But they were much less important in American culture at that point.

The case law, Supreme Court case law in particular, between 1964 and 1978 for the most part recognized the problem of discrimination against black Americans as a serious problem for which legal remedies were necessary, and you see it in cases like *Green, Griggs,* and *Weber*.[8] You see support for a theory of adverse impact discrimination, often called in Europe "indirect discrimination." You see it in support for shifting the burden to the employer to prove nondiscrimination, which exists in Europe and has essentially disappeared in the United States. You see it in support for voluntary affirmative action[9] as a remedy for discrimination.[10] All of that starts to change in the late 1970s and, in some ways, that change is a terrible defeat for those of us who want to enforce civil rights law and those of us who want to promote racial equality.

But there is at least to some extent an explanation of that change as a reflection of transformation having worked, having happened, and the Court wanting to move on because it views the civil rights revolution as a success.

MM-B: *Do you use the term* revolution *voluntarily?*

DO: Yes. It was a revolution, a cultural revolution and a legal revolution in the United States. Not a revolution in the sense of overthrowing the state but a revolution in the sense of changing the state in a very fundamental way, changing the society in a fundamental way.

But you don't have to be very cynical to see the changes that have more recently occurred in the Supreme Court's jurisprudence as reflecting the success of a conservative ideology that was essentially anti–civil rights. It continues to be more and more anti–civil rights to this day.

MM-B: *All the judges?*

DO: No, but a majority of the judges. One of the things that is interesting about following civil rights law and the Supreme Court is that sometimes we are looking at the question of whether Congress or the executive operated with sufficient authority, and other times we are looking at whether the states in their antidiscrimination legislation have acted with proper authority.

The Court's majority asserts that the underlying principles that drive its jurisprudence really concern states' rights, and often the rhetoric focuses on states' rights. But when we look at the outcome of a civil rights case, what we find is that whatever the underlying principles are, the conservative judges who generally claim they believe in deferring to the states are ready to change their rhetoric in order to find that the state had exceeded its constitutional authority if the state passes antidiscrimination legislation.

MM-B: *So they base their reasoning more on the authority of state and federal rights rather than looking in depth at the question of discrimination that's at hand?*

DO: That's what you would expect if the court was not result-oriented and was acting on principle, but instead I can usually predict at least eight votes out of nine based on who wins and who loses: there are four members of the court, and often a fifth, who almost always will vote to oppose any expansion of civil rights for black Americans.

MM-B: *Are you saying that it is hard to evaluate the recent effects of the civil rights legislation because there has been a more conservative Court, that its impact has been skewed as a result? Perhaps you can't really answer that question because the outcome of the law has been hindered by the Court.*

DO: One, and I will come back to this: in 1978, we started moving in a whole new direction because of the diversity justification for civil rights law.

MM-B: *So this will be your second point: transformation through diversity.*

DO: Yes. Continuing with the first point a little longer—

MM-B: *The question was whether the Court is interpreting the laws restrictively, and you said there had been progress.*

DO: Yes, there has been essentially an ongoing dispute between the Congress and the Court, in which the Congress writes a civil rights law, and the Court interprets it narrowly, saying the Congress could not have intended a broad interpretation despite the fact that often the administrative interpretations suggest a broad interpretation. Then Congress says, "We really meant it," and the Court says, "Well, no, you didn't." And so we continue to see legislation on behalf of the expansion of civil rights and on behalf of the enforcement of civil rights.

This raises for me the fundamental question about motivation. Take the issue of color blindness; color blindness goes right to the heart of the problem. Color blindness is the idea that any action by the state which recognizes race is illegitimate, even when the intent is to use race to reduce racial inequality. There are four or five members of the Court who always have the same position (a very French position) that any recognition of race by the state is illegitimate: they are Justices Thomas, Scalia, Roberts, Alito, and sometimes Kennedy.

There are four, and sometimes five, members of the Court who believe that it is proper for the state to recognize race (that is, to be conscious of race and to act on behalf of race) under certain limited circumstances, which are narrowly construed to support a compelling legitimate government purpose: this is true of Justices Ginsburg, Breyer, Souter, and Stevens. It is likely to be true of Justice Sotomayor (though it is always dangerous to predict) and is sometimes true of Justice Kennedy. (And, editing in 2014, it is true of Justice Kagan. —DO)

Do the four who have this absolutist view on color blindness take that position because they believe as a matter of principle in color blindness? Do they believe that this would help promote a better society and would help promote equality in our society? That is what they say. Should they be taken at their word? Or are they laughing behind our backs? Is it the excuse they use to vote against opportunities, progress, and equality for black Americans, because they do not share the goal of equality?

MM-B: *What do you think?*

DO: The polite answer to that question is of course they act on principle.

MM-B: *So they have a large responsibility in the status quo.*

DO: I think they have an enormous responsibility, and I am suspicious of their claim to believe in equality, but a form of equality built on color blindness.

Let me give you two examples of judges who believed in color blindness and therefore were opposed to affirmative action, where I believe they were expressing a principle they really believed in, rather than being strategic and pragmatic.

William O. Douglas was on the Supreme Court for forty years. He took courageous positions on the Supreme Court in support of civil rights. But he did believe in color blindness. In the *Defunis* case,[11] he took a position against affirmative action, even though that meant joining the conservatives with whom he usually disagreed on civil rights issues, because it was consistent with the principles he believed in.

Stanley Mosk served as the attorney general of California and then for many years on the California Supreme Court. He was a great liberal but strongly opposed to affirmative action. It conflicted with his long-expressed views that the Constitution and the law should be color-blind.

I did not doubt their commitment to color blindness, even though I disagreed with them.

But there is no reason to conclude that the conservatives on this Court are acting based on a principle of support for equality, but through color blindness. They have never supported efforts to provide opportunity and equality for black Americans. That leads me to believe their opposition to affirmative action and other civil rights remedies and other civil rights claims is not based on a position of favoring equality for black Americans.

MM-B: *Did you want to show how diversity transforms?*

DO: Sure. The diversity transformation is the second transformation and involves race, religion, and culture.

This was the most remarkable result of Justice Powell's opinion in *Bakke*,[12] which was joined by four justices in one part of his opinion and joined by the other four justices in the other part. Therefore five votes on one part and five votes on the other. So, on the one hand, the Court held that remedial affirmative action is subject to strict scrutiny,[13] and is highly suspicious because it is a race-based decision being made by the government. As a result, racial quotas in admissions violate the Constitution. But on the other hand, when a university decides that it wants to use race, among other factors, to admit a diverse group of students, this use of race is permissible under the Constitution. So, a university's desire for racial diversity justifies affirmative action.

Before 1977, the principal justification for affirmative action was as a remedy for discrimination. But after *Bakke*, in 1978, we see this shift in American law and society, so the primary justification for affirmative action, and eventually all kinds of civil rights enforcement and remedies, is diversity. That's been the second transformation of American society coming out of the civil rights era: the embracing of diversity, including racial diversity, including cultural diversity, including religious diversity. It is a fundamental change.

When I was growing up in the 1950s and 1960s, the prevailing view on how different kinds of Americans should join together was a model of assimilation. Today the prevailing view is celebrating our differences by embracing diversity. It is a remarkable change. Much of that change came out of the Harvard admissions plan embraced by Justice Powell in the *Bakke* decision. People just turned to that and said, "Wow, here is a justification in which there is no guilt, in which there is no accusation of racism, in which there is no history, so we can completely look forward and say, 'Yes! we want diversity.'"

MM-B: *So you agree with the analysis that the argumentation for diversity since* Bakke *has been to look to the future, whereas the previous logic was to remedy past discrimination?*

DO: There was a fundamental shift from figuring out who did something wrong, and therefore there is compensation for their wrongful act, to seeking diversity. Before *Bakke*, an attempt to engage in affirmative action required an analysis of guilt and remedy and compensation and wrongdoing. It was all looking backwards.

So this shift meant people could stop looking backwards and look forwards towards diversity. And this was a new kind of diversity, an idea of diversity not as simply difference in hobbies or geography or interests, but suddenly race and ethnicity become legitimate forms of identity to be included within a policy favoring diversity. That was transformative and continues to be the driving force behind many of the positive actions taken in the United States to reduce racial inequality.[14]

Comparative Perspectives

In his historical panorama, Oppenheimer describes a certain pattern of Supreme Court decisions, in which the Court's positioning has alternately embraced or rejected more advanced reflection on discrimination. But no matter which way the majority leaned, the Court's action has been decisive in shaping equality and diversity principles and in the interpretation of more specific legislation on these matters, providing a useful lens through which to examine how these concepts were formed in France and Europe and their different trajectories.

In Oppenheimer's view, constitutional case law—that is, the constitutional law decisions of the Supreme Court and its interpretation of the constitution—has helped to establish important milestones for equality and eventually led to the introduction of the concept of diversity. Despite mixed results, in this contribution, Oppenheimer sees a gradual improvement in attitudes toward racial diversity.

In the United States, the Supreme Court justices attempted to establish the idea of diversity as a legal concept: the notion of diversity emerged from a constitutional review of equality in a race discrimination case, outside the realm of employment. In contrast, France's approach to diversity is more recent and does not seem to have originated in a judicial understanding of the issue:[15] it is "not so much a critique of the affirmative action model as a critique of a formal equality model that long remained 'blind' to the inequalities and discriminations it engendered."[16]

What the French achieved, in addition to the enactment of a French law on equal opportunities *(loi sur l'égalité des chances)*,[17] was to bring the issue into the collective bargaining arena. In France, the general provisions of the labor code are supplemented by the provisions of the applicable collective bargaining agreement, which is different for each sector or industry. In this highly context-dependent environment, the reigning uncertainty has less to do with legal ambiguities than with the interpretation of diversity, which is invoked without any clear definition of what it covers.[18]

Since 2010, France has had a new power of judicial review.[19] Has France's Conseil Constitutionnel (Constitutional Council) taken advantage of this new clout to fill in the blanks between diversity and equality? France can now expand its case law, implementing a more proactive idea of substantive equality and thereby address inequalities engendered by the application of the law. The judiciary has shown a relatively high degree of deference to legislation, even though laws based on the principle of equality are frequently subjected to a judicial review.[20] To date, the Conseil Constitutionnel has adhered to the clear-cut but relatively prudent approach to equality originally drawn from decisions of the Conseil d'État, France's administrative supreme court, which selects, with the Cour de Cassation, the cases for judicial review.[21] It seems rather that judicial review has reinforced the French supreme courts' (Conseil d'État, Cour de Cassation) power rather than the Conseil Constitutionnel's sphere of influence in matters of equality. Compared to other constitutional courts or councils, the Conseil Constitutionnel exercises greater self-restraint, limiting its scrutiny of the legal norm to an appreciation of its internal coherence: differences of treatment should reflect objective differences of situation which are directly and sufficiently related to the pursuit of the law.[22]

In the United States, shortcomings in governmental efforts to battle discrimination in the employment field have prompted corporate human resources departments to devise their own strategies aiming to promote diversity and value differences regardless of origin.[23] In France, the campaign to root out discrimination is gaining momentum while, at the same time, diversity talk is expanding. These two policies on antidiscrimination and diversity and the legal instruments used do not interrelate in any systematic, organized fashion. In fact, they sometimes clash, although Oppenheimer shows us how the diversity narrative can be a driving force. Is there a risk that these competing norms in France will create an obstacle to the fight against discrimination (the problem with measuring diversity), as it did in the United States? The fact that European antidiscrimination law exists and continues to grow, combined with the availability of collective bargaining, seem to suggest that diversity and antidiscrimination norms will either complement each other or continue along parallel paths without intersecting or reinforcing each other.[24] Antidiscrimination law, based on evidence and judiciary review, is more operational, while diversity is associated with discourse and stated objectives. This distinction is clearly illustrated in European reports on the search for social cohesion, diversity, and equal opportunities for all.[25]

Affirmative action tools in French law are even proliferating: a constitutional revision has enabled specific mechanisms such as quotas for women board members, first in listed companies, to be introduced into French law, although the purview of these tools must be nuanced.[26] The 2013 law on higher education has adopted a new affirmative action plan, resembling the Texas and California percentage plans, in which a certain percentage of the top-performing high school students earn admission to preparatory programs enabling them to access selective higher education establishments (this includes France's elite *"grandes écoles,"* which represent a much more exclusive track than the French university system).[27]

It is interesting to note that the affirmative action issue has permeated the realm of education as well as employment, simultaneously influencing these two spheres in the United States.

II. MORE ON THE ORIGINS OF ANTIDISCRIMINATION LAW

In our conversation, Linda Krieger commented on the Supreme Court's current position on the use of affirmative action and expressed her apprehension about key Supreme Court decisions to come.

LINDA KRIEGER: In the United States, people today are not talking about affirmative action for anyone because of the current Supreme Court. Everyone I know who is on the employee-women-and-minorities side of the civil rights movement is dreading the next Supreme Court affirmative action case. I think if the current Supreme Court were to get a case involving a preferential form of affirmative action in the employment context, it would overrule all the previous cases permitting affirmative action in certain circumstances and find it violative of Title VII, and if it is a public employer, violative of the Fourteenth Amendment. The swing vote is Justice Kennedy. Justice Kennedy has never voted in favor of an affirmative action program in any case he's ever sat, including when he was in the Ninth Circuit. I think we would have a majority of five justices on any case concerning a preferential form of affirmative action.[28]

As Krieger suggests, the United States is currently moving in the opposite direction from France. The promotion of diversity in the United States has confirmed the unconstitutionality of numerical quotas, found to be incompatible with equal protection of the laws in the *Bakke, Grutter,* and *Parents Involved* decisions on school and university admissions policies.[29] Some states have decided that affirmative action plans based on race are unconstitutional. This is why indirect affirmative action mechanisms, such as the percentage plans used in Texas and California, have been introduced into the field of education.[30] These plans take a geographic approach to diversity. In France, the Sciences Po law school attempted a similar approach, later taken by the previously mentioned 2013 law on access to selective higher education, basing preferential treatment on academic ranking.

These subtler initiatives remain under rigorous scrutiny by the Supreme Court if the programs use race as a factor after having applied the percentage plan. In *Fisher v. University of Texas at Austin,* Fisher did not graduate in the top 10 percent of her high school but could still be admitted to the university by scoring high in a process evaluating applicants' "talents, leadership qualities, family circumstances and race." She was denied admission and filed suit against the university, alleging discrimination on the basis of race in violation of her Fourteenth Amendment right to equal protection. Writing for the majority, Justice Kennedy concluded that the lower court had failed to apply strict scrutiny in its decision affirming the admissions policy: "The Fifth Circuit held petitioner could challenge only whether the University's decision to use race as an admissions factor 'was made in good faith.' It presumed that the school had acted in good faith and gave petitioner the burden of rebutting that presumption." In his argument, Kennedy affirmed the *Grutter v. Bollinger* ruling, placing the burden of persuasion primarily with the university "to prove that its admissions program is narrowly tailored to obtain the educational benefits of diversity."

Reva Siegel recounts the 2012 Supreme Court term and shows us how minority claims in other fields of law are not successful.[31] Recent Supreme Court cases failed to "[address] minority claims of racial profiling in enforcement of criminal and immigration law,"[32] shaping "the Court's unprecedented decision to strike down a key provision of the Voting Rights Act of 1965 in *Shelby County v. Holder.*[33] *Shelby County* interprets equality law with solicitude for Americans who claim they have been injured by laws that protect the rights and opportunities of minorities."[34]

Adding to this historical overview by Oppenheimer and Krieger, Robert Post comments on the foundations of antidiscrimination law.

MARIE MERCAT-BRUNS: *Do you agree with the statement that the basic foundations of antidiscrimination law are in tort, but discrimination law has been inspired by constitutional grounds? How powerful has the constitutional influence on antidiscrimination law been as opposed to the impact of tort law?*

ROBERT POST: The Constitution of the United States requires state action so that a private person, including an employer, cannot violate the Constitution. So the constitutional influence on antidiscrimination law comes up with state action. It is a very powerful norm because courts are quasi-sovereign. To put that sovereignty on the basis of that norm is an extremely powerful statement of national ideals and values.

And this spreads horizontally into the private sphere. It causes the rest of the society to be much more aware of these issues and to want more directives. I think this is a causal matter; the fact that we looked at the state, which is supposed to be supremely neutral, led people to think about the relationship between race and private action and led to legislation. These are complementary. It is not either-or. The Supreme Court has been in retreat on questions of constitutional requirements for antidiscrimination even though the Congress has persistently defended antidiscrimination law. We have some disparities there.

I think people in the United States feel more comfortable making statutes and then revising them. The constitutional matter will be much less likely to be on structural redistribution and structural changes because it's constitutional, so it is taking it away from the legislator. We are more cautious in that area and more cautious to things being taken over by social scientists and their statistics, and we are more comfortable allowing a statutory case of antidiscrimination to be determined by statistics because, in the end, if we don't like that, we can change, whereas constitutional change is harder.

There is an inherent tendency to make constitutional law general, and there is more of an opportunity to make statutory law impact-oriented. Even there, there has been in retreat in the courts.

MM-B: *So what you are saying is that you go farther with the statute: in terms of the symbol, it is very important that you have a constitutional principle.*

RP: Exactly. The symbol is acutely powerful because it stands for the national values. And we argue about that symbol that brings us together in a way the statute doesn't.

Comparative Perspectives

Post points out that constitutional jurisprudence has had, and continues to have, strong symbolic value in the area of discrimination and equality. In the United States, constitutional case law has acted as a catalyst by recognizing the merits of substantive equality,[35] affirmative action, and attempts to promote diversity, while possibly inhibiting the scope of indirect discrimination claims.[36] As a result, the net effect of constitutional case law has not necessarily been favorable to expanding antidiscrimination law. The Supreme Court has been a beacon in many cases, enshrining certain key interpretations of law relating to discrimination or equality, but currently, as Krieger notes, the Court is restricting the development of law in this field.

In comparison, what has been the influence of the formal recognition of equality and nondiscrimination as a fundamental norm in European and national law?[37] Although European courts had to contend with the issue of existing German case law on fundamental rights,[38] it can be said that the idea of nondiscrimination and equal treatment as fundamental rights[39] in European law became more legitimate in France once a review mechanism was actually used for the application of European norms in national law, through the process of preliminary rulings. "The expression 'fundamental rights' is more commonly used by the European Union:[40] the Court of Justice prefers to speak of 'fundamental rights and freedoms' rather than 'human rights' and this vocabulary can also be found in Article 6(2) of the EU Treaty."[41] The use of the term *fundamental rights* makes it possible to extend human rights from physical persons to legal persons, notably companies.[42]

In addition, the scope of these rights is surely being amplified by the cross-fertilization occurring between the Court of Justice of the European Union (CJEU) and the European Court of Human Rights (ECtHR), in their roles of interpreting the fundamental rights of the European Union and the rights set out in the European Convention on Human Rights, respectively. The Strasbourg court [ECtHR] refers increasingly often to the Charter of Fundamental Rights,[43] and the Luxembourg court (CJEU) is traditionally receptive to the influence of the ECtHR, even though the CJEU has recently proposed certain adjustments for the accession of the EU to the European Convention for the Protection of Human Rights and Fundamental Freedoms.[44] The path opened by nondiscrimination or the principle of equal treatment is influential, because it is increasingly used by both courts, which not only employ the same concepts of direct and indirect discrimination, but also apply similar forms of scrutiny: they look for objective justification of a difference in treatment in laws or decisions, as applicable, and also perform the proportionality test required to qualify a difference as indirect discrimination.[45]

In other words, in their approach to nondiscrimination and equal treatment, the ECtHR and the CJEU generally favor either a human rights perspective or an economic perspective. The ECtHR's case law can be rather unpredictable in terms of substantive equality, depending on whether it takes into account the state's margin of appreciation.[46] However, with the formal recognition of the fundamental principles of equal treatment and of antidiscrimination based on age, the CJEU appears to be heading in the opposite direction from the United States. Empowered by the recently binding character of the EU Charter of Fundamental Rights, which is an integral part of the EU treaties since Lisbon,[47] the CJEU is journeying toward a consolidation of the normative legitimacy of antidiscrimination law at the highest level.[48]

Even if Article 14 of the European Convention on Human Rights pertaining to nondiscrimination cannot be invoked alone and Protocol No. 12 to the Convention has not yet proven its efficacy, the EU Charter of Fundamental Rights cites some of the same grounds in its list of prohibited grounds (sex, race, color, language, religion, political or other opinion, national or social origin, association with a national minority, property, birth or other status), showing that economic considerations are no longer the main rationale for fighting discrimination believed to obstruct the market. Furthermore, a diverse legal culture among judges on the ECtHR is helping the recognition of certain problematic concepts such as indirect discrimination, a typically Western notion unfamiliar to the courts in Eastern European countries.[49]

Post confirms the influence of Supreme Court case law due to the symbolic power of the Constitution and to the role of constitutional review in the development of law in general. Can a parallel be drawn with EU case law and its influence in protecting the fundamental rights of member-state citizens?[50] If this reasoning is followed, the fundamental right to equal treatment becomes a defining characteristic of European citizenship.[51] The second part of the Treaty of Lisbon is entitled "Nondiscrimination and Citizenship of the Union."[52] Doesn't the Treaty therefore advance social progress by establishing fundamental rights as the European Union's primary driver of consolidation, notably by incorporating the EU Charter of Fundamental Rights into its body of treaties? The charter plays a role that goes beyond the symbolic value of its enunciation of principles.[53] European judges ensure the interpretation of these principles and have the power to disapply inconsistent norms with horizontal direct effect on national private law.[54]

Yet equal treatment and antidiscrimination are not necessarily the bricks and mortar of a European social model,[55] since the application of these principles does not always lead to the recognition of substantive rights. In fact, the opposite can be true.[56] But sometimes the need to ensure the effectiveness of directives and principles is enough to overcome national resistance to new concepts, such as broader meanings of parenthood and couples.[57] A preliminary ruling from the CJEU even recognized that a French collective bargaining agreement reserving access to employment benefits exclusively to married couples constituted direct discrimination against same-sex couples based on sexual orientation.[58] This decision was handed down before the French law on same-sex marriage was adopted.[59] By effectively fighting indirect discrimination and enforcing equal pay, Europe is improving real access to certain employment rights. If we accept that the components of contemporary European citizenship are, as Richard Bellamy asserts, "membership of a democratic political community, the collective benefits and rights associated with membership, and participation in the community's political, economic and social processes,"[60] then the recognition of equal pay for men and women nevertheless enabled the acquisition of substantive rights.[61]

In the United States, Supreme Court judges have often implied that it is not their role to support a certain model of economic or social policy.[62] Some scholars ascribe an even greater purpose to Europe's fundamental values, considering that a fully fledged "European social program" underlies the Treaty of Lisbon, as seen in its "high social ambitions" and commitment to "human dignity [and] solidarity," the fact that it makes the well-being of the European people one of the Union's aims, and the affirmation in the Charter of Fundamental Rights that the Union "places the individual at the heart of its activities."[63]

For some, branding European principles as "values" serves an ideological function. However, this is potentially undesirable because it portrays the founding principles of the Treaty of Lisbon as "an expression of the ethical convictions of EU citizens" built on "sociological" and "paternalistic" assumptions, instead of focusing on the constitutional dimension of these principles.[64]

At the national level, we can question whether the introduction of a form of judicial review in France (*question prioritaire de constitutionnalité* [QPC]) will shape the path of employment equality case law, as it has in the United States. According to certain scholars, the existence of a posteriori constitutional review is not necessarily synonymous with an enriched body of equality case law. "It will all depend on the level of scrutiny exercised by appeal courts on the seriousness of the grievances, as well as the level of scrutiny to be exercised by the Conseil Constitutionnel on the legislative work."[65] The decision on the full-face veil already reflects the judicial stance on equality and religion in the public sphere, which has been echoed by the high court in the employment sector concerning the head veil.[66] This case law on the principle of equality has followed that of the Conseil d'État (the French administrative supreme court), which often leads to two types of review: a review of the legitimacy of the legislature's infringement of the principle of equality, by identifying differences in circumstances and ways of thinking that led the legislature to treat people in potentially comparable situations differently, and a proportionality test that does not always go by that name.[67]

The Conseil Constitutionnel has "discretionary power in assessing the fit between the aim and the measures implemented by the law, without necessarily examining, however, whether the aim assigned to the legislature could be achieved by other means," but in the past it has not hesitated to "shift the focus of its scrutiny as desired" and "point out a manifest error of assessment or a disproportionate error committed by the legislature,"[68] especially where an infringement of freedom is involved. But QPC, France's judicial review mechanism, can be useful by bringing proportionality testing to the table. The Council is often cautious, stating that "the principle of equal treatment is not opposed to the legislature ruling differently in different situations nor with a departure from equality in order to serve the general interest, provided that, in both cases, the resulting difference in treatment remains directly proportionate to the purpose of the law from which it originates."[69] "The Conseil adjusts the level of its scrutiny" of equality based on the matters under consideration: "greater for civil and political rights and . . . more relaxed for economic and social rights,"[70] upon which employment rights partly depend.[71] Through QPC, the Conseil has nevertheless affirmed, on the issue of retirement pensions paid to Algerian nationals, that "although the legislature can base a difference of treatment on the place of residence, taking into account differences in purchasing power, it cannot establish, with respect to the purpose of the statute, any difference based on nationality between holders of civil or military pensions paid from the budget of the State or of public institutions of the State and residing in the same foreign country."[72] The Conseil ruled in the same direction regarding different pension amounts based on the beneficiary's level of disability.[73]

Since the introduction of QPC, the trajectory of equality case law to date has not yet been significantly altered,[74] and will also be influenced by the screening work of the Cour de cassation, France's supreme court, which has a chamber for employment and labor law.[75] For now, the Conseil continues to exhibit a certain deference to the legislature when the equality issue depends on a certain political maturity, as illustrated by the decision on same-sex marriage,[76] or on a clear orientation of more global social policy reforms, as shown in the QPC decision on the constitutionality of a mandatory retirement age.[77] This reasoning is reminiscent of certain conservative positions of the U.S. Supreme Court, in which the Court took into account the societal issues at play to determine how the equality principle or questions about freedoms would impact the equality of American citizens.[78]

American case law does not apply a proportionality test as such, however, preferring to balance the interests of different groups with federal or state interests in assessing equality.[79] However, for its a posteriori constitutionality reviews of the principle of equality, France can draw inspiration from the proportionality test already used by various courts to determine equal treatment:[80] the CJEU, the Conseil d'État, and even the Cour de Cassation[81] use proportionality to assess the equality principle, the antidiscrimination principle, and numerous legal exceptions, respectively, which must show that they have a legitimate purpose and are proportional to that aim or fall into the category of prohibited discrimination on the basis of age or disability.[82] Proportionality is probably less of a cure-all when used to secure legitimacy for a judicial interpretation or policy orientation than to clearly delineate a principle.[83] But the other prong of the necessity-and-proportionality test, consisting of the search for a less restrictive alternative, can prove to be rewarding, by showing lawmakers the concrete, context-related options that are available to them to differentiate among people.

The proliferation of rulings on the scope of equality arising from different judicial systems makes it necessary to determine a hierarchy: France's organic law of December 10, 2009, gives priority to the QPC decision if a complaint for incompatibility with the convention is submitted at the same time,[84] but the order of authority between the CJEU and the Conseil Constitutionnel is not so clearly defined.[85]

Put simply, should we be comforted or concerned that when applying EU interpretations of community norms and the constitutional principle of equality, national judges may sometimes implicitly incorporate political and separation of powers issues into their determination of equality or nondiscrimination? These judges must also endeavor, in each individual case, to balance the protection of individual and group rights by applying a proportionality test to certain internal social policies considered to be critical, such as retirement and employment. Due to these internal tensions, this jurisprudence does not necessarily contribute in a harmonious manner to the consolidation of European fundamental rights or reinforce the legitimacy of building a coherent European social policy on nondiscrimination.[86]

The same cautiousness regarding the need for high-level constitutional review of nondiscrimination and equality can also be found in the United States, in the assessment of the effectiveness of constitutional norms in a social context. American scholars temper the idea that the influence of constitutional norms in America has been essential in antidiscrimination law. They critique the role of these fundamental rules as a catalyst of social progress, even when they are enshrined in legislation and extensively interpreted by judges.

III. THE LIMITATIONS OF FUNDAMENTAL RIGHTS

Richard Ford, Julie Suk, and Janet Halley clarify certain critiques regarding the application of fundamental rights in the United States contained in the Constitution and implemented in law.

Richard Ford is a Stanford law professor and an expert on civil rights and antidiscrimination law. He has authored an extensive body of legal scholarship on race and social criticism.

RICHARD FORD: Does antidiscrimination law allow the vindication of lofty abstract rights? Many people would say that the Civil Rights Act is a constitutional statute. So there is a tendency to focus a lot on courts applying big principles. But I think that practically speaking on the ground, it is really an administrative remedy and most of the work is getting done by trial courts and by administrative agencies like the EEOC and in settlements. For example, management and HR offices will say, "That is sexual harassment; you need to stop that or you are fired" even if the harassment is not unlawful under Title VII.

MARIE MERCAT-BRUNS: *So are you minimizing the significance of constitutional case law in the construction of antidiscrimination law?*

RF: Yes. I would not say it hasn't any significance. I would say that I am pushing back from the tendency of most American lawyers to look at it primarily in terms of vindication of constitutional rights.

But to be sure, the fact that it is widely understood as a statute vindicating quasi-constitutional rights—that matters. It gives it additional weight. It does affect the way the courts interpret the law.

MM-B: *These statutes are therefore seen as fundamental rights? In European case law, there is a rather specific idea of what a fundamental right is.*

RF: Title VII is not seen as a fundamental right. You have fundamental rights in the Constitution, but that is different.

MM-B: *But equality is a fundamental right?*

RF: But that is equality under the Fourteenth Amendment. Formally speaking, that is a different jurisprudence.

MM-B: *It is just the parties that are different; one, the states, and one, private parties. That is all.*

RF: That is a big distinction. It remains the case that if constitutional lawyers talk about fundamental rights, they would include rights under the Fourteenth Amendment but not under Title VII.

MM-B: *But you are looking at the same mechanism, a difference of treatment. They are just seen through a different light?*

RF: Yes, they are seen through a very different light. In the American jurisprudential tradition and constitutional tradition, your rights against the state and state action are very different from your rights against private actors.

We think that on the one hand, the state, with its monopoly of coercive power, must be held to a higher standard than the private sector, where the argument is made that if you do not like it, you can find a different job. It is a market.

MM-B: *In France, it is almost the opposite. We have an administrative supreme court, the Conseil d'État. When there is a public interest (intérêt général), the state has some power, and it instigates some deference.*

We also have formal equality in France. This is a different jurisprudence. It plays a significant role, and it is rather strictly interpreted.

In the private sector, things are different. The individual contract is often considered inherently unequal because of unequal parties. It is therefore important to compensate for this inequality. There is a presumption that the employer might be wrong in the absence of convincing evidence from the parties. This presumption is implicitly justified by the employer's position of power, and it affects the rules of evidence. If the judge is not convinced by either party, the "doubt benefits the employee" and in that case, he or she prevails. This benefit of the doubt given to the employee does not extend to antidiscrimination rules, in which there is a shift of the burden of proof in favor of the presumed victim of discrimination.

RF: That is almost the opposite in the United States. We have had moments in American jurisprudence where people might say something like "The employment contract is inherently unequal or inherently favors the employer." But for the most part, there is an extremely powerful idea that this is a neutral, reciprocal arms-length relationship between two freely consenting entities. Certainly when you get into things like discrimination, the burden of proof is borne by the employee.

Julie Suk is more radical in her assessment of the scope of antidiscrimination norms, including statutory norms.

JULIE SUK: Regarding the influence of the Age Discrimination in Employment Act (ADEA), which embeds the principle of equality and nondiscrimination in law, my point (which is a larger theme in my work) is this: U.S. law often turns to antidiscrimination as a solution to a wide variety of complex social problems (such as aging at work, work-family balance). It is limited in its ability to address these problems, and sometimes it actually poses barriers to innovative experimentation in policies to address these complex problems.

Before I respond to the thoughts of Ford and Suk, consider Harvard Law School Professor Janet Halley's take on fundamental rights discourse and its shortcomings through her personal experience.

MARIE MERCAT-BRUNS: *How has queer theory[87] inspired your work on law and power? For Europeans, it can be interesting to understand how legal theory can draw from other disciplines, sometimes in a very pragmatic way.*

JANET HALLEY: Let me say a couple of words how I experience the connection between queer theory and legal studies.

While I was in literary studies, we began to see the rise of queer theory in American thought generally.... While I was in law school... there was a decision of the Supreme Court called *Bowers v. Hardwick* that held that it was perfectly constitutional... for a state to prohibit and to criminalize same-sex sodomy.... I was strongly affiliated at that time with the gay rights bar. We were wanting to expand the rights of homosexuals, and it was horrible living under *Bowers v. Hardwick*; it was a terrible decision.... Many of us dedicated ourselves to getting it reversed....

But the lower courts started expanding it, saying, . . . "Well, you can prohibit the conduct, so you can also not hire people in the workplace who are likely to commit the conduct; the greater deprivation of rights includes the lesser." Now that's a move from conduct to identity and that expands *Bowers v. Hardwick*. In a way, the criminalization of sodomy was narrow: who is really going to get punished for committing sodomy? . . . But you do need a job, and so the courts were making *Bowers* much more expansive.

Where I came in was trying to understand the conduct-identity relationship. What was the relationship of an act to an identity? As it happens, the French philosopher Michel Foucault . . . helped me to understand how slippery and contingent the relationship between conduct and identity was.

I came in as a law professor still trying to do gay rights—my stance was we need rights—but I was also dedicated to doing it using French critical theory. I wrote a whole bunch of articles on *Hardwick*; then Congress passed the don't-ask-don't-tell policy that said that you could be kicked out of the military if you showed a propensity to engage in same-sex conduct. . . . So I came in analyzing these contraptions through the tools that were given to me by Foucault.

The thing that really astonished me was that, as I worked my way into these arguments, the rights claims weren't watertight; you could not find absolute decisive rights claims that everybody had to accept. The rights I thought we needed were not logically built into the law. I continually found a gap, a hole, a place where there needed to be a political move, there needed to be an alliance, there needed to be some kind of decision on behalf of the judge or the legislator.

Our Constitution and our rights regime didn't mandate those rights; they just made them possible. That was just a severe surprise to me, and that made me understand how contingent these legal rights are on politics. I had my loss-of-faith moment. That's when I turned from being a rights person to becoming a member of the critical legal studies movement, which understands law as a contingent social network of practices rather than as a mandatory normative order.

Comparative Perspectives

These commentaries reveal the tensions underlying the fundamental rights talk:[88] On the one hand, it attributes great symbolic meaning to equality and nondiscrimination and places these principles high up in the hierarchy of norms. On the other hand, this discourse can also overshadow the difficulties experienced by victims of discrimination in accessing economic and social rights in the broader context of social protection.[89] Most of the critical analysis of American antidiscrimination law has arisen from the development of equality and nondiscrimination rights discourse in constitutional case law and federal law, which is seen as having limited scope. Can this critique be explained by the fact that an extensive body of law has been produced in interpreting the concepts of equality and freedom without any corresponding development of a welfare state? This is what Suk claims when she compares gender equality and antidiscrimination norms, which have undermined the organization of collective solutions to resolve work and family conflicts in the United States.[90] But recognizing the limitations of American antidiscrimination law can open up other avenues to gender equality and nondiscrimination: by expanding the social protection system to better incorporate family interests, while continuing to prohibit discrimination.[91]

Critical thinking on antidiscrimination law in the United States originated as a movement of a group of law professors, members of the critical legal studies (CLS) movement,[92] among others, inspired by the analyses of French philosophers Michel Foucault and Jacques Derrida on the relationship between law and power.[93] Although a similar critical legal movement certainly existed and still exists in Europe, it was more deeply rooted in Marxist-inspired ideological debate, at least in France.[94] What this emphasis on the influence of critical thought in antidiscrimination law in the United States shows is that theoretical work on the effectiveness of law and its political, economic, and sociological imprints is not disconnected from the analysis of legal relationships between private individuals; on the contrary, it can enrich the arguments used by lawyers. For those who construe critical thought as undermining the law, its rigor, and the importance of a dogmatic approach to law and the roles of legal practitioners, these conversations demonstrate that critical thought is neither incompatible with nor detrimental to legal practice and its proper functioning. The opposite is true, since critical thought can inform law.[95]

For example, critical theory produced by feminist lawyers[96] made it possible for the concept of sexual harassment, as conceived by Catharine MacKinnon, to inspire Supreme Court case law; for the notion of reasonable accommodation in disability discrimination laws, as conceived by two rational feminists, Martha Minow and Chai Feldblum, to emerge; for ways to prove systemic gender discrimination—by detecting discriminatory biases, as shown by Christine Jolls, and by identifying bias in employer evaluations of women's performance, as shown by Vicki Schultz and embraced by the courts—to be discovered; and for an analogy to be drawn—thanks to the queer theory promoted by Janet Halley, which deconstructed gender in employment—between the construction of sexual orientation stereotypes, leading to discriminations that are not prohibited by federal law in the United States, and the construction of female stereotypes, a factor of sex discrimination.[97]

Critical thought in law breaks down barriers that compartmentalize legal analysis. In France, in particular, the doctrine is often corralled by disciplinary boundaries between public and private law, between contract law and corporate law on the one hand and employment law on the other. Critical thought is a framework that engages with all of the individual and collective mechanisms established by law, in a similar fashion to the way that international private law and comparative law associate different disciplines to resolve questions about the application of law. Some of the scholars interviewed have not merely set out to deconstruct law; they also offer new readings of the use of legal concepts and mechanisms that can inspired lawmakers, because they place problems like discrimination into the broader sociological context from which they arise. In each discipline of law, vehicles of individual and institutional discrimination can therefore be found.[98] These questions sometimes transcend the inherent limitations of a unidisciplinary reading of law.

For other American scholars, critical theory is especially vital in the area of antidiscrimination law, because it deals with the legal subject; that is, the person. Its ambitions are vast and sometimes considered unrealistic.[99] Who is this person possessing none of the (twenty in France) characteristics that the law is attempting to protect in employment?

Lastly, another way to comprehend the critique of fundamental rights talk is to observe the models produced by this body of law. Certain scholars have embarked on this path, either to identify the purpose of antidiscrimination rules or to associate them with a paradigm, as representations of equality.

2

Antidiscrimination Models and Enforcement

The Constitution and the origins of antidiscrimination legislation in the United States supply a first level of insight into this body of law, but measures to combat discrimination can be grasped from other angles. The influence of constitutional rights and their interpretation in the United States does not appear to be confined to the pursuit of fundamental rights: often this influence can be felt in the models and paradigms reflected in antidiscrimination law, and that constitutes a rich matter for critical theory.

I. MODELS OF ANTIDISCRIMINATION

Antidiscrimination rules can be assessed through the lens of an existing inventory of models. American scholars have taken different paths in isolating these models: Robert Post identifies the various functions of equality law,[1] while Reva Siegel, later in this chapter, choses to define the paradigms of equality that shape this law.

The Functions of Antidiscrimination Law

MARIE MERCAT-BRUNS: *What are the functions of antidiscrimination law?*
ROBERT POST: The first function of antidiscrimination law is to structure
its intervention by creating rules to manipulate people in order to obtain
a desired situation.[2] This is the "social engineering" function of the law.
Antidiscrimination law serves as a regulatory tool instrumentalizing people to
achieve equality.

In my book *Constitutional Domains: Democracy, Community, Management*,
I explain this first function of antidiscrimination law using this idea of
management. Management arranges social life for the achievement of given

objectives. It ignores the independent requirements of community values or identity, following instead the logic of instrumental rationality. The distinction between community and management can be seen in the contrast between a criminal law that seeks to predicate punishment on a moral allocation of blame and responsibility, and a criminal law that attempts instead narrowly and strictly to fulfill the goal of preventing harmful forms of behavior. By seeking to align criminal punishment with relevant cultural norms, the former displays the authority of community; by seeking instead instrumentally to achieve an explicit objective, the latter regulates conduct with the authority of management.[3]

In general, the twentieth century has witnessed a significant shift from the former to the latter. This may be seen in the striking transformation of older forms of duty-based tort law, which attempted to use the normative construction of the reasonable person to infuse legal rules with the values of the ambient community, into more modern forms of strict and efficiency-based liability rules, which seek to use tort law as a means of engineering the accomplishment of discreet objectives such as the achievement of efficient allocations of risk. The triumph of the progressive vision of the administrative state has ensured the increased prominence of management in modern law. The trend toward management compounds itself, because the growing rationalization of society undermines cultural norms that might otherwise sustain the authority of the community.[4]

Laws establishing the social order of management can be controversial. For example, disagreements can arise over the underlying mission of certain educational institutions. Managerial laws may also be challenged because they do not actually achieve their goals. Thus, the authority of the institutions implementing them can be challenged.

When we think of law and economics, it tends to treat people in that way: it creates rules that will conduce to the achievement of instrumental objectives, and it manipulates people to attain a social desire. It ignores the independent requirements of community values or identity, following instead the logic of instrumental rationality.

A second way is to express social norms in a society.[5] Every society has social norms that define what that society is and that defines what is desirable and undesirable. We think about law in that sense as expressing the social norms of a particular culture, of a particular historical moment.

Community, as Philip Selznick writes in *The Moral Commonwealth*, turns on "a framework of shared beliefs, interests, and commitments" that "establish a common faith or fate, a personal identity, a sense of belonging and a supportive structure of activities and relationships."[6] Laws instantiating community seek to reinforce this shared world of common faith and fate. They characteristically articulate and enforce norms that they take to define both individual and social identity.[7]

In *Constitutional Domains,* I also offer an extended account of the common law tort of invasion of privacy, which is an exemplary instance of law organizing itself to instantiate the social order of community. Some have contended that the very existence of legal rights is incompatible with the ability of law to serve this function, because legal rights necessarily imply "an image of the rights-bearer as a self-determining, unencumbered individual, a being connected to others only by choice."[8] But I argue that this contention is inaccurate, for the rights created by the tort of invasion of privacy explicitly serve to define and defend social norms, which the tort conceptualizes as essential for maintaining the stable identity of individuals. Like other legal actions redressing "dignitary harms," the tort conceives personal dignity as subsisting in socially defined forms of respect. The tort protects these forms of respect and thereby safeguards the particular community that makes this dignity possible. The tort rests "not upon a perceived opposition between persons and social life (the interests of individuals against the demands of the community), but rather upon their interdependence. Paradoxically, that very interdependence makes possible a certain kind of human dignity and autonomy which can exist only within the embrace of community norms."[9]

The "reasonable person"[10] is of course a figure who continually reappears in American common law, most especially in the law of torts. The important point about the reasonable person is that he is no one in particular,[11] a representative of "the normal standard of community behavior," who embodies "the general level of moral judgment of the community, what it feels ought ordinarily to be done."[12] The difficulty appears when tort law is subjected to rules of civility that attempt to safeguard the intimacy of individuals from intrusion and consider the demands of public accountability: these civility rules maintained by the tort embody the obligations owed by members of a community to each other, and to that extent define the substance and boundaries of community life.[13]

A third function is to transform social norms. We think about law as merely reflecting the norms of a culture, but we are seeking to transform them. So, here, law is not trying to achieve purely or instrumentally a certain goal. It is instead participating within the culture, as a way of changing the culture so as to alter the norms by which persons act and society functions. This transformation may take the form of a redistribution of rights, but it does not always take the form intended, for example, by the lawmaker.[14]

The fourth function of antidiscrimination law is to facilitate autonomy. Generally speaking, it is to create conditions where persons can create their own doctrine, a realm of autonomy. Antidiscrimination law is not a function of democracy and, in that sense, of autonomy. In my book *Constitutional Domains,* I describe this function.[15]

In contemporary constitutional adjudication, it is most common to find both community and management challenged by the claims of yet a third form of social order, which I call democracy. Democracy entails "a self-determination of the people," in the words of Karl Marx, but it is theoretically inseparable from the question of individual self-determination. The essential problematic of democracy thus lies in the reconciliation of individual and collective autonomy.[16]

The American constitutional tradition understands this reconciliation to take place within an open structure of communication. I call this structure "public discourse." If public discourse is kept free for the autonomous participation of individual citizens, and if government decision making is subordinated to the public opinion produced by public discourse, there is the possibility that citizens will come to identify with the state as representative of their own collective self-determination. Protecting freedom of public discourse thus satisfies a necessary (although not sufficient) condition for the realization of democratic self-government. That is why our constitutional tradition regards the First Amendment as "the guardian of our democracy" even though the amendment is itself frankly anti-majoritarian in purpose and effect.[17]

The reconciliation of individual and collective self-determination entails a serious internal tension. On the one hand, a democratic social structure must provide an appropriate space for individual autonomy. Within that space democracy must function negatively; it must refuse to foreclose the possibility of individual choice and self-development by imposing preexisting community norms or given managerial ends. On the other hand, a democratic social structure must also function positively, to foster an identification with the processes that enable the collective experience of self-determination. These processes presuppose forms of social cohesion that depend on community norms, and these processes also often require strategic managerial intervention.[18]

It is always open to contention whether specific behavior regulated by the law ought to lie outside the boundaries of this sphere and be ordered instead according to the logic of community or management. During the era of *Lochner v. New York*,[19] for example, the sphere of democratic authority was delineated by reference to the will of the individual citizen, as concretely expressed in the institution of private property. It was believed that depriving a citizen of his "property, which is the fruit and badge of his liberty, is to ... leave him a slave." Hence "due protection for the rights of property" was "regarded as a vital principle of republican institutions." Accordingly, property rights were strictly enforced as a bulwark of the struggle of democracy against socialism. But this underlying concept of the person crumbled during the triumph of the New Deal, and a different moral image of the autonomous citizen emerged that focused on the independence of reason rather than of will.[20]

I think antidiscrimination law hovers between these first three functions and discussions within antidiscrimination law.[21]

Sometimes antidiscrimination law seeks to reflect ambient norms of decency, respect and civility and insists that persons of color or women or minorities of various kinds are treated with full respect, the way people in society should generally be treated.

Also more generally in the United States, antidiscrimination law has been associated with the transformative idea of law; that is, norms in which minorities are treated as subordinate and the function of antidiscrimination law is to become a fulcrum by which the norms are being changed in civil society.

One has to ask some very difficult questions: Do you change the law before changing the norms? Do you have the power to change the norms in the society? Where do these new norms come from?

One of the things that tells us is the way that, in various instances, antidiscrimination law in the United States is a function of the elite trying to change working-class culture, particularly in regard to things like affirmative action, and that's a challenge. Why did antidiscrimination law alienate the bulk of the working class close to the Democratic Party and allow a wave of political resentment, better associated with the populist Republican Party, to swell?

So, with this transformative way, we will always have cross-inspection.

Aspects of antidiscrimination law serve the objective of redistribution. We want to have more minority persons within the workplace, so we say we will have quotas in order to achieve this. Aspects of antidiscrimination law do that, although they tend to be very controversial. People feel more comfortable with using antidiscrimination law to reflect norms than to objectively redistribute, but there are aspects of it that indisputably help us capture this.

MM-B: *Do you think the narrow interpretation of antidiscrimination law has focused on one of these functions in particular?*

RP: Yes, I think the Supreme Court has been quite hostile to the transformative notion of antidiscrimination law. It has been hostile toward the redistributive notion of antidiscrimination law, hostile toward the notion of accommodation[22] and disparate impact. And it has tended to think about antidiscrimination law as reducing disparate treatment, treating other people with the forms of civility and respect that we expect all persons to be treated with. I think that has been, speaking globally and roughly, the tendency in the last thirty years.

MM-B: *So you don't think there is the possibility of advancing toward a more transformative law? Do you think that it will be an option later on, through some types of legislation that change norms (through accommodation or disparate impact), or do you think this opportunity has passed and won't come back?*

RP: That is a political question. It is of course possible with the right Congress, judiciary, and politics. It is a real possibility, but what it will need is politicians to push it. At the moment, I would say you don't see that. What you see is the left on the defensive on all of these issues; you don't see robust defenses of it.

Comparative Perspectives
The Functions of Antidiscrimination Law and the Proportionality Test

With his description of the different functions of antidiscrimination law, Post sheds fresh light on the development of this body of law in Europe, its influence and its limits. The first—the instrumental, management function—could be applied to early European antidiscrimination law, whose original economic aim was to eliminate market barriers by proscribing discrimination based on sex or nationality and consequently ensuring the free movement of persons. This was a crucial concern at a time when European institutions were being established and foundational laws enacted. So in its function, this law was different from the discrimination prohibition in Article 14 of the European Convention on Human Rights, in which the nonexhaustive enumeration of grounds reveals an initial attachment to the individual rather than an operational rule. This view is corroborated by the fact that in the beginning, Article 14 could not be invoked alone, but only with regard to another article of the Convention. This is no longer true, however: the European Court of Human Rights has since even recognized cases of indirect discrimination.[23]

The law continues to play this instrumental role at the European level today, but increasingly it also fulfills another, more social function,[24] more closely resembling Post's second function of antidiscrimination law: to express social norms, such as standards of human respect and dignity. This is the direction the CJEU has taken, referring to equal treatment as a fundamental right and to general principles of law in establishing age-based discrimination.

The recognition of discriminatory harassment in Europe and then in France, which extends the definition of discrimination to harassment, also contributes to introducing violation of dignity as a defining component, and not only a consequence, of discrimination. These developments have changed the analytical approach to discrimination. Additionally, the binding character given by the Lisbon Treaty to the EU Charter of Fundamental Rights, which drew on the European Social Charter, among other sources, also reflects an underlying discourse that is more sensitive to human rights issues and the dignity of victims of discrimination.[25]

The third function that antidiscrimination rules might serve, the transformation of social norms, does not seem to fall under the purview of European Union lawmakers, who often defer to national governments in matters where the prohibition of discrimination may conflict with the implementation of social policies to achieve social redistribution. One of the few opportunities open to European or national judges is to assess, under the guise of EU directives, the extent to which any exemptions from the bar on discrimination, allowed for certain social policies, are justified, necessary, and proportionate.[26] This scrutiny does not always lead to a defense of these policies, since the general objective is to promote employment. The CJEU often recognizes the legitimacy of differential treatment to attain national social policy objectives. The application of a proportionality test, however, is where it is more difficult to distinguish the consistency or logic of the Court's adjudications.[27] Its action is unpredictable: if it exercises a low level of scrutiny, then policies will take precedence over the principle of nondiscrimination; if it exercises more stringent control, member states are not always successful in persuading the judges of the necessary and proportionate character of their social policies.[28]

In addition to those pinpointed by Post, other functions of antidiscrimination law have been brought to light by European scholars such as Lisa Waddington and Mark Bell, who offer an analysis of the judicial models that could be reflected in European antidiscrimination law.[29] These academics offer three models of equality—equality as individual justice, equality as group justice, and equality as a positive duty, often imposed by public institutions—to guide and inform effective antidiscrimination policies.

The first model focuses on erasing the traces of an unequal treatment overlooking an individual's merit and skill, regardless of the prohibited ground used; it is similar in ways to the French concept of formal equality. Article 21 of the EU Charter of Fundamental Rights reflects this model,[30] which can also be detected in all of the preambles to antidiscrimination directives evoking equal treatment through the very concept of direct discrimination. It raises questions about the specific characteristics of discrimination, which vary from ground to ground, and the complexity of proving discrimination, finding a comparator, and perpetuating stigma for the individual victim whose case brought the discrimination to light. The benefit of this model is that it promotes the adoption of a general antidiscrimination principle applying to all grounds: such a general principle would require transparency in national and European laws regarding the motives for the decisions or differences in treatment underpinning the rules.[31] This first model can be assimilated with the prescriptive, instrumental function of antidiscrimination law identified by Post and its limits, since this function is realized only through litigation.[32]

The second model identified by Bell and Waddington, the group justice model, attempts to overcome the challenges of the first model by showing that the nature of the discrimination is inherently collective. References to indirect discrimination or to positive action in European directives and case law reflect this collective framework. It can also be detected through litigation, among other means, and resembles the individual justice model on that point. Where the member states differ in their grasp of these discriminations as opposed to those following the individual justice model is tied to the fact that this prohibition of discrimination targets inequalities resulting from the identification of an individual or an employee as a member of a certain group. In France, for certain grounds such as race, antidiscrimination laws do not recognize the existence of predefined groups. This is where the paradigm approach by Bell and Waddington, proposing a group vision of equality, is especially relevant. The issue it raises is whether the lack of any overarching framework or clearly defined, homogeneous group of "victims of discrimination" makes it more difficult, in the context of European norms and their interpretation, to use collective means of proving indirect discrimination.[33]

The last model identified by Bell and Waddington is one in which equality goals are promoted by positive duties and the participation of minority groups. The scholars point to the flurry of incentives in Europe and, in some member countries, the creation of organizations contributing to positive action and the participation of labor unions in developing policies to measure and promote equality. Examples are the EQUAL initiative financed by the European Social Fund, which ran until 2008 and explored new approaches through innovative collective agreements to tackling inequality, and the Equinet program, a network promoting cooperation among the national equality bodies of member states.[34] Member states have also engaged in this equality mainstreaming,[35] which offers an alternative to the litigation process as a remedy for discrimination. This equality model evokes the fourth function of antidiscrimination law, related to the participative rights of citizens and rights organizations, which is to give them a certain autonomy in defending and promoting rights. However, this comes with the risk, as emphasized by Bell and Waddington, of isolating the interests of victims of discrimination based on each prohibited ground and disregarding the existence of victims affected by multiple, simultaneous grounds of discrimination (sexual orientation and disability or age and origin, for example).[36]

Coming back to the functions identified by Post, the fourth function, to facilitate autonomy by establishing the conditions for people to "create their own doctrine," offers an interesting perspective. Post's analysis that "antidiscrimination law is not a function of democracy and in that sense, of autonomy" seems responsive to the first, more traditional recognition of antidiscrimination in national and European law concentrating on flushing out differences in treatment based on specific prohibited grounds.

In comparative law, the identification of models of equality reinforces the idea that a new generation of discrimination is gradually emerging. These forms of discrimination are more closely related to freedoms protected by association than to prohibited differences in treatment. In France for example, except for provisions banning discrimination against persons who exercise their right to strike, the new strands of antidiscrimination law related to parenthood, including family status or the marital status of same-sex or mixed-sex couples, all seem to guarantee a certain degree of autonomy to individuals, based on norms generally accepted by the community at a given point in time. In France, the existence or nonexistence of this quest for individual autonomy was a factor in establishing religious discrimination: conflicting with a desire to uphold secular values were alleged restrictions of employees' freedom, which must be justified, necessary, and proportionate, according to Article L. 1121–1 of the French Labor Code.[37] Also in France, although discrimination by association in relation to parenthood and the care of a disabled family member[38] seems to be increasingly recognized and investigated by judges and the law, inequalities faced by people in same-sex relationships have not yet been brought within the protective reach of antidiscrimination law, although European law is evolving in that direction:[39] the Cour de Cassation has strictly interpreted the right to paternity leave, concluding that the civil-union partner of an employee who has had a baby was not entitled to this benefit.[40] In this context, the fourth function of antidiscrimination law creates new spheres of democracy in which an individual's autonomy can be expressed. This particular function of nondiscrimination seems to more closely represent the French struggle against inequality because it focuses less on the idea of a group disadvantage than the other more complex and indirect forms of discrimination do. The violation of an individual's freedom can constitute a more palpable difference in treatment without challenging the universalist paradigm of equality that is so deeply valued by the republican tradition.

Post's nomenclature describing the functions of antidiscrimination law probably contributes to a better understanding of the relative reluctance of national judges and other stakeholders to incorporate antidiscrimination norms into internal law. This resistance originates, for different reasons, from employers, trade unions, certain political parties, and the legislative and executive branches of government.

Employer Resistance to Antidiscrimination Law and the "Management" Perspective

A first source of internal resistance to the application of antidiscrimination law, brought to light through Post's reading, are employers and certain members of employer associations. Antidiscrimination law is often perceived in the workplace as a management issue. The logic of employment discrimination law in corporate management is to eliminate discrimination as an economic barrier in the labor market and the workplace, set on promoting good work performance and diversity.[41] However, beyond this sphere, the application of criminal sanctions to employers in France has been rather unpopular. These sanctions also perform the "community" and "transformation" functions of antidiscrimination law by punishing violations of the dignity of employee victims of discrimination and providing financial compensation for individual and systemic inequalities, especially in pay, in the form of social redistribution. Meanwhile, civil suits for discrimination, brought with greater ease and success due to the shifting of the burden of the proof, probably have the same cultural and ethical impact as criminal charges. In France, however, litigation does not necessarily lead to the award of large civil remedies as in the United States, where criminal sanctions for workplace conduct do not exist. France's former equality body, the HALDE, which contributed significantly to the broader ambition to deeply transform the behavior of social partners by participating in investigations of discrimination complaints, was perceived as overstepping its authority.[42] Yet the independent administrative authority was merely applying the multiple dimensions of antidiscrimination law across society, a mission conferred by the European employment discrimination directives adopted in 2000, but in insufficiently precise terms. A valid question that can be raised is whether the work of the HALDE was hampered by a general misunderstanding, on the part of the government in particular, of the diverse nature of its activities due to the varied functions of antidiscrimination law, and whether this lack of understanding hastened its demise.

Some opposition to the incorporation of antidiscrimination law is also led by organizations in charge of protecting previously acquired social benefits in France, especially certain members of trade unions or political parties. This criticism is directed at the management rationale of antidiscrimination law, which may threaten the welfare state. Antidiscrimination law has resulted in a series of decisions, mainly by the EU court, on night work for women and can be perceived as undermining certain pension plans implementing measures that are not necessary or not proportionate to the employment or health policies promoted by the member states.[43] This judicial standard can be perceived as driven by a management rationale. However, an approach that seeks to identify sources of indirect discrimination can assign a redistribution function to antidiscrimination law, going beyond a simple examination of torts to instead scrutinize the institutions producing the discrimination. Such scrutiny can consist of exposing certain operating mechanisms of government bodies and businesses and examining laws and norms relating to training, working time, retirement, seniority, and other collective bargaining issues that seem neutral but can unfairly disadvantage certain groups (people who are ill, old, young, female, who work part-time, etc.). The power of antidiscrimination law to transform social norms, even if not always in the intended way, can be seen in these areas.

Finally, the executive and legislative bodies of government show a certain reluctance to apply "imported" aspects of antidiscrimination law, whose interaction with the existing republican dogma on equality is not clearly understood and difficult to implement but offers rich possibilities.[44] Although community and management approaches have been taken by successive governments in laws transposing EU directives[45] and in collective bargaining, the legislative and executive branches nevertheless seem to be a long way away from supporting the idea that antidiscrimination law seeks to change not only individual stereotypes but also facially neutral, uniform, systemic rules implemented by the government that directly or indirectly perpetuate discrimination (based on disability and age, for example).[46] The creation of the Défenseur des droits (Defender of Rights, formerly the HALDE)[47] in France echoes the reaction from employer associations and probably translates a desire to prevent the antidiscrimination organization from treading on the territory of government bodies by limiting its powers, in particular its power of recommendation.[48] What Post's paradigm brings into focus is that antidiscrimination law is simply accomplishing its transformative function, rather than infringing on the separation of powers or overstepping its authority as an independent administrative body.

Once public opinion and government bodies accept that antidiscrimination law and its regulatory authority are not stifling democratic debate, the law can perform its functions of transformation and community (promoting the cultural values of respect and dignity) with no threat to democracy—quite the contrary.[49] If we consider the fourth function identified by Post, which is tied to democracy, antidiscrimination norms can enlighten our understanding of the relationships between equality, liberty, and nondiscrimination, which are fundamental to a well-functioning democracy. This function seems to be shared by France's judicial review process (QPC) in that it incites the various executive, legislative, and judicial powers to each assume their part of responsibility in this area.[50]

Models of Equality

Unlike Post, Reva Siegel focuses mainly on constitutional case law on the equality principle to show how the U.S. Supreme Court has taken three different stances. Each of these positions translates a different concept of equality. Siegel mentions a new concern of the high court in its appraisal of equality: a desire to maintain social cohesion, a theme that is also of capital importance to European courts.

In the following conversation, Reva Siegel describes her three models of interpretation of "the equal protection of the laws."

REVA SIEGEL: In the United States, social struggle over the reach and proper understanding of equal protection in matters of race has been articulated as the struggle between two competing conceptions of equal protection: an anticlassification understanding of equal protection and an antisubordination understanding of equal protection.

In an article called "Equality Talk,"[51] which provides a half-century account of the struggle for the enforcement of *Brown v. Board of Education*, I trace the rise and spread of these competing understandings of the American equal protection tradition and take on a fundamental question about an embodied understanding of our tradition in authoritative legal sources: how courts actually interpreted the meaning of the Fourteenth Amendment's Equal Protection Clause.

The conventional view is that courts have embraced an anticlassification position and that proponents of a so-called antisubordination position have been relegated to a strenuous but dissenting critique of official doctrine. In my "Equality Talk" article, I show how this is an oversimplification of this body of law. I show that cocompeting accounts emerged after *Brown* and that the path the court has picked can be responsive to each of these two understandings of equal protection.

At times, equal protection case law embraces views that are generally associated with anticlassification, validating protection of the individual and concerned with wrongful differentiation. But at other times equal protection case law in fact espouses views that are much more resonant with an antisubordination understanding, which is concerned with issues of group equality. In this article, I trace ways in which American law ambivalently has shifted between these two views of equal protection.[52]

In recent work, I have been exploring whether there might be some third view emerging from conflict between these two conceptions of equal protection articulated by the "centric" judges on the Court: [Justice] Powell, the author of the diversity opinion in Bakke; [retired Justice] O'Connor; and now [Justice] Anthony Kennedy. In this more recent work, which draws on the opinions of these three justices and some of the commentary in the Academy on them, I explore whether the ambivalent embrace of affirmative action that you see in decisions like Powell's Bakke opinion or O'Connor's opinion in *Grutter*[53] might not instead reflect an effort to prevent social division and balkanization.

Justice Kennedy reasons from antibalkanization values in the recent cases of *Parents Involved in Community Schools v. Seattle School District No. 1* and *Ricci v. DeStefano.* There Justice Kennedy affirms race-conscious facially neutral laws that promote equal opportunity (such as disparate impact claims in employment discrimination laws) so long as the enforcement of such laws does not make race salient in ways that affront dignity and threaten divisiveness. . . . Attending to the antibalkanization values that led Justice Kennedy to write separately from conservatives and progressives in *Parents Involved*[54] in turn illuminates these same concerns in the opinion Justice Kennedy authored for five members of the Court in *Ricci*,[55] and so identifies a basis, grounded in the text of the decision and in several decades of constitutional history, for reading *Ricci* as vindicating antibalkanization—rather than colorblindness—values.[56]

More generally, this work helps explain the shape of the Court's equal protection decisions. It highlights points of convergence and disagreement among conservatives and progressives on the Court and explores the questions they pose to one another. Striving to understand disagreements about equality can help to transform the way we understand equality.

If anticlassification is concerned with protecting the individual from the wrong of classification and antisubordination is concerned with protecting groups from subordinating practices, the "third way" is concerned with protecting society from the threat of balkanization. Judges concerned about the threat of balkanization support interventions like affirmative action that seek to alleviate extreme social stratification. Yet their very effort to promote social solidarity also produces concern that remedial interventions like affirmative action might inflame social resentment. So judges who approach equality with attention to social solidarity will at times sanction affirmative action (or indirect versions of it), while imposing stringent limits on the intervention.

What is important to see about this middle position is that it is not embracing colorblindness as such: it is neither a legal formalist position nor only concerned with individuals. Rather, it is concerned with the question of social cohesion. It understands *different* threats to social cohesion—the threat of gross social stratification *and* the threat of heavy-handed rectification of social stratification—as potential harms.

MARIE MERCAT-BRUNS: *In European law and institutions, the discourse on social cohesion is also very prevalent, as illustrated by certain research papers.*[57] *This shared interest in social cohesion calls for a comparison with European law.*

RS: I am working on an essay in which I reflect on the tension between these two views.[58]

Judges committed to this antibalkanization approach talk about diversity rather than inequality. And they promote diversity in ways they hope will diffuse the visibility of race remediation practices, so that race-conscious remedies can function as transformative remedies. The judges following this antibalkanization approach are concerned about interventions that might reinscribe the original categories of injury. They want government to represent the problem of inequality in such a way as to lead people away from the old categories. This is the most progressive interpretation of the antibalkanization decisions of judicial moderates.

The good news is that the judicial moderates do seem to be responsive to concerns about gross social stratification as well as to concerns about the resentment that racial remedies can produce. The bad news is that the exponents of this middle position seem far more attuned to the risk of majority resentment than they are moved by the risk of minority anomie or estrangement. A race-progressive might find some aspects of the moderates' approach attractive. But one wonders whether its exponents on the court are as sensible of the risks to social solidarity caused by gross stratification and minority anomie as they are sensible of the risk to social solidarity caused by race remediation and the estrangement or resentment of majority groups.

This framework is a framework for thinking about why we might adopt terms that are analytically blurry.[59]

Siegel's work[60] offers a new way of modeling the standards of assessment of equality in Supreme Court jurisprudence. Siegel shows that the analysis of the tensions between a formal concept of equality, concerned with individuals and the eradication of categories (anticlassification), and a more substantive concept seeking a more structural remedy for socially excluded groups (antisubordination) can be enriched by a third, middle view taken by certain judges. This view does not lean toward one principle or another: instead, it strives to achieve an equality that preserves social cohesion. Siegel therefore departs from pessimistic commentaries on U.S. constitutional case law, deploring a preference by a majority of judges for the application of the anticlassification principle and limiting any equality debate to the subject of the alarmingly conservative progress made by Supreme Court. In her article "From Colorblindness to Antibalkanization: An Emerging Ground of Decision in Race Quality Cases," she explains this middle stance, using two main examples to illustrate this tendency among certain judges and open a new perspective on the interpretation of equality.

What is interesting about this classification of the positions of each judge is that it clarifies our understanding of certain concepts that are difficult to define, such as diversity, and certain mechanisms that are not easy to employ, such as disparate impact or indirect discrimination. In her article employing this triadic model, the first case examined by Siegel is *Parents Involved*.[61] An association representing parents of schoolchildren in a Seattle school district protested against an affirmative action plan for assigning students to highly popular magnet schools, which used race as a criteria to break the tie in the event of an oversubscription. Justice Kennedy adopted neither an anticlassification nor an antisubordination reading; he applied a strict scrutiny framework to racial classifications but considered that colorblindness could not be interpreted as a rule designed to prevent the government from promoting racial integration in schools.[62]

Governments implement race-conscious but facially neutral policies to promote racial integration, of which Justice Kennedy gives many examples in his concurring opinion in *Parents Involved*.[63] However, a racial classification of individuals raises questions about human dignity and the risk of social divisiveness:

> When the government classifies an individual by race, it must first define what it means to be of a race. Who exactly is white and who is nonwhite? To be forced to live under a state-mandated racial label is inconsistent with the dignity of individuals in our society. And it is a label that an individual is powerless to change. Governmental classifications that command people to march in different directions based on racial typologies can cause a new divisiveness. The practice can lead to corrosive discourse, where race serves not as an element of our diverse heritage but instead as a bargaining chip in the political process. On the other hand, race-conscious measures that

do not rely on differential treatment based on individual classifications present these problems to a lesser degree.[64]

These include strategically selecting the location of new schools, taking neighborhood demographics into account in drawing school attendance zones, allocating resources for special programs, recruiting students and teachers in a more targeted manner, and tracking enrollments, academic performance, and other statistics by race.

These more subtle measures of classification do not require as stringent a level of review with respect to equality. As Justice Kennedy explained, although they are racially sensitive, these types of mechanisms are unlikely to require strict scrutiny to be found permissible by judges: "Executive and legislative branches, which for generations now have considered these types of policies and procedures, should be permitted to employ them with candor and with confidence that a constitutional violation does not occur whenever a decision maker considers the impact a given approach might have on students of different races. Assigning to each student a personal designation according to a crude system of individual racial classifications is quite a different matter; and the legal analysis changes accordingly."[65] If instead of school district maps taking racial data into account, the district schools had used individual applications to determine assignment to magnet schools and promote integration, Justice Kennedy would have considered these practices to be constitutional. Neither the anticlassification reasoning that rejects all race classification nor the antisubordination reasoning that accepts all integration efforts adequately explains Justice Kennedy's position, since he impugned the challenged practice in this case. Siegel therefore describes his perspective as embracing a third vantage point, which she terms "antibalkanization."

Justice Kennedy warns against all race classifications due to the inherent risk of creating racial dividing lines between whites and nonwhites, yet he is reluctant to reject affirmative action. The social cohesion component is the decisive factor.

Comparative Perspectives

Siegel draws inspiration from Justice Kennedy's opinion to propose a new way of understanding the "dilemma of difference":[66] doing nothing at all or doing too much both pose a threat to social cohesion. In its initiatives and hesitations, France's position is comparable and reflects the same ambivalence about the quest for equality: it is deeply attached to a republican, universalist ideal of equality, close to the American anticlassification principle, and rejects the construction of policies based on ethno-racial groups but nevertheless currently allows measures to target certain groups, particularly women, such as the law establishing a quota of 20–40 percent of women on boards of large companies.[67] "Positive discrimination" initiatives like the Priority Education Agreements signed between the elite Sciences Po university in Paris and high schools located in disadvantaged areas take a middle road, applying different rules for access to higher education based on geographic criteria. This intermediate position is not unlike that expressed in the *Parents Involved* opinion written by Justice Kennedy, who did not disapprove of more subtle forms of integration.[68] In the United States, the percentage plans implemented by the states of Texas and California are conceived in the same spirit: they guarantee admission to their state universities to a certain percentage of the best students from disadvantaged geographies.[69]

Can this same framework be used to present the advantages of social cohesion as a hybrid model that supports positive action but tempers the differences in the treatment of one group over another by employing more neutral mechanisms? Can other positive action "dilemmas" be found in Europe—with respect to women, for example? France has a long tradition of implementing pregnancy and maternity protection, which can in turn provide a motive for employment discrimination. On another level, Europe's drive to expand the recognition of parenthood in national laws seems to promote antibalkanization values by avoiding family status distinctions that would pit the interests of men against those of women.

Siegel cites another decision by Justice Kennedy as an example of this social cohesion principle: *Ricci v. DeStefano*.[70] This time, the case involves disparate impact discrimination and reveals a conflict between disparate impact and disparate treatment discrimination frameworks. A group of firefighters, having passed a test used to determine eligibility for promotion, brought suit against the city of New Haven for disparate treatment discrimination after the city decided to throw out the test, which was thought to have a disproportionate discriminatory effect on black firefighters. The disparate impact of this test could establish the city's liability under Title VII of the Civil Rights Act, which prompted the city to discard it. The Court's decision, authored by Justice Kennedy, stated that the withdrawal of the test for race reasons (a potential disparate impact discrimination liability, according to the city) led to disparate treatment discrimination against the white candidates who had passed the test: if an employer takes an intentionally discriminatory decision—discarding the test because white candidates scored significantly higher—to avoid or offset disparate impact discrimination, the employer must have a strong basis in evidence to believe it will be subject to disparate-impact liability. If not, and this is the case here, it constitutes disparate treatment discrimination. According to Siegel, Kennedy's position again illustrates a third reading of equality that seeks to maintain social cohesion, by preventing cause for resentment among those who passed the test and denouncing the reverse discrimination resulting from concerns about disparate impact discrimination against nonwhites. A disparate impact discrimination approach is often supported by antisubordination advocates, while anticlassification proponents tend to interpret discrimination more narrowly as exclusively disparate treatment.

In her article "From Colorblindness to Antibalkanization: An Emerging Ground of Decision in Race Equality Cases," Siegel highlights where this third perspective, emerging from tensions between the antisubordination and the anticlassification standards, breaks with the former view of equality. Antisubordination proponents do not generally view antidiscrimination law as a threat to civil solidarity or see racial repair as triggering resistance to the antisubordination theory. Comparison with antibalkanization concerns may prompt antisubordination advocates to devote more attention to questions about whether and how the law can respond to anger and resentment caused by racial repair. If equality is not abstract or imposed, but inherent to social relations, then equality law must show whether equality has been achieved through the existing social understanding and related social arrangements. The race conservative vision requires law to anticipate and adjust to resistance to the evolution of racial norms in order to preserve social solidarity. Race progressives instinctively balk at this question. Accommodation has a long history. Who should pay the cost, and for how long? This line of questioning leads to further queries about the problems of transitional justice, encouraging antisubordination proponents to share their vision of how equality should be implemented in a racially unequal world.

Race progressives can also prompt race moderates to think about implicit assumptions in the antibalkanization principle. Should the law be concerned with issues of estrangement and mistrust? Can the antibalkanization principle be upheld equitably, and does it respond to the risk of estrangement of minority communities as well as majority communities? If so, then why were the majority of the equality cases reviewed by the Supreme Court in recent years brought by white plaintiffs? Has the Court failed by applying a lower standard of scrutiny of equality for government practices that estrange minority communities, in particular with respect to racial profiling? Do cases alleging reverse discrimination call for the same or a higher level of scrutiny? Will the antibalkanization principle be vindicated in ways that entrench historical injustice—or that forge bonds of identity and empathy that a community needs to transcend historical injustice? Is the concern about social cohesion an alternative to race equality—or a predicate of it?[71]

Siegel shows how Barack Obama's "A More Perfect Union" speech delivered in 2008,[72] offering a universal vision of the race issue, seeks to appease the anger and resentment of black and white Americans alike, conveying an unspoken desire for cohesion and social peace. In "Equality Divided,"[73] Siegel takes a step back showing how the judicial scrutiny of the Equal Protection Clause of the U.S. Constitution reflects the power plays between the different branches of government. Siegel offers a doctrinal and political account of how the Supreme Court changed its interpretation of equal protection from the 1970s to the 2013 term, from a minority-protective understanding of equal protection to a predominantly (though not exclusively) majority-protective understanding of equal protection. The Warren Court saw its role as protecting minorities from majority prejudice. The Burger Court sought to limit the Court's superintendence of politics and handed much of the role of protecting minorities to the political branches (to representative government). The Rehnquist and Roberts Courts began to reassert a judicial role in superintending politics but now are acting increasingly to limit how the political branches can protect minorities—that is, to impose equal protection limits on civil rights initiatives—of the sort expressed in 2013 when the Roberts Court decided *Fisher*, further restricting affirmative action, and *Shelby County*, striking down a crucial provision of the Voting Rights Act.

Social cohesion also figures prominently in the European discourse,[74] but are the reasons for this interest the same? The contemporary debate over the integration of Roma people[75] and the rise of nationalist movements indicate that, outside of the domain of employment discrimination, the emergence of conflicts between social groups is a risk, in spite of the diversity management discourse promoted by the European Union. The September 2015 terrorist attacks in Paris might have fueled more social tension in France and Belgium. The references to fundamental rights in Europe's rejected constitutional treaty and in the Charter of Fundamental Rights of the European Union have not yet won widespread support.

The question posed by Siegel's presentation of antibalkanization is also a procedural one. Aside from the economic dimension of discrimination, isn't it a question of trust and confidence that a selection process is fair to both majority and minority group members and of the transparency of employment practices? If antidiscrimination law based on indirect discrimination principles is perceived as conferring advantages to certain categories of citizens, how can it be supported consensually by all groups unless it is better explained?[76] Against the backdrop of a global economic slowdown, in the United States and even in France,[77] greater attention is being paid to the "social meaning"[78] of antidiscrimination norms and consequently their ricochet effect on society, through which the selection of visible, "protected" groups leads to the emergence of ideas about whiteness, masculinity, singleness, queer theory, and gender deconstruction.[79] Is the lack of a communitarian spirit in France and the absence of organizations drawing attention to race, barring a few exceptions such as Conseil Représentatif des Associations Noires (CRAN),[80] enough to counter the risk of social divisiveness between interest groups? On the possible emergence of a generational conflict, Louis Chauvel does not exclude an interpretation that attributes the tensions to the advantages accorded to certain age groups over others.[81] Does age antidiscrimination law have the power to aggravate or alleviate these tensions?[82]

In any case, Siegel's work underscores the important role of constitutional case law in gaining valuable perspective and analyzing the overall social effects of the different models that can frame equality and its interpretation by judges, making a rich contribution to international comparison.

II. PUBLIC AND PRIVATE ENFORCEMENT OF ANTIDISCRIMINATION LAW

Antidiscrimination law cannot be effectively compared and understood without also contrasting the bodies in charge of enforcing this law: in both France and the

United States, labor unions participate in this enforcement but, most importantly, independent agencies have been established with the sole aim of applying antidiscrimination law. In the United States, this authority is the Equal Employment Opportunity Commission (EEOC).[83] Chai Feldblum, one of the scholars interviewed for this book, has been an EEOC commissioner since 2010. The fact that France's equivalent entity, the HALDE, was dismantled and its authority transferred to the Defender of Rights in 2011, makes a comparison all the more welcome. Employee trade unions also seem to have an ambivalent attitude toward antidiscrimination law, which I will attempt to clarify in the following conversations with American scholars. Another interesting point of comparison between the French and American situations focuses on the civil sanctions available[84] for infringements of antidiscrimination laws:[85] In the United States, the amount of damages awarded in a civil suit can be much higher than in France, especially if punitive damages are included.[86] In both countries, if the employee is not reinstated, judges will strive to redress in full the damages suffered as from the first discriminatory act.[87]

Public Enforcement of Antidiscrimination Law

In the following conversation, David Oppenheimer compares the enforcement of antidiscrimination law in the United States and in France.

MARIE MERCAT-BRUNS: *What means and resources are available for the enforcement of antidiscrimination laws?*

DAVID OPPENHEIMER: One of the things I have been thinking about since I have been coming to France studying comparative antidiscrimination law is why we use the enforcement mechanisms we use in American antidiscrimination law. When I first started asking the question a couple of years ago, I started doing some research on it, which was very revealing to me. I have not published anything on it yet. Some other people have.[88] This is not breaking news, but it's not much discussed.

There are at least five ways that we might enforce antidiscrimination law: criminal sanctions; voluntary mediation and conciliation; government agency with an administrative process; government agency with prosecution functions so it could go into civil courts on behalf of the government; and private enforcement in the courts. Let's take these one at a time.

The penal process: should we make antidiscrimination law part of the penal code, as you have in France?

The only discussion I have seen in the United States is by conservatives who oppose civil rights laws and who proposed it with the knowledge (in my opinion) that it would never be successful, because juries in the United States are not about to convict companies of discrimination except under the most horrendous circumstances.

MM-B: *So it would make discrimination law ineffective?*
DO: Exactly. To my knowledge, there was no discussion in the Congress in 1963 or 1964 about such a method.

Second method: voluntary mediation and conciliation. That's the method that was favored in the 1940s, '50s, and into the '60s by those conservatives in the United States who believed in promoting an antidiscrimination agenda but did not believe in requiring employers to stop discrimination. A sizable group that felt way.

So you could divide the United States in the '40s, '50s, and into the '60s into basically three groups. First: those who were opposed to any kind of civil rights enforcement or civil rights law because they were white supremacists and antigovernment and antilaw; in Congress those were basically the Southern Democrats. The second group: those who favored an antidiscrimination law and one with real teeth; most of whom were Northern Democrats, Western Democrats, and Northern Republicans. There were a few Northern Republicans in that category: John Lindsey, Jake Javitz. The third group, the Midwestern Republicans, did not want a civil rights law but did want companies to start voluntarily adopting civil rights policies. This was the "business roundtable" approach to civil rights, and they were a force until the 1980s. I think President George H. W. Bush (the first Bush) believed in that kind of civil rights enforcement, in a kind of "noblesse oblige" third method.

The third way to enforce antidiscrimination law is through a government agency with administrative hearings. That's the model of the NLRB [National Labor Relations Board] enforcing the NLRA [National Labor Relations Act],[89] and it's a potentially very powerful agency. It's powerful because its decisions can be reviewed only by the Court of Appeals, and they can be reviewed only for mistake of law or abuse of discretion. What that means is that usually the decision of the administrative agency will be the final decision. The administrative agency's lawyers and hearing officers are selected by the Administration, by the government. Sometimes they are civil servants. They work for the State. At the higher levels, they are political appointees selected by the Administration. These agencies are potentially very independent and very powerful.

Many Republicans were concerned that if there were a civil rights enforcement agency with these powers, it would be too powerful and too political. This was the model favored by liberals, who wanted a strong enforcement agency. The CRA [Civil Rights Act] was introduced in 1963.

MM-B: *Wasn't it the EEOC?*
DO: The EEOC, as originally conceived, was going to be just like the NLRB.
MM-B: *But they are not similar?*
DO: No. The NLRB has exclusive jurisdiction, which means if you want to bring a claim for a violation of the NLRA, the only place you can bring it is in front of the Board. And in 1963, Republicans in Congress were upset with the

NLRB because they felt that it had become too liberal, too political, too much of a Democratic Party institution.

They feared the creation of an EEOC just as powerful and just as political. So a compromise solution was to have an EEOC, an antidiscrimination enforcement agency, but its cases would be prosecuted not before the agency but instead in civil court in front of federal judges who have been appointed by the President and confirmed by the Senate—judges who act in a very public forum, judges who reflect broadly the communities they come from. Well, this resulted in the appointment of lots of segregationist judges. In John Kennedy's case, every Southern judge he appointed until very late in his term were pro-segregation because they were Southern Democrats. The Southern Democratic Party "decided" who the President would appoint to the bench in their state. You had to go through the Senators from those states. You didn't have to as a matter of law, but politically you had to. It was politically required, so that the President could have a good relationship with the Senate.

So, back to the negotiations over the Civil Rights Act. At the very end of the process, Everett Dirksen, a conservative Republican from Illinois who served as the Senate minority leader, held the trump card. Was he going to support the Civil Rights Act or not? Well, he was very distressed about government enforcement of the Civil Rights Act. Basically he had the business roundtable point of view about how the law should be enforced. So he proposed a compromise, in which he would weaken the employment enforcement mechanism, providing that enforcement would be strictly through private law suits.

Now, how many private lawyers were there at that time in the United States who could bring plaintiffs' employment discrimination cases? Virtually none. There were a few people with the NAACP [National Association for the Advancement of Colored People],[90] a few people at the ACLU [American Civil Liberties Union][91] (where Ruth Bader Ginsburg led its efforts on women's rights issues), and a few people with the National Lawyers Guild.[92] There were a few such organizations. That was it.

Senator Dirksen never imagined that he would create a whole new career path for American lawyers. There are now thousands of lawyers who make a living representing plaintiffs in employment discrimination cases.

MM-B: *Are there that many representing plaintiffs or employers?*
DO: Many more represent employers, but thousands represent plaintiffs. It was unimaginable at that time. That compromise had really been intended to kill enforcement.
MM-B: *Is private action efficient?*
DO: We are not nearly there yet. That was step one. Step two: in 1972, in broadening the CRA,[93] Congress gave the EEOC power to have hearings and to do some of the things the NLRB does, although not exclusively and not with

review limited to the courts of appeals. But the EEOC was never given the budget needed to do its job in a meaningful way.

MM-B: *Can it already be a party in the case?*

DO: It can bring a case, acting as the complaining party. It has had that authority since 1964, which provided that the Attorney General can bring a pattern and practice case on behalf of the EEOC.

In 1972, the EEOC was given the right to intervene in a civil action, and to conduct its own hearings. That's the fourth way to enforce antidiscrimination law. The fifth way is private enforcement action.

So that really leads to two further questions: Has private enforcement worked? Has EEOC enforcement worked since 1972? I think the answer to both questions comes all the way back to the very first question we discussed: Should we see the glass half empty or half full?

Private enforcement has, in some ways, been terribly disappointing. It turns out that these cases are very hard to win. It turns out that these cases are very expensive. It turns out that most lawyers who go into this area to represent plaintiffs find that they can't survive financially, and if they continue to do it, they do it as only part of their practice, and it is not the part of the practice where they are making money. There are a few notable exceptions.

MM-B: *We are talking about the ones who represent plaintiffs.*

DO: It turns out that there is enormous judicial bias against employment discrimination claims.

MM-B: *And is that also from liberal judges, or is it just because they are conservative judges?*

DO: Conservative judges are very conservative concerning such claims. Even liberal judges are probably more skeptical than they ought to be about such claims because there is a very pervasive rhetoric of skepticism about civil rights claims that has had a social and psychological effect, making people believe that discrimination is something that is easily claimed. I think the opposite is probably true.

MM-B: *Why do you think there is that perception? Because they think the burden of proof in employment discrimination shifts?*

DO: Do people believe that to be true? I doubt many people give much thought to burdens of proof, even judges. I think the problem is racial bias, often unconscious bias, against minorities, which is often expressed as skepticism about discrimination law.

MM-B: *They feel it is hostility towards them?*

DO: Certainly anyone accused of discrimination feels very much accused of something terrible.

MM-B: *Does it trigger something on the part of the judge?*

DO: Yes, there is always discussion about empathy and how much a judge should be empathetic. My sense is that many judges feel empathy for the defendants in discrimination cases. I think they identify with defendants, who tend to be more like them in terms of their social status. They tend to be people who are educated, who are affluent (because there is no point in suing poor people), and as a result, if you observe the courtroom in a typical employment discrimination case and ask who does the judge feel empathy with, all too often you can sense that the judge feels empathy with the defendant, a sense of identification with the defendant. And the Supreme Court decisions make these cases harder and harder to prove.

Now, recall that the glass is half full. There are cases where private enforcement has been wonderfully effective. First of all, the class action area for a period of time was very effective, and that continues to be true although there are new limits on class actions.[94] There are class action practitioners who are plaintiffs' lawyers, who are very skilled, and who have lots of resources available. They bring important cases that really do influence the workplace. Occasionally, cases that involve terrible acts of discrimination get in front of judges who are somewhat sympathetic and juries who are somewhat sympathetic, and that produces big damage awards that get lots of publicity.

As a result, I think there is substantial fear on the part of employers about being sued. If employers were more aware of how hard it is to actually win a discrimination suit, they might be less fearful. But part of what they fear is not losing but the cost of litigation whether they win or lose.

Private enforcement has been a mixed bag. There are lots of examples you can point to where it has been very important. There are industries where it has had a big impact. On the other hand, the cases are very hard to bring, very hard to win, and it is much harder to win a discrimination case than most other kinds of civil cases.

MM-B: *Is it easier to win a race case than a sex case? Does the ground play a role in the success of the litigation? Is it easier to bring a suit alleging race discrimination than one alleging sex discrimination?*

DO: The cases that are more likely to succeed are whistleblower cases and sexual harassment cases. Sexual harassment cases end up in a whole other category. Part of the reason is the sexual harassment cases are actually litigated. They are often the quid pro quo cases, where the behavior is pretty bad. In such cases it is easy to get the judge and the jury angry at the defendant.

I have done a study, which was published in the UC Davis law review, looking at jury verdicts in California in employment cases over a two-year period.[95] What I found is that sexual harassment cases were the most frequently won by plaintiffs. The hardest cases to win were race discrimination cases brought by black women and age discrimination cases brought by women over the age of 50. I also found that sexual harassment cases brought by men claiming harassment by other men were among the easiest cases to win. Perhaps these cases appeal to the jury's homophobia.

MM-B: *Is there a contradiction in saying that antidiscrimination law has transformed society and that private enforcement is not that effective?*

DO: Yes. But even if private enforcement has not been that effective in resolving cases, it does not mean it has not been effective in terms of employer behavior, because employers fear not just liability but the cost of litigation.

MM-B: *In France, we see similar employer reactions to the HALDE's more proactive measures facilitating private enforcement. So you are saying that this enforcement is dissuasive?*

DO: Yes. I used to think the EEOC was an unusually ineffective, highly politicized administrative agency; I was very critical.

MM-B: *Have you written about that?*

DO: No, I haven't written about that. Julie Suk, whom I admire very much, has persuaded me that I need to reexamine that opinion.[96] Let me channel Julie a little bit here, if I may. The EEOC has passed important regulations,[97] which for the most part have been progressive and influential, even though in some instances the Supreme Court has rejected them.[98]

MM-B: *So the EEOC has played a doctrinal role?*

DO: Yes, the EEOC has played an important doctrinal role. They influence government hiring and private-sector hiring through their regulations, their interpretations, and their questions and answers.

They have at times been politicized, and the EEOC under President Reagan took some dreadful positions, especially when Justice Thomas was the chair. The EEOC convinced the Court to interpret sexual harassment law in ways that have hurt women very badly.

MM-B: *According to a former EEOC commissioner whom I met, the fight is clearly based on ideological differences of opinions of commissioners. At the same time, when the majority of the members of the EEOC are liberals, then it can expand the breadth of antidiscrimination law.*

DO: The problem is, how can we accept a system where justice for the victims of discrimination depends on these political questions? The EEOC does process a lot of complaints. But it doesn't fully investigate enough of them, and that's a terrible shame.

MM-B: *Not enough money to investigate?*

DO: Partly it is funding. Partly it has been a lack of leadership and political support. But given the limitations of private enforcement, that agency enforcement becomes more attractive, for all its faults.

Robert Post contributes his views on the relationship between the administrative state and antidiscrimination law and the role of institutions like the EEOC, since the European Equal Equality Employment Directive (Directive 2000/78/EC) invites member states to create or to consolidate the action of antidiscrimination law enforcement bodies.

ROBERT POST: You can think about antidiscrimination law on the model that it polices wrongdoing, so it is like a tort system: it focuses on an employer's act to do a bad thing, to discriminate against a worker ... the antidiscrimination law comes along and it remedies it. So the worker has to bring suit either before an administrative agency or before a court to remedy the wrong. That is one model of antidiscrimination law. It is a remedy for individual wrongs.

But if you think about antidiscrimination law in a more transformative way, or if you think about antidiscrimination law as a mechanism of redistribution, then this account is more or less inadequate. It puts the burden on those who are victims of discrimination to come forward—that is more or less a contingent fact. They are going to be discouraged by transactions costs, by the fact they are going to put their jobs at risk, and so on. So you want to be more proactive. Also you would want to make the systemic aspects of the problem visible. They are not visible when discrimination is treated as a phenomenon that is only cognizable on a case-by-case basis. So it is in that context that the administrative state becomes especially important.

The administrative state (a) is proactive—it prevents the problem before it happens—and (b) is capable of employing mechanisms like statistics that make a problem visible, that are structural, and that are not merely the sum of individual pieces. So what allowed antidiscrimination law to be truly transformative in the United States was the use by the EEOC of administrative law techniques like recording requirements and statistical requirements that make patterns visible. Once you see the patterns, then you can intervene at a different level and much more effectively, rather than a series case-by-case, and you can imagine this in the sense of changing the distribution of what is normal in a society and making the distribution visible first. It is a typical function of the administrative state and the use of statistics.

[Later in the interview, Post comes back to the topic of antidiscrimination enforcement agencies.]

MM-B: *What do you think of the difference between the federal EEOC agency and regional agencies? Is it important? In the United States, state laws on discrimination are less visible, and you have regional administrative bodies.*

RP: Yes, we are not centralized, and there are advantages to local law enforcement agencies which are closer to the ground; they see more of what is happening; they are more in touch with local grievances.

At the same time, local bodies are more subject to capture by local elites, and the national one is less subject to local pressures. They have complicated trade-offs and different vulnerabilities than nationals. By having duplication of enforcement mechanisms, you make up for the characteristic weaknesses of each. Although I am not sure this is true, antidiscrimination commissions began at the state level and then moved to the national level. It is the case that when we think about these questions, local levels might be more subject to innovation. The barrier to entry is higher at the national level, and so it makes sense to have avenues of local experimentation. In antidiscrimination law, you can see what works and what doesn't, and we ban different forms of discrimination in different localities.[99] For example, housing courts ban discrimination if your housing is supported by the federal government. So this allows us to see and to experiment and to learn which forms are best suited to prevent discrimination.

Comparative Perspectives

In Oppenheimer's presentation of the various ways to enforce American antidiscrimination law, a few points are particularly worthy of note. The first is a certain skepticism that can be detected regarding the effectiveness of repressive criminal sanctions and, conversely, of the mediation work of the HALDE. Oppenheimer emphasizes the loftier standard of evidence required in a criminal case—showing guilt beyond a reasonable doubt—combined with the fact that in many cases, discrimination is an unconscious act occurring without discriminatory intent. A second point to be highlighted is the influential role of the regulations issued by the EEOC in the United States if litigation is not intentionally circumvented by deferring to employer grievance mechanisms or limited to summary judgment.[100] Judges often use the regulations promulgated by the EEOC as guidance in identifying admissible evidence in a civil proceeding, grasping the particularities of specific grounds of discrimination (reasonable accommodation in religious discrimination, for example), using statistics to show disparate impact, and so on. The HALDE's annual reports and published decisions also influenced the decisions of French judges.[101] Will the Défenseur des Droits fulfill the same role as a quasi-doctrinal source of expertise?

Like Oppenheimer, other scholars evoke the different forms of antidiscrimination enforcement. They discuss the contribution of collective bargaining to employment discrimination law and to diversity. Robert Post looks at the broader picture of employment law in the context of globalization. The following insights of Post and Frank Dobbin suggest that the interplay between collective bargaining, diversity, and globalization in employment discrimination is a current trend in the United States, but the scholars illustrate the risks, challenges, and potential benefits of this multifaceted approach.

Collective Bargaining, Diversity and Globalization

Robert Post comments on the effectiveness of collective bargaining agreements on diversity.

MARIE MERCAT-BRUNS: *French law encourages trade unions and employer associations to enter into collective agreements on diversity. Do you think that this can be an effective means of promoting equal opportunity? Do you think that collective bargaining agreements on diversity can be a mode of transformative law (according to the models you described earlier) or it is just discourse?*[102]

ROBERT POST: In the United States, collective bargaining is associated with the labor movement, and the labor movement was in tension with antidiscrimination law. When Nixon started introducing goals in affirmative action, he did it self-consciously to split the labor movement from the Democratic Party [which was identified with civil rights and people of color]. So collective bargaining is typically a norm in which the consciousness of the working class is reflected. Antidiscrimination is not, and in the United States, this has been a source of great tension.

MM-B: I think in France it is quite similar. A lot of unions say antidiscrimination law is not labor and employment law in the traditional sense. Antidiscrimination law is seen as a conservative, capitalistic, European-inspired economic law that will destroy the basic rights of the workers. A lot of the unions don't believe in it, actually, in France.

RP: In Europe, in the context that you are talking about—correct me if I am wrong—antidiscrimination law is discrimination law between nationals of the different countries. So what you get is the law of the European Union, which says that countries cannot discriminate against the workers of other member states, and that means it is very hard to have national labor policies. It's neoliberal in the sense that it opens up the labor market and makes it an open market, whereas unionization is often on a national scale. So there is a tension with antidiscrimination law viewed as a matter of discrimination between nationals and a national labor movement. That is different from antidiscrimination law against Muslims, for example. That would not be neoliberal because it would not be market-oriented.

MM-B: *Actually, the European directives adopted in 2000 prohibiting discrimination in employment sought to ensure equal treatment among European Union citizens regardless of their nationality or sex and to promote fundamental EU values by helping to combat race and sex discrimination. The two goals (the removal of market barriers based on nationality and the enshrinement of nondiscrimination in employment as a fundamental right with respect to a certain number of grounds) are often conflated. This makes it difficult to promote within member states the idea that labor rights acquired nationally and those acquired at the EU level must be protected to the same degree. A valid question therefore is whether we are converging toward a level of social protection that represents the lowest common denominator among EU member states, choosing equal treatment at all costs, even if it means a gradual narrowing of the scope of employment rights already acquired in certain countries.*

RP: I think that it is correct to distinguish between discrimination based on nationality and discrimination based on race or sex. The underlying logic of the former is based on the idea of a unified labor market. From the viewpoint of a particular member state, the protection afforded by such a unified market can either raise the bar—increasing worker protection—or lower it to a common denominator—reducing their protection. In contrast, the underlying logic of the prohibition of racial or sex discrimination is based on the idea that all citizens *within* a state must have equal access to national labor market opportunities regardless of their race or sex. This logic is intrinsically hostile to the creation of national protections in labor law. In the United States, there are some unions that see the future of union movement as international. For collective bargaining, they organize at an international level, against multinational corporations, or in countries, through labor courts. So there is beginning to be a different sensibility among organized labor in the United States. Labor is seen as an international commodity; if you have a union, it has to be an international union. This is happening in the United States, but it is a relatively recent development.

MM-B: *What unions are involved?*

RP: The Service Employees International Union (SEIU)[103] is very organized internationally. [In the early 20th century, Samuel] Gompers and the AFL[104] organized Mexican workers because they realized that unless you organize workers on the other side of the border, you could organize all you want in Texas, but it would be undercut and mean nothing. So David Montgomery, a labor historian, wrote that the way to organize labor is to organize it traditionally.[105]

MM-B: *This is really important, because in Europe we should know more about the American organized labor movement. On the international level, do the unions use ILO conventions?*

RP: Yes. The SEIU uses the standards set out in ILO conventions and has filed complaints for violations of the freedom of association affecting the organization of workers in various countries where multinationals are operating. The SEIU also works with the OECD [Organization for Economic Co-operation and Development]. Their strategy is to collaborate with their counterparts, trade unions in other countries, in negotiating global framework agreements with multinational companies to strengthen the enforcement of ILO standards.

For example, within the world's largest employer of security guards, they not only organized in the United States but they organized in the different countries where they operate in the labor market with very successful campaigns. It was not a rights-based campaign. It was a collective bargaining campaign.

MM-B: *I want to come back to the nature of collective bargaining compared to legislative norms. When you use collective bargaining, the production of this norm is very different. Of course, there is a power play, but basically it is putting norm into context. Do you think that if we could use collective bargaining in the United States (I know its influence is quite narrow today in the workplace), it could help to better implement antidiscrimination policies there? That is one aspect of the trend in France: you can't look at antidiscrimination law in the banking sector the way you look at it in the building sector, so we need customized tools, and collective bargaining can help us with that.*

RP: I think about this sociologically: I ask who is the source of authority in collective bargaining, who is the source of authority in legislation, who is the source of authority in judge-made law? And people are making the law in each norm. So collective bargaining is either coming out of a given workplace, so some bargain is struck between the working class and owners, or it is between unions more generally understood to represent the working class and owners, whereas legislation is deemed more populist generally, which can be more progressive or more regressive depending on the political state of the country. Judges are a form of administrative elite, and they are speaking from that language and with that authority.

The first question is, where is the source of authority? And the second question is, over whom does the norm extend? Does it extend over only the workplace or the society at large? These are rather large differences, so I don't think they are susceptible to general answers.

You are going to have to ask, what are the interests and the consciousness of the working class—either a particular plant or particular union—and can that be the instrument or not of progressive antidiscrimination law? In history, it has not been, but maybe things are changing. There are now organizations and unions that are trying to organize immigrants, for example.

Their consciousness is quite different than the traditional working-class consciousness: you have to ask, what is the organizational basis of the union, what union, which plant, and so on? I don't think it is susceptible to generalizations.

Frank Dobbin adds his view on how collective bargaining can be used to achieve diversity.

FRANK DOBBIN: In a system with a wide number of trade unions representing people in different industries, as in France, trade unions probably have very different effects by industry. In service industries where lots of their members are women and minorities, we may expect them to be proponents of equal opportunity. But in some of the skilled manufacturing industries where there are few women and members of minority groups, they may not see a problem to solve and may be inclined to practice what sociologists call "social closure"—cutting off access to these highly paid jobs to groups that are not already well-represented and reserving the best jobs for people like themselves.

Comparative Perspectives

Whether or not labor unions have helped advance the fight against discrimination and the enforcement of antidiscrimination law is a difficult question to answer. In France and the United States, conflicting pulls between the activity of unions and the expansion of antidiscrimination law can be observed.[106] On the one hand, unions are intended to advance workers' rights in this era of globalization, so discrimination, especially discrimination based on trade union membership, is being fought at an international as well as a national level. Unions have actively participated in this combat, as attested by union demands, ILO standards,[107] and the union protection rules in the NLRA. Specific case law generated by national bans on antiunion discrimination has been gradually emerging.[108] It is interesting to note that although the European Social Charter protects collective action,[109] the European Union has only begun to refer to this by incorporating the right to collective action into its Charter of Fundamental Rights. French case law on discrimination based on union membership also contains novel decisions regarding evidence of such discrimination in performance appraisals and career advancement.[110] In addition, the "equal pay for equal work" principle arising from the fight for pay equity between men and women led to a sharper demarcation of the meaning of *equal work* in environments in which discrimination is systemic and results from a historical or stereotyped attribution of occupations or responsibilities that should be remunerated equally.[111]

On the other hand, in seeking to win the support of a broad population of employees, labor unions have not always seen their mission as compatible with championing the claims of minority groups or, in the case of women, specific claims not applicable to all employees. Leaving aside old cases of discrimination by majority unions, such as the Supreme Court case of *Steele v. Louisville*[112] in the United States, will France's recent reforms changing the rules for union representativeness, which is no longer presumed but dependent on the share of votes cast in workplace elections, be any help in addressing claims concerning a minority of employees?[113] Should the existence of a plurality of trade unions in France have facilitated the representation of multiple viewpoints, such as those of people from diverse backgrounds? Although strategic alliances are still being formed between unions based on certain commonalities in their demands, they do not necessarily reflect minority interests. Furthermore, in the past, a presumption of representativeness probably lent legitimacy to the main national confederations, which up to now have traditionally defended those causes that concern all workers (retirement, wages, and working conditions).

Given the ambivalent role of labor union activity in the fight against all forms of discrimination, what are the benefits and drawbacks of organizing workers in a way that reflects their diverse identities? According to Maria Ontiveros, the SEIU and other unions have shaped campaigns and initiatives according to the cultural habits and identities of certain employees, such as Hispanic service workers in California.[114] Such identity-based organizing is possible in a country with a communitarian tradition in which multiethnic and multicultural values intertwine with everyday life. But with the current postmodern rejection of rigidly constructed identities, especially in countries that value universalism and deny the existence of groups, this type of organization focusing on cultural interest groups raises many questions. As observed by Michael Selmi and Molly McUsic,[115] even if there is no longer such a thing as a "universal worker," implicitly embodied by the married, white, male worker in the United States, fears that identity-based unions will lead to dispersion and a fragmentation of the power of its members are valid. Instead, inspired by French theory among others, the scholars turn to the concept of a "cosmopolitan unionism" embracing commonalities while recognizing differences: they envision not a union based on cultural identities but a union that is organized and functions in ways that leave room for identity-based claims to be discussed and debated.[116] In the United States, this would necessarily require a reform of the majority system under the National Labor Relations Act (NLRA). As European labor unions gradually organize, the moment is well chosen to initiate broader reflection on incorporating forums for discussion ensuring the contribution of cultural interest groups to union negotiations, because the implicit, homogenous "universal worker" model is not necessarily still relevant across Europe.

Diversity and Trade Unions

Frank Dobbin continues the conversation on diversity and trade unions.

MARIE MERCAT-BRUNS: *France has developed collective bargaining agreements: do you think using the social partners to create norms on diversity might be a more effective way to promote equal opportunity?*

FRANK DOBBIN: I can say unequivocally that this strategy was a disaster in the United States. For the most part, unions hindered the achievement of equal opportunity. From the very earliest days, unions were segregated by race and gender. Even after they were required to integrate, most union leaders saw no benefit in promoting race and gender equality at work. Perhaps it will be different in France, but in a workplace that is not yet fully integrated, in an economy with high levels of unemployment, it isn't clear to me that the current union members would have a strong interest in promoting diversity. Perhaps some would for ideological reasons, but those who are hoping to get their sons and nephews into the union may be happy if their union doesn't get into the business of social advocacy in favor of equality of opportunity.

Dobbin's book *Inventing Equal Opportunity* traces the history of how companies have integrated antidiscrimination law into their practices through their human resource teams and not their legal departments.[117] Neither labor unions nor the government have been effective in interpreting antidiscrimination laws and diversity norms such as equal employment opportunity (equal access to jobs and promotions). Dobbin assesses these integrated norms and shows how diversity and bias training to raise awareness have tended to minimize the causes of discrimination instead of bringing them to the forefront. Affirmative action tools have proved to be much more effective in actually bringing a critical mass of people representing minorities into different job levels and promoting the benefits of diversified a labor force. These are valuable insights for France, where collective agreements on diversity have been adopted. An analysis of the diversity tools they cover and of the role of labor unions in France can be informed by these comments as well as emerging studies on the reach of these collective agreements.[118]

3

Disparate Treatment Discrimination

Intent, Bias, and the Burden of Proof

Litigating direct or disparate treatment discrimination cases is often a question of proving what is in the mind of the employer.[1] Although the defendant may openly admit to discriminatory intent, in most cases he or she will attempt to hide the prohibited motive,[2] knowing that the adversary system of proof and, in French law, Article 1315 of the French Civil Code[3] places the responsibility on the plaintiff for bringing evidence to the attention of the court. In European law, discriminatory intent seems to carry an even greater weight and is regarded not just as a factor but as the primary component of establishing a discrimination case, to the extent that the existence of intent alone is sufficient to support a claim of direct discrimination, even without a designated victim.[4]

The prohibition of direct discrimination is a norm that employers in the United States have had to comply with since the 1960s, and it provides for a shifting burden of proof in recognition of the difficulty of obtaining direct evidence to prove discriminatory intent. The idea of burden of proof actually encompasses two burdens: the burden of production and the burden of persuasion.[5] The burden of production first lies with the plaintiff, who must establish a prima facie case by producing evidence from which it can be concluded that there was an intention to discriminate. The evidentiary burden then shifts to the employer to articulate a nondiscriminatory reason for his or her adverse employment action.[6] As Richard Ford later illustrates, one difference between French law and U.S. law involves the type of justification that an employer can give. In France, it must be not only nondiscriminatory but also objective.

A second difference lies in the burden of persuasion.[7] In the United States, the nondiscriminatory justification provided by the employer at the rebuttal stage is a simple response to the discrimination claim (burden of production): the burden of persuasion remains with the plaintiff, who must convince the judge that the justification is simply a pretext and that unlawful discrimination nevertheless occurred.[8] In France, the burden of proof allocation provided for in Article L. 1134-1 of the French Labor Code states that when the plaintiff establishes facts that show presumed discrimination, the onus is on the defendant to prove that his or her decision was justified by objective elements unrelated to any form of discrimination. The Code goes on to specify that the judge shall make a decision after having ordered any investigative measures he or she deems useful. It would therefore appear that in France, provided that the plaintiff succeeds in the arduous task of presenting elements of fact to allow the presumption of discrimination, then the final burden is on the employer to prove an objective and nondiscriminatory motive.

French law also seems to be more generous toward plaintiffs in discrimination disputes in they are not systematically required to present data on comparably situated persons in order to establish a prima facie case.[9] As the Cour de Cassation reiterated in overturning a Court of Appeals decision on this point, showing the comparability of situations is not an indispensable prerequisite to establishing discrimination.[10] Recently, direct discrimination in collective bargaining agreements were so blatant in the text itself that comparability was not necessary.[11] The HALDE traditionally played a key role in obtaining the data needed to establish the existence of a discrimination, thanks to its power of investigation, which the Defender of Rights (formerly the HALDE) is presumably continuing to exercise.

In the United States, if the employer articulates a legitimate, nondiscriminatory reason, it is ultimately up to the plaintiff to prove that the articulated reason is not credible regarding the job description or required qualifications or is a pretext for discrimination. Certain employers have demonstrated skill in producing nondiscriminatory pretexts or using disparate impact discrimination to achieve their discriminatory goals.[12] Proving discrimination is an immensely difficult task,[13] prompting legal scholars and even judges to explore how social science evidence[14] can be used to identify discrimination[15] in the form of stereotyping. These stereotypes may even be unconscious, or—to use the term Linda Krieger prefers, which she discusses in her interview—implicit. A person with an implicit bias does not necessarily have any conscious desire or intent to discriminate, sometimes making it difficult for judges, who themselves have implicit biases, to recognize them.

In this chapter, Linda Krieger, Richard Ford, Robert Post, Martha Minow, and Christine Jolls comment on the scope and limitations of this social science research. Devah Pager, whose sociological fieldwork has revealed unconscious bias in hiring practices, discusses her findings. Frank Dobbin, a sociologist as well, shares his thoughts on what social psychology research has to offer.

I. STEREOTYPES, IMPLICIT BIAS, AND INTENTIONAL DISCRIMINATION

A considerable amount of American legal scholarship addresses the relationship between conscious and unconscious biases and discriminatory practices, whereas in France, there is practically no debate about this issue. Some American scholars attempt to use cognitive and social sciences to better understand and define the phenomenon of direct discrimination,[16] which is overwhelmingly hidden, while others warn against the possible excesses that these approaches can lead to.[17]

In the following interview extract, Professor Linda Krieger explains the construction of conscious and implicit biases.

MARIE MERCAT-BRUNS: *Shall we start with implicit bias?*
LINDA KRIEGER: Before we talk specifically about implicit bias, we need to back up and talk about the relationship between social science and law, because much of the discussion about implicit bias is actually about the relationship between legal doctrine on the one hand and advances in social science on the other. So I will start there.

In legal analysis, lawyers and judges use two different categories of facts. In U.S. administrative law, they are sometimes referred to as adjudicative facts and legislative facts.

Adjudicative facts are the local facts that characterize a particular dispute. We are dealing with adjudicative facts when we are sifting through particular bits of evidence, attempting to piece them together to figure out what happened at a particular point in time and place. But most of the time, especially when we are dealing with events that we cannot observe directly—such as mental states, for example—we cannot move directly from a particular bit of evidence to a factual conclusion, what we might call an "ultimate fact." To get to those ultimate facts, we have to draw inferences. In order to draw inferences from particular facts, we have to have some sort of theory of reality. In order to arrive at adjudicative facts, facts that together represent what happened at a particular time and place, we have to filter those facts through our taken-for-granted understandings about how things work in the world. These taken-for-granted understandings about how things work in the world are what administrative law scholars have called "legislative facts." These legislative facts tell us how to interpret ambiguous events, what inferences to draw from the evidentiary facts we can actually observe.

These legislative facts are constantly operating in the cognitive background. So whether we are thinking about social science or not, we are constantly using social science, or I should say, social pseudo-science, to interpret ambiguous information or to draw inferences from observed events. It is unavoidable that judges, lawyers, and jurors will apply taken-for-granted assumptions about how things work in the world when they are reasoning inferentially in deciding legal disputes. These taken-for-granted theories about how things work in the world are what I mean by legislative facts.

If one looks, one can see legislative facts reflected in judicial decisions; one can see them in the arguments of advocates. When you read a lawyer's closing argument after a trial, you will see not just reference to specific bits of testimony in the record; you will also see the lawyers trying to interpret those bits of testimony, using legislative facts to suggest what those bits of testimony should be taken to mean about the ultimate facts of the case.

An example of this: When we speak of intent to discriminate in a disparate treatment discrimination case, we all bring to the resolution of a dispute understandings about how people go about making decisions about other people. What is the extent to which perceptions of other people are necessarily subjective or objective? What are the different ways in which social perceptions and judgments can be distorted? Are those distortions random, or do they tend to fall into certain patterns? Are those patterns easily influenced by the particular context in which the perceiver is situated, or do they remain relatively constant over time, like preferences for things like iced cream flavors? Are people consciously aware of the various influences that are operating on their preferences or their judgments at a given moment in time? If so, to what extent and under what circumstances are they more or less likely to have that awareness? When we are talking about implicit bias, what we are really talking about is whose understanding of the taken-for-granted background knowledge of how people go about forming judgments and making decisions about other people are we going to apply in antidiscrimination adjudications? These understandings, these beliefs about how social perception and judgment works become legislative facts that control the development of antidiscrimination jurisprudence as a whole and shape the adjudication of particular cases. This is unavoidable.

What empirical social scientists who study intergroup perception and judgment and their allies in the legal academy are saying is that the "common sense" understandings of how people react to, make judgments about, and behave toward stereotyped groups are not accurate. And there now exists a virtual mountain of solid, scientific evidence backing them up as they make this claim. The intuitive social science currently underpinning antidiscrimination law is junk science. But it is deeply embedded in antidiscrimination jurisprudence and is proving very difficult to displace.

Antidiscrimination jurisprudence will always incorporate and reflect a set of legislative facts about the nature of intergroup perception and judgment. Unfortunately, what is happening now in the United States is that it is incorporating and reflecting theories that have been definitively disconfirmed by many decades of research in cognitive social psychology and, more recently, cognitive neuroscience.

We are now, as always, applying someone's taken-for-granted understanding of how the world works when we adjudicate discrimination cases. Unfortunately, we tend to apply the understanding of whatever ethnic, racial, socioeconomic class, to the development of the law and the adjudication of disputes. That is not a neutral or heterogeneous group of people. It is a homogeneous group of people, and they tend to share a particular, self-serving set of ideological understandings about how the world works, including understandings that are informed by their own privileged position in society.

In antidiscrimination adjudications as elsewhere in public life, those who control the discourse and the outcomes bring to their activities particular understandings of how things work in the world. They call it "common sense." This is one of the great contributions of empirical psychological research—it often shows us that the common sense is wrong. People, it turns out, often don't know what factors are affecting their judgments about other people. People often don't know that they are biased. Economic decision makers do not always behave as rational maximizers of utility. The list goes on and on. The question is, how do we update legal doctrines, which are by nature backward looking, to incorporate advances in the empirical social sciences, which roll forward?

Stanford law professor Richard Ford responds to Krieger's explanations with his views on the challenges of implicit bias thinking.

RICHARD FORD: The social science [about implicit bias], from what I understand, is a bit more ambiguous than is often suggested. That is one thing.

I think that matters because, if you hang your legal argument on social science, then your legal argument is only as strong as the social science. And particularly when you are also dealing with an issue that is salient in the popular culture and about which ultimately you need to persuade people, you can find yourself worse off than if you had not relied on a social science argument. So that's a risk, I think, because the popular uptake of the implicit bias literature is "you can take a test and it tells you whether you have unconscious bias," but the people working in the field say, "Well, it does not quite prove that; what it really proves is that a group of people in a large statistical sample have some sort of implicit association which may or may not be bias." Already, the conservatives are making these kinds of attacks. For instance, there is a professor at Berkeley, Philip Tetlock, who is on the attack against implicit bias. So you are not going to get a free pass.[18]

But I think the larger question for me as a legal scholar and as someone interested in social theory is this: We, in the modern, technologically advanced societies of the West—and certainly in the United States—tend to put a lot of stock in technical, empirical studies, even when the question that we are ultimately trying to resolve isn't an empirical question. That concerns me. The implicit bias literature feeds into a fetish of social science.

In a sense, the implicit bias theories argue that if the Implicit Association Test shows that the decision maker is "biased," we can conclude that she has made an objectively incorrect decision—as opposed to a normatively repugnant decision. The idea is that the decision maker doesn't know her own mind—she is objectively incorrect about her own subjective preferences—because her decisions are being distorted by biases that she herself is not aware are at work. The false hope is that then I can prove that her decisions are invalid—not just objectionable or socially deleterious but invalid, in the way a rigged election is invalid. If that were true, then there would be no normative conflict involved at all—antidiscrimination laws would not involve contested political issues—instead they would involve only the technical question of how to make sure decision makers make the objectively valid decision and avoid the "biased" decision.

But in fact, what we actually are dealing with here is a normative issue: how should we balance the freedom of the individual to hire who he or she wants, rent to the person he or she wants to rent to, and so forth against the social need for integration and diversity? I don't think that this normative question can be resolved by social science. I just don't think that this is going to resolve the question. I don't think it will resolve the question in individual cases, and I don't think it is going to resolve the broader policy question.

In the 1970s, when the first iteration of the unconscious bias argument was articulated by Charles Lawrence in an article called "The Id, the Ego and Equal Protection,"[19] Lawrence was trying to make an argument for a disparate impact theory in equal protection jurisprudence. The idea was that unconscious bias could be identified only indirectly—through unexplained or unjustified statistical imbalance. But disparate impact theory is not a part of constitutional law and it is under sustained attack in the areas where it exists.

Ever since, people have been trying to develop arguments that ultimately go to that question—the question of disparate impact theory—and I think this is just the latest iteration of it. This is the latest version of trying to make an argument for introducing disparate impact on the equal protection side in constitutional law and for a beefed-up disparate impact in Title VII.

The implicit bias theory is basically an argument in favor of disparate impact, an argument to make it stronger—and it is also an argument for changing the way we distribute the burden of proof in intentional discrimination cases, making the law more friendly to plaintiffs. In both cases, the idea is that implicit biases can't be captured with existing evidentiary standards for proof of intentional discrimination.

Now, all of these are good projects as a matter of law and policy, and I am on Linda Krieger's side of every one of them, but I don't think the social sciences justify it. I think the argument is the same without the social science. It's a normative argument: we should do more to promote inclusion and diversity at the expense of the freedom of employers and other decision makers. That is where my hesitation about the social science justification comes in.

This argument almost makes bias into a medical condition, a kind of mental illness. You hear arguments like that. It medicalizes the issue, and I think the medicalization of social problems is a real pathology in our society. (M. Foucault would have a lot of interesting things to say about that.) This is another aspect of the implicit bias argument that worries me.

A last thing: This project constructs bias in a very broad way. It is not just sexism or racism but bias—when something is cut on the bias, it is "against the weave." There is the idea that a "weave" is straight and narrow, that there is an objectively right way to go about making decisions. So through social sciences and technical means, we can kind of move people to make the "right decisions." That is the line in management sciences, technophilia in general, and, to some extent, the trend toward medicalization of social issues I just mentioned. Management sciences is in the background here in a big way. That is why implicit bias research has caught on so easily in the corporate sector in the United States: a group not really happy to have its biases pointed out, not happy about more government regulation, but implicit bias fits in nicely with the management science paradigm. I don't think it is healthy. I am with Vicki Schultz [who wrote about the risks of a "sanitized workplace"] on this.[20]

For all those reasons, I have misgivings; I don't want to say I am against it in all contexts. I do think that this research, viewed appropriately, provides valuable insights; I am not against the research, but it presents some dangers.

Linda Krieger claims that the courts are ignorant of unconscious biases and that is why the cases are coming out the way they are. But actually the law as it is can easily take into account of unconscious bias.

MARIE MERCAT-BRUNS: *Curiously, some courts mention her work.*

RF: That is not inconsistent with what I am saying: the judges that find it convincing may well say, "We ought to put the burden of proof on the defendant; we ought to think of the evidence in a different way because of unconscious bias." As a matter of evidence, that makes sense.

But I am not convinced that the doctrine is written in such a way that it can't take account of, or necessarily ignores, unconscious bias. When you look at the way the proof structure works in Title VII cases, most discrimination is proven by inference. So there is never a moment where the court is saying, "Now we are going to look into the mind of the defendant to see what he is thinking." Instead, the question is, Did the defendant have a good reason to hire this person over that one? What is the reason he has actually offered? Is that reason convincing? If not, we can infer another motivation. It doesn't matter if the motivation is conscious or unconscious. The courts are quite aware of the fact it is very difficult to actually read state of mind. Some courts have even said things like "direct evidence of state of mind is impossible." In a sense, there can be no direct evidence. The cases are all about indirect evidence. In view of the importance of inference and indirect evidence, the distinction between conscious and unconscious motivation goes away; it just does not matter.

If you are thinking more generally about the design of the law, that is where the social science is useful. It does not get you anywhere in litigation, but it may well be important for policy.

Linda Krieger responds to Ford's critique.

LINDA KREIGER: I can see what Professor Ford is saying about the problematics of "pathologizing" discriminators, but on the other hand, we are influenced by our environments. If we live in an environment that is permeated with toxins of various kinds, those toxins will eventually affect our biochemistry. If we are living in a society in which we are surrounded by ideological toxins or by schematic toxins, those toxins will influence the implicit schematic structures through which we observe other people, through which we encode their behavior, interpret their ambiguous behavior, store memories about their behavior, retrieve those memories from our minds, and combine the information retrieved from memory to make social judgments about these people.[21]

I actually think that a public health model of equality is not a bad model, because it focuses attention on the environment in which people develop, judge, and act. It speaks to the need to change environments as a whole rather than to blame individual people or individual outcomes. This is a more systemic way of thinking about social problems as such, but also social problems influence individual judgments. So this is a place where I think my work and, for example, Susan Sturm's work, speak very productively to each other. Professor Sturm is really talking about the need to look at whole environments rather than attempting to identify some sort of invidious discriminatory animus that resides inside some isolated wrongdoer and then affects, on an individual level, his or her employment decisions. No, that's really not how inequality is structured within a society. That is the main insight of the work I am trying to do—take the focus off the individual decision maker and place that focus on the environment in which that decision maker is developing schematic associations, is interpreting behavior, is encoding behavior, and then is using behavior in judgment and choice.

MARIE MERCAT-BRUNS: *What I find fascinating is that you are talking about the systemic dimension of discrimination, whereas in your work on implicit bias you seemed to focus on the individual level of discrimination, the person and the testing. But this analysis is also systemic and takes the environment into account.*

LK: Let me speak a little more about that, if I may. The basic idea in the implicit bias approach to discrimination and nondiscrimination is that all perception and all judgment is mediated by schemas. Schematic frameworks that we absorb from our social environments structure perception, judgment, and memory. Where does schematic content come from? We are not born with certain schematic structures. They come from our cultural and intellectual environments. So you can think of the development of schematic structures almost like a marinade in which some sort of food item is soaking. The food can't help but absorb what is in the environment.

So, if it is bias that is produced through the mediation of schematic frameworks that are built through exposure to discursive, cultural, experiential contexts, then of course implicit bias is going to be a story about social context. It is a story about culture. It is a story about discourse. I think people have misunderstood this.

In the discrimination context, be it in the United States or in France, if there is a dispute, there is going to have been a decision made—did discrimination occur in this particular case or did it not? To answer this question, we often have to examine one particular decision that was made by one particular decision maker. So of course we have to look at the decision-making process of that one decision maker in that one decision context. My work on cognitive bias comes out of my work as a plaintiff-side antidiscrimination lawyer. I want my work to influence what I see as conceptual flaws in individual disparate treatment doctrine as it has developed in the U.S. legal system. I think is why people tend to look at the implicit bias work as being about individuals. But once you move back and understand that, at its core, the work on implicit bias is really about the effects of schematic information processing more broadly, then the link with culture, the link with context, becomes very clear.

MM-B: *If we come back to the European context, we could apply this analysis of implicit bias and schematic information processing, but do you think we would obtain different results because of cultural differences? Would it be more difficult to apply this analysis and promote systemic change in countries where labeling is more common and categorizing people is not only an intrinsic part of social behavior but also provides a basis for the delivery of benefits in a welfare state?*

LK: What you are describing is a process by which individuals are assigned trait labels very rapidly and then trait labels are used to interpret subsequent behavior, are used to place people in fixed, social roles from which it is very difficult to move once assigned. I assume that you would be arguing that those trait labels are used as ways to understand ambiguous behavior and to predict future behavior?

MM-B: *Yes, some categories that correspond to legal statuses are used to accrue benefits in European welfare states. For example, in France, people who received a minimum income allocation known as the "RMI" came to be called something like "RMI-ers."*

LK: I think you are suggesting that the traits along which people are stereotyped would vary from country to country, that if, for example, receiving the RMI is a salient event in France, that those persons who are labeled "RMI-ers" would more readily be stereotyped, whereas a person, say, one who is of African ethnic descent, would not be as readily stereotyped as "black" as a similar person would be stereotyped in the United States than would people who are not labeled.

That is a testable claim, and it has strong public policy consequence if it is true. But again, it is an empirical question. Are blacks in France *really* less likely to be stereotyped and treated differently because of that stereotype than are RMI-ers? It would not be terribly difficult to design studies to test this hypothesis in a variety of contexts and with various different populations.

What I am arguing is that before France decides whether it wants to structure its antidiscrimination law differently or allocate its antidiscrimination law enforcement resources differently in cases of discrimination based on, say, income source as opposed to ethnicity, it would be good to know whether the theory you posit is correct. Without that research, one can speculate about the question, you can theorize it as much as you want. Anthropologists or sociologists, critical theorists, and economists can debate it, but you are not really going to know if is true.

MM-B: *But once you know it's true, what happens?*

LK: You shape policy around it. To the extent that public policy is driven by instrumentalist goals, you want to make sure that the truth claims on which the policy is built are correct in the particular place where the policy is implemented.

Here is an example. In the United States, we arguably focus too much on incentivizing individuals as individuals. Our focus on the individual as the locus of behavioral "choice" is based on something that our social psychologists have called the "fundamental attribution error." Interestingly, the fundamental attribution error—which is that we overattribute individual internal traits rather than environmental contexts—as it turns out, is not so fundamental after all. In Asia, for example, it has been found that Asians and Indians (not Native Americans) tend not to overattribute to internal dispositional traits but attribute more to environmental factors. So there are cross-cultural differences at play any time you are dealing with social psychology. You can't take an insight from one culture, universalize it, use it to shape policy in another culture, and expect the same policy outputs. We just don't know if, for example, white French are different from white Americans in their tendencies to spontaneously categorize by race. I would sure like to see some of those studies done in France.

In turn, Dean Robert Post discusses the scope and limitations of implicit bias approaches.

MARIE MERCAT-BRUNS: *What do you think of all the work that is done on implicit bias and the tests? Do you think it is useful? Is this an instrumentalization of law? Do you think it can have a transformative effect because people realize they have biases?*

ROBERT POST: I think it prejudges the question to call it prejudice or bias. I think what the tests are showing are interesting facts about the way we classify the world, respond to the world based on views of race and gender, and so it would be missing if we didn't. But again, I think it prejudges the question to call it prejudice or bias. These are reflections of natural classifications; how they affect behavior, I don't know what the work shows.

It is plain that on any of these issues, it make sense to use the law. We have a long way to go: we have structures which enforce these in ways that, when brought to consciousness, would probably say much. I would want to use the law to restructure forms of employment to make them more structurally accessible. I would use this implicit bias stuff in the political efforts to do that. Whether it has immediate legal application is a different question that I am not so clear about.

MM-B: *Some people think that this overutilization of science to help antidiscrimination law can in fact tend to control people. What do you think about voluntary compliance? The way Foucault would look at law in terms of power plays? It would mean that we could put everyone in a box and put a label on each behavior. You seem to be saying the same thing in that sense.*

RP: What I am saying is that this stuff is best used it as an educational tool. Whether it is a legal tool I don't see yet, because that would make legal tools depend upon scientific facts which may be pervasive. It would be out of anyone's control, and it would dehumanize things considerably. So I would be careful about using it as a legal tool.

But certainly it is an educational tool. People really believe they are gender-blind or color-blind and it turns out they are not: they should think about the way it influences their perception of the world. Maybe they would become more open to the ways in which things are happening. That is the way I think about it.

Dean Martha Minow shares some interesting research in the United States on implicit bias, stereotypes, and religion, a subject that is not well developed in France or in Europe in general, outside of the United Kingdom.

MARTHA MINOW: Mahzarin Banaji, a social psychologist who teaches at Harvard, and others have worked on implicit bias. They suggest that bias operates preconsciously, before the rational mind kicks in. But research also suggests that the biases are somewhat malleable; they are affected by context and exposure. Showing white people photographs of highly admired black people (such as Martin Luther King, Jr., and Denzel Washington) can at least briefly reduce anti-black bias that shows up in unconscious ways. It is a hopeful thought that people's unconscious biases can actually be influenced by positive encounters.

Christine Jolls, a pioneer in the field of behavioral law and economics[22] and an employment law scholar, describes the impact of stereotypes and the implicit-association test.

MARIE MERCAT-BRUNS: *In addition to the labor market factors that discourage employment of older individuals, are negative views of older workers' attributes and abilities a factor?*

CHRISTINE JOLLS: There may well be conscious forms of bias against older individuals notwithstanding the fact that most individuals do not consciously revile older workers in the way that some white Americans consciously reviled black Americans a generation ago. But more important are implicit, or subconscious, forms of bias that have recently been rigorously studied using new advances in social psychology. Unlike conscious bias, such implicit bias cannot be captured simply by asking people direct questions about their views or attitudes.

In the context of age, a well-known study using a famous test called the Implicit Association Test (IAT) showed that people have a much harder time making positive associations with older individuals than with younger individuals. The IAT asks people to categorize a series of words or pictures into groups. Two of the groups are "young" and "old," and two of the groups are the categories "pleasant" and "unpleasant." Respondents are asked to press one key on the computer for either "old" or "unpleasant" words or pictures and a different key for either "young" or "pleasant" words or pictures (a stereotype-consistent pairing); in a separate round of the test, respondents are asked to press one key on the computer for either "old" or "pleasant" words or pictures and a different key for either "young" or "unpleasant" words or pictures (a stereotype-inconsistent pairing). Implicit bias against older individuals is defined as significantly faster responses when the "old" and "unpleasant" categories are paired than when the "old" and "pleasant" categories are paired. The IAT is rooted in the very simple hypothesis that people who are biased (perhaps subconsciously) against older individuals will find it easier to associate pleasant words with young faces than with old faces. In fact, implicit age bias as measured by the IAT proves to be substantial. Thus, negative attitudes about older individuals, even among those not conscious of holding such attitudes, may affect behavior by employers.

MM-B: *Do people show implicit bias on the basis of race?*

CJ: Absolutely. IAT results show that white Americans are much quicker at associating pleasant words with white faces (or white-sounding names) and unpleasant words with black faces (or black-sounding names) than the reverse.

Black Americans either show a milder form of implicit bias against their own group or, in some studies, show no implicit racial bias in either direction.[23]

Implicit racial bias bears a direct and important relationship with the earlier topic of disparate impact liability. Even if an employer does not consciously select a hiring measure, such as a no-beard rule, with the explicit desire of reducing the hiring of members of a particular group, it is possible that implicit bias explains why the hiring measure is chosen and, perhaps, why, in the absence of disparate impact liability, it may be retained even when its racial consequences become clear. Implicit bias may explain why a measure that needlessly screens out black Americans may be less likely to be abandoned than a measure that needlessly screens out white Americans.

A more comprehensive understanding of implicit bias can be gained by reading an important article co-authored by Christine Jolls and Cass Sunstein[24] and various analyses published by European and U.S. economists on discrimination.[25]

Testing and Implicit Bias

Devah Pager conducted a groundbreaking field experiment on racial discrimination in hiring. She discusses the role of unconscious bias and how discrimination is less overt today.

DEVAH PAGER: In the past, it was easy to observe discrimination based on overt rejections or hostility on the basis of race, ethnicity, gender, and so on. Today, however, because of laws barring discrimination and social norms that frown upon such behavior, discrimination, to the extent that it continues to take place, is much more difficult to observe.

The method of field experiments provides an opportunity to directly measure discrimination in action by investigating how employers (or other gatekeepers) respond to applicants who are identical apart from their race. This way, even if the discrimination is subtle, or unconscious, we can identify to what extent opportunities are shaped by a single status characteristic.

MARIE MERCAT-BRUNS: *Can you explain how you conduct your field experiments?*

DP: Sure. To conduct my field experiments of employment discrimination, I hire groups of young men to pose as job applicants. These young men (called testers) are carefully selected and matched on the basis of their age, height, weight, physical attractiveness, and interpersonal skills. They are then assigned matched fictitious résumés that present identical levels of education and work experience. Finally, the young men are put through an intensive training program to learn the details of their assumed profile and to practice interacting with employers in comparable ways. We want to make sure that the testers present themselves to employers as truly comparable applicants, apart from their race.

MM-B: *To your knowledge, is this the same testing that has been done in France, by Jean-François Amadieu, for example?*[26]

DP: It's similar. Although my sense is that more of the testing that has taken place in France has used paper applications (e.g., résumés sent by mail) rather than in-person applications. This is a method that's appropriate for some types of employment, but not the low-wage jobs I'm interested in, in the United States.

MM-B: *Your first comment about the overtness of discrimination seems to suggest that employment discrimination law is counterproductive if tends to make discrimination invisible or concealed.*

DP: Overall I think employment discrimination law has been incredibly helpful. But I do think there may be some perverse incentives. In fact, in interviews with employers, some mentioned that because of the risks of being sued for discrimination, they have become wary of hiring blacks at all. This is quite perverse: out of fear of being sued for discrimination, they become all the more likely to discriminate!

MM-B: *Why are you interested in low-skilled rather than high-skilled jobs? Does discrimination take a different form? Is it stronger, or is it easier to identify?*

DP: In the United States, it's in the low-wage labor market where we've seen the most persistent (and on some dimensions, increasing) racial disparities in employment. There's no doubt that discrimination exists in higher levels of employment as well, but these audit methods are less well suited to examining it. Discrimination in access to the networks that affect job placement, mentorship, informal opportunities for advancement, and the allocation of work responsibilities and opportunities within firms all show some evidence of discrimination, but these internal firm dynamics must be studied using different approaches.

MM-B: *Is discrimination hard to grasp?*

DP: One of the limitations of contemporary antidiscrimination law is that it relies on the victims of discrimination being aware that discrimination has taken place and being able to document proof. Given the subtlety of contemporary forms of discrimination, though, many (maybe most) individuals who experience discrimination have no idea that it has taken place. Most of my testers felt they were treated very well by employers, felt they were given serious consideration for the job. But, as it turned out, the black testers were only half as likely to receive a callback or job offer as an equally qualified white applicant. If these individuals had been real job seekers experiencing discrimination, there would have been very little recourse for them under the law.

MM-B: *I was also referring to the fact that the decision-making process might be more complex than just one decision or selection process. You mention this is in your articles.*[27] *Is that true today, or has it always been true?*

DP: Yes, that's true too. Because much of the discrimination taking place seems to be unconscious even to the employer, it's not just a matter of thinking, "He's black so I won't hire him." It's more complicated than that. There is a long sequence of interactions and evaluations which may be subtly colored by race. The rapport may be a little less natural, the skills indicated by the résumé may appear slightly less strong . . . lots of little things that cumulate to an eventual disqualification for the minority applicant.

MM-B: *So it's not because several different individuals interview the applicant.*

DP: In most of the jobs I studied, there was a single employer in charge of hiring. They relied a lot on what they referred to as their "gut instinct" about an applicant, which is the type of assessment that's easily influenced by unconscious bias.

MM-B: *So the way organizations are structured does not influence the decision-making process? In other words, doesn't it seem as though sometimes there might not be just one person responsible for the discrimination, because management and recruitment work is performed by teams?*

DP: I think the way organizations are structured has a huge influence on the decision-making process. Firms that have more formal, systematic hiring protocols in place often do a better job focusing on the more objective, job-relevant characteristics and are less distracted by extraneous characteristics that may affect rapport in an interview, even if irrelevant to the actual job. Organizational reform could do a lot to reduce hiring discrimination, in my opinion.

MM-B: *Do you think your testing methods could be used to test other employment decisions (access to training, promotions)?*

DP: I think this would be difficult, as it would be hard to randomly assign testers to positions within the firm. Without random assignment, it's hard to know whether the unequal outcomes are the result of discrimination or differences in the abilities of the various workers.

MM-B: *I would still like to understand how recruitment processes are interactive, contextual, and very much dependent on interpersonal relations.*

DP: Particularly in these jobs in which hiring is based on an unstructured interview, with employers looking for a "gut feeling" about a candidate, there is much about the decision-making process that gets actively shaped in the course of interaction. As we talked about, very few employers would reject any black candidate outright. But there are subtle ways in which the objective characteristics of a candidate (e.g., their qualifications and experience) takes on different meaning and significance depending on other characteristics of the applicant, the employer, and the job in question. Job experience presented by a white applicant may be viewed and interpreted differently than the exact same type of experience presented by a black applicant. We saw this repeatedly in the experiment. Employers interpreted the qualifications of our applicants differently on the basis of their race, even though their résumés were explicitly constructed to reflect identical skills and experience.

MM-B: *What did you learn about unconscious bias during your studies outside of the influence of a "gut feeling"?*

DP: I've conducted a large number of interviews with employers, and I've come to believe that the vast majority of them really believe they are simply looking for the best person for the job, irrespective of race. They have experience working in diverse groups and don't have any conscious opposition to hiring workers of different races.

Because they believe they're nonbiased, it's even harder for them to recognize the ways that various informal aspects of the evaluation process favor whites and disadvantage minorities.

MM-B: *Have you shared your results with law professors or testified at trials?*

DP: I've presented my research at several law schools (Yale, Stanford, Chicago, UVA . . .) and have testified at hearings before the Equal Employment Opportunity Commission, among others.

Comparative Perspectives

Pager begins by admitting that discrimination is largely hidden or unconscious in the United States today: it is seldom overtly expressed as it was in the past, due to the country's long history battling to eliminate discrimination in social and employment practices. Her comments explain how unconscious bias can pervade the decision-making process and how disparities are not only based on protected traits but also depend on the worker's level of skill, since discrimination seems to be more prevalent among low-skilled jobs. Testing for discrimination in employment practices such as promotions and dismissals is difficult to do, unless the company chooses to organize the testing itself. This practice is currently gaining ground in France.[28] An additional difficulty with implicit bias is the fact that victims of discrimination are themselves often unaware of the bias operating against them, which can explain the lack of litigation or civil suits brought against employers.

Social Science and Bias

Frank Dobbin talks about the role of social science in law.

MARIE MERCAT-BRUNS: *Social framework evidence is becoming a source of expertise in employment discrimination litigation (see* Duke v. Wal-Mart*). What are your thoughts on this role of social science in law? Prevention with respect to enforcement of antidiscrimination law: is it just another way of combating discrimination?*

FRANK DOBBIN: I don't know enough about the law to say whether social framework evidence is the best way for plaintiffs to proceed. In American case law in this area, the courts early on made a distinction between disparate treatment and disparate impact. Disparate treatment occurs when an employer visibly treats one group differently from another—tells African Americans that they are not eligible for management jobs. We see much less of that now in discrimination cases, and much more "disparate impact" in which employer practices or customs or bias lead to different outcomes for two groups: for men and women, or for blacks and whites. Social framework evidence is often used in such cases, where there is evidence that an employer promotes blacks at a lower rate than whites to management jobs, but no evidence of the precise mechanism that leads to the difference. Social framework analysis identifies how bias can be inscribed in the culture and practice of a firm. It is typically used to describe a context in which discrimination can occur.

I would hope that the courts would begin to take more seriously the growing body of evidence about the efficacy of different personnel and diversity practices for promoting equality of opportunity. For instance, there are now quite a few studies showing that antidiscrimination training does not reduce bias (a recent review by Paluck and Green of hundreds of studies in the *Annual Review of Psychology* confirms this).[29] And there are now quite a few studies showing that formal performance evaluations probably introduce bias into the promotion and salary-setting process, because they typically favor white men. Courts still seem to give credit to firms for diversity training and performance evaluation programs.

Our research shows that certain other programs actually have helped firms to improve opportunity for women and minorities. I would hope that firms, and the courts, would begin to recognize the efficacy of these programs.

Comparative Perspectives

In the comments by Linda Krieger and Richard Ford, two different perspectives on the benefits and drawbacks of implicit bias theory can be heard.[30] In France, antidiscrimination law is not deeply anchored in the eradication of bias or in the social sciences; its logic is more closely aligned with that of negligence or tort, as will be mentioned later by David Oppenheimer.

Bias is strongly normative and engenders discriminatory practices. This is a point that has been established beyond doubt and is upheld in the language of several Europe-wide employment promotion policies.[31]

The different viewpoints of the scholars interviewed are enlightening. Krieger sees research on stereotypes as at least a way to move forward in the litigation of individual claims of discrimination,[32] which does not completely contradict what Ford says. He points out the risk involved for the legitimacy of laws based on social science if there is a possibility that the social science can be subsequently called into question. The situation is exactly the opposite in France, where as a principle, legal scholars and practitioners shy away from the other disciplines to emphasize "legal technique" and where even statistical evidence of discrimination is not mandatory.

More globally, Krieger also studies the sources of implicit discrimination found in the work environment where they emerge. She also investigates systemic forms of discrimination in companies that are not just the result of one individual's biased decision making. It is possible to apply the research on stereotypes in social psychology to institutional discrimination.[33] Institutions can promote the creation of stereotypes through mechanisms that appear neutral but produce discriminatory effects. But Ford worries that the recognition of stereotypes will encourage the corporate sector and other stakeholders to instrumentalize antidiscrimination law to promote the management sciences and business goals, straying from the true aim of antidiscrimination. Its goal is to detect and remedy inherent workplace inequality, which is exacerbated by discriminatory practices. This argument has also been advanced in the context of diversity initiatives in France, by those who highlight the ambivalence of these initiatives and the accompanying soft law.[34] In the comments by Post, one can sense a certain skepticism regarding the exploration of bias as a means of fighting discrimination, considering that bias is omnipresent in individuals and does not resolve the systemic causes of discrimination.

Other authors, both sociologists and law professors, such as Minow, Jolls, Pager, and Dobbin, also assess the relevance of social framework evidence[35] gathered from sociology and social psychology findings through the lens of their work. They subscribe to the validity of certain surveys and tests that take implicit bias into account. Monitoring individual bias in an organization seems to be one way to reduce the risk of class action litigation due to an error propagated through uniform human resources management. Such bias can permeate skills assessments at a management level in different branches of a company,[36] as has been observed in France.[37]

All of this seems to indicate a need to achieve that elusive balance between law that remains impermeable to the social sciences and what they can offer in terms of uncovering the bias that causes individual and systemic discrimination, and law that relies too heavily on these social sciences, jeopardizing its stability. How can we reconcile the idea of sanctioning discrimination knowing that some discrimination is unconscious? Inescapably, we come back to the intentional nature of the discriminatory practice.

II. DISCRIMINATION AND TORT

In contrast to the United States, antidiscrimination legislation in France provides for criminal sanctions.[38] How is this divergence reflected in the logic of antidiscrimination law and its relationship with tort law?

In the following interview, David Oppenheimer reacts to Linda Krieger's stance that it does not help people to impose criminal sanctions when there might not be conscious intent.

DAVID OPPENHEIMER: I think [she] is right. The question is, if we made discrimination a crime, would it have the effect of dissuading people from discriminating? I think Linda is correct: most people who make discriminatory decisions do so not with the intent to discriminate but for reasons of unconscious bias. I wrote a piece on this in 1993 called "Negligent Discrimination," in which I argued that most discrimination results from unconscious bias and should be treated as a form of negligence.[39]

MARIE MERCAT-BRUNS: *So we could treat discrimination as a tort? Do you think that employment discrimination law is a liability issue like a tort? For example, you've committed a fault, there is a causal effect, there are damages, and then there's remedy. Are we witnessing the same type of mechanism here?*

This is an interesting question in a comparative perspective with France, because common law has already had an undeniable influence on the legal framework in European employment discrimination law, and it might be easier to understand if tort is at the foundation of the employment discrimination model in the United States.

DO: That is the American model. The American model is to treat employment discrimination as an intentional tort, to treat it like an assault. We look at a decision and ask, Would the employer have made the same decision if the applicant had been white or male or straight or young? We therefore compare the protected characteristic of the plaintiff with a hypothetical majority group member (or alternatively with actual majority group members), and we ask whether we can determine if they had been treated differently because of race or sex or some other prohibited category. If the answer is yes, we ask what damages did that cause.

I have proposed we adopt the negligence model in analyzing discrimination. For example, you drive a car faster than you should, and as a result you cause an accident. Did you have a malicious intent? Absolutely not. Did you intend to drive into the other car? Absolutely not. Did you intend to cause an accident? Absolutely not. Did you intend to hurt somebody? No. Did you intend to hurt their car? No. Did you intend to hurt yourself? No. Are you responsible? Yes.

Why are you responsible? Because you have to drive with particular care in order to avoid accidents. That's why we have speed limits. It's also why we have laws against discrimination. As an employer, you are supposed to pay attention to things like race and gender in order to avoid discriminating. So when you get a batch of résumés, if you hire the good-looking white guy, you should say before you make that commitment, Why am I picking the good-looking white guy? Should I be concerned that every time I get to hire somebody I pick the good-looking white guy? Should I have looked a little more carefully at the résumés of the black man or black woman?

MM-B: *Is it a duty to act?*

DO: Yes, like the duty to drive carefully.
MM-B: *But a duty to act, like reasonable accommodation?*
DO: No, it is a duty to not treat people differently. It is not like reasonable accommodation, which can require a preference. It is a duty to not treat people differently because of race.

Comparative Perspectives

A central theme that seems to emerge from studying antidiscrimination norms is the parallel between the development of this law and that of tort: it is clear that the direct discrimination framework is designed to identify the party guilty of a discriminatory act that has caused harm to the victim of the discrimination. In order to establish direct discrimination, certain elements are required from the start, and these elements are equivalent to the prerequisites for establishing tort, as defined in Article 1382 of the French Civil Code: a wrongdoing—that is, the difference in treatment based a prohibited trait; damage—that is, the disadvantage (a harmful act) suffered by the victim of the discrimination; and the causal effect—that is, the proof that the discriminatory motive was the cause of the discriminatory act. In the same vein, Oppenheimer proposes to draw an analogy with no-fault offenses or strict liability as per Article 1383 of the Civil Code, due to the barrier posed by the difficulty of proving discriminatory intent.[40]

Oppenheimer's reasoning can be extended further. In France, tort law has shifted its focus from finding the fault of the person causing the harm to providing a remedy even where no fault has been committed.[41] It is therefore possible for antidiscrimination law to evolve from a law requiring courts to determine whether a fault has been committed in the form of intentional, direct discrimination to a law whose effective enforcement depends on the judge's ability to detect unconscious, indirect discrimination, even where there is no fault but only a discriminatory impact. This comparison with no-fault strict liability is important because it strengthens the legitimacy of the indirect discrimination mechanism in countries where civil-law tradition is firmly rooted. It can help the judges in these countries understand indirect discrimination because they are familiar with strict liability cases, in which the resulting harm and impact on the victim are also key issues. The development of tort law and that of antidiscrimination law can be said to emerge from the very same foundation: "the rule of the majority and the aspiration of equality that characterize the democratic regime, which naturally provoked a response to the difficulties of remedy: a protective response."[42]

In both cases, the question is, who will bear the liability for the risk? Who would be responsible for systemic discrimination related to an apparently neutral practice? The risk theory of liability is a well-known concept.[43] It seems that in France, when the foundations of tort law and antidiscrimination law are compared, it is easy to comprehend a certain similarity of purpose[44] above and beyond the legal mechanisms involved. The same preventive search for liability—this new function of tort law to "preserve the well-being of future generations"[45]—can be seen in efforts to prevent discrimination and aligns with the diversity discourse found in collective bargaining and social responsibility norms. This precautionary principle is clearly oriented toward proactively managing differences and emerging risks rather than simply offering remedies for past harms[46] and tends to be instrumentalized, along with diversity and corporate social responsibility initiatives. A major stumbling block exists in both tort and antidiscrimination law,[47] revealing yet another similarity in their underlying logic: the proof of causation, which is a prerequisite in both types of disputes. In antidiscrimination law as in tort law, there may be several causes contributing to the injury, and a combination of legitimate and discriminatory reasons can be found for the challenged practice. When multiple correlations exist, how can the causal connection with the final injury be defined? Extensive U.S. case law and research have focused on the challenge of discrimination based on mixed motive (discriminatory and nondiscriminatory motives). The current U.S. standard is to find out whether the ground was a motivating factor,[48] except in age discrimination or retaliation cases.[49] France has not yet debated this issue in discrimination cases, outside the realm of unjust dismissal.

4

From Disparate Impact to Systemic Discrimination

Disparate impact discrimination has been under fire in the United States since the landmark *Ricci v. DeStefano* case in 2009.[1] The debate is equally topical in France, where its supreme court, the Cour de Cassation, more recently handed down several rulings recognizing indirect sex discrimination,[2] in an effort to "flush out more subtle forms of discrimination."

European equality law distinguishes between direct discrimination, that is, intentionally treating a person less favorably because he or she has a protected characteristic, and indirect discrimination, which occurs when a general measure that seems to treat people equally on the surface has a disproportionately prejudicial effect on people with a protected characteristic.[3] Save a few nuances, which will be clarified, these same concepts are referred to as "disparate treatment" and "disparate impact" discrimination in the United States. Systemic discrimination is not defined specifically in French law but is mentioned more and more in the public debate on equality. The Equal Employment Opportunity Commission (EEOC) has given examples of these more structural forms of discrimination, including the glass ceiling effect on women.[4]

I. THE STRENGTHS AND LIMITATIONS OF DISPARATE IMPACT DISCRIMINATION

Ricci v. DeStefano is commonly cited when discussing disparate impact and has been extensively discussed in legal scholarship. The background of the case is as follows: after taking a test that would determine their eligibility for promotion, white firefighters in New Haven, Connecticut, passed at a much higher rate than black firefighters. Concerned about its liability for disparate impact discrimination, the city of New Haven discarded the test. White and Hispanic firefighters, who lost their chance of promotion when the test was thrown out, sued the city for race discrimination. In a five-to-four decision written by Justice Kennedy, the Supreme Court found that the city had committed an act of disparate treatment and failed to show a "strong basis in evidence" that it would have faced disparate impact liability if it had not voided the test. Fear of litigation alone was insufficient justification.[5]

In her dissent, Justice Ginsburg predicted that this ruling would not have "staying power" and would remain an exceptional case.[6] She wrote that the test results showed "stark disparities" that "sufficed to state a prima facie case under Title VII's disparate-impact provision," because the passing rate of minorities fell well below the four-fifths standard set by the EEOC. Justice Ginsburg also criticized the Court for failing to explain the "strong basis in evidence" it requires.[7] Rather than elaborate on the standard of proof of disparate impact liability required to justify a race-conscious remedy, the Court merely stated that crossing a certain significant threshold of statistical disparity was not sufficient in itself.[8] The Court also held that "the City could be liable for disparate impact discrimination only if the examinations were not job-related and consistent with business necessity, or if there existed an equally valid, less-discriminatory alternative that served the City's needs but that the City refused to adopt."[9]

Reactions to the controversial decision were spirited, with some scholars seeing it as a challenge to the very legitimacy of the disparate impact rule, its enforcement, and how it differs from disparate treatment. The *Ricci* outcome continues to occupy the foreground of debate on disparate impact discrimination. Robert Post, Linda Krieger, and Julie Suk comment on the case, but first Christine Jolls, Susan Sturm, David Oppenheimer, Richard Ford, and Julie Suk discuss the application, background, and purpose of disparate impact theory in the United States.

Christine Jolls discusses how today's forms of discrimination are different from in the past.

CHRISTINE JOLLS: One of the most important things to understand about discrimination, I believe, is the way in which some of its forms have changed with time while others have remained relatively constant. If we consider the example of race discrimination, a generation ago in America it was still not uncommon to see direct reference to someone's race in a variety of job settings. And it was not until the 1976 decision of the Supreme Court of the United States in *Runyon v. McCrary* that national law in the United States was applied to prohibit race-based exclusion of black children from private schools and camps.

Today, of course, such explicit discrimination on the basis of race in America is not common—but other forms of race discrimination remain. A prominent illustration is the use of facially neutral selection criteria that disproportionately disadvantage or exclude black Americans and are not "job related and consistent with business necessity," in the words of Title VII of the Civil Rights Act of 1964. In a recent case under this provision of U.S. law, a well-known pizza franchise [Domino's Pizza] was successfully sued for race discrimination after it adopted a policy disallowing beards among its male pizza delivery people.[10] The company argued that some patrons feared bearded delivery people and that its policy was racially neutral, applying to whites and nonwhites alike. The court found, however, that while essentially all white men are able to comply with no-beard requirements, a significant fraction of black men cannot comply because of a skin condition in which facial hair becomes ingrown as a result of shaving. Because, the court concluded, a no-beard rule was not "job related and consistent with business necessity" for the non-food-preparation job of pizza delivery person, the fact that the rule screened out a disproportionate number of black workers meant that it violated Title VII.

This form of liability for race discrimination is called "disparate impact liability." It operates to constrain employers who—because of racial bias or other factors—adopt practices that screen out black workers without good reason. Without disparate impact liability, an employer seeking to avoid having members of a particular group in its workforce might be able clandestinely to achieve that impermissible objective through the use of a facially neutral screening rule.

Disparate impact liability has a wide range of potential applications. Most familiarly, some forms of standardized testing may disproportionately disadvantage nonwhite Americans and, at the same time, may not be well-suited to measuring the skills and attributes actually required for successful performance of a given job. In such cases, Title VII prohibits hiring on the basis of the test scores. Hiring measures that, while facially neutral, disproportionately screen out applicants on the basis of race and are not "job related and consistent with business necessity" represent a form of race discrimination that still occurs in America today and is kept in check by Title VII's disparate impact branch.[11]

David Oppenheimer looks back on the development of disparate impact theory, which preceded Title VII and the Civil Rights Act (CRA) and the *Griggs* decision explicitly citing the concept.

DAVID OPPENHEIMER: Before the Civil Rights Act was passed, there were disparate impact cases litigated in the states. There was a big case against Motorola, and it was discussed in the Congress.

MARIE MERCAT-BRUNS: *So there is an effect of state law on employment discrimination developments?*

DO: Sometimes state law has been influential, mostly because it is an alternative source of law, and sometimes state decisions have influenced either the Congress in passing legislation or the EEOC or the Courts in interpreting legislation. The states have played an important role. State law is often broader in a number of ways. In California, for example, it includes sexual orientation discrimination.[12]

MM-B: *If I were to look at some interesting states in employment discrimination law, what states would you advise I concentrate on?*

DO: California, Illinois, Michigan, New Jersey, New York.

In the early 1960s, there was an important disparate impact case against Motorola in Illinois, and there was debate about the case in the Senate. The Senate actually adjusted the language of Title VII to take account of that. There is a pretty good argument that the Congress intended to prohibit disparate impact discrimination, which is sometimes called indirect discrimination.[13]

Then in the *Griggs* case, the Court said unanimously that the Congress intended to reach disparate impact as well as disparate treatment. There is evidence in the legislative history. It is what the Court said in *Griggs*. It was a unanimous decision. Conservative members of the Court (Justice Harlan, for example, who was quite conservative on civil rights matters) did not dissent.

Congress soon after passed amendments to CRA, and then in 1990–1991, Congress reaffirmed *Griggs*. It is pretty clear that *Griggs* was correctly decided, but now the Court keeps narrowing the concept. This Court is very hostile to the enforcement of civil rights and I think it's fair to say it is because they have an anti-civil rights agenda.

MM-B: *Is this a law and economics position? Let the market play its role and performance will thrive regardless of race or sex?*

DO: First of all, there is a counternarrative to the law and economics model of employment discrimination, which is that even though employment discrimination is an economic inefficiency, there are enough social advantages for whites who are averse to contact with blacks that racial discrimination may be efficient for particular employers. If that's true, then you can't expect employers to stop discriminating for reasons of economic efficiency.

MM-B: *Does the economic argument influence the Court, or is it an argument that some members of the Court will point to justify their decisions?*

DO: There is at least one case where the law and economics argument did influence the Court, where it was used to justify a very bad decision. That was a case against Ford.[14] The case concerned the obligation of a plaintiff to mitigate her damages, and the Court put this terrible burden on the plaintiff and justified it in economic terms. I think they were persuaded because they were following a line of economic reasoning.

MM-B: *Does the fact that you can win extensive damages make the law more efficient in the United States compared to France?*

DO: Yes, in the United States you can potentially be awarded millions of dollars, but it is very, very rare. If you win a jury trial, the median verdict in California is around $200,000, but you have to subtract from that some of the litigation costs and fees. So if you are awarded $200,000, you may actually receive $100,000, and from that $100,000, you may have to pay as much as $50,000 in income tax. The settlements are smaller.

MM-B: *How much?*

DO: I don't have data on that because most settlements are confidential, but the typical settlement amount should be lower than the typical judgment.

MM-B: *Do you have any additional observations on disparate impact and* Griggs? *Where are we now in terms of the judicial interpretation of disparate impact?*

DO: Four members of the Court appear to believe that, at least with regard to a state employer, the entire theory of disparate impact discrimination may violate the Fourteenth Amendment to the U.S. Constitution. This is from the *Ricci* case.[15]

This was a statutory employment discrimination case. They did not reach the Constitutional question. It is suggested that if they had reached the Constitutional question, four of the Justices believe that the State may never take account of race in preventing discrimination. I use the word *State* in the French meaning here, to include what we would describe as "government" employment.

MM-B: *But it can have a symbolic effect on them regarding the interpretation of disparate impact. Now, what are the positive effects of disparate impact discrimination law, pinpointing the structural effects of discrimination?*

DO: The great thing about disparate impact is that you can have liability without fault.

MM-B: *Your negligence theory.*[16]

DO: That is right. It does illustrate the structure of racial inequality. It comports with reality. It is consistent with what we have learned on implicit bias, what we have learned on how people make decisions.

MM-B: *Can it be said that disparate impact has had an effect on employers' selection processes?*

DO: Yes. Employers are probably much more self-conscious about their decision-making process because of the adverse impact model of discrimination law.

After Oppenheimer, Richard Ford shares his assessment of the selection methods that are potentially discriminating and the problems they pose.

MARIE MERCAT-BRUNS: *Does combating discrimination incur a cost for businesses?*

RICHARD FORD: Even when you are dealing with something costly like accommodation, it is understood under the rubric of discrimination that if you don't reasonably accommodate, then that is discriminating against. But the truth is, we are doing something different than that. Something that cannot quite be understood in practice as just getting rid of bias.

What we are really doing, what the courts are doing, and what we want the courts to do ideally is strike a balance between what they have done in the past, what is easy to do because it is familiar, and a social policy that an individual employer might not take up on his or her own but is important to have social harmony between various groups and to help subordinated groups throw off the burden of the past.

It is easy to see in the disability context, when you are often talking about costly accommodations, there is no way of making the case to the employer that he is just as well off making the accommodations as not making the accommodations. But you can certainly make the case that society is better off for making them do it.

You can even see it in the race and sex context to a lesser degree. Disparate impact is a good example: the employer has a standardized test that has a disparate impact and might be using the test as a proxy to get at race or sex. But lots of the time, that is probably not what employers are doing. They are using the test because it is easy and cheap. It is not perfect, but it is cheap and it is what they have always done, so why not use it?

For employers, you could probably make the case, in the balance, that they are better off using the standardized test whether it has a disparate impact or not, because they do not want to spend a lot of money having a more narrowly tailored test that really tests for job-related skills. It is just expensive. They would not get enough benefit out of it to make it worth doing. So if they were just looking "beady-eyed" at the bottom line, employers would say, "No, we are going to keep our standardized test, despite the disparate impact." The law does not allow you to do that. You can see this in both the race and sex context.

With race, it is often a standardized written exam that has a disparate impact. With sex, it is often a physical exam: there are cases of police departments where you had to run an eight-minute mile or lift a certain amount of weight. The police departments said, "It is better to have a physically fit workforce than one that is not physically fit." They were required to revisit that, because it had a disparate impact on women. You could make the following case for the departments: "We have a big field of people who are qualified and we don't care whether they are men or women; it is easier to do this, this way. We are better off using our standardized test." But we won't let them do that, because we have a social goal to integrate the workforce. That is more than saying we are just getting rid of bias.

MM-B: *I understand that, and in France, the virtues of indirect discrimination are gradually getting more press. There is also talk about the company's interests in other circumstances.*[17] *However, the issue of bias with respect to discrimination and its relationship to antidiscrimination law is often not mentioned at all.*

[*Later in the interview, Ford comes back to the topic of proving disparate impact.*]

RF: How much of disparate impact do we need to have before we are worried? The EEOC came up with the four-fifths rule. What you come up with is going to be arbitrary: why four-fifths?

MM-B: *Could you explain the rule?*

RF: In disparate impact doctrine, the challenged practice is presumptively discriminatory if the disparity is more than four-fifths, or 80 percent. So, if the percentage of blacks who pass the test is less than 80 percent of whites, then it is presumptively discriminatory. You have got a number now. The question of what is "job-related" is another one that has been explained by the EEOC. *[These tests for disparate impact will be discussed later.]*

Comparative equality law scholar Julie Suk discusses the role played by judges in sanctioning indirect discrimination.

JULIE SUK: I'm just not sure that the concept of discrimination can be stretched far enough to pursue the normative commitment to substantive equality that is often articulated in the landmark decisions like *Griggs*. I am not sure that courts as institutions are capable of bringing about structural transformation. My doubts are even stronger when it comes to French courts, which, due to the very interesting legal history of the judiciary since the Revolution in France, have never been seen in France as instruments of change. And they don't need to be, largely because the French parliamentary system does not face the same impediments to substantive policy making as our system.

MARIE MERCAT-BRUNS: *Interesting. I do think the French judiciary is evolving under the influence of the HALDE and the CJEU, but I agree that the judge's role is historically different. I also think that judicial reasoning is different: judges do not start with the facts and then proceed to draw analogies, as is the case in common law and antidiscrimination law.*

JS: The French judiciary is evolving, but the differences are vast, and it's not clear to me that the American model is worth emulating, even if we were to assume that an evolution towards the American model is remotely feasible, as a normative matter.

The following commentaries by Robert Post, Linda Krieger, and Julie Suk on the *Ricci* case shed light on the application of the indirect discrimination provision, its scope, and its origins in Europe, without promoting the Supreme Court's interpretation of disparate impact.

Yale dean Robert Post begins by discussing the hostility of the American conservatives to this concept.

ROBERT POST: Disparate impact, as you know, measures antidiscrimination norms in terms of their structural impact on the class. It is inherently redistributive. It will pay attention to the structure of the decision making rather than to any particular discrete acts of prejudice, and the Right in this country has been hostile to it. The Court issued a number of decisions hostile to it in the late eighties,[18] and Congress reaffirmed it in the statute in CRA 1991.

And in its most recent decision in *Ricci,* Kennedy writes for the court that the most important form of antidiscrimination law is disparate treatment. It tells you how deeply hostile the Right is to using disparate impact as a structural tool for fighting against discrimination.

MARIE MERCAT-BRUNS: *How important is Kennedy's reading of disparate impact? He does not eliminate it. He just says the employer did not have to voluntarily comply and anticipate the disparate impact of certain tests.*

RP: Right. It is not a disparate impact case. It is affirmative action case in which the question is in what ways you can rectify the situation of minorities and avoid disparate impact, which, I think, is an incoherent opinion.

We have to understand what that means: it is illegal under the law, under the statute; I am not saying that this means it is unconstitutional to provide an impact standard to the states. I know there are some Justices who might take that line. Could it be what is hinted here?

MM-B: *Since disparate impact is structural, this means that it was made to prevent discrimination. So they are taking away what is great about disparate impact.*

RP: [Justice Kennedy] is writing a very narrow opinion. It is hard to know what he means. What he is saying essentially is that you can't anticipate [disparate impact] by setting aside the result of an otherwise valid test. That is the narrowest statement of the Court. Now, how generalizable is that? What do they mean by an otherwise valid test? It is murky. Technically, you can read it very narrowly. On the other hand, you could read it as a sign as that changes are ahead. It could be subject to multiple interpretations.

William S. Richardson School of Law professor Linda Krieger asserts that the *Ricci* decision will not set a precedent.

MARIE MERCAT-BRUNS: *Does the* Ricci *decision say that companies should not engage in self-criticism and that New Haven should not have chosen voluntary compliance and withdrawn its test, which had a disparate treatment on black minorities? Does this decision mark the end, or a limit, to the fight against disparate impact discrimination?*

LINDA KRIEGER: I actually think a little more is read in the *Ricci* decision than has to be. Here is my take on it: in order to use preferential forms of affirmative action, the Supreme Court has long showed that an employer had to make a prima facie showing that discrimination has occurred in the workplace or there are longstanding barriers to entry that nothing short of these preferences have been able to address. Disparate treatment context has only one level of inquiry: whether discrimination is affecting selection.

There is a predicate that employers have to show before they can use preferential forms of affirmative action. It is to show that controlling for other variables, race, sex, or ethnicity had a significant effect on selection in the past and that group membership was going to be used as one factor among many in selecting among otherwise equally qualified applicants. So the disparity was redressed and the preference would no longer be needed.

In earlier cases, there was a requirement that the employer make a pretty strong prima facie showing that their system was amenable to legal challenge.

Now in disparate impact cases, there is not one level of inquiry; there are two. The first level of inquiry, which is the disparate impact analysis, looks at whether a selection device, like a test, selects members of one group at a rate that is statistically lower than the rate of the selected members of the advantaged group. Let's say the answer is yes. That is not the end of the case. The second stage has to be whether the device that is being used validates or rejects performance on the job.[19] There is a violation of Title VII only if the answer to the first inquiry is positive and second inquiry answers to the negative: no, there is no validity to the test that is being used.

What the Court says in *Ricci* is if you are going to cancel a test (I don't think you can cancel a test once it has been given, but I will come back to that), you have to make a strong evidentiary showing not just on the impact element but also on the lack-of-validity element, and that had not been done. The Court found it had not been done. The case will go back down, and we will see how that plays out. The Court basically says it is not enough to show disparate impact, but you also have to have a showing of lack of test validity.

The other factor here is that the Supreme Court has always been very hesitant, actually unwilling, to permit affirmative action if it takes something away from the group that is not being preferred by the affirmative action. We have more than one decision where the Court says you can't use preferential forms of affirmative action in deciding who to lay off because that imposes too great a burden on the nonpreferred group. I think it really matters here that the test had already been given, that people had already got their test results. I think that if they had run a pilot study and found that it had disparate impact and they had not shown it had validity, they probably could have cancelled the test *ex ante*, but in *Ricci* they cancelled the test *ex post*. I think that made a difference.

MM-B: *Canceling the test created the disparate treatment toward the nonpreferred group of whites and Hispanics?*

LK: Yes, but the dissent said the people who had taken the test did not have a job yet so they didn't have a tangible job detriment. There was, though, a psychological job detriment. So we have to make sure when reading Justice Ginsburg's decision that if the roles were reversed, and African Americans thought they had been disadvantaged and did not have a tangible job detriment, how would we feel about the decision then? I would not have liked it one little bit, because I think that a lot of job detriments are dignitary harms. Studying for a test, taking a test, getting the results of a test, and then having the test cancelled does in fact create a dignitary harm for the group who has passed the test. It is hard enough to know that a test that members of the group have historically done well on is not now being used to make selection decisions. For example, I hope to see the day when the test that French schoolchildren take will no longer be used to "determine" the rest of their lives. Upper-class, bourgeois families are not going to feel so good about that change because historically this system has worked relatively well for them. Imagine that you have been accepted in a prestigious lycée in Paris and now the test gets canceled.

MM-B: *So you agree with the majority in the* Ricci *case?*

LK: I am not sure I disagree with the majority on the legal issue. What I do disagree about is how strong a showing an employer should have to make on that second element in order to be able to cancel a test. When I read the record below, there was evidence of lack of validity, so my view of the decision is that they got the facts wrong, and that's why they got to the wrong legal decision. I do think that in terms of the continuity of the *Ricci* decision with earlier Supreme Court affirmative action cases, there was some doctrinal justification for requiring some predicate on both the disparate impact element and the validity element. Some of my colleagues might have more quarrels with the decision than I have.

Also I think as a practical matter, the danger is that the decision comes to be understood as rejecting disparate impact theory. I don't think that that's what the Court did. I think this Court has been hostile to disparate impact theory for a long time. I think the Rehnquist and Roberts Courts are hostile to all structural theories of discrimination. I think if the majority has their way, we would be like rats in a trap.

MM-B: *Coming back to* Ricci, *I also thought the fact there was voluntary compliance was great. What do you think about voluntary compliance? Don't you think companies will read this as a sign not to go in that direction?*

LK: I am all in favor of voluntary compliance. Companies will react according to how good their legal counsel is. It matters more what people think the law is than what the law is. So if people think that what just happened was that the Supreme Court did away with disparate impact theory or said that employers cannot take affirmative action, then the decision will have an extremely negative effect. That is very real danger. I don't think that is what the Court said, but again what people think matters more than what actually happened.

Julie Suk discusses the impact of *Ricci* on employment practices.

MARIE MERCAT-BRUNS: *How can tools for remedying direct discrimination and those for remedying indirect discrimination be combined?*

JULIE SUK: Sometimes, multiple strategies for combating discrimination on one ground (e.g., race) may conflict with each other, and we have to choose in individual instances which strategy is more valuable, by reference to the normative underpinnings of equality law. The *Ricci* case is a rich illustration of this conflict. (I think, by the way, that the Supreme Court chose wrongly in *Ricci*.)

MM-B: *This is a perfect transition: tell me why the Court chose wrongly and more generally what you think about the decision, its scope, the impact it may have on voluntary compliance by employers in the future, and how disparate treatment and disparate impact interact.*

JS: I will send you a short piece that I wrote for the Florence conference on the Evolution of Equality Law and Theory that answers that question as well as some of the other issues that we have discussed so far.[20] But, very quickly, I think that *Ricci* will make it very hard for employers to pursue diversity or equal opportunity in the future. After this decision, if an employer decides to get rid of an employment practice upon discovering that it benefits whites and disadvantages blacks, the employer could face disparate treatment liability unless it has a strong basis in evidence to believe it would lose a disparate impact suit. As you probably know, it is very hard for plaintiffs to *win* disparate impact suits, so it is only in a pretty narrow set of cases that an employer would have a strong basis in evidence to believe it would *lose* such a suit. Without that strong basis in evidence, the employer *cannot* abandon an employment policy that benefits whites because it denies them of an employment opportunity, or changes their terms or conditions of work, on the basis of race, in violation of Title VII.

Decisions like *Ricci* tend to confirm my view that the concept of discrimination is limited and unhelpful, and possibly even an impediment, to the pursuit of substantive equality understood as the eradication of the lingering effects of past subordination of racial minorities and women.

MM-B: *I see that you do not approve of antidiscrimination law and yet I see exciting avenues for this law, via concepts such as reasonable accommodation, which introduces an obligation to act but has been interpreted differently by the courts. Don't you think that the problem is that the American courts have taken a stance against antidiscrimination law and its concepts, and not that the law or the concepts themselves have failed?*

JS: I wonder if we'd be better off if we repealed Title VII and then tried to rewrite an equality law explicitly pursuing the goal I've articulated above. In 1964, the concept of discrimination converged pretty well with that goal. Today, it doesn't and the strategy thus far is to try to stretch the concept of discrimination, but the concept seems to stretch the same way a rubber band does—it stretches pretty far (to include, say, reasonable accommodation) and then it contracts back to its original tighter configuration.

MM-B: *Interesting. You have responded to my observation about reasonable accommodation, but what do you think about my idea that it is the Supreme Court and conservative federal courts who are to blame, not the concept itself?*

JS: My answer to that question is complicated, and perhaps will not come across quite so clearly in this medium. But in short, I don't think that the judges that are deciding discrimination cases are all conservatives. I think that courts have institutional limits. With regard to discrimination, however we decide to define it legally, it does have a certain colloquial meaning closely connected with a formal conception of equality, and it's not going to disappear as a result of our attempts to broaden the concept. I guess I would turn the question back on you: why do you think discrimination is a useful concept? The main reason we rely on it is path dependence.

MM-B: *I think it is useful because it is contextual. French law is so substantive: it carries a certain view of reality all the time, locking in stereotypes and confining itself to protections that are of course essential but do not always take into account the complexity of individual situations or other sources of expertise in the legal arena, psychology and economics, for example. Everyone realizes that these issues of equality and difference are not simple at all, and I think the principle of antidiscrimination allows for a more procedural way of dealing with the issues case by case. In my research on age and aging, I saw how the issues of employment and the physical aptitude of older workers are all intertwined. This does not mean that I do not appreciate the positive contributions of the welfare state, but I do think it is important to think about and resolve these questions on different levels.*[21]

Comparative Perspectives

France introduced a ban on indirect discrimination in employment in a law dated November 16, 2001, driven by European litigation. Since then, overcoming some initial reservations, French judges have been gradually applying the concept.[22]

In the United States, as Oppenheimer indicates, the appearance of disparate impact theory in antidiscrimination law was less straightforward than is generally described. Its neglected history is worth telling, especially to those who foresee an imminent rejection of disparate impact theory by American judges. It will also provide perspective on the interpretation of this concept by European courts, enabling us to discover whether they started from a different premise.[23] Before engaging in a comparative study of the contours and implications of indirect discrimination, in light of the commentary from American scholars,[24] and how an indirect discrimination strategy can be combined with direct discrimination and other tools to achieve equality such as affirmative action (or positive action, as it is called in Europe), we will chart the development of disparate impact theory in the United States.

The Little-Known History of Disparate Impact in America

The story that is commonly told implies that disparate impact theory appeared with a bang in the Supreme Court's decision in *Griggs*,[25] the Court's first ruling proscribing indirect discrimination. The truth is that although *Griggs* case was emblematic, it reflected an interpretation of discrimination that had been steadily taking hold in the United States. The Court concluded in *Griggs*,

> Nothing in the Act precludes the use of testing or measuring procedures; they are useful. What Congress has forbidden is giving these devices and mechanisms controlling force, unless they are demonstrably a reasonable measure of job performance. Congress has not commanded that the less qualified be preferred over the better qualified simply because of minority origins. Far from disparaging job qualifications as such, Congress has made such qualifications the controlling factor, so that race, religion, nationality, and sex become irrelevant. What Congress has commanded is that any test used must measure the person for the job, not the person in the abstract.[26]

This recognition of disparate impact liability was codified into the language of the amended Civil Rights Act of 1991.[27] However, as David Oppenheimer and Susan Carle[28] assert, states were already using effects-based analysis to address racial discrimination as early as the 1950s. An even more surprising discovery, made when examining the civil rights social movements of the time, is the broader context in which the idea to devise a strategy to fight disparate impact discrimination germinated.

From 1910 to 1930, in response to the conservative jurisprudence on civil rights from the Supreme Court and outside of the initiatives taken by individual states,[29] organizations such as the National Urban League sought to ferret out systemic causes of racial employment discrimination, notably a lack of training opportunities.[30] This conciliatory, and probably more moderate, approach, far removed from the litigation-based handling of direct discrimination claims, paved the way for new antidiscrimination strategies. The objective was to experiment with more flexible regulatory strategies and persuade employers to voluntarily expand employment and training opportunities for racial minorities.

As Oppenheimer and Carle have noted, below the federal level, some pioneering states developed legislation prohibiting discrimination in employment,[31] which included disparate impact analysis from the start. The New York State Commission Against Discrimination, the antidiscrimination enforcement agency established in 1945, the year the Ives-Quinn Anti-Discrimination Bill was enacted, and other minority-rights organizations were confronted with not only issues about intentional discrimination but also the need to detect the causes of the structural exclusion of certain groups in the sphere of employment.[32]

When Congress adopted the Civil Rights Act in 1964, the preparatory work had been largely inspired by this previous thinking, language, and analysis relating to subtler forms of discrimination and by important litigation such as

Myart v. Motorola, as mentioned by Oppenheimer. In this 1963 case, Motorola rejected Leon Myart, a black job applicant, after he failed a general aptitude test for a position as an electrician, despite his previous work experience. However, the company could not produce his test results, and when Myart took the test anew for the Fair Employment Practices Commission, he passed. The examiner's work, which contributed to the subsequent enactment of the federal Civil Rights Act of 1964, showed that the first test, which disregarded Myart's extensive work experience, "did not lend itself to equal opportunity to qualify for the hitherto culturally deprived and the disadvantaged groups."[33] Although the term "disparate impact discrimination" was not yet being used, the concept was already present in the minds of civil rights organizations, judges, and state antidiscrimination agencies. Furthermore, by 1963, half of the American states had already enacted legislation banning discrimination in employment. Therefore, when the CRA of 1964 was adopted, the intentions and goals of the drafters extended far beyond fighting disparate treatment only. The *Griggs* case is simply the clear articulation of this implicit goal,[34] reiterating the fact that Title VII does not only aim to find discriminatory intent but also to remove "built-in headwinds" for minority groups and barriers to equal opportunity.[35]

This assessment of the historic development of disparate impact is particularly important in light of the U.S. Supreme Court's current jurisprudence on discrimination,[36] as illustrated in *Ricci v. DeStefano*[37] and more recently *Lewis v. Chicago*,[38] which is feared by some scholars, including Suk and Oppenheimer, to be a near-fatal blow to disparate impact liability.[39] It serves to counter the argument advanced by the majority of the current Court, who challenge the legitimacy of disparate impact and consider the *Griggs* decision to be an expansive interpretation of equality and nondiscrimination.[40] It is in fact possible to demonstrate that even before the CRA of 1964, there was a move to eradicate structural discrimination in the workplace, in addition to pursuing those guilty of disparate treatment discrimination.[41]

How does this new understanding of the genesis of disparate impact in the United States reframe the European history of indirect discrimination? In Europe as well, the concept existed before the enactment of more recent EU directives.[42] It was developed in CJEU jurisprudence to rectify measures implemented by member states creating barriers to the free movement of people, goods, and services across national markets, before the notion of restriction took over.[43] Antidiscrimination principles did continue to be strenuously enforced in the goods and services industry, as shown in a 2010 ruling *(Test-Achats v. Council of Ministers)*,[44] which had the effect of prohibiting sex discrimination in insurance policies. So it was relatively easy for the concept of indirect discrimination to be adopted in European case law involving discrimination on the grounds of nationality and then sex. In *Sotgiu*,[45] the CJEU held that disadvantaging employees who reside in another member state, with respect to the payment of an allowance, was indirect discrimination based on nationality, borrowing the idea of "effectiveness" from the antidiscrimination principle to reach that conclusion. Far removed from concerns about fundamental rights, the Court used indirect discrimination to identify access barriers to all national markets.

Following this pragmatic approach focusing uniquely on economic concerns, the Court would then recognize indirect discrimination in the employment market in *Jenkins*.[46] Because an overwhelming majority of part-time workers were women, paying a lower hourly wage for part-time work disproportionately affected women over men. The Court of Justice would nevertheless maintain in this case that discriminatory intent was a necessary element of disparate impact discrimination. *Griggs* also suggests that certain acts of disparate impact discrimination are intentional: in this instance, the policy with disparate impact was introduced in the wake of a new law banning disparate treatment discrimination. However, the U.S. Supreme Court did not recognize a need for a discriminatory motive to establish disparate impact. In fact, it is precisely in cases of facially neutral practices,[47] where discriminatory intent is even more elusive, that a disparate impact discrimination theory can prevent attempts to circumvent discrimination law, by considering the effects of these practices rather than their intent.

It was not until *Bilka*[48] that the CJEU definitively abandoned the idea of discriminatory intent as a condition for indirect discrimination and focused on providing concrete proof of the disproportionate impact of the practice or rule on a given population. In this case, the Court clarified other requirements for establishing indirect discrimination: any practices with discriminatory effect must be objectively justified by a legitimate aim, and the means to achieve this aim must be "appropriate and necessary." This wording was later codified in the EU Directive 97/80 on the burden of proof, the Racial Equality Directive 2000/43, and the Employment Equality Framework Directive 2000/78.[49]

In its early decisions, the CJEU does not discernibly seek to explain the purpose of indirect discrimination provisions. It appears to be motivated by a broad effort to eradicate structural discrimination reproduced in a system or in a business activity (to borrow the expression used in *Griggs*, "built-in headwinds"[50]) and a desire to encourage employers to scrutinize their employment practices to root out the causes of their indirect impact. As articulated much later in the *Voss* case,[51] the CJEU's reasoning often seems to be rather mechanical: the idea is to observe, on a case-by-case basis, the consequences of applying a selection mechanism based on an apparently neutral provision, criterion, or practice. In the end, it is up to the national court to assess whether the aim is legitimate and whether the measure is proportionate, which could explain the Court's cautious approach. However, a less supportive attitude toward the value of testing discrimination has come to the surface, as shown first in the joined cases of *Hennigs* and *Mai*.[52] In its decision, the CJEU accepted the "protection of the established rights" of workers as a legitimate aim, ruling that a temporary pay scheme discriminating on the grounds of age was appropriate and necessary because it ensured that employees already in post would not suffer any loss in income in the transition to a new system. Regarding the resulting discrimination, the Court added that "the discriminatory effects will tend to disappear as the pay of employees progresses."[53] The *Brachner* case,[54] involving a measure affecting low pension holders that disproportionately impacted women, shows that indirect discrimination liability can apply, even symmetrically, to system-wide mechanisms in matters of social security.[55] A recent CJEU case extends the scope of indirect discrimination to situations of disadvantage, outside of employment, affecting residents who are not Roma in an urban district mainly inhabited by people of Roma origin.[56] Today, French judges also understand the concept of indirect discrimination, even when the legitimacy of a collective benefit scheme is called into question.[57]

What are the concrete steps to establishing an indirect discrimination case in France or the United States? Before comparing the different approaches, a clarification of the contours of an indirect discrimination strategy is in order.

Establishing Indirect Discrimination: A Two-Step Test and a Reversal of the Burden of Proof

The American scholars interviewed here offer fresh perspectives on "indirect discrimination." In France, the debate on this issue is often a narrow one, because it relies on French and European case law, which does not always afford a comprehensive overview of the prohibition of these seemingly neutral but discriminatory practices.

Among other scholars, Post, Krieger, Jolls, and Ford emphasize the importance of disparate impact discrimination.[58] Ford has pointed out it can help courts to strike a balance between "what they have done in the past—what is easy to do because it is familiar—and a social policy that an individual employer might not take up on his or her own" but that promotes social harmony and helps subordinated groups "throw off the burden of the past." As Jolls explains, a disparate impact discrimination approach eliminates obstacles to integration, whether or not they are conscious attempts to cloak disparate treatment discrimination.

Disparate impact discrimination takes a step forward by widening the spectrum of less noticeable forms of discrimination, a point Jolls has insisted upon, encompassing a broad range of neutral criteria such as no-beard policies and standardized testing. These barriers to equality are not necessarily embodied by an individual personally responsible for a discriminatory policy: disparate impact discrimination does not require the employer to have committed a fault. The mechanism eliminates the need for a discriminatory motive, bringing to mind no-fault liability or involuntary negligence as mentioned by Oppenheimer.[59]

This analogy to strict liability is significant because it facilitates the understanding that in European and, most importantly, national law, the indirect discrimination approach serves to demonstrate a discriminatory effect and provide a systematic remedy, regardless of the intent or frame of mind of the person behind the decision or practice. The organization as a whole is responsible for an error in judgment in selecting the criteria for a difference in treatment, which are indirectly discriminatory. This form of discrimination does not target an individual person, which explains how the identification of facially neutral but discriminatory criteria can then be repeated in other organizations. A powerful vision of equality is inherent to the search to eliminate indirect discrimination, even if this multistep process is an intricate one.[60]

The scholars discuss how disparate impact is established, and how this process is different for disparate treatment discrimination. As Ford, Post, and Krieger have noted, to satisfy a judge of the existence of disparate impact liability, plaintiffs must demonstrate the discriminatory effect of a facially neutral practice, but the practice constitutes discrimination only if it is not job-related or not consistent with business necessity.[61] In Europe, the two conditions set out in the Employment Equality Directive (2000/78) are similar to those codified in the Civil Rights Act of 1991, although worded differently and in a somewhat more roundabout manner: "Indirect discrimination shall be taken to occur when an apparently neutral provision, criterion or practice would put persons having a particular religion or belief, a particular disability, a particular age, or a particular sexual orientation[62] at a particular disadvantage compared with other persons unless: that provision, criterion or practice is objectively justified by a legitimate aim and the means of achieving that aim are appropriate and necessary."[63]

So, even if the discriminatory impact of a neutral practice has been proven, employers can justify the practice by arguing that it achieves an appropriate, necessary, and objective business aim. In the United States, the cornerstone for proving disparate impact discrimination is the employer's defense. As stated in *Griggs*, "The touchstone is business necessity. If an employment practice which operates to exclude Negroes cannot be shown to be related to job performance, the practice is prohibited."[64] The jurisprudence in the United States, where the collection of ethnoracial data is permissible, tends to be relatively sophisticated because statistics can be used to prove the disparate impact on groups.

The amended Civil Rights Act of 1991 and the guidelines published by the EEOC outline the method of proof and where the burden of proof initially lies, which is with the plaintiff. To establish an unlawful employment practice based on disparate impact, a plaintiff must demonstrate that the defendant used "a particular employment practice that causes a disparate impact on the basis of race, color, religion, sex, or national origin" and either failed to "demonstrate that the challenged practice is job-related for the position in question and consistent with business necessity," or refused to adopt "an alternative employment practice" that the plaintiff has shown was available.[65]

A close examination of the method of proof used in the United States reveals the complexity of establishing disparate impact.[66] There are two prevailing standards for showing statistical disparity: the four-fifths rule mentioned by Ford and statistical significance testing.[67] When assessing a selection test using the four-fifths rule, for example, there is a discriminatory difference in selection rates if the pass rate of a minority group is less than four-fifths of that of the group with the highest selection rate.[68] We are therefore comparing people in a protected group with people who are not in a protected group, after application of the selection method; we are not comparing minorities in an applicant pool with minorities who have been hired by a company, for example.[69] When performing statistically significance testing, a difference in selection rates can be challenged when the confidence level is sufficiently high—usually between 80 and 95 percent—that the difference is meaningful and not due to random chance.[70]

The use of statistics is not mandatory in European law. This lower standard of proof offers an opportunity to bypass the difficulties of obtaining statistics for certain categories of employees (in France, statistics on race, for example), but it may also cloud the visibility of certain discriminatory impacts. As evidenced by certain court decisions, the discriminatory impact of an apparently neutral rule can be proven only if it can be shown that its direct effect on disadvantaged groups is disproportionate. This is more problematic when the protected group or category of people is not defined in law, as is the case for age discrimination in Europe, for example.[71] Age is not a yes-or-no criterion determined by inclusion in a defined group.[72]

The notion of the comparability of situations is central to determining discrimination—even indirect discrimination—but the approaches differ. For example, in *Römer*,[73] the CJEU first examined the effect of the rule on certain persons and only then looked at whether they made up the majority of the people who had suffered the disadvantage.[74] On the European level, direct discrimination necessarily begins with a comparison of situations before the reason for this difference of treatment is sought. French courts diverge from European jurisprudence on this point, increasingly taking the stand that comparability is not a determining factor in demonstrating direct discrimination.[75] This does not seem to be true for indirect discrimination, with the exception of one significant case.[76]

The second step in establishing disparate impact in the United States involves the employer's claims regarding the business necessity and job relevance of the challenged practice.[77] In Europe, proof sought is that "this provision, criterion or practice is [not] objectively justified by a legitimate aim and that the means of achieving that aim are [not] appropriate and necessary."[78] The EEOC's Uniform Guidelines on Employee Selection Procedures[79] offer some rules about this defense used by the employer: the employer must show a high correlation between the test or other selection procedure and important elements of job performance, demonstrating a relationship between the selection procedure scores and job performance.[80]

The EEOC's guidelines propose three methods that can be relied on by employers to validate their tests (i.e., to show that the tests are job-related and consistent with business necessity): these methods are known as criterion-related studies, content studies, and construct validity studies. Criterion-related studies are used to validate selection methods tied to certain job criteria and involve providing empirical data demonstrating that the selection procedure is significantly correlated with important aspects of job performance; this implies a statistically significant relationship between passing the test and an objective measurement of work performance.

Content studies are so called because they focus on content and require data showing that the content of the selection procedure is representative of important aspects of performance on the job for which the applicants are to be evaluated. The test can be applied to operationally defined knowledge, skills, or abilities that are a prerequisite to successful job performance (typing, for example, for an administrative assistant).

The third method, the construct validity study, uses specific data to select work behaviors that are important to the job and will be evaluated. This is the most challenging and least used validation test method. It attempts to identify a psychological characteristic or behavior (a construct), such as a warm personality in a receptionist, that underlies job performance. The employer then develops a selection test based on the extent to which this characteristic or behavior is found in the individual.[81] The principal difficulty for employers is that they bear the burden of establishing this justification.[82] This complete reversal of the burden of proof constitutes one of the main differences from disparate treatment discrimination—which provides for a shifting of the burden of proof—and was curtailed for a time by the Supreme Court after its *Wards Cove* ruling.[83]

Due to the various options available to employers to justify their practices, proving disparate impact in the United States appears to be a difficult task. Suk confirms this statement in her interview. In France, the situation is visibly different, as illustrated by the *MSA* case,[84] the first to find that the employer's justification for indirect discrimination failed the proportionality test, with respect to an apparently neutral measure. In European case law involving indirect discrimination, once the discriminatory effect has been identified, the requirement to show legitimate aim and proportionality seems to pose less of an obstacle.[85] Could this relative ease be explained by the absence of specific rules defined in legislation or jurisprudence for validating the employer's justification, unlike in the United States? Or might it reflect the fact that it is already difficult to prove the discriminatory effect of the neutral measure, not only because the use of statistics is optional, but because such data are rarely available? Indirect discrimination is a game of proportion or rather a lack of proportion in the impact of a neutral provision, of which evidence needs to be provided.[86] But French case law shows a certain indulgence toward the ways in which this disproportionate effect can be ascertained: in *MSA*, for example, showing that "the measure affects a significantly higher proportion of people of one sex" has been sufficient.[87]

How is it possible to show that an impact is disproportionate without using statistics? Although tricky, it can be done. The discriminatory effect of the provision must be easy to detect. For example, taking absences into account when calculating compensation directly impacts a large proportion of people who have taken sick leave and share the same characteristic:[88] an absence that translates into an interruption in the performance of their work contracts. This clarity required in European law for indirect discrimination claims not supported by statistics applies only to facially neutral rules such as those involving seniority or experience, which do not always relate to a prohibited ground in the same way. For example, if an employer chooses to make compensation or hiring decisions based on experience or seniority, it is not certain whether the rule will benefit or disadvantage younger or older workers. The answer may depend on the industry or education level.

To prove that discrimination occurred, the first step is to prove that persons in certain age brackets are particularly disadvantaged by the "neutral" rule, which may require the use of statistics, depending on the company involved. Once again, the use of statistics will depend on the type of practice being challenged: if an easily identifiable category, such as part-time workers, is the focus, then statistics are more readily accessible because this is a group of workers already tracked by employers. The criteria used by the defendant in the *MSA* case were objective but determined on a case-by-case basis and difficult to calculate. The high cost of producing statistics may be hindering the implementation of indirect discrimination strategies in Europe. It would appear that the supportive role of providing this information in order to prove or disprove the existence of indirect discrimination falls with the Défenseur des Droits (Defender of Rights), the agency in charge of enforcing antidiscrimination law in France. Since 2012, the Cour de Cassation has asked employers to justify their discriminatory practices using a proportionality test to assess whether the practice is necessary and proportionate. Regarding the refusal by AGIRC (Association générale des institutions de retraite des cadres), the French organization governing supplementary retirement pensions for management-level employees, to assign a management level to certain occupations in which a majority of the positions are held by women, resulting in a disadvantage for this group, the Court found that AGIRC's methods were neither relevant nor consistent. Although the AGIRC's justification was an alignment with industry practice, as attested by closely related collective bargaining agreements, in order to ensure the stability, consistency, and long-term survival of the supplementary retirement program, no consideration was given to the actual management duties performed, which would have been expected in this case.[89]

Cost is also an issue in developing selection methods and evaluating employees, as Ford observed. Given the prohibitive cost of developing and deploying customized selection tests, employers may find it more convenient to administer a standard test using simplified selection criteria with no regard to job description or classification.[90]

Is Indirect Discrimination the Answer to the No-Comparator Dilemma?

Another point deserves attention: in indirect discrimination claims, the need to provide a basis of comparison is not regarded with the same level of importance as in direct discrimination cases. This observation comes to mind when Krieger explains the preliminary step required in the United States to prove disparate treatment discrimination: making a prima facie case. To show that a selection method is explicitly or implicitly based on origin or sex, for example, one must compare the situation of disadvantaged persons with that of other groups. Interestingly, in France, as mentioned earlier, the Cour de Cassation has been less adamant about requiring a comparator to prove direct discrimination.[91] A surprising decision by France's Supreme Court, although unpublished, implicitly suggests that one of the advantages of the indirect discrimination argument may be to overcome the hurdle of a lack of comparability, for instance, in a case where the employee's situation is so extremely disadvantaged that no comparison is possible.[92]

What are we comparing? Under European law, direct discrimination refers to past, present, or potential unfavorable treatment of a person following a discriminatory decision (Article 2 of the Employment Equality Directive 2000/78), unlike French law, which does not accept a hypothetical comparator (using evidence about the treatment of other people in similar but not identical situations).[93] Indirect discrimination looks first at the neutral practice and analyzes it to determine whether it has a discriminatory effect for larger proportions of one group than another. People in very different employment situations can therefore show that they suffer a discriminatory disadvantage. But no element of comparability exists other than the fact that a large proportion of people in the disadvantaged group share a protected characteristic.

The CJEU's decision in the *Römer* case is very enlightening on this point.[94] The question posed was whether a supplementary retirement pension granted exclusively to married couples discriminates against couples in registered civil unions. This case is of particular interest because it shows that the issue of comparability, widely discussed in the decision, is a legal knot in direct discrimination—in Europe, at least—that indirect discrimination can untangle. In *Römer*, the Court found that this difference of treatment constituted direct discrimination against registered same-sex partners because their situation was similar to that of married couples. The refusal to grant them the supplementary pension could not be objectively justified by the need to protect the institution of marriage or the family.

In other EU member countries where there is no civil union alternative to marriage, making it difficult to use married couples as a comparator, claiming indirect discrimination based on sexual orientation could be effective. Rather than focusing on a nonexistent comparator, the debate would focus squarely on the discriminatory effects of a rule restricting eligibility for a benefit to married couples. In France, where comparability is not compulsory, the Cour de Cassation used this reasoning in a direct discrimination case against an illegal immigrant working as a domestic helper, whose employment was terminated without notice or severance pay. Proving direct discrimination was not an option, because as an illegal worker, the plaintiff was not protected by the employment code and did not have the right to claim unfair dismissal or the accompanying antidiscrimination law.[95]

With indirect discrimination, the issue of the comparability of situations, addressed by the Cour de Cassation,[96] depends on the "scope of comparison."[97] According to certain scholars, who refer to Article 157 of the Treaty of the Functioning of the European Union,[98] the comparison will depend on the rule's scope of application, determining the set of people included in the comparison.[99] The size and breadth of the comparator group can vary, encompassing people doing the same job, at the same classification level, at the same work site, or in the same company. Claimants must refrain from choosing too broad of a group, which will make it more difficult to highlight the rule's disproportionate effect. The larger the scope, the harder it will be to show that the unequal distribution of rights can be explained only by the protected ground and not by a different, legitimate factor of differentiation. Although the scope of comparison indicates the set of people affected by the employment rule, lower court judges have the discretion to decide how to assess the comparator. According to some commentators, judges may choose to compare the responsibilities held in the differently treated groups, as in the *MSA* case, or more generally consider the nature of the activities assigned to the employees, their training requirements, and their working conditions,[100] consistent with European case law.[101] In fact, unlike the comparability test used in "equal pay for equal work"[102] claims focusing on the job description, it appears that it is not possible to establish a standard comparison methodology for indirect discrimination cases because the comparison will always hinge on the neutral practice or provision being challenged. As the budding case law in France is beginning to show, in addition to employment status, challenged provisions may also be related to eligibility for employment benefits, opening a much larger field that covers concepts related to the person, such as marriage[103] and parenthood,[104] that control access to rights.

Potential Limitations for Indirect Discrimination: Narrow Interpretation and Conflict with Direct Discrimination

Several of the scholars interviewed have commented on the *Ricci v. DeStefano* decision,[105] which was closely followed by a similar case involving the use of an eligibility test with disparate racial impact.[106] The *Ricci* case is interesting on several levels. First, it could jeopardize the future recognition of disparate impact in the United States, if interpreted narrowly. Suk and Oppenheimer especially refer to this threat. In the opinion of some scholars, certain Supreme Court justices have never accepted the legitimacy of disparate impact theory, due to its structural emphasis, which is absent in intentional discrimination.[107] As Post observed, unlike disparate treatment discrimination, disparate impact discrimination conveys the idea that action should be taken to eliminate institutional mechanisms that seem to be fair on the surface but actually perpetuate the exclusion of minority groups. It is closer to a logic of redistribution and equal opportunity.[108] The Supreme Court has never recognized challenges to the disparate impact of government policies under the equal protection of the laws granted in the Fourteenth Amendment.[109] The *Ricci* opinion, which accentuated the level of evidence that employers must provide to justify any action they volunteer to take to rectify disparate impact, is emblematic of the resistance to disparate impact. In his concurring opinion in *Ricci*, Justice Scalia even seemed to suggest that, inevitably, the "evil day" would come when the Supreme Court would entirely disavow the disparate impact provisions of Title VII in order to satisfy the Fourteenth Amendment.[110]

Suk does not believe that the American judges are effectively fighting discrimination in a systematic manner despite the disparate impact provisions.[111] Echoing Oppenheimer's comments, she explains that proving disparate impact is already an arduous task and that the supplementary proof required will only serve to further reduce the number of disparate impact claims and prevent plaintiffs from succeeding in their cases. According to Suk, additional government policies, programs, or legislation is a prerequisite to achieving any substantial change; the narrow trajectory taken by antidiscrimination law may undermine advances in other areas of public policy to reconcile family and work life.[112] She argues that discrimination concepts are not infinitely expandable and sees a certain appeal in completely rewriting antidiscrimination law. Sanctioning employers who seek to voluntarily avoid disparate impact liability, as the city of New Haven did when it withdrew its discriminatory test, will dissuade employers from making any effort in this area. *Ricci* will therefore also affect attempts to prevent disparate impact, if the Court's interpretation in this case is followed. It is true that there have been relatively few disparate impact cases since the 1991 amendment to the Civil Rights Act, which places the burden of justifying the business necessity of the discrimination on the employer.[113]

If we choose to play the role of doomsayer, at first glance the *Ricci* case is a dead end for the expansion of antidiscrimination law. If the fight against discrimination focuses on disparate impact strategies, leading to the dismantling of measures causing the disparate impact, this can produce other forms of discrimination—involving disparate treatment, additional disparate impact, or even reverse discrimination.[114] Many commentators assert that despite the message of *Ricci*, the United States can hardly be said to have entered a post-racial era.[115] The complexity of reconciling the interests of the different groups and individuals affected by antidiscrimination laws, due to indirect discrimination resulting from "neutral" criteria, has already been illustrated in European law. *Cadman*,[116] in which length of service was found to be a legitimate, neutral criterion for a difference in treatment, even if it adversely impacted women with less experience, and the *Hennigs/Mai* joined cases and subsequent cases,[117] in which age was factored into the pay scale as a measure of experience, underscore the intricacy of identifying the neutral criteria that can have discriminatory effects based on the group in question. The relative strength of direct and indirect discrimination strategies continues to be a hot topic, as attested by recent cases showing that, according to the required qualification, a plaintiff can win or lose a case.[118] If a rule appears to be neutral but systematically excludes a protected category of people, either a direct or indirect discrimination strategy can be used.[119] Success will depend on the justification provided by the employer or lawmakers, because the review of justifications is not the same and does not have the same consequences. An objective justification with a legitimate and proportionate means that the neutral practice is not discriminatory, while no justification is accepted if direct discrimination is found.

But a more optimistic interpretation of *Ricci*, shared by Post and Krieger, exists. As they explain, the *Ricci* decision does not necessarily challenge disparate impact. It can be analyzed from another angle. First, as Krieger noted, disparate treatment discrimination was a valid claim, because the whites and Hispanics who had passed the test would no longer be eligible for promotion. If the test had been withdrawn before it was used, the Court's conclusion may have been different. Second, as Krieger noted, the city did not consider all the aspects of disparate impact theory in its analysis. In addition to showing that the test had a statistically significant disadvantage on a minority group, it should also have determined whether the test was related to the job for which it was designed and consistent with business necessity.[120] But the city did not provide all of these elements and therefore did not establish disparate impact liability, allowing direct discrimination against white and Hispanic firefighters who had passed the test to emerge. Krieger does not, however, agree with the Court's conclusion that the basis of evidence of disparate impact should be more stringent.[121]

Post concurs that *Ricci* is not about disparate impact. It is a decision about *affirmative action* drawn from a disparate treatment discrimination case, and it asks the question: what can an employer do to remedy inequality in the workplace without committing disparate treatment discrimination? This was the issue raised by the plaintiffs who opposed the decision to withdraw the test, which they saw as intentionally discriminatory in favor of minorities. So the decision's effect on disparate impact theory does not directly come into play. The Supreme Court and state courts have already been interpreting the legitimacy of affirmative action narrowly for some time.

It is preferable to refocus on the aim of disparate impact discrimination law, which is to motivate employers to take steps to prevent disparate impact and understand what acts are is admissible, while disparate treatment discrimination pushes employers to avoid action and avoid differences in treatment based on a prohibited ground.

Whichever view one prefers to take of the *Ricci* decision,[122] disparate impact or indirect discrimination poses a particular challenge for judges in any country.

In these cases, the judge must consider a context that is larger than the individual suit, which a tricky task in any situation. It can also be observed that most Supreme Court justices and certain federal judges seem to narrowly interpret the entire corpus of antidiscrimination law, including, of course, disparate impact provisions. Meanwhile, the CJEU, the ECtHR,[123] and the Cour de Cassation, like European judges, seem to be driving novel interpretations of antidiscrimination law. Undoubtedly, this comparison should be nuanced and situated on a theoretical level: what does the indirect discrimination approach ultimately aim to achieve? Is it compatible with positive and affirmative action? In light of the observed retreat from the case law in the United States and the commentary by the interviewed scholars, where do these two equality tools meet or compete?

Indirect Discrimination and Positive Action in the Fight Against Systemic Discrimination: Match or Clash?

Stirring under the surface of the *Ricci* decision, the debate over disparate impact can be felt. The discussion it engenders is useful for the European perspective, because the ban on indirect discrimination in Europe was more heavily based on an understanding that this type of discrimination was intentional, using the neutral measure as a pretext. The insight gained by this comparative study suggests that the prohibition of indirect discrimination can be understood from a new angle, one that is familiar in Europe in the area of disability: there is a duty to accommodate. In disability discrimination, this means making adjustments in the workplace for the individual with the disability. The main difference here is the scale of the measure taken. "Appropriate measures" in the field of disability are often determined on an individual basis depending on the disability in question. But indirect discrimination deals with a different order of magnitude, frequently affecting a group of people, because it results from a rule and not an individual decision.[124]

If Justice Roberts,[125] an ardent supporter of the protection of formal equality, giving discrimination its narrowest meaning—that is, that of disparate treatment, is right in proclaiming that "the way to stop discrimination . . . is to stop discriminating," then what disparate impact discrimination accomplishes is closer to affirmative or positive action. It advocates proactive programs by employers to promote equal opportunity and institution-wide integration.[126] As Jolls has written, the ban on disparate impact discrimination may incite employers to take concrete steps to eliminate the institution-wide, systematic exclusion of minorities.[127] This is precisely what alarms the Supreme Court.[128] As Post notes, once a disparate impact has been identified, one of the ways to offset its effect is to use proactive measures to include minorities.[129] Employers fearful of incurring disparate impact discrimination liability are encouraged to apply numerical quotas, regardless of their illegality, to compensate for the discriminatory effect of their selection methods. In *Connecticut v. Teal*, the Court clearly stated that disparate impact discrimination, like reasonable accommodation, required the employer to not only provide an objective justification of its discriminatory practice but to prevent liability by promoting workforce diversity: this does not imply any obligation to implement affirmative action programs. European law follows the same line of reasoning: the disadvantage produced by indirect discrimination must not be assessed *after* other measures have been taken to counteract it.[130]

In the prevention of disparate impact discrimination, in the United States, where the jurisprudence has a longer history, what encounters the most resistance among judges are the disparate impact testing and the subsequent action taken by employers rather than actually establishing disparate impact discrimination. Affirmative action and, in Europe, positive action are confronted with the same problem. What role should be given to measures of preferential treatment that can lead to "positive" discrimination?[131] The CJEU seems to opt for a restrictive interpretation of positive action, wary of the direct discrimination that can result.[132] How is it possible to reconcile the interests of the various groups or individuals affected by these antidiscrimination rules without committing disparate treatment discrimination, as Ford has questioned?

In the United States, affirmative action has lost its legitimacy; its constitutionality is gauged with respect to its potential for disparate treatment discrimination.[133] Is indirect discrimination jurisprudence following the same path? Reverse discrimination, which has garnered little attention in France, is a form of direct discrimination. Given the symmetric nature of sex and race discrimination provisions, it is easy to see how they can be used by persons outside of the minority groups, when these persons suffer an economic prejudice due to preferential treatment for minorities. One has only to imagine the consequences of a deteriorated economy, even in Europe, to comprehend that employment discrimination can become an issue for anyone, even those not initially perceived by the law to be potential victims.

Indirect discrimination jurisprudence raises one last question: what types of rules or practices are targeted by the ban on indirect discrimination? Do some facilitate the detection and justification of indirect discrimination? An openly communicated selection test or method is likely to be scrutinized by job applicants or judges, although the CJEU has shown some indulgence toward trade unions, giving them a certain leeway with respect to potentially discriminatory categories used in their collective bargaining agreements.[134]

It is probably for this reason that in the United States, and France as well, legal requirements to combat discrimination have been translated into best practices and other soft law. Measures to promote diversity through training and management techniques are not easily reached by law: sociologists like Frank Dobbin and Lauren Edelman[135] explain the fascinating ability of organizations to internalize legal norms relating to antidiscrimination and diversity. The outcomes may be mixed,[136] but the approach is a valid consideration. Equality of outcome and equal opportunity in recruitment and promotion and access to fair pay increases are the shared goals of disparate impact discrimination provisions, positive action, and affirmative action. Which of these legal instruments are the most flexible and best suited to help employers achieve the necessary temporary and longer-term adjustments?

Some commentators see a contradiction[137] in attempts to combine positive action measures with a prohibition of disparate impact discrimination to protect the rights of groups with protected characteristics, but as Post notes, employers can always choose to simply measure the objective relevance and transparency of their selection methods against the job's requirements and its potential evolution.[138] All of these tools allow employers to justify their acts, whether they are proactive or not.

In the next part of this chapter, American scholars share their thoughts on other subtle practices implemented by companies to address systemic discrimination, in an environment where collective bargaining is rarer than in France and Europe.

II. DIVERSITY AND PREVENTION OF SYSTEMIC DISCRIMINATION

Disparate impact litigation targets internal company policies and practices such as working hours, physical tests, and dress codes. Although seemingly neutral, these practices can be unintentionally alienating and inherently discriminatory in terms of recruitment, pay, and promotion—against women, older workers, or people with gender identity issues, for example. The scholars' commentary on disparate impact leads naturally to a broader questioning about the implementation of structural measures, in addition to the prohibition of direct and indirect discrimination, to prevent unfair distinctions. Looking back at what has been accomplished, some consider that these two bans, essentially designed to discourage employers from taking certain types of action, are not achieving enough. As Suk observed in recent informal discussions, plaintiffs in the United States are also encountering procedural challenges in antidiscrimination litigation because some cases raised the burden of pleading on plaintiffs and the requirements for class actions are more restrictive.[139] Although litigation is important for bringing to light purportedly objective requirements perpetuating workforce segregation, prevention is key to eliminating systemic discrimination.[140] The scholars express an interest in institutional change focusing on mechanisms of inclusion over causes of exclusion: exploring other measures inciting people to take preventive action against the causes of discrimination or to establish institution-wide safeguards.

Is diversity one such measure? Diversity, achieved through affirmative action or other strategies, is an especially important concept in the United States: its Supreme Court has accepted to rule on the compliance of certain affirmative action measures with the Constitution's equal protection guarantee. Some commentators fear, given the opinion of the majority of Supreme Court justices on the issue, as seen in the *Fisher* case, that the principle of affirmative action will lose its credibility in the United States.[141] Fisher was denied admission to the University of Texas and challenged the selection methods used by the school, a combination of neutral provisions (the top 10 percent of each high school graduating class was automatically admitted, regardless of ethnic, racial origin, or residence)[142] and an affirmative action program (other applicants could still gain admission by scoring highly in a process that took race into account). She filed suit, alleging discrimination on the basis of race in violation of her Fourteenth Amendment right to equal protection.

Writing for the majority, Justice Kennedy concluded that the Fifth Circuit failed to apply strict scrutiny in its decision affirming the admissions policy. "Strict scrutiny does not permit a court to accept a school's assertion that its admissions process uses race in a permissible way without closely examining how the process works in practice."[143] Kennedy argued that, since *Grutter v. Bollinger*, the courts "must assess whether the University has offered sufficient evidence to prove that its admissions program is narrowly tailored to obtain the educational benefits of diversity." Quoting Reva Siegel:

> Today, the strict scrutiny framework recognizes differences in social position among racial groups as a reason for allowing affirmative action.[144] . . . The opinions of Justices Powell, O'Connor, and Kennedy understand concerns about social cohesion as a reason to allow, as well as to limit, race-conscious state action. In various ways, their opinions recognize that in a racially divided society, allowing government to engage in some forms of race-conscious state action may actually transform the experience of race sufficiently to promote social cohesion.[145] . . . Even if government has compelling reasons to take race into account to promote diversity in education[146] and to promote equal opportunity and end racial isolation,[147] Justice Kennedy is insistent that courts oversee the means by which government pursues these ends because of the many harms that racial classifications inflict on all citizens and society as a whole.[148]

In the conversations that follow, some scholars, such as Julie Suk, Richard Ford, and Frank Dobbin, comment on the variable effectiveness of diversity programs in employment. Others discuss how diversity and equal opportunity can be approached differently by exploring the inner workings of the institutions producing the discrimination and the interests of groups other than the victims of the discrimination and by taking into account other factors of exclusion, such as employment level or complex decision-making processes. The scholars also respond to indispensable social science input in evaluating the internalization of law in the workplace, as organizations move to comply with changing regulations, and comment on the implications of focusing on groups versus individuals, a core issue in the fight against discrimination. Lastly, they consider how the reasonable accommodation requirement, with respect to disabilities, and anti-harassment laws are the only legal mechanisms that contain an obligation to act.

Diversity Policies: Scope and Limits

Julie Suk begins by looking at diversity from a comparative approach.

MARIE MERCAT-BRUNS: *What do you think of the concept of diversity?*

JULIE SUK: A few thoughts about diversity: In the United States we're talking about a few different things. First, the need for diversity arises as a way of undoing the effects of past discrimination. In this formulation, it appears that diversity is really just a means of getting to a world in which Americans cease to see the differences between each other. Second, American diversity embodies a commitment to pluralism—the idea that a variety of incompatible cultures, religions, world views should all find a home in our democracy. On this model, the differences should last forever. They're two very different concepts. France has traditionally been very skeptical of the second model, especially when it comes to schools. So I am still trying to make sense of the new diversity talk in France.

MM-B: *Yes. We can come back to France later. I do not necessarily agree that France is skeptical about diversity. Probably a certain amount of skepticism is due to the fact that the diversity discourse is sometimes used for political aims. But I would like to come back to what you said: I think the first meaning of diversity is in a way distinct from the context from which diversity emerged and is actually closer to formal equality? What do you think?*

JS: The project of pursuing diversity as a means to integration suggests that the concept is being shaped by the historical, social, and political context in which it is being deployed.

MM-B: *What I mean refers back to diversity in the* Bakke *and* Grutter *opinions: diversity that is not linked to racial imbalance. So I guess my observation is more about your second definition of diversity as a very individualistic way of looking at differences as what makes a person unique: each individual has his or her own talents and contributes in his or her own way, so groups and their contexts seem to be forgotten. This idea seems to be closer to formal equality, which is blind to differences and upholds the principle that each individual citizen has the same rights.*

JS: On the one hand, *Grutter* seems to invoke a concept of diversity as pluralism; on the other hand, the twenty-five-year time limit on affirmative action as a means of achieving diversity suggests that the diversity concept is really being used to achieve old-fashioned racial integration. Closer to formal equality than to what?

MM-B: *In France we distinguish between two forms of equality: formal equality, that is, treating everyone the same way, and a more substantial, "concrete" equality, that is, treating people in different situations differently.*

JS: It's not a uniquely French conception. American political and legal theorists are also very preoccupied with the distinction between formal and substantive equality, which is elaborated in Rawls's *Theory of Justice*. But I think that the ways in which the two are opposed to each other vary from country to country.

For instance, in the United States, we oppose "formal" equality of opportunity to "substantive" equality of opportunity; in France, the very idea of "equality of opportunity" is linked to formal equality, whereas substantive equality requires more than equal opportunity alone; it seems to be measured in terms of equal outcomes.

MM-B: *So you think that equal opportunity in France means equal outcomes? I'm not so sure about that, personally. In the same spirit, do you think that French law recognizes systemic discrimination, whether it results from disparate treatment of a group or from norms that have a disparate effect?*

JS: I am talking about *égalité des chances* in France, which I would translate as equality of opportunity in the United States. The French far left is somewhat critical of the emphasis on equality of opportunity or égalité des chances, on the grounds that substantive equality requires more. The question of systemic discrimination in France is complicated. On the one hand, I don't think there is any resistance to the idea in France that there are "systemic" and "structural" features of institutions that tend to exclude certain classes of people—the resistance is to the idea that such people be identified as members of racial or ethnic groups rather than as the social underclass.

MM-B: *So it not just a question of not understanding the instruments used like disparate impact/indirect discrimination which do not rely on intentional discrimination?*

JS: I think that the concept of discrimination, and antidiscrimination law by extension, is very limited in addressing what we call structural discrimination or institutional racism or systemic inequalities. We put a lot of hope in concepts like disparate impact or indirect discrimination and tend to be disappointed with the results.

Suk's reflections seem to resonate with Richard Ford's thoughts about strategies other than repression to prevent discrimination.

MARIE MERCAT-BRUNS: *There are both criminal and civil sanctions in French law for discrimination. Linda Krieger showed us that criminal sanctions are not effective in instances where there is unconscious bias.*

What do you think about the whole discourse on preventing discrimination, especially in career advancement? In France, collective bargaining agreements have been signed requiring employers above a certain size to implement policies to promote diversity. In your opinion, is this merely rhetoric and soft law?

RICHARD FORD: I am sure it helps, if it is done right.

MM-B: *For example, they are having managers undergo diversity awareness training, using role-playing and case studies.*

RF: I have mixed feelings. On the one hand, I think that it makes a big difference. That that is where the interaction happens. When you wind up in court, everyone has already lost. It is a way to create incentive for the employer to take proactive measures. I have a few misgivings about it because of the touchy-feely aspect of a lot of this: diversity consulting for example. Everybody has diversity training and they come back and do what they would have done before. The president of L'Oréal says "We have a great diversity program" because of five hours of training a year. I also worry about the management science aspect. Management science is not bad, but it does have its peculiarities.

MM-B: *In creating other norms?*

RF: That is good. It can make a difference if it is done right. Having said all of that, I still think—to get back to statistics in a way—I am for benchmarks. I am for objective measures. Diversity training is great, but I want to be able to see some real improvement too. See more women in the workforce. People react and say, "Oh my God, we are going to have quotas!" You can distinguish benchmarks and quotas in a lot of ways. Statistics are evidence. You can say to an employer, "We think you are consistently behind where you ought to be."

MM-B: *In France, there is a law that requires employers to show that, over time, the difference in wages by sex has diminished to a certain point. That is something you can measure.*

RF: I think you need that.

Comparative Perspectives

The commentary by Suk and Ford tends to confirm certain limitations to the diversity rationale in the United States, which often promotes cultural differences or a temporary remedy for past discrimination with the overarching objective of achieving equal opportunity. This is what emerges from Supreme Court jurisprudence on the issue.[149] However, Julie Suk has explained recently that "properly understood, the consequences of quotas should not justify the categorical rejection of quotas."[150] What diversity does not do is seek to address economic inequality in the labor market and how it intersects with employment discrimination based on origin or sex, the two forms most often addressed by the redistributive positive discrimination policies implemented in France.[151] In all countries, diversity remains an unclear concept,[152] chiefly associated with the pursuit of equality and coupled with other ideas. In Canada, for example, diversity and equity are often cited together.[153]

What is interesting about diversity is that it turns the logic of antidiscrimination law on its head: it considers the enumerated grounds of discrimination as factors of inclusion of people into the workplace rather than factors of exclusion.[154] A person's identity is one way to challenge legal classifications, by showing that one individual—a black disabled person, an elderly woman, an obese gay person, and so on—can belong to more than one protected category,[155] literally embodying diversity. Recognizing the problems of equality that can be faced by individuals who do not fall within strictly defined categories can be one step toward designing strategies for integration that dispense with stereotyped ideas about the needs of victims of discrimination.[156]

But outside of the relatively rare case of fighting multiple discrimination, what are the benefits of affirmative action—or positive action as it is known in Europe—taken by employers in implementing diversity initiatives, above and beyond any stratagems used to avoid discrimination liability suits?[157]

According to some American scholars, concrete benefits have been observed when companies take conscious and voluntary steps to include people with diverse characteristics, but without using quotas. The first benefit, which has already been mentioned, is the reduction of implicit biases. Social psychology research[158] and behavioral economics studies applying American cognitive theory to economics[159] show that the appointment of a person representing a minority or other protected group (a woman, for example) to an executive position can contribute to diminishing implicit biases against this group among other employees or managers.[160] Knowing that a discriminatory motive can be unconscious, positive actions such as these can send out a positive signal that is intuitively received by employees at all levels of the company and by the company's customers.[161] The basis for these measures is the observation that, because of implicit biases,[162] even if employees seem to consciously accept diversity as a valid principle and internalize it in the company, it cannot be promoted from within the company. The movement must flow in the other direction, from the outside to the inside, by giving preference to certain groups in order to establish a new normative standard. This positive action will lead to more equitable decision-making processes and in turn enable the company to effectively promote diversity.

Other American scholars consider that this artificial improvement of the condition of disadvantaged groups will perpetuate the stereotypical assumption that the affirmative action process systematically disregards skills and abilities. They fear that the backlash produced by such programs is just as destructive as the initial inequality.[163]

Still others object to this "showcasing" of diversity and the detrimental message it conveys about the individuals being exhibited due to their origin, age, or sex, for example.[164] To assign a position to a person based on his or her value as a message-sender and instrument of implicit communication is to undermine that person's legitimate status in the organization. The employee is perceived as a mere token used to obtain recognition outside of the company, with no regard for the competitiveness of the employment market or the person's real assets. Being used in this way is degrading in itself and undercuts the logic of nondiscrimination. Instead of an achievement of diversity, the individual represents a means to accomplish a business goal.[165] Within the organization, people hired in the name of diversity face a tougher struggle to earn respect for their merits and, if they are seen to be privileged, are less likely to benefit from shared attitudes of mutual respect and concern in the workplace.[166]

In fact, the real question is not whether diversity is justified but rather how this rationale can be used in legal settings to amalgamate correlation and causality. American courts have found affirmative action in employment to be permissible under the Title VII prohibition of discrimination, in limited circumstances.[167] There may therefore be a correlation between employers that promote diversity in hiring and employers that do not discriminate, but this relationship is not necessarily one of cause and effect. It is interesting to note that within French organizations, the actors implementing diversity are not necessarily those in charge of handling discrimination:[168] although companies may not overtly claim diversity measures as a defense against discrimination allegations, employers accused of discriminating have often riposted with a generous display of diversity measures.[169] So diversity initiatives are at times used to circumvent antidiscrimination law and at times considered to be catalyzers and drivers of emulation, producing organic, institution-wide change rather than a response to an individual incident.

All this diversity debate has a crucial role today in France,[170] where it is illegal to discriminate based on race but where the government chose to introduce the constitutional notion of gender parity[171] on company boards[172] in the law adopted on January 27, 2011, extended in 2014.[173] This law does send out a signal, but it may have been received differently[174] than intended and, as we have seen, not necessarily in a positive way. The conclusions of American studies, regarding the impact of diversity, are mixed. Certain cognitive and anthropological investigations show that risk perceptions related to diversity vary based on the individual's values and worldviews: researchers at Yale[175] developed a four-dimension framework showing a possible correlation between an individual's beliefs and his or her position within this framework.[176]

Alternatively, France's gender parity law may indicate that governance practices in large companies worldwide are changing. In the United States, since the crisis in confidence in the financial markets, laws were passed, in particular the Dodd-Frank Act,[177] requiring boards to better assess risks faced by companies. Board diversity could have an effect on the decisions made to take into account changes in corporate law and new systems of governance.[178] Some scholars,[179] inspired by critical race theory,[180] offer a different, more nuanced analysis, putting forward the idea that no law can truly modify the power relations between board members and individual shareholders and employees with their diverse backgrounds, but that one way to better align the interests of management and the group of employees and individual shareholders would be to effectively diversify the composition of boards of directors.[181]

A closer look at the board decision-making processes rather than structure, however, calls for some prudence in assessing the influence that the positions of board members representing minority groups have on the board majority. Boards negotiate a delicate balance between seeking a consensus and stimulating debate when a difference of opinion arises from the discussion. Studies show that minority or women members, for example, are expected to contribute in more ways than white male executives, of whom only the power of persuasion is required, before they can earn credibility; but if there are at least three board members that represent their minority, then this goal is easier to achieve.[182]

The reach of the French law on gender parity on corporate boards is limited in several ways and can be further restricted simply by the weakness of the "signal" it sends. The first limitation is the scope of application of the law, which does not apply to smaller companies operating as a limited-liability *société à responsabilité limitée*, the most common corporation form in France.[183] Although it gives the illusion of being widespread, the scope of the law could be significantly expanded by including other legal forms of companies. Nevertheless, the recent law of August 4, 2014, on real equality between women and men has extended the parity requirement to unlisted companies, but only to large, profit-making companies.[184] Benchmarking tools must be clearly defined once the law comes into effect.[185]

The second limitation relates to the decision-making powers within a company. The gender parity requirement does not apply to many strategic committees and circles of power in companies, despite the fact that a large number of important decisions are made by these bodies and not just boards of directors, not to mention the numerous management levels where women should be better represented to achieve critical mass in positions of power within the company. Third, some commentators are skeptical about racial diversity measures that reach only the highest echelons of the company without bringing change for minorities at the bottom.[186] The same reasoning can be applied to the empowerment of women in general. Broader consideration should be given to the effect of antidiscrimination law on employees at different skill levels and the decision-making processes that influence employee selections.

Sociological Views of Diversity Policies

Devah Pager discusses diversity awareness-raising programs in organizations from her viewpoint as a sociologist.

MARIE MERCAT-BRUNS: *I have one last question on diversity training: as a sociologist, do you think it can help to modify hiring practices? And do you think the law or other norms, like collective bargaining agreements in France on diversity, can make a difference?*

DEVAH PAGER: My sense is that the evidence is fairly pessimistic about the impact of diversity training. Frank Dobbin would be the one to answer this. But my sense of his and other research on the topic is that diversity training does very little to change actual behavior. If you want to change behavior, you have to focus on outcomes. Policies that actively encourage diversity can have a huge impact, provides that "diversity" is clearly defined and evaluated as an outcome, not just a fuzzy ideal. Ironically, some forms of diversity training can backfire, as they make hiring managers feel that they've done their part, without having actually achieved any real change.

These reflections are enriched by Frank Dobbin's thoughts on certain diversity policies that can detract attention from the real issues of discrimination and maintain a status quo in terms of antidiscrimination measures.

MARIE MERCAT-BRUNS: *What do social scientists and lawyers have to learn from each other about fighting discrimination?*

FRANK DOBBIN: Social scientists have a lot to learn from lawyers about how courts react to corporate antidiscrimination measures. What kinds of measures do they like to see, and what kind do they actually give employers credit for? In some areas of the law, for instance sexual harassment, this is crystal clear. We know that the courts like to see training and other educational efforts, and they like to see clear antiharassment policies at the firm level, and clear mechanisms for dealing with grievances. The Supreme Court set out these standards. But in the case of gender and race and ethnic discrimination in hiring, promotion, and firing, we don't have a clear idea of what the courts favor. Lauren Edelman at Berkeley and her colleagues are doing some very interesting work on that front right now.

Social scientists also have much to learn from lawyers on two fronts. First, there are a few lawyers, such as Susan Sturm at Columbia, who are doing social-scientific studies of corporate and academic diversity programs, adding qualitative evidence about how programs work. Sturm gives us some new hypotheses to test, and confirms a lot that we know from organizational sociology about putting someone in charge of promoting diversity and using professional expertise to design management systems.

Second, a number of lawyers, such as Linda Krieger, have written reviews of the social scientific research from the perspective of the law. Krieger's work explores what has been found in psychology and psychology about discrimination, in the context of how this is relevant to court cases. This helps us to see what kinds of social scientific evidence might be relevant to legal cases.

Going in the other direction, from social science to the law, I would hope that lawyers would be more attentive to the kind of evidence now available on the efficacy of diversity training, performance evaluations, and other programs and would push in legal settlements to get firms to commit to putting their efforts into the kinds of programs—recruitment, mentoring, taskforces—that have proven effective and to cut their expenditures on the kinds of programs—diversity training, diversity performance evaluations, affinity networks—that have not proven effective at increasing opportunity.

Comparative Perspectives

American sociologists cite legal scholarship on the same subjects with fascinating ease. The ideas mentioned by Frank Dobbin in his interview are discussed more extensively in his book *Inventing Equal Opportunity*.[187] His sociological analysis is based on the way that companies have interpreted the law to apply it within their organizations: the perceived constraints of antidiscrimination law may not match the intended scope of the norms as they were written. As Dobbin explains, "the personnel profession's favorite compliance strategies came to define equal opportunity and discrimination.[188] . . . Judges were not empowered to invent new compliance standards from scratch. So judges looked to leading employers when asked how firms should comply with fair employment laws. . . . The executive branch agencies charged with overseeing equal employment and affirmative action likewise looked to private employers to develop guidelines and their own best-practices lists."[189]

In other words, human resource managers translated the legal constraints as they saw fit to protect their employers from discrimination liability. It should be noted that the financial stakes for companies accused of discrimination are high.[190] Confronted with a lack of specific guidelines emanating from the government on how to implement the norms, each company developed its own internal regulations and employee handbooks, with the encouragement of the public authorities.

At first, the companies' strategy was to show that diversity efforts could serve as a defense in the event of litigation: for example, companies developed methodologies to validate selection tests or appointed consultants to protect themselves from disparate impact liability.[191] Then, as affirmative action programs came under attack during the Reagan Administration, companies focused on building a business case for diversity as a factor of economic efficiency.[192] Again, human resource managers, not lawyers, were the ones to pilot this change and rename their equal opportunity efforts as diversity management.[193] Programs and policies developed in the 1970s adopted new designations in the '80s and '90s—mentoring for women and minorities, career planning, diversity task forces, diversity culture audits, and diversity training—but continued to pursue the same aim. What is striking about the new rhetoric is what it produced. Internal diversity norms and best practices not only protected companies from lawsuits but provided a replacement for affirmative action, construed by some to equate with arbitrary preferential treatment for a group.[194] This shift in corporate terminology follows the same pattern as the language of the Supreme Court: the legal qualification of equal opportunity changed from affirmative action to diversity in the field of education; redressing past discrimination was abandoned in favor of promoting the diversity reflected by individual talents.[195]

As human resources turned away from the pursuit of equality to instead aspire for social justice, they did more than redirect the goal of antidiscrimination law.

In some cases, they sparked an organizational impulse in the workplace, transforming certain structural policies and ways of functioning such as work-family policies, fueled by the growing presence of women in the human resources profession.[196] The change of language poses a problem only if, under the guise of fighting for diversity and eradicating bias, it camouflages harmful discrimination:[197] how can it still be evidenced in certain instances in court when, at the same time, proactive policies of employers seem to show their good faith efforts to change things?

Dobbin is not the only scholar to have analyzed how antidiscrimination law has been integrated, interpreted, and transformed by companies. Berkeley professor Lauren Edelman has conducted in-depth research on how legal norms such as antidiscrimination law[198] and diversity rules are interpreted by companies and therefore transformed when applied to real situations to prevent litigation: this is what she calls the "internalization of law."[199] Edelman's postulate is that the relationship between law and corporate governance in the United States has undergone four major phases: the first is the legalization of corporate governance; the second is the growth of private dispute resolution; the third is the development of in-house counsel; and the fourth is the rebirth of private policing. According to Edelman, these processes have interacted with each other to transform large bureaucratic organizations:[200] from being relegated to the role of players within the public legal system, they have grown into private regulators in their own right.[201] Although certain disadvantaged groups, the "have-nots,"[202] may in the short term benefit from the introduction of "citizenship norms" into the workplace, the internalization of law by organizations can in subtle ways tip the balance between democratic[203] and bureaucratic forces in all of society, potentially reinforcing elite power and control.[204]

The legalization of organizational rules can transform many companies into private political spaces with a large number of "citizenship rights," but often these rights do not include the right to vote or even the freedom of speech. Likewise, even if the dispute resolution processes[205] in place provide a forum for reporting grievances, they tend to favor "therapeutic" remedial solutions rather than access to a formal complaints procedure. In-house counsels themselves follow managerial guidelines and the organization's basic orientations, rarely offering pro bono advice to employees voicing complaints or defending the public interest, which is nevertheless one mission of their profession. Lastly, although private policing uses the same rational methods as the public police, the standards and protections applied with regard to searches, surveillance, and secrecy are not the same. Ultimately, "internalization benefits the 'haves' not so much because it undercuts legal neutrality or formality, as because it undercuts democratic governance."[206]

Diversity and Institutional Change

Susan Sturm explores the concept of "institutional citizenship" and diversity.

MARIE MERCAT-BRUNS: *Could you add your views about the effectiveness of Title VII and the diversity rationale?*

SUSAN STURM: I prefer generally to talk about my scholarship on these questions, and you can complete this by looking at the website of the Center for Institutional and Social Change.[207]

We can look at the way institutions/organizations interact with the larger community, the way in which they deliver their services, the way in which they in fact do advance or impede full participation of people. So this is really thinking very much about the relationship between organizations, as in workplaces, and institutions that have a project in a larger system.

MM-B: *Do the norms you are looking at all come from the same sources? I suppose you also look at how they interact?*

SS: Legal norms?

MM-B: *Right.*

SS: You cannot just think about legal norms; you need to think about legal norms in interaction with other norms. If what you are really interested in is creating change in conditions, in the way they are experienced, and in opportunities, you can't just think about the legal norms.

Legal norms are important. One of the big moves that I have made is to suggest that is really important to situate legal norms quite explicitly in a normative and institutional framework and that it is quite different to think about problems or barriers to discrimination in the context of a larger affirmative project than to define the project solely in the terms of discrimination.

So the substantive piece I am writing now and the frame I am developing is the frame of institutional citizenship[208] as one example of what it looks like to articulate a positive, normative vision that requires, as part of it, antidiscrimination norms and apparatus but that is not fully defined by antidiscrimination.

MM-B: *Can antidiscrimination legal norms be counterproductive because they set up oppositions?*

SS: They can be counterproductive but even so are necessary. Part of the real work, which is not really done, is to explicitly navigate the relationship between the systems. So you are asking the questions, What is the relationship? Who are the primary actors? That is a very different stance for public law than the norm, but it is necessary if you are going to influence how norms actually shape practice and the ultimate goal of affecting the conditions of people's lives. I have also become really clear that institutions are a focal point of this work, because institutions shape the micro-level and because institutions are a location where you can get traction at the level of policy.

MM-B: *Don't you think institutions can create resistance?*

SS: That is why they need to be engaged, because they create the conditions that are going to determine whether you are advancing or impeding participation.

MM-B: *Is the EEOC necessarily directly linked to norms and diversity practices and therefore involved in this process? Do you study what the EEOC does?*

SS: Yes. The EEOC is an example of a government intermediary and institutional intermediaries are important. This is actually the subject of a big project on institutional intermediaries. We have looked at some government intermediaries, but we have looked primarily at regulators or compliance organizations as one form of intermediary. The EEOC is a compliance intermediary that is enabling but can be limited in terms of what it can do. Even in the proactive work that the EEOC is doing, organized around building capacity, is limited as is the core mission of the organization, which is compliance. That is the kind of information that they collect and also the way institutions interact with the EEOC. All that is extremely important, but it also means that you are talking about projects that are targeting the cutting edge of the positive deviance. The organizations, the institutions are constructing the vision: what positive institutional citizenship actually looks like. There are organizations that are likely to be doing that in the context of a compliance model.

MM-B: *What is limiting about the compliance model?*

SS: Apparently, it is the way in which the norm is defined. If you are talking about compliance, you are talking about compliance in relation to a norm that you are in a position to mandate. So the norms requiring the EEOC, for example, to advance are limited to the antidiscrimination project. You can go beyond that, but the more the EEOC goes beyond the antidiscrimination project, the less legitimacy it has as an institution. So its purview is limited by the scope of the project that it can ultimately pursue. It is also limited by the fact that it has enforcement powers in the form of being able to litigate or on behalf of classes of people.

MM-B: *How is that limiting?*

SS: It is enabling and limiting. It is enabling in the sense that it can actually mobilize state resources to induce change that can be subject to mandate, particularly before organizations that are negative outliers, that are not up to the norm, as defined by the legal norm. So it has that capability to mobilize resources and attention to try to get the problematic actors in relation to the norm, engaging in intentional discrimination or that have systemic patterns of discrimination that are subject to proof. It can in that context actually mobilize institutional transformation through the remedial project.

MM-B: *You mean financial compensation and the like?*

SS: I mean sanctions ... that also prompt consent decrees, that also give rise to an impetus at all levels for more global organizational change.

Damages also prompt negative publicity and get attention at the top, so they can actually have an impact: the Texaco situation or Wal-Mart[209] are instances in which litigation—sex litigation—has really had an impact, one that we have not really fully appreciated. So it is true that the EEOC has a really important role. The EEOC has a lot of underdeveloped roles that it could advance and that it doesn't now. That is one intermediary.

My take is that the way the EOOC thinks about its work, it doesn't really construct itself as an intermediary: it's actively engaging with other intermediaries, some of which are not compliance agency intermediaries, and it thinks about itself (this is true of a lot of intermediaries) as being part of a system.

MM-B: *Is it due to confidentiality rules or power plays? Is it about a lack of recognition of this part of its role?*

SS: Organizations tend to be siloed and to develop the mission of organization itself as the goal. This is not to say they are entirely self-serving, but they are internally self-referential. This is changing: organizations are now more networked and have that possibility, especially the big organizations. There are other intermediaries, even government intermediaries like the NSF [National Science Foundation], which I wrote about in the architecture of inclusion. It is one example of a public intermediary that is in a position to do things that the EEOC can't do, but there are also things the NSF cannot do.

A whole set of intermediaries are in a position to mobilize norms of different kinds and that architecture to move towards those norms and accountability in relation to that architecture. In order to think about that in a multifarious way, one must have a set of overarching frames that provide a way to link the different sets of norms and systems of projects. That is where institutional citizenship (I am not suggesting it is the only one)—if you thought about the project of employment as advancing institutional citizenship—would lead to a very different way of defining the problem with attention to what the work is.

MM-B: *Could you say that this boils down to looking at the problem rather than the person, which would be stigmatizing?*

SS: You are looking at the problem, but you are also looking at the intentions. Part of the recognition is to only eliminate the problem even if you do it in a structural way. You might even plague the institutional arrangements that re-create the problem. You are not required to envision what it is you actually want in the workplace. All you need to do is to articulate what you think the problem is and you want to eliminate it. You can do that as part of the larger question; it is not that you can avoid doing the problem identification.

But if you want to transform institutional conditions, you have to ask what do you want to transform them towards? People tend to participate differently when they are participating to create something than when they are participating to correct something.

MM-B: *This seems slightly contradictory. Won't you be formatting people to think about participation in a certain way and perpetuating the attitudes that you are actually trying to combat?*

SS: If you don't have a way to deal with entrenched problems for which there is no incentive for change, any effort to do any affirmative social work will be in vain. *[Later in the interview, Sturm comes back to the issue of diversity.]*

MM-B: *If one adopts your perspective of full participation, what would be the employer's incentive to act differently?*

SS: The whole business case for diversity. There is much more motivation to do that; there are intersecting motivations. There is the positive deviance: the small group that is doing it because of the way it defines responsibility in the larger community. I said that even though it is a very small group, it is very important to have that as a frame.

Because it is important and that is where we would like institutions to move to. But you can't base your regulatory system around that because it is too small a group. There are incentives around proactivity as companies define them: What relationship with the capacity to do the work in different companies? There are various things happening to differential degrees in many companies. There is consumer pressure and public pressure coming from the authority intermediaries to ensure positive and negative compliance.

Comparative Perspectives

Susan Sturm recognizes the need to combine litigation of disparate treatment and impact cases with voluntary processes that directly engage institutions at multiple levels in order to change internal social practices engendering discrimination. This overarching approach seems to diverge from European litigation solutions but may be echoed in practices such as the gender mainstreaming promoted by the European Union. This EU initiative is similar to Sturm's model in that it operates at several levels to include and integrate women, engaging both structural and individual aspects in employment, housing, services, and benefits. Unlike Sturm's architecture of inclusion, however, it applies to only one ground, sex.

The European Union has not adopted mainstreaming as a general approach to diversity issues[210] because of the difficulty of employing this technique simultaneously for multiple protected classes, some of which are not identifiable in all countries, such as victims of racial discrimination.[211] Concern about territorial cohesion has been growing, however, as Europe continues to be enlarged and questions have emerged regarding migrant populations, such as the Roma people.[212] As a result, the diversity issue is being pushed to center stage. A multilevel approach is not a new idea, as seen in initiatives such as Equal or other programs supported by the European Social Fund (ESF).[213] Like the architecture-of-inclusion framework, these programs seek to empower those who indirectly advance diversity goals through "soft" law (such as agreements or charters) by highlighting corporate best practices. The European Union seems to insert questions about workplace diversity into these broader concerns about cohesion; for example, in its green paper on territorial cohesion called "Turning Territorial Diversity into Strength": "The European Employment Strategy, an integral part of the Lisbon strategy, makes an important contribution to the development of human capital through better education and the acquiring of new skills in different territories. In addition, the Employment Guidelines include territorial cohesion as one of their three overarching objectives."[214]

European initiatives to promote gender parity are monitored and assessed on a regular basis, but this equality goal focuses only on discrimination based on sex. The European Commission also takes action to combat discrimination on the basis of race and age. But what is unique about Sturm's theory is that it targets many groups of people suffering from discrimination: it emphasizes the causes of exclusion and factors of integration rather than the individual, stigmatizing injuries to each protected group.

Sturm seems to indicate that it is useful to act through law as well as outside of the law and on multiple levels, because the law does not always reach every root source of discrimination. This is a crucial issue and probably points to an added dimension in Europe: equal opportunity must be ensured for employees, as well as the self-employed, and apply to the provision of goods and services. The rapid growth of workers under France's recently introduced *auto-entrepreneur* status for the self-employed glaringly evidences the breadth of the problem.

The definition of *worker* is of primary importance in European law[215] and plays a role in acquiring certain social benefits.[216] Too much emphasis cannot be placed on the need for directives extending the principle of equal treatment and equal opportunity to the self-employed and the liberal professions, in particular with respect to pregnancy,[217] as well as a functional approach to the needs of family workers.[218] Nondiscrimination and equal opportunity take on a systemic form due to a paradigm shift in the worker's access to fundamental rights, considered to be a human right, without attention to the status of the worker. The focus here is no longer on the application of an economic law simply based on the traditional vision of the risk of discrimination inherent in the employee's role as a subordinate.

In the European framework, legal norms are still being used to expand the reach of discrimination law, rather than nonlegal, behavioral norms as Sturm recommends. The EU's flexicurity strategy, rarely mentioned recently,[219] aiming to improve employment security while providing employers with workforce flexibility, seems to be the only structural mechanism addressing gaps in the social and legal protection of workers. Regrettably, it maintains the normative, binary distinction between salaried employees and self-employed workers, adopting a somewhat neoliberal vision of the labor market.[220] The Working Time Directive defines the worker more broadly, indirectly offering a more functional interpretation of workplace issues and work-family balance. The directive on parental leave and the proposed revision of the directive pertaining to pregnant workers, which has been stalled, appear to more closely follow the reasoning of labor unions, providing for a suspension of the employment contract and maternity protection for salaried employees.[221]

Sturm's analysis of the architecture of inclusion and the preceding commentaries on indirect or systemic discrimination consistently look at norms or practices from a group perspective. The concept of diversity encompasses both an individual and a collective approach to difference. This bifurcation is a recurring issue in an international comparison, as seen in the following conversations. The way that groups are perceived seems to be a key element in a comparison of antidiscrimination law.

*Diversity Policies, the Individual, and the Group:
Finding Common Ground?*

Chai Feldblum considers whether discrimination is an individual or a group issue, and how the needs of people with intersectional identities, such as LGBT people, can be reconciled.

MARIE MERCAT-BRUNS: *Is the conflict between the needs of intersectional groups even perceived? If so, how is it resolved? When I tried to flesh out this conflict of interests, I was accused of violating religious freedom.*

CHAI FELDBLUM: A common theme throughout my scholarship has been the notion that the classical liberal notion of equality is not sufficiently robust to allow us to achieve complete equality for marginalized groups, such as LGBT people. That is because the basis for denying equality to such groups is a very sincerely held and deeply experienced feeling and belief that such individuals are not morally equivalent to those who are not LGBT.

Because of that simple fact, I believe we need to address head-on the public's moral assessment of LGBT people—and indeed, to change the majority's moral view of such individuals. From 1996 to 2004, I argued that we should start this conversation solely within scholarly and internal advocacy circles. After the American elections in 2004, however, when "moral values" was used quite destructively in the public rhetoric, I argued that that we should move this conversation into the public domain.

I created a website called The Moral Values Project (MVP)[222] and wrote a chapter explaining the goals and premises of that project.[223] An important outcome of the MVP analysis is that it helps us understand why people who feel homosexuality is immoral may feel attacked when legislatures enact pro-gay-rights legislation. As I wrote recently in an unpublished piece, "Conversations about substantive moral values along these lines could also help raise the consciousness of LGBT people themselves. I believe many people who believe homosexuality is immoral (either because of their religious or secular beliefs) experience themselves as 'under siege' today as society begins to extend equal protection to its LGBT citizens.[224] Perhaps if LGBT people understood the reasons why such individuals felt besieged in today's environment, they might do better in responding to such fears."

This approach of trying to put oneself in the shoes of others who are experiencing themselves "on a tilt" from society is something that I began in my "Rectifying the Tilt" work.[225] Given the complexity and richness of our modern society, and the good that I believe exists in supporting pluralism in our society, it seems essential to me to keep pushing ourselves to understand how both the absence of civil rights for some groups and the acquisition of civil rights for previously marginalized groups will affect different people in society differently.

Susan Sturm contrasts the individual or the group approach.

MARIE MERCAT-BRUNS: *In your work, you refer to different actors and different institutions as part of a more global approach to diversity.*

SUSAN STURM: I may add, there must be explicit attention to the theory of action, to the relationship among the different actors. There is a complicated idea, which is part of the problem, that whatever your location, you think in relation to a much larger picture, and you act differently when you are thinking about what you are doing in relation to a bigger picture. There are things you don't do, because there are other actors that are better located to do those things. Also, there may be people you bring to the table because they do something different, even though they are not the primary participant in what you are doing.

MM-B: *Where does the individual stand in all this? It seems to me that the individual is excluded from this analysis.*

SS: The individual is positioned in part through the ways in which institutions structure the possibility of individuals to express and participate and have their issues addressed. That is one way. Then, individuals experiencing a problem are able to access the legal system to obtain remedies for conduct that is sufficiently problematic that it violates the legal norms.

I haven't exactly decided what I think about trying to expand the antidiscrimination norm to include individualized sanctions for behaviors that are systemically rigged, unless individuals are part of a class.

Comparative Perspectives

From these various comments about the group, a common idea emerges of the group as subjected to, and a beneficiary of, antidiscrimination law and reflected in the diversity initiatives taken in the United States. They also convey a different idea of the role of group identification in U.S. antidiscrimination law. These observations must be weighed against European law and French law in particular, which also classify workers, but the nature and origin of the classifications are different.

In France, a consensus exists to reject the idea of groups as categories of the population whose members are identified based on their origin or defined by racial characteristics they are assumed to have in common,[226] even if this definition does not apply to women,[227] older workers,[228] or workers with disabilities[229] whose numbers are recorded. The broader base on which this negation of groups rests is France's republican tenet by which all citizens regardless of origin[230] enjoy equal rights. French republicanism posits that citizens enter into a contract under which they delegate their political power directly to the government, whose role is to define and promote the common good.[231] This situation is to be contrasted with the European employment context. Inspired by Durkheim's ideas on the division of labor in society and Weber's theory of status groups, the social sciences in continental Europe have built on classifications based on recognized occupational categories formally defined by national institutions and not on racial or religious categories.[232]

Some clarification must also be made regarding the treatment of personal characteristics. In France, legal rules in labor and employment law focus squarely on certain categories of people based on characteristics other than those related to origin. Status, profession, occupational classification, age, and sex are often used to place workers or job seekers into rigidly divided groups. Such groups are even used to determine nonemployability: for example, employment vulnerability and family situation are criteria used in the selection of employees for layoff.

These examples are provided to support the position that a comparative perspective of diversity must not be limited by the debate on groups based on ethnic or racial divisions. Identification with a group can be stigmatizing and corrosive. But if the role of group identification is to pull systemic levers to fight against discrimination, as Sturm describes, then recognizing the incomplete "participation of people" provides an immediate understanding of the institutional causes of this exclusion and precludes preoccupation solely with assessing the injury suffered and counting the number of victims. The division of employees into functional categories used in every source of labor law, especially the occupational classification system, enables access to keys to integration held only by the institution.[233]

In France, however, these same institutional mechanisms can more subtly perpetuate the exclusion of certain employees by placing them in occupational categories. Case law on the principle of equality demonstrates the importance of occupational categories in a varying light: judges follow a logic of deconstruction in their assessment of equal treatment when they consider whether the categories used to divide employees and to determine access to certain rights are justified. There are two paths by which judges can take this approach: the review of equality through the lens of the facially neutral, functional principle of "equal pay for equal work" and the assessment of equal treatment in the grant of benefits to different categories of employees in collective bargaining agreements.[234] The sole risk is an excessive deference shown by judges to established occupational categories defined by the French social partners (labor unions and employers' organizations), but case law reveals that judges often assess a category's relevance case by case. It seems, for example, that the Cour de Cassation requires lower court judges to subject differences in treatment to strict scrutiny with respect to the objective or purpose of the categorization, which must reflect specific aspects of the situation of employees in a given category, in particular aspects related to working conditions, career advancement, compensation, and even social benefits.[235]

So the key question is, what are the objective, relevant[236] justifications for historical occupational categories, given that the legal classification itself engenders differences in treatment that can be more or less favorable? These differences can indirectly reveal occupational segregation or a glass ceiling effect hindering the promotion of certain categories and preventing diversity within employee groups inside the organization. This approach has already been taken with respect to discrimination based on union membership, as the case law shows, because union activity is often closely tied to occupation, making it easier to compare and to detect situations involving stalled careers or wages.[237] Equal treatment litigation seeking to compare "equal value" situations may have temporarily neglected to look at analogous situations between men and women, as illustrated by equal pay claims.[238] However, some cases target specifically work of comparable worth.[239]

In equality case law, once the barrier of comparability of situations has been removed, a more thorough examination of the proportionality of the differential treatment yields a deeper understanding of the systemic coherence of organizational rules or practices. As Sturm pointed out, it is important to know what the goal is: is it possible to judge the extent to which the purpose of the differential treatment based on occupational category acts against the interest of the group, while at the same time validating the existence of the category and therefore its value for all of its members?[240] Whether the category is relevant depends on the specifics of the employees' situation, but these particularities must be objectively assessed. Following such an assessment, the act of eliminating categories that are no longer relevant can indirectly help to integrate people with protected traits. This is illustrated in another approach taken by judges in assessing the inequality of differential treatment based on an occupational category: judicial scrutiny of professional assessment systems, which can reveal quotas that an analysis of the employees' skills and performance fail to justify[241] and the presumption of discrimination in the absence of any professional assessment.[242]

Workplace Flexibility for Diverse Groups

Outside of the debate on the relevance of a group rationale, scholars consider the opportunity for lawmakers and employee and employer organizations to promote diversity in a more systemic manner.

Chai Feldblum is a commissioner of the EEOC, nominated by President Barack Obama. She helped to implement two of the Obama administration's priorities in fighting systemic discrimination. The first is to directly monitor and enforce antidiscrimination norms, which she contributes to through her role on the EEOC. The other is to engage in a more general reflection on the production of norms to promote workplace flexibility. In this context, flexibility should not be construed as it is commonly used, as a certain elasticity introduced into norms to theoretically increase the economic efficiency of businesses. Feldblum has thought about how to shift the frame of reference showing the differences among people targeted by diversity programs. What measures could be taken to better integrate LGBT people, religious people, parents, and people with disabilities, among others? In the following conversation, Feldblum considers diversity and the "flexibility" of the employment market.

MARIE MERCAT-BRUNS: *You mentioned the need for new types of norms applying to companies in the United States. (In France, companies have moved toward the adoption of collective agreements on diversity.)*

CHAI FELDBLUM: The concept that we need a new normal is key to my theory of change and to my theory of equality, "disrupting the normal." The new normal would address disability, religion, sexual orientation, gender, parenting, gender orientation, and gender roles. I didn't have race in my original model, but I will add that: the issue of affirmative action versus color blindness.

We must, as a society, value the caregiving that is given to kids and to aging parents more than we do right now. We need a new cultural norm so that people who are doing caregiving—not to biological kids or parents, but to society overall—are respected as well. It should be understood that people like that have had full lives.

We need both men and women to recognize what kid caregiving requires. We need society overall to be more engaged. I'm referring to Kathleen Gerson's new book, *The Unfinished Revolution*.[243] Her previous book was *The Time Divide,* with Jerry Jacobs (Harvard University Press, 2004). Her new book covers the younger generation's views of caregiving equality. Her theme is the tension between changing individuals and resistant institutions.

We need to change the frame—this is still an individual choice.

Women are in a bind, a catch-22: if you contest the norm, as long as the norm still reigns supreme, then you can be devalued. So we need to disrupt the normal. First we need to disrupt the norm with a wide range of stakeholders.

We have a cultural norm that tells us not be disconnected individuals, like George Clooney's isolated character in *Up in the Air.* But, as a society, we have no structures to help us out in being connected: it's all your problem; go deal with it.

About Workplace Flexibility 2010[244] and the six-circles theory of advocacy. This was Paula Rubin's proposal:[245] comp time instead of overtime pay. Assume you're covered under the FLSA [Fair Labor Standards Act]:[246] for any hours over forty hours a week worked, you get time-and-a-half pay. The Republican proposal was to amend the FLSA so it would be like it is in the government sector, where you work overtime and take it in compensatory time: work three hours overtime and get four and a half hours off.

There was a diet of ideas and it constipated; it was employer versus employee: nothing moved. There was no perceived alignment of interests. But there were common interests to be achieved for both employers and employees, so we expanded the table.

Our first Congressional briefing was on aging workers; we explained that they want to work differently. We want to ride the wave. Workplace flexibility is key for aging baby boomers—that's the wave. We had to move the conversation away from just women! It requires a larger group saying we need to change. It can't just be women saying it.

Comparative Perspectives

Having participated in drafting the Americans with Disabilities Act,[247] Feldblum observes that as long as the implicit norm framing employment relationships does not include all individuals, then any effort to defend the rights of victims of discrimination will be considered as a deviation from the norm that requires compensation or an alignment with standards.

In France, with the current debate on taking work hardship—difficult working conditions—into account, reflection on how norms can translate the adaptation of work to people is an increasingly urgent matter.[248] Feldblum suggests that work needs to be thought out to include vulnerable and marginalized people from the start. What's new about the idea is how it builds around the needs of workers who are not the traditionally imagined mid-career white men. Instead, she suggests organizing work to accommodate workers with specific issues to be resolved to allow them to perform their work. As a result, everyone's work would be transformed, improving general well-being at work, the recognition of work hardship, work-life balance, ergonomic work conditions, and psychosocial risk management and prevention. Some conflicts of interest may arise, as Feldblum mentions, between accommodating religious beliefs and the protecting the rights of gay employees, for example, but in her opinion these issues are not insurmountable when the initial premise in producing these norms is to defend certain values, such as caregiving. All employees ultimately benefit from an employer's efforts to offer them work-life balance and take their nonwork concerns into account. The workplace flexibility[249] campaign supported the development of tools to achieve this ambition through national debate, dialogue about workplace flexibility policies, and proposals for legal mechanisms involving leave entitlements, workplace accommodation, and flexible working hours.

III. SYSTEMIC DISCRIMINATION, REASONABLE ACCOMMODATION, AND HARASSMENT

This discussion on systemic discrimination would not be complete without examining two concrete mechanisms enabling a more structural approach to the causes and manifestations of unequal treatment. One is reasonable accommodation, emerging from the Americans with Disabilities Act prohibiting discrimination based on disability, and the other is harassment. How are these two mechanisms encompassed by or separate from positive action? Outside of their vital role in fighting discrimination based on disability and sex, how does the individual or group view promoted by these mechanisms provide an alternative way to perceive differences?

Reasonable accommodation and harassment do not typically occupy the foreground in discussions of systemic discrimination. The following interviews will show why they should: these legal concepts emerge when a discriminatory difference in treatment is identified, but they often evoke a need to investigate flaws in the organization of employment relationships within the company at a more structural level than the individual work situation.

Discrimination and Reasonable Accommodation

Robert Post discusses antidiscrimination law and reasonable accommodation,[250] a term drawn from the Americans with Disabilities Act, which requires employers to take appropriate measures[251] to fight discrimination based on disability.

ROBERT POST: Accommodation, to my mind, is the same structure as disparate impact. Only now we are applying it to what are considered normal working conditions. Just like antidiscrimination law presupposes a certain concept of what a person is—a male, a single person—the workplace is designed around the needs of what is imagined to be the typical, normal person. What accommodation does is to say, "No, maybe you shouldn't design it around this image; the person can also be a woman who has children." What counts as the normal person, around which the workplace is designed, is up for grabs under accommodation law.

Under accommodation law, you have to redesign the workplace to change the notion of what is normal, to accommodate this enlarged picture of what a person is. It has basically the same redistributive properties that disparate impact has.

MARIE MERCAT-BRUNS: *It actually takes a functional view of the person because it understands that the conflict arises from relationships and the context, not the disability. I have a hard time seeing where the liability falls. Are both the worker and the employer responsible for making the adjustments, or is it solely up to the employer to redesign the workplace to make it accessible?*

RP: It depends whether you are talking substantive law or normative law. For example, there are technical requirements to mediate on accommodations. But let me talk not of the technical requirements of ADA[252] and accommodation but how we want to think of the problem normatively. The problem is that the workplace is created and structured by management, and it is structured in order to attain the goals of the workplace. One of the responsibilities of management is to make employees work in ways that are suited to attain the goals of the workplace. So there isn't this opposition between workers and management; workers are, in the eyes of the law, the instrumentalities of management.

When you impose a duty of accommodation of the workplace, you are saying that people responsible for structuring the workplace are responsible for the accommodation. As a technical legal matter, that means it is the responsibility of the employer to affect the behavior of employees such that they make the accommodation effective. So I would reject that it is only the responsibility of employers.

MM-B: *So there is a kind of dialogue there.*

RP: There has to be. What is ultimately important is that the workplace be accommodated. The responsibility of accommodation applies to the workplace. The workplace is the product of the people; the workplace consists of what employees do, and what employees do is under the responsibility of employers.

Ruth Colker discusses the means available to enforce reasonable accommodation and affirmative action.

MARIE MERCAT-BRUNS: *What means are available to enforce the reasonable accommodation requirement?*

RUTH COLKER: In disability cases, rarely do you have compensatory or punitive damages. That is only if you can prove intentional discrimination. If you have a case about accommodation and you have an employer who acted in good faith and made a suggestion and the court agrees with the plaintiff, the employer will not pay compensatory damages. So very rarely do you get compensatory damages.

For people earning eight to ten dollars an hour, it is not worth it for lawyers to take their case on a contingency basis. It is true that a lawyer can get money as the "prevailing party," but that is only if the lawyer actually goes to trial and gets a judgment from the judge or jury. If a case settles, it is not possible to go to a judge and get money for representing the prevailing party. Most cases settle, and therefore the lawyer is stuck with a contingency award, which would usually be very low. Plaintiffs have a low chance of winning, and some lawyers can't afford to take these cases where the plaintiff is not going to pay the bill.

MM-B: *Just to go a little bit farther on that. So you are saying that this is not a group issue; the way it plays out in litigation is an individual issue. Wouldn't it be better to have proactive measures of diversity? For example, in France, there are more and more collective bargaining agreements on diversity issues, applying to people with disabilities and implementing voluntary compliance to do something different. This type of initiative would be less costly because the focus is on the group, the various forms of disabilities, and how the workplace can adjust to integrate several types of groups into the workforce—but this is a larger issue.*

You seem to be saying that the way the litigation plays out is not very effective, because no one wants to take the pay cases. In addition, these are individual cases, so the change they bring about in the workplace is slow.

RC: Your alternative would be what we call in the United States "affirmative action." Many people in the United States are not very fond of affirmative action (a four-letter word in the United States). Do you see the semantical difference? The United States favors reasonable accommodations but not affirmative action.

Diversity initiatives in France are not necessarily seen as measures of affirmative action, where you have two individuals with similar qualifications and you select the person who is a member of a protected group even if that person is less qualified. In France, diversity is really about preventing discrimination. The workplace is organized in a certain way so that, before employers make any selection decision, they are prepared to welcome people with disabilities. This is different from affirmative action in France, where it is associated with quotas. In fact, quotas exist for the hiring of people with disabilities.[253]

MM-B: *As you said, the underlying principle is different, but collective bargaining agreements on diversity, mainly to address the integration of workers with disabilities, cannot be called affirmative action. There may be a need for a certain financial investment to promote this diversity, but it is not an order, as in some litigation in the United States.*

RC: The analogy in the United States would be the Title III[254] approach, which is that buildings should be made accessible. Proactive approaches do make perfect sense. It is less expensive to make building accessible to begin with rather than retrofitting.

In the workplace, efforts have been made for physical accessibility, but that is not good enough. For people with a mobility impairment, the world has been transformed because they can get around better than they could twenty years ago. Young people with disabilities are getting in and out of buildings much better than when I was a young person. That helps the workplace because it allows some people to work, but that is just the tip of the iceberg. It does not deal with all the problems that people with disabilities face.

MM-B: *So you could say we have the European approach in Title III.*

Could you not anticipate problems and apply a similar logic to other workers, such as older workers, parents with strollers, workers needing more flexible work hours due to work hardship or caregiving duties, for example? This is one direction we're moving in in France: diversity initiatives that focus on shared needs of workers.[255] *Employers accommodating workers with disabilities could also analyze the jobs of other categories of workers requiring accommodation (workstation adaptations, flexible working hours and leave, greater access to training and career opportunities by improving the circulation of information in the company, etc.).*

RC: You couldn't have the logic in the United States: the idea that people could take leave and not have their employment terminated. The problem in the United States is you are not compensated for that medical leave. So, how many people can afford to take leave? Obviously not receiving a salary is very problematic in most people's lives. The very key is not losing your job for people who are in chemotherapy, for example, or recovering from giving birth. The FMLA [Family Medical Leave Act] was one of the first laws passed during the Clinton Administration.[256] That is more like the European approach to find the commonalities between parents, pregnant women, disabled workers, and older workers. (Interestingly, some parts of this law have been struck down as unconstitutional; it is hard to impose these kinds of rules on the public workplace in the United States.)

[Later in the interview, Colker comes back to the topic of reasonable accommodation.]

RC: I have not said much on voluntary compliance. There are many employers that go out of their way to hire people with disabilities and accommodate them. I have worked with a fabulous university coordinator on disability issues. I think my employer does fabulous things to accommodate people with disabilities. So I do not mean to say that all employers do not comply and discriminate. I think, in the end, the ADA amendments will be taken seriously and will cause them to take a stand on their willingness to accommodate people with disabilities.[257] So I do think the 2008 amendments have had a meaningful effect on people's lives.

The harder question is for those people who do not work in institutions like that and are subject to discrimination: do I think the amendments will have an effect on their lives? My answer is that I doubt it. They will face the same hurdles they always face—even worse in a recessionary economy—finding lawyers who can afford to take their cases and fight for them in a way that will let them prevail. With the recession, it will be harder to arrive at settlements.

MM-B: *Will employers use the undue burden defense, if accommodation creates this undue burden?*

RC: Employers have less money: their finances are tight, and they might choose not to spend money. You don't see this at the trial level in front of judges and juries. It is the argument the employer makes who then offers a settlement to plaintiff and the plaintiff agrees. So I am not optimistic for those plaintiffs who pursue litigation that the 2008 amendments will make a meaningful difference in their lives. But I do think that the amendments will give room for employers engaging in good faith to make a difference in their lives. So it is a mixed bag.

MM-B: *So has the ADA sometimes prevented employers from hiring workers with disabilities?*

RC: With the recession, it is hard for everyone right now and even more so for people with disabilities, even with the 2008 amendments. I don't think the ADA can do anything about that. I find it difficult to tackle an employment rate through an antidiscrimination law. You are going to need another model if you want to tackle a higher unemployment rate: an entitlement model or court-ordered model or civil action model. And that is not going to happen in the United States. It isn't going to happen anywhere.

Comparative Perspectives

Like disparate impact, the concept of reasonable accommodation created somewhat of a revolution in American antidiscrimination law:[258] it introduced an obligation for the employer to take action and accommodate qualified employees or applicants with disabilities who needed certain adjustments to perform the essential functions of a job.[259] A similar obligation to accommodate had already made its appearance in the United States in cases of religious discrimination, although it was not defined in Title VII of the CRA of 1964.[260]

The Americans with Disabilities Act (ADA) of 1990 not only bans discrimination against "a qualified individual, with or without a reasonable accommodation,"[261] it provides a nonexhaustive list of concrete examples of such accommodation, which include "making existing facilities used by employees readily accessible and usable by individuals with disabilities," "job restructuring, part-time or modified work schedules, reassignment to a vacant position, acquisition or modification of equipment or devices, appropriate adjustment or modifications of examinations, training materials or policies," and "the provision of qualified readers or interpreters." So the statute is pragmatic and precise in this respect.

The ADA was also ambitious in spirit.[262] The lawmaker's intention was, as Post mentioned, to define a framework integrating the differences arising from disabilities. Instead of attributing differences to individuals,[263] the law acknowledges that the work environment and working conditions are often designed around a certain perception of the standard, typical worker.[264] Once it has been established that an individual with a disability is qualified for a position, the employer and employee should agree on how to adapt the employment relationship to absorb differences impacting job performance, which the employer had failed to take into account. This is different from affirmative action, which as Colker explains is perceived in an increasingly negative light in the United States. The aim is not to benefit less-qualified candidates to promote equal opportunity.[265] Nor is the goal to compensate for an imagined inability for individuals with disabilities to perform to standards. The ambitious new vision of disabilities in the workplace proposed with the reasonable accommodation concept consists in assessing and remedying the shortcomings of the employment relationship. Although the mechanism tends to address individual situations, it undeniably has a systemic dimension as well.

Employers may balk at making an accommodation if the associated cost[266] is excessive.[267] As Colker explains, individuals with disabilities struggle to even reach the litigation stage, because the amount at stake is often too small to find lawyers who are prepared to take their case.[268] According to Colker, the ADA Amendments Act of 2008, which broadened the definition of *disability* after it was narrowly interpreted in a series of Supreme Court decisions, will not necessarily brighten the situation.[269] On the other hand, she says, for employers with a sincere desire to eliminate discrimination by accommodating individuals with disabilities, the amendments are helpful. Reasonable accommodation offers a functional view of disability discrimination, transforming a sanction into a mechanism urging employers to meet their employees' needs (and not those identified by the occupational physicians). The new approach can overcome the perception of individuals with disabilities as perpetual victims.

The challenge here is to compare the U.S. definition of *reasonable accommodation* with its European equivalent[270] and the "appropriate measures"[271] referred to in French labor law, usually in the context of a reassignment requirement.[272] In the private sector, case law rarely refers uniquely to the appropriate measures requirement or the nondiscrimination principle.[273] This is particularly true in hiring, as more clearly shown in the deliberations of the HALDE:[274] most often, litigation is based on the fact that employers violate their reassignment obligation, and the discrimination sanction is added. When employers do not accommodate, they pay a fine for not reaching the quota and having less than 6 percent of workers with disabilities among their employees.

In European law,[275] "instead of requiring people with disabilities to conform to existing norms," the aim of the appropriate measures requirement is "to develop a concept of equality which requires adaptation and change."[276] Eliminating the obstacles arising from the interaction between individuals with disabilities and their physical and social environments that prevent them from performing a specific task or job in a standardized manner[277] is an unfamiliar concept in many EU countries and is not explicitly stated in EU law.[278] The United Kingdom, Ireland, and Sweden are the only countries to have enacted law incorporating this idea prior to the passing of the Employment Equality Framework Directive 2000/78 and the development of case law on the subject.[279] Recent European case law, inspired by the UN Convention on the Rights of Persons with Disabilities, has been more vigilant concerning the scope of the European obligation to provide "appropriate measures"[280] and its implementation by Member States.[281]

The concept of appropriate measures, however, does not fully reflect the controversy over reasonable accommodation. The two main problems arising in enforcement involve the scope of the requirement and the meaning of the term *reasonable*, which is not necessarily synonymous with *appropriate*: what extent of accommodation is considered to place a "nonexcessive" burden on the employer, and what type of accommodation is necessary or effective? When considered under the lens of contract law, *appropriate* seems to carry a less precise meaning. In assessing the balance of contractual obligations, both the employer's commitment to adjust the job and the adaptation required by the employee with a disability must be executed in good faith. This evaluation could be based on the legal reference to the "reasonable" nature of the accommodation.

In addition to "appropriate measures," employers in France must comply with a requirement to reassign employees who are unable to perform their job due to an accident or illness, whether or not it was tied to their work. Is the legal basis the same for these two obligations, which both aim to protect employment?[282] Outside of those cases where a dismissal is found after the fact to be discriminatory and must be sanctioned by reinstatement,[283] appropriate measures such as the reassignment requirement primarily seek the continuity of the employment relationship.[284] However, unlike the failure to take appropriate measures, a failure to reassign employees who are unfit for their jobs[285] does not always produce the same consequences. Some courts classify this failure to reassign as a dismissal without genuine and serious cause,[286] while others pronounce the dismissal void.[287] Some terminations of employment are voided when employers have not followed the proper procedure in reassigning the employee, in particular regarding mandatory medical examinations,[288] or when employees have been subjected to harassment due to their incapacity for work[289] or have been pressured to resign due to this inability.[290]

The application of both norms (a discriminatory violation of the duty to reassign) would constitute the appeal of this sanction—voiding the dismissal—for failure to reassign a qualified employee with a temporary, partial, relative, or permanent disability. The two obligations—to reassign and to take appropriate measures[291]—could be combined and definitively abolish the idea that the inability to perform is a fault on the part of the challenged employee.[292] According to some scholars, the duty to reassign would amount to an obligation to combat discrimination.[293] Some courts are clearly progressing in this direction, even if other elements are often presented to reveal the discrimination, such as a disciplinary sanction.[294]

The difficulty posed by this combination of concepts is that assessing whether an employer has fulfilled the duty to reassign depends on the recommendations of the occupational physician and compliance with the proper procedure documenting the inability to work.[295] This medical view of the inability[296] as a deficiency with respect to employability[297] is the basis on which reassignments[298] are proposed. A preferable approach would be to examine how the work relationship is inadequately adapted to the qualified employee's needs.[299]

Is the difficulty caused by the fact that employability and, consequently, unemployability are not legally defined? An occupational physician determines whether an employee is fit for work by comparing the employee's ability with the position to be filled. There is no room here for a quantitative assessment of invalidity or reference to objective criteria. Full responsibility for the decision is borne by the physician, unless a labor inspector is called in. This is a performative procedure because there is no reference to a preexisting category.[300] Does this "flexibility" afforded by the law, in allowing for case-by-case assessments, also create a risk of discrimination in assessing what measures are appropriate?

It is only when the employment relationship has been terminated that antidiscrimination law comes back into play.[301] A judge will pronounce void a dismissal that does not specify the impossibility of reassigning the employee to another position,[302] if the employee's health is given as justification of the dismissal,[303] or a dismissal pronounced following an examination of the financial consequences of replacing the employee considered unfit for the job.[304] So rather than promoting work arrangements enabling the moderate presence of certain more vulnerable workers in the organization through remote work, antidiscrimination law tends to focus only on the absence of these workers from the workplace. Its vision of the unfit employee is implicitly negative, in comparison to conceiving work adjustments as part of the appropriate measures required by antidiscrimination law. The Cour de Cassation is patently aware of this difference, since the Court ruled for the first time, in a case where the employer calculated working time on a less favorable basis for the employee who was absent on sick leave, that indirect discrimination on the basis of sickness had occurred.[305]

Finally, a comparison of "appropriate measures" and "reasonable accommodation"[306] should not be confined to commonalities in the nature of the requirements they impose—an obligation to take action—while antidiscrimination law generally indicates a prohibition of action. Reasonable accommodation requires the employer, the judge, and the plaintiff alike to focus on an aspect that is increasingly discussed: the assessment of "capability"[307] as the potential[308] of a salaried employee with any form of disability or incapacity for work.[309] This approach assesses the employee's freedom to access rights rather than promoting equality. In other words, the focus is on the individual's capability or potential to choose to perform a job rather than an inability or lack of freedom to choose to perform the job as others do. The logic is that since the work environment has not been set up to capture the potential of qualified (and only qualified) workers who can perform the essential (and not the marginal, nonessential) functions of the job, employers then propose adaptations to the work or the work environment to benefit from the employee's potential, in accordance with the extent of the employee's needs and the company's resources. This balancing of interests does not stigmatize individuals by highlighting an inability to perform: from an antidiscrimination perspective, the duty to adapt should not fall solely on the employee's shoulders.

The French procedure for determining reassignment, based on a medical perspective of disability,[310] is inherently focused on these limitations of ability. A likely reason for this is an administrative desire to align this requirement with allowances and benefits provided for by employment, health care, and social security laws in France. A more explicit reference by judges to appropriate measures beyond the reassignment requirement would probably reinforce the legitimacy of the employee's expectations and rights. The motivation for taking these measures is not only the employee's health, protected by the social security regime, but the employee's inherent professional skills, which can be potentially enhanced by the "disability." However, recent French case law seems to maintain the focus on smoking out discrimination in collective bargaining agreements based on compensation for employees unfit to work.[311]

Discrimination and Harassment

Harassment can be a sign of individual and systemic discrimination,[312] so by detecting harassment, employers can prevent some forms of discrimination. In France, the concepts of moral harassment and sexual harassment first developed outside the realm of discrimination law.[313]

In the United States, harassment is inextricably tied to discrimination. As a judicial concept, it emerged in the context of racial discrimination[314] and was then expanded to include sexual harassment[315] and unwelcome conduct based on sex and other discriminatory grounds. The following conversations with scholars reveal the systemic nature of harassment, regardless of the ground of discrimination. Sexual harassment in the United States is not limited to quid pro quo harassment, in which a superior offers employment benefits in exchange for sexual favors, but also covers same-sex harassment.[316] Litigation also considers the later repercussions of harassment on employment,[317] whether or not the sexual relationship was consensual at a given time.

An evolution has been observed in French case law before the enactment of the new law of 2012,[318] which now addresses harassment incidents between colleagues occurring outside the workplace. France's definition of sexual harassment has been inspired by European law[319] and is also included in its criminal code.[320] Article 2 of Directive 2006/54/EC defines sexual harassment as "where any form of unwanted verbal,[321] non-verbal or physical conduct of a sexual nature occurs, with the purpose or effect of violating the dignity of a person, in particular when creating an intimidating, hostile, degrading, humiliating or offensive environment." No repeat conduct is required. Since France adopted Law No. 2012-954 of August 6, 2012, Article L.1153-1 of the French Labor Code addresses two scenarios: (1) sexual harassment consisting of repeated words or behavior with sexual connotations that violate the dignity of a person due to their degrading or humiliating nature or create an intimidating, hostile or offensive situation for the person, or (2) conduct assimilated to sexual harassment, consisting of any serious form of pressure, even where there is no repetition, used with the real or apparent aim of obtaining an act of a sexual nature, whether for the benefit of the person engaging in the conduct or a third party.[322] It is noted that the first prong of the new definition refers deliberately to a "hostile situation" instead of a "hostile environment," explicit in EU law, as if the word *environment* is too vague and reflects resistance on the part of the French legislature regarding the possible systemic nature of sexual harassment.

In French law, it was probably necessary to first take the route of discriminatory harassment based on sex in order to introduce the notion of sexual harassment focusing on the consequences of that harassment: namely, the creation of a hostile environment linked to a particular ground. The law of May 27, 2008, adapting antidiscrimination provisions in the French Labor Code, eliminated the need for harassment to be a repetitive act and included as prohibited discrimination any act based on a protected ground and any act with a sexual connotation suffered by a person with the aim or effect of violating his or her dignity or creating a hostile, degrading, humiliating, or offensive environment. Recent case law distinguishes separate and cumulative remedies for harassment and discrimination.[323]

Despite this cacophony of definitions, French courts have begun to address cases of sexual harassment having the same consequences as psychological harassment.[324] But even at the European level, some commentators question the relevance of Europe's definition of sexual harassment as only a form of sex discrimination.[325] American scholars shine the light on issues such as abuse of authority, individual and institutional causes, and impact on employment relationships for the different forms of sexual harassment.

> Vicki Schultz talks about sex segregation, stereotyping, and sexual harassment.

MARIE MERCAT-BRUNS: *Am I simplifying if I say that you have a structural view of the workplace and how it can exclude women or make it difficult for them to have significant careers, and you contrast that with a very strong focus in the United States on stereotypes? In France, there is less reflection on the impact of stereotypes. There is a criminal sanction for racist insults, but before passing the law, the prohibition of sexist comments was taken out.*

VICKI SCHULTZ: I think there are different ways of understanding stereotyping. I am less interested in things like the IAT Implicit Association test (Harvard) and the sort of cognitive approach to stereotypes, but I am terribly interested in stereotyping as a basic social psychological phenomenon. The way I view it, a focus on the harm of stereotyping is not at all at odds with the focus on the structural forms of discrimination I have mentioned. In fact, the two support each other.

There is a large body of research by both sociologists and psychosociologists that I have drawn on fairly strongly in my own work, which shows the dynamic interaction between these two phenomenons. For example, it's pretty widely understood where women, or any group, are part of numerically rare group; for example, there are very few women among the skilled trades. A handful of women and a zillion men are carpenters. You can expect those women to be stereotyped: stereotyping arises, is more prevalent, in contexts of segregation where a new group is numerically scarce. We don't really understand why this is the case; there are different theories why this would be the case. That is the bad news.

The good news is, in contexts where integration is achieved and there is a fifty-fifty representation of those two groups, the problems that are associated with stereotypes tend to decline. For example, there is research showing that when it comes to sexual harassment and sexual comments, which can be perceived as very threatening by women where they are numerically rare, [in environments] where women are well represented and well integrated, sexualized comments are not even perceived to be harassment. This suggests that segregation creates a background context in which the same behavior can be understood as threatening or sexist in the highly segregated environment or as nonsexist or nonthreatening in the context where women have greater numbers and perhaps more power. So I think it is very important to understand stereotyping both from the perspective of those who do the stereotyping and from the perspective, as social psychology is pursuing, of those who are subjected to stereotypes as well, and to understand the linkage between the cognitive and social phenomena of stereotyping and the larger structural context of segregation in which that conduct appears.

Comparative Perspectives

A comparative analysis of the concept of sexual harassment should begin with a brief look at how American legal scholarship and judicial decisions shaped harassment as a form of sex discrimination.[326] This legal approach has sparked criticism from scholars for its role in crystallizing a certain perception of gendered identities and of sexuality between men and women.[327] United States case law has enshrined two forms of sexual harassment: quid pro quo harassment, involving the solicitation of sexual favors,[328] and harassment creating hostile environment.[329]

Vicki Schultz's ideas on how anti-harassment norms can form the core of a wider reflection on systemic discrimination are echoed in the following comments by employment discrimination expert Susan Sturm:

SUSAN STURM: Think about sexual harassment: sexual harassment is a problem that requires a systemic look—not only looking at the problem, but looking at the workplace you would like to create. There is a need for women of color to be full participants in a workplace: they cannot fully participate if they are located in only one portion of the organization that is stereotyped in a certain way, which makes it more likely they will harassed. You have to be able to ask those types of questions. The question of how to address this requires engaging on what it means to have a workplace environment that is responsive to the needs and interests of women, and employees more generally, even though that is not the employment discrimination question.

In her commentary and in-depth research on sexual harassment, Schultz explains that a correlation can be drawn between sex segregation in an occupation and the likelihood that women performing occupations in which they are a minority will be harassed. She also argues that too much emphasis on sexual conduct in harassment can be harmful to all employees.[330] Her observations, which also draw on other sociological studies, have been used in litigation and challenge the sources and systemic effects of sexual harassment. According to Schultz, sex discrimination in employment tends to condition workplace behavior and is responsible for an occupational segregation by gender in which secretarial tasks are predominantly performed by women and construction site supervision is mainly reserved for men.[331] American scholars have exposed the dissuasive effect of harassment, which can discourage qualified candidates from claiming their rights to training or promotion in certain professional sectors, without any specific discriminatory act committed by the employer against women or minorities.[332]

What is interesting about this American approach, with respect to French and European law, is that it directs the analysis toward the nature of the work relationship and work organization causing the harassment rather than toward the individual injury suffered by the victim of the harassment. This is where the U.S. perspective intersects with new orientations in the French treatment of sexual harassment and psychological harassment,[333] with the latter form involving a difference in treatment that is not necessarily tied to a prohibited ground.

As in the United States, legal definitions of sexual harassment in France and Europe have evolved and are no longer focused on the power imbalance between the harasser and the victim or the sexual nature of the harassing conduct but increasingly on the nature of the work relationship between the two parties.[334] The new law also sanctioning the crime of sexual harassment[335] provides a more explicit vision of the dynamic of sexual harassment. The new provisions filled the gap left when the Constitutional Council ruled on May 4, 2012, that the provisions on sexual harassment (Article 222–33) in the French Criminal Code were insufficiently precise and therefore unconstitutional.[336]

Regarding civil lawsuits, France has taken an important stride forward by moving past the traditional distinction between harassment occurring inside and outside the workplace. In the past, this distinction has allowed certain employers and offenders to go unpunished,[337] even though today the difference in age can contribute to the presumption of sexual harassment.[338] Judicial decisions have enabled certain conduct to be defined as sexual harassment based not on the time or place it occurred but on the work relationship between the people involved.[339]

The fact that the roots of sexual harassment are embedded in the work relationship supports the need for workplace prevention initiatives.[340] These initiatives can include an obligation to act: if both horizontal and vertical gendered segregation in the labor market is a factor of sexual harassment, then individual sexual practices are not being blamed. Instead, one should seek out the structural causes of sexual harassment, such as neglecting the interests of women in male-dominated work environments or favoring the interests of men in a female-dominated work environments. Without venturing into an analysis of occupations by gender, it can be observed that certain work environments are more hostile to women, in terms of meeting organization, working hours, access to training, and promotion, for example.

Psychological harassment, or "moral" harassment as it is known in France, has no legal counterpart in the United States, where harassment must be of a discriminatory nature to be actionable. However, an analysis of the consequences of harassment—harm to the employee's dignity, physical and mental state, and future career—can be a part of a more general search for the causes of differences of treatment of employees.[341] Unlike an isolated act of discrimination, harassment pollutes and contaminates the work environment (the metaphor is important).[342] The development of sexual harassment laws in the United States and Europe crossed paths at this juncture. Laws prohibiting harassment based on race in the United States led to the recognition of sexual harassment as a difference in treatment affecting the work environment. Meanwhile, in France, moral harassment was first used as a framework to appraise the arbitrary deterioration of workplace relationships, before the European lead was followed and harassment was declared to be a form of discrimination.[343]

Where the French have innovated is in incorporating sexual harassment issues into the employer's obligation to provide a safe and healthy workplace:[344] this removes the need to prove the intent to harass and helps to destigmatize employees. There is no need to communicate complaints to the sexual harasser, as the Cour de Cassation has more recently specified.[345] By requiring employees to take preventive action against harassment in the workplace and sanctioning management practices that harass employees, this approach adds a robust structural dimension to the French definition of harassment that seems stronger than its U.S. equivalent. To establish that harassment has occurred, instead of proving that the harasser is at fault, victims can provide more specific evidence of the existence of repeated acts of harassment[346] and their repercussions and more easily obtain compensation. This sends a systemic message to employees: "If you produce this behavior, it is already too late; you have failed to identify working conditions leading to excessive harm to workers, regardless of the specific profile of the harasser." A work environment that is not designed to prevent such arbitrary acts is a hostile environment.[347]

Judges in the United States have invited employers involved in sexual harassment cases to implement measures to prevent such behavior. In instances of both hostile environment harassment and quid pro quo sexual harassment, employers were found guilty if there were no adequate grievance procedure accessible to the victim or to other people having witnessed the harassment. As a result, as the sociologist Frank Dobbin commented, most companies set up procedures to facilitate the in-house complaints process. These procedures were then used as a defense against individual claims of harassment.

As Lauren Edelman[348] comments in her co-authored work and as Dobbin explains in his book on equal opportunity,[349] while this type of bureaucratization of sex harassment claims does not necessarily prevent harassment from happening, it provides a potential defense for employers. The U.S. Supreme Court clearly supports this view: in a case of hostile environment harassment, it asked the lower courts to determine whether the employer had made efforts to prevent harassment by creating an effective grievance procedure for victims.[350] The implication is that, in the United States, employers have an obligation of means, represented by grievance procedures, for example, and not an obligation of results, as is the case in France, in fighting workplace harassment. More generally, this comparison points to a need for caution with respect to company norms or procedures: they propose apparently systemic solutions to individual behaviors that probably have systemic roots. The apparent neutrality of an internal policy such as whistle-blowing procedures do not in themselves guarantee a workplace free of discrimination or harassment. Investigations can lead to intrusive questioning of workers without anticipating some of the consequences of these investigations, as the recent French case law has shown.[351] They serve as evidence of the "good faith" of the employer, seen to have limited power to prevent the risk of occasional deviant acts committed by individuals in the company.

The obligation in France to provide a certain result—a safe, healthy workplace—ensures that the mere existence of possibly superficial initiatives, to prevent psychosocial risks in the case of moral harassment, for example, is insufficient. Because employers have an obligation of result, if harassment is proven, judges can immediately conclude that the initiatives are insufficient. However, in recent cases of moral harassment, judges have considered that remedies can be evaluated separately: those based on a lack of prevention of the employer, on the one hand, and those compensating a personal harm to the worker, on the other.[352]

As a final observation, in Europe, workplace harassment is mainly interpreted as an attack on an employee's dignity, which can also be disempowering.[353] A dignity-oriented strategy might just be less stigmatizing in terms of gender: it emphasizes that the harm can be suffered by individuals regardless of sex. The incorporation of dignity into the definition of harassment was inspired by the

German constitutional tradition and its fundamental rights, although equality strategies were very effective in fighting harassment in the United States. Susanne Baer suggests combining these two concepts, equality and dignity, and promoting "a call for equal respect, for dignified equality.... Sexual harassment law,... from a comparative perspective, seems to be best grounded in this interrelated approach. The question is not 'dignity or equality?' but what features the law has to offer to guarantee individual dignity on an equal basis for all."[354]

The following chapter will look at how these aspects of direct and indirect discrimination can be applied to various grounds of discrimination.

5

The Multiple Grounds of Discrimination

Antidiscrimination legislation in every country contains an enumeration of protected grounds for discrimination, with the list often growing longer with each passing year. This corresponds to the logic of the law, which is rooted in the prohibition of differences in treatment based on specified categories, unlike norms that are derived from the principle of equality. These inventories like the list established by the European Convention for the Protection of Human Rights, are not necessarily exhaustive.[1] And, despite the many grounds listed—more in France than in other countries,[2] such as the United States[3]—rarely do they come accompanied with precise definitions. For example, age and sex. Once considered, perhaps, to be straightforward, objective traits, debate has now arisen about what exactly is meant by these terms. Sex, or gender? Youth, as well as old age? By examining how courts have applied the notions of direct and indirect discrimination, it is possible to obtain some indication of the contours of these grounds. The courts' decisions have expanded the application of these notions, changing the context in which the grounds are invoked in the different countries.[4] But might not the most cogent question be, What person are these prohibited grounds trying to protect and liberate from all forms of workplace discrimination? Is it possible to fight discrimination in this way without inevitably revealing tensions surrounding the identity of the legal subject—the person[5] whose individual characteristics are being eradicated? Doesn't the search for discriminatory impacts, which is the substance of establishing indirect discrimination, necessarily affect individuals? What is this impact? From a different angle, let's imagine how multiple categories of discrimination might apply to the same person.[6] What does this combination of categories say about the very nature of the discrimination and the effectiveness of antidiscrimination norms?

I. WORKPLACE DISCRIMINATION AND THE PERSON

In this conversation, Robert Post illustrates the implicit questions about the definition of a person that are raised by antidiscrimination law.

MARIE MERCAT-BRUNS: *Continuing with other questions outside of collective bargaining, what conceptions of the person does antidiscrimination law presuppose?*

ROBERT POST: Antidiscrimination law presupposes different concepts of law and, as it enforces antidiscrimination rules, it sets forth the notion of what people are and aren't. In some parts of antidiscrimination law, the person has no sex. In some parts of antidiscrimination law, the person has no color. But in other forms of antidiscrimination law, the issue is more complex. This is an example: a bank has men tellers, and the rule says men can't wear dresses. Antidiscrimination law in the United States says that that is not based upon sex. What does it mean logically?

What it means is not a logical point, because antidiscrimination law is not about logic: it is about what sort of persons we want the law to recognize. We want persons who essentially abide by certain dress codes—but not essentially in the sense that the work is given out according to a sex line base, or whatever.

So, as you follow through the various laws, you can reverse engineer the fact that these come from certain conceptions of the person, and these conceptions are what is most often in conflict in debates on antidiscrimination law.

MM-B: *What do you think about dress codes personally?*

RP: I think that you can follow this as a matter of action and not abstract principle: antidiscrimination law is not about abstract principle, so to imagine a form of law that is so disruptive of ordinary social conventions and social norms is utopian and would not be publicly accepted. I myself as a lawyer wouldn't want to go there, although I can see a role for people who are pushing toward a gender-neutral concept of antidiscrimination law, that is, a queer theory of the person.

Comparative Perspectives

The question of the person protected by antidiscrimination law will be reexamined in later discussions of discrimination on the basis of sexual orientation, of queer theory, and of discrimination on the basis of religion. Another crucial question is whether, depending on the ground of discrimination, the antidiscrimination law seeks to promote equality or promote freedom.

II. RACIAL DISCRIMINATION

I will begin by looking at racial discrimination because it largely served as an antidiscrimination model in the United States for all antidiscrimination norms.[7] Since race was quickly understood to be a stigmatizing social construct with no biological or natural basis, evidence of racial discrimination did not involve a definition of this ground.[8] As of the postwar period, international treaties prohibited race discrimination, while sex discrimination served as the model for antidiscrimination in Europe via the Treaty-enshrined principle of equal pay for women and men.[9] Our scholars often highlight the distinctive character of the race ground by showing how analogies with other protected grounds can be problematic. David Oppenheimer has published extensively on antidiscrimination law in the United States and in Europe. In the interview excerpt that follows, he discusses the existence of race as a social construct.

MARIE MERCAT-BRUNS: *If I understand you correctly, in coining the term diversity, you raised the issue of identity, but certain critics say that there is no specific racial identity. What do you think about that?*

It is very hard to define racial identity. Is it diversity in the sense that each one of us is unique, or is there a specific racial cultural identity, or maybe a cultural identity linked to race? Or is the general principle the fact that we are not denying difference when we look at equality but instead promoting difference with specific identities?

DAVID OPPENHEIMER: Race is a social construct. So obviously race has no importance in biology aside from a few diseases that tend to be disproportionate in certain racial groups. Even the existence of a racial group is something we create socially.

But we do create them socially, and sometimes the majority creates minority identities in order to identify others as being "others"—as having another identity. It becomes a tool of discrimination and inequality.

But sometimes people looking for a sense of personal identity and community identify based on race and ethnicity, or religion, and though we deplore discrimination against people because of race, ethnicity, or religion, that does not mean it's illegitimate for people to feel a sense of identity based on those criteria. Sometimes that identity is the result of having a common experience of oppression.

White people are the majority in the U.S. both in terms of being the numerical majority and being the dominant group in terms of power, political influence, and culture. This is particularly true of white Christians. Americans who are members of minority groups often sense their experience—their *outsider* status—as providing them with a common identity based on that status.

It is not simply imposed on them by the majority. They experience it in a positive way. For example, consider the black empowerment movement throughout the 1960s and thereafter.

MM-B: *The Black Panthers?*

DO: Not necessarily. The Black Panthers were part of a much larger social movement for black people to be proud of their identity. "I'm black, I'm proud, I'm beautiful." It opened up recognition that there are cultures of blackness in America.

MM-B: *That's not a problem for you.*

DO: It is not a problem when we are talking about black people self-identifying, recognizing, and legitimizing their own identity.

MM-B: *Is it a question of being a part of?*

DO: Yes, it is a question of being a part of, a question of membership, a question of identity.

MM-B: *Doesn't being a part of also mean "I am part of because I am excluded from something else"?*

DO: I have a sense of identity as a law professor and it gives me a sense of affinity with other professors. Some would say this is a sort of negative identity. They dislike law professors. I would say I am happy to be part of a community of law professors. It is part of my sense of identity.

I also have a sense of identity as someone who loves to ride a bicycle, and that's part of my sense of identity too. I also have a sense of identity as someone who grew up in New York, and I feel a closeness with people who live in New York, who grew up in New York, and when I meet them, we find common ground through our common affection for New York. I am a Francophile. I love France. I feel entitled to be very critical of French racism because I love France, and that's part of my sense of identity.

I am also Jewish although not a religious person, so it is not so much a religious identity, but it is certainly part of my cultural identity. To some extent, that identity is an outsider identity. In France, the grandchildren and great grandchildren of Jews who were French citizens and who were themselves Christians, Catholics, who had been baptized and whose parents had been baptized, were nonetheless identified as Jews under the Vichy regime—as *outsiders* subject to exportation and extermination. That was an identity imposed from outside. But it does not make it illegitimate for Jews or descendants of Jews to have a sense of Jewish identity.

MM-B: *The possibility of a negative cause of exclusion doesn't make the category illegitimate? Is that it? I am more familiar with the idea stated in case law on equal protection of the laws (referred to in the Supreme Court decision of Carolene Prods.[10]) that racial minorities are historically isolated minorities ("discrete and insular minorities"). Is this also what you are talking about when you talk about identity? But your identity, defined by your affection for New York or France or as a faculty member, does not have this historical dimension, other than your Jewish identity, for example.*

DO: Consider the *Bakke*[11] decision, which says a university may use race as one of the diversity criteria in attempting to select a diverse class. Justice Powell says an affinity for music, coming from a small town, speaking multiple languages, or being African American are four examples of the kind of diversity that a university may legitimately consider in its admissions policies.

MM-B: *So there are different forms of diversity?*

DO: One of the tough questions is whether diversity is simply a code word for "racial minority" or a broader concept of wanting multiple points of view and multiple kinds of experience.

I had a conversation a few months ago with a student who signed up for my class, and she told me she was a little worried because she knew I was very liberal, and she was the leader of the Federalist Society.[12] I told her I had read she was active in the Federalist Society and I was thrilled, because it is great to have ideological diversity in the classroom; it means we will have much more interesting discussions because we will have a much wider range of points of view, and we all learn more under those circumstances.

Richard Ford, followed by Julie Suk, responds to the idea that there is a hierarchy of grounds of discrimination.

MARIE MERCAT-BRUNS: *When I listen to you, what seems to underlie your thoughts is the idea that there is a hierarchy among the different types of discrimination. If you can't go that far, it doesn't bother me. Some doctrinal work says there is absolute discrimination.*

For example, spurred by European law, France only recently introduced legal justification for differences in treatment based on any ground, including race, when it constitutes "a genuine and determining occupational requirement, provided that the objective is legitimate and the requirement is proportionate."[13] *Exemptions for other grounds, such as sex, pregnancy, and differences like disability or age, already existed, and it is presumed that in certain cases they can justify a difference in treatment in employment. There is a sort of implicit historical hierarchy.*

I will tell you why this is a big issue in France: our legislation does not differentiate as much as American law between prohibited grounds for discrimination. Even if there are possible differences in treatment in law based on age and disability, if they are legitimate and proportionate, then the concepts of direct and indirect discrimination and the system of proof of discrimination is the same regardless of the ground invoked. In the United States, however, there are different statutes for different criteria: Title VII of the Civil Rights Act of 1964, the Pregnancy Discrimination Act (PDA), the Age Discrimination in Employment Act (ADEA), and the Americans with Disabilities Act (ADA). For example, indirect discrimination based on age was recognized quite late, and the system of proof of discrimination based on age is not exactly the same: the requirements for proving discrimination based on age are higher. So do these legal differences reflect a hierarchy or ranking of cases of discrimination depending on the protected category?

RICHARD FORD: I wouldn't want to say it is more important to eliminate race discrimination than it is to eliminate sex discrimination. That would be wrong. But they are different. The types of social practices that the law is trying to counteract are different. There are different implications, and so there ought to be differences in the way we go about implementing those policies. Unfortunately, sometimes what happens is people draw the analogy too quickly without attending to the differences. You often hear: "Well, if this was race, no one would allow it; therefore you can't allow it here." So in that sense, you can understand why the United States Supreme Court said racial classifications receive strict scrutiny and sex discriminations receive what they used to call when I was in law school intermediate scrutiny.

MM-B: *It is not called that anymore?*

RF: There used to be an idea that there was this kind of three-part standard, but now rational basis standard[14] has kind of merged into intermediate scrutiny in an interesting way.

The idea is we should look to the purposes of the law: for instance, one of the unfortunate consequences of saying that racial classifications get strict scrutiny is that it has been more and more difficult to have things like affirmative action. In my view, that is a perverse result. In that sense, the hierarchy of concern, with race at the "top" has actually made it harder to remedy race discrimination than it is to remedy sex discrimination, for instance, which it is understood not to receive strict scrutiny.

But we can see the way a separate whites-only bathroom and a black bathroom is very different from a separate men's bathroom and women's bathroom. And it is silly to suggest if we would not allow racial segregation in the bathroom, therefore we cannot allow sex segregation in the bathroom. You can make an argument against sex segregation in bathrooms, but it is not the same thing. Yet some people make that argument because they are kind of enraptured with these conceptual approaches and they are not thinking of the practical implications on the ground.

MM-B: *What are the purposes of the law? How are they different?*

RF: In order to understand the law against race discrimination, you need to look at the practices of race in the United States. We are talking about this country and how it has evolved, and there are very specific practices. For instance, it is not an accident that the law tried to invalidate racially segregated bathrooms, because racially segregated bathrooms were one of the major symbols of Jim Crow segregation.[15] They were set up and designed and had the effect of sending a message of contempt for black people. If there had been a different history, maybe no one would care.

MM-B: *So history has a big influence.*

RF: Yes, it should.

MM-B: *So it is not something objective. You are not looking at the difference of treatment, outside of history, and saying there is something wrong about this.*

RF: I don't think you can do that in the abstract. It has got to be embedded in history and social context, and that's how we can understand why a practice is objectionable and deserves the extraordinary condemnation of the law.

Let's face it: for the most part, we let employers and proprietors make distinctions between people on all sorts of bases, and the law doesn't intervene, even when it is arbitrary, even when it is unfair.

There is a list of categories that we think are particularly problematic. There is a reason we picked those. That is because there is a history of discrimination, a history of irrational aversion, and there are social problems and dislocations that result from that.

Now, for sex, there is a different history; there is a different set of practices and a different set of problems—no less severe, but different. So it makes sense that you would have somewhat different interventions.

When you look at disability, when Congress passed the ADA, they had a sociological finding, which is in the Congressional Record, that disabled people were shut out of the labor market and were disproportionately poor, indigent, and unable to be integrated in any significant way in the mainstream economy or social life. That was the reason for the ADA.

Is that in a different place in the hierarchy? I don't know because in fact ADA, unlike Title VII as applied to race and sex, requires accommodations. Title VII requires accommodations in the religious context, too, but only when the cost to the employer is minimal—the ADA requires accommodations that can be quite costly.

So the ADA requires special treatment. Now, why? Not because discrimination against the disabled is more important, but because it is a different kind. In order to integrate disabled people in the workplace, they need accommodations. There are differences. If you are in a wheelchair, you need a ramp; if you are blind you need braille, and we could go on. Now the law is trying to balance the interest of integrating the disabled person with the cost to the business or the enterprise in question.

MM-B: *You seem often to come back to the idea of balancing of interests. To you, norms are often linked to that application.*

RF: As a practical matter, yes. Yes. When you really drill down, that is what we are doing. Lawyers don't like to talk about it in that way. So what we like to say is we are eliminating bias, we are eliminating bad motivations. We are trying to wipe that out. We are setting up an even playing field.

Even when you are dealing with a situation that requires costly accommodation, it is understood under the rubric of discrimination; if you don't reasonably accommodate, then that is discrimination. But the truth is that we are doing something different, something that cannot quite be understood in practice as just getting rid of bias.

What we are really doing, what the courts are doing, and what we want the courts to do ideally, is strike a balance between what the employers have done in the past, what is easy to do because it is familiar, and a social policy that an individual employer might not take up on his or her own but that is important for social harmony between various groups and to help subordinated groups throw off the burden of the past.

It is easy to see that in the disability context, when you are often talking about costly accommodations. There is no way of making the case to the employer that he or she is just as well off making the accommodations as not making the accommodations. The accommodations are expensive and it would often be better for the employer not to make them. But you can certainly make the case that society is better off for making the employer do it.

Julie Suk also considers the idea of a hierarchy of grounds of discrimination.

MARIE MERCAT-BRUNS: *I would like to come to another question and actually tie together two questions: I think a comparison between French and American law is also useful for understanding in what respect there might be a hierarchy between grounds of discrimination. Do you think France and the United States see discriminations based on race, gender, and age differently, in a hierarchy, somewhat like the different standards of scrutiny of the U.S. Supreme Court: suspect classifications, intermediate scrutiny, and rational basis?*

JULIE SUK: I think both legal systems view different grounds of discrimination differently, and how they do so differs. In the United States, equal protection analysis scrutinizes racial classifications more closely than sex classifications, for instance. In France, only racial distinctions are absolutely prohibited by the Constitution, and in fact you have a constitutional clause that permits the recognition of sex difference through that clause essentially allowing parity through language favoring equal access of men and women to political representation.[16] So in effect, the French Constitution is much stricter with regard to racial distinctions than with regard to sex distinctions.

In the employment context, I think U.S. law tends to analogize race and sex much more easily than the French law. For instance, we have a strong antistereotyping doctrine in both race and sex cases under Title VII. In France, by contrast, generalizations about race are highly problematic and illegal, whereas the generalizations about gender that underlie generous maternity protections and differential treatment of maternity and paternity are generally unproblematic. (Of course I recognize that there are debates about this, as well as some pressure from European courts to take a more gender-neutral approach, but by comparison to the United States, this is a significant difference worth noticing.)

And, as I mentioned in our last session, we also have antistereotyping doctrine to age, and we have extended similar (though not identical) protections to older workers as we do to racial minorities. In Europe, including France, there is much more ambivalence about extending antidiscrimination protections to older workers.

Robert Post considers racial discrimination in constitutional law.

MARIE MERCAT-BRUNS: *At what level (federal constitutional or state legislative) is the combat against discrimination being fought?*
ROBERT POST: There is an inherent tendency to make constitutional law general, and there is more of an opportunity to make statutory law impact-oriented. . . . But even in the interpretation of statutory law, there has been a retreat in the courts.
MM-B: *So what you are saying is that in context, you go farther with the statute, but that in symbolic terms, it is very important that you have a constitutional principle.*
RP: Exactly. The symbol is acutely powerful because it stands for the national values. And we argue about that symbol, which brings us together in a way the statute doesn't.
MM-B: *The symbol focuses more on racial questions than gender.*
RP: No. Our gender constitutional law is a little more complicated. We permit discrimination in the military and in marriage.

Ruth Colker examines the historical dimension of racial discrimination.

MARIE MERCAT-BRUNS: *How do you interpret the race criterion?*
RUTH COLKER: Race is odd. What is the anthropological meaning of race? It is also a socially constructed term. From a subordination perspective, we can see that these groups have faced historical discrimination.

Disability is different from the other categories. Mental health issues, cognitive impairment, and those who do not have a visible disability are each quite different and have little in common, and yet they are lumped together as disabled. I wish there were more understanding and historical analysis in the United States because the term *disability* there is very broad.

Reva Siegel explains how racial discrimination has served as a model.

MARIE MERCAT-BRUNS: *So even for race, you think that constitutional case law on equal protection can explain this need for order and social cohesion in the field of discrimination? Does the constitutional analysis justify this third way of looking at equal protection (in addition to anticlassification and antisubordination)? In the French judicial system, constitutional review through individual litigation is recent (in force since 2010), so for now our constitutional case law on equality is not that extensive, although this is not necessarily true of other courts' jurisprudence, such as that of the Council of State or the Cour de Cassation. Some is based on formal equality, but this is changing. Is it perhaps because of your constitutional case law on equal protection that you can have these three perspectives of diversity? Maybe I am going too far.*

REVA SIEGEL: Yes, this is very much judge-made law. We have large bodies of statutory civil rights law in the United States. In fact, most of our equality law is statutory. The Civil Rights Act of 1964 sets down nondiscrimination law in public accommodations, in employment, and in education. We have a Voting Rights Act, and we have a Fair Housing Act, and there are bodies of law on insurance with nondiscrimination with respect to sex. There is much legislation, some of which is near-constitutional in its character: a kind of legislative deliberation with creative judicial interpretation. By contrast, the constitutional jurisprudence is typically associated with the work of courts, although Robert Post and I have written on the role that legislation often plays in importing constitutional law into civil rights laws.[17]

So, yes, these antisubordination, anticlassification, and antibalkanization[18] concerns have emerged with the work of courts.

Later in the interview, Siegel speaks again about race discrimination and her classification of antidiscrimination models.

RS: First, I want to emphasize that if you asked others to describe the antidiscrimination tradition, they would probably talk about a dispute between two principles: anticlassification and antisubordination. These concerns about balkanization are only intermittent in the commentary. What I am doing is drawing together threads of comments and cases and drawing attention to something I have called antibalkanization. I have not published this piece yet,[19] so it would not be so squarely recognized as the American tradition. I have been writing to bring people to see that it is there. This is very new work.

Second, judges express these concerns about balkanization—about the value of social solidarity and the risks of social division—to guide how issues of race and equality are engaged in the political domain. They are advising administrators of affirmative action how to proceed so as to achieve a form of community in which there is less racial division and conflict. These observations are judicial, but they are judicial intuitions about cultivating understandings in the community at large. For example, the affirmative action cases teach educators how they ought to act if they want to be race-conscious without provoking racial conflict. Those who engage in race-conscious interventions have to proceed with extreme caution for a variety of reasons.

Comparative Perspectives

Racial discrimination is not only the most decried form of discrimination; it has served as the model in the United States for the construction of antidiscrimination rules. To this day, it is still a benchmark of society's efforts to integrate minority groups, and the fiftieth anniversary of the Civil Rights Act in 2014 is a useful reminder of what still needs to be done despite court resistance.[20] More recently, two Supreme Court cases, one concerning a doctor of Middle Eastern descent[21] and the other an African American catering assistant,[22] modify two important standards in the employment discrimination context and make it more difficult for a plaintiff to plead and prove racial harassment and retaliation claims.[23] As mentioned by Ford, Suk, Post, Colker, and Siegel, in addition to considerations about the contours of the ground itself, cases involving race have led to the emergence of the disparate treatment and disparate impact discrimination mechanisms, the categorization of antidiscrimination law as being rooted in anticlassification or antisubordination discourse,[24] and different levels of judicial scrutiny of equality. In the United States, racial discrimination has served as a point of reference from which a body of antidiscrimination law has been created, through analogy, although some mutual influence with case law on other grounds can be observed.[25] This does not signify that racial discrimination is more serious than other forms of discrimination, but it seems to be perceived as possessing the greatest ontological weight in the U.S. body of antidiscrimination law.

Because of the deeply personal and odious nature of racial discrimination, a paradox has been created, which exists in France as well. The fight against racial discrimination is highly visible in society and seen as unquestionably legitimate, but by the same token, it has undermined the expansion of norms established to support this fight, through various perverse effects.[26] With the harsh indictment of overtly racist statements[27] and acts of disparate treatment discrimination[28] since the 1960s or 1970s, depending on the country, subtler acts of conscious and unconscious racial discrimination have surfaced. These biased acts have been identified in the United States but are more difficult to prove in court. Meanwhile, fundamental initiatives such as affirmative action have been stifled.[29] In the United States, these measures have gradually come to be perceived as differences in treatment based on race and are subject to strict judicial scrutiny, as Ford and Siegel point out. The high profile of racial discrimination in the United States[30] has been a trap for those endeavoring to fight it, in the sense that other forms of discrimination with fewer political and social stakes have been successfully addressed through the intermediary of law, using more interdisciplinary and sometimes more subversive measures.[31]

Our American scholars' commentary is therefore doubly relevant, because through the examination of racial discrimination cases, it allows us to track the milestones reached in antidiscrimination law and also measure what remains to be achieved within the logic of this law. American scholars can identify and explain the limits of legal norms with respect to this seminal issue of racial discrimination.

The issue of race, when considered in a comparative perspective with regard to antidiscrimination law, is intertwined with three fundamental questions. The first

156   THE MULTIPLE GROUNDS OF DISCRIMINATION

concerns the blurry contours of the ground, noted in particular by Oppenheimer and Colker, which is more problematic in Europe than in the United States. The second question, closely related to the first, is about the effective enforcement of the law and proving racial discrimination in employment as opposed to in other areas of society. The third involves the different ways of maneuvering out of a relative impasse in the treatment of racial discrimination, by playing with the contours of the ground or the manner in which indirect discrimination is used.

What Is Race?

In the United States, we know that ethnoracial statistics can be collected and that people may volunteer self-stated data on their physical characteristics or race, described as white, black, and so on, or a combination of these.[32] However, one should not assume that there has never been any debate in the United States about collecting this data.[33] Controversy flared over the categories used by the U.S. Census Bureau for the 2000 census. In their commentary, Oppenheimer, Ford, and Colker remind us that the reference to race has a fundamentally historical origin in the Jim Crow laws enforcing racial segregation. This distinguishes race, a "suspect classification," from other grounds, as Ford shows with his compelling example of segregated bathrooms.[34] The scholars agree that race is perceived not as a biological reality but as a social construct. The race ground can therefore be interpreted as a subjective—not objective—ground. In fact, it is a ground with a subjective component, used to reveal not any genuine classification of human beings but the result of an odious social perception held by both those who are discriminated against and those who do the discriminating. Is this not the goal of antidiscrimination law?

The debate in the United States centers on how this social construct is used: either we simply develop the idea that the construct can be used to detect discrimination against people from visible minorities, or we take the idea further and consider the existence of a cultural identity that represents the positive aspects of belonging to a group, outside of racial exclusion. This is the choice that Oppenheimer seems to make when he talks about racial diversity, and his idea can be applied to other groups; it is interesting to see how race might be an important factor in fostering a sense of belonging, on the same level as many other descriptive characteristics cited by Oppenheimer, which are not protected grounds (the fact that he lives in New York, for example, and is a law professor). In his book *Racial Culture: A Critique*, Ford is much more reserved about the existence of a cultural dimension to the social construct of race, the emergence of multiculturalism, and the specificity of an "Afro-American culture," which could combine to create other racial stereotypes.[35] He gives cornrows as an example: can this hairstyle be said to partly represent the Afro-American "culture"? One can imagine the potential missteps leading to the identification of certain traits as specific to a "racial culture."[36] In light of the recent U.S. tension about police brutality with regard to the younger black population[37] and the issue of racial profiling, the question of identification of individuals or groups becomes paramount. In this type of criminal case, the debate revolves around other tools to prove the discrimination: video technology rather than statistics.

In European and international law, race is far from being precisely defined. International law[38] provides a very broad definition of racial discrimination, which tends to encompass every category closely or remotely related to race. In the UN Convention on the Elimination of All Forms of Racial Discrimination, "the term 'racial discrimination' shall mean any distinction, exclusion, restriction or preference based on race, color, descent, or national or ethnic origin which has the purpose or effect of nullifying or impairing the recognition, enjoyment or exercise, on an equal footing, of human rights and fundamental freedoms in the political, economic, social, cultural or any other field of public life."[39] The vagueness of this wording masks the multiple causes of racial discrimination, linked to physical traits in particular, and the differences among the protected grounds in various countries with respect to race.

In Europe, due to a lack of consensus in EU countries on the issue, no definition of race was included in Directive 2000/43[40] on racial equality.[41] EU case law is a little more articulate[42] and addresses each question separately, in particular, the question of differences in treatment based on origin and nationality, which has its own body of law.

The treatment of nationality is in fact complex. EU law contains extensive provisions prohibiting discrimination against citizens of an EU Member State on the basis of nationality.[43] Indirect discrimination was explicitly recognized by the European Court of Justice for the first time[44] in a case involving nationality,[45] with the Court holding that indirect discrimination against nationals of other EU countries was prohibited, as well as against EU nationals for whom free movement between countries is a part of their identity, namely, the Roma people.[46] The issue of discrimination against the Roma[47] reveals ambivalent attitudes in the European Union.[48] On the one hand, the European Union prohibits discrimination based on origin and promotes equal treatment of all EU citizens to ensure free movement[49] and has even condemned a Member State based on ethnic origin discrimination by association,[50] but on the other hand, national courts[51] do not consistently sanction differences in the treatment of the Roma.[52]

Under Article 14 of the European Convention on Human Rights,[53] the position of the European Court of Human Rights (ECtHR) is less ambiguous,[54] referring, in certain cases at least, to the UN international convention on the elimination of racial discrimination.[55] The court also addresses the question of the interaction between origin and ethnicity, whether real or perceived. Its approach to interpreting ethnicity[56] is important because of how it prohibits discrimination based on false perceptions that eventually lead to racial discrimination.[57] Is this not the aim of prohibiting discrimination: to fight against unfounded, arbitrary perceptions or perceptions founded on a false reality engendering unjustified differences in treatment? The court considers not only "dissimilar treatment in similar situations" but also "equal treatment of different situations, without objective and reasonable justification" as discrimination.[58]

ECtHR judges leave scant margin of appreciation to the States if a category leads to racial discrimination[59] and is considered to be "suspect" in the meaning of the Supreme Court, since even differential treatment based on a perceived ethnicity would constitute racial discrimination:

> Discrimination on account of one's actual or perceived ethnicity is a form of racial discrimination. . . . Racial discrimination is a particularly invidious kind of discrimination and, in view of its perilous consequences, requires from the authorities special vigilance and a vigorous reaction. It is for this reason that the authorities must use all available means to combat racism, thereby reinforcing democracy's vision of a society in which diversity is not perceived as a threat but as a source of enrichment.[60] . . . In any event, the Court considers that no difference in treatment which is based exclusively or to a significant extent on a person's ethnic origin is capable of being objectively justified in a contemporary democratic society built on the principles of pluralism and respect for different cultures.[61]

Thus the grounds of origin, nationality and race are considered to be implicitly "suspect" ("particularly invidious"), and this translates into a stricter scrutiny of the justification of differential treatment.[62] In some cases, the second prong of the judicial standard—a proportionality test to determine whether the differential treatment is proportional to the means employed and the intended purpose—is not even required; this approach echoes the position held by the U.S. Supreme Court and our scholars that race is a social construct. In 2008, the ECtHR reiterated its commitment to racial discrimination: "In view of the fundamental importance of the prohibition of racial discrimination, no waiver of the right not to be subjected to racial discrimination can be accepted, as it would be counter to an important public interest."[63]

The ECtHR has acknowledged in certain cases that States "enjoy a margin of appreciation in assessing whether and to what extent differences in otherwise similar situations justify a different treatment," but that very weighty reasons must be put forward in the case of a difference in treatment based exclusively on the ground of sex.[64] This varying intensity of scrutiny seems to reinforce the idea of a hierarchy of grounds, at least on a secondary level, depending of course on the context in which they are invoked.[65] Neither ethnicity nor origin define race, but both grounds produce racial discrimination, sometimes in similar situations, and this is the link between the three factors. Furthermore, the issue of perceived membership in an ethnic group does not mean that the judge's scrutiny of the ground of ethnic origin is more subjective than for race; in fact, they can have the same impact. As the court explained in a pedagogical manner, "Ethnicity and race are related and overlapping concepts. Whereas the notion of race is rooted in the idea of biological classification of human beings into subspecies according to morphological features such as skin color or facial characteristics, ethnicity has its origin in the idea of societal groups marked by common nationality, tribal affiliation, religious faith, shared language or cultural and traditional origins and backgrounds."[66] Some ECtHR decisions examine the discriminatory effects of stereotyping: focusing on the bias that racial and ethnic discrimination produces is a way to avoid dwelling on the specific contours of race and ethnicity.[67] Another legal strategy to grasp racial and ethnic discrimination in all its dimensions is to use the concept of indirect discrimination; this solution, however, has recently been less successful.[68] In the United States these definitions seem to merge, describing both origin and race as a social construct based on biological factors coupled with feelings of belonging to an ethnic or cultural group.[69]

Ban on Distinctions Based on an Indefinable "Race" in France

In France, for obvious historical reasons and current racial tensions,[70] the use of race and other personal data is strictly regulated,[71] which has not prevented the identification of racial discrimination in employment.[72] But the inability to collect data on large scale probably makes it more difficult to produce evidence of subtler discriminatory practices[73] (in the United States, it is possible to compare the pool of black applicants hired by a firm with the pool of black job applicants in that region). Criminal cases are more common outside of the employment arena[74] because they are based on established and observable facts such as racist statements[75] or gestures.[76] The contrast between the high numbers of discrimination complaints[77] based on origin and the low number of lawsuits in France is certainly proof of this.[78] Today, the criminalization[79] of racial discrimination in employment[80] is backed by a more ambitious approach in civil law where a shift of the burden of proof is possible.[81] In addition, based on the lack of transparent and coherent selection criteria and the absence of an objective selection method,[82] a presumption of discrimination on the ground of origin can be made, as the Cour de Cassation confirmed.[83] Although authorized, situation testing is unfortunately more commonly used to prevent discrimination than to sanction a discriminatory act after the fact.[84]

Cases of open racial discrimination have been identified in connection to unwise recruitment decisions by an employer[85] or a temporary work agency,[86] but are no longer those frequently encountered in the workplace.[87] Currently, racial discrimination is either based on conscious bias and more or less adroitly dissimulated,[88] or it is unconscious and revealed only through evidence of systemic or indirect discrimination.[89] France demonstrates a strong attachment to the ideology of equal treatment, which can even be labeled as egalitarianism. This seems to negate any difference in treatment of foreign-born French nationals in the workplace, but the facts are that discrimination on the basis of race or origin is a daily occurrence[90] and can even be exploited[91] to justify certain immigration policies.[92]

Furthermore, a form of racial segregation based on origin has undeniably reappeared in sociological studies of the current reality in France, even if analysts disagree somewhat on this issue.[93] This is a salient point because the social classification of populations, a task now often performed by urban sociologists,[94] plays an important role in France and increasingly relies on surveys of the geographic distribution of the population and of occupational categories.[95] A person's individual status based on his or her occupation is widely used in statistical and sociological studies in France. Unlike the United States, France has other significant options for assessing a person's "status." In addition to tracking occupational data, precise records are kept of a person's civil status, and national ID cards are issued. For a comparative approach examining the grounds of discrimination and the norms that categorize people, it is important to consider how, in most cases, it is the nature of this classification that changes from one country to another. In the United States, racial and cultural statistics are gathered; in France, data on occupation, nationality, and civil status are collected. This is the logic that must be understood in order to fight racial discrimination in France and recognize the potential magnitude of the social and professional segregation of certain groups.

Impasse in the Fight Against Racial Discrimination

How can these difficulties be overcome to achieve a more complete eradication of racial discrimination, the cornerstone of all antidiscrimination law? By taking advantage of the lack of precision in France regarding the contours of this protected group and of what constitutes evidence of discrimination. The ground of origin already encompasses the surname.[96] One option is to choose from among the categories cited in Article L.1132–1 of the French Labor Code—which includes perceived differences (origin, *actual or perceived* membership or nonmembership in an ethnic group, nation or race, or a combination of these)—to refine the ground being invoked, relying on decisions demonstrating how these factors are directly or indirectly linked to racial discrimination. For example, in cases of age discrimination, it is common to demonstrate more legitimate, nonprohibited factors assimilated with age, such as seniority or experience. Race is invoked in references to origin, name, ethnic group, and nationality. Furthermore, since economic status is a more "performative" category in France, the addition of place of residence[97] as a protected ground or, more subversively, social origin,[98] as in the European Convention on Human Rights, might help reveal some forms of racial discrimination. A French legal expert has studied discrimination based on social origin in Quebec, where this ground exists in the Quebec Charter of Human Rights and Freedoms (Article 10),[99] and the Senate recently adopted a bill banning discrimination based on social hardship.[100] This is relevant, for example, for overseas territories and areas with a large proportion of foreign-born residents.

Another possible approach to detecting racial discrimination is to invoke grounds of indirect discrimination. If an employer hires someone on the basis of specific educational qualifications, specific schools, specific general culture tests,[101] or specific types of clothing, then there can be a presumption of discrimination against applicants from economically disadvantaged areas who structurally will not have these characteristics and are therefore subject to multiple discriminations. The United States is also moving in this direction with affirmative action programs that increasingly use location as a selection criterion.[102] Since economic hardship affects both whites and minorities alike, this location-based approach helps reduce the risks of racial conflict highlighted by Siegel (such as the risk of balkanization) and meet the tough standards of constitutional review applied to affirmative action.[103]

III. SEX-BASED DISCRIMINATION

Discrimination based on sex is a legal concept with a long history, whose importance can be gauged by the tensions that continue to plague it.[104] Sex discrimination may not be a new concept, but disputes over its boundaries are still strong, whether in relation to other historic grounds of discrimination, such as race, or newly recognized grounds, such as gender. In the class action case against Wal-Mart,[105] Justice Ginsburg's dissent exposed the individual and systemic nature of this type of discrimination. It reads:

> The plaintiffs' evidence, including class members' tales of their own experiences, suggests that gender bias suffused Wal-Mart's company culture. Among illustrations, senior management often refer to female associates as "little Janie Qs."[106] One manager told an employee that "men are here to make a career and women aren't."[107] A committee of female Wal-Mart executives concluded that "stereotypes limit the opportunities offered to women."[108]
>
> Finally, the plaintiffs presented an expert's appraisal to show that the pay and promotions disparities at Wal-Mart "can only be explained by gender discrimination [which encompasses sex discrimination in the United States] and not by . . . neutral variables."[109] Using regression analyses, their expert, Richard Drogin, controlled for factors including, inter alia, job performance, length of time with the company, and the store where an employee worked.[110] The results, the District Court found, were sufficient to raise an "inference of discrimination."

The following conversations with scholars seek to raise the curtain on specific sources of sex-based discrimination, which are found not only in the sphere of employment but also in assumptions made about a woman's reproductive ability as necessarily forming a part of her intrinsic identity, further consolidated by the "protection" bestowed on women in employment law or workplace policies.

To begin, Vicki Schultz looks back at the history of sex discrimination.

MARIE MERCAT-BRUNS: *Has Title VII been effective in fighting sex discrimination in the workplace, as compared with race discrimination? How have sex stereotypes been identified since Price Waterhouse? With respect to steps taken by employers to avoid disparate impact discrimination based on sex, what do you think of the* Ricci v. DeStefano *race discrimination case? Is the decision a blow to voluntary compliance by employers and the interaction of disparate treatment and disparate impact discrimination?*

VICKI SCHULTZ: How receptive has Title VII been in fighting sex discrimination in the workplace as compared to race discrimination? I would say that with respect to both phenomena, although the time period that we are talking about is different, there has been a similar process. In the early period of Title VII (from 1965 to 1978 or 1979), there was very vigorous enforcement of all the antidiscrimination laws on all fronts simultaneously. The federal government played a big part in this, the Department of Justice Civil Rights Division in particular. There is some agreement, I think, among social scientists that initially, for a decade plus a few years, this was very effective, and the degree of racial segregation by job and by occupation declined very significantly during that period, along with the racial wage gap. So very significant strides were made in the wake of the vigorous enforcement of Title VII that occurred initially.

Things began to stagnate in the late 1970s. There is some controversy and disagreement among social scientists on why that occurred. There are a number of factors that people turn to: the decline in manufacturing jobs, for example, where racial minorities (males) had made headway in the wake of Title VII, due to the globalization and the exportation of many of these jobs abroad.

At one point too, the federal government's efforts to enforce the law begin to decline. In the late 1970s, across a variety of areas, we can see that the courts began to relax enforcement and to adopt slightly less pro-plaintiff standards. So there is some question about the extent to which the change in legal enforcement also contributed to the stagnation.

Sex discrimination enforcement didn't get off the ground during the same period. The National Organization for Women (NOW) was born because the EEOC was not enforcing Title VII with respect to sex discrimination, and Betty Friedan and other women decided to get together and do something about this and form NOW.

So the enforcement of sex discrimination does not begin in earnest until sometime in the early 1970s. We do see throughout the seventies and the eighties, for the first time in a century, the decline in sex segregation in the workplace, and that is a very significant achievement. There is also a decline in the attendance disparity, because those things go hand in hand, and a number of practices that plagued women in various industries are successfully challenged. I think of things like the marriage bar (if you were a flight attendant and you got married, you had to resign from your job). If you were larger than a certain weight, you had to resign from your job. All of these things were successfully challenged. The attack on pregnancy discrimination, which was not successful at first in the Supreme Court,[111] found success in Congress in the Pregnancy Discrimination Act.[112]

There were a number of significant achievements in the 1970s and 1980s. What is interesting in terms of the social science is that we begin to see the same thing, which is the stagnation of the progress in the 1990s. Here the work is more preliminary than it has been in race: the evidence has been accumulating for much longer, and it's been studied more robustly by many people. But there are some papers suggesting that sex discrimination or sex segregation does not decline, and indeed there are some suggestions that it is increasing again in the 1990s. So we have a lot to do to understand why that is occurring and again whether there are structural factors (the decline of the manufacturing sector). I think no one really knows whether women themselves have begun to change their minds about of all of this. I shudder to think that's the case.[113] I think, as someone who has been concerned about these issues, all possible explanations need to be on the table.

There is also the question of less rigorous law enforcement. While I think that is possible, it is really too early to tell. So I think the story, in summary, is the same in both cases: a period of vigorous enforcement and great achievement that we should be very proud of, followed by stagnation and the need to figure out what is going on. Then time to try something new or something old (since the old policies are no longer being pursued).

Schultz goes on to discuss sex-based discrimination and segregation in the workplace.

MARIE MERCAT-BRUNS: *When we read your work, you don't only say it is a question of enforcement, you seem to say there are structural reasons why women are excluded from the workforce. Would that be linked to the specific context of certain workplaces?*

VS: Can you rephrase the question to make sure I understand what context?

MM-B: *The context has changed. Not only is there less enforcement of the law, but women are not given opportunities to achieve a work-life balance. In your analysis of the "lack of interest" argument,[114] advancing that employers configure the workforce, you shed a different light on the issue because you are not looking at how an individual is doing his or her job but at the structural resistance of employers in excluding women in the workforce.*

I don't know if this is compatible with what you just said. Would you like to talk about that now or later on?

VS: I'm happy to talk about that now. You bring out the work I have done on the lack-of-interest rationale, and as an example let's take race first. It is always important to consider what's happening in different areas of social bias. One of the things I found in looking at what happened in the race discrimination litigation is that there was a profound shift in the judicial attitude toward cases challenging systemic exclusion, or what I call segregation, in the late 1970s. This period corresponds with the period where we begin to see stagnation in the progress. So for the first time beginning in 1977, judges of all ideological persuasions, supported by Democrats as well as judges appointed by Republicans, begin to accept some version of a lack-of-interest argument as a defense for patterns of fairly extreme segregation in the workforce.

It was very depressing to me to find this result, but it suggested to me that sometime in the 1970s the liberal consensus on race began to break down in the United States and we began to see the rise of neoconservative explanations for racial inequality. These are not structuralist explanations but instead tend to pin the responsibility or assign responsibility for the persistent patterns of inequality to privatized forces, like what's happening in family life, individual work ethic, or things of that kind, as opposed to large-scale public or quasi-public institutions, like what's happening in the workplace or what's happening in the educational sector or the welfare office.

Now, can we point to something like that in sex discrimination? You can see that in sex discrimination the underlying idea has always been and continues to be that sex inequality is really due to privatized forces and not due to anything that employers or governments or schools or large public or quasi-public institutions do. So even among many feminists, I would say—and here is a controversial assertion, but I do think that there are certain strands of feminist discourse and rhetoric about patterns of inequality by sex that, in a way, resonate with neoconservative explanations pinning the responsibility on women themselves, their choices, and privatized forces in the family, as opposed to looking at what large-scale institutions have done to encourage certain family forms and choices that occur within them. So women are consistently seen as creatures of domesticity whose allegiance is primarily to home and heart and for whom everything else is secondary. When you see women in this light, it makes certain explanations of why we are not found at the top of the heap pretty easy to accept. I am not saying there are not patterns of inequality in family life; of course there are. It is a question of how we explain those patterns.

MM-B: *So are you saying it is an interaction between the choices they make at home and the choices they make in the workforce? So the employers impose a "type" of workforce? I have a harder time understanding the liberal stance on the lack-of-interest argument. Are the liberals saying that women first make a decision at home and then react to pressure from employers?*

VS: I would not use the term *liberal* here, per se. I don't wish to be understood as saying it is all a question of what individual employers do. It is a question of whether you look at family formation in the context of the larger political economy. For example, if you take an individualized model—let's start there because this was your example: A family, a heterosexual man and woman, are deciding upon the birth of a child: (a) whether one of them will stay home for six months or a year to be with that child, and (b) if so, which one it will be.

If the male makes more because of the pattern of sex discrimination in job assignment, hiring, wages, and so forth, it is going to seem rational to do this. So you can always look at that decision later and say the woman chose to stay home with her baby and that's why she is not getting ahead in the workplace. But that brackets out, as a natural fact of life, the pervasive pattern of sex discrimination that may have led to a lower wage to begin with, which would be antecedent to that choice for the couple. That is the sort of thing I mean in the sense that women are constantly seen as creatures of the family, and their duty is seen as primarily motherhood whereas men's is not. So that is one example.

There are other kinds of examples, if you looked at this at a macro level, where you could ascribe certain family formations to larger organizations of the economy: the nuclear family itself and the notion of a family wage that reached its zenith in the 1950s was a product of an economy that was growing, the postwar economy in the United States, in which at least for the first time, working-class men who were members of labor unions and so forth and who were able to capture the benefits of that in wages aspired to have a wife at home, the way the upper-middle classes have had.

Now that family form can't emerge: the notion of the wife at home or the notion of a woman who works part-time without the economy producing certain goods and being structured in a certain way. That ideal is no longer alive in the United States today. People are desperate for work: at least 50 percent of all part-time work is involuntary and this is before the Great Recession hit us. Now those numbers must be astronomical because so few people find full-time jobs and the unemployment rate is 10 percent.[115]

We constantly have to be looking at the way in which our private, intimate life is organized and asking how that is affected by the larger structures of politics and the organization of the economy.

Later in the interview, Schultz comes back to the subject of sex discrimination.

MM-B: *Would you go so far as to say that in the context where women are well-represented in certain fields, then it doesn't matter if stereotypes persist? So stereotyping would not be forbidden because basically the aim is for people, regardless of their sex, to feel comfortable in the workplace?*

VS: We are so far from that. Segregation in the workplace is still pretty prevalent in most countries. Certainly it is still in the United States. So it is not so much we have to face that question legally, although I am certainly prepared to face it. It is a more a question of how we understand these links. If there is ever evidence that shows that remarks that would be perceived as sexist or stereotypes in one context are not really perceived that way anymore in another context, it shows that the context really matters. It really does matter for people on the ground. It should matter legally as well.

Look at the *[Price Waterhouse]*[116] case as well. It is no accident that in the case of Ann Hopkins, fewer than 1 percent of the partners at this great accounting job were women. The idea that women would be subjected to remarks like "walk more femininely, talk more femininely, and wear makeup" would not at all be surprising to someone like Susan Fiske, who understands the link between sex segregation and stereotyping. In fact, I think the harder case would be if those remarks had not been made to Ann Hopkins but instead she had simply been denied the partnership. The interesting question is, Would the courts be prepared? Would lawyers understand how to work with social scientists to uncover the more subtle dynamics that she undoubtedly faced in that environment and understand that stereotyping could still be a claim even in the absence of these kinds of overtly sexist remarks?

A stereotype that is very, very prevalent for women is that we are less competent in the workplace. And I suspect less research has been done on this, or at least that I am aware of. I think the same stereotype exists with respect to people of color. Something that would question their intelligence, their competence in the workplace setting. So if Ann Hopkins had been denied a partnership even without those remarks, I would hope we would still have legal and social scientific tools for uncovering the stereotypes that she might as well have faced. But in order to even know to look for that, you have to understand the links between segregation and stereotyping.

Christine Jolls looks at sex discrimination through the lens of behavioral economics.

MARIE MERCAT-BRUNS: *How do other disciplines help in the legal analysis of discrimination?*

CHRISTINE JOLLS: I believe strongly that work from a range of social sciences, including economics and psychology, is essential for understanding and shaping an effective and sensible antidiscrimination regime. The teachings of the IAT [Implicit Association Test][117] provide a perfect example of the important role of psychology.

With respect to economics, a critical contribution is analysis of the effects of particular antidiscrimination measures on the wages and employment of affected groups. The theoretical aspiration of any form of antidiscrimination law is (at least in part) to help the protected group, so it is obviously crucial to ascertain whether in fact this is what happens when the law is put in place. Much of the strongest contemporary research in this area concerns legal limits on discrimination on the basis of sex and disability.

In the case of sex discrimination law, a central chapter in the evolution of American law involved the elimination of health-insurance exclusions for maternity-related hospital and medical expenses. (Such exclusions are prohibited under various state laws and are generally believed to be unlawful under the Pregnancy Discrimination Act of 1978 [PDA], an amendment to Title VII.) Economic analysis suggests that the prohibition on maternity health coverage exclusions may depress the wage levels of female employees, especially those likely to bear children, because of the very high medical cost of maternity health coverage and the substantial degree of occupational segregation by sex, at least until recent years.[118]

A leading empirical study by MIT economist Jonathan Gruber supports the theoretical prediction of declining wages in a period of significant occupation segregation; Gruber found that the legal mandating of maternity health coverage in the 1970s significantly reduced the wages of married women of childbearing age relative to the wages of the workers least likely to be affected by the mandate (workers beyond childbearing age and unmarried male workers of childbearing age). It should be noted, however, that the fact that occupational segregation has decreased over time means it is possible that a health insurance mandate targeted to female workers today would have effects different from what Gruber's study found.

Linda Krieger shares her views on the effects of employment discrimination case law on gender stereotypes.

MARIE MERCAT-BRUNS: *To come back to the employment context and the* Price Waterhouse *case again, some decisions did draw from the arguments of gender stereotypes to recognize rights to transsexuals, right?*

LINDA KRIEGER: Right. There have been some setbacks as well. Have you read the *Harrah's* case?[119] A new Ninth Circuit decision against Harrah's, which is a hotel chain. It involved a woman bartender at a Harrah's hotel in Las Vegas, which had instituted a policy called the "Personal Best" campaign. They brought in a beauty consultant who sat every female and male employee down. I will focus first on the women employees. They did their hair and they did their makeup, and they took a picture of them with their hair all done and then put it on their ID. They had to come to work looking like that. The men had a haircut and they had to clip their nails. So it was like nothing. This woman, who was a bartender and had been a bartender for years, very successful, did not wear makeup. She did not want to wear makeup. She did not want her hair teased and she refused to do it. She was fired. She sued, relying on *Price Waterhouse*. She lost en banc in the Ninth Circuit. The decision was unbelievable. It was as if *Price Waterhouse* had never happened. It is very uneven.

MM-B: *How do you explain it?*

LK: In terms of legal doctrine, it is just wrong. But the way that I explain it logically is that if the Supreme Court does not take certiorari, the Circuit

Court decision stands. I am not sure why the Supreme Court did not take certiorari for a decision that was obviously wrong. Maybe because there is no conflict yet among the circuits, which is one of the factors the Supreme Court uses in deciding what cases to take. Maybe the judge to whom the case was assigned for certiorari review likes gender stereotypes and likes sex roles and did not want this reviewed. I don't really know. It augurs poorly for the utility of Title VII continuing to break down gender norms as they are distinct from sexual categories of male and female.

My view is that employment discrimination to a great extent is sex discrimination in employment. It is all about gender. It is all about the construction of gender: What social roles are appropriate for women? What social roles are not appropriate for women? It gets back to this question of prescriptive or normative stereotypes. A lot of sex discrimination is about that, and a lot of descriptive stereotypes have been influenced by normative stereotypes. So the deconstruction of gender has an important role to play in opening labor markets to women.

I think the struggle of transgender people is extremely important not just for transgendered people themselves but for people who are gendered as male or female or otherwise. This is a very important struggle: these legal issues are very important, and until the world is safe for transgender persons, it will be safe for neither men nor women nor anyone in-between, because ultimately we need to give people the space in which to enact, in which to perform roles that are now coded as either male or female.

MM-B: *Do you think some trends of feminist doctrine created that strong dichotomy of male/female and their opposition and even reinforced it by promoting a view of a liberated woman free from male oppression?*

LK: Actually, I don't. The women's movement played a tremendous role in freeing women from many of the gender stereotypes that had a tremendously negative effect on their lives and to a lesser extent has opened some space for men to be different as well, although I think men have benefited less from the women's movement than women did. I actually see this whole rhetoric of feminists (in the United States at least) as being sex-negative. I don't really buy it. I think that rhetoric is doing a fair amount of damage to many young women. I raised three boys, and when the younger of the boys, who is now twenty-two, was in high school (a hip high school, Berkeley High), he would regularly come home with stories of how at parties the girls would get very drunk, the boys would line up, and the girls would give them blow jobs. To a certain extent, young women who objected to this were called prudes, all these nasty names that you can take as not sexually liberated. The guys when they were by themselves would refer to those girls as whores, and it is the girls giving the boys the blow jobs. It is a negative social consequence when you go in the other direction. I don't see anything particularly liberatory about this, and yet that was one of the tropes that was being used to perpetuate it. So I think it is a much more complex story. Feminists are in flannel shirts, plaids. They are antisex, bigoted prudes. The queer theory people are sexually liberated, and the feminists are doing the damage. I don't really buy it.

IV. DISCRIMINATION ON THE BASIS OF FAMILY STATUS

France singles out family status as a protected characteristic in its own right,[120] a step that has not been taken in American or European law. Sometimes, the prohibition of "family responsibilities discrimination" in the United States and discrimination based on parenthood in Europe can serve the same purpose, expanding the understanding of equality between men and women.[121] In France, granting childbirth or child care allowances or special child-care-related leave to only mothers and not fathers[122] constitutes a discriminatory practice, but work disadvantages following a decision to take maternity leave, due to the absence from work, are suffered only by women, so distinguishing between men and women in compensating for these disadvantages is not discriminatory.[123] In European law, discrimination on the basis of parenthood must be distinguished from distinctions based on pregnancy or maternity, which are protected by specific measures in Europe, whereas no such difference exists in U.S. law.

Comparative equality law scholar Julie Suk discusses family responsibilities discrimination.

MARIE MERCAT-BRUNS: *What I appreciate immensely is the way you have linked stereotypes on an individual level with general norms, as we can see in your article on the work-family conflict.*[124] *However, you seem to say that stereotypes have prevented American law from evolving to better promote a work-family balance. On that point I see that French law may have something to offer but on the other hand it seems to need to recognize the potential interference of stereotypes perpetuated by the rules governing maternity benefits.*

JULIE SUK: I think there are trade-offs. A strong antistereotyping norm increases opportunities for individuals who defy the stereotypes (for example, a woman who does not have children, is not interested in having children, or has a husband who does most of the caregiving) but may prevent employers or the state from adopting policies and practices that address the social reality (however unjust) that underlies the stereotype, namely the fact that women tend to do more caregiving as a result of ingrained cultural norms. The challenge for French law is whether it can protect individuals from these stereotypes without compromising the robust policies that protect women and enable them to balance work and family. I am not sure.

MM-B: *Do you want to tell us what you think about the new form of indirect discrimination, family responsibility discrimination, and maybe other work you are doing?*

JS: Well, there are two issues that I'm afraid we've conflated: first, whether discrimination is a useful concept, and second, whether litigation is the best approach, as ways of addressing the complex set of social problems that tend to reinforce the effects of past racism and sexism.

Which brings me to family responsibilities discrimination. The concept of discrimination is useful only to the degree that it helps an individual supermom to avoid the stereotype that employers (and society at large) may hold, which is that women tend to experience work-family conflict, which undermines their ability to perform as ideal workers. The concept of discrimination does nothing to change the structural problem, which is that the workplace is designed around the assumption that the ideal worker is a person (i.e., a man) with no significant family responsibilities. So it's a trade-off: the concept of discrimination targets some problems and not others. We then have to ask ourselves which of these problems should be the focus of gender equality. If structural transformation of the workplace is the answer to that question, the concept of discrimination is not going to give us a lot of mileage.

Vicki Schultz shares her views about France's thirty-five-hour workweek.

MARIE MERCAT-BRUNS: *In light of a need for work-life balance, how do you view the question of flexible hours and the thirty-five-hour workweek, which was an important turning point in France?*

VICKI SCHULTZ: This is a very complicated issue. People who subscribe to one or another way of understanding of what discrimination means have different views about these matters.

For me, if I look at the U.S. context, the notion of reducing hours in a universal way, not through women only and not through parents only, would be a wonderful move, a utopian aspiration—although interestingly, in the context of the recession now, it is not nearly as utopian as it used to be. Two weeks ago I attended and gave a paper at a conference on the reduced workweek at the University of Connecticut law school.[125] Many employers and state governments are looking at this as an option now because they can't afford to pay all their employees. So they are actually looking at equitable ways to cost costs, and one way to do it is to reduce everyone's working hours. I wrote a paper[126] on this only three years ago, which I think was treated as really ridiculously utopian and irrelevant to anything American feminists might be considering, and now I think this is coming back on the table.

Why do I think it would be interesting and beneficial to pursue legislation of that kind? Because what I always seek to do in my work is to look for and uncover ways in which the broad structural framework limits the choices people can make. It limits the opportunities they have to practice equality. If we are in an economy and in a situation where there is a wage differential treatment between men and women, and the person who earns most of the money for the family is forced to work extremely long hours in order to hold down his or her job and it is a family with care responsibilities (elders or children or lovers or whatnot), then that is going to put pressure on a member of the couple to work fewer hours: there is no question about it. This couple may not be able to practice equality if they want to in terms of achieving an equitable and an equal distribution of employment versus other forms of work, volunteer work and the like, whereas if that person who earned most of the money weren't subject to the demand to work long hours, the couple might be able to practice equality and work reasonably similar hours in the employment market and spend reasonably similar hours in domestic, volunteer work and the like. In the paper that I wrote, I cited evidence from the book *The Time Divide* by Jerry Jacobs and Kathleen Gerson, in which they find that in countries that have a more moderate workweek, couples are more likely to devote equal time to wage work and home work.[127] This is not to say that if we reduced the workweek in the United States, where people work very long hours, equality would be achieved automatically, because it requires a commitment to equality on the part of the couple that [a reduced workweek] alone would certainly not achieve.

MM-B: *Some studies on the thirty-five-hour workweek show that men in France are not necessarily devoting that extra time to the home or volunteer work or responding to emergency situations for the children, but instead develop their hobbies or sport activities.*

VS: The question is what did change since the thirty-five-hour week? This is actually very difficult methodologically. There has been some suggestion in the United States that men have increased their housework over the last generation. They still do far less than women, so you can look at that as, Do men do as much as women? No. But it is still significant that they have increased their housework and their child care over time, and so the question is, What have been the things that have either forced or enabled them to do that, depending upon how you see it? I think if you have more similar workweeks, as members of a heterosexual or gay couple, you're increasing the bargaining power of the person who worked no hours so the other could work long hours. You are now taking an argument off the table: "But I can't do it because I am working eighty hours a week." In that sense, you are creating a more level playing field that allows for the paradigm of equality (the disruption model)[128] even while it enforces it.

MM-B: *There are definitely examples in France of increased commitment of both parents for example to domestic work, but in a lot of cases the women are still supervising the coordination of family activities, for example.*[129]

VS: Changes are slow in coming. Many factors go into this, and what I would say is to not always see men as the villains—as a feminist, to understand that gender constrains men. Gender roles, stereotypes, and segregation constrain men as much as they constrain women. If you look at the United States, there are Generation Y surveys and the younger men say that they don't want to work long hours. They just don't really want to do it. That was not true of the baby boomers: they would have not expressed that preference. Whether they will be able to achieve their preference is another matter, because it is not all what we want; it is what we are permitted to do.

I do think change is possible but it is slow in coming, and it may be that some of those mothers hang on to the family organization because they want to have a certain control. I can understand that, because they have less power and less control in other spheres of life, so it may be very difficult for many women to give up the one source they really have. It is a source of honor and power and control and virtue in many corners of society.

MM-B: *You mentioned the book by Jerry Jacobs and Kathleen Gerson.*

VS: Yes, *The Time Divide*, published by Harvard University Press. I should be pointing out that to talk about a reduced workweek in the United States is a misnomer because one of the things that Jacobs and Gerson show in this book, and it has been shown by other sources as well, is we really have a bifurcated labor force. We have some people who work very long hours, which is a problem where dual degree couples both work very long hours: that is an intense set of issues. But on the other set of issues, there are people who can't get enough hours, so they end up working two or three jobs and they end up working long hours, but a reduced workweek is not the solution for them.

In the paper I coauthored with Allison Hoffman on this, we were arguing for policies that would try to create convergences for a more moderate workweek for everyone. We weren't addressing the need of only the fancy professionals like lawyers who are forced to work long hours. We tackle the problem of contingent work, and I think it is the case in many other countries as well, where people work sporadic hours and don't even know if [their work] is going to be in the same building or at the same time. It is very involuntary. They would like to have more regularized work that is closer to thirty hours as opposed to ten. They have to paste together several menial jobs to manage to make a living.

MM-B: *Do all your theories revolve around work? Do you believe in all these theories about life paths that alternatively provide opportunities for education, training, and sabbaticals all through life without losing social security benefits during these different periods? This is known as "flexicurity" in Europe. Do you believe in these frameworks, or do you ground your analysis always on work as a foundation?*

VS: I believe both things: I believe work is very important because I cannot foresee a future in which the majority of people do not have to engage in some form of remunerative activity, so I think work will continue to be important in the twenty-first century. However, I do think we are living through a profound paradigm shift in the organization of production and the organization of work that we don't fully understand yet. Some people have pointed out its fundamental features, but we don't really know whether they are fundamental features yet. We just know the emergence of newer technology and globalization have created a kind of rapidity of production, just-in-time production, that has led employers to believe they need a more flexible workforce that can be shed on a moment's notice to expand and contract in relation to these new globalized forms of production As a result of this, employment in many sectors, but not in all, does not have the same form of security as it did.

If we take this to be a fundamental paradigm shift in which people are going to be vulnerable to not having access to full-time work or work that will sustain them (it may not be full-time in its traditional sense), then we do have to do something to deal with the "precariousness" (a European expression) or vulnerabilities of people's existence in relation to employment. I think that we should see this as a fundamental form of vulnerability and risk and not celebrated as a wanted, new form of flexibility that is wonderful for workers, as some Americans economists have the inclination to do.

I think we have to protect people from the risk that they will be out of work to give them the opportunity to retrain and change as their sectors of the economy are becoming obsolete and they need to do something else. This does open up the possibility for thinking about the relationship between work and other spheres of life in new ways. But I don't think it is something to be celebrated as much as something to be understood and to be dealt with in its own terms. People at the bottom, people working two or three ten-hour-a-week jobs that don't promise any regularity will be the first to say it is not a form of flexibility that should be celebrated but something to be dealt with and protected against to render their situation more secure.

MM-B: *Do you think it will have a greater impact on women?*
VS: I can speak to only the American context here. There has been some work on who has contingent jobs in the United States. There are different results depending on what definition you give to contingent work. Interestingly, although there is a gender disparity, it is not as great as you might suspect. There are many, many men who are now facing more contingent forms of employment, including people who were forced out of their full-time job and made to work under contractual arrangements, where they no longer have access to benefits and so forth. Are they doing better than the women who work contingent jobs? Maybe yes, because the contract of employment is sort of on top of the hierarchy of contingent work. With something like seasonal work by migrants, you are at the bottom. There are disparities around this, and I do think in some ways the insecurity of employment and the shift of risk onto the individual worker has become a great equalizer. It leaves us a chance to have political coalition and political identification, if you will, that are new.

Perhaps the election of President Obama in the United States represents some understanding of the collective new forms of risks that we all face and the desire to address things in a new way.

Comparative Perspectives

Sex-based discrimination is probably the form of discrimination that most clearly exposes the ambivalent quality of antidiscrimination law, between its scope of application, which is at times quite extensive, and its limits. This observation is true both in the United States and in Europe.

On the one hand, as affirmed by Vicki Schultz, David Oppenheimer, Reva Siegel, and Linda Krieger in their descriptions of the United States context, the protected ground of sex, like race, laid the groundwork for a solid corpus of law on both sides of the Atlantic, which proved to be particularly effective in enforcing prohibitions of disparate treatment and disparate impact discrimination between men and women in many areas of employment. In some cases, legitimate sex-based distinctions can be made when they are linked to motherhood[130] or when sex is a "bona fide occupational qualification."[131] Sex is a very visible trait because it is an important variable in social protection policies, used to determine health insurance coverage, family benefits, and retirement benefits. In France, for example, retirement pension rules have been charged with creating inequalities between men and women, because women are more likely to have interrupted their careers to raise children and are therefore disadvantaged in accumulating sufficient pension rights.[132] Claims based on the sex ground can sometimes reinforce the static image of female identity as necessarily tied to maternity, for example, in the judgment of the CJEU in *Ulrich Hofmann v. Barmer Ersatzkasse* (C-184/83130),[133] where the court found it legitimate to protect a woman's "physiological and mental functions" after childbirth and the "special relationship between a woman and her child."

On the other hand, the sex ground has often proved ineffective in combatting more subtle problems such as gender discrimination,[134] indeterminate sex, and the oppositions instituted between men and women based on sex. Antidiscrimination law has been denounced as crystallizing a rigid binary distinction between men and women, positioning women as "victims" of discrimination and men as the "villains," to borrow the word used by Schultz. Additionally, more complex issues involving men and women exist, such as family responsibilities discrimination in any form, including discrimination against workers who have not founded a family. Can family status be regarded as introducing the notion of freedom to make personal lifestyle choices, in addition to the right to nondiscrimination? In any case, family status (as a prohibited ground covered by Article 1132–1 of the French Labor Code) is not bound to a personal attribute such as sex.[135]

Lastly, the prohibition of sex-based distinctions constantly raises the question of systemic discrimination against women,[136] due to sex segregation in the labor market and the glass ceiling phenomenon. Should we be investigating the workplace to uncover how it influences the career choices made by women in terms of occupations or career development, as Schultz observed? Antidiscrimination law can cover up institutional discrimination and distract us from addressing the broader issue of establishing a more balanced relationship between work and family life, as noted by Suk.

So it is important to examine the tensions intrinsically joined to the sex ground in antidiscrimination law. First, I will take a comparative historical look at the sex ground. Then, having identified the forces pulling at this protected trait and its particularities, I will show how they can raise the curtain on a better grasp of the discriminations caused by the eminently functional nature of the sex ground and how the concept of gender has taken over from sex.

Is Sex Still a Relevant Ground Today?

Challenges to sex discrimination have been successful historically, as the scholars interviewed have intimated. First, analogies between race and sex discrimination have opened up a broad field of action.[137] As mentioned previously, it was in a race discrimination case that the obstacles to proving hidden direct discrimination were first exposed in the United States.[138] Sex discrimination case law has been particularly prolific in Europe and the United States,[139] carving the outlines of indirect discrimination.[140] In Europe, community case law on sex discrimination, recognizing the fundamental nature of the principle of equal treatment of men and women,[141] is part of the community acquis[142] on which court decisions on age discrimination, for example, have been based,[143] without being confined to the indications provided in directives addressing various individual grounds.

But the analogy between race and sex has created a competitive environment that has ultimately constrained as well as liberated women's rights.[144] In the United States, in particular, the women's rights movement was first perceived as supporting mainly the rights of privileged women. The traditional civil rights movement bringing suit in court, a movement typically associated with the lower social classes, tended to subscribe to the idea put forward in the Moynihan Report in 1965 that the matriarchal family structure in "black" households "emasculated" black men and hampered civil rights progress.[145] Groundbreaking women activists such as civil rights lawyer Pauli Murray, who was rejected from Harvard Law School because she was not the "right" sex, advocated for the rights of lower-class black women. These activists showed that sex-based discrimination could have a larger socioeconomic dimension, similar to, and implicitly related to, race discrimination. The largest organization of feminist activists in the United States, the National Organization for Women (NOW), was also created in response to the low enforcement of the Title VII law prohibiting employment discrimination for women (CRA of 1964), as noted by Schultz and other scholars.[146]

In the United States, the sex characteristic resonates across all occupational categories, certainly more so than race or origin, and in terms of pure numbers it affects a larger population, namely, all women and men.[147] In Europe and in the United States, women encounter both vertical resistance (the glass ceiling)[148] and horizontal resistance (occupation-based) in their careers. These issues affect half of the working population and have a much wider scope of application than any other ground except age. Seen from this angle, the ground of sex appears to be effective in revealing overall rigidities in the employment market and in strongly leveraging the purchasing power of women.[149] The growing body of litigation on genuine occupational requirements[150] that exclude women from certain types of jobs illustrates the need for this incompatibility to be assessed on a case-by-case basis and not generalized to the entire occupation. Such exceptions to the antidiscrimination principle can also perpetuate biases, resulting in widespread, systemic impact when these biases are incorporated into an employer's selection criteria.[151] Upon close scrutiny for evidence of discrimination, certain historical occupational requirements, such as physical strength for law enforcement and security jobs, are shown to be obsolete yardsticks based on perceived needs and are now restrictively interpreted by judges.[152] An alternative to systemically excluding one sex from certain jobs could be to apply a proportionality test, as provided for in European law.[153]

Might it be considered that above and beyond the question of discrimination, the ground of sex has a stronger "functional" aspect than other prohibited grounds, because of the important economic impact of discrimination in pay[154] and in the assessment of occupational requirements?[155] There is a financial undercurrent to all sex discrimination cases involving pay equity[156] and the concept of "work of equal value."[157] The "equal pay for equal work" principle is foundational because it obliges employers to proactively rethink their compensation policies.[158] Judges are looking past the individual to focus on the nature of the work being performed.[159] Ultimately, as the Conseil d'État has already done in the past, courts can assess pay equality by testing for the proportionality of the sex-based difference in pay, comparing the purpose and relevance of the pay advantage to the company's business objective.[160] In France, the added appeal of assessing pay discrimination with respect to pay equity is that an initial comparability of jobs is not required to test the objective justification for a difference in treatment.[161] French policy sways between a discourse on combating sex discrimination and one on achieving "real equality between women and men," which is the name of the last piece of legislation in France, covering a wide scope of issues: domestic violence, quotas for women and men in public institutions, equal pay and protection against discrimination for independent workers on maternity leave.[162]

Wage differences between men and women are identifiable and occur throughout a person's career, even if Krieger explains that information proving the discrimination can still be withheld from plaintiffs, despite the discovery procedure used in the United States.[163] Are repeated absences from work for maternity enough to explain the stagnation in pay experienced by women after returning from leave or their less favorable performance appraisals?[164] As Jolls mentions, is maternity protection the reason for the lower wages paid to women in the United States, as some economic research seems to indicate?

Tensions Surrounding the Sex Ground

Sex-based discrimination cannot be grasped simply by evaluating work and its requirements on a job-by-job basis: it is affected by other tensions.[165] Through the prism of equality, the sex ground reveals how society functions. In many court decisions and laws, organizations, families, and women's rights at home and in the workplace are closely correlated. As Schultz suggests, we might wonder why analyses of sex-based distinctions, even in the context of employment discrimination law, so often refer to women's private lifestyle choices. Isn't this the focus of Catharine MacKinnon's criticism of the legal construction of the concept of the right to privacy as a protected space where male domination over women can be more freely expressed without the possibility of an outside judgment?[166]

This leads to the more sensitive issue of the almost symbolic, institutional nature of sex as related to the employee's body. In the fight for equality, the protected ground of race refers to skin color, facial features, and other physical characteristics, but sex extends beyond the confines of the body and touches on reproduction,[167] sexuality, and private life and implicitly permeates all legal debate on equality and women in employment. Women's bodies, extensively discussed by feminist scholars, constitute a source of social oppression and, paradoxically, a space of freedom. Direct or indirect references to women's bodies in U.S. and European law, particularly in the workplace,[168] attract a great deal of attention from those who strive to achieve equality and women's right to make their own decisions.

This can be clearly seen on both sides of the Atlantic,[169] in the genealogy of the acquisition of women's rights[170] as well as equal employment policies,[171] which in France even provide for fines to be paid in the event of noncompliance.[172] Sex is closely tied to norms involving founding social institutions, such as the family, which are perceived as guaranteeing a cohesive society.[173] But focus has gradually shifted from the problem of sex-based inequalities in employment to the scrutiny of the lifestyle choices made by men and women to achieve a work-family balance. Rather than a dispute over equality and identity, battling discrimination in this context resembles a search to ensure that women and men have an equal right to a private life without any undue impact on their career. What often ensues is a systematic linking of employment-related choices and private-life choices, sometimes more for women than for men.

The development of American constitutional case law offers particularly telling insight into the difficulty of distinguishing between sex-based discrimination and the context in which women exercise their rights, often their right to have control over their bodies. The Supreme Court seems to be straddling a fine line: on the one hand, it eases the constitutional principle of equal protection by justifying differences in treatment made to protect the perceived vulnerability of women,[174] and on the other hand, it uses the idea of privacy to enshrine certain rights over their bodies that sometimes ensnare rather than emancipate women.

In the United States, the first employment-related decisions handed down by the Supreme Court, including the landmark *Muller v. Oregon* decision,[175] found that distinctions in employment laws "protecting" women at work by restricting their working hours, like those that had emerged in France a little earlier,[176] were compatible with the equality principle, despite the fact that a few years prior, in *Lochner v. New York*, the Supreme Court chose to guarantee the liberty to contract, invalidating a law, not specifically directed to women, seeking to restrict working hours for the purpose of protecting workers' health.[177]

After *Muller*, the constitutional case law as a whole seems to accept the implicit stance that a woman's foremost role is to bear children. Even though the Supreme Court began to strike down sex-based legislation under the Fourteenth Amendment's Equal Protection Clause in the 1970s, forbidding government from enacting sex-discriminatory laws premised on the belief that women should bear children and men should support the family, the modern equal protection cases have not wholly broken from the *Muller* tradition. A lower standard of scrutiny is applied to laws drawing distinctions between the sexes, especially laws regulating pregnancy. Siegel shows us how, since *Roe v. Wade*, every abortion restriction has been enacted to protect the fetus, on the presumptions that pregnancy can be imposed on women and that to a certain extent the government can regulate the right to terminate a pregnancy.[178] Although *Roe* protects the right to terminate a pregnancy under a line of cases based in liberty and autonomy, rules regulating abortions can contribute to the subordination of women and should also, according to Siegel, be subject to scrutiny under the equal protection clause.[179]

In all equality case law, one can detect a desire to apply a separate set of standards to dissimilar treatment for men and women. This has crystallized, first, in the inability to amend the Constitution and expressly include the principle of equality between men and women[180] and, second, in the more lenient judicial review of sex-based distinctions under the Fourteenth Amendment's Equal Protection Clause. In *Reed v. Reed*,[181] the Supreme Court decided that sex was not a suspect classification subject to strict scrutiny, like race. Because of this, differential treatment based on sex was allowed if it bore a rational relationship with the objective of the law. The court then veered significantly from this decision and held in *Frontiero v. Richardson*[182] that benefits provided to dependents of members of the military could not be based on sex, suggesting that any classification based on sex must be justified by a compelling state interest, indicating a level of scrutiny (strict scrutiny) used for race distinctions. Finally, in *Craig v. Boren*,[183] the court rolled back and opted for an intermediate standard of judicial review of sex-based distinctions that must substantially relate to the achievement of an important government objective. This more lenient level of review continues today—most prominently in United States v. Virginia, 518 U.S. 515 (1996)—and reflects an attachment to sex-differentiating theories. It can justify legitimate differences in treatment between men and women in the United States, despite the absence of more protective maternity laws such as those that exist in France.

French and European[184] laws offering women pregnancy and maternity protection have been in existence for some time[185] and aggravate the risk of discrimination against women when the period of protection, which employers may consider to be inconvenient or costly, comes to an end. Fortunately, inspired by European case law,[186] antidiscrimination can step into the breach: it considers as suspect any adverse action taken by an employer once maternity protection ends,[187] such as postponing training[188] or a promised promotion after maternity leave.[189] In this context, antidiscrimination laws and maternity protection measures are complementary.[190] Unlike French law, which immediately adopted maternity protection for women in employment[191] and even banned night work for a time as a nod to their perceived vulnerability, U.S. law took some time to recognize pregnancy as a source of discrimination.[192] The inclusion of pregnancy as a protected ground of discrimination first had to be enacted by statute.[193] Rather than adopt legal provisions for maternity leave, feminists preferred the more neutral route of incorporating unpaid, job-protected leave for medical reasons or family responsibilities into the Family and Medical Leave Act (FMLA). Extensive case law on family responsibilities discrimination then emerged, converging with European law, which is prolific on parenthood issues[194] not restricted to sex and, along with French law, reinforces legal norms protecting parental rights and supporting family,[195] generally understood to mean dependents in general.[196] French case law, like European law,[197] seeks to ensure that parental leave does not negatively affect employees when they return to the workplace in terms of working conditions and pay: the employee's job before the leave and after the leave must be compared and the jobs must be similar if not identical.[198] Since the EU directive on the application of the principle of equal treatment between men and women to the self-employed,[199] maternity protection has not been reserved for salaried workers.[200] In the *Danosa*[201] decision, the CJEU applied Directive 92/85 on the protection of pregnant workers to a woman executive committee member considered to be a "pregnant worker" and who was revoked due to her pregnancy. The protection applied to her because she was pregnant, regardless of her employment status. The CJEU has even reflected on maternity leave in surrogacy contracts: "EU law does not require that a mother who has had a baby through a surrogacy agreement should be entitled to maternity leave or its equivalent."[202] The court leaves a door open for Member States that support this form of parenting[203]: "The Pregnant Workers Directive merely lays down certain minimum requirements in respect of protection, although the Member States are free to apply more favorable rules for the benefit of such mothers." In France, the budding number of discrimination suits over pregnancy in self-employment has not been successful, because no justification is required for the termination of simple civil law contracts with self-employed workers. The legislature had to recently intervene.[204]

How can the discernment of family responsibilities in the United States[205] and of family status in France, or parenthood, as an extension of sex discrimination in Europe, change the way employment discrimination is perceived? As Suk observes, perhaps antidiscrimination law does not have the financial or legal means to undertake in-depth transformations to establish a better balance between work and home and even obstructs such advances in the United States by redirecting attention to stereotypes. One can also consider, however, how an expansion of the protected characteristic of sex is coupled with assumptions made about how an individual performs: that is, the challenges of having or not having a family.

Antidiscrimination law is therefore undergoing a subtle but subversive transformation.[206] Like discrimination on the basis of trade union activity and discrimination based on sexual orientation, family responsibilities and family status discrimination introduce the issue of liberty beyond the fight against discrimination. The message being conveyed is that a characteristic like sex is not sufficient to describe a person's identity and life choices.[207] This premise, more reminiscent of a quest for personal dignity, reinforces the idea that sex does not indicate a person's performance in the workplace and even less so in his or her private life; sex is relational and must be contextualized in relation to other people. The new generation of prohibited characteristics has not been designed to weaken the role of the welfare state or do away with sex-based positive action.[208] These grounds help shed light on the impact of the collective measures enforced by the state and employer practices: either they overlook work-family dynamics or, on the contrary, they are not neutral and promote certain ideas about the employee and how any conflicts between work and family life should be resolved. In certain cases, the government or employers should be able to justify or explain the lifestyle choices that they are encouraging their employees to make to increase their rights and benefits, and, as required, do away with policies that are not consistent or compatible with changing behaviors: the legal debate on these issues is at the crossroads of concerns about fundamental rights that articulate simultaneous aspirations for equality and freedom. Is this not an inevitable change for antidiscrimination law in a society seeking to reconcile individual and group expectations in the workplace? This transformation begs the question of how to encourage a more systematic recognition of the ground of gender, coupled with sex.

V. DISCRIMINATION AND GENDER DECONSTRUCTION

To begin with, let us consider what we mean by *gender* and *deconstruction*. Certain works on gender deconstruction in various disciplinary fields have evidently reverberated in American doctrinal thought, inspired by queer theory. Although in a different manner, these ideas have also penetrated French thought, which probably sprang from a different paradigm of sex equality and sex differences. If we proceed in stages, then understanding the gender issue follows from a distinction between the terms *gender* and *sex*. Joan Scott clearly addresses this question as she retraces the history of gender construction: "In its most recent usage, *gender* seems to have first appeared among American feminists who wanted to insist on the fundamentally social quality of distinctions based on sex. The word denoted a rejection of the biological determinism implicit in the use of such terms as sex or sexual difference. Gender also stressed the relational aspect of normative definitions of femininity. Those who worried that women's studies scholarship focused too narrowly and separately on women used the term gender to introduce a relational notion into our analytic vocabulary."[209]

In an effort to draw similarities with Europe, an exploration of these disciplinary fields is very useful for comparing U.S. gender studies with the scope of studies in France.[210] French feminist theory is often simplistically perceived. Early on, it took a relational, psychoanalytical approach to sex differences and relationships related to sexuality, symbolized by the MLF movement and Antoinette Fouque's "Psych et Po" group, which foregrounds the feminine symbolic and a form of essentialism found in the work of Luce Irigaray and Hélène Cixous.[211]

In reality, French analysis of the social construction of gender was more complex, as seen in Simone de Beauvoir's writings and the critique of the myth of woman,[212] and in the materialist feminism of Christine Delphy,[213] Colette Guillaumin,[214] and Monique Wittig,[215] who propose, without naming it as such, an avant-garde deconstruction of gender using Marxist analysis. Adding to this complexity is Pierre Bourdieu's work on masculine domination, which got a rather tepid reception by feminists, along with his useful analysis of the workplace and the impact of the rapid entry of women into a hitherto masculine profession, "in a certain way, threatening men's 'sexual identity', the idea that they have of themselves as men."[216]

If we try to portray the contemporary debate on gender in France, Geneviève Fraisse proposes an essential philosophical perspective of gender and how it relates to equality, aptly illustrating the complex relationship between gender and liberty: "Equality is the central theme of feminist thought. An understandable theme, since it expresses the essence of feminist utopia, the critique of masculine domination and a point-by-point equilibrium between men and women. Freedom is therefore an obvious consequence. Conversely, the liberty of women, logically, does not always lead to equality between the sexes. Let's therefore temporarily set aside the question of liberty, which is both the opposite and the complement of the principle of equality."[217] For Françoise Héritier, recognizing the fundamental anthropological dimension to the relationships produced by a distinction between the sexes is key to identifying certain risks of discrimination that are inherent to an ethnocentrist vision of gender. "The study of kinship terminologies in the Omaha, Crow, Iroquois, and Hawaiian systems led me to posit that the kin terms revealed something, not about actual status or roles at different ages in the life of gendered individuals in human societies, but about a certain idea of the relationship between the sexes through the internal framework of their interaction. They do not express nature, but ideology."[218]

More recently, sociologists have also considered the question of gender in employment in France, as seen in the essential analyses of Margaret Maruani,[219] Rachel Silvera,[220] and Jacqueline Laufer,[221] who reexamine the promotion of equality and antidiscrimination despite the sexual division of labor. Economic and legal analyses scrutinizing the effect of norms on the social roles of the sexes offer a systemic vision of discriminations, which are perpetuated from generation to generation, regardless of changes in employment[222] and are related to the way in which social protection was constructed in France, a reality that it must take into account.[223]

Finally, deconstruction of law, as a last step, enriches the legal analysis and forces a reexamination of Judith Butler's fundamental work, *Gender Trouble*.[224] In this critique, based on theories by Michel Foucault, she goes beyond the traditional distinction between sex and gender to question the individual and sexuality at different times and in different places. In addition to Christine Delphy[225] and Bruno Latour,[226] other researchers work on a certain form of gender deconstruction. In France, despite a probable lag with respect to the United States, where gender studies are more deeply anchored, "throughout its development, the sociology of gender has nevertheless maintained a constant dialogue with the major theoretical frameworks, streams of thought, and even 'schools' of sociology."[227]

All of American feminist legal thought has been more or less inspired by the work of Michel Foucault and of law as an instrument of domination and the central premise for all analysis of positive law.[228] Nevertheless this American thinking was expanded and even turned around to critique the feminists themselves as being responsible for a new form of domination replacing masculine domination.[229] Janet Halley,[230] Vicki Schultz, Nan Hunter, Katherine Franke, William Eskridge, and Duncan Kennedy express this view in their analyses of discrimination, as well as of sexual harassment, privacy law, and constitutional law.[231]

In France, through the lens of American law, in which he is well versed, the sociologist Éric Fassin exposes the "reversal of the homosexual question" and explains why France has resisted the theories of Judith Butler for rather ideological reasons.[232] He offers us a transatlantic comparison of gender, describing how sexual questions arose in an indirect fashion in France, in connection with issues involving the country's republican culture, from head veils to the civil union (*pacte civile de solidarité*, or PACS), including gender parity.[233] Marcela Iacub, Caroline Mecary, and Daniel Borillo deepen our understanding of questions regarding sexual orientation, reproduction, and sexuality,[234] departing from traditional positivist studies on the law related to sex.²³⁵ Only very recently, a broader approach was initiated to reexamine every concept of private law²³⁶ and public law²³⁷ and the notions of contract and consent²³⁸ through the lens of power relations.

In the comparative observations made in the wake of these conversations on gender, I endeavor to better understand how these reflections fit in with the wider issue of discrimination in the workplace. What is its impact on the legal interpretation of inequality at work? How can this new light shed on the deconstruction of sex as a protected ground open a new forum for discussion about the identity of the person at work, his or her private life, sexuality, and the extent of freedom on the job? It is possible to explore even further. Why not offer a new reading of autonomy in employment law through a narrative that deconstructs sex and gender, as Janet Halley suggests? This is in fact a necessary step toward better understanding the differences between the category of sex, enshrined in law, and other closely related grounds of discrimination such as sexual orientation, gender, and physical appearance.

Janet Halley shares her analysis of the rights equality claimed by the gay movement in the United States.

JANET HALLEY: To look at the gay movement in the United States, you would think that marriage and military service are purely good institutions and never once caused anybody any harm! Here's a historical fact: Some centrist gay leaders were surprised when gay divorces started happening. Their strategy had been to argue that they were as committed to marital solidarity as straight couples and so should be allowed into the institution. To read their briefs, you would imagine that the only effects of marriage law are those emerging during marriage. But look at any American Family Law course: legally, the institution is mostly about entry and exit rules. That is, it's mostly about who can get married and how—and divorce. The gay agenda has produced a far more conservative image of marriage in the United States than we had when it started.

Later in the interview, Halley offers other analyses from an international perspective.

MARIE MERCAT-BRUNS: *So basically this new generation of researchers is focusing on labor relations and the effects of globalization.*
JH: Let's think about human mobility, smuggling, and trafficking. This new legal order has been hailed as a protection for the vulnerable. But it originated when countries receiving illegal migration started to take an international criminal law enforcement strategy to get the sending countries to stop sending so many illegal migrants; they basically clamped down on the developing world. Under the Palermo Protocols, states agreed to clamp down on labor migration in the forms of smuggling and trafficking.

This is a border control regime; it is about making it harder for people to migrate illegally. It contains a tiny sliver of protection for migrant workers who are coerced at certain points in their migration. Only in this sense is the trafficking regime in any way protective of the worker. If you are smuggled, you can be prosecuted in the receiving country, but if you are trafficked, you must not be punished and you may be repatriated. If the receiving country does not want you, it must send you back to your home country. You might be devastated when you are sent back to your home country; you might be desperate to migrate.

Meanwhile, the people who helped you or forced you to migrate—and at the border, decisions about which class you fall in are made by extremely low-level immigration officers and are in practice not appealable—are subject to intense criminal sanctions. So the price of migrating into countries that enforce the Palermo Protocols goes up because it's riskier for the middlemen; maybe your best second option is not migrating into the North or the West but into another developing state.

So it seems that the regime fosters South-South migration. Migrants who have good claims to refugee protection are swept into the trafficking-smuggling enforcement regime, also at the border and without time to develop their claims. The big Northern developed countries can wash their hands of the resulting movement of people back into the developing world and economic desperation. These are some of the downsides of the trafficking regime.

I see this as very ambivalent success for poor people. American feminists were against trafficking because they regarded women's migration from one country to the other or from one place to engage in sex work as a really bad thing. So they went to the Palermo convention on antitrafficking; they fostered the push for stronger criminalization because they cared so much about the sex worker. Too narrow a focus; too strong an identity politics; too simple an idea of power.

MM-B: *It is enriching to discover this broader perspective on the criminalization of international labor law.*

Coming back to the idea that some feminists might have fueled the constant perception of male domination, would you like to add on anything about gay rights activists proceeding in a similar view of power struggles, victimization, and constructing homosexual identity?

JH: There is fascinating chain of movement-to-movement imitation in which black civil rights constitutes the classic model, and women's and gay rights imitated it. This imitation process is interesting in its own right. One problematic result for the gay rights movement was that it got focused entirely on civil rights. Civil rights had been central for segregated blacks, so they must be central for the subjects of a despised sexuality. But the broader sexuality agenda included a lot more than civil rights. For instance, and here I draw on the recent work of Libby Adler,[239] it included the question of the most sexually vulnerable population in the world: children and teenagers. They have to figure out their sexuality while under almost complete capture by the family and the State. There is almost no place for a kid to go except home and to school—and the bad things that happen to sexually exploratory kids there aren't violations of civil rights. What remedies do we have for them there? There are some legal avenues—and Adler is developing a clinic to help homeless kids through them—but a lot of the remedies aren't even legal; they involve deepening our commitment to sexual exploration. But the gay marriage campaign has been directly contrary to that commitment. It's been a hard piece of history to watch if your basic political instincts are queer.

MM-B: *Could you give me an example on how you could do that though? Would be through the State? Through education?*

JH: Well, here is one that Adler is working on. Homeless kids commit crimes simply to eat and have a place to sleep. The minute they get caught, they have a criminal record. And that record has a huge negative effect on every subsequent contact they have with the state—getting food stamps, getting an identity card, small things that can make the difference between life and death. Can this process be slowed down so that we don't routinely make things worse for these desperate kids? It's a very low-level bureaucratic question.

MM-B: *What do you think of stereotypes, sexuality in the workplace, and then maybe constitutional issues? Why does the United States not have federal protection of sexual orientation discrimination, when there is such a strong awareness of discrimination against gays?*

JH: Why we don't have prohibition of sexual orientation discrimination in Title VII? That is a political question. The political power is not there to include sexual orientation in Title VII. This is a culture war. Conservatives and especially conservative Christians do not want to see legal rights for nondiscrimination on the basis of sexual orientation. Why don't we get it from the Constitution through equal protection? Let me put this simply. Every constitutional right for homosexuals is either going to be an equal protection right or substantive due process right.[240] But those are highly politicized provisions of the Constitution. The way it is in our legal political world, for the Supreme Court to add gay-friendly rulings under those provisions, is to step into a culture war.

As I said at the beginning of this interview, I started my career thinking I could tell the Supreme Court, "You can grant equal protection to gays without acting politically." But then I realized that the Constitution and constitutional doctrine don't mandate such a decision; there is a political choice[241] that must be made. That's the impasse that we face.

MM-B: *You don't think that the United States is more "gay-friendly" than before with Obama?*

JH: Absolutely it is. It is constantly becoming more gay-friendly. I think we have transformed the political stage in the last twenty years. It is a struggle at every level of society, not just in the Supreme Court.

Robert Post discusses queer theory and the limits of law.

MARIE MERCAT-BRUNS: *What do you think about dress codes personally?*

ROBERT POST: I think that you can follow this as a matter of action and not abstract principle: antidiscrimination law is not about abstract principle and so to imagine a form of law that is so disruptive of ordinary social conventions and social norms is utopian and would not be publicly accepted. So I myself as a lawyer wouldn't want to go there, although I can see a role for people who are pushing toward a gender-neutral concept of antidiscrimination law—that is, a queer theory of the person.

MM-B: *Have you thought about the question of cross-dressers in the workplace and the ability to dress the way you like at work? How do you understand this trend?*

RP: There is a debate in Congress now about ENDA [Employment Non-Discrimination Act][242] and antidiscrimination law and about whether it should prohibit discrimination based on sexual orientation or upon gender. Based on sexual orientation, it is a social movement representation of gays as a group and gay rights; where based on gender, it is the notion that the person does not have any gender. We can't allow business to make any rules that reflect gender in the workplace. So one is extremely more difficult and transformational than the other; it requires more distance from ordinary social norms in which people do have stable identities.

MM-B: *What do you think of the self-development idea and the fact that we are all individuals and are entitled to a certain well-being in the workplace?*

RP: You and I have had that idea, but to imagine using law as an instrument to impose it to everyone else is to attribute to law a transformational possibility I don't think it has particularly. One has to have a very strong social system to do that. Right now that social base does not exist, and we are not sure it would work for one. At certain times the law could reflect that, but in my view, as a matter of social fact, we, in history, are at a certain distance from that.

MM-B: *You think that as a premise, we should accept the fact that there are stereotypes and work with them?*

RP: I don't think human beings think without stereotypes, so the notion that we should think without a stereotype is internally incoherent. The question for me is, which stereotypes?

MM-B: *I think we should emphasize this for the European public. For example, age biases are not easily admitted in Europe, and your reasoning takes a step further, saying you don't necessarily look at conscious or unconscious bias; you say, let's work with these biases, and maybe that is a more interesting way to talk to the European public about this.*

There is a sort of cynical European view that considers that people will always have biases, and you have a more pragmatic view of how to work with them. Do you agree?

RP: Do you know the philosopher Hans Georg Gadamer? He wrote *Truth and Method*.[243] He talks about determining the construction of human meaning, and in that book he talks about how humans always have their own understanding before anything else; you don't start with a blank slate. You always start from somewhere and that somewhere corresponds to your experiences interacting in the world. So the idea that there is an Archimedean point where one can see the world without prejudice—in other words, without preformed opinion, stereotypes, or generalization—that's impossible.

Next, Chai Feldblum discusses her Moral Values Project,[244] which she describes in a chapter of a book published in 2009 called *Moral Argument, Religion and Same-Sex Marriage: Advancing the Public Good*.[245] The project has two aims. First, to facilitate a meaningful conversation in the public arena on the moral neutrality of sexual orientation and the moral "benefit" of acting in line with one's sexual orientation and gender identity. Second, to build a legal argument, both in the public and political domains, in which government has a positive obligation to provide its citizens with equal access to the "moral goods" that are safety, happiness, care, and integrity.

MARIE MERCAT-BRUNS: *How does your work incorporate the issues of sexual orientation and gender identity?*

CHAI FELDBLUM: The theory underlying the Moral Values Project is that only by having substantive moral conversations about sexuality (including homosexuality) and about government's responsibilities to the individual can we ultimately shift the public's substantive moral assessments of LGBT people in a manner that will advance true equality and liberty for us.[246] The bulk of my scholarship, since my first legal scholarship article in this field was published in 1996, has focused on the question of whether and how moral reasoning can be used to advance equality for LGBT people.[247]

Linda Krieger also considers discrimination based on sexual orientation, queer theory, and its limitations.

MARIE MERCAT-BRUNS: *What do you think of queer theory and how it questions "traditional" feminist jurisprudence on male-female domination and provides new insights on gender discrimination law? We are looking for answers to issues with regard to transgender discrimination*[248] *and same-sex discrimination. Do you have any comments? As I understand it, sexual orientation discrimination is not recognized by Title VII of the Civil Rights Act of 1964,*[249] *but some states prohibit it.*

LINDA KRIEGER: Right. We still do not have federal protection against discrimination based on sexual orientation.

MM-B: *Cases like* Price Waterhouse *have shed some light on sex, or more specifically, gender stereotypes, and analogies were used to apply this case law to sexual orientation or transgender discrimination cases, right?*

LK: Just in the circuits on this question. There are two circuit court decisions that suggest that, in certain circumstances, sexual orientation can be understood as a form of gender discrimination, but that is a minority view. I think it is pretty much beyond question that if that issue were to reach the Supreme Court, it would hold that Title VII's prohibition against sex discrimination does not equate to protection against sexual orientation discrimination, and as a matter of statutory interpretation, I think that that decision—sadly I have to say this—would be well-founded. Congress has, on numerous occasions, refused to amend Title VII to add sexual orientation to the list of protected grounds.

MM-B: *Why?*

LK: Because the United States as a whole is an extremely homophobic country.

MM-B: *But there is a strong push towards recognition of same-sex marriage and same-sex parenting, so how do you explain this strong resistance on the employment question?*

LK: This is one of the conundrums of federalism: when you have a polity that is a federation rather than a republic, you can have different states doing very different things and have very little happening on the federal level because you still have a majority of the states that are not making social or legal progress on the issue in question. So we have a number of states that have state prohibitions against sexual orientation discrimination in employment and housing. For example, Hawaii does prohibit sexual orientation discrimination in housing and employment, but it does not permit gay marriage or civil unions, and just last spring, we had an extremely acrimonious civil union debate in which the religious right was mind-blowing in its vitriol. It was a nightmare, a homophobic blood bath in the legislature.

MM-B: *Coming back to the grounds of discrimination, I think what is interesting are the arguments used to try to extend the interpretation of the law (from sex to gender) and how grounds like sex can be seen as social constructs, covering other discriminatory situations. Some go further and believe that reconsidering grounds like sex can be a way to understand other grounds like race[250] from a different perspective. Certain categories are hard to define, and in France there is this challenge of fighting race discrimination without recognizing that race exists per se. I think that what is very interesting in the doctrinal debate in the United States is that sex is contingent and cannot be identified that clearly. The other question I had is, What do you think of the idea that feminist jurisprudence, by focusing on the male-female domination question in its analysis of law, has perpetuated a rigid, binary analysis of sex as necessarily male versus female, locking out any other interpretation of gender norms and without taking into consideration other perceptions of sex and other forms of sexual identity?*

LK: All categories are social constructs. The category "chair" is a social construct but we sit on them. We don't look at a chair and say, "I can't sit on you because you are a social construct." So sex is a social construction; sexual orientation is social construction. Social constructions form because they perform certain functions either socially or economically, and some of those uses perpetuate forms of oppression, but we are not going to stop using sexual constructed categories. Many categories, called study categories,[251] have boundaries that are more probabilistic in nature than they are fixed or formal. So sex is a fuzzy category. There are intersexed individuals. Gender is most certainly a fuzzy category, and gender varies from culture to culture. In some cultures, there are three formal genders. Gender constructs change over time, but again I think that, if there are forms of legal, social, cultural, and economic subordination that work because they use a particular category, we reject that category at our peril because we then cannot effectively participate in that social, political struggle to reduce that level of subordination.

My experience in the United States with queer theory is that it is primarily the problem of the educationally, economically advantaged. Ordinary, working-class American people believe that there is sex. They believe there is sexual orientation. They believe that there is race. If too many of the progressive social activists spend all of their time talking to each other on whether these are meaningful categories or whether these are meaningless social constructs that are simply a result of a random play of signifiers, then we are going to get run over by a thousand trucks. There is too much of a Marxist in me to go there. So it is very interesting, but to me, it doesn't work very well in the real world of political struggle or the real world of legal struggle in which I spent my professional and personal life.

MM-B: *Do you think it can be counterproductive?*

LK: Yes, I do think it can be counterproductive, and I think in some ways in the United States it has been counterproductive. But I think there are ways it can productive. For example, I think, in junior high schools and high schools, in many parts of the United States, young people are rejecting rigid gender categories and rigid sexual orientation categories, and that is having a liberatory effect across the board. I do think there is a generational thing happening here and that at the end of the day, this notion of gender, this notion of sexuality as being fluid, as being constructed, contested, may do some good as people now in their teens and twenties and in their early thirties grow up. I don't mean to sound like a bitter old baby boomer, because I think there is something liberating as an individual, as long as it doesn't disengage from dialogue with people who have not jumped on board. Part of the problem is that we are increasingly ending up with people in the United States who are talking across such an unbridgeable and unbridged ideological, cosmological divide that each group is asking of the other total conversion to each way of viewing the world, and that is not going to work. So the concern I have with the queer theory movement is, in some ways, similar to the problem I have with evangelical Christians. They are both asking of each other a kind of total conversion that neither group is going to concede to. So then what do we do?

We still need our "chairs." We still need our categories so that we can talk about these gulfs, so that people are not just shouting across them.

Julie Suk shares her insight on discrimination based on gender.

Marie Mercat-Bruns; What do you think about the impact of antidiscrimination norms on gender stereotypes?

JULIE SUK: I think there are trade-offs. A strong antistereotyping norm increases opportunities for individuals who defy the stereotypes (for example, a woman who does not have children, is not interested in having children, or has a husband who does most of the caregiving) but may prevent employers or the state from adopting policies and practices that address the social reality (however unjust) that underlies the stereotype, namely the fact that women tend to do more caregiving as a result of ingrained cultural norms. I am not sure.

MM-B: *Yes, of course, but now with European law, some wonder whether antidiscrimination law will be as protective of the welfare state in member countries. . . . I would like to come to my second question: Have you considered homosexual or transgender issues when thinking about work-life balance?*

JS: Yes. I do notice that, perhaps as a result of greater tolerance for gendered generalizations and norms, the issue of same-sex parenting has been much more problematic in France than it is in the United States. I think this is due to a much stronger assumption in France that the ideal family includes one male parent and one female parent.

MM-B: *Do you think this could modify your analysis in your article on the work-family conflict?*[252] *I don't think you mention it. This is probably because it is not yet part of the debate in France.*

JS: Well, I think it gets at a much broader question: Is it possible to adopt policies that rest on the assumption that men and women have different valuable things to offer as parents, without excluding families that fail to adhere to the model? I think it is possible to devise policies that attempt to promote both maternal and paternal caregiving for children, on the one hand, without denying benefits to, say, single parents or homosexual parents. But arguably, the danger is that the state will essentialize and valorize the traditional family, which will lead to a culture that implicitly judges the single parent or the homosexual parents to be inadequate.

Comparative Perspectives

These interview excerpts evoke discriminations based on gender and sexual orientation but also touch upon broader questions about same-sex parenting, international prostitution, homosexuality and children constructing an identity, and queer theory[253] applied to law. Without reviewing all of the issues mentioned, I would like to discuss three salient points: the question of discrimination based on homosexuality in a comparative approach; the distinctive nature of discriminations based on gender, homosexuality, and physical appearance, and the sphere of autonomy in the workplace that they affect; and the American doctrinal deconstruction of sex and gender, and whether it helps to better understand the contours of discrimination based on sex.

Discrimination Based on Homosexuality and Gender Identity

In the United States, despite the extensive American doctrine[254] devoted to homosexuality, same-sex parenting, queer theory, and sexual harassment involving persons of the same sex, as explained by Janet Halley, which echoes the public debate,[255] there is still no federal law prohibiting workplace discrimination on the basis of sexual orientation, and all attempts at passing this type of law have failed.[256] However, the EEOC has been instrumental in recognizing transgender rights in employment, and in July 2014 President Obama signed an executive order barring federal contractors from engaging in anti-LGBT workplace discrimination.[257]

Conversely, in Europe, this principle has been enshrined in the Treaty of Amsterdam (Article 19, TFEU) and Directive 2000/78,[258] and in France, legislation was enacted more quickly on this issue, after first introducing lifestyle as a protected ground.[259] European case law is surprising because it invokes direct discrimination based on sexual orientation in cases involving benefits that are related not to sexual orientation but to marital status, where indirect discrimination could have been equally appropriate.[260] This probably reflects the fact that some indirect discrimination involves discriminatory intent and that for the sake of transparency, it is best to highlight, in sexual orientation cases, the question of discriminatory animus. The French Cour de Cassation did ask for a preliminary ruling on the basis of indirect discrimination involving benefits granted to married couples but denied to partners in a registered civil union (*pacte civil de solidarité,* or PACS).[261] The reason may be that the French PACS is entered into by both gay and heterosexual couples, unlike in Germany, where the registered partnerships considered in the *Maruko* and *Römer* cases brought before the CJEU unite only same-sex couples.[262] However, the CJEU rendered its decision on the basis of direct discrimination, arguing that only same-sex couples could not marry. Therefore, excluding them from employment benefits (this was before the new French law allowing gay marriage[263]) was a pretext for discrimination based on sexual orientation.[264] The CJEU has recently expanded its case law on sexual orientation to the health sector in France, considering that forbidding all homosexuals from donating their blood is disproportionate and constitutes discrimination.[265]

This is not to say that this type of discrimination is always visible in the workplace,[266] since sexual orientation continues to be regarded as a private matter, except in rare cases.[267] EU case law has confronted this issue of proof of sexual orientation by sanctioning an "appearance of discrimination" when overt homophobic remarks are made even if their author is not the direct employer.[268] French case law is also developing in this area.[269] It is true that in the United States, twenty-one states and the District of Columbia have laws prohibiting employment discrimination based on sexual orientation,[270] but there is no federal law in place despite efforts to introduce one.[271] The legal debate has raged at the constitutional level, defining the contours of the right to privacy[272] and equal protection following a state attempt to prevent the recognition of homosexuality as a protected ground for discrimination.[273] As Krieger mentioned, homophobia has a strong foothold in the United States, which may be partly attributable to the adherence of a segment of the population to religions that reject homosexuality on principle (even though on June 26, 2015, the U.S. Supreme Court ruled that the U.S. Constitution guaranteed the right for same-sex couples to marry in all fifty U.S. states[274] and, before the decision, same-sex marriage was legal in thirty-seven states).[275] Feldblum has in fact worked on resolving the difficult issue of reconciling "moral values" and homosexuality, particularly in the workplace, and on the possibility of expanding the circumstances in which accommodations for religious people are considered, while respecting gay rights.[276] At the same time, Post expresses reservations as to the value of passing legislation to resolve gender issues and the risks that this would engender for the protected individual at work, for whom all reference to sex or gender has been eradicated.[277]

In fact, this question is central to all efforts made to obtain a more precise legal definition of sex and how it relates to gender,[278] sexuality, and sexual orientation.[279] In the absence of a federal prohibition of discrimination based on sexual orientation, American case law has relied on drawing analogies between sexual orientation, transgender status,[280] and gender nonconformity. Based on the *Price Waterhouse* ruling, in which the Court held that discrimination against a female employee for not behaving in a manner considered to be feminine[281] constitutes sex discrimination under Title VII, transgender and gay plaintiffs sought to establish that the discrimination they experienced was sex discrimination in a broad sense, because it was based on their nonconformity with a masculine gender, masculine behavior, or a masculine appearance, for example.

Using the example of the chair, Krieger illustrates why social constructs are important. The analogy between sex discrimination and discrimination based on transgender status was well accepted,[282] except by some radical feminists,[283] so much so that one court went one step further. It considered that, whether pre- or post-transition, transgender status was not an issue of nonconformity. In fact, transgender persons are indeed endeavoring to conform to the sex to which they are transitioning. Discrimination in these cases is therefore based simply on sex.[284] This line of argument was supported by the EEOC in the recent *Macy v. Holder* decision.[285] Attempts to draw analogies between discrimination against homosexuality and discrimination against gender nonconformity have often failed because courts consider that since Congress has repeatedly refused to pass legislation expanding antidiscrimination protection, sex is not intended to be interpreted more broadly to include sexual orientation.[286]

In France, this type of reasoning, which looks beyond sex to consider gender and the end result of the antidiscrimination law from a more functional perspective,[287] is not pervasive in case law. During the debates prior to the adoption of same-sex marriage in France, there were frequent protests by the Catholic Church and its supporters, not only contesting the passage of legislation but also objecting to "gender theory," which they feared would dismantle French society's strongholds: marriage, education and family.[288] Gender is implicitly referred to in cases of discrimination based on physical appearance, as illustrated in a ruling by the Cour de Cassation.[289] The case involved a waiter who was dismissed for wearing earrings at work. In the termination letter, the employee cited this behavior and the fact that it was seen as effeminate as grounds for dismissal. The court found discrimination based on physical appearance, in relation to sex. Concern for the image of the restaurant, which was not threatened, and subjective statements made by customers expressing value judgments on men who wear earrings were insufficient evidence that the decision was justified by objective elements unrelated to any discrimination. The court concluded:

> Whereas it has been recalled that by virtue of Article L.1132-1 of the Labor Code, no employee may be dismissed on the basis of sex or physical appearance, the appeal court noted that the dismissal was pronounced for the reason, as stated in the dismissal letter, that "your customer-service position does not permit us to tolerate the wearing of earrings by a man, which you are," signifying that the physical appearance of the employee, in relation to his sex, was the reason for dismissal; having observed that the employer did not justify his decision to require the employee to remove his earrings with objective elements unrelated to any discrimination, the Court was able to deduce that the dismissal was based on a discriminatory ground; that this ground, being based on Article L.1121-1 of the Labor Code, which the appeal court did not invoke, is unfounded.

This ruling does not invoke the infringement of the freedom to dress as one chooses, subject to certain work requirements but explores a new way of looking at discrimination based on physical appearance that can constitute gender discrimination.

The Cour de Cassation acknowledged that the employee who was dismissed for wearing earrings at work was the victim of discrimination based on "physical appearance in relation to sex." The notion of physical appearance in this context should be defined: it denotes the general impression that a person presents, not just their manner of dress or their physical characteristics. Case law on the subject is limited;[290] significant cases involve, for example, height.[291] The innovative aspect of this decision was the application of this prohibited ground to include the general impression given by a male employee wearing earrings. The fact that a discrimination was involved meant that the employee faced a more serious sanction: namely, reinstatement of the unfairly dismissed employee.[292] Without the discrimination, since the freedom to dress as one chooses is not a fundamental freedom, arguing this ground would not have led to reinstatement.[293] The advantage of the discrimination charge is the shifting of the burden of proof: the employee provides elements demonstrating direct discrimination. Once this prima facie case has been established, the onus is on the employer to prove that its decision was justified by objective elements unrelated to any discrimination.[294] In this case, the dismissal letter explicitly mentioned two prohibited grounds of discrimination: physical appearance and sex. The Cour de Cassation cited the dismissal letter, which referred specifically to "the wearing of earrings by a man." The employee was therefore in possession of a rare avowal of reliance on a protected ground.[295]

The Cour de Cassation found the employer to be at fault in motivating its termination decision not only by criticizing the waiter's physical appearance, that is, the earrings worn, but also by condemning the employee for not conforming to a male stereotype. By articulating this link between physical appearance and sex, the court looked outside of biological sex and implicitly designated gender:[296] the socially constructed perception of what a man is and how he should behave, the most visible component of this being his physical appearance.[297] Outside of appearance, the ECtHR has recently reaffirmed that the right to a sex change is within the scope of the right to privacy and personal autonomy.[298]

Gender Discrimination

This brings us to our second point: the problem of discrimination based on sexual orientation[299] and gender that involves not only judgments about physical characteristics but also judgments about behaviors or the exercise of freedoms that could result in discrimination at work.[300] In these cases, is the search to identify discrimination very different from a judge's search to justify the restrictions on individual freedoms[301] imposed by dress codes, as shown in the "earring case" in France? Discrimination based on physical appearance in relation to sex is built on the idea that making decisions based on stereotypes of what is a manly appearance for a man or feminine for a woman, when these decisions are unrelated to work performance, is a discriminatory practice. However, beyond appearance, this type of bias can influence how an employee's personal behavior in the workplace is evaluated, in the absence of objective justification, based on that employee's perceived nonconformity with his or her gender. Unlike more traditional claims of discrimination probing motives based on personal traits (e.g., age or origin), the freedom to dress the way one wants, via the ground of physical appearance, has become a standard of nondiscrimination based on sex, as various scholars have predicted.[302]

We can sense how exercising personal autonomy in the workplace might be interpreted in antidiscrimination law and not only with respect to gender discrimination. In the earrings case, would the employee have won his case if his employer had not referred to his status as a man? We cannot be sure, but much attention has been paid to prohibited grounds related to physical appearance, such as origin and a male flight attendant's cornrows.[303]

Can we consider that gender discrimination represents an intersection between the protection of equality and freedom, two concepts that are so difficult to reconcile?[304] We have therefore struck the core of the problems surrounding the protection of workplace human rights, which are becoming increasingly important in French case law;[305] the difference here is the focus, via discrimination, on the person in the work environment, and not on elements of his or her personal life that directly or indirectly cross into work.[306] In the end, a person's appearance is the crystallization of a set of common cultural representations; the fight against discrimination in employment does not seek to eradicate every reaction to manifestations of gender identity, as Post points out, since stereotyping is a part of human nature. But their impact on employment decisions affecting employees is another essential question added to that of an employee's workplace human rights.[307]

Understanding the Sex Ground Through Deconstruction

Finally, the evaluation of discrimination through the lens of individual freedom raises the question of gender deconstruction, rejecting the binary approach to the sexes as a form of verification of behavior intrinsic to the fight against discrimination based on sex, as shown by Halley. Certainly, Krieger expresses the potential need for a class struggle that takes precedence over queer theory, for a segment of the population that is not part of the elite, but the question of the contours of the sex ground nonetheless cut across all social strata. Sex discrimination problems are almost a unifying theme. How can one refuse to adhere to this approach to the extent that far from threatening the fight for women's rights, it informs it?[308] A better understanding of gender, sexuality at work, transgender issues, and sexual orientation would seem to lead to a better delineation of discrimination based on sex.[309] The earring decision illustrates this reality: women benefit from exposing socially constructed sex-stereotypes but also from revealing the law's implicit impact on sexuality, potentially distorting relationships between people of the same sex, or of different sexes, in the work environment.[310] In the absence of thoughtful discussion of these issues, an employer's brutal investigation of sexual harassment can end up creating a hostile environment and be perceived by a presumed female victim negatively affected by ensuing rumors as an infringement on her right to privacy.[311] This critical view of the power plays inherent in the employment contract clarifies the difficulty residing in issues of worker's consent, sex, or sexuality, which do not necessarily affect work relationships in the same way depending on the individual; for example, it helps revisit notions of sexual harassment.[312]

VI. DISABILITY AND AGE DISCRIMINATION

A certain ambivalence surrounds the idea of discrimination based on disability or age, since both grounds are sometimes used in law to attribute, rather than withhold, rights. Judges, legislators, and commentators face the task of determining how to deal with the special relationship to difference cultivated by age and disability.[313] On both grounds, discrimination often stems from a failure to understand the aging process, the manner in which various disabilities impact employment, and the full range of discriminatory situations potentially affecting individuals. Moreover, the legal norms applied in the workplace do not always succeed in filtering out the challenges of using age and disability as conditions for eligibility for employee benefits, introducing an economic dimension that employers must take into account. Unlike race, but in an analogous manner to sex, the grounds of age and disability have always been important markers of the welfare state, especially in Europe. Nevertheless, as working lives are stretched over increasingly long periods in Europe and the United States, the relevance of the age criterion has lost part of its meaning. How should discrimination be understood in this changing environment? What challenges do the aging working population and the aging of workers with disabilities pose, which aggravate the problems of age and disability discrimination?

Disability Discrimination

The scholars interviewed—Ruth Colker, Martha Minow, and Christine Jolls—examine the particularities of disability discrimination in the United States and its ambitious legal framework. With the Americans with Disabilities Act enacted in 1990, the United States was the first to incorporate, into its antidiscrimination legislation, an obligation to act through reasonable accommodations. It is surprising that this innovation should come from the United States, which has traditionally shown a reluctance to impose positive obligations on employers. As American scholars point out, the law has met with resistance, notably due to the financial constraints placed on employers, the special vulnerability of people with disabilities suffering from discrimination, and their effective access to law. Finally, one of the major difficulties encountered in the fight against disability discrimination is the heterogeneous nature of the disabilities that can lead to discrimination.

Ruth Colker offers her insight of the history of the Americans with Disabilities Act (ADA).

MARIE MERCAT-BRUNS: *Could you talk about the legislative history of the ADA?*
RUTH COLKER: I would be happy to talk about the history of the ADA. When I teach my ADA course, I always start with a long discussion of that because to understand the statute, you have to know where it came from.

I think the American perspective is very different than the European because we tend to think of things from a rights perspective, a discrimination perspective, instead of an entitlement perspective. The United States does not have national health insurance (not yet!),[314] but instead of entitlements, as citizens, there are certain rights in order to be free from discrimination.

I know a bit about Australia. I don't know the French situation very well, but in Australia the perspective is very different from the United States, even though they have adopted the nondiscrimination statute.

For your audience, it is important to understand the breadth but also the limits of the antidiscrimination focus. It is a uniquely American way to think about these types of issues.

There are key aspects about how we got to where we were in 1990 (date the ADA was enacted). I am sure you know that we amended the statute in 2008.

MM-B: *We do indeed need to know if the amendments have really changed things. In terms of the entitlements-versus-rights issue, the same dichotomy exists in France, and it causes some problems. The antidiscrimination principle in France also reflects a rights mentality, but French judges are more familiar with the entitlement framework.*

The French perception of disability discrimination seems to be different from the U.S. perception as reflected in the ADA. I'll go into that in more detail later.

RC: The opportunity to compare is fabulous.

To get back to the legislative history, in 1973 we get the Rehabilitation Act. That was adopted during Nixon's presidency. He actually vetoed that statute in 1972 because he considered it to be too costly. Section 504 of the Rehabilitation Act was a small part of a very broad statute for people who were disabled and needed rehabilitation services. So, at the very beginning, it was a blend of nondiscrimination and entitlements ,which is interesting because we have moved so much away from the entitlement perspective. Nixon didn't veto it because of Section 504 but because of the overall costs, and then Congress revised the bill (but retained Section 504), and it was passed in 1973.

Section 504, which guaranteed nondiscrimination, did so only for entities that needed federal financial assistance. It was not a well-known provision. It was snuck in at the last minute with no discussion. The federal agencies charged with promulgating regulations did not do so until litigation was brought to force them to write regulations.

Nineteen seventy-three is an important moment, but it took five or six years for there to be any enforcement at all of that provision. The regulations were written only after a mass protest that started in Berkeley, California. Law enforcement authorities were baffled at how to respond to people in wheelchairs and with other visible disabilities, who started holding sit-ins and protests to spur public officials to action.

Then in 1975, we enacted the Education for All Handicapped Children Act, which is today the Individuals with Disabilities Education Act. That is huge in the United States. This has more of the entitlement focus: all children from ages three to twenty-one are entitled to public and free education if they are disabled. I don't know that Europe has enacted a law as broad as the Individuals with Disabilities Education Act of 1975. The name changed when the ADA (1990) switched to the term *persons with disabilities* instead of *handicapped*. It is federally funded, but states have to promise to offer free public education to all children who are disabled from ages three to twenty-one. That was in 1975 and a very popular statute passed with a broad bipartisan margin.

The next year that was pivotal is 1988. In 1988, the Fair Housing Act, which had been enacted in 1968 to prevent housing discrimination against African Americans who tried to rent or purchase houses in various neighborhoods, was amended to include disability discrimination. People with disabilities were having housing difficulties: if you wanted to provide group housing for people with cognitive impairments or you wanted to put in a group home for people recovering from alcohol or drug addictions, often neighbors complained, so it was hard to get zoning permission. Because of a Supreme Court case on that issue, there was a large national debate about it. The disability community for the very first time, in 1988, worked in coalition with a broader race-based, civil rights community in the United States. They agreed to have the Fair Housing Act amended to ban disability discrimination. This was the first time a disability bill passed not because the disability community was pushing it, but because it became part of a major civil rights agenda.

MM-B: *How do you explain that the race-based community was suddenly sensitive to these issues? Did they realize all of a sudden that it was a civil rights issue?*

RC: Often the African American community itself is very impacted by disabilities. African Americans serve in the armed forces. A lot of veterans are disabled and in need of the kind of help those statutes provide. A lot of people think that the veteran community was pivotal to forge a national consensus on disability discrimination. In the veteran community, there are a lot of African Americans.

It is hard to say. It is give and take. The disability community also favored some amendments that helped to improve enforcement of the race-based aspects of the housing statute.

For the disability community, they thought it was time to get themselves a statute rather than amend another statute. The disability community wanted a statute for people with disabilities that was comparable to the Civil Rights Act of 1964, which was so important for gender and race in the United States.

As a side note, you might want to consider the parallel issue for the gay rights community in the United States. Some early gay rights activists pushed for Title VII to be amended to ban sexual orientation discrimination, but the fear has always been present that opening up Title VII to amendments would hurt that statute for the racial civil rights community (if narrowing amendments were adopted). So, the gay rights community has generally pushed for its own statute. That statute began very narrowly, banning only a small amount of sexual orientation discrimination matters. Subsequent versions (which still have not become law) have become much more comprehensive and are starting to parallel the Civil Rights Act of 1964. So, a big issue in the civil rights community always is whether we should amend an existing statute or create an entirely new one. The disability community has used both approaches.

So in 1988, after the passage of the Fair Housing amendments, a decision in the disability community was made to seek to develop a broader statute.

Interestingly, at that time, Reagan was president and even if we can't say he was particularly interested in such matters, he actually formed a national commission on disability. He appointed people from the disability community to be on this national advisory board on disability. The people were not all Republicans because disability cuts across the Republican-Democratic line: any person can have a disabled child, a disabled parent. You are not "protected" from disability because of your class. Some of this is about the pervasiveness of disability. So one could give Reagan a little bit of credit for starting discussions at the national level.

This advisory group [the National Council on Disability] drafted the first version of the ADA in 1988. It was very radical; it broadened the definition of disability (compared to what was in Section 504). It covered anything imaginable. It provided for very extensive remedies. This version did not pass Congress. That is where we started, with a very radical, sweeping bill.

Another related development was because of a presidential candidate. Michael Dukakis (governor of Massachusetts) was running against George Bush, Sr. (who had been vice president under Reagan). During the presidential campaign, it came out that Michael Dukakis had mental health treatment following several disappointing episodes in his life: his brother had died in a tragic car accident and he sought medical help, and it came out in the media. They thought it would kill his campaign because several years earlier Jimmy Carter's vice presidential candidate (Eagleton) had sought mental health treatment and had been taken off the ticket. There was a fear that this would kill the Dukakis campaign.

At a press conference, a journalist asked President Reagan: "What do you think of the fact that Michael Dukakis sought mental health treatment?" President Reagan said (maybe jokingly), "I would not want to pick on an invalid." The press relayed this information, and the president got criticized in the press for that insensitive comment. Later, he said he was just joking.

That put George Bush (his vice-president and the presumptive presidential candidate) in an odd position. Bush had been moving to the left to win the presidential election, and he was worried that President Reagan's record on civil rights would hurt his presidential campaign. President Reagan had been very conservative on these issues. So at first Bush said nothing. Then he said to the press that there was a disability bill in Congress and as soon as he was elected president, he would support that bill to become law. I am sure he had not read the bill pending bill in Congress at that time. It was a very far-reaching bill, but he did make that promise.

When Bush won with a landslide margin and was elected president, he said to his advisors one way to be reelected is to keep his campaign promises—one of which was this disability bill. So he met with his cabinet and with Richard (Dick) Thornburgh, who was his attorney general. Thornburgh had a son who had been disabled in a car accident in which his first wife was killed. Bush asked Thornburgh to take the lead in getting the disability bill through Congress.

This was the most fortuitous thing that could have happened to the disability community. Thornburgh was a very passionate advocate for disability and he took that charge very seriously. He obviously sought compromises and asked for the bill to be narrowed and cut back. But he worked considerably to get the bill through Congress. He became part of an overwhelming bipartisan majority.

Interestingly, conservative Republicans worked with Democrats and the bill became law. President Reagan's insensitive remark was an important happenstance in this bill becoming law because of the way it forced Bush to make disability rights a priority.

MM-B: *So the disability community's role was not that important in getting the bill passed?*

RC: No, the role of the disability community was huge. It had become empowered and effective at both a grassroots and national level. It played a crucial role at every stage of the legislative process. This fortuity meant the disability community was not facing opposition on the basic principle. The key legislative lobbyist was Chai Feldblum (who is now an EEOC commissioner but, at the time, worked for the ACLU [American Civil Liberties Union]), who worked tirelessly to get the bill through Congress and be acceptable.

In terms of the draft of the bill, as Chai would tell you, the position of the lobbyists was that, to the extent possible, we would use the language found in the 1973 Rehabilitation Act to not reopen those fundamental issues. That's why sections, such as the definition of disability from the 1973 act, were just added hook, line, and sinker into the 1990 bill even though Chai and I knew that there were some limitations with the approach taken in the 1973 act.

Moving forward to the present, I think that it is very interesting once again that a similar combination of fortuities caused a Republican president and Republican presidential candidate to support the 2008 amendments. John McCain was running against Barack Obama, who has a very strong record on civil rights. McCain, a veteran, supported the 2008 amendments. For the 2008 amendments, it was very much like George Bush, Sr. McCain did endorse the bill. The political climate was such that he could not oppose the amendments introduced under the presidency of the second George Bush. McCain made it clear during the campaign that, if he became president, he would the sign the bill if it was passed by Congress. It was actually passed before the presidential election because Republicans worried that Congress would be even more liberal after the 2008 election (and that is exactly what happened).

A lot of people wondered, after so many years of the statute being interpreted strictly, why did this happen in 2008? I think the position among Republicans was they did accept the 2008 bill when it started to look like Barack Obama was going to become the president of the United States and win a possibly heavy Democratic margin in the House and Senate. So the bill that would come in 2009 (if it were not passed in 2008) would be even more proplaintiff than the one being proposed in 2008 before the new members of Congress took office. The Republicans concluded that was the best deal they could get. Therefore, they should accept those amendments, which were very broad in terms of the definition of disability.

What I should say is that, despite the 2008 bill, I am not particularly optimistic that we will see meaningful changes in the courts making it possible for plaintiffs to prevail. I have been doing the research to try to figure out what is going on in the court decisions. The bill became effective in January 2009.

My current research suggests (but I am just beginning this research—it is preliminary) that, going back to 2008 and looking at the cases in the entire U.S. courts in 2008; people are having enormously difficulty finding competent lawyers to take their cases. None of the legal aid organizations can take these cases. I don't think the key problem facing plaintiffs is a narrow definition of disability. I think the chief problem is a lack of access to competent legal counsel.

MM-B: *Is it harder to introduce a class action claim covering disability litigation? We don't have class action in France, and you would think that could foster some impetus to get cases through the ACLU, for example. I also thought that with the juries, you could get significant damages. I know that with age discrimination, that's what attracts the lawyers. In France, the amount of damages is much lower. Is there a specific question of procedure here with the ADA?*

RC: Very rarely can you do a class action with disability. Usually it is a fact-intensive, individual discrimination case. I am speaking right now only about employment and not the other forms of discrimination. Under the law (in employment), you can get back pay, front pay. People with disabilities are among the poorest of our country. They have the lowest hourly wages in our country.

There is rarely a plaintiff who makes enough money that the damages will be very significant. What lawyer will be interested in pursuing that kind of case on a contingency basis? One-third of low back pay is not enough to support legal fees.

MM-B: *Can you get punitive damages?*

RC: In disability cases, rarely do you have compensatory or punitive damages. That is only if you can prove intentional discrimination. If you have a case about accommodation and you have an employer who acted in good faith and made a suggestion and the court agrees with the plaintiff, the employer will not pay compensatory damages. So very rarely do you get compensatory damages.

For people earning eight to ten dollars an hour, it is not worth it for lawyers to take their case on a contingency basis. It is true that a lawyer can get money as the "prevailing party," but that is only if they actually go to trial and get a judgment from the judge or jury. If a case settles, it is not possible to go to a judge and get money for representing the prevailing party. Most cases settle, and therefore the lawyer is stuck with a contingency award that would usually be very low. Plaintiffs have a low chance of winning, and lawyers can't afford to take these cases where the plaintiff is not going to pay the bill. It is just not a good financial decision for some lawyers to take these kinds of cases.

In the following excerpt, Colker discusses the diverse nature of disabilities and the integration of people with disabilities into the workplace.

MARIE MERCAT-BRUNS: *My next question is deliberately provocative. Do you think there is a hierarchy in how different subgroups of the disability community are treated?*

RUTH COLKER: When Congress passed the ADA, specific groups helped pass law and so we have a very good rules for mobility impairment linked to the construction of building from a mobility impaired perspective, and so on.

The hearing impaired felt left out: they would like telephones to be widely available to them. The ADA had none of that—accessible for them in case of emergency calls (with great difficulty) but nothing more than that. Their needs were not prioritized.

When Congress amended the ADA in 2008, it reached a compromise with respect to visual impairment. Unlike other impairments, one would consider whether you are disabled after the use of corrective lenses. So the needs of that community received less priority than for some other groups. That is inevitable with legislation. There are compromises and not everyone's needs are equally represented.

MM-B: *What does the future hold for us? Now that we have the amendments, I suppose we are in a waiting period. How will they be interpreted? But as you said, that is not the main problem. The problem is getting more lawyers to take cases in this field. So the norms are not the question.*

Other professors, commenting on sex discrimination, are saying that the Civil Rights Act does not really grasp the problem: discrimination can be the result of the old boys' network and fewer opportunities to meet the right clients or get that promotion; that is, exclusion is the result of social practice rather than a visible violation of the law, contested in the courts.[315] *Is that you are saying? That this is a financial, not a normative issue?*

At the end of the day, what can Europeans learn from the application of the ADA? Where should they go from here, considering that Europe has similar norms?

RC: I have not said much on voluntary compliance. There are many employers that go out of their way to hire people with disabilities and accommodate them. I have worked with a fabulous university coordinator on disability issues. I think my employer does fabulous things to accommodate people with disabilities.

MM-B: *In France, some collective bargaining agreements try to incite employers to hire people with disabilities. But there are not many candidates with disabilities applying to qualified positions, because few of them have degrees or technical skills. So it is not just about resistance from employers but also the pool of qualified applicants available. Is it the same situation in the States?*

RC: We do not really have those efforts. We don't proactively employ people. We don't run into that issue.

MM-B: *In the empirical data on people with disabilities, what kind of jobs do they have?*

RC: We know their average wage is very low.

MM-B: *Do they go to college?*

RC: I don't have data on that.

MM-B: *I suppose education is also a factor, if there is an education-training-employment continuum.*

RC: I do think the United States might have done a better job integrating people with disabilities in the workforce because they are getting their high school diploma. Maybe Europe can learn from that in terms of higher education.

Harvard Dean Martha Minow shares her perspective on how accommodation can benefit the entire workforce.

MARTHA MINOW: Accommodation for persons with a disability—done under statute—should be understood as another kind of justifiable accommodation. If a government employer accommodates someone with a disability, then it should as a matter of basic fairness accommodate someone with a religious ground needing a similar accommodation. As a sheer policy matter, disability accommodation offers a very instructive method for reviewing the essential elements of a job and permitting accommodations outside those essential elements. This invites employers to resist assuming the job has always been performed in this way by someone who look a particular way, wears particular clothes, and so forth, and may help open up some jobs to people who have never held them in the past.

In this way, individuals and the whole society can be enriched by an inquiry launched by disability law. It can be very instructive to find out the elements that have been burdensome for people with disabilities and find that similar burdens have existed for women or for members of racial or religious minorities. Here is an example where learning from the disability context can have real benefits for other visible minorities.

MARIE MERCAT-BRUNS: *So do you think we can find a common ground of interests to accommodate for different groups?*

MM: I do think that there is much to learn about unnecessary burdens and exclusions that have treated "differences" as inherent in people who do not fit old traditions. Rules can often serve their central purpose while being redesigned so that they do not fall so heavily on one group as opposed to another. For example, computer software developed to accommodate a person who is visually or hearing impaired can help a lot of other people as well.

From architecture, we learn the concept of universal design of workplaces that takes into account the variety of the people who are there. It turns out the adjustable chairs, ramps, and other accommodations help many kinds of people.

MM-B: *In that respect, you have a more structural view of accommodation, but it is also an individual one. It really depends on the context. Ruth Colker made an observation about the ADA: she said that disability discrimination is largely focused on the individual and that that is often the problem.*

MM: I am not sure I totally agree with Ruth Colker on the disability front, and I would have to know more about the particular statement to be clear about my response. I do note that both in the employment and school contexts, statutes are written without listing the categories of diagnosis and instead look at functions, what an individual can or not do. There is a good reason for this: the approach resists reducing an individual to a label or category and focusing on the work or educational challenge at hand. And the same can be done with regard to religion. An individual may be a Sikh or a Christian Scientist, but a requested workplace can pertain to the individual and the individual conscience.

The strength here is focusing on the individual; it is an individual's right being protected. It is not about group rights. It is not about creating new subclasses that have their own rights. It may seem paradoxical, but even the right to be in a group is protected as the right of the individual to affiliate.

This is the way to maximize individual freedom and reduce government imposition. Compare the individual rights approach to the use of personal law in places such as India and Israel—which assign individuals to a package of family laws based on their or their parents' religion. That personal law approach has been rejected by the United States, Canada, and England.

To look at someone and say because your parents are in a given religious group, then you are governed by the marriage and divorce laws of that group is to deprive the individual of the ability to choose. The individual may say, "I don't want my divorce law governed by Islam even though my parents are Muslim, because I have chosen to marry someone who is a Hindu or to be secular." The individual should have that choice.

A big controversy arose in Canada over whether or not religious dispute-resolution methods should be sanctioned by the government. The controversy unfortunately exposed a lot of Islamophobia because it arose when Muslim groups sought government recognition of Islamic arbitration. The government had permitted arbitration by Jewish groups. Ultimately, the government rejected all faith-based arbitration. That result makes some see if allowing people to create separate dispute-resolution systems means that some individuals would be pushed into a religious system against their own choice and lose access to the courts and the rights protections accorded to each individual under the law. Otherwise, there is a risk that the group could oppress individuals, and gender discrimination could ensue that the State itself would not permit directly.

The Limitations of Disability Discrimination Law

Employment law expert Christine Jolls points out some limitations of disability discrimination law from a law and economics perspective.

CHRISTINE JOLLS: With respect to economics, a critical contribution is analysis of the effects of particular antidiscrimination measures on the wages and employment of affected groups. The theoretical aspiration of any form of antidiscrimination law is (at least in part) to help the protected group, so it is obviously crucial to ascertain whether in fact this happens when the law is put in place. Much of the strongest contemporary research in this area concerns legal limits on discrimination on the basis of sex and disability.

In the case of disability discrimination law, economic analysis suggests that the law may depress the employment prospects of individuals with disabilities because of the financial costs of required disability accommodations coupled with the difficulty of enforcing legal prohibitions on the refusal to hire individuals with disabilities.[316]

At least some empirical economics work supports the prediction about disability discrimination law. The best-known study in this area, by MIT economists Daron Acemoglu and Joshua Angrist, compares wage and employment levels of individuals with and without disabilities before and after the effective date of the Americans with Disabilities Act of 1990. Acemoglu and Angrist find that the wages of individuals with disabilities exhibited no change relative to those of individuals without disabilities, while employment levels fell significantly for individuals with disabilities aged twenty-one to thirty-nine, relative to individuals without disabilities in this same age cohort, and may also have fallen for individuals with disabilities aged forty and above, though the picture is more mixed. As Acemoglu and Angrist recognize, other things relevant to the employment situation of individuals with versus without disabilities may have changed at the same time that the ADA went into effect, and this makes it difficult to be certain that the changes in the relative employment situation of individuals with disabilities resulted from the ADA rather than from these other factors. Acemoglu and Angrist offer several tests to distinguish between the effects of the ADA and the effects of other forces. First, they control for increases in federal disability benefits receipts, since such increases could obviously cause reductions in disabled employment levels if some individuals would no longer work with more generous benefit levels. Second, they examine the change in the relative employment levels of individuals with disabilities at small firms (many of which are not subject to the ADA) relative to medium-sized firms that are both subject to the ADA and likely to have relatively high compliance costs (compared to still larger firms), and they find that the employment declines are greater at the medium-sized firms.[317]

A potentially important effect of the ADA not examined by Acemoglu and Angrist's empirical work is the law's possible encouragement of human capital investments by individuals with disabilities—a feature of the law that might lead to negative employment effects for individuals with disabilities, at least in the near-term, wholly apart from the financial costs of required disability accommodations. If the ADA's protection of individuals with disabilities encourages greater human capital investments, and perhaps also greater particularity about job matches, among this group, then the relative employment level of individuals with disabilities might drop after the ADA's enactment for this reason. Preliminary evidence provides some support for the human capital hypothesis, though further research is required before reaching a more definitive conclusion.[318]

Continued work by antidiscrimination lawyers, together with scholars in psychology, economics, and other fields, will, I hope, produce continued progress in our understanding of the diverse forms of discrimination and of the law's response.

Comparative Perspectives

The scholars discuss the definition of disability and its ties to the reasonable accommodation duty,[319] forcing a reexamination of a series of assumptions about American disability discrimination law and helping to evaluate French norms and better understand disability discrimination.

Colker's narrative dispels a first assumption about the origins of the Americans with Disabilities Act (ADA) and its amendments,[320] exposing the role the

Republicans played in getting the law adopted to fulfill a campaign promise and also prevent more radical provisions from being passed by Democratic opposition.

The second assumption put to the test is the belief that enforcement of the ADA was limited by the judges' narrow interpretation of what constituted a disability. The broad ADA definition covered several situations with respect to an individual: "a physical or mental impairment that substantially limits one or more of the major life activities of such individual; a record of such an impairment; or being regarded as having such an impairment."[321] In the initial case law (reversed by the 2008 amendments), judges refused to apply the ADA to several claims alleging disability discrimination in employment, on the basis that the impairment causing the adverse employment action did not meet the ADA definition of disability. As Minow noted, this was the risk taken by the legislator from the start. As she explained, the ADA definition was innovative in that it focused on functions without listing categories of diagnosis, looking at what people could or could not do and refraining from reducing them to a label or category. There is a risk, however, introduced by the 2008 amendments to the ADA. The fact that the act applies to a wide range of disabilities may generate discrimination among categories of disabilities, with some groups receiving less favorable treatment by employers. Less care may be given to individuals whose disabilities are not visible, on whom the impact of work relationships may be more difficult to predict or detect, versus people with physical disabilities that are more familiar to the public, such as those requiring the use of a wheelchair, for example.[322]

In France, the role of the occupational physician influences the manner in which disabilities are perceived in the workplace,[323] departing from the idea of balancing the interests of integrating disabled people with the associated costs for the business.[324] As Jolls explains, the significant financial burden of reasonable accommodation is perceived differently by companies of varying sizes and, according to some research, could deter them from hiring people with disabilities. Colker observes, nevertheless, that many employers voluntarily hire and accommodate people with disabilities.

The third assumption relates to the 2008 amendments enacted to counter the restrictive interpretation of who is covered by the ADA. The amendments clarified and broadened the definition's three prongs—"a physical or mental impairment that substantially limits one or more major life activities of such individual;[325] a record of such impairment; or being regarded as having such an impairment."[326] The supposition is that the precisions brought by the amendments were crucial and gave the law a new reach; Colker is unconvinced, citing the difficulty for workers with disabilities to find representation due to the low wages they earn on average.

Before exploring this idea further, let's look again at the definition of disability in the United States. Above all, it aims to identify qualified individuals with disabilities.[327] The ADA definition of disability did not supply any precise description of groups of disabilities; the legislator's intent[328] was to give the law a transformative function with respect to the protected category, by reframing certain social norms regarding disabilities.[329] The premise was that a disability is constituted not only "in terms of the internal attributes of the arguably disabled individual" but also "in terms of the external attributes of the attitudinal environment in which that person must function."[330] This can be a person who is limited in his or her life activities but also a person who is perceived to have a disability or who has a record of disability. By referring to a "qualified" person with a disability, the law seeks to redefine how the qualification is perceived. A person is "qualified" not only "in terms of a person's ability to perform the functions of a particular job" but "in terms of her ability to perform the job's essential functions." Therefore, a person who cannot function effectively in the "world-as-it-is" is not unqualified unless he or she would also be unable to function effectively in the "world-as-it-could-be," after reasonable accommodations.[331]

Despite this conception, American courts, in particular the Supreme Court, interpreted the ADA of 1990 restrictively. The first decisions whittled away the scope of the definition, excluding impairments that could be corrected (acute myopia, for example) as well as certain perceived impairments (the third prong of the ADA definition of disability) by choosing to very narrowly interpret the meaning of a "substantial limitation" of major life activities and "activities that are of central importance to most people's daily lives."[332] The 2008 amendments explicitly acknowledged the need to reverse this trend and clarified the meaning of major life activities, providing a very broad definition that includes both general physical and mental activities, such as concentrating and thinking, and more specific bodily functions, such as reproductive functions.[333] The act also revised the provision on perceived disabilities, excluding transitory impairments lasting less than six months. Finally, the act specifies that "an impairment that substantially limits one major life activity need not limit other major life activities" in order to be considered a disability and may consist of "an impairment that is episodic or in remission."[334]

This adjustment to the ADA is interesting from an international perspective. In France, a difference in treatment based on a transitory impairment would be considered as discrimination on the basis of health status (a prohibited ground), rather than disability. This is a useful ground in light of the rather restrictive definition of disability in EU law, which does not recognize a sickness as a disability.[335] Recent CJEU case law, though, adopted a more functional meaning of disability, linked to the long-term effects of obesity at work.[336]

Another interesting aspect for international commentators is the manner in which the ADA invites the EEOC to specify the meaning of an impairment that "substantially limits one or more major life activities,"[337] which often involves highly technical and pragmatic considerations based on the type of occupation. The EEOC was quick to act accordingly and continues to implement the ADA and its amendments with Chai Feldblum's assistance.[338] The role given to the EEOC by the ADA underscores the importance of having an independent, external body to assess, unbiased, what the real work limitations of an impairment are and which limitations are secondary. In France, for example, too many employment decisions probably continue to be based on rigid definitions—medical definitions developed from a social protection perspective and vocational definitions emerging from labor law and assessments from occupational physicians. These are combined with overly vague evaluations regarding potential reassignments for workers with disabilities, who are dependent on the discretionary power of employers and their perception of what constitutes a limitation, without concern for distinguishing essential job functions.[339] U.S. case law on what is considered to be an essential job function,[340] determining whether an employee is qualified, could probably be useful for the enforcement of French and European norms,[341] although the risk of assigning employees with disabilities to lower-skilled positions to keep them in employment should be avoided.[342]

As important as the 2008 amendments may have been, their consequences must be nuanced.[343] As Robert Post explained during our conversation, law is not "a rule." The development of statutes and case law must be thought of as "as a dynamic exchange between Congress and a court which has its own views," and exchange that is constantly "in motion." In Post's words, "You shouldn't imagine it as one thing just controlling. Congress has spoken, but whether the court is listening, whether it is going to resist, I don't know enough about it to say." We cannot predict how norms will be interpreted and applied; interacting with each norm is a set of actions that prevent us from anticipating its consequences. Colker shares this sentiment and does not believe that the amendments will produce a radical change. As she observes, in practice, lawyers are not interested in pursuing these cases, because the low wages generally paid to workers with disabilities mean that the damages won would not cover the legal fees.

This leads us to a fourth illusion, which is that disability discrimination is analogous to any other ground of discrimination. Yes, in addition to the concepts of direct and indirect discrimination (or disparate treatment and disparate impact), we have the very different framework of reasonable accommodation. But the particularity of disability discrimination is that proving an intent to discriminate is not the issue, as Colker points out, unlike with race discrimination, for example. The focus is on the adjustments that should be made to the work or the workplace. If the employer acts in good faith and a compromise is found to accommodate the worker with the disability, then the judge is satisfied. Ford believes that disability discrimination has a distinct nature. Commonalities can probably be found with age discrimination. In some respects, disability can be considered to be a relatively functional ground of discrimination, but, as Colker explains, the types of discrimination and the problems with discrimination encountered by people with disabilities vary widely because there are many different forms of disability. In France, various disability rights groups organized to defend the interests of people with different types of disability. Chai Feldblum did the same when she helped to draft the ADA, reusing the language of the Rehabilitation Act. Clearly, the American public does not view disability and racial discrimination in the same light: their histories are dissimilar, even if at one point, as Ruth Colker revealed, civil rights advocates had joined the fight for disability rights, due to the large number of African American veterans with disabilities. As described by Colker, certain illnesses, such as sickle-cell anemia, can especially affect black people, although they are rare. In the United States, health status is not a ground protected by federal law, so what is at stake for people with disabilities is their right to health care and other benefits, in addition to the fight against discrimination.

What can be learned from these American insights on the nature of disability discrimination? Interest groups lobbying for people with disabilities are relatively well organized in France, for a country that does not traditionally incorporate lobbying into its social policies. The Employment Equality Framework Directive 2000/78 played a fundamental role in prohibiting employment discrimination against people with disabilities in France. However, as explained previously on the subject of reasonable accommodations,[344] it does not appear that France is expanding its notion of disability through extensive use of the concept of reasonable accommodation in employment law. Biases against people with disabilities in France seem to be inherently nourished by the attitude that a disability is an illness, a deficiency, a failure to measure up to the standard represented by the healthy employee, and that weakness must be compensated for.[345] Once a person has been assessed as having this characteristic, then the ADA prohibits discrimination in employment, but without addressing certain psychosocial reasons for the differences of treatment. According to certain European scholars,[346] the European proposal for a new directive on equal treatment moving toward an expansion of the application of Article 19 TFEU (the former Article 13) could embrace a more context-sensitive, relationship-oriented perspective of people with disabilities, inspired by Article 1 of the United Nations Convention on the Rights of Persons with Disabilities of December 13, 2006: "Persons with disabilities include those who have long-term physical, mental, intellectual or sensory impairments which in interaction with various barriers may hinder their full and effective participation in society on an equal basis with others."[347] The CJEU has recently been more demanding in its perception of what constitutes reasonable accommodation, including simple worktime adjustments,[348] and condemned Italy for lack of compliance with EU directives.[349]

Yet another unique dimension of disability discrimination emerges through EU case law and the CJEU's decision in *Coleman*.[350] The court found that discrimination by association had occurred when an employee was dismissed because of her caregiving responsibility toward her disabled child: "Directive 2000/78, and, in particular, Articles 1 and 2(1) and (3) thereof, must be interpreted as meaning that the prohibition of harassment laid down by those provisions is not limited only to people who are themselves disabled. Where it is established that the unwanted conduct amounting to harassment which is suffered by an employee who is not himself disabled is related to the disability of his child, whose care is provided primarily by that employee, such conduct is contrary to the prohibition of harassment laid down by Article 2(3)."[351] This decision underscores how the fight against discrimination can even encompass relationships extending outside of the workplace, such as that between an employee and a dependent, as though protecting victims of ricochet. The court goes so far as to reiterate that "the Community Charter of the Fundamental Social Rights of Workers recognizes the importance of combating every form of discrimination, including the need to take appropriate action for the social and economic integration of elderly and disabled people."

Age Discrimination

Age discrimination was recognized more recently than the other forms of discrimination,[352] but is being pushed to the foreground by global demographic trends. The fight against age discrimination brings into direct confrontation the desire to treat people differently based on age, a principle on which social protection systems are based,[353] and the need to disregard age as a reliable indicator of a worker's ability, in accordance with the principle of nondiscrimination. The normative framework that has emerged from this issue in the United States and in Europe often crystallizes through the judicial scrutiny of exceptions to age discrimination.[354] Furthermore, the dual nature of age as an objective as well as a subjective trait, a potential source of bias, creates some difficulty in identifying victims of discrimination and the causes for this treatment, which vary depending on the age cohort in question. In some cases, perceptions of age are responsible for the termination of an employment contract,[355] while in others a young employee may be disadvantaged by a remuneration system that favors older employees without any legitimate justification. The key is often to look at whether the transitional pay schemes, based often on experience, still perpetuate age discrimination indefinitely.[356] In Europe, all age cohorts are protected by law, unlike in the United States, where the law addresses only people forty years of age or older.[357] Finally, like sex, age is a factor on which statistics are collected, so proving indirect discrimination appears, at least on the surface, to be easier. In France, however, it has been more difficult to prove exactly which age cohorts are the most disproportionately impacted by a facially neutral practice.[358]

Christine Jolls discusses age discrimination and its specific characteristics.

MARIE MERCAT-BRUNS: *Have the groups targeted by discrimination changed over time?*
CHRISTINE JOLLS: Well, certainly the groups targeted by antidiscrimination law have changed; American law now prohibits discrimination on the basis of traits such as age and disability, which were not covered when the Civil Rights Act of 1964 was passed.

Consider age discrimination. Employers' desire not to employ older individuals may differ quite a bit in nature from employers' desire not to employ individuals of a particular race. As the Supreme Court of the United States noted in *Massachusetts Board of Retirement v. Murgia*, "Old age does not define a 'discrete and insular' group . . . in need of 'extraordinary protection from the majoritarian political process.' Instead, it marks a stage that each of us will reach if we live out our normal span." Old age has a temporal and most critically a universal element (almost universal at least) that is lacking in the categories covered by Title VII. Old age is unlikely to be targeted by the same forms of bias and disadvantage that accompany race in America.

Yet for a distinct set of reasons, older workers may be as disadvantaged in the workplace as members of racial minorities. A striking empirical regularity in age discrimination cases is that older workers often suffer termination because they commanded far higher wages than younger workers capable of performing the same job. Higher pay based on age—wholly apart from either productivity or seniority at a particular firm—seems to be a fairly robust empirical fact about the American economy, rooted in economic considerations of bonding and incentives. Many employees may earn well below their value marginal product in their younger years and well above this amount in their later years. Accordingly, age discrimination law may be necessary to prevent opportunistic employer firing when older workers' pay exceeds their value marginal product. Specifically, disparate impact liability, which the Supreme Court of the United States has held applicable to age discrimination claims, imposes some, albeit probably quite weak, limits on the firing of older workers in such circumstances.[359]

MM-B: *In addition to the labor market factors that discourage employment of older individuals, are negative views of older workers' attributes and abilities a factor?*

CJ: There may well be conscious forms of bias against older individuals, notwithstanding the suggestion above that most individuals do not consciously revile older workers in the way that some white Americans consciously reviled black Americans a generation ago. But more important are implicit, or subconscious, forms of bias that have recently been rigorously studied using new advances in social psychology. Unlike conscious bias, such implicit bias cannot be captured simply by asking people direct questions about their views or attitudes.

Chai Feldblum examines how age can be a transformative factor in the workplace.

CHAI FELDBLUM: Age is universal! I do age in my workplace flexibility stuff. My main takeaways from Phyllis Moen[360] are that we have to change how we think, structurally, about school, about work, and about retirement.

Kathleen Christensen[361] from the Sloan Foundation[362] devoted $60 million between 1993 and 2001 on academic research in economics, sociology, psychology, linguistics, and anthropology. The main point is that it's not just about women and kids. The Sloan Foundation created the field of work-family policy in the United States and expanded it under the influence of its former president, Ralph Gomery. A number of CEOs participate in the work of the foundation. They focus on research to make business work well. Policy is about social structural change; that's why Sloan came to me. But they're working with businesses as well, and voluntary change. There is a need to change cultural norms; law is only one component.

Comparative Perspectives

Age is part of a "new generation" of discrimination,[363] as confirmed by Jolls. The main difficulty in enforcing this ground stems from the many paradoxes it produces, especially visible in the case law in Europe, where discrimination is prohibited based on any age, young or old.[364]

The first paradox relates to the universal nature of the age ground, mentioned by Feldblum, and its considerable relativity with respect to aging, of which it is an indicator. The biological aspect creates the illusion that age is an objective fact. "How old are you?" There is only one possible answer, but it can be interpreted in many different ways. This is the soil from which age biases grow, whether they focus on the young or old. Age is assumed to indicate ability or incompetence,[365] experience or immaturity, creativity or an inability to learn—all of these ideas can serve as a basis for discrimination. At the same time, age can be a Bona Fide Occupational Qualification (BFOQ)[366] in the United States,[367] even if this exception is narrowly interpreted in North America and in Europe.[368] Antidiscrimination law sometimes serves to distinguish[369] the true reason behind a difference of treatment based on age:[370] is it the employee's physical abilities, or is it his or her cost to the company as a worker with seniority[371], as Jolls believes? Is it because the employee is not qualified? Is it a desire to scrimp on training for workers in their late career[372] or on their right to a sabbatical?[373] Similar questions can be asked concerning discrimination against younger workers, about whom different assumptions are made regarding a lack of experience, qualifications, loyalty, or work ethic. Judges may take a contextual approach to uncover the "judicial truth" behind dismissal decisions or refusals to provide training. The enshrinement of the general principle of nondiscrimination based on age in European law[374] ensures the legitimacy of scrutinizing such decisions for discrimination, even though age is a pivotal criterion regulating access to social protection.[375]

The second paradox resides in the individual and group aspects of age. Age is a personal trait that describes an individual but also places that individual in an age cohort: a generation, as described by Louis Chauvel.[376] Discrimination can affect an entire generation or cohort in the workplace. In these cases, the indirect discrimination model proves useful, as revealed by French supreme court decisions.[377] However, judges are reluctant to apply indirect discrimination strategies to age, as revealed by the case law in France[378] and even the United States, where disparate impact discrimination against older workers has only a recent history.[379] In *Gross v. FBL Financial Services, Inc.*, the Supreme Court held that the Age Discrimination in Employment Act (ADEA) requires proof that age was the "but-for cause" of an adverse employment action, such that a defendant is not liable if it would have taken the same action for other, nondiscriminatory reasons, imposing a higher standard of proof in age discrimination cases.[380] Moreover, ADEA claims can be subjected to compulsory arbitration.[381] Indirect discrimination has been more easily established on the combined grounds of sex and age in France.[382] In the United States, where antidiscrimination law only protects the upper end of the spectrum—workers aged forty and over[383]—this conflict is not felt, but in Europe, how can the interests of different age cohorts be reconciled? Are they not inherently contradictory? Experience works against both younger and older workers, as shown in the joined CJUE cases *Hennigs* and *Mai* in 2011.[384] Interestingly, European judges seem to be more open to the idea that differences in treatment based on age are unlawful and disproportionate when it is the younger workers who are being discriminated against,[385] leading to yet another paradox about age discrimination.

The third paradox is in the fact that age is an ineffective yet core factor in social policy, creating a façade beneath which to address the more cumbersome challenges of effectively combining labor law with employment and retirement policies.[386] Where age is an issue, often the deeper matter is one of social protection.[387] Symbolically, albeit anecdotally, the two areas targeted by the opposition during the French presidential elections in 2012 provided striking examples of attitudes toward age. They were retirement reform (at age sixty for individuals who began working at an early age) and access to employment for young people (emphasis on education and "generation contracts"[388]), key subjects of political debate in Europe.[389] The employment of older workers is a recurring theme in the European Union,[390] and Feldblum considers it to be a central concern for United States public policy as well.[391]

On both sides of the Atlantic, what is striking is the absence of any in-depth reflection on age discrimination. Age is a public policy tool. In France, it is used as a ready-made answer to settling unemployment or retirement issues (by promoting the employment of young people, for example), overlooking the need to uncover the connection between the individual and group aspects of age.[392] The social consequences of early retirement and job-sharing are too quickly forgotten.[393] The use of a ground of discrimination to further political agendas in France has tinges of the use of race by the Hortefeux immigration law—later declared to be unconstitutional by the French Constitutional Council—permitting ethnic and racial data to be collected in France.[394] Does such an approach serve to displace the real issues raised by age discrimination, namely, how work hardship and professional education and training affect the rhythms of work and well-being in the workplace throughout an employee's life: early, middle, and late career?

Simone de Beauvoir's writings, although somewhat pessimistic, are as relevant as ever:

> That is the crime of our society. Its "old-age policy" is scandalous. But even more scandalous still is the treatment that it inflicts upon the majority of men during their youth and maturity. It prefabricates the maimed and wretched state that is theirs when they are old. It is the fault of society that the decline of old age begins too early, that it is rapid, physically painful and, because they enter in upon it with empty hands, morally atrocious. Some exploited individuals inevitably become "throwouts," "rejects," once their strength has failed them.
>
> That is why all the remedies that have been put forward to lessen the distress of the aged are such a mockery: not one of them can possibly repair the systematic destruction that has been inflicted upon some men throughout their lives. Even if they are treated and taken care of, their health cannot be given back. Even if decent houses are built for them, they cannot be provided with the culture, the interests and the responsibilities that would give their life a meaning. I do not say that it would be entirely pointless to improve their condition here and now; but doing so would provide no solution whatsoever to the real problem of old age. What should a society be, so that in his last years a man might still be a man?[395]

Work has evolved since de Beauvoir's time, but difficult and stressful working conditions have only changed outwardly, becoming more subtle in their physical manifestations over a lifetime of work, intensifying psychosocial risks, for example, while shrinking the proportion of manual production-line labor. Rules placing limits on work hardship[396] and studies on working conditions proliferate,[397] enabling the connection between work hardship and retirement benefits more clearly delineated. But the risk of intergenerational conflicts is only partially addressed by agreements on employment for older workers; in France, old versus young stereotypes on age have only been touched upon.[398] We are seeing the emergence of "age management."[399] The enforcement of rules using age as an essential litmus test of the entitlement to cease work is a legitimate desire.[400] However, the dichotomy created by using age to push people into opposing groups covers up more structural questions about well-being in the workplace and changing workplace practices that do not always consider the impact of active aging[401] on intergenerational relationships[402] and relationships between men and women.[403]

The American approach described by Feldblum feels more structural, since it looks beyond categories and asks questions about shaping a labor market that is better adapted to workers with varying needs, about creating a more flexible workplace, and about changing "how we think, structurally, about school, about work, and about retirement."

Is this focus on employment relationships instead of status feasible in Europe? Can it coexist with the age-oriented categories used in social protection policies? It may be more difficult to achieve, but the indirect discrimination model can be used to reveal, alongside the legitimate age-based distinctions, the potential inconsistencies generated by employment practices based on seniority or experience without any other selection criterion.

VII. RELIGIOUS DISCRIMINATION

In this transatlantic comparison, the fight against religious discrimination in the United States can be comprehended only through the lens of the country's religious history.[404] Without denying the cultural importance of religion in American society, its secular underpinnings[405] are often overlooked, as the scholars interviewed will point out.[406] Today, religious pluralism continues to define the United States, creating challenges in educational and professional environments, in which there is a legal obligation[407] to provide reasonable accommodation.[408] In contrast, in France, the reasonable accommodation principle is simply an option that certain collective agreements or employer associations choose to implement to promote religious diversity.[409] At the European level, the issue of religious accommodations in the workplace is more complex. Although the Employment Equality Directive 2000/78/EC prohibits religious discrimination, it does not require reasonable accommodation, despite the fact that the national law of some EU countries provides for such measures.[410] In both France and Europe, debate on religion and, more specifically, religious discrimination, is raising questions about equal access to certain freedoms, shedding light on the state's approach to these issues in the public and private spheres.[411]

Martha Minow shares her views on religious freedom for all, secularism, and balancing the interests of different religious communities. In the following conversation, she begins by examining how religious freedom is protected differently in the United States and Europe and the origins of these differences.

MARTHA MINOW: It is interesting that the First Amendment in the Bill of
 Rights deals with religious freedom and the protection against the establishment of religion. By having both of those dimensions, there is a fascinating commitment to a private-public divide that is committed to encouraging the flourishing of religion in the private sphere but also a separation of the government from religion that is continuous to the present. This line of separation borders what is public and what is private. But the location of the line is up for grabs more than it has ever been before, including such factors as government outsourcing, activities like the provision of social services, even the operation of jails. And so when there is a contract with a private provider and a private provider is a religious provider, have we now crossed the border into establishment of religion? That's a hot issue.

On the other hand, there is a long-standing tradition in the United States ensuring freedom of religious expression for all, including public figures and including ceremonial government actions, like prayers at the opening of a session of Congress. As we are becoming a more diverse society, such events cannot proceed on the assumption that everyone is Protestant; so prayers opening Congress now rotate Jewish, Muslim, Hindu, Catholic, and other religious texts.

To Europeans, this practice may look like a violation of the commitment to keep religion outside of public life. Yet in the American context, it would be viewed as incursion on religious freedom not to preserve the space for ceremonial prayer. Americans want public spaces and public officials to exhibit religious freedom as long as the message embraces diversity and individual freedom to participate and not to do so.

Yet the privatization of government activities—through outsourcing and other methods—has opened up new questions about when and where either religious freedom or preference for one religion can be exhibited and expressed. When the government contracts out its social services to a religious organization, can that organization require prayer? Fire employees who do not abide by a particular set of religious views? The constant commitments are to preserve the individual freedom of religion and making sure that the government is not endorsing or suppressing one religion, and it's not always easy to ensure both of those commitments.

MARIE MERCAT-BRUNS: *What about certain professions where promoting religious freedom might be a more sensitive issue, such as in social work or fields where professionals work with the young and might serve as role models?*[412]

MM: Schools and social services have been sensitive areas in assessing government treatment of religion in the United States. For better or for worse, our legal system has relied on a public-private divide. So, for example, Kentucky Baptist Services, which is the largest single provider of social services in Kentucky, works under a contract with the State. And an employee who was a lesbian working for that organization was fired because her sexual orientation became known to the public. She objected that this firing violated her freedom and her rights; a reviewing court said: no, it is a private religious organization and it can choose a bona fide occupational requirement is comporting with religious tenets even when the organization provides services under a contract with the state.

Funding private religious schools is a subject attracting huge controversy and much litigation in the United States. After decades of court decisions rejecting many efforts to permit public funding to support aspects of religious education, in 2003 the United States Supreme Court reversed several precedents and permitted the City of Cleveland to offer vouchers, allowing low-income parents to select a private religious school rather than send their child to a public school. Importantly, the court emphasized that the City of Cleveland schools were terribly inadequate and also it was parents, not public officials, who would make the choice—and the choice included a variety of options as well as religious schools because there were choices beside the religious schools.

Now a lot of people looked at that decision, named *Zelman v. Simmons-Harris*,[413] and said, "This is the end of the barrier between religion and government or religion and schools." Actually, matters have not developed that way. In fact, as a political matter, despite the constitutional green light, the voucher movement by all accounts is pretty much dead. Americans as a whole do not want to vote for public monies to support religious schools—and especially suburban parents do want to alter support for the public schools.

In an interesting sequel, the idea of school choice has exploded as a technique of innovation within the public schools. Whether styled as magnet schools drawing students district-wide, or neighborhood schools with specialized features, or charter schools—in which entrepreneurial groups of teachers, parents, and community members create new public schools with special themes—states across the country have witnessed the development of special science and technology schools, schools using computer game technology as a pedagogy while teaching students to design their own programs. There are schools that address needs of students with learning disabilities or autism, and Arabic language, Chinese, and Hebrew language schools. There are concerns that some of these schools are really religious schools, and they are monitored closely; there are concerns that some of these schools produce new kinds of segregation, and that's an ongoing inquiry.

On the other hand, no one doubts it would be helpful to have a departure from the American insularity especially with regard to language and culture. We are coming to realize how good it would be for the next generation to have more people who speak multiple languages. In New York City, the public Arabic-language school enrolled over half the students that come from homes where they do not speak Arabic. That is a real contrast with the two public Arabic-language schools in Minneapolis where 98 percent of the students are Somali immigrants who speak Arabic at home; there, the Arabic-language charter school can offer a bridge for immigrants to English and academic excellence. I cannot say that these developments are free of controversy. In Florida, a Hebrew-language charter school was created and it was run by a rabbi. There was an uproar. The rabbi was moved out, and the textbooks were changed so as to eliminate any reference to religion. When the public Arabic-language school opened in New York City, protestors held banners saying, "Stop the Madrassa,"[414] and the initial principal lost her job for failing to condemn the use of the phrase "intifada NYC."

THE MULTIPLE GROUNDS OF DISCRIMINATION   219

MM-B: *Has there been an increase in cases of anti-Arab discrimination since 9/11? Are people wary of this type of educational initiative because they fear they are training future jihad terrorists? Is this a real issue?*

MM: The issue does arise, but not the way it does in Europe. The use of American schools as a melting pot or salad bowl is such a long-standing tradition. Most immigrant students attend public schools; only a tiny proportion of Muslim immigrants attend private Islamic schools (although there are many new private Islamic schools.) Most of the immigrants go to the public schools; most want to be integrated; and most of them are integrated in school and in society. You take an area like Detroit, Michigan which has a high concentration of Muslim immigrants. They are doing better economically on average than people who are born in the United States and their education levels are as good; they are engaged in business, politics, and identified with America as a place of opportunity; they participate in collaborations with Christians and Jews in projects promoting tolerance and community service.

The narrative of America as a land of immigrants offers a context for Muslim immigrants to feel American. I don't want to say there are no problems. Right after 9/11, there were incidents of discrimination and experiences of name-calling that prompted vigilant responses by government and advocacy groups. Most of the reactions are, in the American tradition, of pluralism and tolerance: in mainstream public institutions, how can they be inclusive and not appear to endorse any religion or preferring any group over others? How do we make sure there is a prayer room available in the public schools? How do we make sure that the dress code is revised to make room for head coverings that are religiously mandated? How can students learn about their differences as resources and features of the great American tapestry?

A fascinating story emerged in Maine. Maine is a state that until recently has not had much diversity of any sort except for French Canadians. Yet over the past few years, a big influx of Muslim immigrants have moved to Maine, especially to several towns like, for example, Lewiston, where groups like Catholic charities have played a large role in helping relocate refugees. Unfortunately, there have been some incidents of conflict in public schools, but the officials and the community have tried to work out the conflicts. One conflict involved the school dress code, which had banned all head coverings. Given the desires of many Muslim families to ensure that their girls could cover their hair, one school revised its code to allow head coverings but continued to ban the use of certain fabric—bandana material—associated with certain gangs. One of the young Muslim girls wore to school one day a head covering made out of bandana material and was really testing the line. I think that what this episode showed was two things: one, this student actually had a lot of solidarity with her non-Muslim classmates and her behavior shows a level of social integration; and, two, American adolescents are American adolescents: they like to push the limits set by adults and test the line, and this refugee in this sense fit right in!

MM-B: *Would you like to add anything?*

MM: Some years ago many intellectuals predicted we were watching the end of religion and the triumph of the secular age. Recent trends just go to show how wrong predictions can be. We are living in a period in which religion is not only strong and vibrant in many communities, but we have also seen that in many instances, there are also more extreme, more fundamentalist versions of religious traditions. I think that many people rightly wonder what has happened to Enlightenment values, the values of tolerance, secularism, individual freedom, resistance to authority. What may have shaken up the apparent triumph of the Enlightenment is economic insecurity; also in some parts of the world, political insecurity produces desires for order and security that authoritarian religious leadership may offer. In communities with economic opportunity and political security, we do not see such a rise of religious authoritarianism even when there are revivals of religious practice. So I think it is very important to put these issues in a larger context.

MM-B: *In North Africa, for example, religious groups help out in the poor neighborhoods.*

MM: Religious groups also help the poor in the Middle East. Yes. How could impoverished people not be affected by the offer of material help?

MM-B: *One last question we haven't touched on is the Jewish religion. This is an issue of particular importance in France because its immigration history is linked to Arab countries, while the traumatic experience of the politics of the Vichy regime casts a shadow over France's past and its relationship to Jews. Jewish people often consider themselves as French foremost and not systematically as members of a religious community, but they recognize the suffering of the Jewish population in the past. I don't think the situation is the same in the United States.*

MM: I don't know enough to comment on the situation in France. I am a Jewish person myself so anti-Semitism is a concern to me personally. But in the United States, Jews are well integrated. We are past the days of overt exclusions, and Jews have access to every profession and line of work. I hope that knowledge of past success in struggles for equality and inclusion can produce support among prior generations of immigrants with new immigrant groups of different religious and nationalities.

MM-B: *Has Obama's arrival also helped?*

MM: President Barack Obama had a remarkable personal experience with multiculturalism and pluralism. I wonder how much living in Hawaii, where there is a multicultural society with enormous religious, racial, and cultural diversity, affected his worldview. Living in Indonesia and having a mother who was very committed to multicultural values influenced him, as he has described.

His family is multiracial: his grandparents being white, his half-sister being South Asian. His own family illustrates the diversity of the human experience. His speeches show commitment to celebrating the humanity in all people and recognizing that we are all part of the same family. His leadership offers much to this country going forward, and I hope, for the world community as well, in terms of this understanding of the human experience.

MM-B: *To find out whether religious integration has been successful (in employment or education), can the census be used to gather statistics on religion?*

MM: Not in the United States. The census does ask about ethnicity and race but not about religion. A public law prevents questions about religious affiliation or ancestry.

MM-B: *Has this been a problem in terms of proving religious discrimination?*

MM: The individual focus of American law provides the basis for proof of discrimination claims. An individual claiming employment discrimination on the basis of religious would say, "My belief is I cannot work on a Saturday because I cannot take transportation," or "I cannot engage in the manufacture of munitions due to a religious belief." It doesn't matter if there is a church or a religious group that agrees or disagrees with that view. The government does not turn to an organized authority or group of experts to validate a view as a religious view; it is about the individual's sincere belief. It has to be a sincere belief; it cannot be something that is manufactured for the moment.

MM-B: *It's a subjective view?*

MM: It is a sincere religious belief. It is the individual, not the group, that is protected under the law.

In the next conversation, Minow turns her focus to reasonable accommodation for religion.

MM-B: *You were talking about religious beliefs and practices, and you have mentioned public schools. In the workplace, is pluralism promoted in the same way? Do you have proactive measures to respect Ramadan in company cafeterias or any other diversity initiatives outside of antidiscrimination? I know there is a legal obligation to accommodate religion in the workplace. To what extent to companies comply voluntarily?*

MM: Proactive measures take the form of human relations training about what to say and what not to say, about when to shake hands and when not to shake hands. Compliance officers and diversity programs in large private companies train employees to understand how to work in a diverse workforce.

MM-B: *This is an issue in France. We now have collective bargaining agreements on diversity containing diversity measures that people don't really know how to apply, while reconciling all the religious beliefs in a meaningful way. That is what you were saying. There are many religions, and the work needs to accommodate them all. I was wondering how this is done in the United States. I know you* don't have a lot of collective bargaining agreements, but I have seen many cases in which unions addressed this issue.

MM: It is true that a shrinking percentage of the American workforce is unionized except in the service sector and government workers. So collective bargaining and the union contracts do not provide the organizing framework for most employers in the United States. We have a federal statute, Title VII of the Civil Rights Act; we also have state and local human rights statutes and ordinances that in some instances are more ambitious in some communities than the federal statute.

The developments at the constitutional level apply only to government employers. When it comes to religious freedom, our courts have changed the reasonable accommodation standard so now the government employer just has to be neutral; there may be no constitutional defect when a general, neutral rule with a legitimate purpose has the incidental effect of burdening an employee's exercise of religion.

MM-B: *Where does that come from? Is that a case?*

MM: Yes, in 1990, the Supreme Court decided a case called *Employment Division v. Smith*, which dealt with refusal of unemployment benefits. The facts of the case involved several Native Americans who were fired from their jobs at drug rehabilitation clinic after they engaged in a ritual practice of smoking a substance, and then they sought unemployment benefits. They were denied the unemployment benefits. They saw this as a failure of religious accommodation, but they lost. The Supreme Court said they were being treated the same under a justifiable neutral rule applied to anyone; the rule says that if you are a drug counselor, you cannot use a prohibited substance, and you don't get an exemption from that simply because you have a religious claim. The crucial element there was that the justifiable rule was across the board. It was neutral. It did not single out the Native Americans. It would apply to anybody.

MM-B: *Was it like a BFOQ[415] because they were drug counselors?*

MM: The question did not come in that form, because they were asking for unemployment benefits. It is true that if it was bona fide occupational qualification, an employee would have to show that he or she was drug free as a qualification for the job of drug counselor, but that was not the question here.

That case has had huge impact in all kinds of government agencies where the issues of accommodating people arise with uniforms, dress codes, and work schedules that may conflict with individuals' free exercise of religion.

Congress enacted a law called the Religious Freedom Restoration Act,[416] directing that government shall not substantially burden a person's exercise of religion even if the burden results from a rule of general applicability exception if two conditions are met—first, the burden must be necessary to further a compelling government interest, and second, the rule must be the method that is least restrictive of individual freedom in which to advance that government interest. But the Supreme Court rejected this statute in part—insofar as it applied to the states—as exceeding the power of Congress; hence, the statute restricts the federal government to protect religious liberty.

The Supreme Court also rejected a religious liberty claim by a member of the armed forces who wanted to wear a yarmulke—a kippah, or skullcap—despite the military regulation banning the head covering. The court deferred to the military regulation; Congress responded by allowing accommodations for neat and conservative religious clothing. Recently however, the U.S. Supreme Court construed the Religious Freedom Restoration Act to apply to protect religious beliefs of owners of a certain kind of closely held corporation and hence to require as a statutory matter some kind of accommodation for an employer whose religious beliefs pose an obstacle to providing employees with insurance coverage for certain kinds of contraception.[417] Stay tuned; this will be an area of ongoing debate, litigation, and decisions.

MM-B: *Can this trend be explained by the current conservative slant of the courts?*
MM: We have seen a turn away from judicial protection for individualized minority accommodations, perhaps because of the cost to the government of carving out exemptions.

In addition, there is theory, gaining academic as well as judicial approval, that religious claims should have no greater claim than those of other individuals, and if you have to accommodate one, you should accommodate another. Let me give you an example: a police department rule may say that officers should have no facial hair. If the department accommodates an individual who claims religious reasons for having a beard, shouldn't it also accommodate an African American man who has a health condition that makes it very painful to shave? If the department can make the exemption for the religious group, then it should be able to make the exemption on the health grounds as a matter of basic fairness. It is more controversial to treat this as a constitutional requirement; indeed, the department might refuse—equally—to accommodate both individuals.

Julie Suk shares a comparative perspective on religious discrimination.

MARIE MERCAT-BRUNS: *Could you talk about how religious discrimination occurs in France compared to religious accommodation in the United States? Could it be said that religious and race discrimination are sometimes confused?*
JULIE SUK: Discrimination against the Maghrebin population in France is very complicated and very different from discrimination against African Americans in the United States. Much of the discrimination against Maghrebins is rooted in Islamophobia, especially since Maghrebins are arguably less visible (in terms of different skin color) than African Americans in the United States.

But discrimination against Maghrebins is not really religious discrimination as such. Very often the Maghrebins who are discriminated against are not even religious, and they are not always making accommodation demands. The discrimination is often based on perceived rather than actual religious difference. That's where it starts to look more like race discrimination.

MM-B: *What do you think of the burqa debate in France?*

JS: I find it astounding that one would contemplate banning the burqa in all public places. That said, I do think the issue is an entirely separate matter from the ban on headscarves in the schools, a policy that I think has reasonable justifications in light of the republican purposes of public schools.

Comparative Perspectives

The distinctive place occupied by religion in France, or Europe, and the United States is so specific to each region, and so dependent on the setting in which religion is practiced, that comparing the protection of religious discrimination in these countries at first appears to be a complex task. However, the template of employment discrimination provides a novel mechanism for articulating a few thoughts about the particular nature of this form of discrimination. A brief review of the legal background and framework is therefore of interest to illustrate how, as Minow has pointed out, governments have promoted the principle of religious neutrality even outside of the context of discrimination. Next, an attempt will be made to define the contours of religion, on which discrimination is implicitly based.[418] Widely divergent strategies to prohibit religious discrimination, mentioned by the scholars interviewed, are implemented in France and the United States.[419] These observations conclude with a more general questioning, from a comparative point of view, of the particular nature of this form of discrimination, based on the insights supplied by American academics: how can employers deal concretely with the tensions surrounding disparities in treatment based on religious practices?

Equal Treatment of Religions and the Role of the State

An examination of the legal norms governing the practice of religion in France and the United States sheds light on the interaction between religion and the state, helping to position the victim in the "private" or the "public" sphere when assessing discrimination.

Unlike the discourse often heard,[420] both France and the United States promoted the idea of a certain secularism and a separation between church and state, guaranteeing freedom of worship. To some extent, their starting point was the same: the United States, through the Establishment Clause of the First Amendment,[421] and France, through the constitutional principle of secularism,[422] promoted a religious neutrality of the state. This translated into a promotion of all religions in an equal manner[423] and, above all, a lack of any hostility toward religion.[424] America's history with religious persecution and the heavy influence of religion on France's past help to explain this historical progression and the stance taken by governments in search of legitimacy.[425]

From this shared foundation,[426] the implementation of statutes prohibiting religious discrimination followed a diverging path, reflecting each country's culture and history and later legislative changes. In a recent series of decisions in France, the Conseil d'État confirmed the idea that the state must support the practice of all religions equally,[427] and the U.S. Supreme Court, as Minow indicates, has at times interpreted the Establishment Clause narrowly. However, in the United States, the initial position taken in the Constitution reflects the nation's attitude of tolerance toward the religious diversity of its citizens. This is the source of the difficulty, because isn't the uniform application of this principle of religious neutrality the key to equality?[428] This premise is the reason why the French law banning face coverings in public,[429] the government guidelines implementing the law,[430] and the related French Constitutional Council decision[431] all use equality rather than secularism as their argument to justify this legislation and its constitutionality:[432] the circular, which echoes the language used in the law and by the Council, states that "face coverings are a violation of the minimum requirements of life in society. They place the people who wear them in a position of exclusion and inferiority that is incompatible with the principles of liberty, equality, and human dignity supported by the French Republic."

The main quandary in the battle against discrimination is to determine whether this normative framework enables the government, as the producer of norms and interpreter of the law, to maintain the same neutrality with respect to every religious denomination.[433] The stance openly adopted in the circular on face coverings supports equality for women and fights exclusion: is there not a paradox in, on the one hand, banning a sartorial item worn mainly by a religious minority, as well as preventing women from covering their faces when in public, while, on the other hand, using this ban in an attempt to liberate women who wear a full body-and-face covering, whether or not they do so voluntarily? Despite, or due to, its strong symbolic value, this law[434] has sparked a reaction in the United States, as echoed by Suk. The sphere in which the religious discrimination is assessed must also be taken into consideration: is it public or private? The boundaries between the two can be difficult to distinguish. The ECtHR has found that the principle of secularism does not always justify the infringement of religious freedom resulting from a ban on wearing religious garments in public.[435] In countries with reasonable accommodation, companies must allow wearing a cross if it allows other visible religious symbols like the hijab and turban.[436]

Is this issue of enforcement simply a question of frame of analysis? In France, the law tends to consider the individual, depending on the context in which the person desires to practice his or her religion. In the United States, as Minow explains, religious communities are clearly recognized, but individuals make their own choices. In this manner, the law in the United States differs from other countries. In Israel or India, for example, Minow has reservations about the application of a family law to individuals, determined by group choices, based on the religion to which the family is affiliated and not on the individual.[437] Here we again encounter the issue of the visibility of groups in the United States, which has already been discussed with regard to racial discrimination. Unlike with race, however, in this case, identified and identifiable religious communities do exist in France.[438] This leads us to the slippery task of tracing the contours of religion as a prohibited ground of discrimination, undefined in the law of either country.

Comparing the Contours of Religion as a Prohibited Ground

First, a rapid detour from antidiscrimination norms[439] is required: at the European level, the ECtHR and CJEU interpret a variety of legislation that also protects the freedom of worship, through the freedom of religion.[440] This freedom is a part of the freedom of conscience principle enshrined in the European Convention on Human Rights[441] and is addressed separately in the EU Charter of Fundamental Rights,[442] which has become legally binding since the Treaty of Lisbon. But the language in European law is silent regarding a precise definition of religion, outside of distinctions between individual and group worship. A few clues can be gleaned from European case law, in the courts' appreciation of the scope of religion. The first is that, although the intent is not to limit religion to the major faiths, the alleged religion must be "identifiable."[443] This is an important point of departure from the more subjective American view of religion, limited only to beliefs that are "meaningful" and "sincere."[444] In France, efforts to formulate what constitutes a sect reflects an attempt to objectively define the concept of religion.[445] Meanwhile, the ECtHR sometimes shows a certain indulgence for well-established religions, such as in the *Lautsi v. Italy* decision of March 18, 2011, which did not see any violation of Article 14 of the European Convention on Human Rights, prohibiting discrimination, in the mandatory display of a religious symbol—a crucifix—in public schools.[446]

Most often, the challenge is not the definition of a religion or a religious belief but to understand how state interference can limit the exercise of this freedom of religion[447] or other freedoms such as the freedom of expression.[448] In fact, the case law reveals a need to distinguish between different manifestations of religion: the first involves beliefs, religious or otherwise, that are felt "in the depths of one's conscience"[449] and seem tied to a person's identity. The European Convention on Human Rights fully protects this intimate aspect of religion: "the freedom to believe as you wish, to adhere to the religion of one's choice, embodied in an organized religious group, and to manifest this choice and this belief in speech and/or action."[450] "A belief is different from a personal motivation (however strong) inasmuch as it must be possible to construe it as the expression of a coherent view of basic issues," that is, the freedoms guaranteed by Article 9 of the Convention. "Beliefs are protected against any form of discrimination."[451] A religious belief is individual[452] even if it can be practiced as a group. Another related issue is the need to prove adherence to a religion to justify an absence from work, which may in turn generate discrimination.[453] Lastly, freedom of conscience also includes the freedom to not have a religion,[454] as in the United States.[455]

The external aspects of the freedom of religion are more problematic, resulting in a more relative freedom. Religious manifestations may be subject to limitations, "to reconcile the interests of the various groups and ensure everyone's beliefs are respected."[456] Accordingly, efforts have been made in each country to balance different interests in protecting the freedom of religion in the workplace, in accordance with laws prohibiting discrimination based on religion. Confronted with the seemingly broader, more subjective U.S. interpretation of religion, some French judges have concluded that religion incorporates two elements: an objective element, the existence of a community, however small, and a subjective element, a shared faith.[457] In U.S. law, *religion* and *religious* are not defined, but courts generally employ the definition used to justify exemptions from military service: "a sincere and meaningful belief occupying in the life of its possessor a place parallel to that filled by the God for those admittedly qualified for the exemption."[458] Because "moral and ethical beliefs can function as a religion" in one's life,[459] the EEOC adds that religious practices "include moral or ethical beliefs as to what is right and wrong which are sincerely held with the strength of traditional religious views."[460] Accordingly, a practice resulting from an employee's anti-abortion sentiment, tied to her religion, came within the scope of this protection.[461] However, in order to be recognized as religious, these beliefs must not be so bizarre as to implicitly disrupt the workplace[462] nor may they convey racist or anti-Semitic ideas.[463]

It therefore appears that the concepts of religion and religious belief have a broader, less institutional meaning in the United States, where religion is more closely associated with the individual practice of religious beliefs. A more functional notion of religion and religious beliefs dominates, stemming from the legal obligation to provide reasonable accommodations. What strategies are used to fight employment discrimination based on religion in the United States, in France, and in Europe, and what are the unique challenges of this form of discrimination?

Differences Between French and American Implementation Standards for Laws Against Religious Discrimination

The enforcement of the prohibition of religious discrimination, in the field of employment in particular, is where the greatest differences between French and American law are found, revealing the complex nature of fighting discrimination based on a choice of belief and, sometimes, behavior. In France, the legal framework protecting against religious discrimination is the same as that for discrimination on any other ground, except where businesses of a religious nature are concerned, for which a derogation from ordinary law is applied. Employers may provide objective, nondiscriminatory reasons to justify disparities in treatment of employees, showing that the differences do not depend on an employee's religious beliefs:[464] consequently, they mobilize an arsenal of defenses based on the definition of the job contained in the work contract, whose performance is required by the employer: objective impact on the company's business if the latter is of a religious nature[465] (or if the employee is proselytizing),[466] special requirements for employees in contact with customers,[467] or the company's image,[468] depending on the employee's position.

In France, however, an additional difficulty arises due to the potential application of two other legal norms to evaluate situations of differential treatment involving religion. Despite the fact that the shifting of the burden of proof in antidiscrimination law offers a promising strategy, case law on potential religious discrimination claims mostly challenge restrictions of individual freedoms in the workplace. But the standard of judicial scrutiny applied to infringements of religious freedom is different from that applied to alleged acts of religious discrimination.

As clearly explained in the deliberations of the HALDE regarding the application of Article 1121-1, pertaining to freedoms, and Article L1132-1, on nondiscrimination, of the French Labor Code, the provision on individual freedoms is more frequently used at this stage to justify the employer's objective and proportionate restrictions to religious freedom, as opposed to the nondiscrimination provision, which addresses only the use of religion as a criteria in making decisions relating to an individual's job.[469] The initial intent of Article L1121-1 of the French Labor Code was to protect the freedoms of employees in the workplace by scrutinizing the restrictions imposed by employers. The HALDE deliberations state that "a restriction may be neither general nor absolute. The situation must be concretely assessed, and the terms of the restriction must be open to negotiation by the parties involved, on a case-by-case basis.[470] The employer has the responsibility of providing justification, with regard to the concrete tasks to be performed by each employee, demonstrating that its decision is proportionate and necessary and founded on objective elements unrelated to any form of discrimination."[471]

For example, in the Baby Loup case regarding the dismissal of a day care center employee who wore an Islamic veil at work, the decision confirmed later by the Cour de Cassation "en banc,"[472] the labor relations court (Conseil des prud'hommes)[473] and the first Court of Appeal[474] focused primarily on whether there was an objective justification[475] of the employee's termination. However, the courts did not allow for any detailed investigation, on an individual level, of whether the wearing of an Islamic headscarf hindered the employee in any practical way from performing her child care job (by impeding interaction with adults and children, causing a reaction of fear in children, hampering movement), aside from considering the principle of religious neutrality upheld by the nonprofit day care center, in a position where the employee works with children. The question of an inference of religious discrimination was raised only by the Cour de Cassation in its first decision addressing the issue of the case, which was later reversed.[476]

One of the arguments raised before the Court of Appeal was the need for employees to promote neutrality—a requirement included in the internal rules—in this sensitive environment, namely, where employees are continually in contact with very young children. Considering that the majority of the parents of the children attending this day care center may have been Muslims, given the general characteristics of the population in that area, the same argument could have been used to support the opposite stance, namely, that allowing the employee to wear the headscarf would contribute to a more welcoming environment. The "objective" justification of the incompatibility between the wearing of the head covering and the job therefore centered on the center's public service mission as a child care provider, rather than the employee's specific job requirements or the local environment of the day care center. The latest Supreme Court decision in 2014 reiterated this same argument of neutrality, which justified a specific restriction of the practice of religion in certain activities like day care.[477] A bill to extend the principle of neutrality to private institutions in charge of minors (day care, youth centers, summer camps, etc.) was put on hold after the National Commission on Human Rights considered that this initiative would create social strife.[478]

Private businesses providing public services may do well to incorporate a religious neutrality requirement into their internal regulations: although not yet a legal obligation, proposed laws also supported an expansion of this obligation.[479] In its assessment of the limitation of freedoms in the Baby Loup case, the Conseil des Prud'hommes applied this type of "soft" norm—the principle of secularism articulated in the day care center's staff rules—to justify the nondiscriminatory character of the ban on the Islamic head covering.[480] At first sight, this is a surprising decision, since the principle of religious neutrality does not generally apply to the private sector,[481] despite the desire of some to see this happen.[482] Upon further reflection, however, it is logical for the defense against an employee claiming a freedom (a religious freedom consisting of the right to wear a religious symbol) to be positioned on a constitutional level, claiming the principle of secularism (Article 1 of the French Constitution of 1958 states that France shall be a "secular" republic).

A traditional, functional judicial assessment of objective elements justifying a difference in treatment in employment, carried out on a case-by-case basis, free of any ideological consideration, was simply not performed. The indirect discrimination model was not considered at all. This strategy would nevertheless have been helpful in identifying seemingly neutral working conditions—working hours on Saturdays, dress codes banning head coverings, and grooming rules prohibiting beards—that disadvantage people who practice religions other than the so-called majority religions, as illustrated in American case law,[483] and shatter the pretense of "religious neutrality" in the workplace.

This tendency, even in the private sphere, to scrutinize the exercise of religious freedoms and the application of the principle of secularism, rather than apply antidiscrimination norms, is so prevalent in the French legal system that some are considering establishing such scrutiny as a legislative norm either in certain businesses or in all private sectors.[484] Without formulating any judgment about this potential development, this shift in case law, and now legislation, reveals a certain reluctance to broach the subject of religious discrimination. This disruptive, subversive form of discrimination has both an individual and a group dimension: it is not tied to a specific trait but reflects the individual's desire for autonomy and recognition of his or her identity. It also raises more important concerns about the need to maintain public order and the relations between the state and religious groups. Protecting the religious freedoms of employees seems to threaten, in the minds of those with a nostalgic attachment to certain traditions, the very foundations of social protection rights and its Christian overtones:

> The emerging logic is not risk-free, because it conveys none of the principles of solidarity on which the rights to social protection were established: neither the all-encompassing solidarity of workers, nor the local solidarity so dear to Christian socialism. If religious imperatives no longer underpinning any societal project are too often given precedence over business needs, will they not also supplant social protection? Will the conscientious objector's point of view prevail over the union's perspectives on the interests of the all workers? In this case, will antidiscrimination law based on religion serve as an argument to protect employment, beyond more traditional employment law? Where would the 'common good' be found?[485]

Does the fight against discrimination in employment ultimately threaten secularism or the religion of the majority, namely, Christianity? Does it not challenge ambiguous relationships between employment law and religion?[486]

Since the Baby Loup decision, the courts have continued to shy away from religious discrimination based on the headscarf. They have either denied that it is religious discrimination, preferring to qualify the act as an unjust dismissal,[487] or have asked the CJEU for a preliminary ruling, when customer preference dictates that religion is a condition of employment.[488]

These questions echo certain introductory comments about the normative context in France, attitudes toward certain religious practices, and the assumption that certain religious practices are tied to a struggle for equality between men and women. What is the situation in the United States, where the concept of religious accommodation exists, in the light of the scholars' commentary?

First, a distinction must be made between the constitutional legal framework, which applies to public-sector workers and citizens subject to certain rules in particular in education and on the other hand, the prohibition of discrimination based on religion in Title VII of the CRA of 1964.

In the first instance, as explained by Dean Minow, the Supreme Court applies the Establishment Clause of the First Amendment to the U.S. Constitution, which implies a freedom to establish a religion while affirming the government's neutrality in promoting religious diversity.[489] Minow specifies that the Supreme Court restrictively interpreted the freedom to exercise religion by not obliging the government to grant reasonable accommodations for all religions.[490] Although the legislature attempted to revise this limitation of the scope of the freedoms imposed by the law,[491] the Supreme Court struck down the initiative, considering that it overstepped Congress's enforcement powers.[492]

The same is not true in the private sector. As seen in Canada[493] and certain European Union countries, employers are not only prohibited from practicing direct or indirect discrimination, they also have the obligation to adjust a job to the employee's religious observances.[494] The religious accommodation requirement, which must be reasonable, has certainly been interpreted more narrowly in case law than the reasonable accommodation requirement for a disability.[495] Nonetheless, the current U.S. legal standards are undeniably more demanding than France's legal provisions. As the Supreme Court recently spelled out in *Equal Employment Opportunity Commission v. Abercrombie & Fitch Stores, Inc.*: "To prevail in a disparate-treatment claim, an applicant need show only that his need for an accommodation was a motivating factor in the employer's decision, not that the employer had knowledge of his need."[496] The difficulty lies in identifying what accommodation is possible and necessary, in terms of working time, dress, and place of work, and does not place an undue burden on the employer or cause excessive hardship for other employees. How can certain forms of employee conduct in accordance with religious beliefs, for example, be accommodated while combating discrimination on the ground of sexual orientation? Feldblum examines this potential dilemma, but concludes that the framework of analysis of these different expectations needing to be reconciled in the workplace is sufficiently flexible to overcome such hurdles.[497] What can be observed in U.S. case law, in addition to a case-by-case approach, is that the analysis of accommodations is very concrete: feasibility is assessed without any ideological discussion of legitimacy. The issue of the protection of individual freedom arises more frequently when other employees protest against the undue hardship of accommodation. Beyond considerations about equality, which are paramount in France, the focus is on "the interpersonal impact of religious practices."[498]

In France, employers are not required to provide religious accommodations and can therefore limit such adaptations, when the employee's religious beliefs are made known upon recruitment, based on the type of work, reactions from third parties, or safety issues. Organizations are in the dark about their room for maneuver: a good-faith approach by employers and employees is essential to any adjustment of working hours or days.[499] Once again, a systematic refusal to accommodate can be assessed in France against the yardstick of proportionality to determine whether the prohibition is excessive.[500] Employers who have not taken steps to promote religious diversity from the start often proceed on a case-by-case basis at this point.[501] What are the specific challenges posed in fighting religious discrimination?

Raising the Veil on Clashes and Contradictions Between Identity and Freedom

"Even in the workplace,[502] where the opposite presumption is made, in the sense that the employee's subordination is the rule, an employee has a certain irreducible autonomy and freedom that cannot be infringed upon by the employer."[503] More than ever, on the ground of religion, discrimination against the employee[504] focuses on the employee as a person, regardless of other characteristics.[505] The growing visibility of an employee's religion reflects a change in paradigm for labor law from the "rights of workers" to the "rights of people at work."[506] Many discriminatory motives correspond to facets of private life, like religious beliefs.[507] Religious beliefs can of course remain within the sphere of the employee's private life, and the prohibition of discrimination forbids employers from seeking out the protected information.[508] In French and American litigation, a shared concern is expressed that evokes similar questions about the invasion of employees' privacy: when do eminently personal choices regarding religious beliefs—often related to identity issues in addition to representing an exercise of individual freedoms[509]—come into conflict with the company's business and its interests, the interests of the other employees, and those of the state? The issue surrounding religion is less about content than practices[510] and their "intrusion in the workplace."[511] In France, there is an implicit agreement to respect the employee's religion as long as it remains confined to the private sphere, as explained by the head advisor at the Cour de Cassation, Philippe Waquet, who promotes "a positive secularism that respects religious beliefs but confines them to the employee's personal life."[512] The line separating personal and work life, drawn by law, has become increasingly blurred, however.[513] How can one achieve a "balancing of the interests"[514] of employees with respect to their personal lives (including religion inside and outside the workplace) with the interests of the company and other employees?

Is the antidiscrimination law model strong enough to embrace the conundrums posed by this type de discrimination, regardless of the strategy applied and with or without reasonable accommodation? How can one not see, in the combat against employment discrimination, an incongruity between the promotion of equality for men and women and the prohibition of religious discrimination that the courts, especially in France, have been unable to clarify through litigation? From this perspective, the benefit of antidiscrimination law—consisting in encouraging employers to be transparent in their justification of differences in treatment—loses its appeal, unless the dogmatic approach taken at times by judges and the government to discrimination is clarified and brought to light.

Are diversity agreements and, more generally, positive action[515] effective in proactively promoting such discussion? How can codes of conduct, codes of ethics, and whistleblowing measures directly or indirectly address this question?[516] Categorization prevents human beings from being reduced to abstract entities and is essential to the development of law. A renter, a consumer, an insurer, an employee, and so on each requires protection that is not provided by the Civil Code,[517] but should this categorization also protect an individual's personal characteristics in one way or another? Should work not be adapted to the person,[518] even outside of the antidiscrimination legal framework?

As Minow points out, the global trend is toward the increasing influence of religion in all spheres of society. If a government wishes to expand norms promoting the principles of secularism, even in the workplace, then antidiscrimination law demands at the very least that these norms truly guarantee neutrality toward all religions. An individual judicial review of infringements of religious beliefs should be available to prevent any arbitrary treatment. Failing this, there is the danger of all discrimination being ultimately based on origin.[519]

VIII. MULTIPLE DISCRIMINATION AND THE INTERSECTIONALITY THEORY

In principle, antidiscrimination law works by identifying a prohibited ground of discrimination: the ground of discrimination then determines the applicable legal sanctions. However, an employer may put forward several reasons to justify a decision, adding legitimate, nondiscriminatory reasons to the discriminatory ground. This situation still qualifies as discrimination. But what happens when the decision is based on more than one discriminatory ground? Age as well as race, sex as well as disability[520] ... the same individual can be affected by myriad potential combinations of protected characteristics.[521] Discrimination resulting from a combination of factors is decidedly distinct from that emerging from each component factor, but is it more serious? Does it require a greater remedy? Is it easier or more difficult to prove? These issues mainly arise when it comes to proving the discrimination. In France, after passing over a female employee of ethnic origin for promotion, an employer rebutted her claim of discrimination by showing that it had promoted both blacks (but who were men) and women (but who were white). It has been observed that cases in civil courts brought by plaintiffs claiming discrimination based on multiple grounds tend to be less successful than those involving a single prohibited ground, fostering a desire for a specific remedy for multiple discrimination claims.[522] Sometimes employers may discriminate against different groups simultaneously.[523]

In establishing a multiple discrimination claim, should the addition or the combination of characteristics be considered? After the fight to achieve formal equality, and then substantive equality, between men and women, this line of thinking inspired a new feminist theory of intersectionality,[524] first introduced by Kimberlé Crenshaw, a law professor and significant contributor to the black feminism movement in the United States.[525] Her idea was to show how for the feminist movement, combating discrimination tended to reflect the concerns of white women of certain social classes, while overlooking those of disadvantaged black women.[526] According to Crenshaw, the single-ground approach of antidiscrimination law fails to recognize the discrimination experienced by people who are at the intersection of several grounds and, according to the American conception of discrimination, at the intersection of several classes of workers protected by the law. Consequently, the law does not reflect the unique characteristics of the factors of exclusion burdening these workers. Crenshaw gives the example of black women, whose experiences are very different from those of white women. Rather uniquely, this theory, which began as a legal discourse, was taken up by social sciences disciplines on the whole: sociology,[527] economics, political science, and so on. Intersectionality theory probably contributes to law on several levels: it facilitates the understanding of the nature of multiple discrimination—namely, discrimination resulting from certain behaviors generated by the specific situation of individuals with more than one characteristic—and it also helps to determine whether this situation has particular consequences in litigation, in terms of success or failure in court. Since the diversification of prohibited grounds in the Amsterdam Treaty,[528] multiple discrimination has been included in European directives and explored in European research such as the GendeRace project.[529] Finally, intersectionality theory casts doubt on the very logic of antidiscrimination law, or at least reframes the issues of this law, by revealing the risks of compartmentalization generated by the existence of grounds of discrimination. It also allows us to probe the very causes of discrimination, beyond the contours of identity and of human behavior as performance, in particular in employment.

Sociologist Devah Pager discusses intersectional grounds (race, gender, and class) and stereotypes.

MARIE MERCAT-BRUNS: *You have studied discrimination based on criminal background and race. Have you thought about working on gender? Do you analyze other mixed motives for hiring? For example, could mixed discriminatory motives involving race and disability be brought to light using your testing method?*

DEVAH PAGER: I haven't focused on gender myself, but I think it's an incredibly important area for study. I'd especially like to see some work examining the interaction between race and gender—I suspect racial stereotypes operate very differently for black men and black women. In terms of mixed motives, I do think the concept of statistical discrimination is very relevant here. Many employers don't have anything against black people per se, but believe that on average blacks are less motivated, less reliable, less subservient, and so on. It's likely that these expectations shape the way they evaluate the more objective information on the resumes. Unfortunately, it's very difficult to disprove these expectations. Even when employers have very positive experiences with black employees, they seem to treat this as an exception, rather than as a chance to reevaluate their assumptions.

MM-B: *So you believe intersectionality has some input to offer? In what way?*

DP: I think intersectionality can mean a lot of different things, depending on the context. In the context of low-wage employment, I believe that black men are likely to be at a distinct disadvantage relative to other groups. Because of stereotypes about aggressiveness and criminality, black men are not viewed as appropriate for the growing number of customer service jobs that dominate the low-wage labor market. Though black women experience many disadvantages that compound the effects of race and gender, in this particular setting, I believe that black men are at the bottom of the hiring queue.

Richard Ford also looks at the role of intersectionality.

MARIE MERCAT-BRUNS: *What do you think about the "sex plus" issues?*[530] *Do you think that it is easier to prove discrimination if you have an older black woman or when you accumulate different traits? Could combining these different traits and statistics be useful, too? In other words, not relying on how these people identify with a specific category to take them into account?*

RICHARD FORD: Yes, this is what I would like to do in the United States, and I expect this could be true in France. You can do pretty well using commonsensical forms of identifications.

Maybe this would not true in France, but in the United States, given our history, it is very easy most of the time to identify someone based on race; you get widespread agreement. Now, a person might say "I don't like it" or "I think it is much more complicated" or I am Tiger Woods and I am "CaublanAsian" [a term he coined to reflect his mixed Caucasian, Asian and Black heritage]. But if Tiger Woods wasn't Tiger Woods and just some average guy, everyone would say, "He is black." That's good enough. Then we don't need to have a lot of questions about how he feels about it because the point is he is just part of a statistical aggregate about which we are gathering information: how large the percentage of blacks is in a particular employment pool? Where are blacks living when the state is drawing electoral districts? Things like that. That is the only information we are interested in.

For sex it is even easier. There is almost universal agreement on what counts to identify a women, what counts to identify a man. Yes, there are marginal cases where people are born with ambiguous genitalia but that is statistically insignificant. Even now in the United States, where there is a growing number of biracial people, I can still say that that is true here. Biracial people and people of ambiguous race are not going to be a problem for gathering data that is useful for the purpose of administering civil rights law. That is all we are trying to do with that data.

I suspect you could do that in France. I suspect there would be widespread agreement on whether a particular person is black. You would not have a lot of people saying, "Well, we are not sure." That is what I am talking about. Maybe it would be harder if you were dealing with: "Is this person North African?" "Is this person Arab"? But I suspect not.

MM-B: *This is an important question in France because the population which historically has been discriminated against is not the black population. Blacks have been subject to discrimination of course. But historically, discrimination has been against the North African and Jewish people in France.*

In France, we are authorized to look only at where the parents are from, the place of residence, and family names. Reports commissioned by the French government (the report by Patrick Weil on nationality and immigration in France and the COMEDD report on the use of statistics, for example) do not suggest amending the law to collect ethnoracial statistics. An attempt to do so, via a new immigration law, failed and was thrown out by the Constitutional Council because it was seen as a way to control immigration rather than fight discrimination. It is not possible to gather the statistics you mention outside of a specific claim in litigation (Article 8 of the data privacy law). But outside of that, there is a public consensus on the notion of origin, which is not the case for race.

RF: But that may not be what is triggering the discrimination, and that is the problem.

MM-B: *Interesting.*

RF: You need to focus on what is triggering the discrimination.

MM-B: *But sometimes the name is what is triggering the discrimination.*

RF: Then that makes sense if the name is what is triggering the discrimination, then you should include the name.

MM-B: *And there is also what they call "délit de faciès," a sort of racial profiling. They have noticed that people coming from the south of France that look like the Arabic people are sometimes suffering from the same discrimination. So it does happen. The problem is physical appearance can't be the criteria because these people are also suffering from it and they are not necessarily from the category.*

RF: Right. It seems to me that those are difficulties but they are surmountable difficulties. If you had savvy statisticians, they could work with that. Sometimes you would actually want to include the people from the south of France who are suffering discrimination in that category.

MM-B: *Like the Americans with Disabilities Act, where people who are "perceived as" disabled as also protected against discrimination.*

RF: If they are suffering the same discrimination, I see no reason to exclude them from the category just because their ancestors happen not to be from that region. What you care about is discrimination.

MM-B: *They are accepting studies by statisticians and researchers, but the material is confidential to protect the identities of the people surveyed. They won't let employers or other agencies gather personal data outside of these surveys, so employers in France don't feel equipped to defend themselves against lawsuits like in the United States. Race is included in European antidiscrimination law, so we have a law, but no one has the tools to identify race discrimination or defend themselves.*

RF: That is a really troubling situation. You have a situation where Brussels is telling you, "You have a law against racial discrimination" and you have the local law in France.

MM-B: Brussels is not saying, "Use certain tools against racial discrimination." They are just saying, "Implement the law."

RF: Implement with or without racial statistics.

MM-B: So we are in a sort of impasse. I wanted to move away from recurring issues about the definition of race. That is the core of the problem in France. What you are telling me is that statistics are just a tool. They don't symbolize anything in particular. You are not trying to identify a category with its culture?[531] You don't necessarily think that these tools perpetuate stigma?

RF: No. I think there is a risk, but this is like almost any policy, which can have some unintended consequences. But on balance, the benefits far outweigh the risk. The risk is doing nothing, and therefore, having no way to combat a lot of discrimination, at least the discrimination where you cannot prove the straightforward direct evidence of discrimination. That is much worse. Because if you do nothing, you are unlikely to make any serious headway on countering bias.

Janet Halley discusses the limitations of intersectionality theory.

MARIE MERCAT-BRUNS: *With regards to intersectionality, I would like to come back to your article in the Halley and MacKinnon book on sexual harassment[532] and on a certain shared attitude about sexuality in the workplace. I often think that when you look at people who belong to several protected categories—I have seen this with age, having written my PhD thesis on aging and the law[533]—it can be an interesting approach to take inspiration from intersectionality theories for a perception of the downsides of having distinct categories, or, on the contrary, to focus on the common ground between different situated groups.*

When I read about your views on eroticism in the workplace and how we should capitalize on it instead of crystallizing certain sex roles through theories of domination, it made me think that these approaches are similar: concerned with the issues and not the people or the categories.

Intersectionality seems more focused on the negative side of distinct categories, whereas the plight of some people should allow us to transcend these categories or understand how they produce new categories drawing from different groups. Do you have anything to add about sexuality as an issue that transcends individuals who want to live and work without being labeled?

JANET HALLEY: The way I understand this question: when I was writing about sexual orientation, one of the things that was most bothersome to me was the fact that we had segmented our political space of the discrimination order into blacks, into Latinos, into gays. We never asked ourselves whether white men ever get discriminated against—and there are places this happens—because we developed these columns of thought: one of the words we should be using. They are like silos in a farm standing separate from the other. That's not how life is. Life isn't like that. You go to work one day and you feel like a woman, and you go to work another day and you never think about the fact you are a woman. There is a black guy there and he's making the highest salary, and there is another black guy who can't get a job. We discriminate against white men with equal employment in the United States. You're interesting if you are a women or a person of color, but if you are white guy, you have to be normal. If you are a white guy, you have to be normal in legal scholarship.

I always thought that real justice that would require getting out of these columns, out of these silos and looking at the whole thing. I don't think intersectionality goes quite far enough: it is about the intersections of the different subordinated groups: what about black women? Latino gays? But I want to get out of those vocabularies all together. I ask myself things like who in a particular workplace is, for instance, not being invited to the training session where you pick up a very useful skill. Do we let the janitor come and get that skill? No, we don't; they are just janitors. That discrimination goes down as completely normal. We don't even look at that. It is a broad distributional question.

MM-B: *It is a class question?*

JH: It is simply off the agenda. It is not only a class question because some male distribution isn't uniform in that way either. So it is about trying to get France to examine the justice of distribution without being controlled by these identity frames. Take them into account, but they are not the be-all and end-all: they don't do all the work for you. So, again and again, my articles end on who we get after identity. Can we go to an after identity phase and ask broader questions about justice?

MM-B: *So you refer to sexuality when the gender category gets in your way? Do you look at people's sexuality and their present life situation? I often feel that the promotion of self-development tools and the search for "diverse sexuality" are a reaction to the heterosexual norm.*

JH: I think that the diverse sexuality piece of this is very, very important. I'm committed to the idea we all have diverse sexuality and some of us have diverse sexuality in the following form: fetishists. There is one thing we like, and we really like that one thing. I am into diverse sexualities but without the moral stance that it has to be diverse. You can be the same. One of the things I got disenchanted with was the gay supremacy that people got into. The idea that being gay was better. It is a bit like the cultural feminist idea that being a woman is better, and I don't think that. I think it is fine to be a man; I think it is fine to be straight. The identity thing ended up as a supremacy thing. That's not my thing at all.

Julie Suk responds to the challenges of intersectionality.

MARIE MERCAT-BRUNS: *What do you think about intersectionality theory? Can we consider subgroups that are subject to discrimination (e.g. older workers with disabilities or minority women)? Can we promote the more positive ideas that we can find common ground or interests among groups to fight against their exclusion from the workforce? Maybe that's diversity?*

JULIE SUK: Intersectionality refers to the notion that a person might be discriminated against on multiple grounds (e.g., race and sex). Your positive formulation is interesting because usually the problem with intersectionality is that a person who is discriminated against on multiple grounds has compounded disadvantage, but sometimes the tools for remedying one form of discrimination may be at odds with remedying another form of discrimination.

And adding to this complication is that, sometimes, multiple strategies for combating discrimination on one ground (e.g., race) may conflict with each other, and we have to choose in individual instances which strategy is more valuable, by reference to the normative underpinnings of equality law. The *Ricci* case[534] is a rich illustration of this conflict.

Martha Minow raises the issue of sex and religious discrimination.

MARIE MERCAT-BRUNS: *Can we come to the question of the burqa, because it is a big debate in France? You have done extensive work on women and the law. This is a very sensitive issue in France, where feminists and others are wondering how to reconcile women's rights and the promotion of religious beliefs. The issue seems to involve a certain image of women.*

MARTHA MINOW: It is very difficult to address this kind of question especially if you hold, as I do, that individual freedom is what matters. So I think the important question concerns how to create a context in which the individual woman could choose what to wear. And yet this question of individual choice may itself be impossible where there are group pressures and even threats.

This is why the issue coming out of Turkey seems to be very, very difficult. Prohibition of the head covering in a Turkish university even when there are women who want to cover is necessary, the Turkish Supreme Court and the European Court of Human Rights decided, to preserve the freedom for women who do not want to cover,[535] because if any are allowed to cover, then all will be subject to harassment or physical jeopardy. Hence, forbidding the headscarf in the Turkish university means something different than it does in another context where the question of the protection of the right to cover is itself an expression of freedom. Context can matter enormously.

In the United States, the issue has come up in the context of driver's licenses. Can an individual get a driver's license without having her photograph taken showing her face? Actually, religious accommodations in the

United States for individuals have apparently increased rather than decreased due to heightened understandings of religious claims. Yet arguments against airport scans have less power in a context of heightened security concerns. As long as individuals are not treated differently in the face of the security concerns, greater intrusion on privacy can be justified.

MM-B: *It comes back to the neutral standpoint.*

MM: Yes, even privacy intrusions are more acceptable when they are across- the-board, not singling out members of one group; and of course, they are more acceptable when there is a compelling interest, an interest for public safety.

But even when justified, privacy intrusions can be done sensitively. For example in airport security, I can understand that someone wearing a burqa might need to be searched. But the individual does not need to be forcibly disrobed in public; it could be done in a private setting. There are ways to accommodate all of these interests and not always at the sacrifice of the religious expression.

MM-B: *Let's come back to the burqa and what it means for women in terms of representation and fostering stereotypes. Is the burqa a form of submission or oppression, given the fact you have to cover your face and hair? Is this the question being asked in the United States?*

MM: I have heard that some people are offended in Europe when a woman walks around covered in public. Some may have that view in the United States, but I think the more likely approach is to acknowledge diversity and recognize freedom of religious requires room for variation. Of course, what may affect one's judgment about this is whether the dominant narrative or understanding of the wearing of the burqa is that the women are oppressed and that they are not choosing to dress that way. Then the question comes: hat must society provide to ensure choice? In this country, we have seen some daughters of assimilated Muslims choose to wear head coverings when they go to college, sometimes to the displeasure of their mothers. It may be a way of fitting into American multiculturalism, or dealing with risks of sexual harassment—and yet other Muslim women resist covering and argue that it is not required religiously, or that they do not want to follow the practice. These issues of girls' and women's dress are prompting difficult debates and even legal disputes in England as well as in France.

MM-B: *In France, schoolgirls who wear a burqa can be excluded, adding more oppression to a potential oppression. They become invisible in the public school system with no opportunity to promote their individual rights. So we also have to look at the effect of some of these norms that try to take into account the individual rights of these women.*

MM: I worry about that by being so stringent in refusing accommodation, the result may actually lead some Islamic families to keep their girls outside mainstream schools, with the result of more confinement, less freedom, and fewer options. Coming back to the example of Ontario again, the same risk could happen: by excluding the Islamic arbitration program from public recognition, the government may leave some women in very religious communities cut off from any access to dispute resolution—if these women cannot pay for a lawyer or gain access to court.

It reminds me of difficulties arising with efforts to ban the practice of *sati*, the practice of having a wife immolated after her husband dies. It was banned and yet apparently still going on in some small towns.[536] Many human rights groups around the world have protested against this. But some nongovernmental organizations working closely on the subject indicate that the ban is only a superficial and at times ineffectual response because it does not address the deeper question. The deeper question is not how this practice can happen, but instead how could it seem to a woman that participating in a practice that takes her own life is a better option than continuing to live? What other opportunities for honor and meaning does the society offer the woman? The ban on sati does not itself create avenues for a woman to have better options in her life, other ways to be honored rather than by killing herself upon her husband's death.

MM-B: *This reminds me of the right-to-die issue and hospice care. Ultimately, it's not about an individual right such as the right to die. It's not about choosing whether to end or prolong life, but about offering a person a better quality of life as he or she nears the end. Also, the relationships that the dying person had with the people around her or him seemed to be important in helping to make the "best" choice.*

MM: I have wondered about that kind of analogy as well. The question of "choice" at the end of life is exceedingly challenging. When our Supreme Court considered the question of physician-assisted suicide, I thought both sides were insufficiently in touch with the deep issues involved. Some people that said physician-assisted suicide was illegal as it devalued life; others people said it should be allowed to enhance self-determination. I was impressed by a third side: we need to make available to individuals sufficient access to pain reduction so that they can imagine a life without pain rather than thinking the only option is to die. The American Medical Association offered evidence that when patients have access to pain reduction, the number of people who want to die goes way down.

MM-B: *In what case was that?*

MM: *Washington v. Glucksberg*, 1997.[537]

Comparative Perspectives

Intersectionality theory points to three important avenues to be explored: understanding what constitutes common ground in analyses of multiple discrimination in its various forms and their influence on the plaintiff's chances of winning a case;

identifying the limitations of the logic of antidiscrimination law, as revealed by the theory; and bringing out certain issues relating to identity, which are often the sources of the discrimination.

Multiple discrimination, meaning discrimination based on more than one discriminatory ground, can be best explained by referring to certain studies in particular an article coauthored by Linda Krieger,[538] which describes the distinctive features of this type of discrimination. In the article, the researchers found that in civil courts, plaintiffs alleging discrimination on the basis of more than one ground are less likely to win their case than those who invoke a single ground,[539] supposing that the victims are even aware of the type of specific disadvantage they suffer from with multiple discrimination. Victims do not know how to enforce their rights in long, complex, and often costly procedures, due to their specific political, economic, and social situations, which are the causes or the consequences of the discrimination.

The victim's situation does not necessarily reflect a multiplication of disadvantages; it may show a new and distinct form of discrimination brought on by the person's specific combination of protected characteristics. Krieger gives the example of an employer who hires black men or white women but not black women, due to stereotypes depicting black women as single mothers in poverty.[540]

The multiplication of grounds can affect litigation outcomes in two ways. The first, which Krieger calls "demographic intersectionality," refers to overlapping demographic characteristics that awaken specific prejudices among employers, jurors, attorneys, and judges.[541] These biased perceptions of the plaintiff and the specific stereotypes associated with him or her may pervade the entire litigation process, making it more difficult to determine the source of the discrimination or its impact on the victim. As shown by Krieger, alleging multiple grounds of discrimination in the concluding arguments is sometimes perceived by judges as an implicit avowal of the weakness of the plaintiff's case if it were based on a single ground.[542]

The second possible effect is what Krieger calls "claim intersectionality." It refers to the added difficulty of proving discrimination when several possible grounds are involved, making litigation strategy more complex. This is a very important issue with respect to the comparability of situations. For intersectional claims, showing a difference in treatment in comparison to advantaged individuals can be problematic. This additional difficulty is reflected in the fact that in the United States, white women win more cases than black men, and black men win more cases than black women.

European case law has also addressed cases of multiple discrimination, even if they were not labelled as such. In the *Kücükdeveci* case,[543] the plaintiff, who was laid off, had been working for her employer for ten years. However, in accordance with the German civil code, in determining her notice period, seven of the years she worked were not taken into account because she was under twenty-five at the time.

The German labor court requested a preliminary ruling from the CJEU regarding age discrimination, but the case also points to a difference of treatment due to the employee's Turkish origin. Entering employment at a young age is characteristic of certain low-skilled, Turkish immigrant communities, especially women, who can encounter difficulties in finding new work or advancing professionally. The case also implicitly shows that in terms of strategy, it was probably better to claim the single ground of age or to claim the ground of age rather than origin, even if more recent European case law indicates some hope for taking a multiple-ground approach. In the *Odar* case,[544] the CJEU considered both age and disability discrimination, although it only found discrimination based on disability.

Intersectionality also comes up in the *Coleman* case,[545] in which the court found that Coleman had suffered discrimination by association as the caregiver for her disabled child. Her employer had approved flexible working arrangements for parents of nondisabled children but rejected Coleman's similar request, arguing that her decision to care for her disabled child, as a single mother, was partly to blame for the disadvantages she experienced at work. So the grounds of both disability and family status were at play in this situation.

European[546] and American[547] research has been devoted to intersectionality, but, according to Dagmar Schiek,[548] multiple grounds do not make it easier to handle the legal issue of proving intersecting grounds of discrimination. It is better to reduce the number of criteria to a minimal number covering the main grounds of race, gender, and disability, she explains, since the other motives are often associated with one of these three "nodes." Age, health, and pregnancy are associated with disability (and gender, too, for pregnancy); sexual orientation and sex in general (whether biological or as a social construct) are encompassed by gender; and origin, nationality, physical appearance, and surname can be grouped with race. This approach would make intersecting grounds more transparent: grouped with the main ground, they would help to reveal and prove the discrimination. In cases like *Kücükdeveci,* where the main source of discrimination was not age—a mere secondary issue next to ethnic origin or gender—redirecting attention to the main discrimination node can be salutary. A European ruling acknowledged the combined disadvantages of age and sex in *Brachner,* a case involving old-age pension entitlements.[549] The court recognized that excluding minimum pensions from a special increase in pensions could constitute indirect discrimination, since women were significantly more likely than men to be the recipients of these minimum pensions.

Other European research focuses on specific grounds.[550] Isabelle Carles's study aimed to assess the reach of race antidiscrimination laws from a gender perspective (Germany, Bulgaria, Spain, France, the United Kingdom, and Sweden). The question was whether women use law in the same way as men when faced with racial discrimination, due to different perceptions of law and diverse experiences of discrimination. An analysis of the complaint files and interviews with victims and lawyers showed that social relationships between sex, class, and ethnic origin influence the perception of racial discrimination and the institutional handling of complaints. Studies show that black women who are subject to discrimination tend to claim race discrimination rather than sex. At the EU level and in national law, there is very little visibility as to the relevance of gender in the treatment of race discrimination claims: a coherent set of statistics on the sex of race discrimination victims is lacking. More efficient institutional monitoring of these specific scenarios of multiple discrimination is needed to address social concerns.[551]

In France, some litigation can be qualified as "intersectional" in the sense that several grounds are possible, such as origin and religion, trade union association and sex,[552] race and physical appearance, and age, health, and disability. However, multiple discrimination grounds, the simultaneous consideration of groups of characteristics, and how they can be reconciled in various employment environments are issues that are more likely to be addressed by diversity provisions and collective bargaining agreements. In France as in the United States, litigation is generally restricted to a single ground, even if a 2012 decision relating to physical appearance and sex uses the combination of these two grounds to refer to a third characteristic: gender.[553]

Another case, in 2011,[554] seems to bring the question of intersectionality to the fore: it is the story of a woman from Cape Verde, illegally residing in France, who was hired by a French couple for childcare and housework. After the couple separated, she continued to be employed by both parents, while lodging in a maid's room in the father's residence. Nine years later, her employment was terminated and she was asked to vacate this accommodation. She contested her illegal employment conditions and unfair dismissal before the labor court (Conseil de prud'hommes). The Cour de Cassation upheld the decision of the Paris Court of Appeal, stating that a comparison of situations with other employees was not required to show evidence of discrimination. The Court of Appeal had acknowledged that the couple had exploited the plaintiff's predicament, resulting in a negation of her legal and contractual rights and putting her at a disadvantage in comparison to domestic workers benefiting from the protection of employment law, and resulting in indirect discrimination on the basis of origin.

This decision is essential for several reasons: first, it reveals the special predicament of a certain number of illegal immigrant women. They suffer multiple disadvantages due to their sex, illegal status, and employment as domestic workers dependent on their employer for both income and housing. The subtle reasoning followed by the Cour de Cassation overcame the obstacles preventing these women from claiming their rights, due to the intersectionality of multiple grounds of discrimination. The first obstacle, comparability of situations, was simply bypassed by the court. The court considered that "a comparison of situations with other employees was not essential to establishing discrimination."[555] This is a main difficulty of intersectionality, as Krieger observed: people suffering from several sources of discrimination are not in a comparable situation with people who have only one protected characteristic (sex, origin, or age). A woman of foreign origin cannot simply compare her situation to other women or other foreigners, but only to other women who are also of foreign origin. In this case, the plaintiff was also an illegal resident and a domestic worker. Another strategy was required to show discrimination. The court stated, as it had in previous rulings,[556] that a lack of comparability does not remove the discrimination or cause it to cease to exist. Comparability is not the sine qua non for finding discrimination; it is one modus operandi the plaintiff can use to "present facts indicating the existence of discrimination ... the existence of a discrimination does not necessarily imply a comparison with other workers." Interestingly, the CJEU drew the same conclusion regarding the lack of comparability and pregnancy discrimination,[557] although EU law emphasizes the need for a comparator, as the CJEU reiterated in the *Römer* decision.[558] The Cour de Cassation seems to be taking the CJEU's pragmatic approach in attempting to ensure the "effectiveness" of EU antidiscrimination law.[559]

In the case of the household employee from Cape Verde, the Cour de Cassation then implicitly circumvented the difficulty of recognizing the special vulnerability of people suffering from different factors of exclusion. It approached the issue from a different perspective, one that does not require comparability from the outset: indirect discrimination based on origin. The plaintiff's illegal status, a seemingly neutral characteristic creating a particular vulnerability, was the cause for the aggravated act of discrimination, qualified by the court as "manifest." In so doing, the court targeted systemic discrimination against illegal residents on the grounds of their origin. This state of nonentitlement increases their risk of discrimination. The court added, "Mr. X and Mrs. Y took advantage of Mrs. Z's undocumented status as a foreigner in France without worker's rights, putting her at complete disadvantage compared with local workers sheltered by employment law." The discrimination is therefore generated not only by unfavorable differences in treatment based on origin but also the employee's lack of recourse to law. The psychological hold generated by this situation is characteristic and can be observed in intersectionality cases outside of the employment sphere.[560]

The court overcame the barrier of the presumed lack of employment rights held by illegal workers, referring to workers who "benefit from employment law" and are not at a "total" disadvantage. In the same way that antidiscrimination law applies to recruitment practices prior to hiring and to hypothetical discrimination with no specific victim,[561] it can be enforced in situations beyond the scope of an employment contract.

Not only does intersectionality theory bring to light the limitations of the logic of antidiscrimination law and its silos of protected groups, it also calls into question our ideas of the identity of the person protected by antidiscrimination law. Intersectionality also paves the way to better understanding of Judith Butler's notion of identity as "performance."[562] Grounds of discrimination can be understood in two ways: rigid, unchanging sources of discrimination to be suffered, as they are traditionally seen, or the consequences of the choices made by individuals with protected characteristics regarding the way that they express those characteristics. For example, what clothing, hairstyles, or accents can be chosen by minorities and tolerated in the workplace? What degree of autonomy does the employee have in asserting or minimizing his or her differences? Intersectionality theory is a way to grasp the close relationship between a conception of identity as performance, ensuring a certain respect of the worker's liberties, and the vulnerability caused by exclusion that antidiscrimination law aims to eliminate.[563]

APPENDIX

The appendix first includes the links to the complete official biographies of the academics interviewed. Moreover, for a deeper understanding of the insights offered by these American scholars on employment antidiscrimination law, it is worthwhile to hear, in their words, how and why some of them became involved in antidiscrimination law.[1]

LINKS TO COMPLETE BIOGRAPHIES
Ruth Colker:
http://moritzlaw.osu.edu/faculty/professor/ruth-colker/
and her blog: http://moritzlaw.osu.edu/sites/colker2/
Frank Dobbin:
http://scholar.harvard.edu/dobbin
Chai Feldblum:
http://www.eeoc.gov/eeoc/feldblum.cfm
Richard Ford:
https://law.stanford.edu/directory/richard-thompson-ford/
Janet Halley:
http://www.law.harvard.edu/faculty/directory/10356/Halley
Christine Jolls:
http://www.law.yale.edu/faculty/CJolls.htm
Linda Krieger:
https://www.law.hawaii.edu/personnel/krieger/linda
Martha Minow:
http://hls.harvard.edu/faculty/directory/10589/Minow
David Oppenheimer:
https://www.law.berkeley.edu/php-programs/faculty/facultyProfile.php?facID=135

248 APPENDIX

Devah Pager:
http://sociology.fas.harvard.edu/people/devah-pager
Robert Post:
http://www.law.yale.edu/faculty/RPost.htm
Vicki Schultz:
http://www.law.yale.edu/faculty/VSchultz.htm
Reva Siegel:
http://www.law.yale.edu/faculty/RSiegel.htm
Susan Sturm:
http://www.law.columbia.edu/fac/Susan_Sturm
Julie Suk:
http://www.cardozo.yu.edu/directory/julie-c-suk

PERSONAL NARRATIVES

Some scholars have chosen to share a personal narrative of their research or involvement in antidiscrimination law.

RUTH COLKER

I started out by working in the Civil Rights Division of the Department of Justice. I taught at Tulane University Law School. I met Martha Kegel[2] and worked as a volunteer mainly in gay rights law pre-*Bowers* time.[3] I received an outstanding service award for having won a class action race discrimination lawsuit against the State of Georgia. I wrote to William Bradford, Assistant Attorney General in charge of civil rights, to donate the prize money to a project for the protection of the right to sexual privacy. I then won a Louisiana Attorney of the Year award for my work defending the rights of people with AIDS, based on the Rehabilitation Act, the law in force before the Americans with Disabilities Act (ADA) of 1990. Scott Burris, an expert in the issue of AIDS and law, opened my eyes to the limits of this old disabilities law. I talked to Chai Feldblum about the limits of the concept of disability and how it should introduce the AIDS question. In 1992 I had my first child, and I joined the faculty at the University of Pittsburgh School of Law teaching a course in disability discrimination following the enactment of the new ADA law in 1992. Chai Feldblum, who had helped to draft the act sent me her materials and I then wrote my own materials and published them. I continued my volunteer work defending people with disabilities and people suffering from AIDS and in the area of abortion rights. In 1997, I joined the faculty at Ohio State and became interested in the primary education for children with disabilities, following the birth of my second child in 1997, who has a disability. I ultimately sued on my own school district successfully so that my child could receive the auxiliary aids he needed to follow classroom instruction. Based on my experience and empirical research on the experience of others, I wrote a book about the limitations of the special education laws.

FRANK DOBBIN

I've taught sociology at Harvard since 2003, and before that taught at Princeton for fifteen years. I did my undergraduate degree in sociology at Oberlin College, and my PhD at Stanford. At Stanford I began to study corporate equal opportunity programs when John Meyer,

Dick Scott, and Ann Swidler asked me to join a project on due process protections in organizations. My graduate student collaborator on that project was Laurie Edelman,[4] and she and I traveled around the San Francisco Bay Area interviewing personnel directors on the origins, and structures, or their due process procedures for workers. Those procedures guaranteed that workers had an internal venue for airing complaints about treatment at work, and we discovered that most of them had been implemented as part of an effort to uncover, and prevent, discrimination on the part of managers that contravened U.S. fair employment laws.

I had grown up in a household where the civil rights, anti-war, and feminist movements were part of daily life. We discussed these movements around the dinner table, and went to demonstrations in Boston (I grew up in a suburb), New York, and Washington. Boston itself underwent a contentious school desegregation program while I was growing up in a nearly all-white suburb, which I watched with great interest at close hand. Having seen the heyday of the civil rights movement as a small child, what really sparked my interest in the effects of the movement was the seeming disappearance of visible political action. By the end of the 1970s, the marches, the protests, and the urban conflagrations that had characterized the 1960s were all but gone. The struggle continued as school districts and workplaces sought to desegregate, but it had nearly vanished from the public political arena.

Throughout my career I've been interested in how the civil rights and feminist movements have been institutionalized: brought into organizations and transformed into bureaucratic procedures and corporate cultures. In 2009 I published a book, *Inventing Equal Opportunity* (Princeton University Press) that charts the history of the civil rights movement within the firm. And with my colleague Alexandra Kalev, and several current graduate students, I continue to study the effects of equal opportunity and diversity programs on the workforce.

RICHARD FORD

I went to law school in the 1980 and early 90s—the height of ideological conflict in law schools and at Harvard in particular. Students and faculty split into camps and I found Critical Legal Studies especially compelling, both because I shared the general left political outlook, because I had studied critical social theory in college, and most of all, because I thought the "crits" were the most honest and realistic about the nature of law and legal decision making. Whereas most approaches to law tried to make it seem as if legal decisions were principled and consistent, CLS frankly admitted that a lot of legal decision-making involved highly contested political questions and the law reflected ideological struggle—just as legislative and policy decisions reflected the political struggles of elected officials. My big influences at Harvard were Duncan Kennedy and Jerry Frug.

My study took two distinct paths: one, I wanted to learn to apply "fancy" continental social theory to legal questions and, two, I was very interested in urban issues: the development of cities as what you might call machines of capital formation and accretion, housing patterns, the sorting of labor, residential segregation, cultural production, etc. These diverged and came together in many ways—sometimes I did policy analysis (I worked on housing policy issues for the city of Cambridge) and other times I worked on jurisprudence. They came together in work on the ideological and material effects of territorial boundaries—a set of ideas I developed in several articles in my early career as a law professor.

I was always interested in issues of race, but unsatisfied with the way they were usually addressed in law. In particular, I disliked the identity politics that was all the rage in the '80s and '90s—with its emphasis on emotion and subjectivity, its ideology of authenticity and narrow focus on individual injuries to dignity and status. But I also didn't trust the typical left alternative: class analysis that sought to describe the racial questions as nothing more than symptoms of class struggle. So I address race issues somewhat orthogonally, by looking at the systemic effects of legal rules on racial segregation in my work on local government, cities and territory. This allowed me to avoid a direct conflict with identity politics while developing a subtle critique of it.

My encounters with Janet Halley—my dear friend and former colleague at Stanford—inspired me to take on identity politics more directly. Janet's work had evolved from ambivalently but centrally feminist and gay rights advocacy to a much more skeptical and critical relation to these identity movements—to the point that she eventually would advocate "taking a break" from feminism.[5] As she was developing these ideas, I was working on a similar critique of identity politics and multiculturalism which eventually became my first scholarly monograph—*Racial Culture: A Critique*. Writing *Racial Culture* was cathartic and let me drop a lot of ideological dogma and break a lot of taboos. Writing the book was an important turning point in my work, because for the first time I put critical analysis first and ideology second. I also decided to write in more accessible and less jargony style and discovered—as George Orwell had argued—that trying to say something in the most straightforward and accessible way possible forces one away from obfuscation and bullshit. As a result a lot of ideological dogma that I had either never examined or avoided challenging out of solidarity had to go. Ultimately I decided it was okay to make arguments that might be called "conservative" if that was where my analysis led me. As a result, I wrote a book that was more ideologically eclectic and contrarian than I had intended.

My next book was written for a popular audience. My goal was to bring the insights of critical legal theory to what I thought had become an impoverished discussion of racial justice in the United States.

The Race Card[6] was the result—another ideologically contrarian book, but again, one I think presses the most important critical insights to the hilt: the premise underlying my entire analysis there is that racial injustice is largely the result of deeply imbedded systemic and structural inequities—not simply a matter a of bigots acting with animus. I've continued to write in this vein, drawing on the CLS critique of rights in two new books soon to be published: *Rights Gone Wrong: How Law Corrupts the Struggle for Equality* and *Universal Rights Down to Earth*—which deals with the international human rights movement.[7]

I am currently working on several projects, one of which is a transnational overview of antidiscrimination law. I'm working with David Oppenheimer from U.C. Berkeley to create an online course on equality law, which will include videotaped interviews from various experts from around the world and taped lectures on antidiscrimination concepts. The course will be taught at Stanford and Berkeley in 2015 and we hope to offer it to other schools worldwide shortly thereafter.

JANET HALLEY

MM-B: *How has queer theory*[8] *inspired your work on law and power? For Europeans, it can be interesting to understand how legal theory can draw from other disciplines, sometimes in a very pragmatic way.*

JH: Let me say a couple of words how I experience the connection between queer theory and legal studies.

I came into legal studies having been trained in literary criticism. I got a PhD in English literature and while I was in literary studies we began to see the rise of queer theory in American thought generally.

Later on I went to law school and eventually decided I would be a legal academic. While I was in law school, long before I thought of becoming a law professor, there was a decision of the Supreme Court called *Bowers v. Hardwick*[9] that held that it was perfectly constitutional and not a violation of anyone's rights for a state to prohibit and to criminalize same-sex sodomy. I was strongly affiliated at that time with the gay rights bar. We were wanting to expand the rights of homosexuals and it was horrible living under *Bowers v. Hardwick*; it was a terrible decision. It was really a low point in the jurisprudence of the Supreme Court and many of us dedicated ourselves to getting it reversed.

The first thing that happened, though, was that lower courts started expanding it. The courts began to say: well, you can prohibit the conduct so you can also not hire people in the workplace who are likely to commit the conduct; the greater deprivation of rights includes the lesser. Now that's a move from conduct to identity and that expansion of *Bowers v. Hardwick*. In a way, the criminalization of sodomy was narrow: who is really going to get punished for committing sodomy? The police are never going to see you doing it, right? But you do need a job and so the courts were making *Bowers* much more expansive.

Where I came in was trying to understand the conduct/identity relationship. What was the relationship of an act to an identity? And as it happens, the French philosopher Michel Foucault gave me the key in his book *The History of Sexuality, Volume I*. Foucault helped me to understand how slippery and contingent the relationship between conduct and identity was.

I came in as a law professor still trying to do gay rights—my stance was, we need rights—but I was also dedicated to doing it using French critical theory. I wrote a whole bunch of articles on *Hardwick*; then Congress passed the "don't ask, don't tell policy" that said that you could be kicked out of the military if you showed a propensity to engage in same-sex conduct and created this whole semiotic system in the military, construing troops' behavior to detect manifestations of a propensity. So I came in analyzing these contraptions through the tools that were given to me by Foucault. The result was my book *Don't: A Reader's Guide to the Military's Antigay Policy*.

The thing that really astonished me was that, as I worked my way into these arguments, the rights claims weren't watertight; you could not find absolute decisive rights claims that everybody had to accept. The rights I thought we needed were not logically built into the law. I continually found a gap, a hole, a place where there needed to be a political move, there needed to be an alliance; there need to be some kind of decision on behalf of the judge or the legislator.

Our Constitution and our rights regime didn't mandate those rights; they just made them possible and that was just a severe surprise to me to see that and that made me understand how contingent legal rights are on politics. I had my loss of faith moment. That's when I turned from being a rights person to becoming a member of the critical legal studies movement which understands law as a contingent social network of practices rather than as a mandatory normative order.

So it was a process for me I had to move through these stages; first critical social and discursive theory was necessary and then the critical theory about law was necessary. I hope that was a clear answer.

DAVID OPPENHEIMER

I can't remember when I didn't want to be a civil rights lawyer. I grew up during the height of the Civil Rights movement, and the most heroic people of that time were ministers and lawyers. I knew I wasn't going to be a minister, so that left lawyer, and while I drifted from the path briefly from time to time, and taught high school before going to law school, I always returned to it.

When I graduated from law school (Harvard) I thought I'd open my own civil rights office in Berkeley or Oakland, California. But good luck kept getting in the way. First I was offered a clerkship with Rose Bird, the Chief Justice of the California Supreme Court (and a very courageous woman). Then I went to work for the California state agency that prosecuted civil rights cases, where I tried lots of cases. Then I was invited to design and direct a discrimination law clinic at Berkeley Law. I've been an academic ever since.

I've been teaching employment discrimination law, and then comparative anti-discrimination law, for over twenty-five years now. For several years I also consulted on anti-discrimination cases, and I still sit on the legal committee of the Northern California ACLU, but as my administrative and scholarly work has increased, I've mostly given up any practice. (Though I've kept up my bar membership in case a really righteous case comes along.)

Most of my writing now is on comparative anti-discrimination law, including the first American casebook in the field, which was published by Foundation in 2012, titled *Comparative Equality and Anti-Discrimination Law*.[10] Working with two U.S. coauthors and five contributing authors from Europe has broadened my vision, and I'd like to think our work on equality has helped many of our students enter the field as advocates and scholars. As to the value of studying comparative equality, I hope it helps us all get a little closer to Gandhi's talisman:

> Whenever you are in doubt, or when the self becomes too much with you, apply the following test. Recall the face of the poorest and the weakest man [woman] whom you may have seen, and ask yourself, if the step you contemplate is going to be of any use to him [her]. Will he [she] gain anything by it? Will it restore him [her] to a control over his [her] own life and destiny? In other words, will it lead to swaraj [freedom] for the hungry and spiritually starving millions? Then you will find your doubts and your self melt away.

DEVAH PAGER

I was born and raised on the island of Hawaii, a multiethnic community that boasts the title as the only American state which, in terms of its racial and ethnic composition, is a "majority minority." Hawaii has the highest rate of intermarriage in the United States, and, likewise, there is a tremendous amount of interpersonal mingling among subgroups. It was not until I arrived in Los Angeles for college that I witnessed the tremendous social and spatial segregation characteristic of most American cities. While UCLA was nestled in the western hills, close to the homes of glamorous movie stars, just twenty minutes south and east were areas of concentrated poverty where Latino and African American communities were concentrated. The four years I spent in Los Angeles provided an education far beyond the classroom; it was here that my interest in racial inequality and discrimination first began.

In 1995, I was awarded a Rotary Ambassadorial Scholarship to pursue a master's degree in Sociology at the University of Cape Town in South Africa. During this year, I conducted research on post-apartheid education reform in a black township outside of Cape Town. The eighteen months I spent in South Africa during this critical period of transition (one year after the end of apartheid) provided an opportunity to witness the upheaval of deeply racialized institutions of social and political power. This formative experience abroad gave me new perspective on the issues facing American society, challenging me to consider both the unique and the universal in struggles of racial conflict.

In graduate school at the University of Wisconsin–Madison, I returned to a focus on racial inequality in the United States. But this time a new institution came to my attention. The incarceration rate in the United States had been growing steadily since the early 1970s, with its effects disproportionately felt by African American men. Nearly one in three young black men will spend time in prison by their early thirties. I wanted to understand the implications of this significant institutional intervention. In particular, I wanted to understand how the experience of incarceration affected subsequent employment opportunities, and how race interacted with criminal background in shaping employment trajectories. To study this question, I adopted an experimental approach to study hiring discrimination on the basis of race and criminal record. I hired young men to pose as job seekers and sent them all over the city—with matched resumes reflecting identical levels of education and work experience—to apply for real, low-wage jobs. The results were staggering. Those with criminal records were only half as likely to receive a callback or job offer relative to those with clean records. But even more surprising, a black candidate with a clean record fared no better than a white applicant who reported just having been released from prison. In the minds of these employers, being black seemed equivalent to having a felony conviction.

After completing my dissertation, I was awarded a Fulbright grant to spend the year in Paris. There I conducted research on the French criminal justice system, examining how the concentration of immigrants and their descendants in certain areas shaped the severity of punishment. France is a highly centralized country and it is often assumed that state-level bureaucracies like the criminal justice system function similarly irrespective of geography. By contrast, I found that the severity of punishment—rates of pretrial detention, convictions, and length of sentences—varied significantly across local areas, even after controlling for crime rates. The strongest predictor of this variation was the percentage of North African immigrants. This ecological analysis did not allow me to directly test mechanisms, and can only be considered suggestive of an underlying causal relationship. The difficulties of studying race in France leave one to wonder whether the absence of racial statistics reduces racial inequality or simply makes it harder to document.

At the end of that year I returned to the United States, teaching at Northwestern for two years and Princeton for nine years before moving to Harvard. During that time I resumed my experimental work on hiring discrimination in New York City. Once again, despite the larger and more cosmopolitan context, we see similar rates of discrimination. The experimental method has been helpful in communicating the ongoing problems of discrimination because it produces clear and easy to interpret results. I continue to use these methods, in addition to seeking out complementary strategies for studying discrimination and its longer term consequences both for job seekers and employers.

REVA SIEGEL

Professor Reva Siegel is Nicholas deB. Katzenbach Professor at Yale University. Professor Siegel's writing draws on legal history to explore questions of law and inequality and to analyze how courts interact with representative government and popular movements in interpreting the constitution. Professor Siegel is a member of the American Academy of Arts and Sciences and an honorary fellow of the American Society for Legal History, and serves on the board of the American Constitution Society and on the General Council of the International Society of Public Law. In our interview, Siegel described the focus of her work.

RS: One distinguishing feature of my work on inequality law is that I bring legal historical background to the problem. I look at the way in which law deals with inequality dynamically, that is to say, in history over time. I am very much interested in processes of contestation, modification, and adaptation of regimes of status inequality. This is the framework in which I did much of my early work on the dynamic I call "preservation through transformation."

In that body of work, I sought to understand how persisting forms of group status inequality persist long after the society prohibits discrimination on the basis of race or sex. That was my own historical situation when I came into the legal academy: the society had prohibited race and sex discrimination and yet pervasive forms of social stratification along lines of race and sex persisted. I was fascinated by the coexistence of those two social facts. I became interested in looking at the development of inequality law in the past as a way of thinking about the logic of equality law in the present. I looked in the nineteenth century at how the abolition of slavery was followed by a Jim Crow regime of racial apartheid: a legal order that prohibited slavery and yet sanctioned new social arrangements that preserved the secondary position of African Americans in the United States.[11]

I also considered how the nation eliminated many of the old marital status rules for women and ended the disenfranchisement of women, and how women's social exclusion from politics and employment persisted through other social practices, often with the assistance of law.

Through this process of reflection on the past, I began to explore how status conflict over equality law can modernize the ways a society legitimates continuing forms of inequality.

The claim is not that nothing changes. The claim is not that all is equally bad, but rather only and more modestly that it is possible for much to change and fundamental forms of social stratification to persist in new forms. Looking to the past, we can see that law guaranteeing equality can play a role in rationalizing persisting inequality. The question is, what is the relationship? How might this dynamic persist in the present? It is a critical inquiry that forces us to ask whether laws guaranteeing equality break with the past, or whether the enforcement of equality laws might preserve, and legitimate in new forms, parts of the past we claim to repudiate.

In the past, I have looked at that question as a way to explore the law of domestic violence, the law of harassment, and the law of marital property. And throughout my career questions of this kind have shaped the way I look at the evolution of equal protection doctrine concerning race in the United States.[12] Recently, I have carried these concerns with preservation through transformation into a recently published article that analyzes demands for religious liberty exemptions from laws governing women's health (in the areas of abortion, contraception, and assisted reproduction) and from laws guaranteeing equality to LGBT persons (in marriage and employment).[13]

JULIE SUK

Julie C. Suk is a Professor of Law at the Benjamin N. Cardozo School of Law–Yeshiva University in New York City, where she teaches comparative law, employment law, and civil procedure. She has been a visiting professor at the Harvard Law School, the University of Chicago Law School, and UCLA School of Law, and held research fellowships at Princeton University and the European University Institute. In our interview, Suk described her professional path.

JS: I arrived at law school in 2000 with two experiences that shaped my interest in comparative antidiscrimination law. First, I had begun doctoral work at Oxford in 1997 in political theory, focusing on normative debates about the cultural rights of minority groups. I had arrived as an American in the United Kingdom shortly after the racist murder of a young black teenager, Stephen Lawrence. The suspects were acquitted, after which the Home Secretary launched a public inquiry that eventually concluded that the police had been "institutionally racist." The Stephen Lawrence Report, as it was known, included 70 reform recommendations to address institutional racism, not only in the police, but also in a wide range of public institutions. Although there were many analogues to the Stephen Lawrence case in the United States, the British state's response of opening up a national conversation about the subtle forms of discrimination known as "institutional racism" seemed novel. Years later, I returned to the U.S.-U.K. comparison on race relations in my article, "Antidiscrimination Law in the Administrative State" (*University of Illinois Law Review*).[14]

Second, I had studied English, American, and French literature as an undergraduate in the 1990s, having traveled to Paris to learn about the Négritude movement of the 1930s and its parallels to the Harlem Renaissance in the United States. I was struck by the different historical trajectories of the concept of race-blindness[15] in the two societies, as well as the emerging public consciousness in France of the problem of racial discrimination throughout the 1990s. After I became a law professor, I wrote several articles comparing French and American approaches to race discrimination: "Equal by Comparison: Unsettling Assumptions of Antidiscrimination Law" (*American Journal of Comparative Law*, 2007), "Discrimination at Will: Job Security Protections and Equal Employment Opportunity in Conflict" (*Stanford Law Review*, 2007),[16] and "Procedural Path Dependence: Discrimination and the Civil-Criminal Divide" (*Washington University Law Review*, 2008).[17]

I came to the study of U.S. antidiscrimination law with the critical theoretical perspectives generated by comparison. On the one hand, the United States is often seen as the global pioneer of antidiscrimination law; it was only after 2000 that many European countries passed laws against discrimination due to EU directives adopted in that year, and created administrative agencies to enforce antidiscrimination law. At the same time, these countries had other legal mechanisms for promoting equality, which have had mixed effects on minorities and women. My scholarship has focused on race and gender inequality and the solutions offered by law and public policy in different national context. Differences, however small, in constitutional tradition, institutional design, class structure, the history of religious and ethnic conflict, and social movements, can shape how law and public policy can protect or promote equality, and sometimes undermine it. At Yale Law School, I learned constitutional antidiscrimination law from Reva Siegel and Kenji Yoshino, the American civil justice system from Judith Resnik, and comparative law from Jim Whitman. These experiences put me on the path of trying to highlight the parts of a legal regime that may seem natural to its inhabitants, but turn out not to be universal, and in fact uniquely good or bad, when considered in global perspective.

This method deepened my appreciation for the wide range of institutional, political, and social factors that contribute to, and undermine, the pursuit of equality. In this vein, my research is now focusing on the interaction between laws prohibiting sex discrimination, on the one hand, and social welfare policies that protect the rights of mothers in the workplace, on the other hand, as manifested in my article, "Are Gender Stereotypes Bad for Women?" (*Columbia Law Review*, 2010).[18] My more recent work examines the puzzle of gender and race quotas in several constitutional orders in Europe and Latin America.[19] U.S. antidiscrimination law regards quotas as discrimination; but several other constitutional democracies are reconciling quotas with antidiscrimination law, and embracing them as necessary to legitimize democratic equality. The purpose of my work is to show how the success and failures of antidiscrimination law depend on background conditions that vary across legal cultures, such as the role of the state in providing social welfare, regulating businesses, prohibiting offensive speech, and promoting shared ideas of the good life. Viewing American equality in comparison with European approaches, particularly those arising from strong republican state traditions like the French, can develop a new language for critiquing the current impasse in U.S. antidiscrimination law, without fully embracing European conceptions of equality.

NOTES

PREFACE

1. Some comparative law specialists have already followed this track and interviewed experts in the field. *See, e.g.,* Pierre Legrand, *Questions à Rodolfo Sacco,* 47 REV. INT'L DR. COMP. 943 (1995).
2. JEAN-CLAUDE COMBESSIE, LA MÉTHODE EN SOCIOLOGIE 13, 45 (2007).
3. BILL MOYERS, HEALING AND THE MIND (1995).
4. Susan P. Sturm, *The Architecture of Inclusion: Advancing Workplace Equity in Higher Education,* 29 HARV. J.L. & GENDER 247 (2006).
5. MARTHA MINOW, MAKING ALL THE DIFFERENCE: INCLUSION, EXCLUSION, AND AMERICAN LAW (1991).
6. Robert Post, *Prejudicial Appearances: The Logic of American Antidiscrimination Law,* 88 CAL. L. REV. 1 (2000).
7. Jack M. Balkin & Reva B. Siegel, *Principles, Practices, and Social Movements,* 154 U. PA. L. REV. 927 (2006).
8. David Benjamin Oppenheimer, *Negligent Discrimination,* 141 U. PA. L. REV. 899 (1992).
9. Christine Jolls & Cass R. Sunstein, The Law of *Implicit Bias,* 94 CAL. L. REV. 969 (2006).
10. Linda Hamilton Krieger, *The Content of Our Categories: A Cognitive Bias Approach to Discrimination and Equal Employment Opportunity,* 47 Stan. L. Rev. 1161 (1995).
11. RICHARD T. FORD, RACIAL CULTURE: A CRITIQUE (2005)
12. JANET HALLEY, SPLIT DECISIONS: HOW AND WHY TO TAKE A BREAK FROM FEMINISM (2008).
13. Julie Suk, *Are Gender Stereotypes Bad for Women? Rethinking Antidiscrimination Law and Work-Family Conflict,* 110 COLUM. L. REV. 4 (2010).
14. Vicki Schultz, *Reconceptualizing Sexual Harassment,* 107 YALE L.J. 1683 (1998).
15. RUTH COLKER, The Disability PENDULUM: The First Decade of the Americans With Disabilities Act (2005).

16. Frank Dobbin, Inventing Equal Opportunity (2009).

17. Devah Pager, Bruce Western, and Bart Bonikoswki, *Discrimination in a Low-Wage Labor Market: A Field Experiment*, 74 Am. Sociol. Rev. 777–99 (2009).

18. *See* Ruth Colker's blog, http://moritzlaw.osu.edu/sites/colker2/. Her published work includes Disabled Education: A Critical Analysis of the Individuals with Disabilities Education Act (2013); The Law of Disability Discrimination Handbook: Statutes and Regulatory Guidance (7th ed., 2011); Special Education Advocacy (with Julie Waterstone) (2011); Federal Disability Law in a Nutshell (4th ed., 2010); The Law of Disability Discrimination (7th ed., 2009); When Is Separate Inherently Unequal?: A Disability Perspective (2008); Everyday Law for Individuals with Disabilities (with Adam Milani) (2005); The Disability Pendulum: The First Decade of the Americans with Disabilities Act (2005); American Law in the Age of Hypercapitalism: The Worker, The Family, and the State (1998); Hybrid: Bisexuals, Multiracials, and Other Misfits Under American Law (1996). *Hybrid Revisited*, 100 Geo. L.J. 1069 (2012); *The Learning Disability Mess*, 20 Am. U. J. Gender, Soc. Pol'y & L. 81 (2011) (symposium); *Speculation about Judicial Outcomes Under 2008 ADA Amendments: Cause for Concern*, 4 Utah L. Rev. 1029 (2010) (symposium); *Reflections on Race: The Limits of Formal Equality*, 69 Ohio St. L.J. 1089 (2008); *Extra Time as an Accommodation*, 69 U. Pitt. L. Rev. 413 (2008); *The Mythic 43 Million Americans with Disabilities*, 49 Wm. & Mary L. Rev. 1 (2007); *Anti-Subordination Above All: A Disability Perspective*, 82 Notre Dame L. Rev. 1415 (2007); *Absentee Voting by People with Disabilities: Promoting Access and Integrity* (with Daniel P. Tokaji), 38 McGeorge L. Rev. 1015 (2007); *Justice Sandra Day O'Connor's Friends*, 68 Ohio St. L.J. 517 (2007); *Marriage Mimicry: The Law of Domestic Violence*, 47 Wm. & Mary L. Rev. 1841 (2006); *The Disability Integration Presumption: Thirty Years Later*, 154 U. Pa. L. Rev. 789 (2006); *Homophobia, HIV Hysteria, and the Americans with Disabilities Act*, 8 J. Gender Race & Just. 33 (2004); *The ADA's Journey Through Congress*, 39 Wake Forest L. Rev. 1 (2004); *Empirical Studies: How Do Discrimination Cases Fare in Court? Proceedings of the 2003 Annual Meeting of the Association of American Law Schools, Section on Employment Discrimination*, 7 Employee Rts. & Emp. Pol'y J. 533 (2003).

19. Frank Dobbin's published work includes *Resisting the Iron Cage: The Varied Effects of Bureaucratic Personnel Reforms on Diversity* (with Daniel Schrage & Alexandra Kalev), Am. Sociol. Rev. (forthcoming); *Why Firms Need Diversity Managers and Task Forces* (with Alexandra Kalev), *in* How Global Migration Changes the Workforce Diversity Equation 170–98 (Massimo Pilati et al. eds., 2014); *Institutions and the Economy* (with Carl Gershensen), *in* Emerging Trends in the Behavioral and Social Sciences (forthcoming); *Finance and Institutional Investors* (with Jiwook Jung), *in* The Oxford Handbook of the Sociology of Finance 52–74 (Karin Knorr Cetina & Alex Preda eds., 2012); *Review of Nancy Plankey-Videla, We Are in This Dance Together: Gender, Power, and Globalization at a Mexican Garment Firm*, 59 Admin. Sci. Q. 182–83 (2014); *Review of Virginia Doellgast, Disintegrating Democracy at Work: Labor Unions and the Future of Good Jobs in the Service Economy*, 58 Admin. Sci. Q. 152–54 (2013); *The Origins and Effects of Corporate Diversity Programs* (with Alexandra Kalev), *in* The Oxford Handbook of Diversity and Work 253–81 (Quinetta Roberson ed., 2012); *A Sociology of Institutions: Review of Cathie Jo Martin and Duane Swank: The Political Construction of Business Interests*, Reviews & Critical Comment. (Dec. 10, 2012), available at SSRN: http://ssrn.com/abstract=2278499; *Progressive Corporations at Work: The Case of Diversity Programs* (with Soohan Kim & Alexandra Kalev), 36 N.Y.U. Rev. L. & Soc. Change 171–213 (2012); *Review of J. C. Sharman, The Money Laundry: Regulating Criminal Finance in the Global Economy*, 118 Am. J. Sociology 850–52 (2012); Frank Dobbin, *Industrial Policy* (with Soohan Kim), *in* Palgrave Encyclopedia of Strategic Management (David J. Teece & Mie Augier eds., 2012); *Review of*

Greta Krippner, *Capitalizing on Crisis: The Political Origins of the Rise of Finance*, 23 TRA-JECTORIES 2–4 (2012).

20. Richard Thompson Ford's published work includes *Bias in the Air: Rethinking Employment Discrimination Law*, 66 STAN. L. REV. 1381 (2014); *The Double Secret Danger in the Supreme Court's Affirmative Action Ruling*, SLATE (June 27, 2013); UNIVERSAL RIGHTS DOWN TO EARTH (2011); RIGHTS GONE WRONG: HOW LAW CORRUPTS THE STRUGGLE FOR EQUALITY (2011); THE RACE CARD: HOW BLUFFING ABOUT BIAS MAKES RACE RELATIONS WORSE (2008); RACIAL CULTURE: A CRITIQUE (2005); *Law's Territory (A History of Jurisdiction)*, 97 MICH. L. REV. 843–930 (1999); *The Boundaries of Race: Political Geography in Legal Analysis*, 107 HARV. L. REV. 1841–1921 (1994).

21. Other published work by Janet Halley includes *After Gender: Tools for Progressives in a Shift from Sexual Domination to the Economic Family*, 31 PACE L. REV. 881 (2011); *Le genre critique: Comment (ne pas) genrer le droit?* (Vincent Forray trans.), JURISPRUDENCE: REV. CRITIQUE 109 (2011); *Vergewaltigung in Berlin: Neue Überlegungen zur Kriminalisierung von Vergewaltigung im Kreigsvölkerrecht*, KRITISCHE JUSTIZ (German translation of *Rape in Berlin: Reconsidering the Criminalisation of Rape in the International Law of Armed Conflict*); *Behind the Law of Marriage, Part I: From Status/Contract to the Marriage System*, 6 UNBOUND: J. LEGAL LEFT 1 (2010); *Does Law Have an Outside?* 7 OSGOODE HALL L. SCH. COMP. RES. L. & POL. ECON. RES. PAPER SERIES (2010).; *Tribute to Eve Kosofsky Sedgwick* (Janet Halley ed., with an introduction by Janet Halley, *A Tribute from Legal Studies to Eve Kosofsky Sedgwick: Introduction*) 33 HARV. J.L. & GENDER 309 (2010); *Note sulla Costruzione del Sistema delle Relazioni di Coppia: Un Saggio di Realismo Guiridico*, 27 REVISTA CRITICA DEL DIRITTO PRIVATO 515 (2009); *Rape at Rome: Feminist Interventions in the Criminalization of Sex-Related Violence in Positive International Criminal Law*, 30 MICH. J. INT'L L. 1 (2008); *Rape in Berlin: Reconsidering the Criminalisation of Rape in the International Law of Armed Conflict*, 9 MELBOURNE J. INT'L L. 78 (2008); *My Isaac Royall Legacy*, 24 HARV. BLACKLETTER L.J. 117 (2008). WORDS: FROM THE HLS CREATIVE WRITER'S GROUP, SPRING 2006 (Janet Halley & Rose Moss eds., 2006); SPLIT DECISIONS: HOW AND WHY TO TAKE A BREAK FROM FEMINISM (2006), excerpted in FEMINIST JURISPRUDENCE: CASES AND MATERIALS (Cynthia Grant Bowman, Laura A. Rosenbury, Deborah Tuerkheimer, & Kimberley A. Yuracko, eds., 2010); *From the International to the Local in Feminist Legal Responses to Rape, Prostitution/Sex Work, and Sex Trafficking: Four Studies in Contemporary Governance Feminism* (with Prabha Kotiswaran, Hila Shamir & Chantal Thomas), 29 HARV. J.L. & GENDER 335 (2006); *The Politics of Injury: A Review of Robin West's Caring for Justice*, HARVARD UNBOUND (Spring 2005); *Of Time and the Pedagogy of Critical Legal Studies*, in DUNCAN KENNEDY, LEGAL EDUCATION AND THE REPRODUCTION OF HIERARCHY (2004).

22. Christine Jolls's published work includes *Behavioral Economics Analysis of Employment Law*, in BEHAVIORAL ECONOMICS AND PUBLIC POLICY (2011); *The New Market for Federal Judicial Law Clerks* (with Christopher Avery, Richard A. Posner & Alvin E. Roth), 74 U. CHI. L. REV. 447 (2007); *Employment Law*, in HANDBOOK OF LAW AND ECONOMICS (A. Mitchell Polinsky & Steven Shavell eds., 2007); *The Law of Implicit Bias* (with Cass R. Sunstein), 94 CAL. L. REV. 969 (2006); *Antidiscrimination Law's Effects on Implicit Bias*, in NYU SELECTED ESSAYS ON LABOR AND EMPLOYMENT LAW, VOL. 3, BEHAVIORAL ANALYSES OF WORKPLACE DISCRIMINATION 69 (Mitu Gulati & Michael J. Yelnosky eds., 2007); *Law and the Labor Market*, 2 ANN. REV. L. & SOC. SCI. 359 (2006).

23. Linda Krieger's main publications on employment discrimination law include *Multiple Disadvantages: An Empirical Test of Intersectionality Theory in EEO Litigation*, 45 L. & SOC'Y REV. 991 (2011); *The Watched Variable Improves: On Eliminating Sex Discrimination in Employment*, in SEX DISCRIMINATION IN EMPLOYMENT (Faye J. Crosby et al. eds., 2007); *Implicit Bias: Scientific Foundations* (with Anthony G. Greenwald), 94 CAL. L. REV. 945

(2006); *Socio-Legal Backlash, in* BACKLASH AGAINST THE ADA: REINTERPRETING DISABILITY RIGHTS (Linda Hamilton Krieger ed., 2003); *The Content of Our Categories: A Cognitive Bias Approach to Discrimination and Equal Employment Opportunity,* 47 STAN. L. REV. 1161 (1995), *Civil Rights Perestroika: Equal Employment Opportunity After Affirmative Action,* 86 CAL. L. REV. 1251 (1998); *Behavioral Realism in Employment Discrimination Law: Implicit Bias and Disparate Treatment* (with Susan T. Fiske), 94 CAL. L. REV. 659 (2006). She recently coauthored a book with Paul Brest, PROBLEM SOLVING AND DECISION MAKING: A GUIDE FOR LAWYERS AND POLICY MAKERS (2010).

24. Martha Minow's published work includes IN BROWN'S WAKE: LEGACIES OF AMERICA'S EDUCATIONAL LANDMARK (2010); PARTNERS, NOT RIVALS: PRIVATIZATION AND THE PUBLIC GOOD (2002); *Outsourcing Power: Privatizing Military Efforts and the Risks to Accountability, Professionalism, and Democracy, in* GOVERNMENT BY CONTRACT: OUTSOURCING AND AMERICAN DEMOCRACY 110 (with Jody Freeman eds., 2009); BETWEEN VENGEANCE AND FORGIVENESS: FACING HISTORY AFTER GENOCIDE AND MASS VIOLENCE (1998); NOT ONLY FOR MYSELF: IDENTITY POLITICS AND LAW (1997); MAKING ALL THE DIFFERENCE: INCLUSION, EXCLUSION, AND AMERICAN LAW (1990). She has also edited or coedited the following publications: GOVERNMENT BY CONTRACT: OUTSOURCING AND AMERICAN DEMOCRACY (with Jody Freeman eds., 2009); JUST SCHOOLS: PURSUING EQUALITY IN SOCIETIES OF DIFFERENCE (with Richard A. Shweder & Hazel Markus eds., 2008); IMAGINE CO-EXISTENCE: RESTORING HUMANITY AFTER ETHNIC CONFLICT (with Antonia Chayes eds., 2003). She has also coedited casebooks for law students, including CIVIL PROCEDURE: DOCTRINE, PRACTICE AND CONTEXT (4th ed. 2012) and WOMEN AND THE LAW (4th ed. 2007).

25. David Oppenheimer's published work includes articles in French law reviews: *L'alerte éthique, Etats-Unis,* 3 REV. DR. TRAVAIL 184 (2009); *The Legality of Promoting Inclusiveness: May the University of California Use Race or Ethnicity as Factors in Applicant Outreach?,* 27 CHICANO-LATINO L. REV. 11 (2008); *Why France Needs to Collect Racial Data on Racial Identity . . . In a French Way,* 31 HASTINGS INT'L & COMP. L. REV. 735 (2008); *La rupture conventionnelle* (with Pascal Lokiec et al.), 9 REV. DR. TRAVAIL 550 (2008); *La période d'essai (1re partie)* (with Pascal Lokiec et al.), 4 REV. DR. TRAVAIL 257 (2008); *Mise en oeuvre du droit du travail et cultures nationales* (with Sophie Robin-Olivier et al.), 2 REV. DR. TRAVAIL 124 (2007), *Prise d'acte et rupture du contrat de travail à l'initiative du salarié* (with Pascal Lokiec et al.), 3 REV. DR. TRAVAIL 196 (2006); *Le discours sur la flexibilité, le droit du travail et l'emploi* (with Pascal Lokiec & Sophie Robin-Olivier), 1 REV. DR. TRAVAIL 48 (2006); *Evaluating the U.S. Policy of Using Private Lawsuits to Remedy Employment Discrimination,* 49 DROIT & CULTURES 109 (2005); *Verdicts Matter: An Empirical Study of California Employment Discrimination and Wrongful Discharge Jury Verdicts Reveals Low Success Rates for Women and Minorities,* 37 U.C. DAVIS L. REV. 511 (2003); *McDonnell Douglas Corp. v. Green Revisited: Why Non-Violent Civil Disobedience Should Be Protected From Employer Retaliation by Title VII,* 34 COLUM. HUM. RTS. L. REV. 635 (2003); *Rethinking Equality in the Global Society, Washington University Law* (with Dorsey D. Ellis et al., transcribed conference proceedings), 75 WASH. U. L.Q. 1561 (1997); *From Little Acorns Great Oaks Grow: Neil Gotanda's Contribution to the Law Permitting General & Punitive Damages in Employment Discrimination Cases,* 4 ASIAN AM. L.J. 63 (1997); *Trina Grillo—A Personal Remembrance,* 31 U.S.F. L. REV. 965 (1997); *Inclusiveness, Interrelatedness, and the Affirmative Action Debate in California—Introduction to the GGU School of Law Symposium on Race Relations in America,* 27 GOLDEN GATE U. L. REV. 287 (1997); *Employer Liability for Sexual Harassment by Supervisors: A Comparison of Federal (Title VII) and California (FEHA) Law* (with Mark Vickness), 10 CAL. LAB. & EMP. L.Q. 3 (1997); *Understanding Affirmative Action,* 23 HASTINGS CONST. L.Q. 921 (1996); *Workplace Harassment and the First Amendment: A Reply to*

Professor Volokh, 17 BERKELEY J. EMP. & LAB. L. 321 (1996); *Exacerbating the Exasperating: Title VII Liability of Employers for Sexual Harassment Committed by Their Supervisors*, 81 CORNELL L. REV. 66 (1995); *Negligent Discrimination*, 141 U. PA. L. REV. 899 (1993); *Distinguishing Five Models of Affirmative Action*, 4 BERKELEY WOMEN'S L.J. 42 (1989); *Employment Discrimination and Wrongful Discharge: Does the California Fair Employment and Housing Act Displace Common Law Remedies?* (with Margaret M. Baumgartner), 23 U.S.F. L. REV. 145 (1988); *Boalt Hall's Employment Discrimination Clinic: A Model for Law School/Government Cooperation in Integrating Substance and Practice*, 7 INDUS. REL. L.J. 245 (1985); *Employment Discrimination: Rightful Place Seniority under Title VII and Section 1981, The Teamsters Roadblock May Be Only a Detour*, 1 HAMLINE L. REV. 15 (1979); COMPARATIVE EQUALITY AND ANTI-DISCRIMINATION LAW: CASES, CODES, CONSTITUTIONS, AND COMMENTARY (with SHEILA FOSTER & SORA HAN) (2012).

26. Devah Pager's other published work includes *Race, Self-Selection, and the Job Search Process* (with David Pedulla), 120 AM. J. SOC. 1005 (2015); *Estimating Risk: Stereotype Amplification and the Perceived Risk of Criminal Victimization* (with Lincoln Quillian), 73 SOC. PSYCHOL. Q. 79 (2010); *Discrimination in a Low Wage Labor Market: A Field Experiment* (with Bruce Western & Bart Bonikowski), 74 AM. SOC. REV. 777 (2009); *Sequencing Disadvantage: Barriers to Employment Facing Young Black and White Men with Criminal Records* (with Bruce Western & Naomi Sugie), 623 ANNALS AM. ACAD. POL. & SOC. SCI. 195 (2009); *Bayesian Bigot? Statistical Discrimination, Stereotypes, and Employer Decision-Making* (with Diana Karafin), 621 ANNALS AM. ACAD. POL. & SOC. SCI. 70 (2009); *The Republican Ideal? Ethnic Minorities and the Criminal Justice System in Contemporary France*, 10 PUNISHMENT & SOC. 375 (2008). Her working papers include *Prison As a Social Context: Inmate Trajectories and Their Facility Environments over Time* (with Michelle Phelps) (2012).

27. Robert Post's articles and chapters include *Theorizing Disagreement: Reconceiving the Relationship Between Law and Politics*, 98 CAL. L. REV. 1319 (2010); *Constructing the European Polity: ERTA and the Open Skies Judgments*, in THE PAST AND FUTURE OF EU LAW: THE CLASSICS OF EU LAW REVISITED ON THE 50TH ANNIVERSARY OF THE ROME TREATY (Miguel Poiares Maduro & Loïc Azuolai eds., 2010); *A Progressive Perspective on Freedom of Speech* and *Democratic Constitutionalism* (with Reva B. Siegel), in THE CONSTITUTION IN 2020 (Jack M. Balkin & Reva B. Siegel eds., 2009); *Roe Rage: Democratic Constitutionalism and Backlash* (with Reva B. Siegel), HARV. C.R.-C.L. L. REV. (2007); *Federalism, Positive Law, and the Emergence of the American Administrative State: Prohibition in the Taft Court Era*, WM. & MARY L. REV. (2006); *Foreword: Fashioning the Legal Constitution: Culture, Courts, and Law*, HARV. L. REV. (2003); and *Subsidized Speech*, YALE L.J. (1996).

28. Vicki Schultz's published work includes *The Need for a Reduced Workweek in the United States*, in PRECARIOUS WORK, WOMEN, AND THE NEW ECONOMY: THE CHALLENGE TO LEGAL NORMS (Judith Fudge & Rosemary Owen eds., 2006); *The Sanitized Workplace*, 112 YALE L.J. 2063 (2003); *Life's Work*, 100 COLUM. L. REV. 1881 (2000); and *Reconceptualizing Sexual Harassment*, 107 YALE L.J. 1683 (1998).

29. Reva Siegel's published work on constitutional law and inequality includes Chapters 7–9 of PROCESSES OF CONSTITUTIONAL DECISION-MAKING (with Paul Brest et al. eds., 6th ed., 2014). Her articles include *The Supreme Court, 2012 Term—Foreword: Equality Divided*, 127 Harv. L. Rev. 1 (2013); *From Colorblindness to Antibalkanization: An Emerging Ground of Decision in Race Equality Cases*, 120 YALE L.J. 1278 (2011); and *Remembering How to Do Equality* (with Jack M. Balkin), in THE CONSTITUTION IN 2020 (with Jack M. Balkin eds., 2009). Her writing on reproductive rights includes *Dignity and the Duty to Protect Unborn Life*, in UNDERSTANDING HUMAN DIGNITY (Christopher McCrudden ed., 2014); *The Constitutionalization of Abortion*, in THE OXFORD HANDBOOK OF COMPARATIVE CONSTITUTIONAL LAW 1057 (Michel Rosenfeld & András Sajó eds., 2012); *Dignity and Sexuality:*

Claims on Dignity in Transnational Debates Over Abortion and Same-Sex Marriage, 10 INT'L. J. CONST. L. 335 (2012); BEFORE ROE V. WADE: VOICES THAT SHAPED THE ABORTION DEBATE BEFORE THE SUPREME COURT'S RULING (with LINDA GREENHOUSE, 2nd ed., 2012); *Before (and After) Roe v. Wade: New Questions About Backlash* (with Linda Greenhouse), 120 YALE L.J. 2028 (2011); *Roe's Roots: The Women's Rights Claims That Engendered Roe*, 90 B.U. L. REV. 1875 (2010); *Struck by Stereotype: Ruth Bader Ginsburg on Pregnancy Discrimination as Sex Discrimination* (with Neil S. Siegel) 59 DUKE L.J. 771 (2010); *Pregnancy and Sex-Role Stereotyping, From "Struck" to "Carhart"* (with Neil Siegel), 70 OHIO ST. L.J. 1095 (2009). Her more recent work on antidiscrimination law includes *Conscience Wars: Complicity-Based Conscience Claims in Religion and Politics* (with Douglas NeJaime), 124 YALE L.J. 2516 (2015). For earlier work, see *A Short History of Sexual Harassment*, in DIRECTIONS IN SEXUAL HARASSMENT LAW 1 (Catharine A. MacKinnon & Reva B. Siegel eds., 2004).

30. Susan Sturm's published work includes *Full Participation: Building the Architecture for Diversity and Public Engagement in Higher Education* (with Tim Eatman, John Saltmarsh, & Adam Bush), COLUM. L. SCH. CTR. FOR INSTITUTIONAL & SOC. CHANGE (2011); *Building Pathways of Possibility from Criminal Justice to College* (with Kate Skolnick & Tina Wu), COLUM. L. SCH. CTR. FOR INSTITUTIONAL & SOC. CHANGE (2010); *Scaling Up* (with Lourdes Hernández-Cordero, Kathleen Klink, & Allan J. Formicola), *in* MOBILIZING THE COMMUNITY FOR BETTER HEALTH: WHAT THE REST OF AMERICA CAN LEARN FROM NORTHERN MANHATTAN (Allan Formicola & Lourdes Hernández-Cordero eds., 2010); *Linking Mobilization to Institutional Power: The Faculty-Led Diversity Initiative at Columbia* (with Emma Freudenberger, Jean E. Howard, & Eddie Jauregui), *in* RECONSTRUCTING THE ACADEMY: FACULTY TAKE THE LEAD (Winnifred Brown-Glaude ed., 2008); *Negotiating Workplace Equality*, 2 INT'L ASS'N FOR CONFLICT MGMT. 92–106 (2009); *Conflict Resolution and Systemic Change* (with Howard Gadlin), 2007 J. DISP. RESOL. (2007); *The Architecture of Inclusion: Advancing Workplace Equity in Higher Education*, 29 HARV. J.L. & GENDER 249 (2006); *Law's Role in Addressing Complex Discrimination*, *in* HANDBOOK OF EMPLOYMENT DISCRIMINATION RESEARCH (Laura Beth Nielsen & Robert Nelson eds., 2005); *Equality and the Forms of Justice*, 58 U. MIAMI L. REV. (2003–2004); *Lawyers and the Practice of Workplace Equity*, 2002 WISC. L. REV. 277 (2002); *Second Generation Employment Discrimination: A Structural Approach*, 101 COLUM. L. REV. 458 (2001); and WHO'S QUALIFIED? (with Lani Guinier, 2001). *The Architecture of Inclusion* was the focus of a symposium issue of HARV. J.L. & GENDER (June 2007).

31. Julie Suk's published work includes *Criminal and Civil Approaches to Antidiscrimination Enforcement in Europe*, 14 EUR. ANTI-DISCRIMINATION L. REV. 11 (2012); *Gender Parity and State Legitimacy: From Public Office to Corporate Boards*, 10 INT'L J. CONST. L. (I*CON) 449 (2012); *Are Gender Stereotypes Bad for Women? Rethinking Antidiscrimination Law and Work-Family Conflict*, 110 COLUM. L. REV. 1 (2010); and *Discrimination at Will: Job Security Protections and Equal Employment Opportunity in Conflict*, 60 STAN. L. REV. 73 (2007).

INTRODUCTION

1. See interviews of Devah Pager in this book and her study on discrimination in hiring candidates with criminal records; for example, Devah Pager, *The Mark of a Criminal Record*, 108 AM. J. SOCIOLOGY 937 (2003); *see* Olatunde Johnson, *Leveraging Discrimination*, in A NATION OF WIDENING OPPORTUNITIES? THE CIVIL RIGHTS ACT AT 50 (Samuel Bagenstos & Ellen Katz eds., forthcoming 2015); Tristin K. Green, *Targeting Workplace Context: Title VII as a Tool for Institutional Reform*, 72 FORDHAM L. REV. 659 705–06 (2003); Tristin K. Green, *Discrimination in Workplace Dynamics: Toward a Structural Account of Disparate Treatment Theory*, 38 HARV. C.R.-C.L. L. REV. 91 (2003).

2. Christine Jolls (Yale Law School), Reva Siegel (Yale Law School), Susan Sturm (Columbia Law School), Dean Martha Minow (Harvard Law School), Dean Robert Post (Yale Law School), Linda Krieger (University of Hawaii Law School), Ruth Colker (Ohio State University, Moritz School of Law), Julie Suk (Benjamin Cardozo Law School), Vicki Schultz (Yale Law School), Chai Feldblum (Equal Employment Opportunity Commission), Richard Ford (Stanford Law School), David Oppenheimer (Berkeley Law School), Devah Pager (Harvard Law School), Frank Dobbins (Harvard Law School), Janet Halley (Harvard Law School).

3. Citing *Grutter v. Bollinger*, 539 U.S. 306, 327 (2003), Justice Ginsburg starts her dissent in *Ricci v. DeStefano*, 557 U.S. 557 (2009), with this observation.

4. 570 U.S. ___ (2013).

5. 131 S. Ct. 2541 (2011): sex discrimination case in which the Supreme Court decided the plaintiffs did not have enough issues of law and fact in common to constitute a class: "the existence of a class of persons who have suffered the same injury must be bridged by significant proof that an employer operated under a general policy of discrimination. Such proof is absent here." See Pauline T. Kim, *Addressing Systemic Discrimination: Public Enforcement and the Role of the EEOC*, 95 B.U. L. REV. 2015, 1133. Marie Mercat-Bruns, *Comparaison entre les discriminations fondées sur l'appartenance syndicale, l'âge et le sexe, révélatrice de la discrimination systémique*, 11 REV. DR. TRAVAIL 92 (2015).

6. Burwell v. Hobby Lobby, 573 U.S. ___ (2014).

7. Ian F. Haney-Lopez, *Intentional Blindness*, 87 N.Y.U. L. REV. 1779 (2012).

8. George Yancy & Judith Butler, *What's Wrong With "All Lives Matter"?* N.Y. TIMES: OPINIONATOR, http://opinionator.blogs.nytimes.com/2015/01/12/whats-wrong-with-all-lives-matter.

9. Shelby County v. Holder, 570 U.S. ___ (2013), on voting rights.

10. Ann C. McGinley, *Title VII at Fifty Years: A Symposium*, 14 NEV. L.J. 661 (2014).

11. Theresa M. Beiner, *The Trouble with Torgerson: The Latest Effort to Summarily Adjudicate Employment Discrimination Cases*, 14 NEV. L.J. 673 (2014).

12. *See* CHRISTINE DELPHY, SEPARATE AND DOMINATE: FEMINISM AND RACISM AFTER THE WAR ON TERROR (2015). *See also* Cass. soc., April 9, 2015, No. 13–19855: the Cour de Cassation is asking the Court of Justice of the European Union (CJEU) for preliminary ruling on the question whether banning the veil of an engineer can be an essential and determining requirement for the job because of customer preference.

13. See interviews of Devah Pager in this book.

14. John Fitzgerald Gates, *Microaggression: The New Workplace Bigotry*, HUFFINGTON POST BUSINESS: THE BLOG, http://www.huffingtonpost.com/john-fitzgerald-gates-phd/microaggression-the-new-w_b_5544663.html.

15. *See* John McWhorter, *"Microaggression" Is the New Racism on Campus*, TIME: OPINION, http://time.com/32618/microaggression-is-the-new-racism-on-campus/.

16. See interviews of Susan Sturm in this book. Marie Mercat-Bruns, *L'identification de la discrimination systémique*, 11 REV. DROIT TRAV. 672 (2015) & Marie Mercat-Bruns, Emmanuelle Boussard-Verrecchia, *Appartenance syndicale, sexe, âge et inégalités : vers une reconnaissance de la discrimination systémique ?* 11 REV. DROIT TRAVAIL 660 (2015).

17. See the development of human rights bodies replacing equality bodies in the combat against discrimination in the Netherlands and France, for example.

18. See interviews of Janet Halley and Richard Ford.

19. Samuel R. Bagenstos, *"Rational Discrimination," Accommodation, and the Politics of (Disability) Civil Rights*, 89 VA. L. REV. 825, 837–70 (2003); Samuel Bagenstos, *Employment Law and Social Equality*, 112 MICH. L. REV. 225 (2013).

20. *See generally* JOHN J. DONAHUE III, FOUNDATIONS OF EMPLOYMENT DISCRIMINATION LAW (2002).

21. See interviews of Linda Krieger in this book.

22. See interviews of Christine Jolls in this book.

23. See interviews of Reva Siegel in this book.

24. Marie Mercat-Bruns, *Les discriminations multiples et l'identité au travail au croisement des questions d'égalité et de libertés*, 1 REV. DR. TRAVAIL 28 (2015).

25. *See* AILEEN MCCOLGAN, DISCRIMINATION, EQUALITY AND THE LAW (2014); DAVID OPPENHEIMER ET AL., COMPARATIVE EQUALITY AND ANTI-DISCRIMINATION LAW: CASES, CODES, CONSTITUTIONS AND COMMENTARY (2012); Richard Ford in collaboration with David Oppenheimer, Comparative Antidiscrimination Law (Stanford Law School online course forthcoming in 2015); S. Jagwanth, *Affirmative Action in a Transformative Context: The South African Experience*, 36 CONN. L. REV. 725 (2003–2004).

26. Linda Krieger, *The Watched Variable Improves: On Eliminating Sex Discrimination in Employment*, in SEX DISCRIMINATION IN EMPLOYMENT (Faye Crosby et al. eds., 2007).

27. The law reverses *Ledbetter v. Goodyear Tire & Rubber Co.*, 550 U.S. 618 (2007).

28. See interviews with Julie Suk in this book and her article *Are Gender Stereotypes Bad for Women? Rethinking Antidiscrimination Law and Work-Family Conflict*, 110 COLUM. L. REV. 1 (2010).

29. On the socially constructed aspect of gender performativity, see JUDITH BUTLER, GENDER TROUBLE: FEMINISM AND THE SUBVERSION OF IDENTITY (1990).

30. L. Camille Hebert, *The Disparate Impact of Sexual Harassment: Does Motive Matter?*, 53 U. KAN. L. REV. 341 (2005).

31. See interviews of Vicki Schultz in this book.

32. See the work of the EEOC; for example, *Selected Enforcement Guidances and Other Policy Documents on the ADA*, LAWS, REGULATIONS, GUIDANCE, & MOUs, http://www.eeoc.gov/laws/types/disability_guidance.cfm.

33. See interviews of Ruth Colker in this book.

34. See interviews of Robert Post in this book and ROBERT POST & REVA SIEGEL ET AL., PREJUDICIAL APPEARANCES: THE LOGIC OF AMERICAN ANTI-DISCRIMINATION LAW (2001).

35. See, for example, Sciences Po's "conventions d'éducation prioritaires" and percentage plans in Texas and California, explained in Chapter 2.

36. Parity rules in France and diversity programs in U.S. corporate firms.

37. See, for example, the discriminatory policies against the Roma in Europe and in France, ERIC FASSIN ET AL., ROMS & RIVERAINS: UNE POLITIQUE MUNICIPALE DE LA RACE (2014). See recently CJEU Case C-83/14, *Chez* (July 16, 2015).

38. STÉPHANIE HENNETTE-VAUCHEZ & VINCENT VALENTIN, L'AFFAIRE BABY-LOUP OU LA NOUVELLE LAÏCITÉ (2014).

39. Reva B. Siegel, *From Colorblindness to Antibalkanization: An Emerging Ground of Decision in Race Equality Cases*, 120 YALE L.J. 1278 (2011); Reva B. Siegel, *The Supreme Court, 2012 Term—Foreword: Equality Divided*, 127 HARV. L. REV. 1 (2013).

40. On community values, see Robert C. Post, *The Social Foundations of Privacy: Community and Self in the Common Law of Tort*, 77 CAL. L. REV. 957 (1989).

41. COLLEEN SHEPPARD, INCLUSIVE EQUALITY: THE RELATIONAL DIMENSIONS OF SYSTEMIC DISCRIMINATION IN CANADA (2010).

42. RICHARD THOMPSON FORD, RIGHTS GONE WRONG: HOW LAW CORRUPTS THE STRUGGLE FOR EQUALITY (2012).

43. JANET HALLEY, SPLIT DECISIONS: HOW AND WHY TO TAKE A BREAK FROM FEMINISM (2008).

44. See interviews of Martha Minow and her work MAKING ALL THE DIFFERENCE: INCLUSION, EXCLUSION, AND AMERICAN LAW (1991).

45. See interviews of Minow and MAKING ALL THE DIFFERENCE, *supra* note 44.

46. See interviews of Minow and MAKING ALL THE DIFFERENCE, *supra* note 44; Chai R. Feldblum, *Rectifying the Tilt: Equality Lessons from Religion, Disability, Sexual Orientation, and Transgender,* 54 ME. L. REV.159 (2000).

47. Kimberlé Crenshaw, *Demarginalizing the Intersection of Race and Sex: A Black Feminist Critique of Antidiscrimination Doctrine, Feminist Theory, and Antiracist Politics,* U. CHI. LEGAL F. 138 (1989).

48. See interviews of Frank Dobbin in this book.

49. Susan P. Sturm, *The Architecture of Inclusion: Interdisciplinary Insights on Pursuing Institutional Citizenship,* 30 HARV. J.L. & GENDER 407 (2007).

50. See interviews with Chai Feldblum in this book.

51. Even if American judges, unlike European judges, seem to use proportionality less often than rationality or reasonableness as a requirement for justification. See Moshe Cohen-Eliya, *Proportionality and the Culture of Justification,* 59 AM. J. COMP. L. 463 (2011).

52. See generally global law as a way to rethink the legal norms; NEIL WALKER, INTIMATIONS OF GLOBAL LAW (2014).

53. Matteo Borzaga, *Accommodating Differences: Discrimination and Equality at Work in International Labor Law,* 30 VT. L. REV. 749 (2006); ARTURO BRONSTEIN, INTERNATIONAL AND COMPARATIVE LABOUR LAW: CURRENT CHALLENGES (2009); Faina Milman-Sivan, *Book Review,* reviewing Arturo Bronstein, International and Comparative Labour Law: Current Challenges, 59 AM. J. COMP. L. 289 (2011).

54. Manuela Tomei, *Discrimination and Equality at Work: A Review of the Concepts,* 142 INT'L LAB. REV. 401, 401–05 (2003), in which the author cites in particular Christopher McCrudden, *The New Concept of Equality,* 3 ERA FORUM 9, 13–17 (2003). The models of equality he identifies are the procedural or individual justice model, the social or group justice model, and equality as diversity. For a more transnational grid of analysis to reframe the study of law and society, see TRANSNATIONAL LEGAL ORDERS (Terence Halliday & Gregory Shaffer eds., 2015).

55. See also MATHIAS MÖSCHEL, LAW, LAWYERS, AND RACE: CRITICAL RACE THEORY FROM THE UNITED STATES TO EUROPE (2014).

56. The quotation comes from the following excerpt, which partly illustrates this position:

> Some seek to understand the law as a human phenomenon, as a cultural artifact, as a text; to seek the meaning in law in the way one would seek the deeper meaning in a piece of literature or art or social practice. The commitments here are to the non-instrumental. . . . The scholar's ethical commitment is, in essence, to law itself. . . . But some also seek to understand law as an instrument. Understanding law as an instrument is goal-oriented, directed not to measurement against hermeneutic standards but against practical ones. Law is not (just) a text. . . . Here the scholar's ethical commitment is to the person on whom law operates. . . . How law and legal institutions work systemically to produce people's lives—not in its individual instances but in its often obscure aggregative effects—has not traditionally been the affair of legal education and scholarship. Perhaps this is why the scholar who focuses on the instrumental is so often seen as an interloper doing violence to law itself. It may be true that there is an 'untranslatable abyss' between the law of one place and the law of another—just as there is between one person's experience of a strawberry and another's—but this does not mean that we have no business seeking to understand why law here produces this effect and law there produces that effect. To my mind, the goal of the legal scholar is to be competent across these different perspectives.

Gillian K. Hadfield, *The Strategy of Methodology: The Virtues of Being Reductionist for Comparative Law,* 59 U. TORONTO L.J. 223 (2009).

57. I have chosen the term *antidiscrimination law* to refer to the rather dense body of law made up of rules, procedures, case law, and doctrinal sources dealing exclusively with

the fight against employment discrimination, and the instruments used to prevent and sanction this discrimination. I have emphasized the scope of private law, although public law currently offers very fertile ground for analysis. *See* LUCIE CLUZEL-METAYER & MARIE MERCAT-BRUNS, DISCRIMINATIONS DANS L'EMPLOI: ANALYSE COMPARATIVES DE LA JURISPRUDENCE DU CONSEIL D'ÉTAT ET DE LA COUR DE CASSATION (2011). The new French Labor Code recognizes the importance of antidiscrimination, devoting an entire section (Titre III) to the topic in Book I of Part I. In the United States, where areas of specialization tend to be narrower, it is common to refer to *employment discrimination law*, and the subject is taught in almost every American law school.

58. The question of choosing and assessing a method is central to all international legal research. *See* Steven R. Ratner & Anne-Marie Slaughter, *Appraising the Methods of International Law: A Prospectus for Readers*, 93 AM. J. INT'L L. 291 (1999) ("To elucidate the theoretical underpinnings of contemporary scholarship through recourse to the methods employed by various theories, we decided upon seven methods for appraisal: legal positivism, the New Haven School, international legal process, critical legal studies, international law and international relations, feminist jurisprudence, and law and economics. In our view, they represent the major methods of international legal scholarship today.").

59. Although they have previously been used in comparative law. *See, e.g.,* Pierre Legrand, *Questions à Rodolfo Sacco*, 47 REV. INT'L DR. COMP. 943 (1995).

60. The approach taken in this work, that is, interviews punctuated with comparative observations, cannot be as easily combined with a methodology based on a preestablished taxonomy of orders and norms, as also seen in international law; Boris N. Mamlyuk & Ugo Mattei, *Comparative International Law*, 36 BROOK. J. INT'L L. 385 (2011); Ugo Mattei, *Three Patterns of Law: Taxonomy and Change in the World's Legal Systems*, 45 AM. J. COMP. L. 5 (1997). Interest in a transnational perspective of equality law is nevertheless growing in an era of globalization: see the papers presented at the 2014 American Association of Law Schools (AALS) Workshop on Transnational Perspectives on Equality Law, June 22–24, 2014, in Washington, DC. See also Gregory Shaffer, Transnational Legal Ordering and State Change (2013).

61. Naturally, the author is not implying that American law and American doctrine are the only fields of research worthy of interest in this respect. *See infra* the authors cited in the notes in Chapter 1 on the limits to the reach of constitutional norms and nondiscrimination as a fundamental right.

62. The perspective of the author of a comparative analysis is always present. Here, two perspectives are put forward depending on the interview: a European perspective or a French perspective. For more on the challenges of this dual perspective in comparative employment law, *see* BOB HEPPLE & BRUNO VENEZIANI, THE TRANSFORMATION OF LABOUR LAW IN EUROPE (2009), and Sebastian Krebber, *"The Grand Duchy, Tucked Between Belgium, France and Germany": Some Thoughts Upon the Methodology of Bob Hepple & Bruno Veneziani, the Transformation of Labour Law in Europe*, 32 COMP. LAB. L. & POL'Y J. 811 (2011).

63. Previously Article 13 of the Treaty of Amsterdam. After the European Court of Justice decisions in *Defrenne* I, II, and III (*see infra* Chapter 1, note 36), national courts began to make references for preliminary rulings on the interpretation of European antidiscrimination norms, especially the gender equality directives, and their scope.

64. For an economic assessment of its effectiveness, see page 54 et seq. of *L'évaluation du droit du travail: problèmes et méthodes* (research report by the Institut International pour les études comparatives, supervised by Antoine Lyon-Caen, dated April 11, 2008).

65. *See, e.g.,* PHILIPPE MALINVAUD, INTRODUCTION À L'ÉTUDE DU DROIT 150 (2004).

66. VOCABULAIRE JURIDIQUE 318 (Gérard Cornu ed., 2004).

67. Christophe Jamin and Philippe Jestaz critique the development of doctrine in France, which they liken to a French "school," tracing the origins of this doctrinal tradition. The French doctrine, they say, "was formed around the time of the transition from the 19th to the 20th century, establishing the principles of a science of law closely identified with legal dogmatics." For jurists of the Roman tradition, this was not new, but as Jamin and Jestaz explain, the innovation was that the doctrine was now "theorized by a school that called itself *scientific.*" This theory countered the social sciences, which were gaining ground at the time and threatening the autonomy of the legal system. Consequently, they say, the French notion of doctrine incorporates both "the self-proclaimed authority of a body of jurists and the appeal of well-tempered dogmatics," with a few rare exceptions. In this context, can it truly be said that doctrinal writing in France is characterized by "liberty" and "diversity," as some scholars claim? CHRISTOPHE JAMIN & PHILIPPE JESTAZ, LA DOCTRINE 8, 9, 11 (2004); GÉRARD CORNU, DROIT CIVIL: INTRODUCTION, LES PERSONNES, LES BIENS 153 (8th ed. 1997).

68. See Adhémar Esmein, *La jurisprudence et la doctrine*, 1 REV. TRIM. DR. CIV. 5 (1902); Christian Atias, *La mission de la doctrine universitaire en droit privé*, 1 JCP 2999 (1980); Henri Batiffol, *La responsabilité de la doctrine dans la création du droit*, RD PROSP. 175 (1981); Christian Mouly, *La doctrine, source d'unification internationale du droit*, 38 REV. INT'L DR. COMP. 351 (1986); Christian Atias, *Des réponses sans questions 1804–1899–1999 (quantitatif et qualitatif dans le savoir juridique)*, RECUEIL DALLOZ 406 (1998); Nicolas Molfessis, *Les prédictions doctrinales*, in L'AVENIR DU DROIT: MÉLANGES EN HOMMAGE À FRANÇOIS TERRÉ 141 (1999); Philippe Malaurie, *La pensée juridique du droit civil au XXe siècle*, 1 JCP 283 (2001); Pierre-Yves Gautier, *Les articles fondateurs (réflexions sur la doctrine)*, in ÉTUDES OFFERTES À PIERRE CATALA: "LE DROIT PRIVÉ FRANÇAIS À LA FIN DU XXÈME SIÈCLE" 255 (2001).

69. The case law approach of the common-law system, ever mindful of judges' opinions, is less favorable to the construction of a doctrine. Blackstone's commentaries, which largely influenced the development of American law, provide more of an overview, at times a less than accurate one, of the scope of English jurisprudence, rather than an analysis of underlying dogmatics or principles.

70. See JAMIN & JESTAZ, *supra* note 67, at 269.

71. See the emergence of realism in legal thought in the article by Justice Oliver Wendell Holmes, *The Path of the Law*, 10 HARV. L. REV. 457 (1897) and his famous dissent in the Supreme Court case Lochner v. New York, 198 U.S. 45 (1905).

72. JAMIN & JESTAZ, *supra* note 67, at 11.

73. One of the cardinal functions of comparative law is to gain insight into one's own legal system and its characteristics: Horatia Muir Watt, *La fonction subversive du droit comparé*, 52 REV. INT'L DR. COMP. 503, 518 (2000) ("A better understanding of oneself, facilitated by looking at others"); *see also* Günter Frankenberg, *Critical Comparisons: Re-thinking Comparative Law*, 26 HARV. INT'L L. J. 411 (1985), in which the author observes that the failure of comparatists to critically evaluate their own law explains why comparative law is considered as a second-class discipline. Christopher McCrudden, *Why Compare? The Theory and Practice of Comparative Anti-discrimination Law*, paper presented at the Berkeley Comparative Anti-Discrimination Law Study Group, First Annual Symposium, Sciences-Po in Paris (May 4, 2012).

74. This line of thought is also explored in research on law and economics; Vincy Fon & Francesco Parisi, *Judicial Precedents in Civil Law Systems: a Dynamic Analysis*, 26 INT'L REV. L. & ECON. 519 (2006).

75. Holger Spamann, *Large-Sample, Quantitative Research Designs for Comparative Law?*, 57 AM. J. COMP. 797 (2009).

76. See, e.g., Mathias Reimann, *The Progress and Failure of Comparative Law in the Second Half of the Twentieth Century,* 50 AM. J. COMP. L. 671 (2002).

77. "There is a rather remarkable parallel between what comparatists write about the advantages of comparison and the more massive tendency to engage in subversive activities by the deconstructive trends internal to the American system." Muir Watt, *supra* note 73, at 509.

78. Antidiscrimination law reveals a characteristic shared by the scholars, which is their tendency to "deconstruct" law to varying degrees. They are able not only to unravel the meaning of a rule and how it fits into a body of law but also to connect with thinking from other disciplines to subsequently enrich the legal analysis. At the same time, these academics express their critical opinions, without precluding them from joining interdisciplinary schools of thought permeated by the social sciences.

79. *See* Muir Watt, *supra* note 73, at 506; Edward J. Eberle, *The Methodology of Comparative Law,* 16 ROGER WILLIAMS UNIV. L. REV. 60 (2011).

80. Such as the approach taken by KONRAD ZWEIGERT & HEIN KÖTZ, AN INTRODUCTION TO COMPARATIVE LAW 30 (1992); nor does the American scholar Mary Ann Glendon reject the functional perspective. MARY ANN GLENDON ET AL., COMPARATIVE LEGAL TRADITIONS: TEXT, MATERIALS, AND CASES ON THE CIVIL AND COMMON LAW TRADITIONS, WITH SPECIAL REFERENCE TO FRENCH, GERMAN, ENGLISH AND EUROPEAN LAW 11 (2nd ed. 1994).

81. *Cf.* Nuno Garoupa & Carlos Gómez Ligüerre, *The Syndrome of the Efficiency of the Common Law,* 29 B.U. INT'L L.J. 287 (2011) (defending French civil law); *see also* Vivian Grosswald Curran, *Comparative Law and Legal Origins Thesis: "[N]on scholae sed discimus vitae discimus,"* AM. J. COMP. L. 863 (2009); for the terms of the debate, see Catherine Valcke's introduction to *Focus: Economics and Comparative Law,* 59 U. TORONTO L.J. 179 (2009).

82. "Comparison pursues the goal of underscoring the variety in law and organizing this variety. . . . The comparatist must recognize—and this is the deepest point of convergence of the questions that comparison raises—that difference is not indifferent and include this comparison within the *difference*. This means that the person who is comparing must first overcome the 'particular repugnance to conceiving of difference, to describing separations and dispersions.'" Pierre Legrand, *Comparer,* REV. INT'L DR. COMP. 279, 295 (1996) (quoting MICHEL FOUCAULT, L'ARCHÉOLOGIE DU SAVOIR 21 (1969)). *See also* PIERRE LEGRAND, COMPARER LES DROITS, RÉSOLUMENT (2009).

83. "Arguing that a comparison does not give us insight into one type of law, but into a perspective of law . . . should not undermine the comparative undertaking." Legrand, *Comparer, supra* note 82, at 310.

84. *See* Daniel Berkowitz et al., *The Transplant Effect,* 51 AM. J. COMP. L. 163 (2003); RODOLFO SACCO, LA COMPARAISON JURIDIQUE AU SERVICE DE LA CONNAISSANCE DU DROIT (1991).

85. "Regardless of whether one considers that anthropology or linguistics should or should not contribute to an extended notion of law, the author of a comparison cannot ignore these different fields of knowledge essential to his or her undertaking." Legrand, *Comparer, supra* note 82, at 290.

1. HISTORY OF ANTIDISCRIMINATION LAW: THE CONSTITUTION AND THE SEARCH FOR PARADIGMS OF EQUALITY

1. Dred Scott v. Sandford, 60 U.S. 393 (1857).
2. Plessy v. Ferguson, 163 U.S. 537 (1896).

3. *See* Reva B. Siegel, *Equality Talk: Antisubordination and Anticlassification Values in Constitutional Struggles over Brown*, 117 HARV. L. REV. 1470 (2004).
4. Brown v. Bd. of Education of Topeka, 347 U.S. 483 (1954).
5. LE DÉFENSEUR DES DROITS, http://www.defenseurdesdroits.fr/
6. Title VII of the Civil Rights Act of 1964 prohibits employment discrimination based on race, color, religion, sex, and national origin.
7. Regents of Univ. of Cal. v. Bakke, 438 U.S. 265 (1978).
8. McDonnell Douglas Corp. v. Green, 411 U.S. 792 (1973) (recognizing disparate treatment and introducing the burden-shifting framework (prima facie case) for the first time); Griggs v. Duke Power Co., 401 U.S. 424 (1971) (recognizing disparate impact for the first time); United Steelworkers of Am. v. Weber 443 U.S. 193 (1979) (holding that affirmative action in employment is not incompatible with the nondiscrimination provisions of the Civil Rights Act of 1964).
9. *See* Daniel Sabbagh, *La tentative de l'opacité: le juge américain et l'affirmative action dans l'enseignement supérieur*, 111 POUVOIRS 5 (2004); Gwénaële Calvès, *Les politiques françaises de discrimination positive: trois spécificités*, 111 POUVOIRS 29 (2004).
10. *See* David Benjamin Oppenheimer, *Negligent Discrimination*, 141 U. PA. L. REV. 899 (1992).
11. DeFunis v. Odegaard, 414 U.S. 1038 (1973).
12. Regents of Univ. of Cal. v. Bakke, 438 U.S. 265 (1978).
13. In assessing equal protection, strict scrutiny is the most rigorous form of judicial review, applied to race classifications, which must be justified by a compelling state interest.
14. *See infra* Chapter 4 on diversity.
15. *See* GWÉNAËLE CALVÈS, LA DISCRIMINATION POSITIVE, (2nd ed. 2008); LES POLITIQUES DE LA DIVERSITÉ: EXPÉRIENCES ANGLAISE ET AMÉRICAINE (Emmanuelle Le Texier et al. eds., 2010); DANIEL SABBAGH, L'ÉGALITÉ PAR LE DROIT: LES PARADOXES DE LA DISCRIMINATION POSITIVE AUX ÉTATS-UNIS (2003).
16. Jacqueline Laufer, *L'égalité professionnelle entre les hommes et les femmes: est-elle soluble dans la diversité?*, 21 TRAVAIL, GENRE & SOCIÉTÉS 35 (2009).
17. Act No. 2006-396 of March 31, 2006.
18. Françoise Favennec-Héry, *Non-discrimination, égalité, diversité: la France au milieu du gué*, DR. SOC. 3 (2007).
19. Amendment to the French Constitution adopted on July 23, 2008 (articles 61–1, 62); French Law No. 2009-1523 of Dec. 10, 2009. Judicial review has been available since March 1, 2010, and authorizes the Conseil Constitutionnel to declare null and void any provision that violates the Constitution by infringing on rights and liberties, arising in any litigation before courts under the jurisdiction of the Conseil d'État or the Cour de Cassation. "Equality has been continually affirmed in the first article of its 1958 constitution, in Article 6 of the Declaration of the Rights of Man and of the Citizen and in paragraphs 3 and 5 of the preamble of the French constitution of 1946, and has long ranked as a general principle of law." CE Ass. [Conseil d'État, plenary session], Apr. 1, 1938, Société de l'Alcool dénaturé de Coubert, Rec. Lebon 337, REV. DR. PUB. 487 (1939); CE Sect. [Conseil d'État, section], Mar. 9, 1951, Société des concerts du conservatoire, Rec. Lebon 151, DR. SOC. 168 (1951). It has even been referred to as a constitutional principle (CC [Conseil constitutionnel], July 12, 1979, Ponts à péage, 9 AJDA 38 (1979)). This "founding principle of democracy" (CONSEIL D'ÉTAT, SUR LE PRINCIPE D'ÉGALITÉ 21 (1996) (annual report of the Conseil d'État)), embedded in French law since the Revolution, has long been the subject of substantial judicial interpretation.
20. Bertrand Mathieu, *Neuf mois de jurisprudence relative à la QPC: un bilan*, 137 POUVOIRS 66 (2011); Ferdinand Mélin-Soucramanien, *Le principe d'égalité dans la jurisprudence*

du Conseil constitutionnel: Quelles perspectives pour la question prioritaire de constitutionnalité? 29 CAHIERS DU CONSEIL CONSTITUTIONNEL 5 (2010).

21. "There is no longer any question of a purely formal reading of equality: the administrative courts have long since recognized that different situations may be treated in different ways and that exceptions may be established to serve the general interest." Therefore, "the principle of equality is not opposed to the rule-making authorities ruling differently in different situations or to their departing from equality to serve the general interest, provided that, in either case, the resulting difference in treatment is directly related to the purpose of the law from which it originates and not manifestly disproportionate with respect to the differences in situation or justifying reasons." CE Ass., July 13, 1962, Conseil national de l'ordre des médecins, Rec. 479, REV. DR. PUB. 739 (1962) (conclusion by Guy Braibant). This ruling was later fine-tuned (in particular, CE, May 15, 2000, Barroux, Rec. 172); CE, Jan. 10, 2005, Hardy, Le Cornec, Rec. 9, AJDA 1575 (2005) (note, Jean-Claude Hélin); CE Sect., July 25, 2007, Syndicat des avocats de France, No. 288720; *see* Bertrand Seiller, *Contribution à la résolution de quelques incohérences de la formulation prétorienne du principe d'égalité, in* LE DROIT ADMINISTRATIF: PERMANENCES ET CONVERGENCES, MÉLANGES EN L'HONNEUR DE JEAN-FRANÇOIS LACHAUME 979 *et seq.* (2007). "The principle of equality simply implies that people in the same situation are treated in the same manner." LUCIE CLUZEL-MÉTAYER & MARIE MERCAT-BRUNS, DISCRIMINATIONS DANS L'EMPLOI: ANALYSE COMPARATIVE DE LA JURISPRUDENCE DU CONSEIL D'ÉTAT ET DE LA COUR DE CASSATION (2011) (study submitted to HALDE).

22. CC [Conseil constitutionnel] decision No. 2009-588 DC, Aug. 6, 2009, Rec. 163. It has applied the same standard before and after judicial review. See Morgan Sweeney, *La diversité des sources de l'exigence d'égalité, in* LE DROIT SOCIAL, L'ÉGALITÉ ET LES DISCRIMINATIONS 49 (Georges Borenfreund & Isabelle Vacarie eds., 2013); no violation of the principle of equality: CC decision No. 2014-373 QPC, Apr. 4, 2014 (on night work and equal treatment for employers); CC decision No. 2014-401 QPC, June 13, 2014 (on short-term contracts and violation of equality between workers); CC decision No. 2014-402 QPC, June 13, 2014; CC decision No. 2014-700 DC, July 31, 2014 (declaring constitutional the law on substantive equality between men and women).

23. *See generally* FRANK DOBBIN, INVENTING EQUAL OPPORTUNITY (2009).

24. The French government plans to revamp and simplify the Labor Code in 2018 to give more room to collective bargaining while maintaining antidiscrimination law as a legislative mandate. As an example of this proposed trend, see ROBERT BADINTER & ANTOINE LYON-CAEN, LE TRAVAIL ET LA LOI (2015).

25. *Communication from the European Commission on Renewed Commitment for Non-discrimination and Equal Opportunities,* COM (2008) 420 final (July 2, 2008); *see* Frédérique Michéa, La cohésion sociale en droit communautaire (2003) (unpublished thesis, Université de Rennes, supervised by Daniel Gadbin).

26. Notably, these quotas first did not apply to companies established under a simplified legal form known as an SAS, of which there are a large number in France, nor to other types of executive committees. See Philippe Reigné, *Les femmes et les conseils d'administration: réponse à un éditorial de M. François-Xavier Lucas,* 3 JCP 27 (2010). See *infra* Chapter 4. Considering this limit of the 2011 law, the new law on "substantive equality between women and men" of August 4, 2014, extended this parity requirement of 40 percent to executive boards of larger companies (more than 500 employees), covering listed and unlisted companies, which must be implemented by January 1, 2017. This obligation now also targets companies with 250–499 employees that make more than €50 million in annual sales.

27. French Law 2013-660 of July 22, 2013 (on higher education and research). The percentage of students benefitting from this right to access preparatory programs is set each

year by executive order. For example, if the measure applies to 7 percent of high school students, 3,700 students are affected. Executive Order [Décret] 2014-610 of June 11, 2014, set this percentage at 10 percent for 2014.

28. Since this interview, in Fisher v. University of Texas, 570 U.S.___(2013), No. 11-345, decided June 24, 2013, Justice Kennedy wrote the opinion on the affirmative action admissions policy of the University of Texas at Austin. In a 7-1 decision, the Court vacated and remanded the Fifth Circuit's ruling.

29. In the academic sphere, see Regents of Univ. of Cal. v. Bakke, 438 U.S. 265 (1978); Grutter v. Bollinger 539 U.S. 306 (2003) (No. 02-241); Parents Involved in Cmty. Sch. v. Seattle Sch. Dist. No. 1, 551 U.S. 701 (2007) (striking down affirmative action in schools).

30. Daniel Sabbagh, *Vertus et limites de la discrimination positive indirecte dans l'enseignement supérieur: l'expérience du Texas et de la Californie*, 3-4 MOUVEMENTS 102 (2008).

31. Reva B. Siegel, *The Supreme Court, 2012 Term—Foreword: Equality Divided*, 127 HARV. L. REV. 1 (2013).

32. Monroe v. City of Charlottesville, 579 F.3d 380 (2009), *cert. denied; see also* United States v. Brignoni-Ponce, 422 U.S. 873 (1975); *see* Melendres v. Arpaio, 2013 WL2297173, § 19.

33. Shelby Cnty. v. Holder, 133 S. Ct. 2612 (2013); see Jon Greenbaum, Alan Martinson, & Sonia Gill, Shelby County v. Holder: *When the Rational Becomes Irrational*, 57 HOWARD L. J. 811 (2014)

34. Siegel, *supra* note 31, at 67.

35. When arguments combine references to standards of equality and liberty, *see recently* Obergefell v. Hodges, 576 U.S.__(2015).

36. *See* Ricci v. DeStefano, 129 S. Ct. 2658, 2671, 174 L. Ed. 2d 490 (2009).

37. *See* Étienne Picard, *L'émergence des droits fondamentaux en France*, AJDA (SPECIAL ISSUE) 6 (1998); LOUIS FAVOREU ET AL., DROIT DES LIBERTÉS FONDAMENTALES 13 (2005). *See also* DROITS FONDAMENTAUX ET DROIT SOCIAL (Antoine Lyon-Caen & Pascal Lokiec eds., 2004);. ISABELLE MEYRAT, DROITS FONDAMENTAUX ET DROIT DU TRAVAIL (1998).

38. Community case law developed only in the 1970s; see Case 80/70, Defrenne v. Belgian State, 1971 E.C.R. 445 [hereinafter *Defrenne* I]; Case 43/75, Defrenne v. Sabena, 1976 E.C.R. 455 [hereinafter *Defrenne* II]; 149/77, Case 149/77, Defrenne v. Sabena, 1978 E.C.R. 1365 [hereinafter *Defrenne* III]; Case 152/73, Sotgiu v. Deutsche Bundespost, 1974 E.C.R. 153; Case 96/80, Jenkins v. Kingsgate Ltd., 1981 E.C.R. 911.

39. A fundamental right can be defined as "a legal norm, able to be set forth in a constitution (German constitutional law) or an international treaty (European Convention on Human Rights), unable to be overridden by a constitutional court." DICTIONNAIRE DU VOCABULAIRE JURIDIQUE 152 (2nd ed. 2004).

40. In 2010, the European Commission published a communication called *Strategy for the Effective Implementation of the Charter of Fundamental Rights by the European Union* (COM (2010) 573/4). *See* Bruno Nascimbene, *Les droits fondamentaux vingt ans après le traité de Maastricht*, 2 LAW & EUR. AFF. 267 (2012).

41. JEAN-SYLVESTRE BERGÉ & SOPHIE ROBIN-OLIVIER, INTRODUCTION AU DROIT EUROPÉEN 209 (2008).

42. "By referring to fundamental rights, the category can be enlarged to include economic rights and freedoms indisposed to being qualified as 'human rights.'" *Id.* at 208.

43. For example, Demir and Baykara v. Turkey, App. No. 34503/97, Eur. Ct. H.R. (2008); Eskelinen v. Finland, App. No. 63235/00, 45 Eur. H.R. Rep. 43 (2007).

44. Court of Justice of the European Union [CJEU], Dec. 18, 2014, Opinion 2/13; *and see* David Szymczak, *Juridictions européennes et principe de non-discrimination: analyse croisée à l'aune de la garantie des droits fondamentaux*, 2 LAW & EUR. AFF. 217 (2009-2010).

45. Although indirect discrimination was not found in this case, *see* Jordan v. United Kingdom, App. No. 24746/94, 37 Eur. H.R. Rep. 2 (2001); *see* JEAN-FRANÇOIS RENUCCI, DROIT EUROPÉEN DES DROITS DE L'HOMME: DROITS ET LIBERTÉS FONDAMENTAUX GARANTIS PAR LA CEDH (2010). On indirect discrimination, D.H. v. Czech Republic, No. 57325/00, 47 Eur. H.R. Rep. 3 (2008). On religious discrimination where indirect discrimination was rejected: Eweida v. The United Kingdom, Nos. 48420/10, 59842/10, 51671/10, 36516/10, Eur. Ct. H.R. (Jan. 15, 2013).

46. Sometimes its decisions are progressive, as in Goodwin v. the United Kingdom, No. 28957/95, 35 Eur. H.R. Rep. 18 (2002) (on transgender rights). But the Court has also complied with strong national sentiment and accepted state justifications for restrictions, disregarding the risks of discrimination based on religion or sex: *see* S.A.S. v. France, No. 43835/11, Eur. Ct. H.R. (July 1, 2014) (upholding France's ban on full-face veils in public) (*infra* Chapter 5); ABC v. Ireland, Eur. Ct. H.R. (December 16, 2010) (holding that Ireland's ban on abortion does not violate the Convention) In other instances, the ECtHR does not refer to Article 14 but has still condemned the country, as in Winterstein v. France, No. 27013/07, Eur. Ct. H.R. (October 17, 2013) (in a case of eviction of French travelers from private land where they had been living for many years), and in Y.Y. v. Turkey, No. 14793/08, Eur. Ct. H.R. (Mar. 10, 2015), the Court unanimously ruled that by barring a transsexual man from access to gender reassignment surgery for several years, Turkey violated his right to privacy (ECHR, Article 8).

47. Indeed, following Case C-144/04, Mangold v. Helm, 2005 E.C.R. I-9981 and Case C-555/07, Kücükdeveci v. Swedex, 2010 E.C.R. I-365, Case C-147/08, Römer v. City of Hamburg, 2011 E.C.R. I-3591, explicitly consecrates the principle of equal treatment as a general principle of European Union law. This status has been reinforced by the now legally binding character of the Charter of Fundamental Rights of the European Union. The Court of Justice considers that access to EU citizenship is becoming the foundational status of member-state citizens, crystallized by "broad access to social security benefits by mobile citizens," with certain moderations nonetheless, reflected in Community case law. *See* Caroline Picheral, *Du droit des citoyens de l'Union européenne à la non-discrimination en matière de prestations sociales*, 2 LAW & EUR. AFF. 294 (2009–2010); *see* Article 21 of the Charter, which prohibits "any discrimination based on sex, race, colour, ethnic or social origin, genetic features, language, religion or belief, political or any other opinion, membership of a national minority, property, birth, disability, age or sexual orientation."

48. This is not always the case regarding its interpretation of directives pertaining to employment. *See* Mark Bell, *Flexicurity and Fundamental Social Rights: The EU Directives on Atypical Work*, 37 EUR. L. REV. 31 (2012).

49. Zdeněk Kühn, *Nina-Louisa Arold, The Legal Culture of the European Court of Human Rights*, 58 AM. J. COMP. L. 205 (2010) (book review).

50. Some scholars believe there is a correlation between European citizenship and antidiscrimination, where combating all illegal discrimination enlarges the social content of European citizenship, uncovering new protected grounds for discrimination, such as age. *See* Case C-555/07, Kücükdeveci v. Swedex, 2010 E.C.R. I-365; *see* Anastasia Iliopoulou, *Citoyenneté européenne et principe de non-discrimination*, 1 LAW & EUR. AFF. 58 (2011).

51. Sonia Morano-Foadi, *EU Citizenship and Religious Liberty in an Enlarged Europe*, 16 EUR. L.J. 420 (2010).

52. Nondiscrimination is a necessary step toward citizenship. *See* Jürgen Habermas, *Bringing the Integration of Citizens into Line with the Integration of States*, 18 EUR. L.J. 485 (2012).

53. Jo Shaw, *The Many Pasts and Futures of Citizenship in the European Union*, 22 EUR. L. REV. 554 (1997) (showing how the symbolic value of these principles is nevertheless important in the construction of EU citizenship).

54. *See* Case C-555/07, Kücükdeveci v. Swedex, 2010 E.C.R. I-365, ¶¶ 22, 55; and Case C-147/08, Römer v. City of Hamburg, 2011 E.C.R. I-3591, ¶ 60, referring to pt. 23 of CJEU *Kücükdeveci*.

55. On the visibility of disputes in this area involving European Union staff, *see* Siofra O'Leary, *Applying Principles of EU Social and Employment Law in EU Staff Cases*, 36 EUR. L. REV. 769, 769, 782 (2011).

56. *See* Case C-345/89, Criminal Proceedings against Stoeckel, 1991 E.C.R. I-4047 (condemning the ban on women's night work in France as a violation of the equal treatment principle, leading to the ban being removed) (regardless of the judgment that may be made on the opportunity of this withdrawal). For decisions involving other possible infringements of rights, *see* Case C-438/05, International Transport Workers' Federation v. Viking Line, 2007 E.C.R. I-10,779; Case C-341/05, Laval v. Svenska Byggnadsarbetareförbundet, 2007 E.C.R. I-11,767; Case C-346/06, Rüffert v. Land Niedersachsen, 2008 E.C.R. I-1989.

57. Case C-147/08, Römer v. City of Hamburg, 2011 E.C.R. I-3591; Case C-267/06, Maruko v. Versorgungsanstalt der deutschen Bühnen, 2008 E.C.R. I-1757 (showing a functional approach to the comparability of married couples and couples in other forms of union in terms of access to a specific social benefit and its nature).

([from Paragraph 42] . . . It should be pointed out that, as is apparent from the judgment in Maruko (paragraphs 67 to 73), first, it is required not that the situations be identical, but only that they be comparable and, second, the assessment of that comparability must be carried out not in a global and abstract manner, but in a specific and concrete manner in the light of the benefit concerned. In that judgment, concerning the refusal to grant a survivor's pension to the life partner of a deceased member of an occupational pension scheme, the Court did not carry out an overall comparison between marriage and registered life partnership under German law, but, on the basis of the analysis of German law carried out by the court which made the reference for a preliminary ruling, according to which there was a gradual harmonisation in German law of the regime put in place for registered life partnerships with that applicable to marriage, it made it clear that registered life partnership is to be treated as equivalent to marriage as regards the widow's or widower's pension.

([Paragraph 43] Thus, the comparison of the situations must be based on an analysis focusing on the rights and obligations of the spouses and registered life partners as they result from the applicable domestic provisions, which are relevant taking account of the purpose and the conditions for granting the benefit at issue in the main proceedings, and must not consist in examining whether national law generally and comprehensively treats registered life partnership as legally equivalent to marriage.)

58. Case C-267/12, Hay v. Crédit Agricole Mutuel de Charente-Maritime et des Deux-Sèvres, 2013 E.C.R. I-0000.

59. Law No. 2013-404 of May 17, 2013 (extending marriage to same-sex couples).

60. RICHARD BELLAMY, CITIZENSHIP: A VERY SHORT INTRODUCTION 12 (2008); recently, indirect discrimination has been used to vindicate men's pension rights, Case C-173/13, Leone, Leone v. Garde des Sceaux et Caisse nationale de retraites des agents des collectivités locales (July 17, 2014), and concerning citizens indirectly discriminated against by association because they lived in Roma districts, Case C-83/14, *CHEZ Razpredelenie Bulgaria AD (July 16, 2015)*.

61. *See* Article 157 of the Treaty on the Functioning of the European Union (TFUE) and the *Defrenne* I, *Defrenne* II, and *Defrenne* III judgments.

62. *See* Justice Oliver Wendell Holmes's celebrated dissenting opinion in Lochner v. New York, 198 U.S. 45 (1905) (upholding this view).

63. *See* the preamble to the Charter, paragraph 2; and Mélanie Schmitt, *La dimension sociale du traité de Lisbonne*, 6 DR. SOC. 682, 684, 685 (2010).
64. Armin Von Bogandy, *Founding Principles of EU Law: A Theoretical and Doctrinal Sketch*, 16 EUR. L.J. 95, 103–04 (2010).
65. Christophe Radé, *La question prioritaire de constitutionnalité et le droit du travail: a-t-on ouvert la boîte de Pandore?*, 9/10 DR. SOC. 873, 881 (2010).
66. *See* CC [Conseil constitutionnel] decision No. 2010-613 DC, Oct. 7, 2010 (declaring the full-face veil ban constitutional and no violation of principle of equality); *see also* the 2014 Baby Loup case on the veil in employment, Cass. soc., June 25, 2014, No. 13-28369, *infra* Chapter 5, and the Cour de Cassation has recently asked the CJEU for a preliminary ruling on the legality of a company ban of the veil imposed on a female engineer seen as an essential requirement for the job because of customer preference, Cass. soc., Apr. 9, 2015, No. 13-19855.
67. *See* FERDINAND MÉLIN-SOUCRAMANIEN, LE PRINCIPE D'ÉGALITÉ DANS LA JURISPRUDENCE DU CONSEIL CONSTITUTIONNEL 194 (1997).
68. JEAN GICQUEL & JEAN-ERIC GICQUEL, DROIT CONSTITUTIONNEL ET INSTITUTIONS POLITIQUES, MONTCHRESTIEN 746 (2010).
69. CC [Conseil constitutionnel] decision, No. 2008-568 DC, Aug. 7, 2008 (reforming working hours) (recitals 7 and 8, referring to CC decision No. 87-232 DC, Jan. 7, 1988).
70. *See* commentary on CC [Conseil constitutionnel] decision, No. 2009-588 DC, Aug. 6, 2009, in 27 LES CAHIERS DU CONSEIL CONSTITUTIONNEL (2009). This was confirmed recently concerning the regulation of night work (Code du travail [C. Trav.] [Labor code] arts. 3122-32, 3122-33, 3122-36): the Conseil Constitutionnel decided the protection of health, security, rest, and leisure in the Preamble of the Constitution of 1946 should prevail over the right to freedom of enterprise. *See* CC decision No. 2014-373 QPC, Apr. 4, 2014.
71. Recent decisions do not often favor employees. *See* CC [Conseil constitutionnel] decision No. 2012-232 QPC, Apr. 13, 2012 (ruling no violation of the Constitution because of a difference of treatment concerning employees with under two years of seniority).
72. CC [Conseil constitutionnel] decision No. 2010-1 QPC, May 28, 2010.
73. CC [Conseil constitutionnel] decision No. 2010-83 QPC, Jan. 13, 2011, holds that Article 28 of the Civil and Military Retirement Pensions Code is unconstitutional, considering that it creates a difference in treatment "with regard to the increase in pension to include a family allowance among retired disabled civil servants who have raised at least three children and retired civil servants who are not disabled and have raised at least three children" and that "the difference in treatment thus created is not justified by the purpose of the law."
74. The same observation can be made with respect to applications for preliminary rulings (QPC) relating to nondiscrimination issues that were not transmitted to the Conseil Constitutionnel: *see* Cass. ass. plén., June 25, 2010, No. 10-40.009 (on whether Labor Code art. 3245-1 infringes the principle of accessibility and comprehensibility of the law, the principle of equality, the right to ownership, the right to employment, and the antidiscrimination principle because it applies a five-year statute of limitations for wage claims made pursuant to Labor Code arts. L.7321-1 to L.7321-5). The Court declined to refer the application to the Conseil Constitutionnel, stating that "the issue raised, relating to the statute of limitations for wage claims, is not of a serious nature."
75. On the role of the QPC in labor law, Jean-François Cesaro, *La QPC sociale: l'Eldorado des causes perdues?*, 22–23 JCP S. 17 (2011).
76. CC [Conseil constitutionnel] decision No. 2010-92 QPC, Jan. 28, 2011, considering "that by maintaining the principle according to which marriage is the union of a man and a woman, the legislature has, in exercising its power under Article 34 of the Constitution,

deemed that the difference in situation between couples of the same sex and those composed of a man and a woman can justify a difference in treatment with regard to the rules regarding the right to a family; that it is not for the Conseil Constitutionnel to substitute its judgment for that of the legislator regarding the consideration of this difference of situation" (recital 9).

77. Taking age into account does not infringe on the right to employment or the principle of equality. See Art. L. 1237-5 of the French Labor Code; CC [Conseil constitutionnel] decision No. 2010-98 QPC, Feb. 4, 2011. See also CC decision No. 2010-617 DC, Nov. 9, 2010 (on the law reforming retirement pensions).

78. See Dred Scott v. Sandford, 60 U.S. 393 (1857); Bowers v. Hardwick, 478 U.S. 186 (1986).

79. See, e.g., the reasoning in Lawrence v Texas, 539 U.S. 558 (2003). See also Roozbeh (Rudy) B. Baker, *Balancing Competing Priorities: Affirmative Action in the United States and Canada*, 18 TRANSNAT'L L. & CONTEMP. PROBS. 527 (2009).

80. See Matthias Herdegen, *The Relation Between the Principles of Equality and Proportionality*, 22 COMMON MKT. L. REV. 683 (1985).

81. See Cass. soc., May 11, 2010, No. 08-45307 and No. 08-43681, Bull. civ. V, No. 105; Marie Mercat-Bruns, *Retour sur la discrimination fondée sur l'âge*, 10 REV. DR. TRAVAIL 587 (2010); Marie Mercat-Bruns, *Age and Disability Differential Treatment in France: Contrasting EU and National Courts Approaches to the Inner Limits of Anti-discrimination Law*, INT'L J. DISCRIMINATION L. (Nov. 12, 2014).

82. See Nicolas Moizard, *Quelques observations sur les méthodes d'interprétation de la Cour de justice en matière de droit social*, 12 DR. SOC. 1216, 1218 (2010); Frédérique Michéa, *Le traitement judiciaire du critère discriminatoire de l'âge: retour sur la jurisprudence récente de la CJUE*, 11 DR. SOC. 1060, 1068 (2010). See examples of recent CJEU age discrimination case law on legitimacy and proportionality test: Case C-20/13, Daniel Unland (Sept. 9 2015); Case C-515/13, Landin (Feb. 26, 2015), C-417/13, Starjakob (Jan. 28, 2015)

83. See the comparison between the proportionality tests in German and in EU law, Tor-Inge Harbo, *The Function of the Proportionality Principle in EU Law*, 16 EUR. L.J. 185 (2010).

84. See § 23-2 of Ordinance No. 58-1067, Constituting an Institutional Act on the Constitutional Council.

85. Case C-188/10, Melki v. France, and Case C-189/10, Abdeli v. France, 2010 E.C.R. I-5667; Xavier Prétot, *La Constitution, la loi et le droit de l'Union européenne*, 11 REV. JURIS. SOC. 734 (2010).

86. See supra notes 63, 64, 83.

87. See JUDITH BUTLER, GENDER TROUBLE: FEMINISM AND THE SUBVERSION OF IDENTITY (1990).

88. MARY ANN GLENDON, RIGHTS TALK: THE IMPOVERISHMENT OF POLITICAL DISCOURSE (1991). See also MARIE MERCAT-BRUNS, VIEILLISSEMENT ET DROIT À LA LUMIÈRE DU DROIT FRANÇAIS ET DU DROIT AMÉRICAIN (2001); RONALD DWORKIN, TAKING RIGHTS SERIOUSLY (1977) (providing an almost contrary critical reading considering fundamental rights to be cardinal rights); JOHN RAWLS, A THEORY OF JUSTICE (1971) (providing a critical reading with a different understanding that values courts).

89. See RICHARD T. FORD, RACIAL CULTURE: A CRITIQUE (2005).

90. Julie C. Suk, *Are Gender Stereotypes Bad for Women? Rethinking Antidiscrimination Law and Work-Family Conflict*, 110 COLUM. L. REV. 1, 54 (2010).

91. Infra Chapter 4 and Chapter 5 on gender discrimination.

92. Inspired by American legal realism, the CLS movement emerged in the 1970s. See MARK KELMAN, A GUIDE TO CRITICAL LEGAL STUDIES (1987); COSTA DOUZINAS &

Adam Gearey, Critical Jurisprudence: The Political Philosophy of Justice (2005); Roberto Mangabeira Unger, The Critical Legal Studies Movement (1983); Left Legalism / Left Critique (Wendy Brown & Janet Halley eds., 2003); Duncan Kennedy, Legal Education and the Reproduction of Hierarchy: A Polemic Against the System, A Critical Edition (2004); Duncan Kennedy, A Critique of Adjudication: Fin de Siècle (1997).

93. Michel Foucault, Surveiller et punir (1975); Jacques Derrida, Introduction, in Edmund Husserl, L'origine de la géométrie (1962); Jacques Derrida, Force de loi (1994); Jacques Derrida, L'écriture et la différence (1967).

94. See François Ewald, *Le droit du travail: une légalité sans droit?*, 11 Dr. soc. 723, 723–28 (1985); Antoine Jeammaud, *Propositions pour une compréhension matérialiste du droit du travail*, 11 Dr. soc. 337, 337–45 (1978); Antoine Jeammaud, *La règle de droit comme modèle*, Recueil Dalloz 199, 199–210 (1990); Antoine Jeammaud & Evelyne Serverin, *Evaluer le droit*, Recueil Dalloz 263, 263–68 (1992); Antoine Jeammaud, *Les règles juridiques et l'action*, Recueil Dalloz 207, 207–12 (1993); Antoine Jeammaud et al., *L'ordonnancement des relations du travail*, Recueil Dalloz 359, 359–68 (1998). On legal sociology, *see* Jean Carbonnier, Flexible droit (2001). See critical thought in other countries: Birkbeck (University of London), University of Melbourne, University of Kent, Keele University, University of Glasgow, and University of East London. There is also a strong critical legal tradition of course in Belgium. *See also* the law reviews Law and Critique and Australian Feminist Law Journal, among others.

95. *See* Marie Mercat-Bruns, *La doctrine américaine sur les discriminations et le genre: dialogue entre la critique du droit et la pratique*, 2 Juris. Rev. Crit. 93 (2011).

96. *See generally* Libby S. Adler et al., Women and the Law (4th ed. 2008); and William N. Eskridge & Nan D. Hunter, Sexuality, Gender, and the Law (2nd ed. 2004).

97. For all of these issues, *see infra* Chapter 5, Sections III, IV, and V.

98. Chapter 4 will look at the contours of "institutional" discrimination found in disparate impact cases, for example.

99. *See generally* Robert C. Post et al., Prejudicial Appearances: The Logic of American Antidiscrimination Law 1 (2001).

2. ANTIDISCRIMINATION MODELS AND ENFORCEMENT

1. This interview has been enriched, at the request of Robert Post, with excerpts from his publications.

2. Robert C. Post, Constitutional Domains: Democracy, Community, Management 4 (1995).

3. *Id.* at 4–5.

4. *Id.*

5. Robert C. Post, *The Social Foundations of Privacy: Community and Self in the Common Law of Tort*, 77 Cal. L. Rev. 957 (1989).

6. Philip Selznick, The Moral Commonwealth: Social Theory and the Promise of Community 358 (1994).

7. Post, *supra* note 2, at 3.

8. *Id.*

9. Post, *supra* note 5.

10. Post, *supra* note 2, at 3.

11. Post, *supra* note 5, at 961.
12. FOWLER V. HARPER & FLEMING JAMES, JR., THE LAW OF TORTS, § 16.2 (1956).
13. POST, *supra* note 2, at 27.
14. *See* ROBERT POST ET AL., PREJUDICIAL APPEARANCES: THE LOGIC OF AMERICAN ANTIDISCRIMINATION LAW 1 (2001).
15. POST, *supra* note 2, at 6.
16. *Id.* at 7.
17. *Id.*
18. *Id.* at 7–8.
19. Lochner v. New York, 198 U.S 45 (1905) (Supreme Court decision holding that the Fourteenth Amendment protects an individual's "general right to make a contract in relation to his business" and striking down a New York law prohibiting individuals from working in bakeries for more than ten hours per day or sixty hours per week).
20. POST, *supra* note 2, at 8.
21. For a better understanding of the first, second, and fourth functions, see POST, *supra* note 2, at 1.
22. *See infra* Chapter 4, for reflections on the concept of reasonable accommodation and systemic discrimination.
23. *See* Jordan v. United Kingdom, App. No. 24746/94, 2001-III Eur. Ct. H.R. 537; Zarb Adami v. Malta, App. No. 17209/02, Eur. Ct. H.R. 305 (2006-VIII); D. H. v. Czech Republic, App. No. 57325/00, Eur. Ct. H.R. (2007); Oršuš v. Croatia, App. No. 15766/03, Eur. Ct. H.R. (2010); and see JEAN-FRANÇOIS RENUCCI, DROIT EUROPÉEN DES DROITS DE L'HOMME 82 (2010). On the other hand, no indirect discrimination based on religion in S.A.S. v. France, No. 43835/11, Eur. Ct. H.R. (2014).
24. See Sophie Robin-Olivier, *Politique sociale de l'Union européenne*, 3 RTD EUR. 673 (2010).
25. Especially when the notion of harassment as it affects the dignity of the person is considered as a form of discrimination. *See, e.g.,* Directive 2000/78/EC.
26. *See also* Alec Stone Sweet & Jud Mathews, *Proportionality Balancing and Global Constitutionalism*, 47 COLUM. J. TRANSNAT'L L. 73 (2008).
27. Tor-Inge Harbo, *The Function of the Proportionality Principle in EU Law*, 16 EUR. L.J. 158 (2010).
28. On the employment of older workers, see Case C-144/04, Mangold v. Helm, 2005 E.C.R. I-9981, even though today the CJEU is more often deferent when scrutinizing, for example, retirement policies targeting older workers, see Case C-141/11, Torsten Hörnfeldt v. Posten Meddelande AB, 2012 E.C.R I-00000, or pay grading schemes if they are transitional; see, for example, Case C-501/12, Specht (June 19, 2014); Case C-20/13, Daniel Unland (Sept. 9, 2015).
29. *See* Mark Bell & Lisa Waddington, *Reflecting on Inequalities in European Equality Law*, 28 EUR. L. REV. 349, 351 (2003).
30. *Id.* at 351–52.
31. *See also* Moshe Cohen-Eliya, *Proportionality and the Culture of Justification*, 59 AM. J. COMP. L. 463 (2011).
32. Mark Bell & Lisa Waddington, *More Equal Than Others: Distinguishing European Union Equality Directives*, 38 COMMON MKT. L. REV. 587 (2001).
33. *See* Marie Mercat-Bruns, *Âge et discrimination indirecte: une jurisprudence en gestation (Soc. 19 octobre 2010, 2 arrêts)*, 7–8 REV. DR. TRAVAIL 441, 443 (2011). The challenges of disparate impact discrimination in the United States have let some American scholars to provide another, more global view of equality norms: "Antidiscrimination law is best

justified as a policy tool that aims to dismantle patterns of group-based social subordination, and that does so principally by integrating members of previously excluded, socially salient groups throughout important positions in society. . . . I recognize that my definition of 'antidiscrimination' leaves out an important aspect of what we usually call antidiscrimination law—the prohibition on practices that have a disparate impact on members of protected classes and that lack a sufficient business justification." Samuel Bagenstos, *Rational Discrimination, Accommodation and the Politics of Disability (Civil) Rights* 89 VA. L. REV. 833, 839 (2003) ; Samuel Bagenstos, *Employment Law and Social Equality* 112 MICH. L. REV. 226 (2013); Tristin Green, *Discrimination in Workplace Dynamics : Toward a Structural Account of Disparate Treatment Theory* 38 HARV. C.R.-C.L. L. REV. 91 (2003).

34. *See* EQUAL, http://ec.europa.eu/employment_social/equal_consolidated/ (archived Mar. 24, 2011); EQUINET, EUROPEAN NETWORK OF EQUALITY BODIES, http://www.equineteurope.org/.

35. Christopher McCrudden, Theorizing European Equality Law and the Role of Mainstreaming, *in* Equality Authority Conference on Equality Law, Dublin (2001); AILEEN MCCOLGAN, DISCRIMINATION, EQUALITY AND THE LAW 6 (2014).

36. Bell & Waddington, *supra* note 32, at 358.

37. *See* from the lower court case Conseil de Prud'hommes [CP] [labor court] Mantes la Jolie, Dec. 13, 2010, Association Baby-Loup, No. 10–00587, to the last decision of the Cour de Cassation upholding a restriction of religious practice (veil) in a day care center, Cass. soc., June 25, 2014, No. 13–28369, on the dilemmas of equality and liberty in the workplace; *see also* Cass. soc., Apr. 9 2015, No. 13–19855: the Cour de Cassation is asking the CJEU for preliminary ruling on the question whether banning the veil of an engineer can be an essential and determining requirement for the job because of customer preference; *see* Marie Mercat-Bruns, *Les discriminations multiples au croisement des questions d'égalité et de libertés*, 1 REV. DR. TRAVAIL 28 (2015).

38. Case C-303/06, Coleman v. Attridge Law & Steve Law, 2008 E.C.R. I-5603; for a more recent decision on indirect discrimination by association, see *supra* Chapter 1, note 60: Case C-83/14, CHEZ Razpredelenie Bulgaria AD (July 16, 2015).

39. Case C-267/06, Maruko v. Versorgungsanstalt der deutschen Bühnen, 2008 E.C.R. I-1757; Case C-147/08 Jürgen Römer v. Freie und Hansestadt Hamburg 2011 E.C.R. I-03591; Case C-267/12, Hay v. Crédit Agricole Mutuel de Charente-Maritime et des Deux-Sèvres, 2013 E.C.R. I-0000 (Dec. 12, 2013) ; Case C-81/12 25 Accept (Apr. 25, 2013).

40. "Under article L.331-8 and D.331-4 of the Social Security Code, paternity leave is linked to the father because of the legal parent-child relationship; these provisions exclude any discrimination based on sex or sexual orientation and do not infringe on the right to a family life. Considering the Court of Appeals rightly decided that Miss X could not benefit from the paternity leave . . . ," Cass. 2e civ., Mar. 11, 2010, No. 09–65.853, Bull. civ., II, No. 57. This contrasts with the CJEU's consideration of cases involving leave for mothers who use surrogates, although it has not recognized the right at this point: see recently Cases C-167/12, C. D. v S. T., 2014 E.C.R. I-000 and C-363/12, Z. v. A Government Department, E.C.R. I-000.

41. *See* Laure Bereni, *Faire de la diversité une richesse pour l'entreprise: La transformation d'une contrainte juridique en catégorie managériale*, 35 RAISONS POLITIQUES 87 (2009).

42. See the unsuccessful litigation of an employer contesting the investigations of the HALDE, which were seen as favoring the employee and violating the principle of equality of arms at trial under article 6 of the European Convention, Cass. soc., June 2, 2010, No. 08–40.628, Bull. civ. V, No. 124.

43. See proportionality test in art. 6 of Directive 2000/78/EC.

44. *See generally* LUCIE CLUZEL-MÉTAYER & MARIE MERCAT-BRUNS, DISCRIMINATIONS DANS L'EMPLOI: ANALYSE COMPARATIVE DE LA JURISPRUDENCE DU CONSEIL D'ÉTAT ET DE LA COUR DE CASSATION (2011).

45. Law 2001-1066 of Nov. 16, 2001 (against discrimination); Law 2008-496 of May 27, 2008 (on adjustments to EU law to combat discrimination).

46. The concept of systemic discrimination is not included in French law, whereas the United States refers to systemic disparate treatment, and case law in Canada defines systemic discrimination; *see* decision of the Supreme Court of Canada, ATF c. C.N. (25 juin 1987, RCS 1114).The EEOC describes it on its website (http://www.eeoc.gov/eeoc/systemic/):

> Systemic discrimination involves a pattern or practice, policy, or class case where the alleged discrimination has a broad impact on an industry, profession, company or geographic area. [. . .] Examples of systemic practices include: discriminatory barriers in recruitment and hiring; discriminatorily restricted access to management trainee programs and to high level jobs; exclusion of qualified women from traditionally male dominated fields of work; disability discrimination such as unlawful pre-employment inquiries; age discrimination in reductions in force and retirement benefits; and compliance with customer preferences that result in discriminatory placement or assignments.

The French class action bill still pending in Parliament (http://www.legifrance.gouv.fr/affichLoiPreparation.do?idDocument=JORFDOLE000030962821&type=general&typeLoi=proj&legislature=14) might lead to further reflection on structural discrimination; *see* Marie Mercat-Bruns & Emmanuelle Boussard Verrecchia, *Appartenance syndicale, sexe, âge et inégalités: vers une reconnaissance de la discrimination systémique*, REV. DR. TRAVAIL 91 (2015); Marie Mercat-Bruns, *Comparaison entre les discriminations fondée sur l'appartenance syndicale, l'âge et le sexe, révélatrice de la discrimination systémique* REV. DR. TRAVAIL 103 (2015).

47. See the reports from the HALDE (the last annual report was submitted by Éric Molinié for 2010) and the current reports from the Defender of Rights, http://www.defenseurdesdroits.fr/documentation.

48. It is necessary to compare, for example, the decision making of the HALDE in the public sphere and that of the Defender of Rights; see art. 1 of Organic Law 2011-333 of Mar. 29, 2011 (describing the organization of the Defender of Rights): the Defender of Rights is not the competent authority for claims between public persons and institutions with public service missions, but it is a constitutional body.

49. The recent introduction of a French bill to promote a form of class action *(action de groupe)* against discrimination reflects the increasing political momentum to encourage broader litigation against discrimination through NGOs and unions. See link for legislative history of bill still pending: http://www.legifrance.gouv.fr/affichLoiPreparation.do?idDocument=JORFDOLE000030962821&type=general&typeLoi=proj&legislature=14.

Two different versions of the bill passed in the National Assembly and Senate, which are going to be merged by legislative committee into a final version of the law, submitted for adoption in January 2016.

50. At this point, it looks like the French judicial review *(question prioritaire de constitutionnalité* [QPC]) serves more to legitimize the changes brought about exclusively by the legislative branch, without applying its own substantive equality standard. Consider the way the Constitutional Council decided, before the French law of 2013 on same-sex marriage, that treating people in different situations (same-sex couples) differently did not violate the principle of equality: CC decision No. 2010-92 QPC, Jan. 28, 2011. Following the adoption of the same-sex marriage law, the Conseil Constitutionnel reversed its position: CC decision No. 2013-669 DC, May 17, 2013. Compare with the more progressive recent

U.S. Supreme Court decision on same-sex marriage: Obergefell v. Hodges, 576 U.S. ___ (2015).

51. *See* Reva B. Siegel, *Equality Talk: Antisubordination and Anticlassification Values in Constitutional Struggles over* Brown, 117 HARV. L. REV. 1470 (2004) [hereinafter Siegel, *Equality Talk*]; Reva B. Siegel, *From Colorblindness to Antibalkanization: An Emerging Ground of Decision in Race Equality Cases*, 120 YALE L. J. 1278 (2011) [hereinafter Siegel, *Colorblindness to Antibalkanization*]; Reva B. Siegel, *The Supreme Court, 2012 Term—Foreword: Equality Divided*, 127 HARV. L. REV. 1 (2013) [hereinafter Siegel, *Equality Divided*].

52. Siegel, *Colorblindness to Antibalkanization, supra* note 51.

53. Grutter v. Bollinger, 539 U.S. 306 (2003).

54. Parents Involved in Cmty. Sch. v. Seattle Sch. Dist. No. 1, 551 U.S. 701 (2007).

55. Ricci v. DeStefano, 129 S. Ct. 2658, 2671, 174 L. Ed. 2d 490 (2009).

56. Siegel, *Colorblindness to Antibalkanization, supra* note 51, at 1278, 1282.

57. *See* Frédérique Michéa, La cohésion sociale en droit communautaire (2003) (unpublished thesis, Université de Rennes, supervised by Daniel Gadbin).

58. The article has since been published: Siegel, *Colorblindness to Antibalkanization, supra* note 51.

59. *See infra* Chapter 3 on systemic discrimination.

60. Siegel, *Colorblindness to Antibalkanization, supra* note 51.

61. Parents Involved in Cmty. Sch. v. Seattle Sch. Dist. No. 1, 551 U.S. 701 (2007).

62. "The plurality opinion is too dismissive of the legitimate interest government has in ensuring all people have equal opportunity regardless of their race. The plurality's postulate that '[t]he way to stop discrimination on the basis of race is to stop discriminating on the basis of race' . . . is not sufficient to decide these cases. . . . The enduring hope is that race should not matter; the reality is that too often it does." *Parents Involved*, 551 U.S. at 787–88 (Kennedy, J., concurring in part and concurring in the judgment).

63. *Id.* at 789.

64. *Id.* at 797.

65. *Id.* at 789.

66. *See* MARTHA MINOW, MAKING THE DIFFERENCE : INCLUSION, EXCLUSION, AND AMERICAN LAW (1990).

67. Law 2011–103 of Jan. 27, 2011 (on the balanced representation of women and men in executive boards and professional equality). Its scope was extended to other institutions within the public sector by Law 2014–873 of Aug. 4, 2014 (on real equality between men and women), http://www.legifrance.gouv.fr/eli/loi/2014/8/4/FVJX1313602L/jo/article_61; *Commission Proposal for a Directive of the European Parliament and of the Council on Improving the Gender Balance among Non-executive Directors of Companies Listed on Stock Exchanges and Related Measures*, COM (2012) 614 final (Nov. 14, 2012)

68. The HALDE also recommended adding place of residence as a prohibited ground of discrimination in its decision No. 2011–121 of Apr. 18, 2011; this proposal was adopted in a recent law on urbanization, Law 2014–173 of Feb. 21, 2014.

69. See FRENCH AMERICAN FOUNDATION, PROMOUVOIR L'EGALITÉ DES CHANCES DANS L'ENSEIGNEMENT SUPERIEUR SELECTIF: L'EXPÉRIENCE AMERICAINE DES PERCENTAGES PLANS ET SA PERTINENCE DANS LE CONTEXTE FRANÇAIS (2008).

70. Ricci v. DeStefano, 129 S. Ct. 2658, 2671, 174 L. Ed. 2d 490 (2009).

71. Siegel, *Colorblindness to Antibalkanization, supra* note 51, at 1365–66.

72. Senator Barack Obama, A More Perfect Union, Address at the National Constitution Center (Mar. 18, 2008), http://constitutioncenter.org/amoreperfectunion/docs/Race_Speech_Transcript.pdf.

73. Siegel, *Equality Divided*, supra note 51.

74. Michéa, *supra* note 57.

75. Jean-Philippe Lhernould, *L'éloignement des Roms et la directive 2004/38 relative au droit de séjour des citoyens de l'UE*, 11 Dr. Soc. 1024 (2010) ; Serge Slama, *Roms, Go Home*, Recueil Dalloz 2056 (2010); Jean-Pierre Margénaud & Jean Mouly, *Délogement et relogement des Roms: la France dans le collimateur de la CEDH*, Recueil Dalloz 2678 (2013).

76. See infra Chapter 4 on indirect discrimination.

77. See on gender, Éric Fassin, L'inversion de la question homosexuelle (2005); Éric Fassin, *Statistiques raciales ou racistes? Histoire et actualité d'une controverse française*, in Les nouvelles frontières de la société française 427 (Didier Fassin ed., 2010); Éric Fassin et al., Roms et riverains, une politique municipale de la race (2014).

78. See Siegel, *Colorblindness to Antibalkanization*, supra note 51, at 1346 ("managing the 'public social meaning'").

79. Janet Halley, Split Decisions: How and Why to Take a Break from Feminism (2006).

80. See Conseil représentatif des associations noires, http://lecran.org/.

81. See Louis Chauvel, Le destin des générations: structure sociale et cohortes en France du xxième siècle aux années 2010 (2011).

82. See the growing body of case law on age discrimination, Marie Mercat-Bruns, *Retour sur la discrimination fondée sur l'âge*, 10 Rev. Dr. Travail 587 (2010) and infra Chapter 5; Marie Mercat-Bruns, *Age and disability differential treatment in France—Contrasting EU and national courts approaches to the inner limits of anti-discrimination law*, Int'l J. Discrimination & L. (Nov. 12, 2014), http://jdi.sagepub.com/content/early/2014/11/12/135822 9114558383.abstract. See more recently for example, CJEU Case C-529/13, Felber, (Jan. 21, 2015); Case C-417/13, Starjakob (Jan. 28, 2015); Case C-20/13, Daniel Unland (Sept. 9, 2015); Case C-432/14, Bio Philippe Auguste SARL (Oct. 1, 2015).

83. See EEOC, http://www.eeoc.gov/; Margo Schlanger & Pauline Kim, *The Equal Employment Opportunity Commission and structural reform of the American workplace*, 91 Wash. U.L. Rev. 1519 (2014); Pauline T. Kim , *Addressing Systemic Discrimination: Public Enforcement and the Role of the EEOC* 95 B.U. L. Rev. 1133 (2015).

84. See also Julie C. Suk, *Criminal and Civil Enforcement of Antidiscrimination Law in Europe*, 14 Eur. Anti-discrimination L. Rev. 11 (2012).

85. The comparative outlooks in this work do not dwell on remedies, but the interviewed scholars cover this point.

86. Punitive damages do not exist in France, and in the United States these damages do not exist for age discrimination.

87. Even though a statute of limitations exists in claims for discrimination, the "reality" of the discrimination, as the Cour de Cassation calls it, can cover periods of time prior to that specified by this statute of limitations to acknowledge the difference of treatment with colleagues hired at the same time with the same qualifications. See Cass. soc., Jan. 26, 2010, No. 08-44397; Cass. soc., Feb. 4, 2009, No. 07-42697; see also Cass. soc., June 12, 2012, No. 10-14632; Cass. soc., Jan. 15, 2014, No. 12-24860 and No. 12-24966 (after reinstatement, on the calculation of remedies in a case of discrimination based on health status).

88. See Julie C. Suk, *Equal by Comparison: Unsettling Assumptions of Antidiscrimination Law*, 55 Am. J. Comp. L. 295 (2007).

89. National Labor Relations Act of 1935, 29 U.S.C. §§ 151–69.

90. National Association for the Advancement of Colored People, http://www.naacp.org/content/main.

91. American Civil Liberties Union, http://www.aclu.org/.

92. NATIONAL LAWYERS GUILD, https://www.nlg.org/.
93. On the prohibition of discrimination based on race, color, religion, sex, and national origin in employment, Title VII of the Civil Rights Act of 1964, 42 U.S.C. § 2000e, et seq., and its amendments with the Civil Rights Act of 1991 (Pub. L. 102–166).
94. *See* Wal-Mart v. Dukes, 131 S. Ct. 2541 (2011) (No. 10–277) on June 20, 2011, limiting the scope of class action lawsuits in cases of discrimination under civil procedure Rule 23(b)(2). It does not apply to equal pay class action cases (Equal Pay Act): Allen Smith, *Pay Class Actions Will Survive*, Jun. 1, 2011, http://www.shrm.org/legalissues/federalresources/pages/payclassactions.aspx.
95. David Benjamin Oppenheimer, *Verdicts Matter : An Empirical Study of California Employment Discrimination and Wrongful Discharge Jury Verdicts Reveals Low Success Rates for Women and Minorities*, 37 U.C. DAVIS L. REV. 511 (2003).
96. Julie C. Suk, *supra* notes 84 and 88.
97. See laws and guidelines of the EEOC: http://www.eeoc.gov/laws/regulations/index.cfm; http://www.eeoc.gov/laws/guidance/index.cfm.
98. See *infra* Chapter 5 for case law on the concept of disability in the Americans with Disability Act (ADA), reversed by the 2008 amendments of the ADA, http://www.ada.gov/pubs/ada.htm.
99. On physical appearance discrimination, see ROBERT POST ET AL., PREJUDICIAL APPEARANCES: THE LOGIC OF AMERICAN ANTIDISCRIMINATION LAW 1 (2001).
100. Thereza M. Beiner, *The Many Lanes Out of Court : Against Privatization of Employment Discrimination Disputes*, 73 MD. L. REV. 837 (2014).
101. On pregnancy discrimination, Marie Mercat-Bruns, *La portée de l'interdiction de licenciement au moment du congé maternité*, 1 REV. DR. TRAVAIL 31 (2011).
102. Although today, experts like Julie Suk observe that the challenge is more often that cases like *Bell Atlantic v. Twombly* 550 U.S. 544 (2007) have raised the burden of pleading for plaintiffs in civil proceedings; the burden of proof of discrimination has not been raised, but it is harder for plaintiffs to vindicate rights in court.
103. SERVICE EMPLOYEES INTERNATIONAL UNION, http://www.seiu.org/.
104. AMERICAN FEDERATION OF LABOR, http://www.aflcio.org/.
105. Montgomery passed away in 2011. DAVID MONTGOMERY, BEYOND EQUALITY: LABOR AND RADICAL REPUBLICANS 1862–1872 (1981); DAVID MONTGOMERY, BLACK WORKERS' STRUGGLE FOR EQUALITY IN BIRMINGHAM (2004); DAVID MONTGOMERY, CITIZEN WORKER: THE EXPERIENCE OF WORKERS IN THE UNITED STATES WITH DEMOCRACY AND THE FREE MARKET DURING THE NINETEENTH CENTURY (1994).
106. Even though case law on union discrimination is extensive; see recently an interesting case on indirect discrimination based on different wage calculations after participation in a strike, Cass. soc., *July 9, 2015*, 14–12779.
107. Despite the challenges the ILO is facing in the global context, which is less favorable to social norms. *See* Jean-Michel Servais, *L'incontournable besoin d'une agence de régulation sociale*, REV. DR. TRAVAIL 530 (2012).
108. *See* Cass. soc., July 10, 2001, Bull. No. 261: under article L.412–2 of the French Labor Code, the dismissal of an employee based on union discrimination is null and void; *see also* Cass. soc., July 9, 2014, No. 13–16434 and No. 13–16805.
109. Outside of European collective bargaining agreements, see MICHEL MINÉ ET AL., DROIT SOCIAL INTERNATIONAL ET EUROPÉEN EN PRATIQUE 73 (2013).
110. *See* CLUZEL-MÉTAYER & MERCAT-BRUNS, *supra* note 44, at 65; *see recently* Cass. soc., Jan. 15, 2014, No. 12–24860; Cass. soc., Oct. 8, 2014, No. 13–18342; Cass. soc., Nov. 26, 2014, No. 13–21379.

111. CLUZEL-MÉTAYER & MERCAT-BRUNS, *supra* note 44, at 23. Recent decisions on equal pay demonstrate that diplomas still play a role to identify work of comparable value, Cass. soc., Sept. 30, 2015, No. 14-17748.

112. Steele v. Louisville & N.R. Co., 323 U.S. 192 (1944).

113. *See* Law 2008-789 of Aug. 20, 2008 (on the renovation of social democracy and reform of worktime), and Law 2013-504 of June 14, 2013 (on securing employment).

114. On the "Justice for Janitors" campaign by Latino immigrants, see Maria Ontiveros, *A New Course for Labour Unions: Identity-Based Organizing as a Response to Globalization*, in LABOUR LAW IN AN ERA OF GLOBALIZATION: TRANSFORMATIVE PRACTICES AND POSSIBILITIES 418 (Joanne Conaghan et al. eds., 2002).

115. Michael Selmi & Molly S. McUsic, *Difference and Solidarity: Unions in a Postmodern Age*, in LABOUR LAW IN AN ERA OF GLOBALIZATION, *supra* note 114, at 430.

116. *Id.* at 443.

117. FRANK DOBBIN, INVENTING EQUAL OPPORTUNITY (2009).

118. *See* Morgan Sweeney, L'égalité en droit social au prisme de la diversité et du dialogue des juges (2010) (unpublished thesis on diversity, Université Paris Ouest Nanterre).

3. DISPARATE TREATMENT DISCRIMINATION: INTENT, BIAS, AND THE BURDEN OF PROOF

1. *See* Watson v. Fort Worth Bank & Trust, 487 U.S. 977, at 986.

2. In the absence of overt discrimination, a "smoking gun." *See* Fuller v. Phipps, 67 F.3d 1137 (4th Cir. 1995); Tyler v. Bethlehem Steel Corp., 958 F.2d 1176 (2d Cir. 1992); Price Waterhouse v. Hopkins, 490 U.S. 228 (1989). But overt discrimination is not always required in mixed motive cases; *see* Desert Palace, Inc. v. Costa, 539 U.S. 90 (2003).

3. On the difficulty of obtaining access to proof in discrimination cases in France, see LUCIE CLUZEL-MÉTAYER & MARIE MERCAT-BRUNS, DISCRIMINATIONS DANS L'EMPLOI: ANALYSE COMPARATIVE DE LA JURISPRUDENCE DU CONSEIL D'ÉTAT ET DE LA COUR DE CASSATION 69 (2011).

4. Case C-54/07, Centrum voor gelijkheid van kansen en voor racismebestrijding v. Feryn, 2008 E.C.R. I-5187 (discriminatory statements made to a newspaper by a Belgian employer who said he could not hire persons from the Maghreb to sell gates door-to-door because customers would not open to them).

5. *See* McDonnell Douglas Corp. v. Green, 411 U.S. 792 (1973).

6. *See McDonnell*, 411 U.S.; and Texas Dep't of Cmty. Affairs v. Burdine, 450 U.S. 253 (1981) ("the plaintiff has the burden of establishing a prima facie case, which he/she can satisfy by showing that (i) he belongs to a racial minority; (ii) he applied and was qualified for a job the employer was trying to fill; (iii) though qualified, he was rejected; and (iv) thereafter the employer continued to seek applicants with plaintiff's qualifications"); and subsequent cases: St. Mary's Honor Ctr. v. Hicks, 509 U.S. 502 (1993); Reeves v. Sanderson Plumbing Prods., Inc., 530 U.S. 133 (2000). *See also* later cases on the prima facie framework, not necessarily on hiring: Fisher v. Pharmacia & Upjohn, 225 F.3d 915, 918-19 (8th Cir. 2000); Brown v. McLean, 159 F.3d 898, 905 (4th Cir. 1998); Silvera v. Orange Cnty. Sch. Bd., 244 F.3d 1253, 1259 (11th Cir. 2001); Jones v. Bessemer Carraway Med. Ctr., 137 F.3d 1306, 1311 (11th Cir. 1998).

7. Cécile Michaud, *La preuve des discriminations en droit du travail*, 46 JCP S 11 (2012); *generally*, on rules of evidence in France, see ETIENNE VERGES, GERALDINE VIAL, & OLIVIER LECLERC, DROIT DE LA PREUVE (2015).

8. *McDonnell*, 411 U.S. at 807; Lindahl v. Air France, 930 F.2d 1437 (1991); Lowe v. City of Monrovia, 775 F.2d 1008 (1985); *see* Deborah C. Malamud, *The Last Minuet: Disparate*

Treatment After Hicks, 93 MICH. L. REV. 2229 (1995); Note, *Title VII—Burden of Persuasion in Disparate Treatment Cases,* 107 HARV. L. REV. 342, 348 (1993).

9. *See* Cass. soc., Nov. 10, 2009, No. 07-42849; Cass. soc., Mar. 23, 2011, No. 09-42666 FSPB; Cass. soc., Jun. 29, 2011, No. 10-14067; Cass, soc., June 12, 2013, No. 12-14.153; Cass. soc., Feb. 20, 2013, No. 10-30028.

10. In this case, it was simpler to prove indirect discrimination; proof of direct discrimination was harder without a comparator. *See* Cass. soc., Nov. 3, 2011, No. 10-20765 ("To characterize discrimination does not require a comparison with the situation of other workers").

11. Cass. soc., Oct. 8, 2014, No. 13-11789. *See* Marie Mercat-Bruns, *Inaptitude physique non professionnelle et discrimination directe dans une convention collective,* 2 REV. DR. TRAVAIL 119 (2015).

12. Griggs v. Duke Power Co., 401 U.S. 424 (1971).

13. Susan P. Sturm, *The Architecture of Inclusion: Interdisciplinary Insights on Pursuing Institutional Citizenship,* 30 HARV. J.L. & GENDER 407 (2007).

14. Marie Mercat-Bruns, *Sciences sociales et discrimination dans l'emploi: leçons de l'expérience américaine,* 2 LAW & EUR. AFF. 185 (2010).

15. Research on this field is prolific outside of the work by L. Krieger and C. Jolls. For example, see Richard Thompson Ford, *Bias in the Air: Rethinking Employment Discrimination Law,* 66 STAN. L. REV. 1381 (2014); Samuel Bagenstos, *The Structural Turn and Limits of Antidiscrimination Law,* 94 CAL. L. REV. 1 (2006); Barbara Flagg, *Was Blind But Now I See: White Race Consciousness and the Requirement of Discriminatory Intent,* 91 MICH. L. REV. 953 (1993); Tristin Green, *Discrimination in the Workplace Dynamics: Toward a Structural Account of Disparate Treatment Theory,* 38 HARV. C.R.-C.L. REV. 91 (2003); Anton Page, *Batson's Blind-Spot: Unconscious Stereotyping and the Peremptory Challenge,* 85 B.U. L. REV. 155 (2005); Kevin Clermont & Stewart Schwab, *Employment Discrimination Plaintiffs in Federal Court: From Bad to Worse?,* 3 HARV. L. & POL'Y REV 103 (2009); R. A. Nagareda, *Class Certification in the Age of Aggregate Proof,* 84 N.Y.U. L. REV. 97 (2009); Gregory Mitchell & Philip E. Tetlock, *Antidiscrimination Law and the Perils of Mindreading,* 67 OHIO ST. L.J. 1023 (2006); Jerry Kang & Mazahrin Banaji, *Fair Measures: A Behavioral Realist Revision of "Affirmative Action,"* 94 CAL. L. REV. 1063 (2006).

16. Anthony Greenwald & Linda Krieger, *Implicit Bias: Scientific Foundations,* 94 CAL. L. REV. 945 (2006). *See* PROJECT IMPLICIT, https://implicit.harvard.edu/implicit/. It is still difficult to win a case on gender bias within a certain profession; *see* the 2015 Ellen Pao v. Kleiner Perkins case: http://www.npr.org/sections/thetwo-way/2015/09/10/439232954/ellen-pao-former-reddit-ceo-drops-appeal-in-gender-discrimination-lawsuit.

17. Amy Wax, *The Discriminating Mind: Find It, Prove It,* 40 CONN. L. REV. 979 (2009).

18. Richard T. Ford, *Lutter contre les discriminations raciales: les vertus de la mesure statistique, in* DIVERSITÉ ET DISCRIMINATIONS RACIALES: UNE PERSPECTIVE TRANSATLANTIQUE 76, 83 (Frédéric Guiomard & Sophie Robin-Olivier eds., 2009).

19. *See* Charles R. Lawrence III, *The Id, the Ego and Equal Protection: Reckoning with Unconscious Racism,* 39 STAN. L. REV. 317 (1987).

20. Vicki Schultz, *The Sanitized Workplace,* 112 YALE L.J. 2061 (2003).

21. Greenwald & Krieger, *supra* note 16, at 945.

22. Christine Jolls, *Behavioral Economics Analysis of Employment Law, in* THE BEHAVIORAL FOUNDATIONS OF PUBLIC POLICY 264 (Eldar Shafir ed., 2013).

23. For further discussion of empirical evidence of implicit racial and other bias, see Christine Jolls & Cass R. Sunstein, *The Law of Implicit Bias,* 94 CAL. L. REV. 969 (2006).

24. *Id.*

25. GARY BECKER, THE ECONOMICS OF DISCRIMINATION (1957); Edmund Phelps, *The Statistical Theory of Racism and Sexism*, 62 AM. ECON. REV. 659 (1972); Ariane Ghirardello, *Pour une analyse économique positive de la discrimination*, 11 ECON. & SOC. 1891 (2004); Stéphane Carcillo & Etienne Wasmer, *Discrimination and Bilateral Human Capital Investments Decisions*, 71–72 ANNALES D'ÉCONOMIE & STATISTIQUES 317 (2003).

26. *La validité méthodologique du testing*, OBSERVATOIRE DES DISCRIMINATIONS, UNIVERSITÉ PARIS 1 PANTHÉON SORBONNE, http://www.observatoiredesdiscriminations.fr/#!testing/c1d3j.

27. *See* Devah Pager, *Estimating Risk: Stereotype Amplification and the Perceived Risk of Criminal Victimization*, 73 SOC. PSYCHOL. Q. 79 (2010); Devah Pager et al., *Discrimination in a Low-Wage Labor Market: A Field Experiment*, 74 AM. SOC. REV. 777 (2009).

28. A new report came out on May 19, 2015, from France's Ministry of Labor, Ministry of Justice, and Ministry of Youth and Sports, recommending eighteen measures to fight discrimination in employment: among them, the report recommends auto-testing measures that encourage companies to participate in external evaluations and verify résumé selection to check for biases in recruitment. The report also advises introducing into law a type of class-action type procedure against discrimination. *See infra* Chapter 2, note 47. *See also Trois ministres engagés contre les discriminations au travail*, MINISTRY OF JUSTICE (May 19, 2015), http://www.justice.gouv.fr/la-garde-des-sceaux-10016/trois-ministres-engages-contre-les-discriminations-au-travail-28097.html.

29. Elizabeth Levy Paluck & Donald P. Green, *Prejudice Reduction: What Works? A Critical Look at Evidence from the Field and the Laboratory*, 60 ANN. REV. PSYCHOL. 339 (2009).

30. Linda Hamilton Krieger & Susan T. Fiske, *Behavioral Realism in Employment Discrimination Law: Implicit Bias and Disparate Treatment*, 94 CAL. L. REV. 997 (2006).

31. Rep. from the European Commission to the European Parliament and the Council on the Application of the Racial Equality Directive 2000/43/EC and Employment Equality Directive 2000/78/EC, at 10, COM (2014) 2 final (Jan. 17, 2014), http://ec.europa.eu/justice/discrimination/files/com_2014_2_en.pdf.

32. Linda Krieger, *The Watched Variable Improves: On Eliminating Sex Discrimination in Employment*, *in* SEX DISCRIMINATION IN EMPLOYMENT 295, 310 (Faye Crosby et al. eds, 2007).

33. *See* Tristin Green, *Discrimination in Workplace Dynamics: Toward a Structural Account of Disparate Treatment Theory*, 38 HARV. C.R.-C.L. L. REV. 91 (2003); Tristin Green, *The Future of Systemic Disparate Treatment Law* 32 BERKELEY J. EMP. & LAB. L. 387(2011).

34. Gwénaële Calvès, *Reflecting the Diversity of the French Population*, 57 INT'L. SOC. SCI. J. 165 (2005); REJANE SENAC, L'INVENTION DE LA DIVERSITÉ (2012).

35. Definition of *social framework evidence*: "In employment litigation, an expert offering social framework testimony will explain the general social science research on the operation of stereotyping and bias in decision making and will examine the policies and practices operating in the workplace at issue to identify those that research has shown will tend to increase or limit the likely impact of these factors." Melissa Hart & Paul M. Secunda, *A Matter of Context: Social Framework Evidence in Employment Discrimination Class Actions*, 78 FORDHAM L. REV. 39 (2009).

36. *See* Marie Mercat-Bruns, *Égalité salariale, discriminations individuelles et systémiques: un éclairage de la jurisprudence américaine*, 114 REVUE DE L'OFCE 95 (2010).

37. Marie Mercat-Bruns, *Sciences sociales et discrimination dans l'emploi: leçons de l'expérience américaine*, 2 LAW & EUR. AFF. 185 (2010).

38. Criminal sanctions are found in arts. 225–1 and 225–2 of the French Penal Code. The articles prohibit (intentional) direct discrimination but not indirect discrimination.

There is no shift in the burden of proof in criminal procedure. On the limits of proving discrimination through criminal sanctions, see Elisabeth Fortis, *Réprimer les discriminations depuis la loi du 27 novembre 2008: entre incertitudes et impossibilités*, ACTUALITÉS JURIDIQUES PÉNAL 303 (2008). For a recent example of a criminal case in which discrimination based on disability was rejected, see Cass. crim., *Mar. 17, 2015, No. 13-88062*.

The French version of this book also goes into more depth to explain the scope of criminal law prohibiting antidiscrimination and the limited case law in the employment sector because of the standard of proof in criminal proceedings: MARIE MERCAT-BRUNS, DISCRIMINATIONS AU TRAVAIL: DIALOGUE AVEC LA DOCTRINE AMÉRICAINE 210 (2013).

39. David Benjamin Oppenheimer, *Negligent Discrimination*, 141 U. PA L. REV. 899 (1993).

40. *Id.* at 899–978.

41. This development in tort law stems from a broad interpretation of art. 1384 of the Civil Code; *see* Matthieu Poumarède, *L'avenement de la responsabilité du fait d'autrui, in* MÉLANGES EN L'HONNEUR DE PHILIPPE LE TOURNEAU 839 (2008).

42. JACQUES FLOUR ET AL., LES OBLIGATIONS: 2. LE FAIT JURIDIQUE 80 (2011).

43. *See* RAYMOND SALEILLES, LES ACCIDENTS DE TRAVAIL ET LA RESPONSABILITÉ CIVILE: ESSAI D'UNE THÉORIE OBJECTIVE DE LA RESPONSABILITÉ DÉLICTUELLE (1897), http://gallica.bnf.fr/ark:/12148/bpt6k5455257c.

44. Yvonne Lambert-Faivre, *L'éthique de la responsabilité*, REV. TRIM. DR. CIV. 1 (1998).

45. *See* PHILIPPE BRUN, RESPONSABILITÉ CIVILE EXTRACONTRACTUELLE 11 (2009).

46. *See* PHILIPPE KOURILSKY & GENEVIÈVE VINEY, LE PRINCIPE DE PRÉCAUTION: RAPPORT AU PREMIER MINISTRE (2000).

47. Some authors are worried that there is a progressive tortification of employment discrimination law in the United States; *see* William Corbett, *What Is Troubling About the Tortification of Employment Discrimination Law?* 75 OHIO ST. L.J. 1027 (2014) (following Supreme Court decisions like Staub v. Proctor Hospital, 131 S. Ct. 1186, 1191 (2011)).

48. Price Waterhouse v. Hopkins, 490 U.S. 228 (1989), was the first case to confront the issue directly. Then the Civil Rights Act of 1991 (Pub. L. No. 102-166, 105 Stat. 1071, § 2 (1991) (codified as amended at 42 U.S.C. § 1981 (2008)) made it easier on the plaintiff in these types of cases.

49. Gross v. FBL Fin. Servs., Inc., 557 U.S. 167, 180 (2009) ; Univ. of Tex. Sw. Med. Ctr. v. Nassar, 133 S. Ct. 2517, 2532–33 (2013).

4. FROM DISPARATE IMPACT TO SYSTEMIC DISCRIMINATION

1. Ricci v. DeStefano, 129 S. Ct. 2658, 2681 (2009). *See* Charles A. Sullivan, *Ricci v. DeStefano: End of the Line or Just Another Turn on the Disparate Impact Road?*, 104 NW. U. L. REV. 411 (2010) ; Richard Primus, *The Future of Disparate Impact*, 108 MICH. L. REV. 1341, 1345 (2010); for a critical view of disparate impact discrimination, see Amy L. Wax, *Disparate Impact Realism*, 53 WM. & MARY L. REV. 621, 625 (2011).

2. *See, for example,* Cass. soc., June 6, 2012, No. 10-21489; Cass. soc., July 3, 2012, No. 10-23013; Cass. soc., May 23, 2012, No. 10-18.341; Cass. soc., Feb. 12, 2013, No. 11-27689; Cass. soc., Sept. 30, 2013, No. 12-14752; *see* Marie Mercat-Bruns, *Pourquoi certains métiers féminisés ne rentrent pas dans le "cadre"?* 35 JCP 908 (2012) [hereinafter Mercat-Bruns, *Métiers féminisés*]. After asking the CJEU whether it was indirect discrimination to treat married and civil union couples differently with regard to a collective bargaining right, the court followed the CJEU and concluded that it was direct discrimination, *See* Cass. soc., July 9, 2014, No. 10-18341; Cass. soc., Sept. 24, 2014, Nos. 13-10233, 13-10234; Cass. soc.,

Oct. 22, 2014, joined cases No. 13-16936 and No. 13-17209 (a case rejecting indirect sex discrimination).

3. *See* CHRISTA TOBLER, INDIRECT DISCRIMINATION: A CASE STUDY IN THE DEVELOPMENT OF THE LEGAL CONCEPT OF INDIRECT DISCRIMINATION UNDER EC LAW 424 (2005).

4. According to the EEOC, "systemic practices include: discriminatory barriers in recruitment and hiring; discriminatorily restricted access to management trainee programs and to high level jobs; exclusion of qualified women from traditionally male dominated fields of work; disability discrimination such as unlawful pre-employment inquiries; age discrimination in reductions in force and retirement benefits; and compliance with customer preferences that result in discriminatory placement or assignments.... The identification, investigation and litigation of systemic discrimination cases, along with efforts to educate employers and encourage prevention, are integral to the mission of the EEOC." *Systemic Discrimination*, EEOC (n.d.), http://www1.eeoc.gov/eeoc/systemic/index.cfm. The Ministry of Justice and the Defender of Rights have also ordered a report on the implementation of antidiscrimination law in France that will cover the issue of systemic discrimination, headed by the Sciences Po law school/political research center and CERSA (Centre d'Études et de Recherches de Sciences Administratives et Politiques): *see* MARIE MERCAT-BRUNS & JEREMY PERELMAN, LES JURIDICTIONS ET LES INSTANCES PUBLIQUES DANS LA MISE EN OEUVRE DU PRINCIPE DE NON-DISCRIMINATION: PERSPECTIVES PLURIDISCIPLINAIRES ET COMPARÉES (forthcoming 2016); *see also infra* note 140. *See also* Marie Mercat-Bruns & Emmanuelle Boussard Verrecchia, *Appartenance syndicale, sexe, âge et inégalités: vers une reconnaissance de la discrimination systémique* 11 REV. DR. TRAVAIL 660 (2015) ; Marie Mercat-Bruns, *Comparaison entre les discriminations fondée sur l'appartenance syndicale, l'âge et le sexe, L'identification de la discrimination systémique*, REV. DR. TRAVAIL 672 (2015).

5. *Ricci*, 129 S. Ct. at 2677 ("We hold only that, under Title VII, before an employer can engage in intentional discrimination for the asserted purpose of avoiding or remedying an unintentional disparate impact, the employer must have a strong basis in evidence to believe it will be subject to disparate-impact liability if it fails to take the race-conscious, discriminatory action").

6. *Id.* at 2690.

7. *Id.* at 2700.

8. *Id.* at 2678.

9. *Id.*

10. Bradley v. Pizzaco of Nebraska, Inc., 7 F.3d 795 (8th Cir. 1993).

11. See also on disparate impact, Christine Jolls, *Antidiscrimination and Accommodation*, 115 HARV. L. REV. 642 (2001).

12. Twenty-one states and the District of Columbia have passed laws prohibiting employment discrimination based on sexual orientation. Attempts to prohibit discrimination on a federal level include the Employment Non-Discrimination Act (ENDA), H.R. 1755; S. 815 was approved by the Senate on November 7, 2013, by a bipartisan vote of 64-32.

13. *See* Griggs v. Duke Power Co. 401 U.S. 424 (1971) (recognizing disparate impact discrimination for the first time); David Garrow, *Toward a Definitive History of* Griggs v. Duke Power Co., 67 VAND. L. REV. 197 (2014); ROBERT BELTON, THE CRUSADE FOR EQUALITY IN THE WORKPLACE: THE *GRIGGS V. DUKE POWER* STORY (2014).

14. Ford Motor Co. v. EEOC, 458 U.S. 219 (1982).

15. Ricci v. DeStefano, 129 S. Ct. 2658 (2009).

16. David Benjamin Oppenheimer, *Negligent Discrimination*, 141 U. PA. L. REV. 899 (1993).

17. On judicial scrutiny on just cause of economic layoffs (CODE DU TRAVAIL [LABOR CODE] art. L. 1233-3); the justification can be the need to restructure the company to stay competitive (Cass. soc., Mar. 24, 2010, 494 REV. JURIS. SOC. 2010).

18. Wards Cove Packing Co. v. Atonio, 490 U.S. 642 (1989).

19. The requirement of business necessity: *see infra* "Establishing Indirect Discrimination: A Two-Step Test and a Reversal of the Burden of Proof."

20. Julie Suk, U.S. Equality Law, *in* Workshop on Evolution of Equality Law and Theory, European University Institute, Florence (Jan. 29, 2010).

21. One of the assets of employment discrimination law is the shift of the burden of proof of discrimination.

22. *See* Marie Mercat-Bruns, *Âge et discrimination indirecte: une jurisprudence en gestation (Soc. 19 octobre 2010, 2 arrêts)*, 7–8 REV. DR. TRAVAIL 441 (2011) [hereinafter Mercat-Bruns, *Âge et discrimination indirecte*]; Cass. soc., Mar. 30, 1994, Dr. Soc. 561 (1994); Cass. soc., Apr. 9, 1996, Dr. Ouvrier 10 (1988); Cass. soc., Jan. 9, 2007, No. 05–43962; Cass. soc., June 6, 2012, No. 10–21489; Mercat-Bruns, *Métiers féminisés, supra* note 2, at 908; Cass. soc., July 3, 2012, No. 10–23013; Cass. soc., Nov. 3, 2011, No. 10–20765; Cass. soc., Feb 12, 2013, No. 11–27689; Cass. soc., Sept. 30, 2013, No. 12–14752; Cass. soc., July 9, 2014, No. 10–18341 (finally preferring direct to indirect discrimination in light of CJEU preliminary ruling); Cass. soc., Sept. 24, 2014, No. 13–10233, 13–10234; Cass. 2e civ., July 12, 2012, No. 10–24661 (no indirect discrimination in a case before the Second Civil Chamber of the Cour de Cassation); *see* Cass. soc. *July 9, 2015, No. 14–12779* (more recently recognizing indirect discrimination after participation in a strike).

23. *See* Julie Suk, *Disparate Impact Abroad*, *in* A NATION OF WIDENING OPPORTUNITIES? THE CIVIL RIGHTS ACT AT 50 (Samuel Bagenstos & Ellen Katz eds., forthcoming 2015).

24. Michael Selmi, *Was the Disparate Impact Theory a Mistake?* 53 UCLA L. REV. 701 (2006).

25. Griggs v. Duke Power Co., 401 U.S. 424 (1971), and research on its impact: Michael Evan Gold, Griggs' *Folly: An Essay on the Theory, Problems, and Origins of the Adverse Impact Definition of Employment Discrimination and a Recommendation for Reform*, 7 INDUS. REL. L.J. 429 (1985); George Rutherglen, *Disparate Impact Under Title VII: An Objective Theory of Discrimination*, 73 VA. L. REV. 1297 (1987); Amy Wax, *Disparate Impact Realism*, 53 WM. & MARY L. REV. 621 (2011).

26. *Griggs*, 401 U.S. at 437.

27. Pub. L. 102–166, 105 Stat. 1072 (Nov. 21, 1991). It was, among other things, to counter the effects of a Supreme Court that had heightened the burden of proof of plaintiffs in a disparate impact case, Ward's Cove Packing v. Atonio, 490 U.S. 642 (1989).

28. Susan Carle, *A New Look at the History of Title VII Disparate Impact Doctrine*, 63 FLA. L. REV. 251 (2011).

29. *Id.*

30. William L. Bulkley, *The Industrial Condition of the Negro in New York City*, 27 ANNALS AM. ACAD. POL. & SOC. SCI. 128 (May 1906).

31. New York State's Ives-Quinn Act, 1945 N.Y. Laws 457.

32. *See* Carle, *supra* note 28, at 283; Holland v. Edwards, 307 N.Y. 38, 119 N.E.2d 581, 584 (1954): this was almost disparate impact discrimination based on religion, looking systematically at maiden names, and the judges observed that there are ways to discriminate in a more subtle and discreet manner.

33. Myart. v. Motorola, Inc. No. 636–27, reprinted in 110 Cong. Rec. 5662 (1964).

34. *See* Carle, *supra* note 28, at 292.

35. 401 U.S. 424, 430 (1971), 420 F.2d at 1232; Melissa Hart, *From* Wards Cove *to* Ricci: *Struggling Against the "Built-In Headwinds" of a Skeptical Court*, 46 WAKE FOREST L. REV. 262 (2011).

36. *See* McClain v. Lufkin Indus., Inc., 519 F.3d 264, 275–79 (5th Cir. 2008); EEOC v. Joe's Stone Crab, Inc., 220 F.3d 1263, 1275, 1288 (11th Cir. 2000); Davis v. Cintas Corp., 717 F.3d 476, 497 (6th Cir. 2013).

37. Ricci v. DeStefano, 129 S. Ct. 2658 (2009).

38. Lewis v. City of Chicago, 130 S. Ct. 2191 (2010).
39. Erica E. Hoodhood, *The Quintessential Employer's Dilemma: Combating Title VII Litigation by Meeting the Elusive Strong Basis in Evidence Standard*, 45 VALPARAISO U. L. REV. 111 (2010); Lindsey E. Sacher, *Through the Looking Glass and Beyond: The Future of Disparate Impact Doctrine under Title VII*, 61 CASE W. RESERVE L. REV. 603 (2010).
40. Especially in view of the fact the disparate impact theory does not apply to the equal protection clause: *see* Washington v. Davis, 426 U.S. 229 (1976); Pers. Adm'r of Mass. v. Feeney, 442 U.S. 256 (1979).
41. Antidiscrimination law is not just a blame game.
42. *See* Equal Treatment Directive 1976/207, art. 2 (1), and Directive 97/80/EC of Dec. 15, 1997, on the Burden of Proof in Cases of Discrimination Based on Sex, art. 2.
43. PETER OLIVER, FREE MOVEMENT OF GOODS IN THE EUROPEAN COMMUNITY (2003); even though some authors still rely on the notion of indirect discrimination in their analysis of the free circulation of goods and services in Europe; GARETH DAVIES, NATIONALITY DISCRIMINATION IN THE EUROPEAN INTERNAL MARKET (2003).
44. Case C-236/09, Test-Achats v. Council of Ministers, 2010 E.C.R. I-773.
45. Case C-152/73, Sotgiu v. Deutsche Bundespost, 1974 E.C.R. I-153.
46. Case C-96/80, Jenkins v Kingsgate, 1981 E.C.R. 911.
47. Christine Jolls describes the subtle nature of disparate impact discrimination; *see* Jolls, *supra* note 11, at 670.
48. Case C-170/84, Bilka-Kaufhaus v. Hartz, 1986 E.C.R. 1607.
49. See the first definition in Article 2, Directive 97/80/EC of Dec. 15, 1997 on the burden of proof in cases of discrimination based on sex; Directive 2000/43/EC of June 29, 2000 implementing the principle of equal treatment between persons irrespective of racial or ethnic origin; Directive 2000/78/EC of Nov. 27, 2000, establishing a general framework for equal treatment in employment and occupation. Regarding the direct influence of British politicians and lawyers on the adoption of an indirect discrimination framework in Europe, see Suk, *supra* note 23, at 5.
50. Griggs v. Duke Power Co., 401 U.S. 424 (1971).
51. Case C-300/06, Voss v. Land Berlin, 2007 E.C.R. I-10573.
52. Joined Cases C-297/10 and C-298/10, Hennigs v. Eisenbahn-Bundesamt and Land Berlin v. Mai, 2011 E.C.R. I-7965, pt. 101; *see* Marie Mercat-Bruns, *La CJUE et les présomptions sur l'âge*, 12 REV. JURIS. SOC. 815 (2011). See more recently for example of acquired rights and transitional pay schemes based on experience but still linked to age, Case C-501/12 to Case C-506/12, Case C-540/12 and Case C-541/12, Specht (June 19, 2014); Case C-20/13, Daniel Unland (Sept. 9, 2015)
53. In the most recent cases on discriminatory pay schemes, see *supra* 52, transitional pay systems that still refer to age produce differential treatment based on age but are justified and proportionate if not indefinite in perpetuating discrimination for disfavored categories under old pay schemes. The debate focuses on admissibility of exception to direct discrimination based on age and not indirect discrimination.
54. Case C-123/10, Brachner v. Pensionsversicherungsanstalt, 2011 E.C.R. I-000. A more recent decision on law pertaining to disability pensions for part-time workers in Spain did not consider that the legal norm statistically disadvantaged part-time workers, particularly women, and ruled out indirect discrimination: Case C-527/13, Fernandez v. Instituto Nacional de la Seguridad Social, CJEU (Apr. 14, 2015).
55. Indirect discrimination based on sex can favor men; concerning pension rights for men, see Case C-173/13, Leone and Leone v. Garde des Sceaux (July 17, 2014) (on indirect discrimination based on age discrimination), and Case C-152/11, Odar v. Baxter Deutschland GmbH, 2012 E.C.R. I-0000.

56. Case C-83/14 *CHEZ Razpredelenie Bulgaria AD (July 16, 2015)*:

The concept of "discrimination on the grounds of ethnic origin," . . . [in] . . . Directive 2000/43/EC of 29 June 2000 . . . must be interpreted as being intended to apply in circumstances such as those at issue before the referring court—in which, in an urban district mainly lived in by inhabitants of Roma origin, all the electricity meters are placed on pylons forming part of the overhead electricity supply network at a height of between six and seven metres, whereas such meters are placed at a height of less than two metres in the other districts—irrespective of whether that collective measure affects persons who have a certain ethnic origin or those who, without possessing that origin, suffer, together with the former, the less favourable treatment or particular disadvantage resulting from that measure.

57. *See* Jean-Philippe Lhernould, *Les discriminations fondées sur le sexe et la Cour de cassation*, 11 REV. JURIS. SOC. 731 (2012); *see infra* "Establishing Indirect Discrimination: A Two-Step Test and a Reversal of the Burden of Proof."

58. Alfred W. Blumrosen, *The Legacy of* Griggs: *Social Progress and Subjective Judgments*, 63 CHI.-KENT L. REV. 3–5 (1987).

59. *See* Oppenheimer, *supra* note 16.

60. Hart, *supra* note 35, at 262.

61. Civil Rights Act (CRA) of 1991, SEC. 2000e-2; Section 105: (a); Section 703, CRA of 1964, Title VII (42 U.S.C. 2000e-2). *See* Susan Grover, *The Business Necessity Defense in Disparate Impact Discrimination Cases*, 30 GA. L. REV. 387 (1996).

62. The other directives focus on nationality, race, origin, and sex.

63. *See* Lhernould, *supra* note 57, at 731.

64. Outside of *Griggs*, see other cases on selection processes and whether they are job-related: Conn. v. Teal, 457 US 440 (1982); N.Y. City Transit Auth. v. Beazer, 523 US 83 (1979); Dothard v. Rawlinson, 433 US 321 (1977); Albermarle Paper Co. v. Moody, 422 US 405 (1975); after the CRA of 1991, *see also* Lanning v. Southeastern Pa. Transp. Auth., 181 F.3d 478 (Ed Cir 1999); Bryant v. City of Chicago, 200 F.3d 1092 (7th Cir. 2000).

65. 42 U.S.C. § 2000e-2(k)(1) (2006). Congress amended Title VII of the CRA of 1991 to counter the Supreme Court's holding in Wards Cove Packing Co. v. Atonio, 490 U.S. 642 (1989): an employer whose practice is found to have such an impact may avoid liability by proving that the challenged discriminatory practice is required by "business necessity."

66. The plaintiffs must designate the specific employment practice that caused the disparate impact. *See* McClain v. Lufkin Indus., Inc., 519 F.3d 264, 275–79 (5th Cir. 2008); EEOC v. Joe's Stone Crab, Inc., 220 F.3d 1263, 1275, 1288 (11th Cir. 2000); Davis v. Cintas Corp., 717 F.3d 476, 497 (6th Cir. 2013).

67. Hoodhood, *supra* note 39, at 111, 122.

68. The Supreme Court acknowledges the importance of this rule: Eang L. Ngov, *When the "Evil Day" Comes, Will Title VII's Disparate Impact Provision Be Narrowly Tailored to Survive an Equal Protection Clause Challenge?* 60 AM. U. L. REV. 543 (2011).

69. This calculation is also essential to prove systemic disparate treatment discrimination; *see* Teamsters v. United States, 431 U.S. 324 (1977).

70. Jennifer L. Peresie, *Toward a Coherent Test for Disparate Impact Discrimination*, 84 IND. L. REV. 773–74 (2009).

71. Mercat-Bruns, *Âge et discrimination indirecte*, *supra* note 22, at 441. Cases on direct age discrimination towards younger workers are emerging more and more on the EU level; *see recently* Case C-432/14, Bio Philippe Auguste SARL, Oct. 1, 2015.

72. CRA of 1991, SEC. 2000e-2.; Section 105: (a); Section 703, CRA of 1964, Title VII (42 U.S.C. 2000e-2). But in the United States, the contours of the protected age group are

limited to those over 40 (see Chapter 5 on age discrimination) whereas in France, all ages are covered.

73. Case C-147/08, Römer v. City of Hamburg, 2011 E.C.R. I-3591.

74. This point can be crucial if the scope of the apparently neutral law is not explicit. It is then easier to show that the law benefits a certain type of people and that the discriminatory impact of the law targets the majority of the protected group.

75. *See, for example,* Cass. soc., Nov. 10, 2009, No. 07-42849; Cass. soc., Mar. 23, 2011, No. 09-42666; Cass. soc., June 29, 2011, No. 10-14067; Cass. soc., Feb. 20, 2013, No. 10-30028.

76. Cass. soc., Nov. 3, 2011, No. 10-20765.

77. 42 U.S. Code § 2000e-2 (k); respondent must demonstrate that the challenged practice is job related for the position in question and consistent with business necessity. Courts have often accepted employer justifications for their practices; see some earlier decisions: Lanning v. Se. Pa. Transp. Auth., 308 F.3d 286 (3d Cir. 2002); Ass'n of Mexican-Am. Educators v. Cal., 231 F.3d 572 (9th Cir. 2000).

78. The French Cour de Cassation examined this second prong of the indirect discrimination test in 2012 for the first time; Mercat-Bruns, *Métiers féminisés, supra* note 2, at 908.

79. EEOC Uniform Guidelines on Employee Selection Procedures, 29 CFR § 1607.1 and 1607.4.

80. *Id.* at 29 CFR § 1607.4.

81. Mark J. Simeon, *Symposium: Perspectives on Equal Employment Opportunity Litigation: Title VII Defenses: An Overview,* 27 HOWARD L.J. 479, 486 (1984).

82. *See* Griggs v. Duke Power Co., 401 U.S. 424, 431 (1971); or the plaintiff can show there was a possible alternative selection process with no disparate impact, as in Albemarle v. Moody, 422 U.S. 405, 425 (1975).

83. Wards Cove Packing Co. v. Atonio, 490 U.S. 642 (1989), reversed by the Civil Rights Act (CRA) of 1991 (Pub. L. 102-166).

84. Cass. soc., June 6, 2012, No. 10-21489.

85. *See* Case C-96/80, Jenkins v Kingsgate, 1981 E.C.R. 911; Case C-300/06, Voss v. Land Berlin, 2007 E.C.R. I-10573.

86. Mercat-Bruns, *Âge et discrimination indirecte, supra* note 22, at 443.

87. Cass. soc., June 6, 2012, No. 10-21489.

88. Cass. soc., Jan. 9, 2007, No. 05-43962. *See also* Cass. soc., Feb. 12, 2013, No. 11-27689.

89. *See* Mercat-Bruns, *Métiers féminisés, supra* note 2, at 908.

90. See similar discussion on modes of evaluation of wage standards in joined cases C-297/10 and C-298/10, Hennigs v. Eisenbahn-Bundesamt and Land Berlin v. Mai, 2011 E.C.R. I-07965, and subsequent cases *supra* note 52.

91. *See, e.g.,* Cass. soc., Nov. 10, 2009, No. 07-42849: proof of discrimination does not necessarily require a comparison with the status of other employees.

92. Cass. soc., Nov. 3, 2011, No. 10-20765.

93. CODE DU TRAVAIL [LABOR CODE] art. 1132-1.

94. Case C-147/08, Römer v. City of Hamburg, 2011 E.C.R. I-3591.

95. Cass. soc., Nov. 3, 2011, No. 10-20765.

96. *See* Cass. soc., July 3, 2012, No. 10-23013; Cass. 2e civ., July 12, 2012, No. 10-24661.

97. Cass. soc., Nov. 3, 2011, No. 10-20765: this undocumented domestic worker was not in a comparable situation with workers legally protected by law who can contest their dismissal in court.

98. Treaty on the Functioning of the European Union [TFEU] art. 157, § 1.

99. Lhernould, *supra* note 57, at 734, 735.

100. Lhernould, *supra* note 57, at 737.

101. Case C-381/99, Brunnhofer v. Bank der österreichischen Postsparkasse, 2002 E.C.R. I-4961.
102. CODE DU TRAVAIL [LABOR CODE] art. L.3221–4.
103. Case C-147/08, Römer v. City of Hamburg, 2011 E.C.R. I-3591; Case C-267/12, Hay v. Crédit Agricole Mutuel de Charente-Maritime et des Deux-Sèvres, 2013 E.C.R. I-0000, §37.
104. Cass. 2e civ., July 12, 2012, No. 10–24661.
105. Julie Suk, Robert Post, and David Oppenheimer.
106. Lewis v. City of Chicago, 130 S. Ct. 2191 (2010).
107. Michael Selmi, *Was the Disparate Impact Theory a Mistake?* 53 UCLA L. REV. 701, 705 (2006).
108. Owen M. Fiss, *Groups and the Equal Protection Clause*, 5 PHIL. & PUB. AFF. 107, 147–57 (1976); John Donohue, *Employment Discrimination Law in Perspective: Three Concepts of Equality*, 92 MICH. L. REV. 2609 (1994); Samuel Bagenstos, *Employment Law and Social Equality*, 112 MICH. L. REV. 225, 228 (2013).
109. Washington v. Davis, 426 U.S. 229 (1976); Pers. Adm'r v. Feeney, 442 U.S. 256 (1979). For an excellent analysis of the case law, see Reva B. Siegel, *The Supreme Court, 2012 Term—Foreword: Equality Divided*, 127 HARV. L. REV. 16 (2013) [hereinafter Siegel, *Equality Divided*].
110. Ricci v. DeStefano, 129 S. Ct. 2658, 2682 (2009) (Scalia, J., concurring); Richard Primus, *The Future of Disparate Impact*, 108 MICH. L. REV. 1341 (2010).
111. See Suk, *supra* note 23, at 1.
112. Julie Suk, *Are Gender Stereotypes Bad for Women? Rethinking Antidiscrimination Law and Work-Family Conflict*, 110 COLUM. L. REV. 4 (2010).
113. Hart, *supra* note 35, at 271.
114. Cheryl Harris & Kimberly West-Faulcon, *Reading* Ricci: *Whitening Discrimination, Racing Test Fairness*, 58 UCLA L. REV. 73, 163–65 (2010).
115. Helen Norton, *The Supreme Court's Post-Racial Turn Towards a Zero-Sum Understanding of Equality*, 52 WM. & MARY L. REV. 224 (2010).
116. Case C-17/05, Cadman v. Health and Safety Executive, 2006 E.C.R. I-9583.
117. Case C-297/10 and C-298/10, Hennigs v. Eisenbahn-Bundesamt and Land Berlin v. Mai, 2011 E.C.R. I-07965. See subsequent cases, *supra* note 52.
118. See more recently Case C-173/13, Leone v. Garde des Sceaux, July 17, 2014, which extends retirement rights to men based on indirect discrimination.
119. In Case C-83/14, *CHEZ Razpredelenie Bulgaria AD, July 16, 2015 (see supra note 56), the Court combines indirect discrimination with discrimination by association (which is a form of direct discrimination; see CJEU Coleman described infra in Chapter 5, "VI. Disability and Age Discrimination").
120. See *supra* note 77.
121. Strong basis evidence.
122. See Marie Mercat-Bruns, *Sciences sociales et discrimination dans l'emploi: leçons de l'expérience américaine*, 2 LAW & EUR. AFF. 185 (2010).
123. Cases on indirect discrimination at the European Court of Human Rights: D.H. v. Czech Republic, App. No. 57325/00, Eur. Ct. H.R. 2007; Jordan v. United Kingdom, App. No. 24746/94, 2001-III Eur. Ct. H.R. 537, § 154; Zarb Adami v. Malta, App. No. 17209/02, 2006-VIII Eur. Ct. H.R. 305; Oršuš v. Croatia, App. No. 15766/03, Eur. Ct. H.R. 2010.
124. Jolls, *supra* note 11, at 642.
125. "The way to stop discrimination on the basis of race is to stop discriminating on the basis of race," Parents Involved in Cmty. Sch. v. Seattle Sch. Dist. No. 1, 551 U.S. 701, 748 (2007) (Roberts, J., concurring).
126. Strong *critics* of this view: RICHARD EPSTEIN, FORBIDDEN GROUNDS: THE CASE AGAINST EMPLOYMENT DISCRIMINATION LAWS 234–36 (1992); Deborah Malamud, *Values, Symbols, and Facts in the Affirmative Action Debate*, 95 MICH. L. REV. 1668, 1693 (1997).

127. Jolls, *supra* note 11, at 642.

128. Herbert Bernhardt, Griggs v. Duke Power Co.: *The Implications for Private and Public Employers,* 50 TEX. L. REV. 901, 928 (1972); Alfred W. Blumrosen, *The Legacy of Griggs: Social Progress and Subjective Judgments* 63 CHI.-KENT L. REV. 3–5 (1987).

129. *See also* Julie Suk, *Quotas and Consequences: A Transnational Re-evaluation, in* PHILOSOPHICAL FOUNDATIONS OF DISCRIMINATION LAW 228 (Deborah Hellman & Sophia Moreau eds., 2013).

130. Rejection of the "bottom line analysis" in *Conn. v. Teale,* 457 US 1982, p. 440; The same analysis is implicit in Directive 2000/78/EC ("indirect discrimination shall be taken to occur where an apparently neutral provision, criterion or practice would put persons . . . at a particular disadvantage").

131. Ambivalent term sometimes used in France.

132. Flexible quotas with saving clause required: Case C-450/93, Kalanke v. Freie Hansestadt Bremen, 1995 E.C.R. I-3051; Case C-409/95, Marschall v. Land Nordrhein Westfalen 1997 E.C.R. I-6363; Case C-158/97, Badeck v. Landesanwalt beim Staatsgerichtshof des Landes Hessen, 1999 E.C.R. I-1875; Case C-407/98, Abrahamsson v. Fogelqvist, 2000 E.C.R. I-5539. For a reevaluation of quotas in light of European initiatives, see Suk, *supra* note 129, at 237.

133. Grutter v. Bollinger, 539 U.S. 306, 311 (2003); Regents of the Univ. of Calif. v. Bakke, 438 U.S. 265, 269–70 (1978); Fisher v. Univ. of Texas, 570 U.S. ___ (2013); see also state bans on state preferential treatment on the basis of race among other grounds (Arizona, Oklahoma, New Hampshire, etc.).

134. Case C-411/05, Palacios de la Villa v. Cortefiel Servicios SA, 2007 E.C.R. I-8531; Case C-447/09, Prigge v. Deutsche Lufthansa AG 2011 E.C.R. I-8003; joined Cases C-297/10 and C-298/10, Hennigs v. Eisenbahn-Bundesamt and Land Berlin v. Mai, 2011 E.C.R. I-7965; see Marie Mercat-Bruns, *La CJUE et les présomptions sur l'âge,* 12 REV. JURIS. SOC. 815 (2011), *supra* note 52, especially Case C-501/14 to C-506/12, Specht (June 19, 2014). Also compare with two cases that consider a legislative norm: Case C-530/13, Schmitzer (Nov. 11, 2014) (where budgetary considerations alone cannot justify a discriminatory pay scheme but deference of the Court concerning pension grading scheme based on a law); Case-529/13, Felber (Jan. 21, 2015).

135. Lauren B. Edelman & Mark C. Suchman, *When the Haves Hold Court: Speculations on the Organizational Internalization of Law,* 33 LAW & SOC'Y REV. 941 (1999).

136. *See* FRANK DOBBIN, INVENTING EQUAL OPPORTUNITY (2009).

137. In France, a similar debate exists on employment policies that conflict because they favor one category of unemployed workers over another. Companies then take advantage of these subsidies strategically, which implies that the interests of all vulnerable workers in employment cannot be taken into account.

138. HR in companies invites employers to review their job profiles and selection processes to avoid liability based on disparate impact discrimination; *see* DOBBIN, *supra* note 136, at 129.

139. See Bell Atlantic v. Twombly, 550 U.S. 544 (2007), which involved antitrust law and civil procedure; Ashcroft v. Iqbal 556 U.S. 662 (2009) explicitly extended the *Twombly* holding to constitutional civil rights/discrimination cases, but the lower courts had already begun to apply *Twombly* to Title VII plaintiffs. As Suk also mentions, the Supreme Court decision Walmart Stores, Inc. v. Dukes, 564 U.S. ___ (2011), considered one of the requirements of the procedural rules was not fulfilled (commonality; Federal Rule of Civil Procedure, Rule 23(a)), and so smaller-scale, regionally based class actions have been filed, in which the plaintiffs have more commonality.

140. The idea of systemic discrimination is increasingly present in the debate on discrimination in France. It is referred to in one of the former reports for the Ministry of

Justice on a possible class action to fight against collective discrimination: Laurence Pecaut-Rivolier, LUTTER CONTRE LA DISCRIMINATION AU TRAVAIL: UN DEFI COLLECTIF 27 (2013). Outside of systemic disparate treatment in U.S. case law, this form of discrimination has already been recognized by the Supreme Court of Canada in Action Travail des Femmes v. Canadian National Railway, [1987] S.C.R. 1114, 1139 (Can.), 8 C.H.R.R. D/4210 (S.C.C.). The French class action bill still pending in Parliament (http://www.legifrance.gouv.fr/affichLoiPreparation.do?idDocument=JORFDOLE000030962821&type=general&typeLoi=proj&legislature=14) might lead to further reflection on structural discrimination. *See* Marie Mercat-Bruns & Emmanuelle Boussard Verrecchia, *Appartenance syndicale, sexe, âge et inégalités : vers une reconnaissance de la discrimination systémique ?* 11 REV. DR. TRAVAIL 660 (2015) ; Marie Mercat-Bruns, *L'identification de la discrimination systémique* 11 REV. DR. TRAVAIL 672 (2015).

141. Fisher v. University of Texas 570 U.S. ___ (2013), June 24, 2013; Siegel, *Equality Divided*, supra note 109.

142. See CATHERINE L. HORN & STELLA M. FLORES, PERCENT PLANS IN COLLEGE ADMISSIONS: A COMPARATIVE ANALYSIS OF THREE STATES' EXPERIENCES 11 (The Civil Rights Project at Harvard University, 2003) ("Percent plans by state universities . . . guarantee admission for a fixed percentage of the top students from every high school in the state").

143. *Fisher,* supra note 141, at 8–13.

144. Siegel, *supra* note 109, at 1.

145. *See* Reva B. Siegel, *From Colorblindness to Antibalkanization: An Emerging Ground of Decision in Race Equality Cases*, 120 YALE L. J. 1278, 1300–08 (2011).

146. *See* Grutter v. Bollinger 539 U.S. 306 (2003), at 387–88, 395 (Kennedy, J., dissenting).

147. *See* Parents Involved in Cmty. Sch. v. Seattle Sch. Dist. No. 1, 551 U.S. 701 (2007) at 787–90, 797–98 (Kennedy, J., concurring).

148. Siegel, *supra* note 109, at 44.

149. *See, for example,* Regents of Univ. of Cal. v. Bakke, 438 U.S. 265 (1978); Grutter v. Bollinger 539 U.S. 306 (2003) (No. 02-241).

150. Suk, *supra* note 129, at 228.

151. Gwénaële Calvès, *Les politiques françaises de discrimination positive: trois spécificités,* 111 POUVOIRS 29 (2004).

152. *See* Mitu Gulati & Patrick S. Shin, *Showcasing Diversity,* 89 N.C. L. REV. 1031 (2011).

153. Beth Bilson, *A Dividend of Diversity: The Impact of Diversity on Organizational Decision Making,* 44 U.B.C. L. REV. 9 (2011).

154. Jennifer K. Brooke & Tom R. Tyler, *Diversity and Corporate Performance: A Review of the Psychological Literature,* 89 N.C. L. REV., 715, 745 (2011): "The best diversity management practices are rooted in procedural justice principles. Interpersonal respect, a proactive attitude towards diversity, the promotion of an overarching organizational identity, and respect for subgroup identities all play an important role in a positive diversity climate."

155. *See* Colleen Sheppard, *Grounds of Discrimination: Towards an Inclusive and Contextual Approach,* 80 CANADIAN BAR REV. 893, 911 (2001).

156. *See* RICHARD T. FORD, RACIAL CULTURE: A CRITIQUE 48 (2005).

157. Lauren B. Edelman et al., *Diversity Rhetoric and the Managerialization of Law,* 106 AM. J. SOC. 1589, 1590 (2001); Tristin Green, *Race and Sex in Organizing Work: "Diversity," Discrimination, and Integration,* 59 EMORY L. J. 595 (2010); Erin L. Kelly & Frank Dobbin, *How Affirmative Action Became Diversity Management: Employer Response to Antidiscrimination Law, 1961–1996,* 41 AM. BEHAV. SCI. 972 (1998).

158. Jerry Kang & Mahzarin R. Banaji, *Fair Measures: A Behavioral Realist Revision of "Affirmative Action,"* 94 CAL. L. REV. 1063, 1072–75 (2006).

159. Stephen A. Ross, *The Determination of Financial Structure: The Incentive Signaling Approach*, 8 BELL J. ECON. 35 (1977).

160. For a critique of this perspective, see Richard Delgado, *Affirmative Action as a Majoritarian Device: Or, Do You Really Want to Be a Role Model?* 89 MICH. L. REV. 1222, 1226–29 (1991).

161. Katharine Bartlett, *Making Good and Good Intentions: The Critical Role of Motivation in Reducing Implicit Workplace Discrimination*, 95 VA. L. REV. 1893, 1895–98 (2009); Linda Krieger, *The Content of Our Categories: A Cognitive Bias Approach to Discrimination and Equal Employment Opportunity*, 47 STAN. L. REV. 1161, 1213–16 (1995).

162. Christine Jolls & Cass R. Sunstein, *The Law of Implicit Bias*, 94 CAL. L. REV. 969, 988 (2006).

163. Angela Onwuachi-Willig, *Cracking the Egg: Which Came First—Stigma or Affirmative Action?* 96 CAL. L. REV. 1299 (2008).

164. *See* Gulati & Shin, *supra* note 152, at 1040.

165. *Id.* at 1041.

166. *See* David B. Wilkins, *From "Separate Is Inherently Equal" to "Diversity Is Good for Business": The Rise of Market-Based Diversity Arguments and the Fate of the Black Corporate Bar*, 117 HARV. L. REV. 1548, 1597–98 (2004).

167. *See* United Steelworkers of Am. v. Weber 443 U.S. 193 (1979); Johnson v. Transp. Agency of Santa Clara Cnty., 480 U.S. 616 (1986).

168. Laure Bereni, *Faire de la diversité une richesse pour l'entreprise: la transformation d'une contrainte juridique en catégorie managériale*, 35 RAISONS POLITIQUES 87, 104 (2009).

169. For example, this was the reaction of Renault and Ikea.

170. Same importance and ambivalence of diversity measures in the United States: Sung Hui Kim, *The Diversity Double Standard*, 89 N.C. L. REV. 945 (2011); James Fanto et al., *Justifying Board Diversity*, 89 N.C. L. REV. 901 (2011).

171. Through the "business case" of diversity, employers try to attract more women to their companies. *See* Wendy C. Schmidt, *Deloitte's Initiative for the Retention and Advancement of Women 2009 Brochure*, *in* DIVERSITY IN LAW PRACTICE 2010: STRATEGIES AND BEST PRACTICES IN CHALLENGING TIMES (Practising Law Institute, 2010).

172. CODE DE COMMERCE [COMMERCIAL CODE] art. L.225-18-1 as amended by Law 2014-873 of Aug. 4, 2014:

> The proportion of directors of each sex must not be less than forty percent in companies whose shares are admitted for trading on a regulated market and, at the close of the next general meeting called to appoint directors, in companies that, for the third consecutive year, employ an average of at least two hundred fifty permanent employees and have net revenues or a balance sheet total of at least fifty million euros. In these same companies, when there are more than eight members on the board of directors, the difference between the numbers of members of each sex must not be more than two. . . . Any appointment made in violation of the first paragraph that does not have the effect of remedying the irregularity of the composition of the board shall be null and void. This nullity does not invalidate the deliberations in which the irregularly appointed director may have participated.

As stated in art. 5 of Loi 2011-103 du 27 janvier 2011 relative à la représentation équilibrée des femmes et des hommes au sein des conseils d'administration et de surveillance et à l'égalité professionnelle [Law 2011-103 of January 27, 2011 on the balanced representation of women and men on boards of directors and supervisory boards and on equality in the workplace], JOURNAL OFFICIEL DE LA RÉPUBLIQUE FRANÇAISE [J.O.] [OFFICIAL GAZETTE OF FRANCE], Jan. 28, 2011, p. 1680:

> I. Sections II to VI and VIII of article 1, sections III to VII of article 2 and section II of article 4 come into force as of January 1 of the sixth year following the year of publication of this law. The

compliance of the boards of directors and supervisory boards of the companies concerned will be assessed at the close of the first ordinary general meeting following this date. The third consecutive year referred to in the first paragraph of articles L.225–18–1, L.225–69–1 and L.226–4–1 of the French Commercial Code is understood as from January 1 of the sixth year following the year of publication of this law. II. In the companies mentioned in Chapters V and VI of Title II of Book II of the Commercial Code whose shares are admitted for trading on a regulated market, the proportion of directors or supervisory board members of each sex must not be less than twenty percent at the close of the first ordinary general meeting following January 1 of the third year following the year of publication of this law. If one of the two sexes is not represented on the board of directors or supervisory board on the date of publication of this law, at least one representative of this sex must be appointed at the next ordinary general meeting held to appoint directors or supervisory board members.

Art. 7 of Law 2011–103:

By December 31, 2015, the government shall establish a report for the Parliament assessing the role of women on the boards of directors or equivalent bodies of public administrative establishments or publicly owned industrial and commercial establishments and presenting the State's efforts to achieve a representation of at least forty percent of each sex in these bodies.

173. *See* Law 2011–103 of Jan. 27, 2011 on the balanced representation of women and men on boards of directors and supervisory boards and on equality in the workplace, *supra* note 172; in the United States, Darren Rosenblum, *Feminizing Capital: A Corporate Imperative*, 6 BERKELEY BUS. L.J. 55 (2009); *see also* Law 2014–873 of Aug. 4, 2014 on "real equality" between men and women (extends parity rules to certain institutions of the public sector, sport organizations and unlisted companies employing, for three consecutive years, at least 500 employees and reporting profits of at least €50 million), *supra* note 172.

174. Julia Redenius-Hoevermann & Daniela Weber-Rey, *La représentation des femmes dans les conseils d'administration et de surveillance en France et en Allemagne*, 4 REV. SOCIÉTÉS 203 (2011); Véronique Martineau-Bourgninaud, *L'obligation de mixité dans les conseils d'administration et de surveillance*, 10 RECUEIL DALLOZ 599 (2010). See Anne-Françoise Bender, Isabelle Berrebi-Hoffmann, & Philippe Reigné, *Les quotas de femmes dans les conseils d'administration*, 34 TRAVAIL GENRE SOCIÉTÉ 169 (2015).

175. *See* Dan Kahan, *The Cultural Cognition of Risk: Theory, Evidence and Implications*, Cultural Cognition Project (Oct. 8, 2009); THE CULTURAL COGNITION PROJECT AT YALE LAW SCHOOL, http://www.culturalcognition.net.

176. Using a typology established by anthropologist Mary Douglas and cultural theorist Aaron Wildavsky, these Yale researchers have tested the hypothesis that worldviews (i.e., individual views of an "ideal society") can explain variations in individual perceptions of what is risky despite available facts on these risks: Dan M. Kahan et al., *Fear of Democracy: A Cultural Evaluation of Sunstein on Risk*, 119 HARV. L. REV. 1071, 1072 (2006). According to Douglas and Wildavsky's typology, there are four worldviews: communautarian, individualistic, egalitarian, and hierachist. *See* Mary Douglas, A History of Grid and Group Culture Theory, *available at* http://projects.chass.utoronto.ca/semiotics/cyber/douglas1.pdf.

177. Dodd-Frank Wall Street Reform and Consumer Protection Act, Pub. L. No. 111–203, 124 Stat. 1376 (2010); *see* Regina F. Burch, *Worldview Diversity in the Boardroom: A Law and Social Equity Rationale*, 42 LOY. U. CHI. L.J. 585, 621 (2011). In her article, Burch discusses risk in corporate law before and after the 2008 financial crisis and the passage of the Dodd-Frank Act, and argues that "corporate fiduciary duty law is sparse with respect to holding directors liable for taking unreasonable risks. Further, the Dodd-Frank Act contains risk management provisions, but does not go far enough." *See* Dodd-Frank Act, tit. I, § 165,124 Stat. 1376, 1423 (requiring large, interconnected financial institutions to set up risk

committees) and tit. IX, § 956 (requiring that certain financial institutions report information about incentive-based compensation programs and that corporate governance systems balance risks and financial rewards).

178. The Dodd-Frank Act requires listed financial companies to form risk management committees within boards of directors to "prevent or mitigate risks to the financial stability of the United States that could arise from material financial distress or failure, or ongoing activities, of large, interconnected financial institutions."

179. See Burch, *supra* note 177, at 585, 621.

180. Steven A. Ramirez, *Games CEOs Play and Interest Convergence Theory: Why Diversity Lags in America's Boardrooms and What to Do About It*, 61 WASH. & LEE L. REV. 1583, 1584 (2004).

181. See Theresa A. Gabaldon, *Like a Fish Needs a Bicycle: Public Corporations and Their Shareholders*, 65 MD. L. REV. 538 538, 547 (2006).

182. *See* RICHARD LEBLANC & JAMES GILLIES, INSIDE THE BOARDROOM: HOW BOARDS REALLY WORK AND THE COMING REVOLUTION IN CORPORATE GOVERNANCE 8 (2005) (advancing the thesis that "board decision-making is a function of the competencies and behavioural characteristics of the individual directors and how they fit together"); Burch, *supra* note 177, at 585, 625 ("Creative tension must also exist in the boardroom. This chemistry results from the interaction of directors who bring different interpersonal skills to the boardroom"); LEBLANC & GILLIES, at 143 ("A board cannot work, that is, reach good decisions, unless there are directors who, through credibility, leadership and interpersonal and communication skills, are on occasion able to persuade other directors and management of their point of view or of a particular course of action. At the same time, a board cannot work unless there are directors who can find common themes within dissenting views and bring about a consensus"). *See also* DOUGLAS BRANSON, NO SEAT AT THE TABLE: HOW CORPORATE GOVERNANCE KEEPS WOMEN OUT OF AMERICA'S BOARDROOMS 167–75 (2007) (describing how stereotyping and tokenism prevent women from reaching and remaining in the top corporate echelons) ("Research on the experience of women and people of color on boards indicates that these directors must prove their qualification to serve on the board and build credibility in a way that is qualitatively different from the experience of white male directors"); Burch, *supra* note 177, at 585, 625 (referring to the idea of critical mass) ("Research suggests that a minimum of three directors who are women or people of color increases the credibility of the directors and facilitates the directors' ability to build consensus around ideas that may conflict with established behavioral norms"); ALISON M. KONRAD ET AL., CRITICAL MASS ON CORPORATE BOARDS: WHY THREE OR MORE WOMEN ENHANCE GOVERNANCE 3–4, Wellesley Ctrs. for Women, Report No. WCW 11 (2006), http://www.wcwonline.org/pdf/CriticalMassExecSummary.pdf (finding that achieving a critical mass of women in the boardroom broadens discussions and enhances decision-making); Marleen A. O'Connor, *The Enron Board: The Perils of Groupthink*, 71 U. CIN. L. REV., 1233, 1309 (2003) (contending that greater diversity improves the ability of a group to make decisions").

183. Philippe Reigné, *Les femmes et les conseils d'administration: réponse à un éditorial de M. François-Xavier Lucas*, 3 JCP E. 27 (2010); François-Xavier Lucas, *La 'modernitude' s'invite dans les conseils d'administration*, BULL. JOLY 945 (2009). Moreover, there is a move to transform listed corporations into simplified joint-stock companies (Société par Action Simplifiée) with no executive boards; see Bender, Berrebi-Hoffmann, & Reigné, *supra* note 174.

184. See *supra* note 172: Law of Aug. 4, 2014.

185. Report to Signatories of the Statement of Diversity Principles, *Beyond Diversity 101: Navigating the New Opportunities 2008*, PRACTISING LAW INSTITUTE CORPORATE LAW AND PRACTICE COURSE HANDBOOK SERIES, PLI No. 14119 (Feb.27, 2008).

186. Mitu Gulati & Devon W. Carbado, *Race to the Top of the Corporate Ladder: What Minorities Do When They Get There*, 61 WASH. & LEE L. REV. 1645, 1662 (2004).
187. *See* FRANK DOBBIN, INVENTING EQUAL OPPORTUNITY (2009).
188. *Id.*, at 222.
189. *Id.*
190. In 1996, Texaco settled a racial discrimination case for $176 million, and in 2001, Coca-Cola settled for $193 million; see DOBBIN, *supra* note 187, at 232.
191. DOBBIN, *supra* note 187, at 222.
192. *See* Robert W. Ackerman, *How Companies Respond to Social Demands*, 51 HARV. BUS. REV. 92 (1973).
193. DOBBIN, *supra* note 187, at 138.
194. *See* DOBBIN, *supra* note 187, at 157; R. Roosevelt Thomas, Jr., *From Affirmative Action to Affirming Diversity*, *in* DIFFERENCES THAT WORK: ORGANIZATIONAL EXCELLENCE THROUGH DIVERSITY 29 (Mary C. Gentile ed., 1994).
195. Regents of Univ. of Cal. v. Bakke, 438 U.S. 265 (1978); Grutter v. Bollinger 539 U.S. 306 (2003) (No. 02-241).
196. DOBBIN, *supra* note 187, at 161.
197. *Id.* at 232.
198. Lauren B. Edelman et al., *Internal Dispute Resolution: The Transformation of Civil Rights in the Workplace*, 27 LAW & SOC'Y REV. 497 (1993).
199. Lauren B. Edelman & Mark C. Suchman, *When the Haves Hold Court: Speculations on the Organizational Internalization of Law*, 33 LAW & SOC'Y REV. 941 (1999).
200. Mark C. Suchman & Lauren B. Edelman, *Legal Rational Myths: The New Institutionalism and the Law Society Tradition*, 21 LAW & SOC. INQUIRY 903 (1996).
201. *See also* LES ENGAGEMENTS DANS LES SYSTÈMES DE REGULATION (Marie-Anne Frison Roche ed., 2006).
202. *See also* Mark Galanter, *Why the "Haves" Come Out Ahead: Speculations on the Limits of Legal Change*, 9 LAW & SOC'Y REV. 95–160 (1974).
203. Lauren B. Edelman, *Legal Environments and Organizational Governance: The Expansion of Due Process in the American Workplace*, 95 AM. J. SOCIOLOGY 1401–40 (1990).
204. Marie Mercat-Bruns, *Les discriminations multiples et l'identité au travail au croisement de l'égalité et des libertés*, 1 REV. DR. TRAVAIL 28, 36 (2015).
205. Edelman et al., *supra* note 198.
206. Edelman & Suchman, supra note 199, at 982. See also Linda Hamilton Krieger, Rachel Kahn Best, & Lauren B. Edelman,*When "Best Practices" Win, Employees Lose: Symbolic Compliance and Judicial Inference in Federal Equal Employment Opportunity Cases* 40 LAW & SOCIAL INQUIRY 843 (2015).
207. CENTER FOR INSTITUTIONAL AND SOCIAL CHANGE: http://www.changecenter.org/.
208. Susan P. Sturm, *The Architecture of Inclusion: Interdisciplinary Insights on Pursuing Institutional Citizenship*, 30 HARV. J.L. & GENDER 409 (2007); Susan P. Sturm, *The Architecture of Inclusion: Advancing Workplace Equality in Higher Education*, 29 HARV. J.L. & GENDER 249 (2006).
209. Marie Mercat-Bruns, *Égalité salariale, discriminations individuelles et systémiques: un éclairage de la jurisprudence américaine*, 114 REV. OFCE 95 (2010).
210. *See generally* JÉRÔME PORTA, LA RÉALISATION DU DROIT COMMUNAUTAIRE: ESSAI SUR LE GOUVERNMENT JURIDIQUE DE LA DIVERSITÉ (2007).
211. *See* Commission Green Paper on Equality and Non-discrimination in an Enlarged European Union, COM (2004) 379 final.
212. *Id.* See recently the global work of the the European Platform for Roma inclusion (http://ec.europa.eu/justice/events/roma-platform-2015/index_en.htm), a forum

for concerted thinking and discussion of all relevant stakeholders for the integration of Roma people in Europe. It aims to contribute to making both European and national policies more sensitive to Roma needs. See, for example, the meeting of the European Roma Platform on March 16–17, 2015, which had two aims. On the one hand, it was to provide the possibility for operational-level discussions among all types of stakeholders of Roma integration on topics that are considered as particularly relevant for the way forward for Roma integration policies and practices. On the other hand, it was to reflect the policy commitment and the high position of Roma integration on the EU member states' national political agendas. Based on the operational-level and policy reflections, meetings contribute to set the agenda for the future steps of the European Platform for Roma inclusion.

213. Equal opportunity was one of the priorities of France's Regional Competitiveness and Employment Operational programs funded by the European Social Fund (ESF) for 2007–2013. The ESF finances national, regional, and local policy in the fields of employment, training, and an inclusive labor market. France defined four priority themes facilitating initiatives to anticipate and respond to economic change, fight unemployment, increase social inclusion, combat discrimination in the workplace, and promote human capital, innovation, and equal opportunity for all.

214. Communication from the Commission to the Council, the European Parliament, the Committee of the Regions, and the European Economic and Social Committee of 6 October 2008, Green paper on territorial cohesion: *Turning Territorial Diversity into Strength*, COM (2008) 616 final (not published in the *Official Journal*). *See more recently*, Communication from the Commmission to the European Parliament, the Council, the European Economic and Social Committee, and the Committee of the Regions, *Sixth Report on Economic, Social and Territorial Cohesion: Investment for Jobs and Growth* (ECO/370, EESC-2014–4756), COM (2014) 473 final (Jan. 21, 2015).

215. See how the CJEU makes an analogy between employees and those independent workers who are in fact under economic subordination: Case C-256/01, Allonby v. Accrington & Rossendale Coll., 2004 E.C.R. I-873; Catherine Barnard, *Discrimination Law, Self-Employment and the Liberal Professions*, 12 EUR. ANTI-DISCRIMINATION L. REV. 29 (2011); extending rights to workers from non–EU Member States: C-311/13, Tümer v. Raad van bestuur van het Uitvoeringsinstituut werknemersverzekeringen, CJEU, Nov. 5, 2014. See also efforts to define workers to allow them to acquire child care benefits: C-516/09, Borger v. Tiroler Gebietskrankenkasse, 2011 E.C.R. I-1493; to acquire pension rights: C-379/09, Casteels v. British Airways plc, 2011 E.C.R. I-1379; to avoid abuse with renewed short-term workers: C-109/09, Deutsche Lufthansa AG v. Kumpan, 2011 E.C.R. I-1309 (without referring to age discrimination in this case).

216. Case C-333/13, Dano v. Jobcenter Leipzig, CJEU, Nov. 11, 2014: "economically inactive EU citizens who go to another Member State solely in order to obtain social assistance may be excluded from certain social benefits."

217. Directive 2010/41/EU of the European Parliament and of the Council of July 7, 2010, on the application of the principle of equal treatment between men and women engaged in an activity in a self-employed capacity and repealing Council Directive 86/613/EEC.

218. *See* Recital 3 of Directive 2010/41/EU ("In its conclusions of 5 and 6 December 2007 on 'Balanced roles of women and men for jobs, growth and social cohesion,' the Council called on the Commission to consider the need to revise, if necessary, Directive 86/613/EEC in order to safeguard the rights related to motherhood and fatherhood of self-employed workers and their helping spouses.")

219. Communication from the Commission to the European Parliament, the Council, the European Economic and Social Committee, and the Committee of the Regions,

Towards Common Principles of Flexicurity: More and Better Jobs Through Flexibility and Security, COM (2007) 0359 final.

220. On the less favorable plight of workers hired by subcontractors, see CJEU, September 18 2014, aff. 549/13, Bundesdruckerei GmbH c/ Stadt Dortmund.

221. Council Directive 2010/18/EU of 8 March 2010, implementing the revised Framework Agreement on parental leave concluded by BUSINESSEUROPE, UEAPME, CEEP and ETUC and repealing Directive 96/34/EC (Text with EEA relevance).

222. MORAL VALUES PROJECT, http://www.law.georgetown.edu/moralvaluesproject/.

223. Chai R. Feldblum, *The Moral Values Project: A Call to Moral Action in Politics,* in MORAL ARGUMENT, RELIGION, AND SAME-SEX MARRIAGE: ADVANCING THE PUBLIC GOOD 205 (Gordon A. Babst et al eds., 2009).

224. According to Feldblum, those who oppose gays and lesbians feel under siege in today's world. This is reflected in the discourse of organizations like the Traditional Values Coalition, Focus on the Family, and Concerned Women for America. *See* Chai R. Feldblum, *The Moral Values Project: A Call to Moral Action in Politics,* in MORAL ARGUMENT, RELIGION, AND SAME-SEX MARRIAGE: ADVANCING THE PUBLIC GOOD 205 (Gordon A. Babst et al. eds., 2009); Chai R. Feldblum, *Gay Is Good: The Moral Case for Marriage Equality and More,* 17 YALE J. L. & FEMINISM 139 (2005); Chai R. Feldblum, *The Moral Rhetoric of Legislation,* 72 NYU. L. REV. 992, 994 (1997); Chai R. Feldblum, *Sexual Orientation, Morality, and the Law: Devlin Revisited,* 57 U. PITT. L. REV. 237 (1996).

225. Chai R. Feldblum, *Rectifying the Tilt: Equality Lessons From Religion, Disability, Sexual Orientation, and Transgender,* 54 ME. L. REV. 159 (2000).

226. Gwénaële Calvès, *Les politiques de discrimination positive,* 111 POUVOIRS 30 (2004).

227. *See* Laure Bereni & Eléonore Lépinard, *Parité, mythe d'une exception française,* 111 POUVOIRS (2004).

228. There are collective bargaining agreements in France for "seniors" without precisely defining the age group.

229. A 6-percent quota exists for the recruitment of workers with a disability; if the quota is not filled, employers must pay a fine into a fund for people with disabilities.

230. This implicitly excludes immigrants who are noncitizens: "The democratic system requires that all groups of society be able to participate in the public debate, exchange arguments and controversies by way of their representatives. By refusing this opportunity to immigrants, a category stigmatized by those who construct public opinion, the French Republic has opened the door, in the twentieth century, to a flow of racist and nationalist discourse." GERARD NOIRIEL, IMMIGRATION, ANTISÉMITISME ET RACISME (XIX—XXÈME SIÈCLE): DISCOURS PUBLICS, HUMILIATIONS PRIVÉES 134 (2007).

231. *See* Michèle Lamont, *Le rôle de l'immigration, de la race et de la pauvreté, in* LES CODES DE LA DIFFÉRENCE: RACE, ORIGINE, RELIGION, FRANCE—ALLEMAGNE—ÉTATS-UNIS 258 (Riva Kastoryano ed., 2005); CLAUDE NICOLET, LA RÉPUBLIQUE EN FRANCE, ÉTAT DES LIEUX 122–68 (1992). A similar attitude resembling an "injunction to integrate" extends to immigrants. *See* Danièle Loschak, *L'intégration comme injonction: enjeux idéologiques et politiques liés à l'immigration,* 64 CULTURES & CONFLITS 131 (2006).

232. Riva Kastoryano, *Définir l'autre: en France, en Allemagne et aux États-Unis, in* LES CODES DE LA DIFFÉRENCE (Kastoryano ed.), *supra* note 231, at 14.

233. "The Welfare State ignores people to promote categories: social insurance replaces individual responsibility and the notion of fault is replaced by the concept of risk. It was no longer people who were concerned but representatives of collective categories (labeled later as 'management' and 'labor')." NOIRIEL, *supra* note 230, at 118. *See also* FRANÇOIS EWALD, L'ÉTAT PROVIDENCE (1986).

234. Jérôme Porta, *Égalité, non-discrimination et égalité de traitement: à propos des sens de l'égalité dans le droit de la non-discrimination (1re partie)*, 5 REV. DR. TRAV. 290 (2011); Jérôme Porta, *Égalité, non-discrimination et égalité de traitement: à propos des sens de l'égalité dans le droit de la non-discrimination (2ème partie)*, 6 REV. DR. TRAV. 354 (2011).

235. Cass. soc., Oct. 12, 2011, No. 10–15101; Cass. soc., June 8, 2011, Nos. 10–14725 and 10–11933.

236. Cass. soc., June 8, 2011, No. 10–30162; Cass. soc., Mar. 23, 2011, No. 09–42666; Cass. soc., July 6, 2011, No. 09–65554 (considering advantages given to employee representatives); Cass. soc., Oct. 14, 2009, No. 08–40161 (differences of treatment between part-time and full-time workers); Cass. soc., July 1, 2009, RJS 10/09, No. 760 (differences between managers and nonmanagers); Cass. soc., Jan. 11, 2012, No. 10–14614; *see also* Cass. soc., Mar. 13, 2013, No. 11–20490; Cass. soc., Mar. 13, 203, No. 10–28022; Cass. soc., Mar. 13, 2013, No. 11–23761. More recently, another case presumes justified differences of treatment in collective bargaining agreements between more qualified (engineers and managers) and lower-level professionals adopted by the employee representatives and the burden of proof thus lies with the party that questions this difference of treatment: Cass. soc., Jan. 27, 2015, No. 13–22179. See also Jean-François Césaro, *L'ascension du principe jurisprudentiel d'égalité*, 26 JCP S 44 (June 30, 2015).

237. Cass. soc., Nov. 10, 2009, No. 07–42489; Cass. soc., Jan. 19, 2011, No. 09–42541; Court of Appeals Paris, May 5, 2010, Niel No. 08–08694; Court of Appeals Versailles, Jan. 5, 2011, No. 10–01866. It is nevertheless harder for female union members to prove unequal pay because male union members have higher wages: Cass. soc., Apr. 10, 2013, No. 11–26986; *see also* Marie Mercat-Bruns, *Discrimination multiple: le défi de la preuve, Panorama Droit et Genre*, 16 RECUEIL DALLOZ 963 (2014).

238. See RACHEL SILVERAS & SÉVERINE LEMIÈRE, COMPARER LES EMPLOIS ENTRE LES FEMMES ET LES HOMMES: DE NOUVELLES PISTES VERS L'ÉGALITÉ SALARIALE (2010) (for the HALDE).

239. See recently Cass. soc., Oct. 22, 2014, No. 13–18362.

240. Cass. soc., June 8, 2011, Nos. 10–30162, 10–30163, 10–30164, 10–30165, 10–30166, 10–30167, 10–30168, 10–30169, 10–30170, and 10–30171.

241. Judicial scrutiny of differential treatment based on the system's aim, in accordance with CODE DU TRAVAIL [LABOR CODE] art. L.1222-3; Court of Appeals Versailles, Sept. 8, 2011, No. 10–00567.

242. Cass. soc., Feb. 20, 2008, No. 06–40085; Cass. soc., Mar. 31, 2009, No. 07–45522.

243. KATHLEEN GERSON, THE UNFINISHED REVOLUTION: HOW A NEW GENERATION IS RESHAPING FAMILY, WORK, AND GENDER IN AMERICA (2009).

244. *See* WHITE HOUSE FORUM ON WORKPLACE FLEXIBILITY, http://www.workplaceflexibility2010.org/index.php/whats_new/white_house_forum.

245. See Rubin's biography at Paula N. Rubin & Susan W. McCampbell, *The Americans With Disabilities Act and Criminal Justice: Mental Disabilities and Corrections*, Research in Action, National Institute of Justice, NCJ 155061 (July 1995), 7, https://www.ncjrs.gov/pdffiles/amdisact.pdf, and her work cited by Center for Innovative Public Policies, http://www.cipp.org/workforce/index.htm.

246. Fair Labor Standards Act, Pub. L. 75–718, ch. 676, 52 Stat. 1060, June 25, 1938, 29 U.S.C. ch. 8.

247. Americans with Disabilities Act of 1990, Pub. L. 101–336, 104 Stat. 328 (1990).

248. *See* Report on the reform of employee councils on working conditions: Pierre-Yves Verkindt, *Les C.H.S.C.T. au milieu du gué: Trente-trois propositions en faveur d'une instance de représentation du personnel dédiée à la protection de la santé au travail*, Report to the

Minister of Labor and Employment (Feb. 2014); *and see* Loïc Lerouge & Camille Hebert, *The Law of Workplace Harassment of the United States, France, and the European Union: Comparative Analysis After the Adoption of France's New Sexual Harassment Law*, 35 COMP. LAB. L. & POL'Y J. 93 (2013).

249. WORKPLACE FLEXIBILITY 2010, http://workplaceflexibility2010.org/, and KATHLEEN CHRISTENSEN & BARBARA SCHNEIDER, WORKPLACE FLEXIBILITY: REALIGNING 20th-CENTURY JOBS FOR A 21ST-CENTURY WORKFORCE (2010).

250. Same terminology in art. 5 of Directive 2000/78/EC.

251. Preferred term in CODE DU TRAVAIL [LABOR CODE] art. L.1226-2–L.1226-4; Law 2005-102 of Feb. 11, 2005 on equal treatment, equal opportunity, participation, and citizenship of people with disabilities.

252. Americans with Disabilities Act (ADA) (Pub. L. 101-336, 104 Stat. 327), 42 U.S.C. § 12101 (July 26, 1990); Amendments to the ADA (Pub. L. 110-325), 42 U.S.C.A. §§ 12101, 12102, 12111–12114, 12210, 12206–12213 (Sept. 25, 2008).

253. The quota requiring companies to employ 6 percent of people with disabilities can be regarded as equivalent to a form of affirmative action, and now there is also a quota for gender parity on the boards of directors of listed companies. Law 2011-103 of Jan. 27, 2011, on the balanced representation of women and men on boards of directors and supervisory boards and on equality in the workplace; *see* Julia Redenius-Hoevermann & Daniela Weber-Rey, *La représentation des femmes dans les conseils d'administration et de surveillance en France et en Allemagne*, 4 REV. SOCIÉTÉS 203 (2011); Véronique Martineau-Bourgninaud, *L'obligation de mixité dans les conseils d'administration et de surveillance*, 10 RECUEIL DALLOZ 599 (2010).

254. ADA, *supra* note 252, Title III.

255. Marie Mercat-Bruns, *Discrimination fondée sur l'âge: un exemple d'une nouvelle génération de critères discriminatoires*, 6 REV. DR. TRAVAIL 360 (2007).

256. The Family Medical Leave Act (FMLA) (Pub. L. 103–3, 29 CFR 825) 29 U.S.C. § 2601 (Feb. 5, 1993) entitles eligible employees of covered employers to take unpaid, job-protected leave for specified family and medical reasons with continuation of group health insurance coverage under the same terms and conditions as if the employee had not taken leave.

257. The 2008 ADA amendments (*supra* note 252) reversed case law restrictively interpreting the concept of disability: *see infra* Chapter 5.

258. Some authors are skeptical: Samuel Issacharoff & Justin Nelson, *Discrimination with a Difference: Can Employment Discrimination Law Accommodate the Americans with Disabilities Act?* 79 N.C. L. REV. 307 (2001).

259. The ADA defines a qualified individual as one "who, with or without reasonable accommodation, can perform the essential functions of the employment position that such individual holds or desires," 42 U.S.C. 12111(8). *See infra* Chapter 5.

260. *See* Title VII, § 701 (j), on religious discrimination; and see case law: TWA v. Hardison, 432 U.S. 63, 97 S.Ct. 2264, 53 L.Ed.2d 113. *See also infra* Chapter 5.

261. *See* 42 U.S.C. 12111(8).

262. On legislative history, see Ruth Colker, *The ADA's Journey Through Congress*, 39 WAKE FOREST L. REV. 1 (2004); RUTH COLKER, THE DISABILITY PENDULUM: THE FIRST DECADE OF THE AMERICANS WITH DISABILITIES ACT (2007).

263. *See generally* MARTHA MINOW, MAKING A DIFFERENCE: INCLUSION, EXCLUSION AND AMERICAN LAW (1990).

264. *See* Sharona Hoffman et al., *The Definition of Disability in the Americans with Disabilities Act: Its Successes and Shortcomings*, 9 EMP. RTS. & EMP. POL'Y J. 473 (2005) (proceedings of the 2005 Annual Meeting, Association of American Law Schools Sections on Employment Discrimination Law; Labor Relations and Employment Law; and Law, Medicine and Health).

265. See Christine Jolls, *Antidiscrimination and Accommodation*, 115 Harv. L. Rev. 642 (2001); Mathew Diller, *Judicial Backlash, the ADA and the Civil Rights Model*, 21 Berkeley J. Emp. & Lab. L. 19, 41 (2000).

266. For opposing arguments on the economic cost of employing people with disabilities, inspired by supporters of Law and Economics theory and the neoclassic theory, Michael Ashley Stein, *Labor Markets, Rationality and Workers with Disabilities*, 21 Berkeley J. Emp. & Lab. L. 193 (2000).

267. On the notion of "undue hardship": a response that requires difficulty and expense, § 101(10(A)), which seems more extensive than the one applied to religious accommodation: U.S. Airways, Inc. v. Barnett, 535 U.S. 391, 122 S.Ct. 1516, 152 L.Ed.2d, 257: "Undue hardship means that the accommodation would be too difficult or too expensive to provide, in light of the employer's size, financial resources, and the needs of the business." See also Samuel Bagenstos, *Rational discrimination, Accommodation and the politics of (disability) rights*, 89 Va. L. Rev. 825 (2003).

268. Ruth Colker, *The Americans with Disabilities Act: A Windfall for Defendants*, Harv. C.R.-C.L. L. Rev. 99, 100 (1999).

269. See Chai Feldblum et al., *The ADA Amendments Act of 2008*, 13 Tex. J. C.L. & C.R., 187 (2008).

270. Art. 5 of Directive 2000/78/EC:

Reasonable accommodation for disabled persons: In order to guarantee compliance with the principle of equal treatment in relation to persons with disabilities, reasonable accommodation shall be provided. This means that employers shall take appropriate measures, where needed in a particular case, to enable a person with a disability to have access to, participate in, or advance in employment, or to undergo training, unless such measures would impose a disproportionate burden on the employer. This burden shall not be disproportionate when it is sufficiently remedied by measures existing within the framework of the disability policy of the Member State concerned.

271. Code du travail [Labor Code] art. L.5213-6 provides that to guarantee the respect of equal treatment with regard to people with disabilities, the employer must take the appropriate measures, according to the needs in a concrete situation, to allow the workers mentioned in art. L.5212-13 to be employed or keep their employment reflecting their qualifications, to perform their work, progress, or gain access to training if needed. These measures are taken except if they involve in their implementation an undue burden which is disproportionate, despite of the financial support provided by art. L.5213-10 to compensate all or part of the designated expense. The refusal to take these measures can constitute discrimination according to § 1 of art. L.1133-2. The Defender of Rights (French equality body—*see supra* Chapter 2) has recommended an amendment in the bill pending on class action (*supra* note 140), which would include adding reasonable accommodation as a form of discrimination by modifying art. 1 of Law No. 2008-496 of May 27, 2008 on discrimination; see Opinion of Defender of Rights No. 15-23 (October 28, 2015). This would expand the scope of reasonable accommodation outside of employment (housing, contract law, goods and services).

272. Most cases that apply the notion of "appropriate measures" have been decided by the Conseil d'État, not the Cour de Cassation.

273. CE, July 11, 2012, No. 347703 on appropriate measures taken for a judge; in the private sector, Labor Court of Nantes, Apr. 22, 2010, No. 09/00440, case followed by the HALDE (in which an employee was dismissed on the basis of her disability after the occupational physician suggested an accommodation of work time following sick leave; the employer was fined €42,000, of which €33,000 were in damages); *see also* CPH Nîmes,

Dec. 13, 2010 (in which an employer took disciplinary measures against a person with a disability who had requested accommodation, but the occupational physician suggested that the employer refuse to accommodate, based on allegations of an undue burden for the workshop; the employer lost the case and was ordered to pay €15,000 in damages).

274. See also the HALDE decision for refusing to accommodate an applicant for a job as salesman after confirmation by the occupational physician that the candidate is qualified with accommodation. The application was rejected based on the justification that the applicant no longer fit the job profile. The HALDE proved that this was a pretext to avoid accommodation and constitutes discrimination, according to CODE DU TRAVAIL [LABOR CODE] art 5213-6: Decision No. 2009-128 of Apr. 27, 2009.

275. Francis Kessler, *Droit européen, handicap et intégration à l'emploi*, RDSS 806 (2011). See on the EU concept of disability, Case C-13/045, Chacon Navas v. Eurest Colectividades, July 11, 2006, RDSS 75 (2007), note Augustin Boujeka.

276. *See* Sandra Fredman, *Disability Equality: A Challenge to the Existing Anti-Discrimination Paradigm? in* DISABILITY RIGHTS IN EUROPE; FROM THEORY TO PRACTICE 199-203 (Anna Lawson & Caroline Gooding eds., 2005).

277. *See* CASES, MATERIALS AND TEXT ON NATIONAL, SUPRANATIONAL AND INTERNATIONAL NONDISCRIMINATION LAW 631 (Dagmar Schiek et al. eds., 2007); Lisa Waddington & Aart Hendriks, *The Expanding Concept of Employment Discrimination in Europe: From Direct and Indirect Discrimination to Reasonable Accommodation Discrimination*, INT. J. COMP. LAB. L. IND. REL. 403-27 (2002).

278. Olivier De Schutter, *Reasonable Accommodations and Positive Obligations in the European Convention of Human Rights, in* DISABILITY RIGHTS IN EUROPE; FROM THEORY TO PRACTICE 35-63 (Anna Lawson & Caroline Gooding eds., 2005).

279. United Kingdom, Disability Discrimination Act de 1995, s. 3A(2); Ireland, Employment Equality Act 1998, s. 16, and Equal Status Act 2000, s. 4; Sweden, Disability Discrimination Act, s. 6.

280. Case C-335/11, Ring v. Dansk (2013) and on the need to reasonably accommodate someone affected by obesity. National courts must decide whether obesity amounts to a disability in the particular circumstances of a case where the worker's obesity caused reduced mobility or other medical conditions. If an obese worker is disabled, then the employer would have to make "reasonable accommodation" to allow that person to "have access to, participate in or advance in employment." Case C-354/13, Fag og Arbejde (FOA), acting on behalf of Kaltoft v. Kommunernes Landsforening (KL) (Dec. 18, 2014).

281. Case C-312/11, Commission v. Italy, 2013 E.C.R. I-000.

282. Bernadette Pélissier, *L'obligation de reclassement*, I RECUEIL DALLOZ 399 (1998). For the worker with a disability that is recognized officially (as a handicap, a word still used in France), other obligations prior to reassignment, such as retraining, can be required outside of reasonable accommodation: Cass. soc., Feb. 17, 2010, No. 08-45476.

283. *See* Cass. soc., Jan. 31, 2007, No. 05-42855.

284. Pélissier, *supra* note 282.

285. Cass. soc., Mar. 24, 2010, No. 09-40339; Cass. soc., Mar. 21, 2012, No. 10-12068; Cass. soc., July 9, 2008, No. 07-41318; Cass. soc., Jan. 26, 2011, No. 09-43193; Cass. soc., Feb. 17, 2010, No. 08-43725; Cass. soc., Feb. 20, 2013, No. 11-26793.

286. *See* Cass. soc., Feb. 6, 2001, RJS 2001, No. 433; Cass. soc., Oct. 12, 2011, No. 10-18038. See also when Court considers dismissal without just cause when the right procedure is not followed, Cass. soc., Dec. 5 2012, No. 11-17913

287. CODE DU TRAVAIL [LABOR CODE] art. L.1132-4; some authors suggest that if the employer does not provide the necessary readjustment, the dismissal is not only without just cause, but it is null and void, according to the prohibition of discrimination in CODE

DU TRAVAIL [LABOR CODE] art. L.1132. *See* JEAN PÉLISSIER ET AL., LES GRANDS ARRÊTS DU DROIT DU TRAVAIL 367 (2008); but some cases maintain that the dismissal is without cause, Cass soc., May 21, 2008, No. 07–41277.

288. Cass. soc., May 21, 2008, No. 07–41380; *see recently,* Cass. soc., Jan. 7, 2015, No. 10–27105; Cass. soc., Oct. 15, 2014, No. 13–16113.

289. Cass. soc., Jan. 28, 2010, No. 08–42616.

290. Cass. soc., Mar. 30, 2011, No. 09–71542.

291. CODE DU TRAVAIL [LABOR CODE] art. L.1133–2.

292. Serge Frossard, *Les contextes de l'obligation de reclassement,* DR. SOC. 963 (2010).

293. Pélissier, *supra* note 282, at 400–01; *see also* Cass. soc., Feb. 16, 1999, No. 96–45394.

294. Labor Court CPH Nîmes, Dec. 13, 2010.

295. On the positive side, if the occupational physician certifies the state of disability, and if the employer does not follow the procedure required to show that dismissal is unavoidable, after two medical examinations and no work adjustment possible, the violation of this formality could constitute discrimination, Cass. soc., Feb. 16, 1999, No. 96–45394. *See* Marie Mercat-Bruns, *Les contours de la discrimination professionnelle en raison de l'état de santé à la lumière du droit américain,* 11 LES CAHIERS DE DR. DE LA SANTÉ 16 (2010).

296. See Mathilde Caron & Pierre-Yves Verkindt, *Inaptitude, invalidité, handicap: l'image du "manque" en droit social,* RDSS 862 (2011) (to illustrate "the inadequacy in labor law, one must imagine being at the center of a triangle with angles named disability, handicap and inability"); *see also* Cass. soc., Jan. 25, 2011, No. 09–42766; Cass. soc., Feb. 15, 2011, No. 09–43172; Cass. soc., Apr. 28, 2011, No. 09–70845.

297. Frédéric Tallier, *L'évaluation du handicap et de l'aptitude à l'emploi,* RDSS 821(2011):

> The term *employability* is increasingly used but remains controversial. Like the term disability, people tend to take advantage of the vagueness of the concept to define it as they choose. Employability refers to a person's capability of obtaining and maintaining employment: in other words, it means that the person can demonstrate the skills required to perform the job duties. This is a multidimensional concept that varies according to level of training, whether prior to employment or on-the-job, work experience, time away from a job, functional abilities, social and family environment, and the adaptability of the person and his/her environment.

298. Cass. soc., Feb. 6 2008, No. 06–44413; this implies that the employee accepts the work adjustment, Cass. soc., Feb. 20 2008, No. 06–44867.

299. Caron & Verkindt, *supra* note 296 ("The centrality of the concept of inadequacy is at the heart of welfare schemes and reflect the idea of need").

300. *Id.*

301. Cass. soc., Oct. 6, 2015, No. 13–26052 *(it is difficult to prove discrimination after dismissal of a worker who is put on disability and who also contends discrimination based on union membership).*

302. Cass. soc., Apr. 9, 2008, No. 07–40356 (physical disability without a possible work adjustment does not constitute a specific cause of dismissal).

303. Cass. soc., Jan. 13, 1998, No. 95–44301; Cass. soc., July 3, 2001, No. 99–41738.

304. Cass. soc., Feb. 20, 2008, No. 06–44712; Court of Appeals Paris, Sept. 7, 2010, No. S07/07628 (declaring null and void the dismissal of a worker based on the disruptive effect that her absence had on the work team, given that this effect and the need to replace the worker were not proven); *see also* Cass. soc., Sept. 16, 2009, No. 08–41879 (finding that the dismissal of a sick worker whose absence is disruptive to the work in the department cannot be justified seventeen months after the position has been filled by a replacement).

305. Cass. soc., Jan. 9, 2007, No. 05–43962. Indirect discrimination based on health status was also found in a more recent case in which an employer imposed an interview with

employees after their absence from work, regardless of the cause of that absence, Cass. soc., Feb.12, 2013, No. 11-27689.

306. Pierre Verge & Dominic Roux, *Personnes handicapées: l'obligation d'accommodement raisonnable selon le droit international et le droit canadien*, DR. SOC. 965 (2010): this notion in Canadian law is closer to a global concept of the person and discrimination as an infringement of dignity.

307. See the work of Amartya Sen cited by Philippe Pédrot, *Handicap, aptitude à l'emploi et vulnérabilité*, RDSS 791 (2011) ("With the aging of people with disabilities, the increase in long-term care, and the tightening of the labor market, the idea is to integrate in our legal thinking the notion of 'capabilities' coined by Nobel prize economist Amartya Sen, to allow people with disabilities to effectively exercise their right to citizenship"). Through the idea of capability, the vindication of individual rights is not determined by resources or assets but based on the freedom people really have in choosing the life they value. Equality of income can leave behind great inequalities in our ability to act. An individual with a disability cannot act in the same way as a person without a disability. Level of education, work environment, capacity for resilience are the parameters which influence his/her action. Principles of justice, based on capabilities, stem from the idea of varying needs of individuals according to their ability to benefit from their resources. Amartya Sen considers the freedom of choice as an integral part of well-being. "Capability reflects the freedom of an individual to choose between different ways of living": AMARTYA SEN, ÉTHIQUE, ÉCONOMIE ET AUTRES ESSAIS 189 (1993).

308. The idea is not to identify the potential of an individual to act to compensate incapacity but to identify his or her potential to respect the freedom of each person as a source of dignity. *See also* Martha Nussbaum and her philosophy of "care," also inspired by Amartya Sen's work, and how the French law of 2005 reflects this way of thinking; Pédrot, *supra* note 307.

309. Nussbaum suggests that the capabilities approach can justify a core of human entitlements that should be respected and implemented by the governments of all nations, as a bare minimum of what respect for human dignity requires. She identifies a list of "central human capabilities" (including life; bodily health; bodily integrity; senses, imagination and thought; emotions; practical reason; affiliation; and control over one's political and material environment), arguing that all of them are implicit in the idea of a life worthy of dignity. The approach uses the idea of a threshold level of each capability, beneath which it is held that truly human functioning is not available to citizens. *See* MARTHA NUSSBAUM, FRONTIERS OF JUSTICE 70 (2006).

310. *See* Sophie Fantoni-Quinton et al., *Un avenir pour la santé au travail sans "aptitude périodique" est possible*, 48 JCP S 10, 11 (2011) (showing the limits of the mechanism focused on medically certified disability).

311. Cass. soc., Oct. 8, 2014, No. 13-11789.

312. Sexual harassment can even be reconceptualized in the workplace as a form of disparate impact discrimination; see the excellent work of L. Camille Hebert, *The Disparate Impact of Sexual Harassment: Does Motive Matter?* 53 U. KAN. L. REV. 341 (2005).

313. See generally Marie Mercat-Bruns, *Harcèlement sexuel au travail en France: entre rupture et continuité*, in LA LOI ET LE GENRE 201 (Stéphanie Hennette-Vauchez et al. eds, 2014) [hereinafter Mercat-Bruns, *Harcèlement sexuel*]. See also Loïc Lerouge & Camille Hebert, *The Law of Workplace Harassment of the United States, France, and the European Union: Comparative Analysis After the Adoption of France's New Sexual Harassment Law*, 35 COMP. LAB. L. & POL'Y J. 93 (2013).

314. Rogers v. EEOC, 454 F.2d 234 (CA5 1971), cert. denied, 406 U.S. 957 (1972) which involved a Hispanic and was apparently the first case to recognize a cause of action based on a discriminatory environment.

315. See for example, the Supreme Court case Meritor Savings Bank v. Vinson, 477 U.S. 57 (1986), and the EEOC regulations, 45 Fed. Reg. 74676 (1980), mentioned in the case to consider that hostile environment harassment violates Title VII antidiscrimination law as sex discrimination.

316. Oncale v. Sundowner Offshore Services, 523 U.S. 75 (1998); Vance v. Ball State Univ. 570 U.S. ___(2013).

317. The harassment becomes severe and pervasive, See Harris v. Forklift Systems Inc, 510 U.S. 17 (1993).

318. See, for example, *infra* note 339, where Cass. soc., Oct. 19, 2011, No. 09–72672, is explained.

319. For a European comparison of sexual harassment, see Sophie Robin-Olivier et al., *Le harcèlement sexuel: droit italien, droit anglais, droit espagnol*, 5 REV. DR. TRAVAIL 353 (2013).

320. The Constitutional Court decided the criminal code definition of sexual harassment was not precise enough (CC, May 4, 2012, No. 2012–240); *see* Béatrice Lapérou-Scheneider, *L'éclipse du harcèlement sexuel*, 7/8 DR. SOC. 714 (2012). The new definition of sexual harassment applies to criminal and labor law and is more expansive: see Law 2012–954 of Aug. 6, 2012; CODE PÉNAL [PENAL CODE] art. 222-33.I and CODE DU TRAVAIL [LABOR CODE] art. L.1153-1, defining sexual harassment as the act of repeatedly subjecting a person to unwelcome verbal or physical conduct of a sexual nature that either compromises the victim's dignity through its degrading or humiliating nature or that creates an intimidating, hostile or offensive situation for the victim ("II.: is assimilated as sexual harassment, even nonrepeated acts, using all forms of strong pressure to obtain, in a real or apparent way, acts of sexual nature, regardless of the fact this is to benefit the author of the acts or a third party"). See the guidelines of the Minister of Justice of Aug. 7, 2012 (circulaire CRIM 2012 -15 / E8) explaining what the definition covers and how to implement the law.

321. The European definition covers verbal harassment and does not imply a request for sexual favors. Curiously, sexist comments were not sufficient to characterize sexual harassment justifying dismissal of the perpetrator before the new law of 2012 (Cass. soc., Feb. 27, 1992, No. 91–41057).

322. Before the 2012 law, case law was already covering situations outside of quid pro quo harassment to obtain sexual favors (Cass. soc., Nov. 14, 2007, No. 06–45.263), even though these situations of sexual favors do exist: see Cass. soc., Mar. 3, 2009, No. 07- 4082; Court of Appeals Paris, Oct. 6, 1995 (involving a manager who promised to promote an intern in exchange for sexual favors); Cass. soc., Sept. 24, 2008 (involving a manager who tried to kiss an underage coworker in the workplace and made repeated attempts to accompany her home, triggering anxiety and depression).

323. For a case of harassment of a journalist during her maternity leave, see Cass. soc., Mar. 3, 2015, No. 13–23521.

324. Cass. soc., Oct. 25, 2007, No. 06–41806 (involving a company manager who used inappropriate language and behavior toward an employee who informed the union representatives and filed complaints with the human resources department and the local police); Cass. soc., Feb. 9, 2010, No. 08–44632 (involving the dismissal of an employee who had offended his female colleagues and an intern by sending them inappropriate messages and inviting them to see pornographic films on his computer); Cass. soc., Dec. 15, 2009, No. 08–44848 (involving an employee's inappropriate behavior and language despite objections from female employees who found it offensive); Cass. soc., Oct. 11, 2006, No. 04–45719. The employer is liable for sexual harassment when he ignores a complaint of sexual assault from one of his employees in a fixed term contract, see *Cass. soc., May 6, 2015, No. 13–24261*. However, the employer has no liability if the complaint of the employee

concerns only nostalgic text messages from her boss, the rejected lover, Cass. soc., Sept. 23, 2015, No. 14-17143.

325. *See* Rikki Holtmaat, *Sexual Harassment and Harassment on the Ground of Sex in EU Law: A Conceptual Clarification*, 2 EUR. GENDER EQUALITY L. REV. 4 (2011) (observing that there are forms of sexual harassment that are not linked to sex, but to sexuality as a way of abusing power, and showing a possible causal relationship between sexual harassment and inequality, in cases of abuse based on an employee's homosexuality or religion, for example).

326. *See* Reva B. Siegel, *Introduction: A Short History of Sexual Harassment, in* DIRECTIONS IN SEXUAL HARASSMENT L. 1 (Reva B. Siegel & Catharine A. MacKinnon eds., 2003); Catharine A. MacKinnon, *Afterword, in* DIRECTIONS IN SEXUAL HARASSMENT L. 672 (2003).

327. *See* William N. Eskridge, Jr., *Theories of Harassment "Because of Sex," in* DIRECTIONS IN SEXUAL HARASSMENT LAW 155 (2003); Katherine M. Franke, *What's Wrong with Sexual Harassment, in* DIRECTIONS IN SEXUAL HARASSMENT LAW 169 (2003); Janet Halley, *Sexuality Harassment, in* DIRECTIONS IN SEXUAL HARASSMENT LAW 182 (2003); Mark Spindelman, *Discriminating Pleasures*, cited, *in* DIRECTIONS IN SEXUAL HARASSMENT LAW 201 (2003); *see also* Marie Mercat-Bruns, *La doctrine américaine sur les discriminations et le genre: dialogue entre la critique du droit et la pratique?* 2 Juris.Rev. CRIT. 93 (2011); Mercat-Bruns, *Harcèlement sexuel, supra* note 313, at 201.

328. *See* Barnes v. Costle, 561 F. 2d 983, 990 (DC Cir. 1977).

329. Meritor Savings Bank v. Vinson, 477 U.S. 57 (1986).

330. Vicki Schultz, *Telling Stories About Women and Work: Judicial Interpretation of Sex Segregation in the Workplace in Title VII Cases Raising the Lack of Interest Argument*, 103 HARV. L. REV. 1749, 1832 (1990); *see also* Vicki Schultz, *The Sanitized Workplace*, 112 YALE L. J. 2063 (2003).

331. Comparative studies between U.S. and European legal frameworks already existed: *see* Abigail Saguy, *Employment Discrimination or Sexual Violence? Defining Sexual Harassment in American and French Law*, 34 LAW & SOC'Y REV. 1091 (2000); Gabrielle S. Friedman & James Q. Whitman, *The European Transformation of Harassment Law: Discrimination versus Dignity*, 9 COLUM. J. EUR. L. 241 (2003); *see generally* KATHRIN ZIPPEL, THE POLITICS OF SEXUAL HARASSMENT: A COMPARATIVE STUDY OF THE UNITED STATES, THE EUROPEAN UNION, AND GERMANY (2006).

332. The institutional environment and the type of company and job can increase the risk of sexual harassment, which can be combined with other sources of vulnerability, such as religion or origin. *See* Holtmaat, *supra* note 325, at 9.

333. *Cass. soc., Mar., 11 2015, No. 13-18603 (some cases condemn the employer for moral harassment and sexual harassment when moral harassment from other workers is triggered by rumors of complaint to employer who did not respect rules of confidentiality).*

334. Neither the EU directives nor French law (CODE DU TRAVAIL [LABOR CODE] arts. L.1153 and L.1132-1) refer to an abuse of authority. Instead, they use a hostile environment as a basis for assessment, although the definition refers to a hostile situation, not environment. See the EEOC's guidelines.

335. Journal Officiel of Aug. 7, 2012.

336. This decision of the Constitutional Council interrupted all criminal suits that were pending. The criminal sanction is two years of imprisonment and a fine of €30,000, increased to three years of imprisonment and a fine of €45,000 if the offender has abused his or her authority or targeted a victim who is fifteen years of age or whose particular vulnerability, due to age, illness, infirmity, physical or mental deficiency, or pregnancy, is apparent or known to the offender. These increased sanctions also apply if the victim's

particular vulnerability or subordination is due to economic or social status and is apparent or known to the offender or an accomplice.

337. A parallel can be drawn with the development of the concept of privacy in family law to protect the immunity of couples in domestic violence cases and thwart plans to incriminate the abuser.

338. *Recently* Cass. soc., Jan. 28, 2014, No. 12–20497 (an older worker sexually harassing a young intern).

339. Cass. soc., Oct. 19, 2011, No. 09–72672:

> Considering on the one hand, the employee had used sexual explicit language with two female colleagues in his messages on MSN sent outside of office hours and outside of the office between noon and 1:30 PM, because he worked from 3 PM to 11 PM or during events organized after work, and on the other hand, that he had, during work time, made inappropriate comments to another female employee about her physical appearance and had followed a third female colleague into the bathroom, the Court of Appeals decided that the initial facts were part of the personal life of the male employee and hence could not constitute a breach in the performance of the contract and that the second series of facts were not sufficient to constitute acts of sexual harassment. By adopting this line of argument, despite the fact that his verbal comments of a sexual nature and his inappropriate attitude towards female employees, with whom the concerned employee interacts because of his work, are not part of his personal life, the Court of Appeals has violated the cited rules . . .

See also Cass.soc., Jan. 11, 2012, No. 10–12930. In addition, Cass. soc., Mar. 3, 2009, No. 07–44082 (demonstrating the same trend in case law, in a case in which sexual harassment in a person's private life causes a disability at work, also constituting moral harassment); for prior case law in which privacy is used as a defense for the alleged harasser, see Cass. soc., Nov. 30, 2005, No. 04–13877.

340. Cass. soc., Feb. 3, 2010, No. 08–44019 (the employer cannot justify the lack of preventive measures because the harasser resigns).

341. The attitude of the victim of moral harassment cannot limit the responsiblity of harasser, Cass. Crim., May 27, 2015, No. 14–81489; Cass. soc., May 13, 2015, No. 14–10854. It is only if the employee knows the acts are untrue that the employer can argue bad faith, Cass. soc., June 10, 2015, Nos. 14–13338 and 13–25554.

342. The Court reminds the finder of fact that he or she must consider all the facts together, (the humiliation and mistreatment) which contribute to presume harassment is present: *see recently* Cass soc., Sept. 24, 2014, No. 13–12073; Cass. soc., Apr. 30, 2009, No. 07–43219; Cass. soc., Jan. 25, 2011, No. 09–42766; this includes what is called managerial harassment, Cass. soc., Nov. 10, 2009, No. 07–45321 ("methods of management adopted by supervisor if, directed against one specific employee, involve repeated acts which constitute or have the effect of deteriorating working conditions to the point of violating the rights of the person, his dignity, his physical and mental state or compromise his career").

343. Law 2008–496 of May 27, 2008 introduced harassment as a form of discrimination (CODE DU TRAVAIL [LABOR CODE] art. L.1132–1). However the Defender of Rights (Opinion of Defender of Rights, No. 15–23, Oct. 28, 2015) recommends introducing more clearly in the law of 2008 (amendment to art. 1) that harassment based on discrimination can be linked to an isolated act (no repetition need like moral harassment). Introduction in the pending bill on class action: *see supra* note 140.

344. *See* Cass. soc., Oct. 19, 2011, No. 09–68272 (involving moral harassment committed by a third party exercising an authority, in fact, over employees); *see also* Cass. soc. 1er, Mar. 1, 2011, No. 09–69616; Cass. soc., Feb. 3, 2010, No. 08–40144.

345. See one of the first cases on environmental sexual harassment since the law of 2012: Cass. soc, Feb. 18, 2014, No. 12-17557 (proof of sexual harassment through witnesses of sexually explicit remarks, and the Court reminds us that the employer must protect workers for health reasons from sexual harassment; there is no need to communicate complaints to presumed harasser).

346. Except it is linked to a prohibited ground; if that is the case, one act is sufficient because it is qualified as discriminatory harassment.

347. Cass. soc., June 21, 2006, No. 05-43914.

348. *See* Lauren B. Edelman et al., *The Endogeneity of Legal Regulation: Grievance Procedures as Rational Myth*, 105 AM. J. SOCIOLOGY 406-54 (1999).

349. DOBBIN, *supra* note 187, at 213.

350. Burlington Industries v. Ellerth, 118 S. Ct 1998, 2263.

351. Cass. soc., May 21, 2014, No. 13-12666; Marie Mercat-Bruns, *Enquête interne, atteinte à la vie privée et obligation de sécurité*, 9 REV. DR. TRAVAIL 554 (2014).

352. Cass. soc., Nov. 19, 2014, No. 13-17729. The Cour de cassation has recently applied a lower standard in its scrutiny of the employer's obligation to protect the health and security of employees, Cass. soc. Nov. 25 2015 No. 14-24444.

353. It all depends on how dignity is defined: is it a subjective or an objective standard? Who decides? What is the implicit norm in the workplace? See DUNCAN KENNEDY, SEXY DRESSING ETC. (1995). In France, dignity can often be linked to vulnerability, and it begs the question of agency linked to harassment. *See* Kathryn Abrams, *Subordination and Agency in Sexual Harassment Law, in* DIRECTIONS IN SEXUAL HARASSMENT LAW 111 (Reva B. Siegel & Catharine A. MacKinnon eds., 2003). The Court has also recently distinguished damages linked to moral harassment from those linked to discrimination based on maternity: *see* Cass. soc., March 3, 2015, No. 13-23521.

354. Susanne Baer, *Dignity or Equality? Responses to Workplace Harassment in European, German, and U.S Law, in* DIRECTIONS IN SEXUAL HARASSMENT LAW 595 (Reva B. Siegel & Catharine A. MacKinnon eds., 2003).

5. THE MULTIPLE GROUNDS OF DISCRIMINATION

1. European Convention on Human Rights art. 14 uses the term *notably* to indicate this nonexhaustivity.

2. Despite numerous prohibited grounds in France, most discrimination litigation in France is based on union membership, a more traditional and legitimate ground in labor law. The supreme court has stated that violations of union rights are not systematically discriminatory acts: see Cass. soc., Oct. 8, 2014, No. 13-16720. See Marie Mercat-Bruns & Emmanuelle Boussard Verrecchia, *Appartenance syndicale, sexe, âge et inégalités: vers une reconnaissance de la discrimination systémique?* 11 Rev. Dr. Travail 660 (2015).

3. Prohibited grounds in federal law can be different from the prohibited grounds in each state (which may be more numerous).

4. See two more recent studies of French employment discrimination case law for the Ministry of Justice: EVELYN SERVERIN & FRÉDÉRIC GUIOMARD, DES REVENDICATIONS DES SALARIÉS EN MATIÈRE DE DISCRIMINATIONS ET D'ÉGALITÉ: LES ENSEIGNEMENTS D'UN ÉCHANTILLON D'ARRÊTS EXTRAIT DE LA BASE JURICA (2007-2010) (2013); BERNARD BOSSU, LES DISCRIMINATIONS DANS LES RELATIONS DE TRAVAIL DEVANT LES COURS D'APPEL: LA RÉALISATION CONTENTIEUSE D'UN DROIT FONDAMENTAL (2014). For another study on the implementation of discrimination law, see MARIE MERCAT-BRUNS & JEREMY PERELMAN (EDS.), LES JURIDICTIONS ET LES INSTANCES PUBLIQUES DANS LA MISE EN OEUVRE DU PRINCIPE DE NON-DISCRIMINATION: PERSPECTIVES PLURIDISCIPLINAIRES ET COMPARÉES (forthcoming 2016).

5. Marie Mercat-Bruns, *La personne au prisme des discriminations indirectes*, 37 RECUEIL DALLOZ 2475 (2013).

6. Marie Mercat-Bruns, *Les discriminations multiples et l'identité au travail au croisement des questions d'égalité et de libertés*, 1 REV. DR. TRAVAIL 28 (2015) [hereinafter Mercat-Bruns, *Les discriminations multiples et l'identité au travail*].

7. Even if, in the United States, the fight against sex discrimination also helped the fight against race discrimination. *See generally* SERENA MAYERI, REASONING FROM RACE: FEMINISM, LAW AND CIVIL RIGHTS REVOLUTION (2011) [hereinafter MAYERI, REASONING FROM RACE]; Marie Mercat-Bruns, *La discrimination professionnelle fondée sur le sexe aux États-Unis: une notion juridique sous tension*, 28 TRAVAIL GENRE SOCIÉTÉ 63 (2012) [hereinafter Mercat-Bruns, *La discrimination professionnelle fondée sur le sexe aux États-Unis*].

8. Which does not signify that the use of ethnoracial statistics was not contested in the United States as early as 1954, with the segregation of schools. *See* Reva B. Siegel, *Equality Talk: Antisubordination and Anticlassification Values in Constitutional Struggles over* Brown, 117 HARV. L. REV. 1470, 1471 (2004).

9. Now, Treaty on the Functioning of the European Union [TFEU] art. 157.

10. *See* United States v. Carolene Prods. Co., 304 U.S. 144, 153 n.4 (1938).

11. Regents of Univ. of Cal. v. Bakke, 438 U.S. 265 (1978) (referring to the idea of diversity for the first time).

12. The Federalist Society is a group of conservatives and libertarians seeking to reform the American judiciary system to adhere to an originalist interpretation of the U.S. Constitution, placing emphasis on the original intent of those who drafted the law.

13. Act No. 2008-496 of May 27, 2008, art. 2 (introducing several measures for adapting to community antidiscrimination law).

14. Applicable to differences in treatment based on age.

15. *See generally* MICHAEL J. KLARMAN, FROM JIM CROW TO CIVIL RIGHTS: THE SUPREME COURT AND THE STRUGGLE FOR RACIAL EQUALITY (2004). *See also* MICHELLE ALEXANDER, THE NEW JIM CROW: MASS INCARCERATION IN THE AGE OF COLORBLINDNESS (2012).

16. And in the representative bodies of listed companies (Act No. 2011-103 of Jan. 27, 2011, on the balanced representation of women and men on boards of directors and supervisory boards and workplace equality). See also Law of 2014 on real equality (*Loi 2014-873 du 4 août 2014 (pour l'égalité réelle entre les femmes et les hommes)*), which extends the parity rule in the public sector, *supra* Chapter 4.

17. Robert C. Post & Reva B. Siegel, *Legislative Constitutionalism and Section Five Power: Policentric Interpretation of the Family and Medical Leave Act*, 112 YALE L.J. 1943 (2003).

18. *See supra* the developments in Chapter 2, "Models of Equality."

19. The article has since been published. Reva B. Siegel, *From Colorblindness to Antibalkanization: An Emerging Ground of Decision in Race Equality Cases*, 120 YALE L. J. 1278 (2011).

20. *See supra* Chapter 1, "I. The Origins of Antidiscrimination Law," David Oppenheimer interview, and Chapter 4, "I. The Strengths and Limitations of Disparate Impact Discrimination," Robert Post interview, on Supreme Court cases with regard to race and equal protection.

21. University of Texas Southwestern Medical Center v. Nassar, 133 S. Ct. 2517 (2013).

22. Vance v. Ball State University, 570 U.S.___ (2013).

23. Since the *Vance* case, a plaintiff must now show that an individual committing harassment had the ability to take a tangible employment action against the plaintiff in order for that individual to be considered a "supervisor" in the context of a hostile work environment claim. After the *Nassar* case related to retaliation under Title VII, an employee must now demonstrate that retaliatory motivation was the but-for cause of an adverse

employment action and not simply a motivating factor. In other words, the plaintiff must prove that the unlawful retaliation would not have occurred in the absence of the alleged wrongful action of the employer.

24. See Reva Siegel's observations in Chapter 2 describing these different conceptions of equality through constitutional case law.

25. *See* MAYERI, REASONING FROM RACE, *supra* note 7 (examining the influence of sex discrimination case law on racial discrimination case law, in particular in disparate impact cases).

26. On the reasons why the United States has not yet achieved a postracial society, see generally JOHN A. POWELL, RACING TO JUSTICE: TRANSFORMING OUR CONCEPTIONS OF SELF AND OTHER TO BUILD AN INCLUSIVE SOCIETY (2012).

27. This repression of discrimination first began in the United States in response to "smoking gun" evidence in the form of discriminatory comments that reveal the proximity of an act of discrimination. In Europe, *see* C-54/07, Centrum voor gelijkheid van kansen en voor racismebestrijding v. Firma Feryn, 2008 E.C.R. I-5187. The many recent decisions in France deal more frequently with incitement to racial hatred or racist statements; *see, e.g.*, Cass. crim., June 19, 2001, JCP 2002, II; Cass. crim., June 7, 2011, No. 10-85.179.

28. *See* Slack v. Havens, 522 F.2d 1091 (1975) ("Colored folks . . . clean better"). *See also* Ash v. Tyson Foods, 546 U.S. 454 (2006) (discussing the significance of the use of comments, names, or expressions conveying stereotyped images). The case involved the use of the term *boy* without any reference to color. The court found this sufficient, from a legal point of view, to establish discriminatory intent: *Ash*, 546 U.S. at 556 ("Although it is true the disputed word will not always be evidence of racial animus, it does not follow that the term, standing alone, is always benign. The speaker's meaning may depend on various factors including context, inflection, tone of voice, local custom, and historical usage").

29. *See supra* Chapter 1 and Chapter 4.

30. It must be understood that European Union law, in principle, does not distinguish between discrimination grounds: *see* Directive 2000/78. This is not the case in the United States, where a series of different legal regimes exists; *see infra* sections on the grounds of age and disability.

31. Compare the fierce debates on affirmative action with those on the Americans with Disabilities Act (*see infra* Chapter 5, "VI. Disability and Age Discrimination," and Chapter 5, "IV. Discrimination on the Basis of Family Status,"on the statutes and case law on discrimination based on sex, pregnancy, and age).

32. See the guidelines on collecting race data since 2000, U.S. Census Bureau, http://www.census.gov/topics/population/race.html.

33. See the essay by Jack M. Balkin & Reva B. Siegel, *Principles, Practices, and Social Movements*, 154 U. PA. L. REV. 927, 937–38 (2006) (relating that racial data collection was not always authorized in the United States either) ("During the 1950s and 1960s, however, the civil rights movement was quite wary of government collection of racial data, viewing it as a practice likely to entrench segregation. After *Brown*, the Supreme Court [suggested that] government collection of racial data—for example, [the compulsory designation of race] on ballots—either manifested or stimulated racial prejudice, and therefore violated the antidiscrimination principle.") *See* Anderson v. Martin, 375 U.S. 399, 402 (1963), and Tancil v. Woolls, 379 U.S. 19 (1964) (confirming the lower court decision from Hamm v. Virginia State Bd. of Elections, 230 F.Supp. 156, 158 (E.D. Va. 1964) invalidating laws that separated voting and property records based on race, but upholding a law requiring that divorce decrees designate the race of the divorcees). *See also* Whitus v. Georgia, 385 U.S. 545, 551 (1967) (holding that the practice of selecting jury members from tax records indicating race is discrimi-

natory). Certain state fair-employment laws even prohibited employers from keeping ethnoracial statistics on their employees. For a thorough interpretation of "color blindness," see Owen M. Fiss, *A Theory of Fair Employment Laws,* 38 U. CHI. L. REV. 235, 265 (1971). "Views about the constitutionality of racial data collection began to shift with the enactment of the 1964 Civil Rights Act, which incorporated racial data collection into the enforcement apparatus of the nation's new antidiscrimination legislation. With passage of the 1964 Act, racial record-keeping was not only permitted, it was now required by federal antidiscrimination law." Balkin & Siegel, *supra* note 33, at 938. *See, e.g.,* Civil Rights Act of 1964, Pub. L. No. 88–352, tit. IV, § 402, 78 Stat. 247 (codified as amended at 42 U.S.C. § 2000c-1 (2000)) (requiring a survey of race to determine equal opportunity in education). "Passage of the Act prompted reassessment of the purposes for which government or employers might be collecting racial data, and so altered assumptions about the compatibility of racial data collection practices with the antidiscrimination principle. During the 1960s, as government began to change the form and function of racial data collection, the attitude of the civil rights movement toward the practice shifted markedly." Balkin & Siegel, *supra* note 33, at 938.

34. The Supreme Court has reiterated this point on many occasions. As expressed in the Justice Stone's famous footnote 4 in *Carolene,* 304 U.S., at 153 n.4:

> It is unnecessary to consider now whether legislation which restricts those political processes which can ordinarily be expected to bring about repeal of undesirable legislation, is to be subjected to more exacting judicial scrutiny under the general prohibitions of the Fourteenth Amendment that are most other types of legislation [...]. Nor need we inquire whether similar considerations enter into the review of statutes directed at particular religious [...] or national [...] or racial minorities, [...] whether prejudice against discrete and insular minorities may be a special condition, which tends to seriously curtail the operation of those political processes ordinarily to be relied upon to protect minorities, and which may call for a correspondingly more searching judicial inquiry.

35. RICHARD T. FORD, RACIAL CULTURE: A CRITIQUE 31 (2005).

36. *Id.,* at 25.

37. In reference to the riots that followed the death of Michael Brown, an eighteen-year-old black man who was shot and killed by police officer Darren Wilson in Ferguson, Missouri, on August 9, 2014, and Baltimore protests in reaction to the death of Freddie Gray following police custody on April 19, 2015. Debate also arose after the death, linked to the use of a police choke hold, of Eric Garner in New York on July 17, 2014.

38. *See* International Convention on the Elimination of All Forms of Racial Discrimination, adopted and opened for signature and ratification by General Assembly Resolution 2106 (XX) on Dec. 21, 1965 (entering into force on Jan. 4, 1969), art. 1.

39. This international convention on racial discrimination drew inspiration from the Universal Declaration of Human Rights art. 2; *see also* International Covenant on Civil and Political Rights art. 2.

40. But as observed by Marie-Thérèse Lanquetin, the directive mentions the difficulty of referring to race in recital 6 ("The European Union rejects theories which attempt to determine the existence of separate human races. The use of the term 'racial origin' in this Directive does not imply an acceptance of these theories."), which may explain why the term *ethnic origin* is included. Marie-Thérèse Lanquetin, *Discrimination,* 109 RÉPERTOIRE DE DROIT DU TRAVAIL 6 (2010).

41. The race category is a real challenge for CJEU judges. *See* DENIS MARTIN, ÉGALITÉ ET NON-DISCRIMINATION DANS LA JURISPRUDENCE COMMUNAUTAIRE: ÉTUDE CRITIQUE À LA LUMIÈRE D'UNE APPROCHE COMPARATISTE 199 (2006).

42. *See* the innovation brought by C-54/07, Centrum voor gelijkheid van kansen en voor racismebestrijding v. Firma Feryn, 2008 E.C.R. I-5187 (condemning discriminatory statements relating to origin in a case without a specific victim).
43. Treaty Establishing the European Community (TEC) arts. 12, 39.
44. Case 152/73, Sotgiu v. Deutsche Bundespost, 1974 E.C.R. 153.
45. Julie C. Suk, Disparate Impact Abroad (paper presented at the University of Michigan Law School symposium on the Civil Rights Act at fifty, Oct. 11, 2013).
46. Anastasia Iliopoulou, *"Le temps des gitans": à propos de la libre circulation des Roms dans l'Union*, *in* 1 EUROPE (Jan. 2011).
47. In France, *see* Cass. crim., June 7, 2011, No. 10-85.179 (on statements labeling the Roma people as dangerous); see the controversial 2012 guidelines by the French Minister of the Interior on the dismantling of Roma camps, signed also by the Ministers of Housing and Labor and a department head of the Ministry of Education.
48. Jean-Philippe Lhernould, *L'éloignement des Roms et la directive 2004/38 relative au droit de séjour des citoyens de l'UE*, 11 DR. SOC. 1024 (2010).
49. For a study of the functional conception of equal treatment with respect to nationality, *see* JEAN-SYLVESTRE BERGÉ & SOPHIE ROBIN-OLIVIER, INTRODUCTION AU DROIT EUROPÉEN 138 (2008).
50. Case C-83/14 CHEZ Razpredelenie Bulgaria AD (July 16 2015):

> The concept of "discrimination on the grounds of ethnic origin," ... [in] ... Directive 2000/43/EC of 29 June 2000 ... must be interpreted as being intended to apply in circumstances such as those at issue before the referring court—in which, in an urban district mainly lived in by inhabitants of Roma origin, all the electricity meters are placed on pylons forming part of the overhead electricity supply network at a height of between six and seven metres, whereas such meters are placed at a height of less than two metres in the other districts—irrespective of whether that collective measure affects persons who have a certain ethnic origin or those who, without possessing that origin, suffer, together with the former, the less favourable treatment or particular disadvantage resulting from that measure.

51. *See* Zéhina Aït-El-Kadi, *Traitement des demandes d'asile de citoyens européens*, AJDA 14 (2010) (note under CE, Dec. 30, 2009, OFPRA v. Covaciu, No. 305226): "The Council of State considers that a citizen of a Member State of the European Union may only seek asylum in another Member State of the European Union in limitatively listed cases." In this case, OFPRA (Office français de protection des réfugiés et apatrides) challenged a Refugee Appeals Board (Commission des recours des réfugiés [CRR]) decision recognizing the refugee status of a Romanian national of Roma origin because of the persecution he faced due to his membership in the Roma community and his father's political militantism in Romania. As of the date of the board's decision, Romania had become a member of the European Union. The Conseil d'État, pursuant to Protocol No. 29 appended to the treaty establishing the European Community, recalled that Member States of the European Union are by definition considered to be safe countries of origin in matters of asylum.
52. *See* Thien Uyen Do, *A Case Odyssey into 10 Years of Anti-Discrimination Law*, 12 EUR. ANTI-DISCRIMINATION L. REV. 11, 14–15 (2011). This article describes discrimination against the Roma people, outside of the field of employment, involving racist remarks, access to the same quality of education, the right to housing, and even immigration control by British officers operating at the Prague airport (R. v. Immigration Officer at Prague Airport (2004), UKHL 55).
53. European Convention art. 14 lists thirteen grounds for prohibited distinction or discrimination, and this list is not exhaustive: sex, race, color, language, religion, political

or other opinion, national or social origin, association with a national minority, property, birth or other status. Except for association with a national minority, these grounds are the same as those listed in the Universal Declaration of Human Rights and the International Covenants on Human Rights.

54. By applying European Convention on Human Rights [ECHR] art. 14 (on discrimination) in conjunction with ECHR Protocol 1, art. 1 (on the right to peaceful enjoyment of possessions) (Gaygusuz v. Austria, App. No. 17371/90, 23 Eur. H.R. Rep. 364 (1996); Koua Poirrez v. France, App. No. 40892/98, 40 Eur. H.R. Rep. 34 (2003)) or with ECHR art. 8 (on the right to private and family life) (Petrovic v. Austria, App. No. 20458/92, 33 Eur. H.R. Rep. 307 (1998); Niedzwiecki v. Germany, App. No. 58453/00, 42 Eur. H.R. Rep. 33 (2006), and Okpisz v. Germany, App. No. 59140/00, 42 Eur. H.R. Rep. 32 (2006); Wagner v. Luxembourg, App. No. 76240/01, Eur. Ct. H.R. (2007)), the European Court was able to expand the application of the antidiscrimination principle to property rights and thereby the right of access to social benefits.

55. See Jersild v. Denmark, App. No. 15890/89, 19 Eur. H.R. Rep. 1 (1994); Timishev v. Russia, App. Nos. 55762/00 and 55974/00, 44 Eur. H.R. Rep. 37 (2005). However, the ECtHR does not prohibit contracting parties from treating groups differently in order to correct factual inequalities, although it has accepted that in certain circumstances, to compensate factual inequalities, it is legitimate to allow differences of treatment on the basis of ethnic origin. In Orsus v. Croatia, App. No. 15766/03, judgment of Mar. 16, 2010, § 157, the court took the view that "temporary placement of Roma children in a separate class on the grounds they lack adequate command of the language is not, as such, automatically contrary to ECHR art. 14. It might be said that in certain circumstances such placement would pursue the legitimate aim of adapting the education system to the specific needs of the children. However, when such measure disproportionately or even, as in the present case, affects members of a specific ethnic group, then appropriate safeguards have to be put in place." Olivier de Schutter, EUROPEAN COMMISSION, THE PROHIBITION OF DISCRIMINATION UNDER EUROPEAN HUMAN RIGHTS LAW 19 (2011).

56. The court can take account of the particular circumstances of applicants. See Aksu v. Turkey, App. Nos. 4149/04 and 41029/04, 56 Eur. H.R. Rep. 4 (2010) (applying to Roma people).

57. The benefit of the court's intervention is to identify discrimination based on ethnic origin in all areas where it is revealed, with respect to the condemnation of Spain for nonpayment of a survivor's pension to a widow who had married in accordance with Roma rites (Muñoz-Díaz v. Spain, App. No. 49151/07, 50 Eur. H.R. Rep. 1244 (2009); however, more recently no violation of ECHR art. 14 was found in conjunction with art. 1 of Protocol 1 for a difference in treatment between civil and Islamic marriages. Şerife Yiğit v. Turkey, App. No. 3976/05, Nov. 2, 2010. Compare with the EU Court of Justice reflexion on stereotypes associated with Roma, CJEU *CHEZ*, point 82, *supra* note 50: "Observations submitted to the Court that, in various cases [. . .] CHEZ RB asserted that in its view the damage and unlawful connections are perpetrated mainly by Bulgarian nationals of Roma origin. Such assertions could in fact suggest that the practice at issue is based on ethnic stereotypes or prejudices, the racial grounds thus combining with other grounds."

58. *See generally* Abdulaziz v. United Kingdom, App. Nos. 9214/80, 9473/81, and 9474/81, 7 Eur. H.R. Rep. 471 (1985); Pretty v. United Kingdom, App. No. 2346/02, 35 Eur. H.R. Rep. 1 (2002).

59. See more recently a case of police brutality motivated by racism and strong biases against the Roma people: Ciorcan and Others v. Romania, App. Nos. 29414/09 and 44841/09, Eur. Ct. H.R., Jan. 27, 2015.

60. *Timishev, supra* note 55, at § 56. Timishev, an ethnic Chechen lawyer living as a forced migrant, was refused entry at one checkpoint and forced to make a 300-kilometer detour to another checkpoint, based on oral instructions from the Minister of the Interior not to admit people of Chechen origin. The court held that there was a violation of ECHR art. 14 (on discrimination) taken conjunction with art. 2 of Protocol No. 4 (on the right to freedom of movement).

61. *Timishev, supra* note 55, at § 58.

62. The ECtHR considers that, in view of the fundamental importance of the prohibition of discrimination on grounds of race, no waiver of the right not to be subjected to discrimination on such grounds can be accepted as it would be counter to an important public interest; *see* D.H. v. Czech Republic, App. No. 57325/00, 47 Eur. H.R. Rep. 59 (2007), § 204 (concerning the education of Roma children).

63. Dimitrescu v. Romania, App. No. 3028/04, Eur. Ct. H.R. (2008) (on schooling for Roma children).

64. *See* Van Raalte v. Netherlands, App. No. 20060/92, 24 Eur. H.R. Rep. 503 (1997) (on the obligation for unmarried childless men to pay contributions to child benefits). *See also* in this direction, Larkos v. Cyprus, App. No. 29515/95, 30 Eur. H.R. Rep. 597 (1999); Thlimmenos v. Greece, App. No. 34369/97, 31 Eur. H.R. Rep. 411 (2000); Koua Poirrez v. France, App. No. 40892/98, 40 Eur. H.R. Rep. 34 (2003).

65. Even if technically in European law there is no hierarchy among prohibited grounds.

66. Timishev v. Russia, App. Nos. 55762/00 and 55974/00, 44 Eur. H.R. Rep. 37 (2005), § 55.

67. *See* Aksu v. Turkey, App. Nos. 4149/04 and 41029/04, Mar. 15, 2012; the applicant alleged that three publications—a book and two dictionaries—having received government funding included remarks and expressions that reflected anti-Roma sentiment. The author had stated that Gypsies were engaged in illegal activities, lived as "thieves, pickpockets, swindlers, robbers, usurers, beggars, drug dealers, prostitutes and brothel keepers," and were polygamist and aggressive. The applicant relied on ECHR art. 14 taken in conjunction with art. 8. Although art. 14 was applicable and, as a Roma, he considered that these statements constituted an attack on his Roma identity, the court observed that "the case does not concern a difference in treatment, and in particular ethnic discrimination, as the applicant has not succeeded in producing prima facie evidence that the impugned publications had a discriminatory intent or effect." But other grounds have led the way in pointing out stereotyping: see Konstantin Markin v. Russia (App. No. 30078/06) (pertaining to sex); Alexandra Timmer, *Towards an Anti-Stereotyping Approach for the European Court of Human Rights*, 4 Hum. Rts. L. Rev. 707 (2011); Kiyutin v. Russia, App. No. 2700/10, 53 Eur. H.R. Rep. 908 (2011) (pertaining to disability). It was held to be unlawful discrimination under the European Convention on Human Rights for a government to refuse to grant a residence permit on the basis of HIV-positive status. Since it was dealing with a vulnerable group, the State had only a narrow margin of appreciation.

68. See decisions on indirect discrimination after D.H. v. Czech Republic, App. No. 57325/00, 47 Eur. H.R. Rep 59 (2007), § 204. Relying on ECHR art. 8 in conjunction with art. 14, applicants from Ghana submitted that it amounted to indirect discrimination against them when applying for family reunion, that persons who were born Danish citizens were exempt from the attachment requirement altogether, whereas persons who had acquired Danish citizenship at a later point in life had to comply with the twenty-eight-year rule before being exempted from the attachment requirement. In the present case that would entail that the first applicant could not be exempted from the attachment requirement until 2030, thus after twenty-eight years of Danish citizenship, and after having reached the age of fifty-nine. The ECtHR ruled no violation. A refusal to exempt the applicant from the attachment requirement after such a short time (first applicant, no ties to Denmark) cannot

in the Court's view be considered disproportionate to the aim of the twenty-eight-year rule; namely, to exempt from the attachment requirement a group of nationals who, seen from a general perspective, had lasting and long ties with Denmark. Biao v. Denmark, App. No. 38590/10, Eur. Ct. H.R., Mar. 25, 2014, request for referral to the Grand Chamber pending.

69. Even though origin is a tricky ground: The Supreme Court decided that an employer's refusal to hire a person because he or she is not a United States citizen does not constitute employment discrimination on the basis of "national origin" in violation of § 703 of the Civil Rights Act of 1964. *See* Espinoza v. Farah Mfg. Co., 414 U.S. 86 (1973). Marie Mercat-Bruns & Louis Imbert, *Les discriminations fondées sur la nationalité: Perspectives américaines*, 103 PLEIN DROIT 60 (2014).

70. *See generally* DANIÈLE LOCHAK, LE DROIT ET LES JUIFS, EN FRANCE DEPUIS LA RÉVOLUTION (2009). See guidelines by Minister of Justice Christiane Taubira for quicker and harsher prosecution of racist or xenophobic acts, Jan. 12, 2015, following the *Charlie Hebdo* and kosher supermarket attacks. However, the kamikaze attacks in Paris on Nov. 13, 2015, were followed by the adoption of a state of emergency for three months, which facilitates a wide scope of criminal investigations to prevent future terrorist attacks: *Law 55-385 of Apr. 3, 1955, on the State of Emergency* (http://www.legifrance.gouv.fr/affichTexte.do?cidT exte=JORFTEXT000000695350).

71. *See* art. 1 of the French Constitution of 1958; art. 31, Act No. 78-17 of Jan. 6, 1978 (on information technology, data files and civil liberties), and art. 8 (applying specific restrictions on the collection of personal data); HALDE decision No. 2006-31 of Feb. 27, 2007; Versailles, June 17, 2009, No. 08/03751 (against the use of keeping "ethnic" data). *See also* art. 63 of the draft legislation on immigration and integration, known as the "loi Hortefeu," Sept. 2007 (authorizing the collection of ethnic statistics), and CC [Conseil constitutionnel] decision No. 2007–557 DC, Nov. 15, 2007 (holding art. 63 unconstitutional); Veil Report, released in December 2008 by the committee headed by Simone Veil, refusing to revise the Preamble to the French Constitution to introduce the idea of diversity; report by the Committee for the Measurement of Diversity and Discrimination (Comité pour la mesure de la diversité et des discriminations [COMEDD]), released in February 2010.

72. *See* Katell Berthou, *La preuve des discriminations à l'embauche en raison de l'origine*, 11 REV. DR. TRAVAIL 635 (2010) (commenting on the Toulouse Court of Appeal decision of Feb. 19, 2010, on the ban (or limitation) of the use of ethnoracial statistics). It is possible to approach the issue from a different angle, showing a contradiction in the logic in France: if "race" as a social construct does not exist, why have a law (1978) to prohibit something that does not exist? This is the question posed by Professor Randall Kennedy at Harvard Law School in a 2010 conversation with the author in preparation for this book.

73. The judges reason by default. A lack of objective evidence explaining an arbitrary difference in treatment enables them to infer the possibility of discrimination based on origin, if no other factor exists to explain such delayed career development, Cass. soc., Feb. 7, 2012, No. 10–19505. The Défenseur des Droits (successor to HALDE), to combat this lack of evidence, helped create a website to allow citizens to alert directly a platform of organizations if they are victim of racial comments or racial micro-agressions (including in employment); see http://www.egalitecontreracisme.fr/.

74. An increase in cases involving racist statements made outside of the workplace has been observed. *See* Cass. crim., Mar. 15, 2011, No. 11–1738; Cass. crim., June 7, 2011, No. 11–2763; Cass. crim., June 19, 2001, No. 98-83.954 (involving a French mayor who, in an exclusive interview given to a German journalist, made comments constituting incitement to racial hatred and violence). The mayor was found guilty of aiding an act of defamation when, without her knowledge, the interview was published in a French newspaper. The journalist was prosecuted as the principal offender. With this decision, the Criminal

Chamber overturned the Aix-en-Provence Court of Appeal's decision of Mar. 9, 1998, in which the trial courts considered that "by granting an interview to the journalist for publication, [the mayor] intended to make her comments public and obtained the means to do so" and that "although her consent was materially given only to this journalist, it must be considered applicable to any publication, provided that her comments are faithfully reproduced."

75. Michel Danti-Juan, *Discriminations,* 41 RÉPERTOIRE DR. PÉNAL (1996). "Evidence of intent to discriminate, indispensable to the demonstration of the offense, presents notable practical difficulties whenever this intent has not been manifested by written or oral statements or other expressions enabling judges to perceive the frame of mind of the person denying a good, service or employment." *See* CRIMINAL CODE [CODE PÉNAL] art. 225-1.

76. On Jan. 8, 2014, France's administrative supreme court (Conseil d'État) declared null and void a lower court's injunction suspending the effects of a mayor's ban on stand-up comedian Dieudonné's show because of anti-Semitic comments. The court's reasoning is based on the infringement of dignity of the human person as part of public order, Ordonnance No. 374508. On Dieudonné's being fined €22,500 on Mar. 19, 2015, because of racist comments against a Jewish journalist made during his show, see *Propos antisémites de Dieudonné : le jugement mis en délibéré au 19 mars,* LE MONDE, http://www.lemonde.fr/societe/art/2015/01/28/dieudonne-comparait-en-justice-pour-ses-propos-sur-patrick-cohen_4564674_3224.html; http://www.francebleu.fr/infos/dieudonne-condamne-22-500-euros-d-amende-pour-des-propos-contre-patrick-cohen-2228721.

77. *See* the 2010 annual report of the HALDE (former equality body, succeeded by Défenseur des Droits), *available at* http://www.halde.fr/IMG/pdf/DP_RA_HALDE_2010.pdf. Origin was consistently the leading factor of discrimination claims. The breakdown by ground of discrimination has remained relatively constant since 2005, with origin accounting for 27–29 percent since 2007, handicap and health 19 percent, sex (including pregnancy) 9 percent, age 6 percent, and union activity 5 percent. The annual report of the Défenseur des Droits mentions a few cases involving racial discrimination, racial comments, use of foreign surnames, and progress in using a "panel" method of comparison to prove discrimination; see decision No. MLD-2013-98 of July 1, 2013, http://www.defenseurdesdroits.fr/decisions/ddd/MLD-2013-98.pdf.

78. The figures have hardly changed in criminal law, despite this 2008 testimonial by a legal practitioner: Thierry Sagardoytho, *Le droit pénal de la discrimination, un droit à construire,* 7–8 ACTUALITÉ JURIDIQUE PÉNAL 313 (2008). See also the 2014 annual report of the Défenseur des Droits (in French), RAPPORT ANNUEL D'ACTIVITÉ 15 (2014).

79. Cass. crim., Dec. 1, 1992, No. 89–82.689, Bull. crim., No. 398 (finding that an employer is not criminally liable for publishing a racially discriminatory job offer where it has been established that the offer was published after outsourcing the recruitment mission to a service provider). The director of publication may not be held responsible as the principal offender or as an accomplice unless materiality and intent elements have been established, or a knowing participation in the punishable principal act, which was not the case here.

80. For example, Cass. crim., Nov. 14, 1989, No. 88–81.817, Bull. crim. No. 416; Paris, 11th Ch. B, Oct. 17, 2003, *Moulin Rouge,* No. 03–00.387, REV. JURIS. SOC. (2004), No. 171; Michel Miné, note under TGI Paris, 31st Ch. corr., Nov. 22, 2002, 660 DR. OUVRIER 270 (2003); Paris, 11th Ch. A, June 7, 2004; Nantes criminal court of July 17, 2006; Cass. crim., June 23, 2009, Adecco, No. 07–85.109, Bull. crim., No. 126; ACTUALITÉ JURIDIQUE PÉNAL 408 (2009) (note by Jérôme Lasserre Capdeville); Jean-Baptiste Thierry, *Parce qu'elles ne le valaient pas bien,* 12 REV. DR. TRAVAIL 722 (2009).

81. On the limitations of criminal proceedings: "Although the arsenal of repression may seem impressive, the criminal approach to discrimination remains largely unsatisfactory. This widely shared observation has several causes, the main ones being a complex delineation of the contours of the discrimination offense, the difficulties of proving discrimination and the relatively feeble financial sanctions ordered." Elisabeth Fortis, *Réprimer les discriminations depuis la loi du 27 mai 2008: entre incertitudes et impossibilités*, 7 ACTUALITÉ JURIDIQUE PÉNAL 303 (2008). For the difference between civil and criminal proceedings in terms of evidence of discrimination, *see* CC decision No. 2011-455 DC, Jan. 12, 2002, J.O. 1053 (Jan. 18, 2002); Cass. crim., Apr. 3, 2007, No. 870, REV. JURIS. SOC. (2007).

82. See a very rare labor court decision refusing a promotion "because of inexperience." The employee considered, because of highly positive appraisals, that the refusal was discriminatory, based on "origin" and "skin color." The court observed that the employee was qualified for the promotion and that three colleagues with similar or lower qualifications were hired as risk analysts. Conseil des prud'hommes de Paris (decided by professional judge after a tie vote between union and employer acting as judges), Dec. 27, 2012, No. 11–01105, Natixis Corporation. Sometimes no objective justification is produced by employer for the direct discrimination; *see* Court of Appeal, Colmar, Apr. 24, 2008, No. 1020765. In other instances, candidates of a certain origin were probably selected because of their place of residence, but at that time, place of residence was not a ground for discrimination, and anonymity of selection process was used to reject discrimination claim; see Cass. soc., *June 16, 2015, No. 13–28129*.

83. Cass. soc., Dec. 15, 2011, No. 10–15873, Airbus (considering that since the lower court had held that the plaintiff has presented elements suggesting discrimination upon recruitment and that it had noted the employer's failure to demonstrate that its selection of another applicant was based on that applicant's level of education or work experience, it had legally justified its decision).

84. Jérôme Lasserre Capdeville, *Le testing*, ACTUALITÉ JURIDIQUE PÉNAL 310 (2008) ("the legal recognition of testing did not greatly affect the fight against discrimination, especially repressive criminal sanctions in this area. In fact, testing currently only plays a subsidiary role in criminal law, which is not expected to develop in the future, given that this approach can be easily disputed in the absence of outside corroborating evidence. Testing can, however, be useful to measure discriminatory mechanisms before the fact"). This is why the current government is pushing to generalize testing procedures; see the recommendations made in the May 19, 2015, report by the French Ministry of Labor, *supra* Chapter 3, note 28.

85. Cass. soc., Jan. 18, 2012, No. 10–16926 (finding discrimination in a case where a deputy HR manager asked a highly recommended job candidate to return in two weeks when her boss, who "does not trust women from the Maghreb," would be on vacation); Cass. soc., Nov. 10, 2009, No. 08–42.286 (holding that an employer's request that an employee change his name from Mohamed to Laurent, particularly at the time of hiring, constitute discrimination on the basis of origin). In the latter case, the circumstantial fact that several employees in the company or department are also named Mohamed was not in itself an objective justification of such as request. The appellate court's decision to reject the plaintiff's claim for damages for discrimination, arguing that the employee had accepted the change of name at the time of hiring and that at the time the employment contract was signed, there were four other employees in the company with the same first name, was struck down.

86. Cass. crim., June 23, 2009, No. 07–85.109, BULL. CRIM. 2009, No. 126 (ruling that the recruitment campaign conducted by two companies, excluding non-European or nonwhite

people from their search for women to promote a hair care product, unjustified by the nature of the product being promoted, was discriminatory on the basis of origin). Candidates were sought to meet these requirements: aged 18 to 22, size 40 maximum (U.S. size 8–10), and BBR, an abbreviation standing for "bleu, blanc, rouge" (blue, white, red, the colors of the French flag).

87. Racial discrimination in promotion or job transfer decisions is harder to prove unless the job opportunities are given to less-experienced or less-skilled nonminority workers. See Conseil des prud'hommes de Paris, Dec. 27, 2012, Natixis Corporation, No. 11–01105.

88. In a case where educational qualifications were presented as selection criterion only after hiring, an assumption could be made that that the unsuccessful applicant's name of North African origin was the cause for the denial of recruitment. This was the reasoning of the Cour de cassation, Cass. soc., Dec. 5, 2011, No. 10–15873, confirming the decision of the Toulouse Court of Appeal of Feb. 19, 2010, sentencing Airbus to a €18,000 fine for damages for discrimination on the ground of origin.

89. Cass. soc., Dec. 15, 2011, No. 10–15873. A short-term worker was not recruited for a long-term position and the employer could not justify that the refusal decision was based on education or work experience. In the absence of an objective justification, the court recognized discrimination based on origin and surname. The French supreme court is encouraging judges to infer discrimination in cases of unequal treatment of workers, if employers refuse to produce objective evidence. For a case of unequal pay, see Cass. soc., June 12, 2013, No. 11–14458.

90. The European Commission against Racism and Intolerance (ECRI), the human rights body of the Conseil de l'Europe, made up of independent experts, published its Fourth Report on France on June 15, 2010. Improvements were observed, such as reinforced legal provisions to combat discrimination, thanks in particular to the role played by the HALDE, especially against racism. The ECRI, however, pointed out the persistence of discrimination on the basis of "race," color, language, religion, nationality, and national or ethnic origin in access to employment, education, housing, and goods and services. Likewise, the report denounced the unacceptable living conditions of Roma and Travelers, with the number of stopping places still insufficient. See the summary in 25 JCP G 706 (2010). See also LA LUTTE CONTRE LE RACISME, L'ANTISÉMITISME ET LA XÉNOPHOBIE, the 2014 report on racism, xenophobia, and antisemitism, by the French Commission on Human Rights (Commission nationale consultative des droits de l'homme [CNCDH]) and the interview of its president, *available at* http://www.cncdh.fr/fr/actualite/rapport-annuel-sur-le-racisme-lantisemitisme-et-la-xenophobie (the 2015 report is forthcoming), and the 2015 report on discrimination by the ILO and the Défenseur des Droits, describing the types of discrimination in recruitment faced by workers of foreign origin, *available at* http://www.ilo.org/public/french/region/eurpro/paris/actualites/download/barom8synthese.pdf. Recently certain cases have prevailed in the courts with regard to racial profiling of police during routine ID checks; *see* Court of Appeals, Paris June 24 2015, 13/24261.

91. Éric Fassin, *Statistiques raciales ou racistes? Histoire et actualité d'une controverse française, in* LES NOUVELLES FRONTIÈRES DE LA SOCIÉTÉ FRANÇAISE 430 (Éric Fassin ed., 2010): "In particular, what delineates the battlefield in the recent controversy is the problematic relationship between the race question and the immigration question. Do ethnic statistics refer to origin, i.e., once again to immigration? Or, on the contrary: does the dispute over statistics signify a new recognition of racial discrimination?" *See also* the Constitutional Council's censorship of the introduction of ethnic statistics in the act relating to the control of immigration, integration, and asylum, CC decision No. 2007–557 DC, Nov. 15, 2007:

> Section 63 of the statute referred for review, which is the results of an amendment passed by the National Assembly on first reading, amends II of section 8 and I of section 25 of the Act

of January 6, 1978 referred to hereinabove. It is designed to allow processing of personal data "indicating, directly or indirectly, the racial or ethnic origins" of persons for the carrying out of studies on diversity of origin, discrimination and integration, and subject to the authorization of the National Committee of Data Processing and Individual Liberties.

92. See Law 211–672 of June 16, 2011, on immigration, integration, and citizenship, J.O., June 17, 2011, p. 10290, which focuses on procedures for returning illegally staying third-country nationals, reinforces the means by which the government can monitor third-country nationals pending their return and plans amendments to the administrative return procedure, which also includes community nationals under certain conditions (art. L. 511-3-1); these measures can impact Roma people. See Olivier Lecucq, *L'éloignement des étrangers sous l'empire de la loi du 16 juin 2011*, 34 AJDA 1936 (2011).

93. See DE LA QUESTION SOCIALE À LA QUESTION RACIALE? REPRÉSENTER LA SOCIÉTÉ FRANÇAISE (Didier Fassin & Éric Fassin eds., 2009); ERIC MAURIN, LE GHETTO FRANÇAIS: ENQUÊTE SUR LE SÉPARATISME SOCIAL 61 (2004); HUGUES LAGRANGE, LE DÉNI DES CULTURES 115 (2010); ERIC FASSIN ET AL., ROMS & RIVERAINS: UNE POLITIQUE MUNICIPALE DE LA RACE (2014).

94. Edmond Preteceille, *La ségrégation ethno-raciale a-t-elle augmenté dans la métropole parisienne?*, 50 REV. FR. DE SOCIOLOGIE 489 (2009); MARCO OBERTI, L'ÉCOLE DANS LA VILLE, SÉGRÉGATION—MIXITÉ—CARTE SCOLAIRE (2007); ÉMEUTES URBAINES ET PROTESTATIONS: UNE SINGULARITÉ FRANÇAISE (Hugues Lagrange & Marco Oberti eds., 2006).

95. See the occupational categories used by France's national statistics body, INSEE, http://www.insee.fr/fr/methodes/default.asp?page=nomenclatures/pcs2003/pcs2003. htm. This classification is fundamental to all sociological studies in France. The new version of these Occupations and Socio-occupational Categories [Professions et Catégories Socioprofessionnelles] introduced in 2003 is the result of work in progress since 1982. The updated version groups occupations for which the distinction has now become obsolete and similarly breaks down other categories to reflect the appearance of new occupations (in the fields of the environment and new information and communication technologies, for example), as well as occupations that are not specific to a particular industry (methods, quality control, logistics).

96. Since French Law No. 2012–954 of Aug. 6, 2012, the list of grounds refers to family name instead of name. See Cass. soc., Nov. 10, 2009, No. 08–42286: "By deciding that requesting that the employee change his name from Mohamed to Laurent constitutes discrimination on the basis of origin and that the circumstance that several employees were named Mohamed was not an objective element justifying the decision, the appellate court violated the statute referred to hereinabove." See also the analysis by Thérèse Aubert-Monpeyssen, *Vous avez dit 'Laurent'?*, 3 REV. DR. TRAVAIL 169 (2010): "By finding discrimination based on origin, the Social Chamber interprets the law with emphasis on its actual end purpose, demonstrating the coherence of the list of protected grounds and their nonexhaustive nature. In so doing, it widens the spectrum of behavior that can be sanctioned based on this ground. In particular, it makes it possible to fight forms of discrimination of which, according to the Fauroux report, "the offenders themselves are not always aware" but that "harshly affect victims [and] participate in the disintegration of society, undermining it from within." ROGER FAUROUX, MINISTÈRE DE L'EMPLOI, DE LA COHÉSION SOCIALE ET DU LOGEMENT, LA LUTTE CONTRE LES DISCRIMINATIONS ETHNIQUES DANS LE DOMAINE DE L'EMPLOI 8 (2005).

97. The ground of place of residence was added to LABOR CODE [CODE DU TRAVAIL] art. L.1132–1 by Law 2014–173 of Feb. 21, 2014, enforced since Feb. 23, 2014, on city planning and urban cohesion. The HALDE had published a deliberation on Apr. 18, 2011, on discrimina-

tion based on place of residence, calling for the adoption of a legislative measure adding "residential address as a prohibited ground of discrimination without legitimate reason" to the list of prohibited criteria in the Labor Code (Délibération relative aux discriminations à raison du lieu de résidence: un nouveau critère à inscrire dans la loi no 2011–121 du 18 avril 2011); *see* Emmanuel Duguet et al., *Les effets du lieu de résidence sur l'accès à l'emploi: une expérience contrôlée sur des jeunes qualifiés en Île-de-France, in* 128 DOCUMENT DE TRAVAIL 17 (Centre d'études de l'emploi, 2010) (observing that discrimination on the basis of place of residence particularly affects women).

98. *See* Marie-Thérèse Lanquetin, *Discriminations*, 109 RÉPERTOIRE DE DROIT DU TRAVAIL: "Furthermore, origin can also refer to social origin, a ground not explicitly listed in art. L. 1134–2, but that has been included in Convention No. 111 of the ILO, ratified by France in 1981 and in force since 1982. This ground has also been included in the EU Charter on Fundamental Rights." Case law in employment involving this ground is still not abundant. *See* Cass. soc., Apr. 8, 1992, No. 90–41.276, RECUEIL DALLOZ 293 (1992) (note by Antoine Lyon-Caen).

99. The author reflects on the difference between social origin and social condition and the difficulty in using standards to identify the ground. Diane Roman, *La discrimination fondée sur la condition sociale, une catégorie manquante du droit français*, RECUEIL DALLOZ 1911 (2013).

100. Proposition de loi visant à lutter contre la discrimination à raison de la précarité sociale [draft legislation aiming to fight discrimination based on social insecurity], Bill No. 378, introduced by Socialist senator Yannick Vaugrenard and adopted unanimously with some abstentions by the conservatives on June 18, 2015, *available at* http://www.senat.fr/leg/ppl14-378.html. The bill must now be passed by the National Assembly; see http://www.assemblee-nationale.fr/14/propositions/pion2885.asp; the grounds cover "a particular vulnerability caused by an apparent or known economic situation."

101. See the decision to remove the general culture test from the entrance examination to Sciences Po law school, *available at* http://www.sciencespo.fr/node/8952.

102. On percentage plans seen from a French perspective, see the report published by the French-American Foundation in November 2007 on the findings of the study tour conducted by the Foundation to the University of California at Berkeley and the University of Texas at Austin, *available at* http://www.frenchamerican.org/sites/default/files/documents/media_reports/percentageplans_report_fr.pdf, and new measures similar to the Texas percentage plans adopted in France in 2013.

103. *See supra* Chapter 2, and the work by Daniel Sabbagh on his classification of "indirect positive discrimination" and the threat of the Supreme Court's *Fisher v. University of Texas* decision on affirmative action programs.

104. Mercat-Bruns, *La discrimination professionnelle fondée sur le sexe aux États-Unis*, supra note 7, at 63.

105. Wal-Mart v. Dukes, 131 S. Ct. 2541 (2011) (No. 10–277) on June 20, 2011 ("The certification of the nationwide class of female employees was not consistent with Federal Rule of Civil Procedure 23(a), which requires the party seeking class certification to prove that the class has common questions of law or fact"): The nationwide class alleging discrimination in pay and promotions by Wal-Mart failed to satisfy commonality prerequisite for class action certification under method requiring "significant proof" of general policy of discrimination, despite social framework analysis by expert who testified that employer has "strong corporate culture" that makes it "vulnerable" to gender bias, where he conceded that he could not calculate whether 0.5 percent or 95 percent of employment decisions might be determined by stereotyped thinking.

106. Plaintiffs' Motion for Class Certification in No. 3: 01-cv-02252-CRB (ND Cal.), Doc. 99, p. 13.
107. 222 F.R.D. 137, 166.
108. Plaintiffs' Motion for Class Certification in No. 3, *supra* note 105, at 16.
109. 222 F.R.D. 137, 155.
110. *Id.* at 159.
111. Two cases justify the adoption of the Pregnancy Discrimination Act (P.L. 95–555) of 1978. In 1974, in Geduldig v. Aiello, 417 U.S. 484 (1974), the U.S. Supreme Court held that pregnancy was not a sex-based classification and therefore California was permitted to exclude pregnancy-related disability from its temporary disability benefits program under the Equal Protection Clause. In 1976, in General Electric v. Gilbert, 429 U.S. 125 (1976), the U.S. Supreme Court held that denying disability benefits to pregnant workers was also not sex discrimination under Title VII. In light of the Pregnancy Discrimination Act, the Supreme Court has held recently that the courts must evaluate the extent to which an employer's policy treats pregnant workers less favorably than nonpregnant workers with similar inabilities to work and determine whether there are any legitimate reasons for such differences; see Young v. United Parcel Services, Inc., 575 US __ (2015).
112. Pregnancy Discrimination Act (P.L. 95–555) of 1978.
113. ELISABETH BADINTER, LE CONFLIT: LA FEMME ET LA MÈRE (2011).
114. On the "lack of interest argument," see Vicki Schultz, *Telling Stories About Women and Work: Judicial Interpretation of Sex Segregation in the Workplace in Title VII Cases Raising the Lack of Interest Argument*, 103 HARV. L. REV. 1749 (1990).
115. Today, the unemployment rate is much lower, e.g., 5.6 percent in December 2014.
116. Price Waterhouse v. Hopkins, 490 U.S. 228 (1989).
117. *See supra* Chapter 3, interview with Christine Jolls, for more about the Implicit Association Test (IAT).
118. See also on the economic analysis of accommodation, Christine Jolls, *Accommodation Mandates*, 53 STAN. L. REV. 223 (2000); Christine Jolls, *Antidiscrimination and Accommodation*, 115 HARV. L. REV. 642 (2001).
119. Jespersen v. Harrah's, 2004 U.S. App. LEXIS 26892 (9th Cir).
120. Family status discrimination can be linked to the couple: Cass. soc., Feb. 10, 1999, No. 96–42998 (finding it discriminatory to prohibit access to departments with "sensitive" information to prevent leaks because the husband of the employee works for a competitor); Cass. soc., June 30, 2010, No. 08–41936 (finding it discriminatory to fire an employee who had not prevented his spouse from insulting the employer). HALDE decision. No. 2011–13, Jan. 31, 2011 (finding family status discrimination when an employer reserves summer jobs for children of employees); HALDE decision No. 2007–366, Feb. 11, 2008 (finding a collective bargaining agreement providing leave for family events exclusively for married employees to be discriminatory); HALDE decision No. 2011–62, Apr. 18, 2011 (finding discriminatory a refusal to offer training to a play stage technician because of a maternity leave). However, specific benefits can be offered to women when the difference of situation can be justified with other workers—*see* Cass. soc., Feb. 26, 2002, No. 99–44671 (involving pay advantages given to head of households)—as long as these differences do not conceal differences of treatment based on sex (Case C-173/13, Leone and Leone, Feb. 27, 2014) or sexual orientation (Cass. soc., July 9, 2014, No. 10–18341, finding discriminatory based on sexual orientation to give an advantage in a collective bargaining agreement only to married couples).
121. Case C-243/95, Kathleen Hill, June 17, 1998, point 42 ("Community policy in this area is to encourage and, if possible, adapt working conditions to family responsibilities.

Protection of women within family life and in the course of their professional activities is, in the same way as for men, a principle which is widely regarded in the legal systems of the Member States as being the natural corollary of the equality between men and women, and which is recognised by Community law").

122. Cass. soc., Oct. 8, 1996, No. 92-42291; Cass. soc., Feb. 27, 1991, No. 90-42239; Cass. soc., May 4, 2011, No. 09-72206.

123. Disadvantages that can stem from living far away from the workplace: Cass. soc., Oct. 11, 2000, No. 98-46.433.

124. Julie Suk, *Are Gender Stereotypes Bad for Women? Rethinking Antidiscrimination Law and Work-Family Conflict*, 111 COLUM. L. REV. 1 (2010).

125. Vicki Schultz, *Feminism and Workplace Flexibility*," 42 Conn. L. Rev. 1203 (2010).

126. Vicki Schultz & Allison Hoffman, *The Need for a Reduced Work Week in the United States*, in JUDITH FUDGE & ROSEMARY OWEN EDS., PRECARIOUS WORK, WOMEN, AND THE NEW ECONOMY: THE CHALLENGE TO LEGAL NORMS (2006).

127. JERRY JACOB & KATHLEEN GERSON, THE TIME DIVIDE: WORK, FAMILY AND GENDER INEQUALITY (2004).

128. See interview with Vicki Schultz in MARIE MERCAT-BRUNS, DISCRIMINATIONS EN DROIT DU TRAVAIL: DIALOGUE AVEC LA DOCTRINE AMERICAINE 109-111 (2013), in which she identifies four models of antidiscrimination based on a historical analysis:

> At the moment, probably all four frameworks are in competition with each other. [. . .] You can have a notion of discrimination as a violation of a kind of norm of impartiality. [. . .] There is a conservative view of this that says that any time you take race into account or sex, that is a violation of the norm of impartiality, and so this is close to the majority view in the *Ricci v. DeStefano* Supreme Court case. So the disparate impact principle itself becomes a violation of the norm of impartiality. [. . .] You could have a different understanding of discrimination: I call this one the perpetuation of past discrimination. What's wrong with a standardized test is that it projects into one sphere, the sphere of the workplace, the degradation and insubordination and inequality that was practiced elsewhere. So if you understood that the reason why Afro-Americans did less well on standardized tests was their history of inferior schooling, then you would say the antidiscrimination principle is violated when you allow one sphere to be infected with the discrimination in another sphere, without a really compelling justification for the violation of the "Rawlsian" spheres of justice principle. [. . .] Now each of these models developed a critique which leads to the birth of the next, so the third model I call the diversity model. It comes out of the critique of the past discrimination model, and those critiques are that there is a notion that a cumulative disadvantage is practiced upon historically subordinated groups. So the focus is always: what is wrong with them? . . . Wouldn't it be a good thing to have diversity, because it would recognize that there is something about us as women that we bring to the table, maybe because we have historically been discriminated against? There is something virtuous that should be celebrated and accommodated in the workplace. This is the essence of the diversity model: one could also call it an accommodation model; it is more a multicultural model. In a way, it seeks to promote integration, but through a notion of accommodating difference—exogenous difference produced outside the workplace sphere under investigation. The proponents of the fourth model, which I call the disruption model, are wary about these globalizing claims of exogenous difference and want to be very careful about making them. The disruption model, I think, in contrast to the diversity model, looks for both structural and micro-level interactions within institutions that actually produce difference, so that difference is not treated as exogenously given to the institution, but is taken as a phenomenon to be investigated. So you're like a detective trying to figure out whether or not there is something the employer or the union or the interaction between the employees is doing that is actually creating sex in a very context-specific way.

129. Hélène Périvier & Rachel Silvera, *Maudite conciliation*, 24 TRAVAIL GENRE SOCIÉTÉS 25 (2010).

130. Reference to pregnancy, giving birth, and breastfeeding.

131. Bona Fide Occupational Qualification (BFOQ): *see* Title VII of the Civil Rights Act of 1964 (Pub. L. 88-352) (Title VII), as amended, section 703(e) ("It shall not be an unlawful employment practice for an employer to hire and employ employees, for an employment agency to classify, or refer for employment any individual, for a labor organization to classify its membership or to classify or refer for employment any individual, or for an employer, labor organization, or joint labor management committee controlling apprenticeship or other training or retraining programs to admit or employ any individual in any such program, on the basis of his religion, sex, or national origin in those certain instances where religion, sex, or national origin is a bona fide occupational qualification reasonably necessary to the normal operation of that particular business or enterprise"); art. 14 of Directive 2006/54/EC of the European Parliament and of the Council of July 5, 2006 (on the implementation of the principle of equal opportunities and equal treatment of men and women in matters of employment and occupation ("Member States may provide, as regards access to employment including the training leading thereto, that a difference of treatment which is based on a characteristic related to sex shall not constitute discrimination where, by reason of the nature of the particular occupational activities concerned or of the context in which they are carried out, such a characteristic constitutes a genuine and determining occupational requirement, provided that its objective is legitimate and the requirement is proportionate")); Case C-273/97, Sirdar v. Army Board, 1999 E.C.R. I-7403.

132. There is a very important issue in France concerning equal access to retirement for men and women who have raised their children full-time and therefore paid fewer contributions into the retirement system. *See* Annie Junter & Caroline Ressot, *La discrimination sexiste: les regards du droit*, 114 REVUE DE L'OFCE 106 (2010). The CJEU has found that the apparently neutral French rule benefitting employees who have taken leave from work to raise children must not indirectly disadvantage men: *see* Case C-173/13, Leone and Leone, Feb. 27, 2014. The CJEU also found no indirect discrimination against women because of part-time work in the level of disability pensions: C-527/13, Fernandez v. Instituto Nacional de la Seguridad Social, Apr. 14, 2015.

133. Case 184/83, Hofmann v. Barmer Ersatzkasse, 1984 E.C.R. 3047; Directive 92/85/EEC of Oct. 19, 1992, on the introduction of measures to encourage improvements in the safety and health at work of pregnant workers and workers who have recently given birth or are breastfeeding.

134. On a brief definition of gender as a social construct and the role assigned to men and women based on their sex, see GENEVIÈVE FRAISSE, À CÔTÉ DU GENRE: SEXE ET PHILOSOPHIE DE L'ÉGALITÉ 299 (2010); *see also* ELSA DORLIN, SEXE, GENRE ET SEXUALITÉS: INTRODUCTION À LA THÉORIE FÉMINISTE (2008) [hereinafter DORLIN, SEXE, GENRE ET SEXUALITÉS]. In the United States, the fight continues. For a description of the pending Silicon Valley case, see Audrey Dilling, *Sex Discrimination Trial Puts Silicon Valley Under the Microscope*, *available at* http://www.npr.org/2015/03/17/393347548/sex-discrimination-trial-puts-silicon-valley-under-the-microscope, in which Joan Williams, professor at the University of California, Hastings College of Law, questions whether, in the world of venture capital, you can be seen as "too masculine to be likeable" and "too feminine to be competent."

135. Family status is mentioned as a ground in LABOR CODE [CODE DU TRAVAIL] art. 1132-1. See recently, a case involving a father on parental leave, who claimed unequal treatment rather than discrimination based on family status: Cass. soc., Sept. 24, 2014, No. 13-14226.

136. Wal-Mart v. Dukes, 131 S. Ct. 2541 (2011) (No. 10-277) illustrates the risk of systemic sex discrimination: *see* Dukes v. Wal-Mart , Memorandum of Points and Authorities in Support of Plaintiffs' Motion for Class in Wal-Mart Certification (n.d.; retrieved May 17, 2006, from http://www.walmartclass.com/staticdata/walmartclass/brief2.html), in which it is described how Wal-Mart does not give objective guidelines to select its employees for training, allowing them to use subjective grounds; Wal-Mart does not systematically circulate training opportunities to all staff; and there is no policy in place for monitoring gender disparities in pay and promotion. *See also* Mercat-Bruns & Boussard Verrecchia, *supra* note 2, at 660; Marie Mercat-Bruns, *Comparaison entre les discriminations fondée sur l'appartenance syndicale, l'âge et le sexe, révélatrice de la discrimination systémique* 11 REV. DR. TRAVAIL 672 (2015).

137. *See* Linda Krieger, *The Watched Variable Improves: On Eliminating Sex Discrimination in Employment, in* SEX DISCRIMINATION IN EMPLOYMENT 295, 304 (Faye Crosby et al. eds., 2007).

138. McDonnell Douglas Corp. v. Green, 411 U.S.792 (1973) (establishes the prima facie case of discrimination). *See supra* Chapter 3.

139. *See* MAYERI, REASONING FROM RACE, *supra* note 7 at 9.

140. *See* Case C-96/80, Jenkins v. Kingsgate, 1981 E.C.R. 911; Case C-300/06, Voss v. Land Berlin, 2007 E.C.R. I-10573.

141. Case C-144/04, Mangold v. Helm, 2005 E.C.R. I-9981, and Case C-555/07, Kücükdeveci v. Swedex, 2010 E.C.R. I-365, refer to this.

142. These are acquired rights that stem from CJEU case law, incorporated subsequently in EU directives; *see, for example,* CJCE Defrenne I, II, III.

143. Case C-144/04, Mangold v. Helm, 2005 E.C.R. I-9981.

144. *See* MAYERI, REASONING FROM RACE, *supra* note 7, at 9, citing ELLEN DUBOIS, FEMINISM AND SUFFRAGE: THE EMERGENCE OF AN INDEPENDENT WOMEN'S MOVEMENT IN AMERICA, 1848–1869 (1999); Mercat-Bruns, *La discrimination professionnelle fondée sur le sexe aux États-Unis, supra* note 7, at 63.

145. *See* DANIEL MOYNIHAN, THE NEGRO FAMILY: A CASE FOR NATIONAL ACTION, OFFICE OF PLANNING AND POLICY RESEARCH 5–14, 29–31, 35–36 (1965), cited by MAYERI, REASONING FROM RACE, *supra* note 7, at 24.

146. MAYERI, REASONING FROM RACE, *supra* note 7, at 29.

147. When the HALDE (now the Defender of Rights) was created, half of the sex discrimination claims brought before it were by men. In the United States; *see* Diaz v. Pan American Airways, 442 F.2d 385.

148. For a recent potential glass ceiling case, see Court of Appeal, Orléans, Apr. 23, 2015, 14/00500. In this case, a female employee introduced a complaint based on sex discrimination because all of the executive jobs were held by men in comparable situations. The court considered this insufficient to prove sex discrimination. Among the court's arguments was this one, based on the employer's defense: more and more women are climbing the corporate ladder, and the employee in question had neither requested a promotion nor been refused one.

149. DOMINIQUE MÉDA & HÉLÈNE PÉRIVIER, LE DEUXIÈME ÂGE DE L'ÉMANCIPATION: LA SOCIÉTÉ, LES FEMMES ET L'EMPLOI (2007); MARGARET MARUANI, TRAVAIL ET EMPLOI DES FEMMES (2011).

150. See LABOR CODE [CODE DU TRAVAIL] art. L.1142-2, para. 1 ("If a member of one or the other sex is an essential and determining requirement and if the aim is legitimate and the requirement proportionate, the prohibition of discrimination of art. L.1142-2 is not applicable. LABOR CODE [CODE DU TRAVAIL] art. L.1142-2, para. 2 refers to a decree validated by the Conseil d'État. It determines, after consulting unions and employers on a national level,

a list of jobs that require one of the sex as a determining condition for employment. This list is reexamined regularly"). French law turns to EU law, which sets a judicial standard to determine the scope of this exception to sex discrimination. *See* Case C-248/83, Commission v. Germany, 1985 E.C.R. 1459; Case C-222/84, Johnston v. Chief Constable of the Royal Ulster Constabulary, 1986 E.C.R. 1651; Case C-285/98, Kreil v. Germany, 2000 E.C.R. I-69. Generally, from this case law, it seems that the Member States have a certain "margin of appreciation" to exclude certain jobs on the grounds of sex if the jobs are specifically listed and the Member States review their list regularly to narrow the targeted professions so that these exclusions can be temporary and exceptional.

151. On the United States, see Leslie Wexler, *Wal-Mart Matters*, 46 WAKE FOREST L. REV. 96 (2011).

152. U.S. and EU case law seem to follow the same standard of scrutiny toward a more concrete evaluation of the skills required for the job: *see* Case C-222/84, Johnston v. Chief Constable of the Royal Ulster Constabulary, 1986 E.C.R. 1651; Case C-318/86, Commission v. France, 1988 E.C.R. 3559; Case C-285/98, Kreil v. Germany, 2000 E.C.R. I-69. For U.S. law, *see* Dothard v. Rawlinson, 433 U.S. 321 (1977); Diaz v. Pan American World Airways, 311 F. Supp. 559 (S.D. Fla. 1970); Wilson v. Southwest Airlines, 517 F. Supp. 292 (N.D. Tex. 1981).

153. Katell Berthou, *Différences de traitement: esquisse des exigences professionnelles déterminantes après la loi du 27 mai 2008*, DR. SOC. 410 (2009).

154. More recently, indirect discrimination based on unequal pay in the French postal service between employees with a public status and a private short-term contract status was not considered as creating a particular disadvantage towards women. The court showed a rather narrow appreciation of indirect discrimination, looking only at the fact that there are still more women in long-term contracts compared to short-term contracts instead of globally comparing the professional status of men and women. *See* Cass. soc., Oct. 22, 2014, No. 13–16936.

155. See the impetus of EU law, Case C-127/92, Enderby v. Frenchay Health Authority, 1993 E.C.R. I-5535.

156. In the United States, Wal-Mart v. Dukes, 131 S. Ct. 2541 (2011) (No. 10–277), demonstrated that certain human resources strategies in multinational corporations could be challenged through discrimination law, even though litigation could be unsuccessful. *See* Wexler, *supra* note 151; Marie Mercat-Bruns, *Égalité salariale, discriminations individuelles et systémiques: un éclairage de la jurisprudence américaine*, 114 REV. DE L'OFCE 129 (2010).

157. SÉVERINE LEMIÈRE & RACHEL SILVERA, COMPARER LES EMPLOIS ENTRE LES FEMMES ET LES HOMMES: DE NOUVELLES PISTES VERS L'ÉGALITÉ SALARIALE 11 (2010) [hereinafter LEMIÈRE & SILVERA, COMPARER LES EMPLOIS ENTRE LES FEMMES ET LES HOMMES].

158. Thérèse Aubert-Monpeyssen & Nicolas Moizard, *Égalité: des exigences trop fortes?* 3 REV. DR. TRAVAIL 128 (2012).

159. In equal pay cases, the Cour de Cassation first rejected the comparability of two jobs of equal value, considering the work was not the same; the comparison was between male executives and a female executive; *see* Cass. soc., June 26, 2008, No. 06–46204. In a very similar case, the court reversed its standard and considered that the "Court of Appeals must appreciate a comparable amount of professional knowledge, attested by a title, a degree or professional practice, skills acquired through experience, responsibilities and endured nervous or physical hardship." *See* Cass. soc., July 1, 2009, No. 07–42691; *see also* Cass. soc., July 6, 2010, No. 09–40021; Cass. soc., Oct. 22, 2014, No. 13–18362.

160. Conseil d'Etat, Jan. 30, 2008, No. 273438, AJDA 2008 IR 1223; Isabelle Meyrat, *L'égalité de traitement à la croisée des chemins*, 11 REV. DR. TRAVAIL 648 (2008); LUCIE CLUZEL-MÉTAYER & MARIE MERCAT-BRUNS, DISCRIMINATIONS DANS L'EMPLOI: ANALYSE COMPARATIVE DE LA JURISPRUDENCE DU CONSEIL D'ÉTAT ET DE LA COUR DE CASSATION 24 (2011).

161. Cass. soc., Mar. 17, 2010, No. 08–43088.

162. Law 2014-873 of Aug. 4, 2014 (on real equality between women and men). This is the last of a series of laws that also attempted to promote equal pay through mandatory collective bargaining and monitoring of wage disparities: Law 2010-1330 of Nov. 9, 2010, implemented through Decree 2011-822 of July 7, 2011; Law 2006-340 of Mar. 23, 2006.

163. Krieger, *supra* note 137, at 317. Three mechanisms—mandatory arbitration agreements with confidentiality clauses as conditions of recruitment, confidential clauses in settlements, and court orders to prohibit disclosing to the EEOC and OFCCP information obtained through discovery—prevent the public from obtaining data on employers who violate their obligations with respect to discrimination. Individual women in the job market and women's associations are unable to find out which employers treat women less favorably than men or vice versa.

164. On recent cases of dismissal following maternity leave in France, see Cass. soc., Apr. 30, 2014, No. 13-12321; Cass. soc., July 2, 2014, No. 12-29385; Cass. soc., July 2, 2014, No. 13-12496; Cass. soc. Mar. 3, 2015, No. 13-23521. Some cases are not favorable to women out on sick leave, after maternity leave; see Cass. soc. July 8, 2015, No. 14-15979.

165. LEMIÈRE & SILVERA, COMPARER LES EMPLOIS ENTRE LES FEMMES ET LES HOMMES, *supra* note 157, at 25.

166. Catharine MacKinnon, *Privacy v. Equality: Beyond Roe v. Wade*, in FEMINISM UNMODIFIED: DISCOURSES ON LIFE AND LAW (Catharine A. MacKinnon ed.) (1987).

167. See Reva B. Siegel, *Sex Equality Arguments for Reproductive Rights: Their Critical Basis and Evolving Constitutional Expression*, 56 EMORY L. J. 815 (2007). See also Reva B. Siegel, *The Constitutionalization of Abortion*, in THE OXFORD HANDBOOK OF COMPARATIVE CONSTITUTIONAL LAW 1057 (Michel Rosenfeld & Andras Sajo eds., 2012).

168. See recently on pregnancy discrimination and work accommodations, Young v. United Parcel Service, Docket No. 11-2078, Argument on Dec. 3, 2014, *available at* http://www.supremecourt.gov/Search.aspx?FileName = /docketfiles/12-1226.htm.

169. Frances Olsen, *The Myth of State Intervention in the Family*, 18 U. MICH J.L. REFORM 835 (1985).

170. For a general view of the law, see FRANCIS CABALLERO, DROIT DU SEXE (2010). For a more critical view of the law, see DANIEL BORILLO, DROIT DES SEXUALITÉS (2009).

171. In the United States, see diversity programs for women and Frank Dobbin's remarks on systemic discrimination, *supra* Chapter 4.

172. See Law 2006-340 of Mar. 23, 2006 (on equal pay between men and women), which sought to eliminate pay disparities between men and women by Dec. 31, 2010; it was amended by Law 2010-1330 of Nov. 9, 2010 (on retirement). Decree 2011-822 of July 7, 2011, established a fine for the failure of any company with more than fifty employees to implement a plan or collective bargaining agreement on equality at work (law entering into force on Jan. 1, 2012) or, where a plan or agreement does exist, for the termination of said plan or agreement. See also on the report on sexism in the workplace in France, CONSEIL SUPERIEUR DE L'ÉGALITÉ PROFESSIONNELLE ENTRE HOMMES ET FEMMES, LE SEXISME DANS LE MONDE DU TRAVAIL: ENTRE DENI ET REALITÉ (2015).

173. See, on the origins of the Family and Medical Leave Act (FMLA) and true equality between men and women, Robert C. Post & Reva B. Siegel, *Legislative Constitutionalism and Section Five Power: Policentric Interpretation of the Family and Medical Leave Act*, 112 YALE L.J. 1943, 1986-1987 (2003).

174. *Vulnerable* has different meanings: vulnerable because of her pregnancy and maternity, because she is the only link with the fetus in gestation, and because she can represent, according to her choices, a danger for the viability of the fetus. Reva B. Siegel, *Reasoning from the Body: A Historical Perspective on Abortion Regulation and Questions of Equal Protection*, 44 STAN. L. REV. 261, 342 (1992) [hereinafter Siegel, *Reasoning from the Body*].

175. Muller v. Oregon, 208 U.S. 412 (1908).

176. Law of Nov. 2, 1892 (limiting the working hours of women and children and organizing the profession of labor inspectors). From the 1860s, there are declarations on rights of women that cover the private and professional sphere (core civil rights, access to education, work and equal pay). *See* MICHELE RIOT-SARCEY, HISTOIRE DU FEMINISME 53 (2008).

177. Lochner v. New York, 198 U.S. 45 (1905); *see generally* CATHARINE A. MACKINNON, FEMINISM UNMODIFIED: DISCOURSES ON LIFE AND LAW (1987).

178. Siegel, *Reasoning from the Body, supra* note 174, at 366:

> Regulators may adopt particular means for protecting unborn life because stereotypical assumptions about the maternal role lead them to underestimate the impact of fetal-protective regulation on women. If one examines the conventional structure of abortion-restrictive regulation, it does indeed appear that such regulation must rest on traditional assumptions about women's natural obligations or instrumental uses as mothers. Absent such attitudes about women, it is reasonable to assume that legislatures would adopt at least some measures to offset the consequences of compelled motherhood for women, whether by compensating them, or by protecting their employment and education opportunities, or by affording them needed medical services and child care. Normally, some remuneration reward, support, and/or recognition is offered to those asked to perform services for the community, whether they are asked to provide foster care for children, volunteer or are drafted for military service, or are compelled to alienate property to the state. If no offsetting or compensating measures are adopted or even contemplated when the state engages in fetal life-saving by compelled pregnancy, it is clear that abortion-restrictive regulation is indeed premised on certain views about women as well as the unborn: that women's physical and intellectual and emotional energies as mothers can be publicly appropriated without recompense, that their lives can be subordinated to the work of gestation and nurturance without consequence.

179. Siegel, *Reasoning from the Body, supra* note 174, at 369:

> Abortion-restrictive regulation has several characteristics that make it particularly suitable for analysis under even the most constrained application of antisubordination principles. . . . The clearest illustration of this orientation is the requirement that plaintiffs challenging the discriminatory impact of facially neutral state action must show that state actors adopted the challenged policy with discriminatory purpose. *See* Personnel Adm'r of Mass. v. Feeney, 442 U.S. 256, 274, 279 (1979). . . . The results in many of the Court's gender discrimination cases might well be different if the Court inquired, not whether the state's decision to regulate on the basis of sex was substantially related to important governmental ends, but instead: Has the challenged action harmed women in ways that enforce, perpetuate, or aggravate their subordinate social status?

See CATHARINE A. MACKINNON, SEXUAL HARASSMENT OF WORKING WOMEN 117 (1979); Owen M. Fiss, *Groups and the Equal Protection Clause*, 5 PHIL. & PUB. AFF. 107, 157 (1976); Charles R. Lawrence, III, *The Id, the Ego, and Equal Protection: Reckoning with Unconscious Racism*, 39 STAN. L. REV. 317 (1987). We are reminded that in the United States, constitutional case law does not recognize indirect discrimination under the principle of the equal protection of the laws. In Washington v. Davis, 426 U.S. 229, 248 (1976), the Court considered that the contrary would "perhaps invalidate . . . a whole range of tax, welfare, public service, regulatory, and licensing statutes that may be more burdensome to the poor and average black than the more affluent white." According to Siegel, *supra* note 174, at 369-70:

> First, abortion-restrictive regulation is sex-based state action: It is regulation directed at women as a class, and not dispersed across the citizenry at large. Second, the most dramatic and vis-

ible of its effects—the continuation of an unwanted pregnancy—is an intended consequence of social policy. Indeed, as I have already argued, it is fair to characterize forced childbearing as the principal purpose of abortion-restrictive regulation. Third, abortion-restrictive regulation has historically functioned as caste legislation. Finally, today, as in the past, the injury inflicted on women by compelling them to bear children is a specific form of status harm, one that plays a central role in women's subordination.

180. The Equal Rights Amendment (ERA) was never adopted.

181. Reed v. Reed, 404 U.S. 71 (1971).

182. Frontiero v. Richardson, 411 U.S. 677 (1973).

183. Craig v. Boren, 429 U.S. 190 (1976).

184. Directive 92/85/EEC of 19 October 1992 on the introduction of measures to encourage improvements in the safety and health at work of pregnant workers and workers who have recently given birth or are breastfeeding.

185. *See* LABOR CODE [CODE DU TRAVAIL] art. L.1225–1 and following ("The Labor Code protects the pregnant woman once she has informed her employer and produced a medical certificate attesting the pregnancy, detailing dates of departure and return from maternity leave. The pregnant employee can then request accommodations of her working conditions, temporary reassignment to a different job because of a medical risk or night work. The pregnant employee can also request authorizations to miss work and to be present at mandatory medical exams.").

186. *See* Case C-136/95, Caisse nationale d'assurance vieillesse des travailleurs salariés v. Thibault, 1998 E.C.R. I-2011; Case C-471/08, Parviainen v. Finnair Oyj, 2010 E.C.R. I-6533.

187. Cass. soc., Sept. 15, 2010, No. 08–43299, Marie Mercat-Bruns, *La portée de l'interdiction de licenciement au moment du congé maternité*, 1 REV. DR. TRAVAIL 31 (2011). Or discrimination can begin before maternity leave and continue after the leave; see recently a series of cases: Cass. soc., July 2, 2014, No. 12–29385; Cass. soc., Apr. 2, 2014, No. 12–27849; and Cass. soc., Jan. 15, 2014, No. 12–22751, after a parental leave.

188. *See* Case C-595/12, Napoli v. Ministero della Giustizia, Mar. 6, 2014 (postponing training without giving any new date because of maternity leave, delaying promotion, and affecting wages and conditions of employment).

189. Cass. soc., Dec. 16, 2008, No. 06–45262.

190. This is the case at the European level: Case C-177/88, Dekker v. VJV Centrum, 1990 E.C.R. I-3941.

191. On maternity leave, LABOR CODE [CODE DU TRAVAIL] arts. L.1225–16 to L.1225–34, L.1225–66 to L.1225- 69, D.1225–4-1, R.1225–18, and R.1225–19; on specific paternity leave, LABOR CODE [CODE DU TRAVAIL] arts. L.1225–35, L.1225–36, and D.1225–8.

192. After two cases, Geduldig v. Aiello, 417 U.S. 484 (1974), and General Electric v. Gilbert, 429 U.S. 125 (1976), the Pregnancy Discrimination Act (P.L. 95–555) of 1978 extended protection from discrimination to pregnant women.

193. Pregnancy Discrimination Act (P.L. 95–555) of 1978.

194. In France, parental leave (LABOR CODE [CODE DU TRAVAIL] arts. L.1225–47 to L.1225–60, R.1225–12, and R.1225–13, recently amended): To be entitled to the full period of leave, three months cannot be transferred to the spouse, in accordance with the revised parental leave, Directive 2010/18.EU. See also the extension of rights from women to men: Case C-104/09, Roca Alvarez, 2010 E.C.R. I-08661 (involving the grant of breastfeeding leave to a spouse for bottle feeding); Case C149/10, Chatzi, 2010 E.C.R. I-8489 (holding that parental leave is not a right of the child but a right of the parent).

195. LABOR CODE [CODE DU TRAVAIL] arts. L.3142–1 and L.3142–2: leave for family events.

196. Since Law No. 2010-209, Mar. 2, 2010, a leave for solidarity can be taken by any employee who needs to assist a loved one suffering from a terminal illness (the leave can be arranged rapidly, is only for a limited time, and is taken without pay (unless more favorable measures are provided for in the collective bargaining agreement)) (LABOR CODE [CODE DU TRAVAIL] arts. L. 3142–16 to L. 3142–21 and LABOR CODE [CODE DU TRAVAIL] Decree 3142–6 to D. 3142–8).

197. Case C-116/08, Meerts, 2009 E.C.R. I-10063 (involving parental leave). *See also recently* CJEU Case C-222/14, Maïstrellis, July 16, 2015.

198. Cass. soc., Mar. 17, 2010, No. 09–44127 (when the position offered to the employee returning from parental leave is not equivalent to the job level held before the leave). Even calculation of redundancy payment after illegal dismissal following parental leave must take into account previous full-time work: recently, CJEU Case C-588/12, Lyreco Belgium NV v. Rogiers, Feb. 27 2014.

199. Directive 2010/41/EU of the European Parliament and of the Council of July 7, 2010 (on the application of the principle of equal treatment between men and women engaged in an activity in a self-employed capacity and repealing Council Directive 86/613/EEC).

200. The CJEU is also focused on facilitating State income support to women without work because of pregnancy and maternity: "art. 45 TFEU must be interpreted as meaning that a woman who gives up work, or seeking work, because of the physical constraints of the late stages of pregnancy and the aftermath of childbirth *retains the status of 'worker'*, within the meaning of that article, provided she returns to work or finds another job within a reasonable period after the birth of her child." *See* CJEU Case C-507/12, Saint Prix v. Secretary of State for Work and Pensions, June 19, 2014, point 48.

201. Case C-232/09, Danosa v. LKB Lizings SIA, 2010 E.C.R. I-11405.

202. CJEU Cases C-167/12, C.D. v. S.T., and C-363/12, Z. v. A Gov't Dep't and the Board of Mgmt. of a Community Sch., Mar. 18, 2014.

203. The European Court of Human Rights has decided to protect the citizenship rights of children of surrogates for those coming from a country like France that bans surrogacy contracts. If the children's nationality is not registered despite the father's French citizenship, "[t]he Court considers, having regard to the consequences of this serious restriction on the identity and right to respect for private life of the third and fourth applicants [children], that by thus preventing both the recognition and establishment under domestic law of their legal relationship with their biological father, the respondent State overstepped the permissible limits of its margin of appreciation." ECtHR, Mennesson v. France, App. No. 65192/11, June 26, 2015.

204. See litigation on breach of contract involving women lawyers returning from maternity leave who could not be protected by rules on unjust dismissal because they were independent workers: Court of Appeals, Paris, Oct. 11, 2011, No. 11–10802. Under the impetus of Directive 92/85/EEC (protecting pregnancy and maternity discrimination) and Directive 2010/41/EU (on the application of the principle of equal treatment between men and women engaged in an activity in a self-employed capacity), the new law on "real equality between women and men" (Law No. 2014-873 of Aug. 4, 2014) reversed the case law and awarded protection against discrimination, even for the self-employed.

205. Joan C. Williams, *Family Responsibilities Discrimination: The Next Generation of Employment Discrimination Cases*, PLI Order No. 11091, October 2007, Hastings College of Law; regarding family responsibility discrimination and discrimination based on caregiving, both can be considered as either sex or disability discrimination; *see* ENFORCEMENT GUIDANCE: UNLAWFUL DISPARATE TREATMENT OF WORKERS WITH CAREGIVING RESPONSIBILITIES, www.eeoc.gov/policy/docs/caregiving.html.

206. Sylvaine Laulom, *La protection de la parentalité*, 1489 SEM. SOC. LAMY, Supp. 22 (2011).

207. On the interaction of sex and age, see Jourdan Day, *Closing the Loophole—Why Intersectional Claims Are Needed to Address Discrimination Against Older Women*, 75 OHIO ST. L.J. 447 (2014).

208. On positive action: art. 3 of Directive 2006/54/EC and art. 7 of Directive 2000/78/EC; Case C-450/93, Kalanke v. Freie Hansestadt Bremen, 1995 E.C.R. I-3051; Case C-409/95, Marschall v. Land Nordrhein Westfalen, 1997 E.C.R. I-6363; Case C-158/97, Badeck v. Landesanwalt beim Staatsgerichtshof des Landes Hessen, 1999 E.C.R. I-1875; Case C-407/98, Abrahamsson Fogelqvist, 2000 E.C.R. I-5539.

209. Joan Scott, *Gender: A Useful Category of Historical Analysis*, 91 AM. HIST. REV. 1054 (1986).

210. *See* DORLIN, SEXE, GENRE ET SEXUALITÉS, *supra* note 134, at 7.

211. *See* Kelly Oliver, *French Feminism in an American Context*, *in* FRENCH FEMINISM READER vii, ix (Kelly Oliver ed., 2000).

212. *See generally* SIMONE DE BEAUVOIR, LE DEUXIÈME SEXE, tomes I et II (1949).

213. *See* Christine Delphy, *The Invention of French Feminism: An Essential Move*, 87 YALE FRENCH STUD. 190 (1995); CHRISTINE DELPHY, L'ENNEMI PRINCIPAL, 2. PENSER LE GENRE (2001).

214. *See generally* COLETTE GUILLAUMIN, SEXE, RACE ET PRATIQUE DU POUVOIR: L'IDÉE DE NATURE (1992).

215. *See generally* MONIQUE WITTIG, LA PENSÉE STRAIGHT (2001).

216. *See* PIERRE BOURDIEU, LA DOMINATION MASCULINE 103 (1998).

217. GENEVIÈVE FRAISSE, À CÔTÉ DU GENRE: SEXE ET PHILOSOPHIE DE L'ÉGALITÉ 299 (2010).

218. Françoise Héritier, *La valeur différentielle des sexes*, *in* FEMMES, GENRE ET SOCIÉTÉS: L'ÉTAT DES SAVOIRS 54 (Margaret Maruani ed., 2005).

219. *See generally* MARGARET MARUANI, TRAVAIL ET EMPLOI DES FEMMES (4th ed. 2011).

220. *See generally* LEMIÈRE & SILVERA, COMPARER LES EMPLOIS ENTRE LES FEMMES ET LES HOMMES, *supra* note 157.

221. Jacqueline Laufer, *Entre égalité et inégalités: les droits des femmes dans la sphère professionnelle*, 53 L'ANNÉE SOCIOLOGIQUE (2003) 143; Jacqueline Laufer, *Égalité professionnelle, principes et pratiques*, 12 DR. SOC. 736 (1984); Jacqueline Laufer, *L'égalité professionnelle*, *in* FEMMES, GENRE ET SOCIÉTÉS: L'ÉTAT DES SAVOIRS 239 (Margaret Maruani ed., 2005).

222. *See generally* 114 REV. DE L'OFCE (2010), LES DISCRIMINATIONS ENTRE LES FEMMES ET LES HOMMES (Françoise Milewski & Hélène Périvier eds., 2011); Hélène Périvier, *La logique sexuée de la réciprocité dans l'assistance*, 114 REV. DE L'OFCE 237 (2010); Annie Junter & Caroline Ressot, *La discrimination sexiste: les regards du droit*, 114 REV. DE L'OFCE 65 (2010); Marie-Thérèse Lanquetin, *Discriminations: la loi d'adaptation au droit communautaire du 27 mai 2008*, 7/8 DR. SOC. 778 (2008); Marie-Thérèse Lanquetin, *L'égalité des rémunérations entre les femmes et les hommes, réalisée en cinq ans?* 6 DR. SOC. 624 (2006).

223. Périvier, *supra* note 222, at 281.

224. JUDITH BUTLER, GENDER TROUBLE: FEMINISM AND THE SUBVERSION OF IDENTITY (1990); JUDITH BUTLER, BODIES THAT MATTER: ON THE DISCURSIVE LIMITS OF "SEX" (1993).

225. Christine Delphy, *Rethinking Sex and Gender*, *in* FRENCH FEMINISM READER 63 (Kelly Oliver ed., 2000).

226. *See* Delphine Gardey, *Bruno Latour, guerre et paix, tours et détours féministes*, *in* SOUS LES SCIENCES SOCIALES, LE GENRE: RELECTURES CRITIQUES DE MAX WEBER À

MICHEL FOUCAULT 203 (Danielle Chabaud-Rychter et al. eds, 2010) [hereinafter SOUS LES SCIENCES SOCIALES, LE GENRE (Chabaud-Rychter et al. eds.)].

227. Danielle Chabaud-Rychter, Introduction, *Question de genre aux sciences sociales normales, in* SOUS LES SCIENCES SOCIALES, LE GENRE (Chabaud-Rychter et al. eds.), *supra* note 226, at 9.

228. FEMINIST LEGAL THEORY: AN ANTI-ESSENTIALIST READER 9 (Nancy E. Dowd & Michelle S. Jacobs eds., 2003).

229. JANET HALLEY, SPLIT DECISIONS: HOW AND WHY TO TAKE A BREAK FROM FEMINISM (2006).

230. Janet Halley, *Sexual Orientation and the Politics of Biology: A Critique of the Argument from Immutability,* 46 STAN. L. REV. 503 (1994); Toni M. Massaro, *Gay Rights, Thick and Thin,* 49 STAN. L. REV. 45 (1996).

231. *See* DUNCAN KENNEDY, SEXY DRESSING ETC.: ESSAYS ON THE POWER AND POLITICS OF CULTURAL IDENTITY 145 (1993); WILLIAM N. ESKRIDGE & NAN D. HUNTER, SEXUALITY, GENDER AND THE LAW 65, 22, 584 (2004).

232. ÉRIC FASSIN, L'INVERSION DE LA QUESTION HOMOSEXUELLE 218 (2008).

233. ÉRIC FASSIN, LE SEXE POLITIQUE: GENRE ET SEXUALITÉ AU MIROIR TRANSATLANTIQUE 238 (2009).

234. DANIEL BORILLO, LE DROIT DES SEXUALITÉS (2009); CAROLINE MÉCARY, DROIT ET HOMOSEXUALITÉ 2 (2000); MARCELA IACUB, LE CRIME ÉTAIT PRESQUE SEXUEL ET AUTRES ESSAIS DE CASUISTIQUE JURIDIQUE 20 (2009).

235. *See generally* FRANCIS CABALLERO, DROIT DU SEXE (2010).

236. See 2 Rev. Juris. Critique (2011) (focusing on the theme of gender); *see also* La loi & le genre: études critiques de droit Français (Stéphanie Hennette-Vauchez, Marc Pichard, & Diane Roman eds., 2014).

237. Stéphanie Hennette-Vauchez, *Vademecum à l'usage de la Cour européenne des droits de l'homme: La théorie féministe du droit au secours d'une juridiction menacée "splendide isolement,"* 20 RECUEIL DALLOZ 1360 (2011).

238. Geneviève Pignarre, Les frontières du consentement: de la confrontation du pouvoir aux marges de l'autonomie, 2 REV. DES CONTRATS 611 (2011).

239. *See* Libby Adler, *Teaching Sexuality and Gender as Distributional Issues, in* VULNERABLE POPULATIONS AND TRANSFORMATIVE LAW TEACHING: A CRITICAL READER (Society of American Law Teachers ed., 2011).

240. No deprivation of personal freedom without due process. Both rights are rooted in interpretation of the Fourteenth Amendment to the Constitution.

241. During his second presidential campaign, Obama declared support for same-sex marriage.

242. The Employment Non-Discrimination Act (ENDA) is a bill that has been proposed every year since 1994 to prohibit employment discrimination on the basis of sexual orientation and gender identity at the federal level, but has never passed. An amended version of the ENDA was approved by the Senate on Nov. 7, 2013, by a bipartisan vote of 64–32, but the House never brought up the measure for a vote. On Nov. 26, 2014, a Republican-controlled panel in the U.S. House rejected a last effort to pass a version of ENDA as part of major defense legislation before Congress adjourned. This latest version of ENDA had a religious exemption along the lines of Title VII of the Civil Rights Act of 1964. Unlike the version of ENDA the Senate passed in 2013, the new version of ENDA would bar LGBT discrimination at religious-affiliated businesses for nonministerial positions. However on July 21, 2014, President Obama signed an executive order barring federal contractors from engaging in anti-LGBT workplace discrimination. The new rule for the executive order was signed on December 3, 2014.

243. HANS-GEORG GADAMER, TRUTH AND METHOD (Joel Weinsheimer & Donald G. Marshall trans., 2004).

244. MORAL VALUES PROJECT, http://www.law.georgetown.edu/moralvaluesproject.

245. Chai R. Feldblum, *The Moral Values Project, in* MORAL ARGUMENT, RELIGION, AND SAME-SEX MARRIAGE: ADVANCING THE PUBLIC GOOD 205 (Gordon A. Babst et al. eds., 2009).

246. LGBT stands for "lesbian, gay, bisexual, and transgender."

247. *See* Chai R. Feldblum, *Sexual Orientation, Morality, and the Law: Devlin Revisited,* 57 U. PITT. L. REV. 237 (1996); Chai R. Feldblum, *The Moral Rhetoric of Legislation,* 72 N.Y.U. L. REV. 992 (1997); Chai R. Feldblum, *Gay Is Good: The Moral Case for Marriage Equality and More,* 17 YALE J.L. & FEMINISM 139, 147–48 (2005).

248. The EEOC has since recognized, in a landmark decision, that anti-transgender discrimination is covered under the ban on sex discrimination found in Title VII. *See* Macy v. Holder, No. 0120120821, 2012 WL 1435995 (E.E.O.C. Apr. 20, 2012), *available at* http://www.eeoc.gov/decisions/0120120821%20Macy%20v%20DOJ%20ATF.txt.

249. Since this interview, the EEOC has confirmed that discrimination based on sexual orientation, when resulting from stereotypes or assumptions about certain sexes, also falls under the ban on sex discrimination. *See* Veretto v. U.S. Postal Service, No. 0120110873, 2011 WL 2663401 (E.E.O.C. July 1, 2011); Castello v. U.S. Postal Service, No. 0520110649 (E.E.O.C. Dec. 20, 2011), *available at* http://www.eeoc.gov/decisions/0520110649.txt.

250. *See* MAYERI, REASONING FROM RACE, *supra* note 7, at 106.

251. As explained by Krieger, research categories based on mathematical research conducted, for example, at the University of California, Berkeley.

252. Julie C. Suk, *Are Gender Stereotypes Bad for Women? Rethinking Antidiscrimination Law and Work-Family Conflict,* 110 COLUM. L. REV. 54 (2010).

253. Queer theory, as it is generally defined, considers gender as a construct and not a biological fact and therefore enables an understanding of identity that is not restricted by the normative standards of a society built around a binary division of human beings and around the idea that the heterosexual couple is the main manifestation of this complementarity of sexual difference. *See* Butler, *supra* note 224; E.K. Sedgwick, *Queer Performativity: Henry James's The Art of the Novel,* 1 GLQ 1 (1993); MICHAEL WARNER, FEAR OF A QUEER PLANET: QUEER POLITICS AND SOCIAL THEORY (1994).

254. *See* Janet Halley, *What Is Family Law?: A Genealogy, Part II,* 23 YALE J.L. & HUMAN. 189 (2011); Janet Halley, *What Is Family Law?: A Genealogy, Part I,* 23 YALE J.L. & HUMAN. 1 (2011).

255. Debate reopened, for example, by Obama's support of same-sex marriage during his reelection campaign and by the adoption of same-sex marriage in additional states at that time.

256. *See supra* note 242 on the last failed attempt in 2014 to pass ENDA.

257. The Equal Employment Opportunity Commission (EEOC) has determined that a transgender woman's claim of employment discrimination based on gender identity, change of sex and/or transgender status is viable under Title VII of the Civil Rights Act. The case, Macy v. Holder, No. 0120120821, 2012 WL 1435995 (E.E.O.C. Apr. 20, 2012) was brought by Mia Macy, a former male police detective who contends she was denied a job as a ballistics technician with the Department of Justice's Bureau of Alcohol, Tobacco, Firearms, and Explosives (the "Agency") on account of her decision to become a woman. The EEOC's finding that Macy may proceed with this cause of action could have an influence on the private sector, in the absence of a federal law like ENDA. On President Obama's executive order concerning public contracts, *see supra* note 242.

258. And European case law recognizing an increasing of gay rights. *See* Case C-267/06, Maruko v. Versorgungsanstalt der deutschen Bühnen, 2008 E.C.R. I-1757 (concerning a

survivor's pension); Case C-147/08, Römer v. City of Hamburg, 2011 E.C.R. I-3591 (concerning a supplementary retirement pension paid to married couples); Case C-81/12, Asociaţia Accept v. Consiliul Naţional pentru Combaterea Discriminării, 2013 (concerning homophobic comments); *see also* Jean-Philippe Lhernould, *La discrimination en raison de l'orientation sexuelle: essai de synthèse en attendant Römer, in* REV. JURIS. SOC. 261 (2011).

259. *See* Lhernould, *supra* note 258.

260. Nicolas Moizard, *Clarifier le cadre juridique de la lutte contre les discriminations au travail, in* Thérèse Aubert-Montpeysson & Nicolas Moizard, *Égalité: des exigences trop fortes?*, 3 REV. DR. TRAVAIL 128, 131 (2012).

261. Case C-267/12, Hay v. Crédit Agricole Mutuel de Charente-Maritime et des Deux-Sèvres, 2013 E.C.R. I-0000; Cass. soc., May 23, 2012, No. 10-18.341. The question referred to the CJEU for a preliminary ruling was whether a collective bargaining agreement granting days off work and a bonus for married employees constituted indirect discrimination against employees in a registered civil union.

262. *See* Jean-Philippe Lhernould, *Les discriminations indirectes fondées sur le sexe et la Cour de Cassation*, 11 REV. JURIS. SOC. 731, 733 (2012).

263. Law 2013-404 of May 17, 2013 (extending marriage to same-sex couples).

264. Case C-267/12, Hay v. Crédit Agricole Mutuel de Charente-Maritime et des Deux-Sèvres, CJEU, judgment of Dec. 12, 2013, at § 44: "The difference in treatment based on the employees' marital status and not expressly on their sexual orientation is still direct discrimination because only persons of different sexes may marry and homosexual employees are therefore unable to meet the condition required for obtaining the benefit claimed." See French decision handed down to conform to the CJEU interpretation, Cass. soc., July 9, 2014, No. 10-18341.

265. *See* Case C-528/13, Geoffrey Léger v Ministre des Affaires sociales, de la Santé et des Droits des femmes and Établissement français du sang.

266. *See* HOMOPHOBIE DANS L'ENTREPRISE (Christophe Falcoz ed. 2008) (study on homophobia in the workplace, conducted for the HALDE).

267. Cass. soc., Apr. 17, 1991, No. 90-42.636, DR. SOC. 485 (1991) (sexton fired because he was gay). See, *e.g.*, Court of Appeal, Versailles, Jan. 10, 2012, B. v. Sitel France, 10/04996, 6th Ch. An employee was denied a promotion in Morocco due to his sexual orientation (a letter clearly stated that the reason for the refusal was his homosexuality). The court recognized the discriminatory nature of the denial of promotion. However, the employee also claimed to have been subjected to homophobic insults from colleagues and his direct manager, using a feminine-sounding nickname. For the judges, this abusive behavior did not constitute discrimination, although it did demonstrate a breach of the employer's obligation to ensure the safety of its employees. But this breach was not sanctioned by the judge, who awarded only damages for discrimination to the employee.

268. C-81/12, Asociaţia Accept v. Consiliul Naţional pentru Combaterea Discriminării, 2013, at § 49: "A defendant employer cannot deny the existence of facts from which it may be inferred that it has a discriminatory recruitment policy merely by asserting that statements suggestive of the existence of a homophobic recruitment policy come from a person who, while claiming and appearing to play an important role in the management of that employer, is not legally capable of binding it in recruitment matters."

269. Cass. soc., Nov. 6 2013, No. 12-22.270 (finding that taking an account away from an employee after he revealed his homosexuality and then dismissing him for serious misconduct constitutes possible evidence of discrimination based on sexual orientation). *See also* Cass. soc., Apr. 24, 2014, No. 11-15204 (presumption of discrimination raised after several refused promotions).

270. Eighteen states and Washington, D.C., also prohibit discrimination based on gender identity. Although these laws provide protection, according to a 2013 General Accounting Office (GAO) report, relatively few complaints of discrimination based on sexual orientation have been filed in these states. For California civil rights law and legislation, see http://oag.ca.gov/civil.

271. See *supra* note 242 on the latest attempt to pass ENDA, in 2014. Some authors believe Title VII would be more favorable to LGBT rights than the adoption of ENDA; *see* Alex Reed, *Abandoning ENDA*, HARV. J. ON LEGIS. 277 (Summer 2014).

272. See the progression of case law from Bowers v. Hardwick, 478 U.S. 186 (1986) to Lawrence v. Texas, 539 U.S. 558 (2003). *See also* Janet Halley, *Reasoning about Sodomy: Act and Identity in and after* Bowers v. Hardwick, 79 VA. L. REV. 1721 (1993).

273. *See* Romer v. Evans, 517 U.S. 620 (1996) (declaring unconstitutional an amendment to the Constitution of the State of Colorado, adopted in a referendum, prohibiting Colorado cities and counties from enacting laws affording protection from discrimination based on sexual orientation and thereby preventing the treatment of sexual orientation as a protected category, like race).

274. Obergefell v. Hodges, 576 U.S. ___ (2015).

275. Twenty-six by court decision: Alabama (Feb. 9, 2015), Alaska (Oct. 17, 2014), Arizona (Oct. 17, 2014), California (June 28, 2013), Colorado (Oct. 7, 2014), Connecticut (Nov. 12, 2008), Florida (Jan. 6, 2015), Idaho (Oct. 13, 2014), Indiana (Oct. 6, 2014), Iowa (Apr. 24, 2009), Kansas (Nov. 12, 2014), Massachusetts (May 17, 2004), Montana (Nov. 19, 2014), Nevada (Oct. 9, 2014), New Jersey (Oct. 21, 2013), New Mexico (Dec. 19, 2013), North Carolina (Oct. 10, 2014), Oklahoma (Oct. 6, 2014), Oregon (May 19, 2014), Pennsylvania (May 20, 2014), South Carolina (Nov. 20, 2014), Utah (Oct. 6, 2014), Virginia (Oct. 6, 2014), West Virginia (Oct. 9, 2014), Wisconsin (Oct. 6, 2014), Wyoming (Oct. 21, 2014). Eight by state legislature : Delaware (July 1, 2013), Hawaii (Dec. 2, 2013), Illinois (June 1, 2014), Minnesota (Aug. 1, 2013), New Hampshire (Jan. 1, 2010), New York (July 24, 2011), Rhode Island (Aug. 1, 2013), Vermont (Sept. 1, 2009). Three by popular vote : Maine (Dec. 29, 2012), Maryland (Jan. 1, 2013), Washington (Dec. 9, 2012). Washington, DC legalized gay marriage on Mar. 3, 2010, the date marriage licenses became available to same-sex couples. The governors of Puerto Rico, of the Northern Mariana Islands, and the Virgin Islands announced after the Supreme Court's June 26, 2015, ruling that same-sex marriage would begin in their territory within a certain time frame.

276. See Chai R. Feldblum, *Rectifying the Tilt: Equality Lessons from Religion, Disability, Sexual Orientation, and Transgender*, 54 ME. L. REV. 159 (2002).

277. *See* ROBERT C. POST ET AL., PREJUDICIAL APPEARANCES: THE LOGIC OF AMERICAN ANTIDISCRIMINATION LAW 27 (2001) (exposing an element of absurdity in attempts to prohibit discrimination based on appearance).

278. See Katherine M. Franke, *The Central Mistake of Sex Discrimination Law: The Disaggregation of Sex from Gender*, 144 U. PENN. L. REV. 1 (1995).

279. See Mary Anne Case, *Disaggregating Gender from Sex and Sexual Orientation: The Effeminate Man in the Law and Feminist Jurisprudence*, 105 YALE L.J. 1 (1995).

280. Transgender in its popular use appeared in Québec and describes people whose gender (personal and social identity, related to concepts about men and women) does not correlate with their biological sex.

281. Price Waterhouse v. Hopkins, 490 U.S. 228 (1989) (holding discriminatory the refusal to promote a female employee as partner due to her behavior that did not correspond to her employer's idea of womanly behavior). The employer's argument was also based on physical appearance: he advised Hopkins to "walk more femininely, talk

more femininely, dress more femininely, wear make-up, have her hair styled, and wear jewelry."

282. Courts have found that discrimination based on certain stereotyped ideas of sex-appropriate behavior constitutes sex discrimination. *See* Schwenk v. Hartford, 204 F.3d. 1187, 1202 (9th Cir. 2000); Rosa v. Park West Bank & Trust Co., 214 F.3d 213 (1st Cir. 2000); Smith v. City of Salem, 378 F.3d 566, 568 (6th Cir. 2004) (a transsexual firefighter suspended after dressing as a woman); Schroer v. Billington, 424 F.Sup.2d 203 (D.D.C. 2006) (in which a counterterrorism expert and retired U.S. Army colonel, having been offered a research position at the Library of Congress, saw the job offer withdrawn after revealing her intention to transition from male to female); Mitchell v. Axcan Scandipharm, Inc., Civ. A., No. 05-243, 2006 WL 456173 (W.D. Pa., Feb. 17, 2006) (a similar case of termination of employment after the employee announced his intention to make a gender transition). These cases of discrimination for gender nonconformity often involve occupations with a particularly masculine image (e.g., firefighting or counterterrorism).

283. Michelle Goldberg, *What Is a Woman? The Dispute Between Radical Feminism and Transgenderism,* NEW YORKER (Aug. 4, 2014), http://www.newyorker.com/magazine/2014/08/04/woman-2.

284. The *Schroer* case goes a step further because rather than using the sex-stereotyping theory to qualify sex discrimination, the Court took a direct approach, considering that discrimination against transsexuality is in fact sex discrimination: "Schroer is not seeking acceptance as a man with feminine traits. She seeks to express her female identity, not as an effeminate male, but as a woman. She does not wish to go against the gender grain, but with it." According to certain judges, Title VII (prohibiting discrimination in employment because of sex) protects against discrimination based on sex and gender, in particular the failure to "conform to socially constructed gender expectations." *See Schwenk,* F.3d, *supra* note 282.

285. The EEOC's position is important not only because it recognizes Macy's particular situation as sex discrimination, but also because it emphasizes that any discrimination based on "gender identity, change of sex, and/or transgender status" (Macy's complaint) is entitled to the protections of Title VII. That kind of discrimination inherently takes sex into account: "That Title VII's prohibition on sex discrimination proscribes gender discrimination, and not just discrimination on the basis of biological sex, is important. If Title VII proscribed only discrimination on the basis of biological sex, the only prohibited gender-based disparate treatment would be when an employer prefers a man over a woman, or vice versa. But the statute's protections sweep far broader than that, in part because the term 'gender' encompasses not only a person's biological sex but also the cultural and social aspects associated with masculinity and femininity." EEOC Decision No. 0120120821, Macy v. Holder, 2012 WL 1435995 (Apr. 20, 2012).

286. Hamm v. Weyauwega Milk Prod., 332 F.3d 1058 (7th Cir. 2003); DeSantis v. Pacific Tel. and Telegraph, 608 F.2d 327 (9th Cir. 1979).

287. Sex being more closely related to sexual identity and self-perception on this level.

288. See, for example, Christine Bard, *La peur rancie de l'indifférenciation sexuelle,* LE MONDE (Feb. 7, 2014), http://www.lemonde.fr/idees/art/2014/02/07/la-peur-rancie-de-l-indifferenciation-sexuelle_4361425_3232.html. In the academic world, a petition of law professors followed suit against the same-sex marriage legislation; however, other schools have promoted reflection on law and gender: http://etudiant.lefigaro.fr/les-news/actu/detail/art/a-sciences-po-on-enseigne-le-gender-depuis-trois-ans-4284/.

289. Cass. soc., Jan. 11, 2012, No. 10-28.213, JurisData No. 2012-000191. *See* Marie Mercat-Bruns, *L'apparence physique du salarié rapportée à son sexe: l'émergence de la discrimination fondée sur le genre?,* 10 JCP 281 (2012).

290. Cass. soc., Mar. 5, 2014, No. 12-27701: in this recent case, the court rejected the claim of discrimination based on the employer's refusal to retrain an employee returning from parental leave, whose "esthetic capacities" were called into question by a choreographer. The EU is turning to disability to protect discrimination associated with weight, since physical appearance is not a protected ground. The European Equal Treatment in Employment Directive of 2000 prohibits discrimination based on disability. The Advocate General stated on July 23, 2014, that obesity may meet the definition of "disability" for the purposes of discrimination law, if it has reached such a degree that "it plainly hinders participation in professional life." The CJEU decision is pending as of October 2015. See the Advocate General's opinion in C-354/13, Kaltoft v. Municipality of Billund, Denmark.

291. HALDE decision No. 2010-272, Dec. 13, 2010. Other characteristics are weight (HALDE decision No. 2007-251, Oct. 1, 2007) and hairstyle (Court of Appeal, Rennes, Ch. Prud'h. 5, Sept. 6, 2005, 04/00583, Chalot v. SAS; Court of Appeal, Reims, Mar. 6, 1996, JCP E 350 (1997); JurisData No. 1996-043654).

292. LABOR CODE [CODE DU TRAVAIL] art. L. 1132-4.

293. Since the case of the employee who was dismissed for wearing Bermuda shorts to work: Cass. soc., May 28, 2003, No. 02-40.273.

294. LABOR CODE [CODE DU TRAVAIL] art. L. 1134-1.

295. Case C-54/07, Centrum voor gelijkheid van kansen en voor racismebestrijding v. Firma Feryn, 2008 E.C.R. I-5187.

296. Philippe Reigné, *Sexe, genre et état des personnes,* 42 JCP G 1140 (2011).

297. In the ECtHR, gender discrimination and stereotypes are often mentioned. *See, for example,* Goodwin v. the United Kingdom, No. 28957/95, 35 Eur. H.R. Rep. 18 (2002); and on gender stereotypes and men, Konstantin Markin v. Russia, App. No. 30078/06, judgment of Mar. 22, 2012.

298. See Y.Y. v. Turkey, App. No. 14793/08, Mar. 10, 2015.

299. We note the difficult question of bisexuality and the pros and cons of its invisibility: *see* Kenji Yoshino, *The Epistemic Contract of Bisexual Erasure,* 1 STAN. L. REV. 353 (2000).

300. *See* Jean-Yves Frouin, *La protection des droits de la personne et des libertés du salarié,* 99 CAHIERS SOC. DU BARREAU DE PARIS 123 (1998).

301. The potential implications of antidiscrimination law can be seen the issue of drug and alcohol testing in the workplace for health-related reasons. *See* Alexia Gardin, *Consommation d'alcool et de drogues en milieu de travail: entre impératifs sécuritaires et considérations sanitaires,* 8-9 REV. JURIS. SOC. 593, 597 (2011).

302. As of the "Bermuda shorts" decision, some scholars predicted that "the respect due to clothing choices may be claimed on the basis of principles other than 'freedom of dress,' notably, certain protected grounds of discrimination. And, in that case, it is not certain that the employer can provide legitimate justification." LES GRANDS ARRÊTS DU DROIT DU TRAVAIL 332 (Jean Pélissier et al. eds., 2008) at § 69.

303. *See* HALDE decision No. 2011-16, Apr. 4, 2011 (on appearance and religious dress) (Court of Appeal, Paris, Ch. 18, Sect. C, June 19, 2003, Tahli v. Téléperformance, No. 03/30212, JurisData No. 2003-219940); or HALDE decision No. 2007-107, Apr. 2, 2007 (on appearance and skin color).

304. See also on religious discrimination, *infra* Chapter 5, Part VII.

305. Lise Casaux-Labrunée, *La confrontation des libertés dans l'entreprise,* 11 DR. SOC. 1032, 1033 (2008).

306. *See* Agathe Lepage, *La vie privée du salarié: une notion civiliste en droit du travail,* 4 DR. SOC. 364 (2006).

307. Antoine Lyon-Caen & Isabelle Vacarie, *Droits fondamentaux et droit du travail*, *in* DROIT SYNDICAL ET DROITS DE L'HOMME À L'AUBE DU XXIE SIÈCLE: MÉLANGES EN L'HONNEUR DE JEAN-MAURICE VERDIER 421 (2000).

308. See Mercat-Bruns, *La discrimination professionnelle fondée sur le sexe aux États-Unis*, *supra* note 7, at 63.

309. See Marie Mercat-Bruns, *La doctrine américaine sur les discriminations et le genre: dialogue entre la critique du droit et la pratique*, 3 JURIS. CRITIQUE 93, 97 (2011).

310. See Janet Halley, *Sexuality Harassment*, *in* Directions in Sexual Harassment Law 182, 189, 193 (Reva B. Siegel & Catharine A. MacKinnon eds., 2003). *See in France*, Cass. soc., Sept. 23, 2015, No. 14-17143 (love notes in text messages do not constitute sexual harassment). There is an increase in litigation on sexual harassment since the new French law of 2012 (duty to protect employee from repeated sexual assault), Cass. soc., Jan. 15, 2015, No. 13-17374 (liability of employer if no prevention of harassment is organized). Dismissing harasser does not avoid liability: Cass. soc., Mar. 11, 2015, No. 13-18603; no sanction for claiming sexual or moral harassment by apprentice except if bad faith of plaintiff is proven, *see* Cass. soc., June 10, 2015, No. 14-13318.

311. In this case, the female employee lost before France's supreme court: Cass. soc., May 21, 2014, No. 13-12666. *See* Marie Mercat-Bruns, *Enquête interne, atteinte à la vie privée et obligation de sécurité*, 9 REV. DR. TRAVAIL 554 (2014).

312. Marie Mercat-Bruns, *Harcèlement sexuel au travail en France: entre rupture et continuité*, *in* LA LOI ET LE GENRE 201 (Stéphanie Hennette-Vauchez et al. eds, 2014).

313. For the first time, the CJEU examined discrimination based on two grounds, age and disability, in the same decision, rejecting direct discrimination based on age but acknowledging indirect discrimination based on disability. The claim involved a reduction in severance pay for laid-off employees as they neared retirement age (the age at which they were entitled to a state pension). Because workers with disabilities retire at an earlier age, they received less severance pay than nondisabled employees in the same situation. Case C-152/11, Odar v. Baxter Deutschland GmbH, E.C.R. I-0000. Today the Convention on the Rights of Persons with Disabilities offers a perspective on persons with disabilities who encounter barriers to inclusion in society. *See* http://www.un.org/disabilities/convention/signature.shtml and art. 1: "The purpose of the present Convention is to promote, protect and ensure the full and equal enjoyment of all human rights and fundamental freedoms by all persons with disabilities, and to promote respect for their inherent dignity. Persons with disabilities include those who have long-term physical, mental, intellectual or sensory impairments which in interaction with various barriers may hinder their full and effective participation in society on an equal basis with others."

314. This interview was conducted just before the adoption of the Patient Protection and Affordable Care Act, Public Law 111–148, May 1, 2010.

315. See Susan Sturm's work, *supra* Chapter 4.

316. *See also* Christine Jolls, *Accommodation Mandates*, 53 STAN. L. REV. 223 (2000). Some authors disagree with this analysis: "Those who wish to defend civil rights laws must defend them as the interventions into the economy that they are, rather than treating them as beyond challenge or defense," Samuel R. Bagenstos, *Rational discrimination, Accommodation, and the Politics of (Disability) Civil Rights*, 89 VA. L. REV., 825, 832 (2003).

317. Daron Acemoglu & Joshua D. Angrist, *Consequences of Employment Protection? The Case of the Americans with Disabilities Act*, 109 J. Pol. Econ. 915, 917 (2001).

318. I present preliminary evidence in Christine Jolls, Identifying the Effects of the Americans with Disabilities Act Using State-Law Variation: Preliminary Evidence on Educational Participation Effects, AMERICAN ECONOMIC REVIEW, Papers and Proceedings, 2004.

319. See *supra* Chapter 4.

320. Americans with Disabilities Act, July 26, 1990, Pub L. 101–336, 104 Stat. 327, 42 U.S.C. § 12101; ADA Amendments, Sept. 25, 2008, PL 110–325, 42 USCA § 12101, 12102, 12111 to 12114, 12210, 12206 to 12213.

321. Americans with Disabilities Act, Title 42, § 12102.

322. Jeannette Cox, *Disability Stigma and Intraclass Discrimination*, 62 FLA. L. REV. 429 (2010).

323. See *supra* Chapter 4 on reasonable accommodation.

324. However, some case law has proven to be discriminatory when a collective bargaining agreement gives advantages based on the cause of the physical inability (work-related or not). See Marie Mercat-Bruns, *Inaptitude physique non professionnelle et discrimination directe dans une convention collective*, 2 REV. DR. TRAVAIL 119 (2015).

325. ADA, Title 42, § 12102 (2) ("For purposes of paragraph (1), major life activities include, but are not limited to, caring for oneself, performing manual tasks, seeing, hearing, eating, sleeping, walking, standing, lifting, bending, speaking, breathing, learning, reading, concentrating, thinking, communicating, and working . . . For purposes of paragraph (1), a major life activity also includes the operation of a major bodily function, including but not limited to, functions of the immune system, normal cell growth, digestive, bowel, bladder, neurological, brain, respiratory, circulatory, endocrine, and reproductive functions").

326. ADA, Title 42, § 12102 (1).

327. ADA, Title 42, § 12112 (A) ("No covered entity shall discriminate against a qualified individual on the basis of disability in regard to job application procedures, the hiring, advancement, or discharge of employees, employee compensation, job training, and other terms, conditions, and privileges of employment").

328. See Ruth B. Colker, *The ADA's Journey through Congress*, 39 WAKE FOREST L. REV. 1 (2004).

329. Sec. 12101, ADA Amendments Act of 2008, Pub. L. 110–325, § 2, Sept. 25, 2008, 122 Stat. 3553 ("Congress finds that (2) in enacting the ADA, Congress recognized that physical and mental disabilities in no way diminish a person's right to fully participate in all aspects of society, but that people with physical or mental disabilities are frequently precluded from doing so because of prejudice, antiquated attitudes, or the failure to remove societal and institutional barriers").

330. Linda Krieger, *Afterword: Socio-Legal Backlash*, 21 BERKELEY J. EMP. & LAB. L. 481 (2000).

331. *Id.*

332. ADA § 12101 (B):

The purposes of this Act are (1) to carry out the ADA's objectives of providing 'a clear and comprehensive national mandate for the elimination of discrimination' and 'clear, strong, consistent, enforceable standards addressing discrimination' by reinstating a broad scope of protection to be available under the ADA; (2) to reject the requirement enunciated by the Supreme Court in Sutton v. United Air Lines, Inc., 527 U.S. 471 (1999) and its companion cases that whether an impairment substantially limits a major life activity is to be determined with reference to the ameliorative effects of mitigating measures; (3) to reject the Supreme Court's reasoning in Sutton v. United Air Lines, Inc., 527 U.S. 471 (1999) with regard to coverage under the third prong of the definition of disability and to reinstate the reasoning of the Supreme Court in School Board of Nassau County v. Arline, 480 U.S. 273 (1987) which set forth a broad view of the third prong of the definition of handicap under the Rehabilitation Act of 1973; (4) to reject the standards enunciated by the Supreme Court in Toyota Motor Manufacturing, Kentucky, Inc. v. Williams, 534 U.S. 184 (2002), that the terms 'substantially' and 'major' in the definition of disability under the ADA 'need to be interpreted strictly to create a demanding standard for qualifying as disabled,' and that to be substantially limited in performing a major life activity under the ADA 'an individual must have an impairment that prevents or severely restricts the individual from doing activities that are of central importance to most people's daily lives'; (5) to convey congressional intent that the standard created by the Supreme Court in the case of Toyota Motor Manufacturing, Kentucky, Inc. v. Williams, 534 U.S. 184 (2002) for 'substantially limits', and applied by lower courts in numerous decisions, has created an inappropriately high level of limitation necessary to obtain coverage under the ADA, to convey that it is the intent of Congress that the primary object of attention in cases brought under the ADA should be whether entities covered under the ADA have complied with their obligations, and to convey that the question of whether an individual's impairment is a disability under the ADA should not demand extensive analysis; and (6) to express Congress' expectation that the Equal Employment Opportunity Commission will revise that portion of its current regulations that defines the term 'substantially limits' as 'significantly restricted' to be consistent with this Act, including the amendments made by this Act.

333. Before the 2008 amendments reversed more restrictive case law, Bragdon v. Abbott, 524 U.S. 624 (1998) recognized that the reproductive function was a major life activity.

334. In § 12102 ("The term 'substantially limits' shall be interpreted consistently with the findings and purposes of the ADA Amendments Act of 2008. (C) An impairment that substantially limits one major life activity need not limit other major life activities in order to be considered a disability. (D) An impairment that is episodic or in remission is a disability if it would substantially limit a major life activity when active").

335. It excludes illness: Case C-13/05, Chacón Navas v. Eurest Colectividades, 2006 E.C.R. I-6467.

336. Case C-354/13, Fag og Arbejde (FOA), pt. 65 (ruling that "the obesity of a worker constitutes a 'disability' within the meaning of [Council Directive 2000/78/EC] where it entails a limitation resulting in particular from long-term physical, mental or psychological impairments which in interaction with various barriers may hinder the full and effective participation of the person concerned in professional life on an equal basis with other workers.").

337. Sec. 12101 note: Findings and Purposes of ADA Amendments Act of 2008, Pub. L. 110-325, § 2, Sept. 25, 2008, 122 Stat. 3553, provided that one of the purposes of the ADA is "to express Congress' expectation that the Equal Employment Opportunity Commission will revise that portion of its current regulations that defines the term 'substantially limits' as 'significantly restricted' to be consistent with this Act, including the amendments made by this Act."

338. Chai R. Feldblum, *Following in Paul Miller's (Very Large) Footsteps*, 86 WASH. L. REV. 702 (2011).

339. In looking to reassign workers, sometimes employers limit themselves to equivalent jobs and do not consider how some jobs can be modified to eliminate nonessential tasks that cannot be performed by workers with disabilities.

340. Rehrs v. Iams Co., 486 F.3d 353 (8th Cir. May 15, 2007): the essential functions of a job can include the ability to work rotating shifts.

341. For example, the employer justifies the essential nature of the task by looking at the job profile, the time spent on the task, the consequences if the task is not completed, definitions of tasks and jobs in collective bargaining agreements, the experience workers can share about the job, and the current experience at the job.

342. Huber v. Wal-Mart, 486 F.3d 480 (8th Cir. May 30, 2007) (No. 06-2238): A Wal-Mart employee, disabled after an accident at work, sought as a reasonable accommodation to be reassigned to a vacant and equivalent position. Ultimately, Wal-Mart filled that position

with a nondisabled applicant, stipulating that Huber was not the most qualified candidate. She was eventually placed at another facility in a lower-level job as a maintenance associate (a janitorial position). The Court concluded that the ADA is not an affirmative action statute and does not require an employer to reassign a qualified disabled employee to a vacant position when such a reassignment would violate a legitimate nondiscriminatory policy of the employer to hire the most qualified candidate.

343. Chai Feldblum, Kevin Barry, & Emily A. Benfer, *The ADA Amendments Act of 2008*, 13 TEX. J. C.L. & C.R. 187–240 (2008).

344. *See supra* Chapter 4, even if recent EU case law seems a little more favorable to expand disability to cases of obesity, *supra* note 336, and reasonable accommodations to worktime adjustments, *see infra* note 345.

345. *See* Law 2005–102 of Feb. 11, 2005 (on equal treatment, equal opportunity, participation, and citizenship of people with disabilities). An amendment to add "loss of autonomy" as a ground for discrimination was introduced on Sept. 16, 2015 in Parliament to the bill entitled "Adjusting law to aging." See Marie Mercat-Bruns, *Lutte contre les discriminations: nouveau critère tiré de la perte d'autonomie*, RECUEIL DALLOZ 1957 (2015).

346. Lisa Waddington, *Future Prospects for EU Equality Law: Lessons to Be Learnt from the Proposed Equal Treatment Directive*, 36 EUR. L. REV. 163, 174 (2011).

347. *See also* Preamble (e) to the Convention ("Recognizing that disability is an evolving concept and that disability results from the interaction between persons with impairments and attitudinal and environmental barriers that hinders their full and effective participation in society on an equal basis with others"). The Convention on the Rights of Persons with Disabilities and its Optional Protocol (A/RES/61/106) was adopted on Dec. 13, 2006.

348. Joined Cases C-335/11 and C-337/11, Ring v. Dansk, 2013.

349. Case C-312/11, Commission v. Italy, 2013 E.C.R. I-000.

350. Case C-303/06, Coleman v. Attridge Law & Steve Law, 2008 E.C.R. I-5603.

351. *Id.* at point 64.

352. Marie Mercat-Bruns, *La discrimination fondée sur l'âge: un exemple d'une nouvelle génération de critères discriminatoires?* 6 REV. DR. TRAVAIL 360 (2007) [hereinafter Mercat-Bruns, *La discrimination fondée sur l'âge*].

353. Reducing severance pay for older workers based on their retirement age does not constitute direct discrimination: Case C-152/11, Odar v. Baxter Deutschland GmbH, E.C.R. I-0000.

354. Case C-144/04, Mangold v. Helm, 2005 E.C.R. I-9981; C-388/07, Age Concern England, 2009, I-01569; Case C-88/08 Hütter v. Technische Universität Graz, 2009 E.C.R. I-5325; Case C-341/08, Petersen, 2010 E.C.R. I-47; Case C-45/09, Rosenbladt, 2010 E.C.R. I-09391; Case C-499/08, Andersen, 2010 E.C.R. I-9343; Case C-159/10, Fuchs, 2011 E.C.R. I-6919; joined Cases C-297/10 and C-298/10, Hennigs v. Eisenbahn-Bundesamt and Land Berlin v. Mai, 2011 E.C.R. I-0796; Case C-447/09, Prigge v. Deutsche Lufthansa AG, 2011 E.C.R. I-8003. In French case law, see Marie Mercat-Bruns, *Retour sur la discrimination fondée sur l'âge*, 10 REV. DR. TRAVAIL 587 (2010); Marie Mercat-Bruns, *Age and disability differential treatment in France—Contrasting EU and national courts' approaches to the inner limits of anti-discrimination law*, INT'L J. DISCRIMINATION & L. (Nov. 12, 2014), http://jdi.sagepub.com/content/early/2014/11/12/1358229114558383.abstract. *See more recently, for example,* CJEU Case-C529/13, Felber (Jan. 21, 2015); Case C-417/13, Starjakob (Jan. 28, 2015); Case C-20/13, Daniel Unland (Sept. 9, 2015); Case C-432/14, Bio Philippe Auguste SARL (Oct. 1, 2015).

355. Cass. soc., Apr. 4, 1990, No. 88–43555 (Folies Bergères case).

356. *See* Marie Mercat-Bruns, *La CJUE et les présomptions sur l'âge*, 12 REV. JURIS. SOC. 815, 817 (2011) [hereinafter Mercat-Bruns, *La CJUE et les présomptions sur l'âge*]; joined

Cases C-297/10 and C-298/10, Hennigs v. Eisenbahn-Bundesamt and Land Berlin v. Mai, 2011 E.C.R. I-0796; Case C-530/13, Schmitzer (Nov. 11 2014).

357. Age Discrimination in Employment Act of 1967 (ADEA), Pub. L. 90–202. EU cases on younger workers are starting to come up and are not necessarily more favorable to younger workers; for example, the CJEU decided that the grant of a payment on the expiry of a fixed-term employment contract is intended to compensate for insecurity and justifies the exclusion of young people working during their school holidays or university vacations who necessarily go back to school, Case C-432/14, O. v. Bio Philippe Auguste SARL (Oct. 1, 2015).

358. See Cass. soc., Apr. 30, 2009, No. 07–43945 (rejecting the claim of indirect discrimination resulting from the introduction of a cap on the length of service (twelve years) taken into account to calculate redundancy payments upon dismissal).

359. For further discussion of age discrimination, see Christine Jolls, *Hands-Tying and the Age Discrimination in Employment Act*, 74 TEX. L. REV. 1813 (1996).

360. Phyllis Moen, professor, McKnight Presidential Chair in Sociology University of Minnesota. She and Professor Erin Kelly codirect the Flexible Work and Well-Being Center. Her works include Phyllis Moen, *A Life-Course Approach to the Third Age*, in DAWN CARR & KATHRIN KOMP, GERONTOLOGY IN THE ERA OF THE THIRD AGE: IMPLICATIONS AND NEXT STEPS 13 (2011).

361. See WORKPLACE FLEXIBILITY: REALIGNING 20TH-CENTURY JOBS FOR A 21ST-CENTURY WORKFORCE (Kathleen Christensen & Barbara Schneider, eds., 2010).

362. Major program areas of the Alfred P. Sloan Foundation, *available at* http://www.sloan.org/major-program-areas/.

363. See Mercat-Bruns, *La discrimination fondée sur l'âge*, *supra* note 352, at 360.

364. MARIE MERCAT-BRUNS, VIEILLISSEMENT ET DROIT À LA LUMIÈRE DU DROIT FRANÇAIS ET DU DROIT AMÉRICAIN (2001) [hereinafter MERCAT-BRUNS, VIEILLISSEMENT ET DROIT].

365. See a case of the Conseil d'Etat that explains why mandatory retirement for air traffic controllers is "justified" and proportionate: "age can affect endurance, vigilance and performance," CE, Apr. 4, 2014, App. No. 362785.

366. Case C-229/08, Wolf, 2010 E.C.R. I-1.

367. Age Discrimination in Employment Act of 1967 (ADEA), Pub. L. No. 90–202, 81 Stat. 602 and § 623; for case law on Bona Fide Occupational Qualification, see Western Airlines v. Criswell, 472 U.S. 400 (1985).

368. In EU law, there is a narrow interpretation of this exception: *see* C-447/09, Prigge v. Deutsche Lufthansa AG 2011 E.C.R. I-8003, Pt. 74 (to invoke this defense, one must prove that its application is legitimate and proportionate); C-416/13, Vital Pérez v. Ayuntamiento de Oviedo, EU:C:2014:2371, Nov. 13, 2014 (recently rejecting an age limit of thirty to recruit policemen). In France, an exception was also recently rejected because it was applied to refuse the recruitment of older ski instructors: Cass. soc., Mar. 17, 2015, No. 13–27142.

369. See Mercat-Bruns, *La CJUE et les présomptions sur l'âge*, *supra* note 356, at 817.

370. The specific nature of litigation on age discrimination in EU law and American law is that it often focuses on the application of the exceptions to age discrimination (in EU, the legitimacy and proportionality test of art. 4 and art. 6 of Directive 2000/78/EC). See Marie Mercat-Bruns, *Retour sur la discrimination fondée sur l'âge*, 10 REV. DR. TRAVAIL 587 (2010); Marie Mercat-Bruns, *Age and Disability Differential Treatment in France—Contrasting EU and National Courts' Approaches to the Inner Limits of Anti-discrimination Law*, INT'L J. DISCRIMINATION & L. (Nov. 12, 2014), *available at* http://jdi.sagepub.com/content/early/201 4/11/12/1358229114558383.abstract [hereinafter Mercat-Bruns, *Age and Disability Differential Treatment in France*].

371. Some authors refer to the "life cycle" theory based on the "economic structure of career employment" to justify the disadvantages of older workers: see Samuel Issacharoff & Erica Worth Harris, *Is Age Discrimination Really Age Discrimination?: The ADEA's Unnatural Solution*, 72 N.Y.U. L. REV. 780 (1997).

372. The French Cour de Cassation recently held that it was discriminatory to refuse an employee access to training because he or she is close to retirement age: Cass. soc., Feb. 18, 2014, No. 13-10294.

373. Cass. soc., Apr. 9, 2015, No. 13-27550.

374. *See* Case C-555/07, Kücükdeveci v. Swedex, 2010 E.C.R. I-365.

375. *See* Case C-152/11, Odar v. Baxter Deutschland GmbH, E.C.R. I-0000.

376. LOUIS CHAUVEL, LE DESTIN DES GÉNÉRATIONS: STRUCTURE SOCIALE ET COHORTES EN FRANCE DU XXE SIÈCLE AUX ANNÉES 2010 15 (2011).

377. Indirect discrimination based on health status: *see* Cass. soc., July 3, 2012, No. 10-230013; Cass. soc., June 6, 2012, No. 10-21489; Cass. soc., Feb. 12, 2013, No. 11-27689.

378. Cass. soc., Apr. 30, 2009, No. 07-43945; Cass. soc., Oct. 19, 2010, No. 08-45254.

379. In Smith v. City of Jackson, 544 U.S. 228 (2005), the Supreme Court extended disparate impact discrimination in an age discrimination case; the ADEA did not provide for this protection. Indirect discrimination based on age is explicitly prohibited in French law (Law 2001-1066 of Nov. 16, 2001, amended by Law 2008-496 of May 27, 2008).

380. Gross v. FBL Financial Services, Inc., 557 U.S. 167 (2009): in mixed motive cases, since the CRA of 1991 does not concern age discrimination, the motivating-factor instruction does not apply to age. See also the legislative attempts to improve older workers' protection in the United States, Protecting Older Workers Against Discrimination Act, H.R. 3721, 111th Cong. (1st Sess. 2009), and on the proposed bill, see David Sherwyn et al., *Experimental Evidence That Retaliation Claims Are Unlike Other Employment Discrimination Claims*, 44 SETON HALL L. REV. 455 (2014).

381. See Gilmer v. Interstate/Johnson Lane Corporation, 500 U.S. 20, 35 (1991); extending to all employment discrimination cases, Staub v. Proctor Hosp., 131 S. Ct. 1186, 1191 (2011).

382. See Case C-123/10, Brachner v. Pensionsversicherungsanstalt, 2011 E.C.R. I-000. In France: Cass. soc., Sept. 30, 2013, Nos. 12-14752 and 12-14964.

383. The ADEA protects workers over forty; when both workers are over forty, the law protects only older workers over younger workers: *General Dynamics Land Systems, Inc. v. Dennis Cline*, 2004 WL 329956.

384. Joined Cases C-297/10 and C-298/10, Hennigs v. Eisenbahn-Bundesamt and Land Berlin v. Mai, 2011 E.C.R. I-0796; Case C-499/08, Ingeniørforeningen i Danmark on behalf of Ole Andersen v. Region Syddanmark, 2010 E.C.R. I-9343 (Oct. 12, 2010); Case C-159/10, Fuchs, 2011 E.C.R. I-6919.

385. Case C-88/08, Hütter v. Technische Universität Graz, 2009 E.C.R. I-5325; joined Cases C-501/12 to C-506/12, C-540/12 and C-541/12, Thomas Specht et al. (2014). *In France recently*, Cass. soc., May 20, 2014, No. 12-29565 (in which the mandatory retirement of a worker was justified by an exception to age discrimination: the benefit of a full pension and the recruitment of younger workers to promote younger generations in this job category).

386. *See* Case C-141/11, Hörnfeldt v. Posten Meddelande AB, 2012 E.C.R. I-0000; *see more recently* Case C-515/13, Ingeniørforeningen i Danmark acting on behalf Landin (Feb. 26, 2015).

387. See EU case law, which considers that intergenerational fairness in the workplace is a legitimate exception to age discrimination, joined Cases C-250/09 and C-268/09, Georgiev, 2010 E.C.R. I-11869; Frédérique Rolin, *Quelques précisions quant à la nature et au régime de justification des discriminations fondées sur l'âge*, 3 RAE 610 (2011); Mercat-Bruns, *Age and Disability Differential Treatment in France*, *supra* note 370.

388. See Law 2013-185 of Mar. 1, 2013 (on the "generation contract") and amendments in Law 2014-288 of Mar. 5, 2014. It aims to promote the hiring of young people under twenty-six and the continued employment of older employees by creating junior-senior pairs to support transfer of know-how from the older worker to the younger worker. The mechanism includes a government subsidy for small- and medium-sized companies (fewer than three hundred employees): €4,000 a year for three years for each young worker hired under an intergenerational agreement. In companies with more than fifty employees, a collective bargaining agreement may be negotiated but is no longer a prerequisite.

389. But this right to retirement can be less favorable for workers with disabilities who are required to retire earlier than workers without a disability; in this case, the rule disproportionately disadvantages older workers with disabilities: Case C-152/11, Odar v. Baxter Deutschland GmbH, E.C.R. I-0000, Pt. 72.

390. 2012 was the European Year for Active Ageing: EUROPEAN YEAR FOR ACTIVE AGEING AND SOLIDARITY BETWEEN GENERATIONS, http://ec.europa.eu/archives/ey2012/.

391. See one of the federal reports on aging, Report of the Taskforce on the Aging of the American Workforce (2008).

392. As the case law shows, economic layoffs can justify limited redundancy for older workers about to retire as well as the legitimate aim to balance the workforce. Judicial scrutiny of these exceptions to age discrimination was harsher in the past: Cass. soc., June 27, 2012, No. 10-27220; Cass. soc., Oct. 9, 2012, Nos. 11-23142 to 11-23146; Cass. soc., May 11, 2010, No. 08-45307; Cass. soc., Feb. 16, 2011, No. 09-72061; Cass. soc., Dec. 21, 2006, No. 05-12816, examining the individual situations of the older workers involved. Now the judges are more deferent to the need to cater to the young unemployed generation (Cass. soc., Nov. 26, 2013, Nos. 12-21758 and 12-22200, 12-24690, 12-22208; Cass. soc., May 20, 2014, No. 12-29565; Cass. soc., May 13, 2014, No. 13-10781; Cass. soc., Apr. 15, 2015, No. 13-18849; Cass. soc. July 9, 2015, No. 14-16009 (financial advantages linked to a severance pay plan cannot be refused to employees who do not consent to early retirement plan) and follow the CJEU's more lenient standard of appreciation of national age policies; *see recently* CJEU Cases C-515/13, Ingeniorforeningen i Danmark (Feb. 26, 2015), and C-529/13, Georg Felber v. Bundesministerin für Unterricht, Kunst und Kultur (Jan. 21, 2015) (finding that a civil servant retirement system that does not take into account years of service before the age of eighteen because of the technical obstacle of contributing to a public scheme is not discriminatory); Case C-20/13, Daniel Unland (Sept. 9, 2015) (concerning a transitional pay scheme); there is no valid point of reference under the old pay scheme of civil servants and, contrary to the argument by the applicant, neither a category of "young judges" are at a disadvantage as a result of that law nor a category of "older judges" who are placed in a more favourable position as a result of those laws; a transitional pay scheme does not perpetuate discriminatory categories.

393. MERCAT-BRUNS, VIEILLISSEMENT ET DROIT, *supra* note 364, at 257.

394. Conseil Constitutionnel decision No. 2007-557 DC, Nov. 15, 2007, striking down art. 63 of the Act of Oct. 25, 2007 (on the control of immigration, integration, and asylum).

395. SIMONE DE BEAUVOIR, OLD AGE 602-603 (Patrick O'Brien, trans., 1977).

396. Law 2010-1330 of Nov. 9, 2010, and Decree No. 2011-823 of July 7, 2011 (on the obligation to negotiate an action plan or a collective bargaining agreement on work hardship factors), and Decree No. 2014-1156 of Oct. 9, 2014 (creating a points system to keep track of hardship factors and enable workers exposed to these factors to retire earlier).

397. See PIERRE-YVES VERKINDT, LES C.H.S.C.T. AU MILIEU DU GUÉ, Feb. 28, 2014 (report to the French government on the representative body in charge of working conditions), *available at* http://www.travailler-mieux.gouv.fr/Rapport-etabli-par-le-professeur.html.

398. For more emphasis on this issue in the United States, see HOWARD EGLIT, ELDERS ON TRIAL: AGE AND AGEISM IN THE AMERICAN LEGAL SYSTEM 23 (2004).

399. Nicole Catala, L'emploi des seniors: enquete d'entreprises 35 (2005).

400. Samia Benallah, *La surcote: premiers éléments de bilan d'une mésure emblématique de la réforme des retraites de 2003*, 60 Retraite et société 43 (2011).

401. *See* Pierre Bailly & Jean-Philippe Lhernould, *Discrimination en raison de l'âge: sources européennes et mise en oeuvre en droit interne*, 3 Dr. soc. 223 (2012); Sylvaine Laulom, *L'interdiction des discriminations fondées sur l'âge*, 1489 Semaine Sociale Lamy 25 (2011); Frédérique Michéa, *Le traitement judiciaire du critère discriminatoire de l'âge*, 11 Dr. Soc. 1060 (2010).

402. For sociological accounts on age cohorts, see Evelyne Sullerot, L'âge de travailler 47 (1986); Anne-Marie Guillemard, L'âge de l'emploi: les sociétés à l'épreuve du vieillissement (2003). In management, see Eléonore Marbot & Jean-Marie Peretti, Les seniors dans l'entreprise 93 (2004).

403. Without dwelling on the damaging effects of extensive early retirement policies in France from the late 1960s onward, see Mercat-Bruns, Vieillissement et droit, *supra* note 364, at 98.

404. *See generally* Isabelle Richet, La religion aux États-Unis (2001).

405. Kent Greenawalt, *Common Sense About Original and Subsequent Understandings of the Religion Clauses*, 8 U. Pa. J. Const. L. 479, 511 (2005)

406. *See* Camille Froidevaux-Metterie, Politique et religion aux États-Unis (2009); Denis Lacorne, De la religion en Amerique: essai d'histoire politique (2007).

407. See the EEOC guidelines on religious accommodation according to Title VII, offering a narrower definition than the one applied to reasonable accommodation for persons with disabilities, *available at* http://www.eeoc.gov/policy/docs/religion.html#_Toc203359518.

408. *See generally* Kent Greenawalt, *Five Questions About Religion Judges Are Afraid to Ask*, *in* Obligations of Citizenship and Demands of Faith: Religious Accommodations in Pluralist Democracies 196–244 (Nancy Rosenblum ed., 2000).

409. For an example of a French company having decided to provide reasonable accommodation, see *Capitalising on the Rich Diversity of Our Workforce*, Groupe Casino, http://www.groupe-casino.fr/en/committed-employer/capitalising-on-the-rich-diversity-of-our-workforce/ (last visited on Jan. 27, 2015).

410. *See* Emmanuelle Bribosia et al., *Reasonable Accommodation for Religious Minorities: A Promising Concept for European Antidiscrimination Law?*, 17 Maastricht J. Eur. & Comp. L. 137 (2010).

411. See the novel by Abd Al Malik, L'islam au secours de la République (2013).

412. On activities such as day care, see the saga of the French *Baby Loup* case, which ended with a Cour de Cassation case justifying the dismissal of a day care deputy manager who wanted to wear her hijab to work. The court based its argument on the nature of the activity: taking care of children required workers to not wear conspicuous religious symbols: *see* Cass. ass. plén., June 25, 2014, No. 13-28369.

413. Zelman v. Simmons-Harris, 536 U.S. 639 (2002).

414. A madrassa is an Islamic school.

415. 42 U.S.C. § 2000e-2(e) (2010):

> It shall not be an unlawful employment practice for an employer to hire and employ employees, for an employment agency to classify, or refer for employment any individual, for a labor organization to classify its membership or to classify or refer for employment any individual, or for an employer, labor organization, or joint labor-management committee controlling apprenticeship or other training or retraining programs to admit or employ any individual in any such

program, on the basis of his religion, sex, or national origin in those certain instances where religion, sex, or national origin is a bona fide occupational qualification reasonably necessary to the normal operation of that particular business or enterprise.

416. Pub. L. No. 103–141, 107 Stat. 1488, 42 U.S.C. § 2000bb (Nov. 16, 1993).
417. Burwell v. Hobby Lobby Stores, Inc., 573 U.S. ___ (2014).
418. Legal experts have not reflected on religion as much as experts in other fields: *see* Nancy Green, *La religion aux États-Unis comme catégorie d'analyse; la religion en France comme catégorie d'analyse, in* LES CODES DE LA DIFFÉRENCE 74, 80 (Riva Kastoryano ed., 2005); MAX WEBER, SOCIOLOGIE DES RÉLIGIONS (Jean-Pierre Grossein ed. & trans., Gallimard, 1996); OLIVIER BOBINEAU & SÉBASTIEN TANK-STORPER, SOCIOLOGIE DES RÉLIGIONS (2007).
419. *See* RICHARD FORD, HEADSCARVES, HAIRSTYLES AND CULTURE AS A CIVIL RIGHT 9 (French-American Foundation & Sciences Po, 2011), http://www.frenchamerican.org/sites/default/files/documents/media_reports/ford_headscarves_report_en.pdf (expressing qualms about religious accommodations):

> The headscarves controversy in France and elsewhere has captured world-wide attention and provoked a great deal of criticism from defenders of religious liberty. Many American commentators insist that European nations—France in particular—should adopt an American approach to religious liberty and accommodate distinctive religious practices as a matter of civil rights. These criticisms overstate the extent to which American law requires the accommodation of religious practices and unfairly dismiss the concerns that underlay rules prohibiting conspicuous religious symbols. Indeed, the American experience with civil rights requiring the accommodation of distinctive group practices and cultural affections largely vindicates the concerns of the French. Often the supposedly authentic practices of a minority group are in fact imposed by more powerful members of the group on others who prefer a less conspicuous or less traditional way of expressing their racial, ethnic or religious identifications—here, a right to accommodation reinforces the power of these dominant group members. Legal rights to accommodation can also encourage the most divisive and illiberal aspects of a minority group's culture, since these are precisely the aspects of any group culture that would be subject to censure in the absence of rights to accommodation.

420. *See* François Gaudu, *La religion dans l'entreprise*, 1 DR. SOC. 65 (2010).
421. Reference to the First Amendment of the U.S. Constitution ("Congress shall make no law respecting an establishment of religion").
422. Art. 1 of the 1958 French Constitution ("France is a secular, democratic and undividable republic. It ensures equality before the law to all its citizens regardless of their origin, race or religion"); Decision No. 2004–505 DC, Nov. 19, 2004, and CE, Mar. 16, 2005, Rec. Lebon 168 (recognizing the constitutional principle of *"laïcité"*); Law of Dec. 9, 1905 (on the separation of church and state).
423. This is the translation of the neutrality of *laïcité*. We might be overlooking "its essence": *see* Patrice Adam, *La crèche et l'au-delà*, 1527 SEM. SOC. LAMY 30 (2012). See on the distortion of the concept, STÉPHANIE HENNETTE-VAUCHEZ & VINCENT VALENTIN, L'AFFAIRE BABY LOUP OU LA NOUVELLE LAÏCITÉ (2014).
424. Jean Rivero, *La notion juridique de laïcité*, 31 RECUEIL DALLOZ 137 (1949); see also the recommendation of the Conseil d'État on the wearing of a veil at school, Nov. 27, 1989, RFD ADM. 1 (1990).
425. For a description of the important role of the Catholic Church, especially during the prerevolutionary period, see HISTOIRE DE LA FRANCE RELIGIEUSE (Jacques Le Goff & Réné Remond eds., 1988); for an essay relating how the United States was founded by

groups seeking religious freedom, see DENIS LACORNE, DE LA RELIGION EN AMERIQUE: ESSAI D'HISTOIRE POLITIQUE (2007).

426. See Appel-Irrgang v. Germany, App. No. 45216/07, Eur. Ct. H.R. (2009) (defending the idea of the state's neutrality with regard to religion).

427. See the five decisions by the Conseil d'État, July 19, 2011, No. 308544, on the compatibility of laïcité and financial support of local government to religion institutions.

428. On the production of norms to reinforce or justify the principle of laïcité, see Remy Libchaber, À la croisée des interprétations: le voile et la loi, RTD CIV. 161 (2004).

429. Law 2010–1192 of Oct. 11, 2010.

430. Circular of Mar. 2, 2011, J.O. 4128 (Mar. 3, 2011) (on the implementation of the law of 2010).

431. CC decision No. 2010-613 DC, Oct. 7, 2010 (the Conseil Constitutionnel applies a narrow proportionality test balancing principles of religious freedom with the principle of equality in the aim of preserving public order, which is constitutionally protected).

432. Anne-Marie Leroyer, La circulaire et le voile: interrogations sur une notion émergente: les exigences minimales en société, RTD CIV. 399 (2011).

433. See Dahlab v. Switzerland, 2001-V, Eur. Ct. H.R. 447 (2001) (supporting the principle of laïcité in conformity with the European convention, regarding a veil ban for Swiss teachers); see also Karaduman v. Turkey, App. No. 16278/90, 74, Eur. Com. H.R. Dec. & Rep. 93 (1993).

434. See Libchaber, supra note 428.

435. Arslan v. Turkey, App. No. 41135/98 § 2, Eur. H.R. Rep. (2010); Jean-Pierre Marguénaud, La liberté de porter des vêtements religieux dans les lieux publics ouverts à tous, RTD CIV. 682 (2010). But recently, in SAS v. France, App. No. 43835/11, Eur. Ct. H.R. (2014), the French law on the burqa ban was considered justified by the French government's attachment to the ability to "live together" (vivre ensemble).

436. For example, in Eweida v. United Kingdom, Nos. 48420/10, 59842/10, 51671/10, and 36516/10, Eur. Ct. H.R. (2013), British Airways uniform code must allow wearing a cross if it also allows other visible religious symbols like the hijab and turban.

437. See Minow's interview, supra Chapter 5, Part VI:

> This is the way to maximize individual freedom and reduce government imposition. Compare the individual rights approach to the use of personal law in places such as India and Israel—which assign individuals to a package of family laws based on their or their parents' religion. That personal law approach has been rejected by the United States, Canada, and England. To look at someone and say because your parents are in a given religious group, then you are governed by the marriage and divorce laws of that group is to deprive the individual of the ability to choose. The individual may say, "I don't want my divorce law governed by Islam even though my parents are Muslim because I have chosen to marry someone who is a Hindu or to be secular." The individual should have that choice.

438. Law 2001–504 of June 12, 2001 (to reinforce the prevention and suppression of sects).

439. Art. 14 of the HRC and art. 2 of Directive 2000/78/EC.

440. The Strasbourg Court recognizes freedom of religion as a substantive right of the convention. Gérard Gonzalez, LA CONVENTION EUROPÉENE DES DROITS DE L'HOMME ET LA LIBERTÉ DES RELIGIONS 42 (1997)

441. ECHR art. 9.

442. See Charter of Fundamental Rights of the European Union art. 10.

443. JEAN-FRANÇOIS RENUCCI, DROIT EUROPÉEN DES DROITS DE L'HOMME 134 (2010); X v. United Kingdom, App. No. 7291/75, Eur. Cm. H.R., Oct. 4, 1977, 11 DR 55.

444. Welsh v. United States, 398 U.S. 333, 339 (1970).

445. See Law 2001–504 of June 12, 2001 (on sects), unsuccessfully contested before the ECtHR: Nov. 6, 2001, Fédération chrétienne des témoins de Jéhovah de France v. France, Rec. 2001-XI, 15.

446. Lautsi v. Italy, App. No. 30814/06, 2011 Eur. Ct. H.R. (G.C.).

447. RENUCCI, *supra* note 443, at 28.

448. Giniewski v. France, 2006-I Eur. Ct. H.R. 468 (2006) (holding that criticism against Pope John Paul II was a form of freedom of expression).

449. RENUCCI, *supra* note 443, at 132.

450. Gérard Gonzalez, *Liberté de pensée, de conscience et de religion*, in DICTIONNAIRE DES DROITS DE L'HOMME 636 (Joel Andriantsimbazovina et al. eds, 2008)

451. RENUCCI, *supra* note 443, at 133: no deadline can be imposed to recognize the status of a religious faith, Jehovas v. Austria, No. 40825/98, Eur. Ct. H.R., July 31, 2008; Verein der Freunde des Christengemeinschaft v. Austria, No. 76581/01, Eur. Ct. H.R., Feb. 26, 2009.

452. Corporations do not have religious rights: Comm. EDH, Feb. 27, 1979, X v. Switzerland, D. 16/85. In the United States, this position is different: *see recently* Burwell v. Hobby Lobby Stores, 573 U.S. ___ (2014) (the first time the Supreme Court has recognized a closely held for-profit corporation's claim of religious belief).

453. Kosteski v. Former Yugoslav Republic of Macedonia, App. No. 55170/00, 2006 Eur. Ct. H.R. 403.

454. Buscarini v. San Marino, 1999-I Eur. Ct. H.R. 605.

455. See legislative history of law of 1964 (Title VII), which covers religion: 110 Cong. Rec. 2548, 2607 (1964).

456. RENUCCI, *supra* note 443, at 136; Kokkinakis v. Greece, 260 Eur. Ct. H.R. (ser. A) (1993); Church of Bessarabia v. Moldova, App. No. 45701/99, 2001-XII Eur. Ct. H.R. (2001).

457. Court of Appeal, Lyon, July 28, 1997, Ministère public v. Veau; *see also* Claire Brisseau, *La religion du salarié*, 9–10 DR. SOC. 969 (2008).

458. Welsh v. United States, 398 U.S. 333, 339 (1970).

459. *Welsh*, 398 U.S. at 339; THOMAS HAGGARD, UNDERSTANDING EMPLOYMENT DISCRIMINATION LAW 144 (2008).

460. 29 C.F.R. § 1605.1 (EEOC guidelines on discrimination because of religion).

461. Wilson v. U.S. West Communications, 58 F.3d 1337 (8th Cir. 1995); the constitutional standard applied to religious freedom is more restrictive when applied in the context of abortion rights.

462. No discrimination in the case of denying an employee the right to eat cat food in the company cafeteria due to the employee's personal beliefs: Brown v. Pena 441 F.Supp. 1382 (S.D.Fla. 1977).

463. *See* Young v. Southwestern Savings & Loan, 509 F.2d 140 (5th Cir. 1975) ("The racist and anti-Semitic philosophy of the Ku Klux Klan has been held not to qualify as a *religion*, even though it allegedly derives from Biblical sources"); THOMAS HAGGARD, UNDERSTANDING EMPLOYMENT DISCRIMINATION LAW 144 (2008).

464. Cass. soc., Mar. 24, 241998, DR. SOC. 614 (1998): a Muslim butcher who, after two years, made a request to stop working with pork, which the employer refused. The Cour de Cassation found no fault in requesting that an employee perform the job he was hired to do. In France, an employer has no duty to accommodate, similar to the United States; *see also* Cass. soc., June 2, 1993, No. 91–44476 (involving a request to not work on Fridays).

465. *See also* Siebenhaar v. Germany, Eur. Ct. H.R. (2011), 5 RJS 357 (2011); Obst v. Germany, App. No. 4205/03, Eur. Ct. H.R. (2010); Schüth v. Germany, Eur. Ct. H.R. (2010), 1 RJS 11 (2011).

466. Court of Appeal, Versailles, Jan. 23, 1998, No. 95–9736; Court of Appeal, Nancy, June 30, 2006, No. 04–1847.

467. Even though the "justification that the employer has to deal with customers can be considered more or less legitimate, . . . it is up to the judge of the employment contract to examine, on a case by case basis, the type of market targeted by the company and the type of product sold, which could require a restriction of religious freedom (fashion apparel? home appliances?)." *See* Adam, *supra* note 423, at 33; Court of Appeal, Saint Denis de la Reunion, Sept. 9, 1997, RECUEIL DALLOZ 546 (1998) (involving a requirement for elegant attire and a veiled salesperson); Labor Court (CPH), Paris, Dec. 17, 2002, DR. SOC. 360 (2004). And the Cour de Cassation has recently asked the CJEU for a preliminary ruling on the legality of a company ban of the veil imposed on a female engineer seen as an essential requirement for the job because of customer preference, Cass. soc. Apr. 9, 2015, No. 13–19855.

468. The behavior of the employee cannot affect the image of the company that supports a certain religious faith. Court of Appeal, Toulouse, Aug. 17, 1995, DR. OUVRIER 369 (1996).

469. *See* HALDE deliberation No. 2011–67, Mar. 28, 2011, and the lack of an adequate legal framework to regulate religious practices in the private sector.

470. In some cases, the veiled Muslim employee has won at the Labor Court level based on LABOR CODE [CODE DU TRAVAIL] art. L.1121–1 (employer's references to surveys of public opinion disapproving the veil cannot justify a ban of the veil based on customer preference). However, the court rejected the argument based on religious discrimination: Labor Court of Lyon (Conseil de prud'hommes de Lyon en départage), Sept. 18, 2014.

471. *Id.,* at 9.

472. Cass. ass. plén., June 25, 2014, No. 13–28369. This was the second time the French supreme court heard the case: this decision emanated from the plenary assembly because the court of appeal, on remand, considered a second time that the dismissal of the veiled employee was for just cause. In Assemblée Plénière, the judges are in a sort of en banc composition, one from each chamber. The first decision of the Cour de Cassation on this case had sided with the employee, considering that the principle of neutrality did not apply to the private sector. *See* Cass. soc., Mar. 19, 2013, No. 11–28.845; *see also* PATRICE ADAM, L'INDIVIDUALISATION DU DROIT DU TRAVAIL (2005); Patrice Adam, *Baby Loup: horizons et défense d'une jurisprudence anathème*, 6 REV. DR. TRAVAIL 385 (2013); Patrice Adam, *L'affaire Baby Loup: vues du sommet*, 10 REV. DR. TRAVAIL 607 (2014); STÉPHANIE HENNETTE-VAUCHEZ & VINCENT VALENTIN, L'AFFAIRE BABY LOUP OU LA NOUVELLE LAÏCITÉ (2014).

473. Labor Court (CPH) of Mantes La Jolie, Dec. 13, 2010.

474. Court of Appeal, Versailles, Oct. 27, 2011, No. 10–05642.

475. No objective justification, foreign to any discrimination.

476. *See supra* note 472.

477. *Id.*

478. Adopted by the Senate in 2012, the bill was supposed to be debated in March. On Mar. 19, 2015, the Commission on Human Rights intervened and suggested its withdrawal from the agenda: see *Laïcité dans les crèches: la CNCDH veut le retrait de la proposition de loi,* VOUSNOUSILS: L'E-MAG DE L'ÉDUCATION (Mar. 23, 2015), http://www.vousnousils.fr/2015/03/23/laicite-dans-les-creches-la-cncdh-veut-le-retrait-de-la-proposition-de-loi-565704.

479. François Gaudu, *L'entreprise de tendance laïque,* 12 DR. SOC. 1186, 1188 (2011), and the amended bill in the French Senate of Oct. 25, 2011, No. 56, and Report by High Council on Integration, opinion given on Sept. 1, 2011.

480. On the astonished reactions of public law experts on the application by the Labor Court of the principle of *laïcité* to the private sector, see Halima Boualili, *Laïcité et port du foulard islamique au travail,* 7–8 DR. SOC. 779, 781 (2011).

481. It was an NGO: see HALDE deliberation No. 2009-117, Apr. 6, 2009 ("*laïcité* imposes upon civil servants a strict neutrality in the performance of their work") ("there is no equivalent in labor law" applying to the private sector).

482. Gaudu, *supra* note 479, at 1188.

483. In the United States, amendments to Title VII in the CRA 1991 (Pub. L. 102-166) confirmed that disparate impact discrimination applies to religious discrimination reversing previous case law; EEOC v. Sambo's of Georgia, 530 F. Supp. 86 (N.D. Ga. 1981).

484. *See supra* note 479.

485. François Gaudu, *Droit du travail et religion*, 9-10 DR. SOC. 959 (2008).

486. *Id.* at 959: "French labor law and religion are maintaining armed peace."

487. The Labor Court of Lyon, Sept. 18, 2014, decided a case where a supermarket cashier was fired for not removing her veil, as required by the company's internal dress code. The labor court viewed this as an unjust dismissal but refused to qualify the act as religious discrimination. It did, however, reject the employer's argument that the dismissal decision was based on survey results showing that clients were hostile to the veil.

488. For a case in which a consultant was dismissed for refusing to take off her Islamic veil while working at a client's site (Cass. soc., Apr. 9, 2015, No. 13-19855), a referral was made to the CJEU. The CJEU will have to say whether Directive 2000/78 considers a requirement to not expose religious clothing as a condition of employment.

489. First Amendment to the U.S. Constitution ("Congress shall make no law respecting an establishment of religion, or prohibiting the free exercise thereof").

490. Strict interpretation of reasonable accommodation in the public sector, Sherbert v. Verner 374 U.S. 398 (1963), Emp't Div., Dep't. of Human Res. of Oregon v. Smith, 494 U.S. 872 (1990); Goldman v. Weinberger, 475 U.S. 503 (1986).

491. Religious Freedom Restoration Act, 42 U.S.C. § 2000bb (1988).

492. City of Boerne v. Flores, 521 U.S. 507 (1997).

493. Isabelle Desbarats, *De la diversité religieuse en milieu de travail. Regards croisés en droit français et en droit canadien*, 3 REV. RECHERCHE JUR. DROIT PROSPECTIF 1447 (2010).

494. 31 Fed. Reg. 8370 (1966); *see also* Ansonia Board of Education v. Philbrook 479 U.S. 60 (1986).

495. Under 703 (a) (1) Title VII, an employer can justify undue hardship to refuse to make reasonable accommodations for the religious practices of his employees and prospective employees; *see* TWA Inc. v. Hardison, 432 U.S. 63 (1977).

496. 575 US _ (2015); see also Marie Mercat-Bruns, EEOC v. Abercrombie & Fitch Stores, Inc: *l'image de l'entreprise dévoilée*, 2 REV. DR. TRAVAIL 2016 (forthcoming).

497. Chai R. Feldblum, *Rectifying the Tilt: Equality Lessons from Religion, Disability, Sexual Orientation, and Transgender*, 54 ME. L. REV. 159 (2002).

498. *See* Gaudu, *supra* note 420, at 71.

499. Jean Savatier, *Liberté religieuse et relations de travail*, *in* DROIT SYNDICAL ET DROITS DE L'HOMME À L'AUBE DU XXIE SIÈCLE: MÉLANGES EN L'HONNEUR DE JEAN-MAURICE VERDIER 455 (2001).

500. Cass. soc., Dec. 16, 1981, Bull. No. 968 (finding that the dismissal of an employee who did not report to work because of the Muslim feast of Eid-el-Kabir was for just cause, without serious misconduct).

501. Jean-Christophe Sciberras, *Travail et religion: une cohabitation sous tension*, 1 DR. SOC. 72, 74 (2010).

502. The issue of the employee's "personal life" refers to the worker as a person: it is a better qualifier than the one chosen by Michel Despax, "life outside the workplace," which seems to indicate an application outside of the workplace: see Michel Despax, *Life outside the workplace and its effect on the employment contract*, JCP I 1776 (1963).

503. Jean-Yves Frouin, *La protection des droits de la personne et des libertés du salarié*, 99 CAH. SOC. DU BARREAU DE PARIS 123 (1998).

504. Antidiscrimination law targets the person beyond the employee: Antoine Lyon-Caen, *Droit du travail et protection sociale: brèves observations sur un couple*, 11 DR. SOC. 1014 (2009) ("The process of generalization reaches its ultimate phase when labor law selects the person as its subject, a universal being encompassing all individuals, whether salaried or independent, working or not working, a citizen or a foreigner . . . As universal rights distinct from the employment contract, fundamental rights play a central role here"). See Patrice Adam, *La dignité du salarié (deuxième partie)*, 4 REV. DR. TRAVAIL 244 (2014).

505. Even if the grounds of religion and race often intersect: see *infra* Chapter 5, VIII, on intersectionality.

506. Jean-Emmanuel Ray, *D'un droit des travailleurs aux droits de la personne au travail*, 1 DR. SOC. 3 (2010).

507. Lepage, *supra* note 306, at 4.

508. *Id.* at 376.

509. PHILIPPE WAQUET, L'ENTREPRISE ET LES LIBERTÉS DU SALARIÉ 174 (2003).

510. Lepage, *supra* note 306, at 376 ("the standard of relevancy of information and the prohibition of discrimination restricts the use of information more than its access").

511. Natacha Gavalda, *La liberté de la correspondance ou l'intrusion de la vie privée dans l'entreprise*, JCP S 1194 (2010) (discussing the notion of intrusion "as an element of representation of workers").

512. Philippe Waquet, *La vie personnelle du salarié, in* DROIT SYNDICAL ET DROITS DE L'HOMME À L'AUBE DU XXIE SIÈCLE: MÉLANGES EN L'HONNEUR DE JEAN-MAURICE VERDIER 181 (2001).

513. *See* Cass. soc., May 3, 2011, No. 09-67464; *note* Danielle Corrignan-Carsin, *Vie personnelle-vie professionnelle: la cloison est-elle étanche?*, JCP S 1311 (2011); Cass. soc., May 21, 2014, No. 13-12666; Marie Mercat-Bruns, *Enquête interne, atteinte à la vie privée et obligation de sécurité*, 9 REV. DR. TRAVAIL 554 (2014).

514. It is the judge's role: *see* Evelyne Collomp, *La vie personnelle au travail, Dernières évolutions jurisprudentielles*, 1 DR. SOC. 43 (2010).

515. If we adopt Morgan Sweeney's definition: "Positive actions are measures based on prohibited grounds of discrimination (age, sex, real or presumed membership of and ethnic or racial group, disability, religion, sexual orientation, etc.) in order to remedy, compensate, or prevent discrimination suffered by a particular population (women, homosexuals, etc.). Subsequently this membership determines access to an advantage." Morgan Sweeney, *Les actions positives à l'épreuve des règles de non-discrimination*, 2 REV. DR. TRAVAIL 88 (2012).

516. On the same issue regarding freedom of expression: Cass. soc., Dec. 8, 2009, No. 08-17191, JCP S 1213 (2010).

517. Pascal Lokiec, *Le travailleur et l'actif*, 11 DR. SOC. 1018 (2009).

518. Pascal Lokiec, *L'adaptation du travail à l'homme*, 7-8 DR. SOC. 755 (2009).

519. By analogy, when one discrimination hides another: Cass. soc., Jan. 28, 2010, No. 08-44486, JCP S 1196 (2010).

520. For cases involving an older woman, see Court of Appeal, Poitiers, Feb. 17, 2009, 08/00461; Court of Appeals, Versailles, May 7, 2014, 13/03766, Madame L. v. SAS ERES: refusal of job transfer to another lingerie shop cannot be justified by female employee's age and physical appearance.

521. Multiple discrimination encompasses different experiences. Marie-Thérèse Lanquetin shows the variety of forms it can take. She refers to the idea of multiple discrimination as "sequential discrimination." For example, a woman with a disability can be affected by employment decisions her whole life. She will have a harder time finding a first job

because of the required reasonable accommodation linked to her disability. Then, during her career, if she takes time off for maternity leave, she is more likely to be discriminated against in promotion decisions because of family responsibilities. Lanquetin also describes multiple discrimination as "combined discrimination" affecting subordination at different levels, associated with the meshing of different grounds. For instance, compared to nonimmigrant women, immigrant women might have access only to fixed-term, less-qualified employment, such as domestic work, and be paid less than immigrant men. European scholarship also embraces the idea of "intersectional" discrimination, drawing directly from Kimberlé Crenshaw's work *infra* note 523: in this case, new stereotypes are perceived as emerging as a result not simply of additive forms of discrimination but assumptions, for example, made about women of certain origins. They can be associated with certain types of biases influencing the employer's evaluation of the employee's conduct at work: Muslim workers wearing veils may be seen as subordinated to their spouses, or black women may be assumed to be single mothers with less flexibility in terms of working hours. See Marie-Thérèse Lanquetin, *Égalité, diversité et discriminations multiples*, 21 TRAVAIL, GENRE ET SOCIÉTÉS 91 (2009); Marie Mercat-Bruns, *Le jeu des discriminations multiples*, 4 REV. DR. TRAVAIL 254 (2013); Marie Mercat-Bruns, *Discrimination multiple: le défi de la preuve, in Droit et Genre*, 16 RECUEIL DALLOZ 954 (2014); Mercat-Bruns, *Les discriminations multiples et l'identité au travail*, supra note 6, at 28.

522. GENDERACE: THE USE OF RACIAL ANTIDISCRIMINATION LAWS: GENDER AND CITIZENSHIP IN A MULTICULTURAL CONTEXT, FINAL REPORT 2010 (Isabelle Carles & Olga Jubany-Baucells eds., 2010), available at http://genderace.ulb.ac.be/rapports/GENDERACE%20FINAL%20REPORT%20sent.pdf.

523. "The U.S. Equal Employment Opportunity Commission (EEOC) and private plaintiffs today announced their mutual resolution of the lawsuit EEOC v. Abercrombie & Fitch Stores, Inc., Case No. CV-04-4731 SI, which was filed on November 10, 2004, in the United States District Court for the Northern District of California in San Francisco. The lawsuit alleged that Abercrombie & Fitch violated Title VII of the Civil Rights Act of 1964 by maintaining recruiting and hiring practices that excluded minorities and women and adopting a restrictive marketing image, and other policies, which limited minority and female employment." EEOC Agrees to Landmark Resolution of Discrimination Case Against Abercrombie & Fitch, http://www.eeoc.gov/eeoc/newsroom/release/11-18-04.cfm.

524. Kimberlé Crenshaw, *Demarginalizing the Intersection of Race and Sex: A Black Feminist Critique of Antidiscrimination Doctrine, Feminist Theory, and Antiracist Politics*, U. CHI. LEGAL F. 139, 149 (1989) [hereinafter Crenshaw, *Demarginalizing the Intersection of Race and Sex*]:

> Consider an analogy to traffic in an intersection, coming and going in all four directions. Discrimination, like traffic through an intersection, may flow in one direction, and it may flow in another. If an accident happens in an intersection, it can be caused by cars traveling from any number of directions and, sometimes, from all of them. Similarly, if a Black woman is harmed because she is in an intersection, her injury could result from sex discrimination or race discrimination.... But it is not always easy to reconstruct an accident: Sometimes the skid marks and the injuries simply indicate that they occurred simultaneously, frustrating efforts to determine which driver caused the harm.

In social science, the theory of intersectionality was then used to analyze how forms of oppression, such as race and gender, work together in producing injustice. For a French description of the theory, see LAURE BERENI ET AL., INTRODUCTION AUX ÉTUDES SUR LE GENRE 280 (2012). See also Alexandre Jaunait & Sébastien Chauvin, *Représenter l'intersection*, 62 REV. FRANÇAISE SCIENCES POLITIQUES 5 (2012); Eleonore Lepinard, *Doing*

Intersectionality: Repertoires of Feminist Practices in France and Canada, 28 GENDER & SOCIETY 877 (2014).

525. Crenshaw, *Demarginalizing the Intersection of Race and Sex, supra* note 523, at 139; Kimberlé Crenshaw, *Mapping the Margins: Intersectionality, Identity Politics, and Violence Against Women of Color*, 43 STAN. L. REV. 1241 (1991) [hereinafter Crenshaw, *Mapping the Margins*]; Kimberlé Crenshaw, *Race, Gender, and Sexual Harassment*, 65 S. CAL. L. REV. 1467 (1992).

526. PATRICIA HILL COLLINS, BLACK FEMINIST THOUGHT: KNOWLEDGE, CONSCIOUSNESS AND THE POLITICS OF EMPOWERMENT 11–12 (1990):

> If women are allegedly passive and fragile, then why are Black women treated as "mules" and assigned heavy cleaning chores? If good mothers are supposed to stay at home with their children, then why are US Black women on public assistance forced to find jobs and leave their children in day care? If women's highest calling is to become mothers, then why are Black teen mothers pressured to use Norplant and Depo Provera? In the absence of a viable Black feminism that investigates how intersecting oppressions of race, gender, and class foster these contradictions, the angle of vision created by being deemed devalued workers and failed mothers could easily be turned inward, leading to internalized oppression. But the legacy of struggle among U.S. Black women suggests that a collectively shared Black women's oppositional knowledge has long existed. This collective wisdom in turn has spurred U.S. Black women to generate a more specialized knowledge, namely, Black feminist thought as critical social theory.

527. *Id.*; *see also* ANGELA DAVIS, WOMEN, RACE, AND CLASS (1983).

528. Directive 2000/43/EC (Recital 3) and Directive 2000/78/EC (Recital 3); Decision of Parliament and of the Council, May 17, 2006, European Year of Equal Opportunities for All (point 10); ACTION OF THE COMMISSION: STRATEGY FOR EQUALITY BETWEEN MEN AND WOMEN (2010–2020).

529. *See supra* note 521.

530. "Sex +" cases are U.S. antidiscrimination cases involving at least one ground of discrimination outside of sex.

531. RICHARD T. FORD, RACIAL CULTURE: A CRITIQUE 125 (2005).

532. Janet Halley, *Sexuality Harassment*, *in* DIRECTIONS IN SEXUAL HARASSMENT LAW 182 (Reva B. Siegel & Catharine A. MacKinnon eds., 2003).

533. MERCAT-BRUNS, VIEILLISSEMENT ET DROIT, *supra* note 364.

534. *See infra* Chapter 4 on indirect discrimination.

535. *See infra* Chapter 5, Part VII.

536. In India, for example.

537. Washington v. Glucksberg, 521 U.S. 702 (1997).

538. Rachel Kahn Best et al., *Multiple Disadvantages: An Empirical Test of Intersectionality Theory in EEO Litigation*, 45 L. & SOC'Y REV. 991 (2011).

539. Paulette Caldwell, *A Hair Piece: Perspectives on the Intersection of Race and Gender*, 2 DUKE L.J. 365 (1991); Devon W. Carbado & Mitu Gulati, *The Fifth Black Woman*, 11 J. CONTEMP. LEGAL ISSUES 701 (2011) [hereinafter Carbado & Gulati, *The Fifth Black Woman*]; Cheryl Harris, *Finding Sojourner's Truth: Race, Gender and the Institution of Property*, 18 CARDOZO L. REV. 309 (1997); Peggy Smith, *Separate Identities: Black Women, Work, and Title VII*, 14 HARV. WOMEN'S LAW J. 21 (1991); Virginia Wei, *Asian Women and Employment Discrimination: Using Intersectionality Theory to Address Title VII Claims Based on Combined Factors of Race, Gender and National Origin*, 37 B.C. L. REV. 771 (1996); PATRICIA WILLIAMS, THE ALCHEMY OF RACE AND RIGHTS (1991).

540. Ivy Kennelly, *That Single Mother Element: How White Employers Typify Black Women*, 13 GENDER & SOC'Y 168 (1999).

541. Carwina Weng, *Individual and Intergroup Processes to Address Racial Discrimination in Lawyering Relationships, in* CRITICAL RACE REALISM: INTERSECTIONS OF PSYCHOLOGY, RACE AND LAW 64 (Shayne Jones ed., 2008).
542. Rachel Kahn Best et al., *supra* note 534, at 991.
543. Case C-555/07, Kücükdeveci v. Swedex, 2010 E.C.R. I-365.
544. Case C-152/11, Odar v. Baxter Deutschland GmbH, E.C.R. I-0000.
545. Case C-303/06, Coleman v. Attridge Law & Steve Law, 2008 E.C.R. I-5603.
546. Sieglinde Rosenberger & Birgit Sauer, *Governing Muslim Headscarves: Regulations and Debates in Europe, in* THE LIMITS OF GENDERED CITIZENSHIP: CONTEXTS AND COMPLEXITIES 159 (Elzbieta H. Olesky et al. eds., 2011)
547. DENISE M. HORN, WOMEN, CIVIL SOCIETY AND THE GEOPOLITICS OF DEMOCRATIZATION 3 (2010).
548. Dagmar Schiek, *Organizing EU Equality Law Around the Nodes of "Race," Gender and Disability, in* EUROPEAN UNION NON-DISCRIMINATION LAW AND INTERSECTIONALITY: INVESTIGATING THE TRIANGLE OF RACIAL, GENDER AND DISABILITY DISCRIMINATION 12 (Dagmar Schiek & Anna Lawson eds., 2011).
549. Case C-123/10, Brachner v. Pensionsversicherungsanstalt, 2011 E.C.R. I-000.
550. *See* GENDERACE, *supra* note 521.
551. *Id.*, at 274–76.
552. *See* Malha Naab, *De la place des femmes dans le syndicalisme français à une négociation collective à travers le prisme du genre*, 2 JURIS. CRITIQUE 173 (2011); Cécile Guillaume et al., *Genre, féminisme et syndicalisme*, 30 TRAVAIL, GENRE & SOCIÉTÉ 29 (2013). *See also* Cass. soc., May 19 2015, No. 13-27.763 (on an older male union member).
553. Cass. soc., Jan. 11, 2012, No. 10-28.213.
554. Cass. soc., Nov. 3, 2011, No. 10-20765.
555. *Id.*
556. See the first case where the Cour de Cassation set aside the requirement of comparability, involving a woman who was discriminated against in promotion decisions after taking part in a strike but who could not produce any elements to compare her status with that of coworkers with the same qualifications: Cass. soc., Nov. 10, 2009, No. 07-42849. The court simply compared her career path before and after the strike. Multiple discrimination in this case offers a way to analyze the effects of the combination between the ground of sex and the freedom to strike.
557. Case C-177/88, Dekker v. VJV Centrum, 1990 E.C.R. I-3941.
558. Case C-147/08, Römer v. City of Hamburg, 2011 E.C.R. I-3591.
559. *See* Cass. soc., May 11, 2010, No. 08-45307, and No. 08-43681, in which the Cour de Cassation attempted to apply the principle of effectiveness of the EU directives to France.
560. For examples outside of employment, see Crenshaw, *Mapping the Margins, supra* note 524, at 1241.
561. C-54/07, Centrum voor gelijkheid van kansen en voor racismebestrijding v. Firma Feryn, 2008 E.C.R. I-5187.
562. Carbado & Gulati, *The Fifth Black Woman, supra* note 538, at 701.; See also recent examples of identity performance in French case law, Mercat-Bruns, *Les discriminations multiples et l'identité au travail, supra* note 6, at 28.
563. Carbado & Gulati, *The Fifth Black Woman, supra* note 538, at 711.

APPENDIX

1. I interviewed thirteen professors of law (Martha Minow, Dean of Harvard Law School; Robert Post, Dean of Yale Law School; Janet Halley, Professor at Harvard; Richard Ford,

Professor at Stanford; Linda Krieger, Professor at the University of Hawaii; Vicki Schultz, Professor at Yale; Susan Sturm, Professor at Columbia; Julie Suk, Professor at Cardozo; Chai Feldblum, on leave as Professor at Georgetown while serving on the Equal Employment Opportunity Commission; Ruth Colker, Professor at Ohio State; David Oppenheimer, Professor at Berkeley, Christine Jolls, Professor at Yale, Reva Siegel, Professor at Yale) and two sociologists (Frank Dobbin, Professor at Harvard; and Devah Pager, Professor at Princeton).

2. Martha Kegel was the president of the American Civil Liberties Union (ACLU) in Louisiana. She is currently an attorney and Executive Director of UNITY, an award-winning nonprofit providing housing and services to the homeless in New Orleans.

3. Bowers v. Hardwick, 478 U.S. 186 (1986), in which the Supreme Court ruled that a Georgia law criminalizing private, consensual sodomy between gay adults was constitutional; this decision was overturned in Lawrence v. Texas, 539 U.S. 558 (2003).

4. Lauren Edelman is a professor of law and sociology at the Berkeley Law. She has conducted fascinating work on the internalization of law in organizations: see *When The Haves Hold Court: Speculations on the Organizational Internalization of Law* (with Mark C. Suchman), 33 LAW & SOC'Y REV. 941 (1999); *The Endogeneity of Legal Regulation: Grievance Procedures as Rational Myth* (with Christopher Uggen & Howard S. Erlanger), 105 AM. J. SOCIOLOGY 406 (1999); *Constructed Legalities: Socio-Legal Fields and the Endogeneity of Law, in* HOW INSTITUTIONS CHANGE: INSTITUTIONAL DYNAMICS AND PROCESSES (Walter W. Powell & Daniel L. Jones eds., forthcoming); *Symbols and Substance in Organizational Response to Civil Rights Law* (with Stephen M. Petterson), *in* 17 RESEARCH IN SOC. STRATIFICATION & MOBILITY 107 (1999); *Legal Readings: Employee Interpretation and Enactment of Civil Rights Law* (with Sally Riggs Fuller & Sharon F. Matusik), 25 ACAD. MGMT. REV. 200 (2000).

5. A reference to Halley's book SPLIT DECISIONS: HOW AND WHY TO TAKE A BREAK FROM FEMINISM (2006).

6. RICHARD THOMPSON FORD, THE RACE CARD: HOW BLUFFING ABOUT BIAS MAKES RACE RELATIONS WORSE (2008).

7. These books have since been published: RICHARD THOMPSON FORD, RIGHTS GONE WRONG: HOW LAW CORRUPTS THE STRUGGLE FOR EQUALITY (2011); and RICHARD THOMPSON FORD, UNIVERSAL RIGHTS DOWN TO EARTH (2011).

8. In relation to queer theory, see *supra* Chapter 1 on the limitations of constitutional norms and nondiscrimination as fundamental rights.

9. Bowers v. Hardwick, 478 U.S. 186 (1986).

10. DAVID B. OPPENHEIMER ET AL., COMPARATIVE EQUALITY AND ANTI-DISCRIMINATION LAW: CASES, CODES, CONSTITUTIONS, AND COMMENTARY (2012).

11. Jim Crow laws mandated racial segregation in public facilities from the end of the Civil War to the mid-1960s.

12. *See supra*, Chapter 2.

13. Douglas NeJaime & Reva B. Siegel, *Conscience Wars: Complicity-Based Conscience Claims in Religion and Politics*, 124 YALE L.J. 2516 (2015).

14. Julie Chi-hye Suk, *Antidiscrimination Law in the Administrative State*, 2006 U. ILL. L. REV. 405.

15. Color blindness.

16. Julie C. Suk, *Discrimination at Will: Job Security Protections and Equal Employment Opportunity in Conflict*, 60 STAN. L. REV. 73 (2007).

17. Julie C. Suk, *Procedural Path Dependence: Discrimination and the Civil-Criminal Divide*, 85 WASH. U. L. REV. 1315 (2008).

18. Julie C. Suk, *Are Gender Stereotypes Bad for Women? Rethinking Antidiscrimination Law and Work-Family Conflict*, 110 COLUM. L. REV. 1 (2010).

19. Julie C. Suk, *Quotas and Consequences: A Transnational Re-evaluation*, in PHILOSOPHICAL FOUNDATIONS OF DISCRIMINATION LAW (Deborah Hellman & Sophia Moreau eds., 2013); Julie C. Suk, *Gender Quotas After the End of Men*, 93 B.U. L. REV. 1123 (2013); Julie C. Suk, *Work-Family Conflict and the Pipeline to Power: Lessons from European Gender Quotas*, 2012 MICH. ST. L. REV. 1797; Julie C. Suk, *Gender Parity and State Legitimacy: From Public Office to Corporate Boards*, 10 INT'L J. CONST. L. (I*CON) (2012).

INDEX

abortion, 178, 227, 248, 255
accommodation, 33–34, 45, 86–87, 130–33, 151–52, 192, 202–206, 239–40 ; reasonable, 3, 27, 54, 80, 92–93, 106, 109, 133–37, 196, 206–210, 216, 221–25, 227, 230–32
ADA (Americans with Disability Act), xvi, 131, 133–35, 149, 151, 196–210, 248
ADEA (Age Discrimination in Employment Act), 25, 149, 214
affirmative action, xxi, 3, 11, 13–17, 33, 40–43, 46, 55, 60, 89–91, 93, 105–10, 113–14, 117, 128, 131–32, 135, 150, 154–55, 161
African American, 77, 90, 148, 155, 198, 210, 223, 253–54
aging, xiv, 25, 93, 128–29, 196, 213, 215, 237
Americans with Disabilities Act, 129–30, 236. See also ADA
Antibalkanization, 40–46, 154
Antisubordination, 39–45, 153–55
appearance, 192; physical, 183, 191, 193–95, 236, 243–44; prejudicial, xv, xix
autonomy, 31–32, 36–37, 178, 183, 191, 194, 230, 232, 246

Behavioral Economics, xv, xviii, 2, 113, 166
belief : 10, 30, 64, 98, 114, 124, 129, 178, 207, 221, 223, 226–27, 231–33, 239
BFOQ (Bona fide occupational qualifications): 213, 222. See Bona fide occupational requirements

bias, 1, 2–3, 7, 10, 27, 50, 60–61, 77–78, 118, 151–52, 155, 159, 161, 163, 176, 186–87, 194, 210–12, 212–13, 237, 242; implicit, xv, 62–73, 76–77, 86, 113, 212; racial, xv, 50, 72–73, 84, 159; unconscious, 3, 50, 62–73, 75–79, 111, 155, 159
birth : 20, 133, 165, 169, 174
black: 10–13, 44–45, 51, 70–75, 77, 79, 82–85, 88–89, 92, 95, 112, 147–48, 150, 156, 159, 175, 184, 210, 212, 233–38, 242, 244, 253, 255, 353n520,523, 354n525
bona fide occupational requirements, 174, 217
burden of proof, 25, 50, 61–62, 66, 67, 96–98, 100, 159, 194, 228, 282n102, 286n38; of persuasion, 17, 61–62; of production, 61–62, 67, 98
burqa, 224, 239–40
business necessity, 83–84, 98–100, 104–5

catholic, 148, 193, 217, 219
Charter of Fundamental Rights of the European Union, 46
child care, 169, 171, 228–229
christian, xvii, 147–148, 185, 190, 204, 219, 230
citizen, xi-xii, 4, 20–22, 32–33, 36, 46, 55–56, 109–110, 125–26, 148, 157, 187, 197, 225; citizenship, xii, 20–21, 118–21
civil rights, xv-xvii, xx, 1–2, 9–14, 17, 23, 44, 46–50, 55, 84–85, 94–95, 98, 104, 125, 149, 154–55, 162, 175, 184–85, 187–89, 198–200, 202, 210–11, 222, 235, 248–49, 252

359

CJEU, 19, 20, 22–23, 34–35, 88, 95–97, 99, 102, 106–7, 174, 179, 191, 208, 210, 226, 230, 243, 245
class: action, 1, 51, 78, 88, 108, 161, 201, 248; social, xxi, 33, 55, 57, 65, 91, 111, 165, 175, 189, 195, 199, 233–34, 238, 244, 250, 256
cognitive, 63–64, 69, 113–14, 139–40, 153, 198
colorblindness, 40–42, 44
community, 4, 6, 21, 23, 30–32, 37–40, 45, 119, 122, 147–48, 154, 175, 198–200, 202, 211, 219–21, 227, 252, 271n38, 321n92
comparative law, xiii, xxi, 6–8, 28, 36, 255–56
comparative perspectives, xiv, 15, 19, 26, 34, 43, 54, 58, 76–77, 80, 93, 112, 117, 122, 125, 129, 134, 140, 146, 154, 174, 190, 206, 213, 224, 241
constitutional law, xv, xix, 8, 15, 18, 66, 153–154, 182
corporate board, 115
Council of Europe, 10
Court of Justice of the European Union, 19. *See* CJEU
criminal, xxi, 4, 18, 38, 138, 141, 157, 159, 183, 185, 234, 253, 255; justice system, xix, 253; sanctions, 30, 37, 47, 54, 78, 111, 139, 184
critical legal studies, xv, 26–27, 249, 251
critical race theory, 114
critical theory, xvii, 26–29, 251–52

deconstruction, 46, 126, 168, 180–83, 191, 195
Defender of Rights, 9, 39, 47, 62, 101, 279n48, 303n271, 309n343, 326n147. *See also* HALDE
dignity, 3, 21, 31, 34, 37, 39, 40, 42, 138–39, 142–44, 180, 225, 250, 306n308,309, 307n320, 310n353, 318n76
disability, xv-xvi, 1, 3, 22, 27, 36, 39, 87, 98, 106, 128, 130–31, 133–38, 149, 151–53, 166, 196–211, 231, 233–34, 243–44, 248, 303n270, 306n307, 323n111, 338n290, 339n313
Discrimination: age, 3, 20, 22, 34, 46, 51, 81, 96–97, 99, 149, 152, 160, 175, 194, 196, 201, 209, 211–15, 243; direct, 6, 19–20, 35, 61–63, 80, 82, 91, 93–94, 99, 102–3, 105, 107–8, 144–45, 149, 175, 194, 209, 231; disparate impact, xiv, 33–34, 44, 42, 44, 54, 62, 66, 73, 77, 82–144, 155, 161–62, 174, 209, 212, 214; disparate treatment, xiv, 33, 44, 61–107, 111, 122, 155, 162, 174, 209, 231; family responsibilities, 36–37, 104, 164–65, 169–172, 174, 179, 180, 243; grounds, 2, 18, 20, 34–35, 36, 54, 145–246; indirect, 2, 6, 11, 19–21, 34–38, 42, 46, 80, 82, 85, 87–88, 93–101, 102–8, 111, 124, 137, 144–45, 149, 156–57, 159–60, 169, 175, 191, 209, 211, 214, 216, 229, 231, 243–45; multiple, 2, 4, 36, 113, 145–246, 352n520, 353n523; race, 15, 17, 36, 51, 55, 83–84, 107, 109, 114, 123, 142, 147, 150, 152, 154, 159, 161–63, 175, 188, 209, 223–24, 236, 244, 248, 253–255; religion, 37, 54, 134, 146, 216, 221, 223–25, 227–28, 230–32, 239; sex, 1, 27, 34, 51, 55–56, 82, 95, 123, 138–41, 147, 150, 161–66, 168, 175–76, 178, 180, 188, 191–93, 195, 202, 205, 254, 256; diversity, 2, 10, 12–17, 19, 37, 40–42, 46, 54, 66, 78, 108, 109–115, 119–122, 124–128, 132, 147–49, 154, 156, 158, 216–17, 219–21, 225, 230–31, 239–40; agreements, 54–55, 57, 59–60, 81, 92, 132, 221, 232, 244; higher education, xx-xxi, 1, 17, 109, 149; programs, 115–17, 128, 221, 249; training, xvi, 60, 77, 107, 111–12, 115–17
domestic violence, 176, 255
dress codes, 3, 108, 146, 186, 194, 219, 222, 229, 351n487

EEOC, 24, 48–50, 52–54, 82–84, 88, 98–99, 120–21, 128, 162, 191–92, 200, 208, 227. *See* Equal Employment Opportunity Comission
empowerment, 1, 115, 147; empowered, 200
enforcement, xiv, xxi, 2, 8, 12, 14, 17, 29–60, 70, 76, 80, 83, 85, 94, 120, 136, 156, 162, 163, 175–76, 183–84, 197–98, 207, 209, 215, 225, 227, 231, 255
Equal Employment Opportunity Commission, xvi, 9, 47, 76, 82, 231. *See* EEOC
equal pay, 1, 3, 21, 58, 103, 126–27, 147, 176, 283n111, 327n154,159, 328n172
equal protection, xv, xix, 17, 39–40, 45–46, 66, 104, 108–9, 125, 148, 152–54, 178, 185, 192, 255
equal treatment, 19–20, 22, 34–35, 55, 123, 126–27, 130, 157–59, 175, 179, 210, 224, 272n47
essentialism, 181
ethnicity, 14, 43, 70, 73, 90, 147, 157–59, 221
European Convention on Human Rights, 19–20, 34, 157, 160, 226

Family Medical Leave Act, 133, 179
feminism, xv, xvii, 181, 233, 250, 354n525; feminist, xix, 27, 164, 168–71, 175, 177, 179, 181–82, 184, 187–88, 192, 233, 238–39, 249–50
FMLA (Family Medical Leave Act), 133, 179
freedom, 19, 22, 27, 32, 36–37, 66–67, 137, 146, 157, 160, 174, 177, 180–81, 183, 193, 194–95, 204, 216–17, 220, 231–32, 239–40, 252; of association, 56; religious, 124, 216–17, 222–30, 40; of speech, 118, 226

INDEX

gender, xvii, xix, xxi, 1–4, 8, 27, 46, 59, 71, 73, 79, 108, 114–16, 122–23, 127–28, 140–43, 145–46, 152–53, 157, 161, 167–68, 170–71, 173–75, 180–83, 186–95, 198, 205, 234–35, 238, 243–44, 256, 337n284,285
globalization, 5, 54, 58, 162, 173, 183

HALDE, 9, 38–39, 47, 52, 54, 62, 88, 135, 228, 280n68, 320n90. *See also* Defender of Rights
hate speech, xxi
history, xv, xix-xx, 7, 10–28, 40, 57, 59, 76, 85, 88, 93–95, 107, 150–51, 161, 181, 185–86, 196–97, 214, 216, 220, 224–25, 235, 249, 251, 254, 256
homophobia, 51, 192
homosexual, 25, 182, 184–85, 190, 251; homosexuality, 124, 187, 191–92
hostile environment, 3, 139–40, 143, 195
human rights, xviii, xix, 2, 10, 19–20, 34, 145, 157, 160, 195, 222, 226, 229, 239, 241, 250, 263n17, 271n42, 313n39

identity, xi, 8, 14, 26, 30–31, 45, 59, 108, 122, 145, 147–48, 156–57, 161, 174, 177, 180–81, 183–85, 187–88, 191, 195, 226, 230–32, 234, 238, 242, 245–46, 249–51, 316n67, 334n253, 336n280, 337n284,285
impairment, 132, 153, 198, 202, 207–10
inclusion, xv, xx-xxi, 4, 66, 99, 108, 112, 121–22, 124, 220, 298n212
institutional change, xv, xx, 4, 108, 118
intergenerational, 215
intersectionality, 2, 233–35, 237–39, 241–46, 353n523

Jews, 148, 219; jewish, 148, 205, 217, 220, 236
Jim Crow, 150, 156, 254, 356n11
judicial review, 10, 15, 21–22, 39, 178, 233
justice, 2, 52, 117, 238; forms, 35–36; theories, xviii, 45, 111

labor, xii, xvii, xx, 22, 48, 55–56, 59–60, 126, 129, 135, 137, 172, 182–84, 209, 214–15, 232, 243–44; code, 15, 37, 62, 135, 139, 160, 174, 193, 228; market, xix, 37, 55–56, 72, 74, 112, 123, 142, 151, 168, 212, 215, 235; movement, 55; unions, 36, 47, 58–60, 124, 127, 165. *See also* trade union
LGBT, 124–25, 128, 187, 191, 255
liberty, xiv, 1, 4, 32, 39, 178, 180–81, 187, 223, 225, 255, 347n419

marriage, 21–22, 102–3, 153, 162, 183, 185, 187–88, 191–93, 205, 252, 255

maternity, 44, 124, 152, 167, 169, 174, 176–77, 179
methodology, xiii, 7–8, 103
Middle Eastern, 155
multiculturalism, xvii, 4, 156, 220, 240, 250
muslim, 205, 217, 219, 229, 240; Muslims, 55

nationality, 22, 34, 55, 94–96, 157–60, 236, 243
negligent, 79

parental leave, 123, 179
parity, 114–15, 123, 152, 182
paternity, 37, 152
part-time, 38, 96, 101, 134, 165
percentage plans, 16–17, 44
police brutality, 1, 156
policy, social, 21–23, 35, 87, 97, 152, 214
pregnancy, 1, 44, 123, 149, 162–63, 167, 169, 178–79, 243, 245
prima facie, 61–62, 83, 89–90, 102, 194
privacy, xvi, xviii, 31, 177–78, 182, 192, 194–95, 232, 236, 240, 248, 309n337
proportionality test, 19, 21–23, 34–35, 100–101, 158, 176
prostitution, 191

QPC (Question prioritaire de constitutionnalité), 10, 21–23, 39. *See also* judicial review
queer theory, xvii, 25, 27, 46, 146, 169, 181, 186–87, 189–91, 195, 250–51, 334n253
quotas, xxi, 14, 16–17, 33, 43, 106, 112–113, 127, 132, 135, 176, 256

race, xi, xvii, xix, xx-xxi, 1, 3, 12–15, 17–18, 20, 23, 27, 31, 35–36, 39–46, 51, 55–56, 59, 70–73, 75, 79–80, 83–87, 90–92, 94, 98–99, 107, 109, 114, 116, 123, 128, 142, 146–64, 174–75, 177–78, 181, 188–89, 196, 198, 209–10, 212, 214, 217, 221, 223–24, 226, 232–37, 239, 243–44, 248–50, 253–56
rape, xvii
recruitment, xv-xvi, 75, 107–8, 116, 159, 231, 245
religious, xi, xviii, 1, 3, 14, 124, 126, 128–29, 148, 151, 159, 188, 192, 203–5, 216–233, 240–41, 255–56; discrimination, 37, 54, 216, 221, 223–25, 228, 230, 239
reproduction, 177, 182, 255
republicanism, xii, 126
roma, 46, 97, 122, 157

same-sex marriage, 21–22, 187–88, 192–93, 333n241

scrutiny, 16–17, 19, 21–22, 35, 38, 127, 152, 176, 178, 211, 228–29, 269n13; intermediate, 150, 152; strict, 14, 17, 42–43, 45, 109, 127, 150, 155, 158, 178
seniority, 38, 101, 160, 212–13, 216
sex segregation, xv, xix, 139, 141, 150, 162–63, 166, 174
sexual harrassment, xv, 1, 24, 27, 51–52, 116, 138–44, 182, 191, 195, 237, 240
sexual orientation, xvi, 20, 27, 36, 85, 98, 102, 128, 146, 180, 182–83, 185–95, 198–99, 217, 231, 237, 243, 333n242
snowball sampling, xiv
social psychology, xv, 2, 62, 64, 70, 72, 78, 113, 140, 212
social science, xiii, xiv, xix-xx, 6, 62–68, 76–78, 109, 126, 166, 234; evidence, 62, 116, 163
sociology, xiii, xvi, xix, 7–8, 78, 116, 182, 213, 234, 248, 253
statistics, 53–54, 99–101, 112, 157, 211, 221, 235–36, 244; ethnoracial, 98–99, 156, 160, 236, 236–37, 253, 311n8
stereotypes, xv, 27, 39, 62, 71–72, 77–78, 93, 139–40, 156, 161, 165–69, 171, 180, 185–88, 190, 194–95, 215, 234–35, 140, 242, 256
structural, xx, 3–4, 18, 42, 53, 71, 88–91, 94, 103, 108, 111, 118, 122–23, 130, 139, 142, 163–64, 170, 204, 212, 215, 250; change, 18, 213, 88; discrimination, 82, 86, 95–96, 111, 140, 142, 161. *See also* systemic
suspect classification, 152, 156, 178
symbol, 18, 150, 225–26, 229; symbolic, 19, 20, 26, 86, 153, 177, 181, 214, 225

systemic, 37, 39, 53, 68, 164, 182, 250; change, 69; discrimination, 2–3, 27, 58, 68, 78, 80, 82–144, 159, 161, 174, 245. *See also* structural

test, 3, 19, 21–23, 34–35, 44, 65–66, 68, 71–76, 82–84, 89, 90–91, 94–95, 97, 99–101, 105, 107–108, 116–17, 139, 158, 160, 166, 176, 252; standardized, 84, 87–88, 97, 324n128
trade union, 9–10, 37–38, 47, 54, 56–59, 107, 180, 244. *See also* labor
transnational, xvii, xxi, 2, 6, 250
transsexual, 167

veil, 1, 21, 182, 228
voluntary compliance, 71, 89, 91–92, 132–33, 162, 203

wage, xix, 58, 74, 96, 112, 127, 162, 165–67, 170–71, 176–77, 201, 203, 205, 207, 209, 212, 234–35, 253
welfare state, 2, 5, 27, 38, 69, 93, 180, 190, 196
woman, 79, 112–13, 130, 161, 164–65, 167–69, 174, 178–79, 181, 190, 194, 235, 238–41, 244–45, 252
work-family: balance, 25, 123, 177; conflict, xv, xxi, 169, 170; issues, xx; policy, 118, 213
worker, xi, 3, 53, 55–56, 58–59, 72, 75–76, 84, 93, 96, 101, 103, 108, 123–26, 129, 131–37, 143, 153, 167, 170, 173–74, 176, 178–80, 184, 195–96, 207, 209, 211–15, 222, 230, 232, 234, 239, 244–46, 249
workplace flexibility, xvi, 127–29, 212

www.ingramcontent.com/pod-product-compliance
Lightning Source LLC
Chambersburg PA
CBHW031416230426
43668CB00007B/330